CW01374024

Catalonia
A Guide
to Modern
Architecture
1880-2007

£36·00p

Catalonia
A Guide
to Modern
Architecture
1880-2007

Maurici Pla
Photographs by **José Hevia**

▶ **Triangle** editorial

Col·legi d'Arquitectes
de Catalunya

The guide, simply

The publication of *Catalonia. A Guide to Modern Architecture. 1880-2007* forms an integral part of the desire to serve society expressed so abundantly and in many ways by the Col·legi d'Arquitectes de Catalunya (Architects' Institute of Catalonia) in the course of its many years of existence (75 years is a long time). With it, once more, we present an initiative that reaches beyond the exclusive world of professionals, filling an obvious gap, to meet a need and the intellectual curiosity of everyone—in Catalonia and the rest of the world, experts and amateurs alike—who is attracted by architecture as a cultural and artistic phenomenon of great import, with an influence that goes beyond its technical particularities. The book, published in Catalan, Spanish and English, therefore aims to disseminate with clarity, simplicity and consistency the values of Catalonia's modern architecture in all its magnitude. To do this, it draws on a broad-based body of artistic, historical, urbanistic, political, economic and aesthetic documentation.

Yet this is not just one more architecture guide. This is the first published guide of modern Catalan architecture, centring exclusively on Catalonia, covering all the styles, trends and movements in architecture constructed between the late 19th century and 2007. This makes a total of 417 buildings, presented in the form of files with a descriptive text, illustrated by photographs and, in some cases, plans and drawings. The other new feature is the regional division of these 417 files, never previously used in a guide to architecture or any other kind. The map used covers all of Catalonia, divided into three main parts (Coast, Inland and Mountains) and 10 areas: Figueres, Girona, Barcelona, Tarragona, Tortosa, Olot, Vic, Manresa, Lleida and La Seu d'Urgell. Catalan architecture is thereby structured into a constellation of municipalities that is quite independent of the regional organization of provinces and *comarques*, or counties.

In addition to providing a catalogue of the foremost buildings to have been constructed in Catalonia in the last 120 years, the guide aims to constitute a tribute to the individuals and the institutions, including even the youngest generations, who have placed Catalan architecture among the best known, most prestigious and highly valued in the world. However, the continuity of this extraordinary heritage would probably still be in danger unless all of us, individuals and institutions, firmly renew our commitment to and our faith in architecture, for all that it represents culturally and socially. This is very much to the point today; the development of our country's physical environment is at stake, as are its social cohesion and competitiveness.

It only remains to commend the splendid work carried out by Maurici Pla and his team, by the photographer José Hevia and by the COAC's Publications Service, and to voice our congratulations. There can be no doubt that *Catalonia. A Guide to Modern Architecture. 1880-2007* represents a new landmark in the editorial achievements of the Col·legi d'Arquitectes de Catalunya.

Jordi Ludevid i Anglada
President of the Col·legi d'Arquitectes de Catalunya

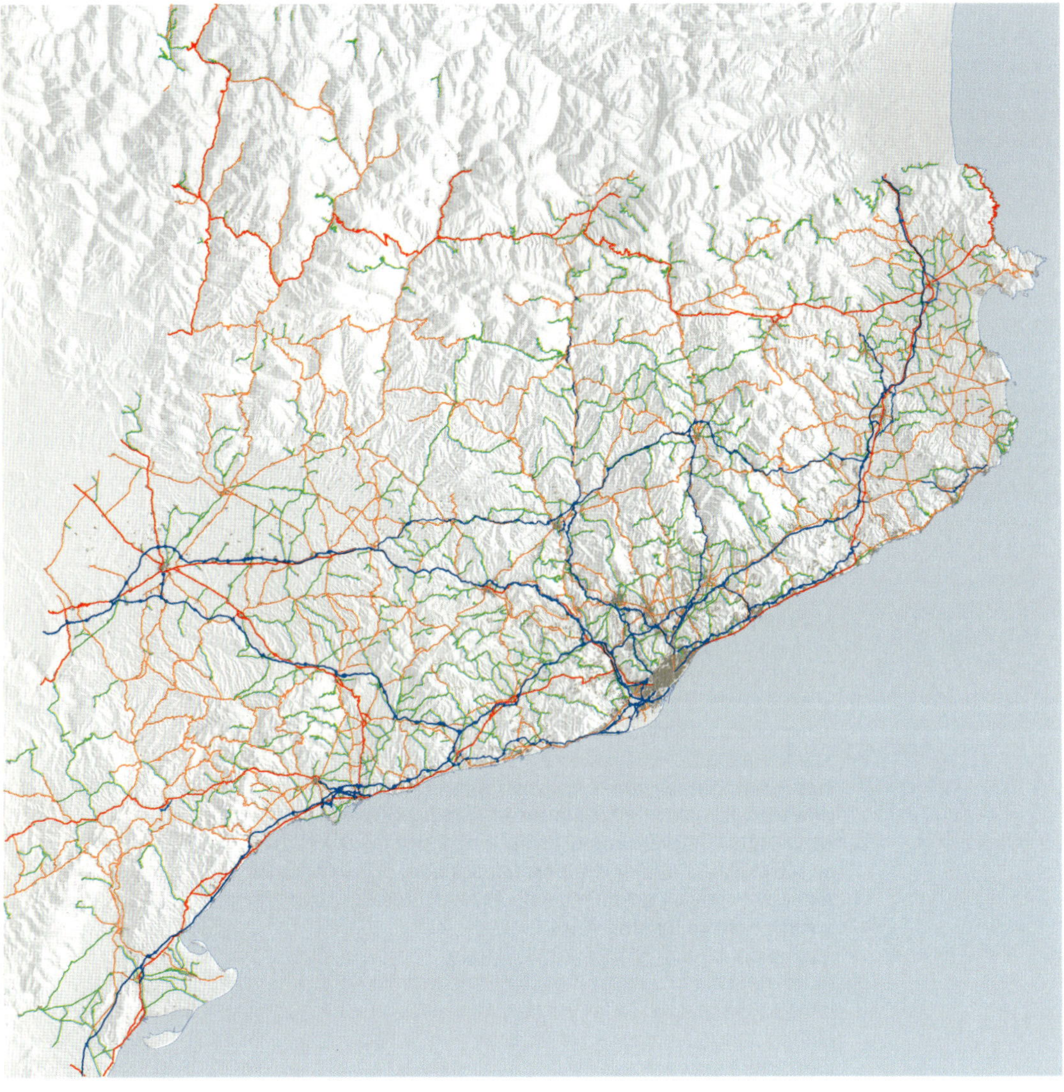

The Modern Architecture of Catalonia

This guide appears in response to a generalized demand that has grown in recent decades for aids that bring an ordered, systematic approach to the architecture of various towns and cities in the broader scope of a territorial culture. This demand is the consequence of the interest that architecture excites among the public, but also of the changes that have occurred in the practice of analysis and criticism in more specialized fields, among students and professionals. Widespread speculation about architecture-related issues has been replaced by interest and curiosity directed at individual buildings. Accordingly, recent years have seen the publication in many of the world's countries and cities of guides that set out to establish an order and criteria for a visit, and occupy a place somewhere between the traditional tourist guide model and more discipline-based works of a historiographic, theoretical or critical nature. As a result, the culture of architecture chose to present a documentary basis that acquainted users with buildings *in situ*, temporally waiving more elaborate or conclusive analyses which, prior to the 1970s, had been expressed in text form, generating some confusion and, above all, consolidating systematically negative thinking about architecture. Between the 1970s and 1980s, architecture ceased to be an object of systematic criticism and became an object of prestige and consumption, the best possible ornament to offer a new world in the process of transformation. This phenomenon spread throughout the Western world, marking the change from a culture in which criticism was pre-eminent to a critical culture in crisis, a culture in which the project and the architecture phenomenon once again rose to supremacy, an acritical culture of anti-crisis.

Direct interest in architecture has not only contributed to its newly acquired prestige, it has also completed displaced, rather than suppressing, instruments of analysis and criticism. This formed the context for the proliferation of guides to the architecture of many of the world's cities and countries, offering a rigorous documentary base that encouraged new forms of analysis and critical guidelines. This approach to architecture was identified with leisure and holidays; travel was a means of direct familiarization with many buildings that previously had been presented in fragmentary form in manuals. This generated a new field of opportunities to become familiar with architecture, to analyse it, enjoy it, appreciate it—and also to consume it. Today's new consumer of architecture may be an attentive observer, a traveller, an enthusiast, a student or an expert. Whatever the case, their instruments for exploring the architecture phenomenon have changed, and students and the public alike have assimilated this change. Guides have become more useful than monographic studies, many of which offer a fragmented view of each work and seem to serve only to identify and build up the architect. Guides offer comprehensive documentary bases about a given city or territory and, as travel handbooks, they are instruments of order, selection and hands-on knowledge. As works of reference, they establish norms and hierarchies for these cities or territories. They constitute documentary compilations containing information which would otherwise remain dispersed in dozens of journals and archives, or be lost and forgotten in the territory. The prestige enjoyed by guides can be identified with the prevalence of information and description as the most important data when approaching architecture, representing the pinnacle of the theory and speculation that dragged on throughout the 19th and into the 20th century, when they ceased to represent any further contribution to real development of the discipline.

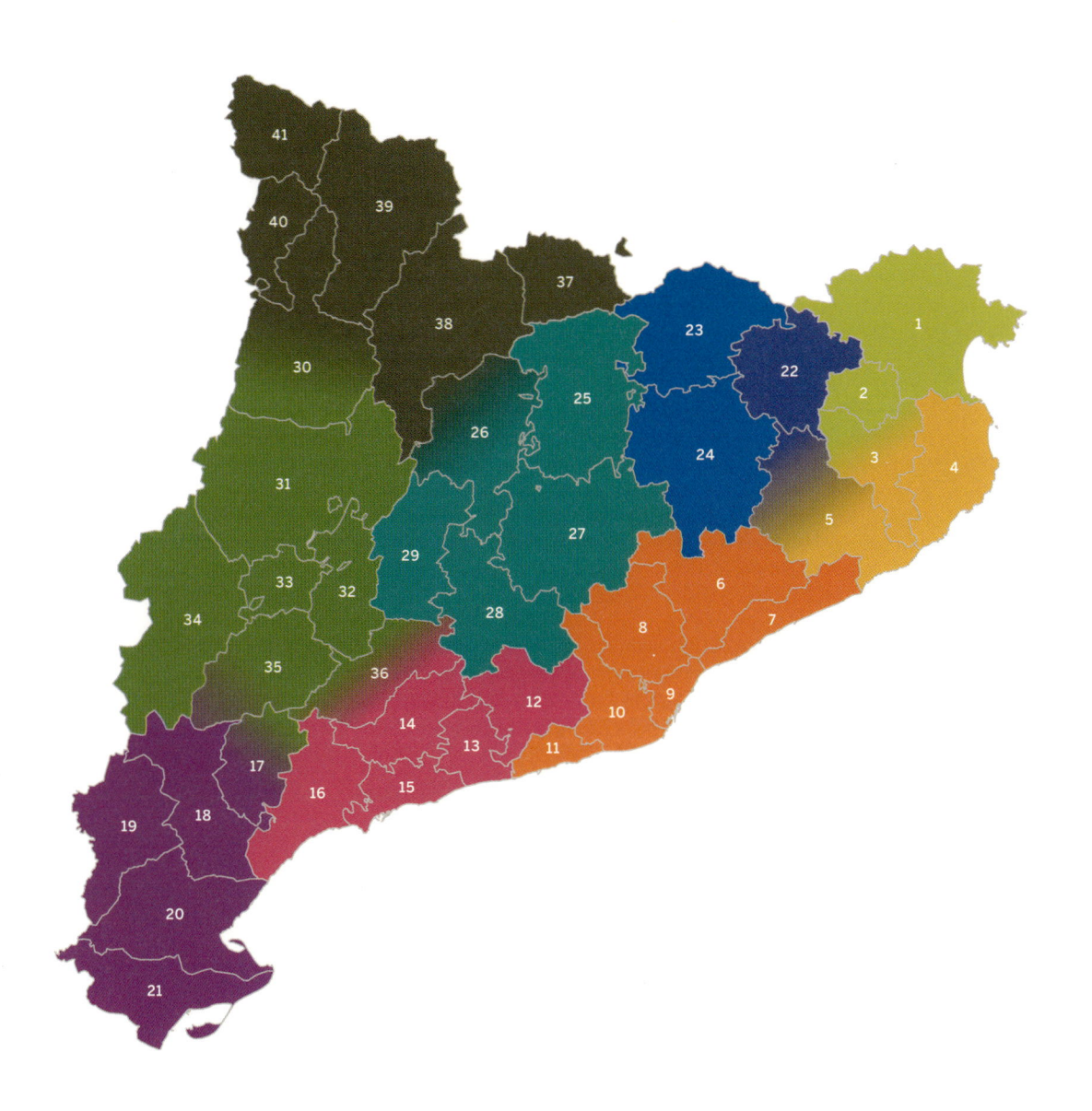

1 Alt Empordà **2** Pla de l'Estany **3** Gironès **4** Baix Empordà **5** Selva **6** Vallès Oriental **7** Maresme **8** Vallès Occidental **9** Barcelonès
10 Baix Llobregat **11** Garraf **12** Alt Penedès **13** Baix Penedès **14** Alt Camp **15** Tarragonès **16** Baix Camp **17** Priorat **18** Ribera d'Ebre
19 Terra Alta **20** Baix Ebre **21** Montsià **22** Garrotxa **23** Ripollès **24** Osona **25** Berguedà **26** Solsonès **27** Bages **28** Anoia **29** Segarra
30 Pallars Jussà **31** Noguera **32** Urgell **33** Pla d'Urgell **34** Segrià **35** Garrigues **36** Conca de Barberà **37** Cerdanya **38** Alt Urgell
39 Pallars Sobirà **40** Alta Ribagorça **41** Val d'Aran

Catalonia. A Guide to the Modern Architecture. 1880-2007 fills the gap that used to exist for Catalan territory. In recent years, numerous guides have been published about specific regions of this territory, with particular attention to the city of Barcelona. The reader will find a comprehensive list of these guides in the bibliography at the end of this book. Yet the Catalan territory as a whole has never before been taken as a theme, which immediately raised the issue of methodology. At present, the identity and scope of this territory is the subject of political debate and struggle, marked furthermore by strong cultural implications, which consequently have a direct affect on the phenomenon of architecture itself. This guide takes Catalonia as a consolidated administrative area that reflects a state of affairs in the political and cultural fields, but it also adopts a historical viewpoint. This provides the point of departure and, within the territory, some forms of organization are prioritized at the expense of others. For reasons of history, Catalonia should be seen as a complex organization of urban cultures rather than as a single territorial culture. In terms of organization, this guide is therefore based on municipalities rather than the structure of provinces (administrative forms associated with the system of organization of the Spanish state) or even that of *comarques*, or counties, linked with the landscape, topography, qualities of the land, and farming and stock-keeping. Provincial organization continues to be the subject of political debate, and county organization is subject to constant change, even today. The municipal structure of Catalonia, however, is apparently consolidated and immovable, as it reflects very clear identities that have been defined by recent history. For this reason, the municipal structure is ideal as a basis for the organization of architecture through Catalan territory, despite the location in the countryside of a few significant works. This guide therefore addresses Catalonia as an overall constellation of municipalities, a reading that enables us to establish very clear correspondences between each building and the history, economy, urban form and identity of each village, town or city.

As regards historical and cultural scope, this guide identifies the culture of modern architecture as manifested in recent decades, since the emergence of the innovations associated with Modernisme, the Catalan Art Nouveau. It therefore also represents an exploration of the distinguishing features of modernity and a search for a series of constants that serve to outline this term and assign it a clear historiographic content. Practically all the examples included in the guide are characterized by their association with some form of progress, be it political, economic or aesthetic, since this association constitutes the essence of modernity and, by extension, modern architecture. Many Modernista architects remodelled old structures, aspiring to a new image and new aesthetic parameters associated with the country's economic progress and the need for new forms of representation. But it is also true that the foremost Modernista architects found an opening to design new constructions that gave them the opportunity to work with spatial concepts that prefigured modern architecture. The architecture of the Second Republic is clearly associated with democratic and social progress, giving rise to organisms with characteristic aesthetic features, but not totally dissociated from previous achievements. In the 1950s, the heroic work of small groups of architects not only managed to break with the habits imposed by the academic culture of Francoism, but these architects were actually capable of producing a new and critical reading of the modern movement, which also generated a series of characteristic forms and procedures. School and health-care buildings built in the 1980s are directly linked to democratic achievements and the new political programmes associated with them. There was a vein of architectures that accurately defined the tastes of

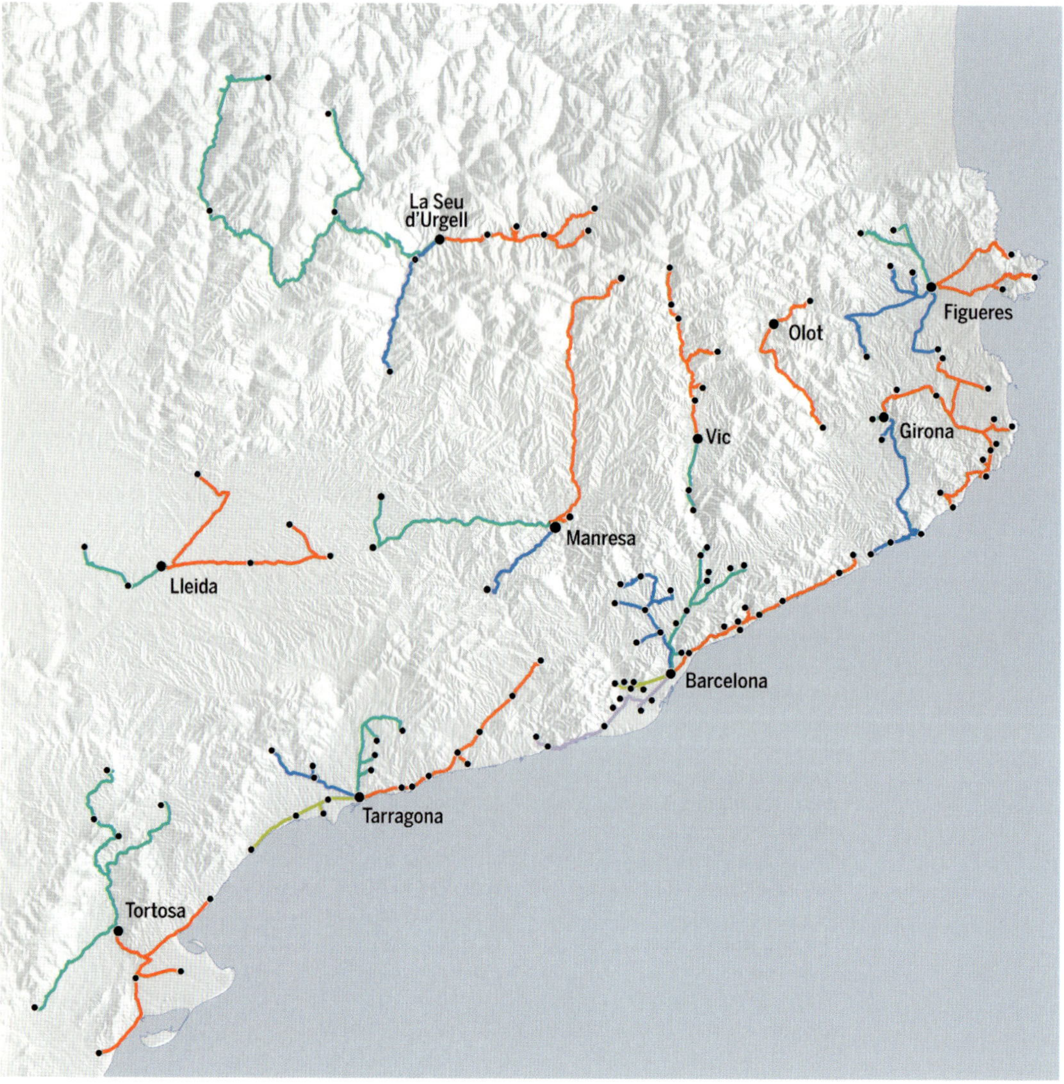
La Seu d'Urgell
Figueres
Olot
Vic
Girona
Lleida
Manresa
Barcelona
Tarragona
Tortosa

their times, though in each case associated with some form of progress. For this reason, the guide leaves out the architecture of the post-war period and certain post-modern manifestations by contemporary architects, more closely associated with an approach that was either backward-looking or else sterile from the viewpoint of architectural progress. The clear identification of modernity is a good critical instrument for identifying the progress of architecture with political or economic progress, or progress in terms of sensibility and taste. This constitutes one of the principal criteria of selection applied in this guide. With the chosen buildings bought together in a single volume, suggesting specific itineraries to visit or study, it is easier to reconstruct an image of architectural modernity in Catalonia, as the study of each building generates connections with the country's cultural, political and economic history.

A systematized approach to the overall Catalan territory is based on a series of topographic maps made on a very small scale. These maps show an image of Catalonia in which it is not possible to identify the most characteristic geographic features of each place, instead offering a series of general lines that allow us to construct a more abstract image of Catalan topography. This summarized image takes the coastline as a datum point, with the highest level situated in the northwest extreme of the triangle, in the Pyrenees of Lleida. On the basis of these elementary data, it is easy to reconstruct an ascending topography that rises to the northwest, forming parallel strips. The capacity for abstraction of these small-scale maps allows an understanding of Catalan relief that is impossible with more detailed topographic maps which record the territory in a more rigorous, particularized way.

The superposition of the structure of municipalities over this general scheme produces three main zones that sweep across Catalonia from the coastline to its highest point. Each of these zones has its own hierarchy of municipalities that define different areas. These areas are described in relation to the capital and its area of influence, served by a system of roads following a dendritic structure. Finally, Catalonia is divided into three zones and 10 areas following the structure of the municipalities and the general features of topographical configuration. The internal structure of this approach defines the index to the guide, divided into 10 chapters. The final structure is outlined below:

The coastal zone. 5 areas
FGR – Figueres area
GRN – Girona area
BCN – Barcelona area
TGN – Tarragona area
TTS – Tortosa area

The inland zone. 4 areas
OLT – Olot area
VIC – Vic area
MNR – Manresa area
LLD – Lleida area

The mountain zone. 1 area
SGL – La Seu d'Urgell area

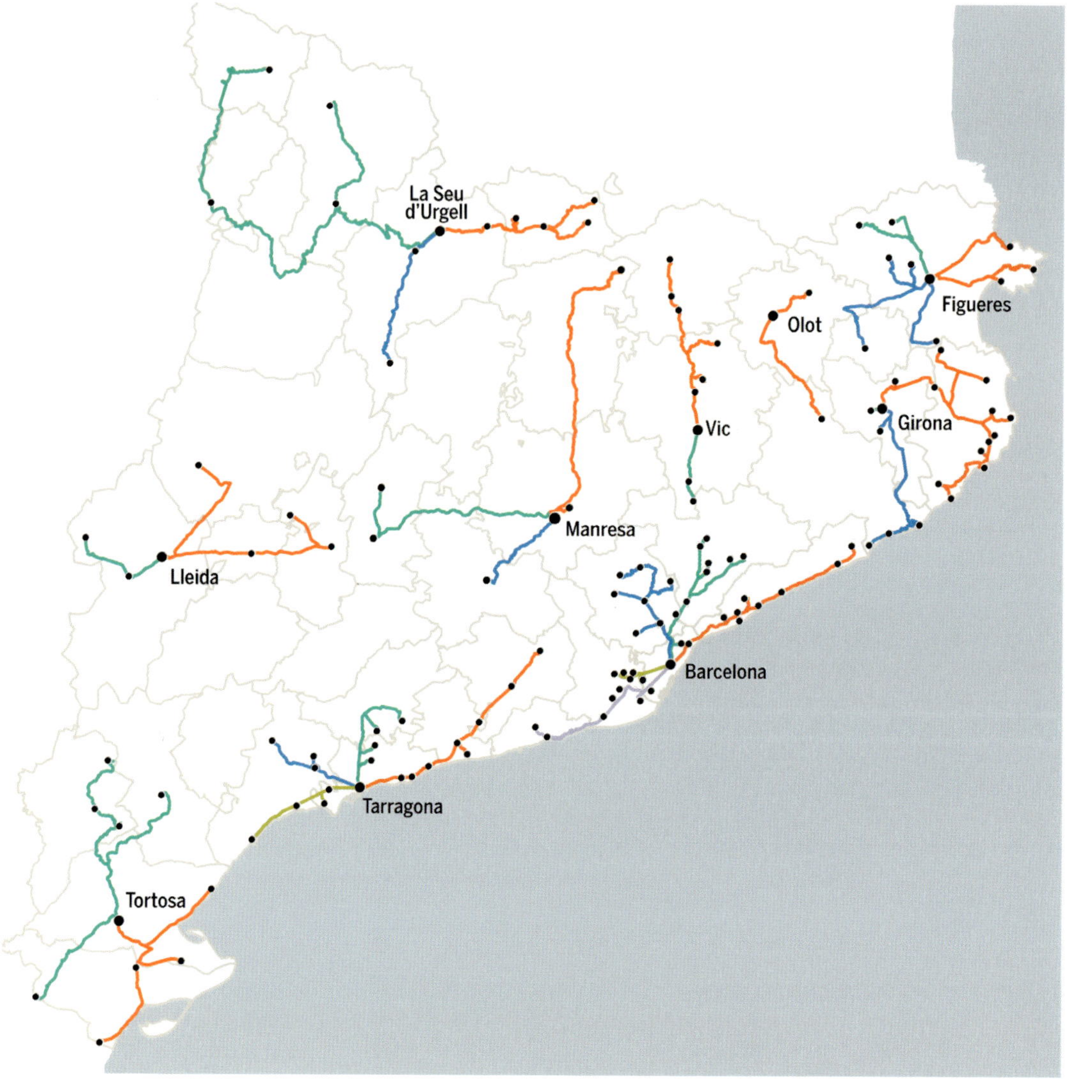
La Seu d'Urgell
Olot
Figueres
Vic
Girona
Lleida
Manresa
Barcelona
Tarragona
Tortosa

This structure covers the entire extension of the territory with ten interlocking cogwheels, if we take into account the road system based around each major town or city. The reader or user of the guide is presented with an ordered reading of the territory that is neither arbitrary nor organized according to conventional divisions; it is designed to produce the optimum organization of the 417 buildings that make up the guide. Travellers can use this structure to orient themselves in Catalan territory, using the recommendations to move about with complete freedom and invent countless itineraries.

The resulting guide constitutes a great documentary database, ordered and brought together into a single volume, taking into account historical factors without going into explicit detail and offering an instrument that provides a structured, selective approach to the best buildings to have been built in Catalonia in the course of a century or more. Any guide should be seen as a valuable source of information rather than a study that completes a jigsaw made up of architecture, geography and history. This guide presents a selection of architecture with a specific geography and history. If the study of architecture starts with the specific and leads up to the general, this guide, as all guides should, provides the scholar with a point of departure to a whole constellation of specific events. And, having reached the end of the volume, made the visits and studied the buildings, the reader or scholar will be well placed to approach a more comprehensive critical study that allows him or her, with full knowledge of the facts, to reach more general theories and conclusions.

Maurici Pla

Maçanet de
Cabrenys
Agullana
El Port
de la Selva
Terrades
Llers
Cadaqués
Figueres
Roses
Saus
Banyoles

FGR – The Figueres area

Territorial scope

The Figueres area practically coincides with the outline of the *comarca* of Alt Empordà, though it includes incursions into Pla de l'Estany and Gironès. It verges to the north on the French border, where the main crossing points are Portbou and La Jonquera. Its eastern edge is the northern coastline of the Costa Brava, where the Gulf of Roses and Cap de Creus are the principal geographic features. To the south, it borders on Gironès and Baix Empordà, two counties beyond the influence of the Pyrenees, and to the west on Garrotxa, which corresponds roughly with the Olot Area in this guide.

Road structure

If you are driving from France, the most direct route to Figueres is via the border crossing point at La Jonquera, on the AP-7 motorway. If you are coming from Portbou, take the N-260 trunk road, a more winding route. The AP-7 motorway continues to Barcelona and the south of Catalonia.

ROUTE 1 of this area, towards the coast, has two branches: one leading to Cadaqués and another to El Port de la Selva. For Cadaqués, take the C-260 via Castelló d'Empúries and then a local road, the GI-614, to Cadaqués. For El Port de la Selva, take the N-260 to Llançà, then the GI-614, which also leads to Cadaqués.

ROUTE 2, heading north, starts out on the N-II trunk road to Maçanet de Cabrenys and Agullana, and then takes the local roads GI-502 and GI-501. This route follows the layout of the AP-7 motorway towards La Jonquera, though the motorway has no turnoffs to the local roads.

ROUTE 3, which heads west, has four different branches, leading to Llers, Terrades, Banyoles and Saus. Llers is very close to Figueres, and both Llers and Terrades are on the GI-510. For Banyoles, take the N-260, via Besalú. For Saus, take the AP-7 motorway that continues to Barcelona, turning off near Orriols.

If you are heading for Girona, south of Figueres, take the AP-7 motorway, and for Olot, to the west, take the N-260. The AP-7 motorway and the N-260 form the basis of the road network throughout the area and are references on all the routes.

Maçanet de Cabrenys
Agullana
El Port de la Selva
Terrades
Llers
Cadaqués
Figueres
Roses
Olot
Saus
Banyoles
Girona

Municipalities	Comarca	Surface area (municipality)	Population (2001)
FIGUERES	Alt Empordà	19.3 km²	33,064 inhabitants
ROUTE 1			
ROSES	Alt Empordà	45.9 km²	12,726 inhabitants
CADAQUÉS	Alt Empordà	26.4 km²	2,024 inhabitants
EL PORT DE LA SELVA	Alt Empordà	41.6 km²	760 inhabitants
ROUTE 2			
MAÇANET DE CABRENYS	Alt Empordà	67.9 km²	666 inhabitants
AGULLANA	Alt Empordà	27.7 km²	668 inhabitants
ROUTE 3			
LLERS	Alt Empordà	21.3 km²	1,012 inhabitants
TERRADES	Alt Empordà	21.0 km²	210 inhabitants
BANYOLES	Pla de l'Estany	11.1 km²	14,232 inhabitants
SAUS	Alt Empordà	11.4 km²	686 inhabitants

001

ROGER HOUSE
PRIVATE DWELLING

Josep Azemar i Pont
1896

C/ Monturiol, 9 - Figueres

Josep Azemar trained at the Escola Provincial d'Arquitectura de Barcelona, under the direction of Elies Rogent, at a time of widespread ideological cohesion in the field of modern construction and compositional proceedings, and a firm rejection of the Neo-Classical tradition. Roger House, one of Azemar's early works, responds to the programme for a private dwelling in a central street in Figueres. The house demonstrates Azemar's interest in highlighting the central volume of the building by means of a projecting tribune supported by two slender stone columns that continue in the composition of the railings. The window frames and the rusticated ashlars at the ends reflect a desire to simplify the constructional solutions and their expression. The crown presents a glazed gallery that marks a brief, accelerated cadence from one side to the other. The upper cornice displays corbels and the silhouette of the tiles, marking the upper edge of the façade.

SALLERAS HOUSE
CAFÉ-RESTAURANT CONTINENTAL

Josep Azemar i Pont
1904

Rambla, 16 - Figueres

Situated at the northern end of the Rambla Nova in Figueres, Salleras House responds to a programme for a three-storey private dwelling. Azemar adapted his design to the client's requirements, emphasizing the central part of the façade with a glazed tribune on the first floor, which is compensated by the visible crown elements at the ends. The order of the first floor is quite different to that of the second, though the two are unified by the plane of the façade, ornamented with floral motifs. The crown unifies the breadth of the whole building by means of a succession of small pinnacles. Azemar plays constantly with the balance between the centre and the edges, constructing a composition of two principal hierarchies. The Café-restaurant Continental remains intact on the ground floor with its painted and gilt decoration, conserving many small-scale elements of the original building.

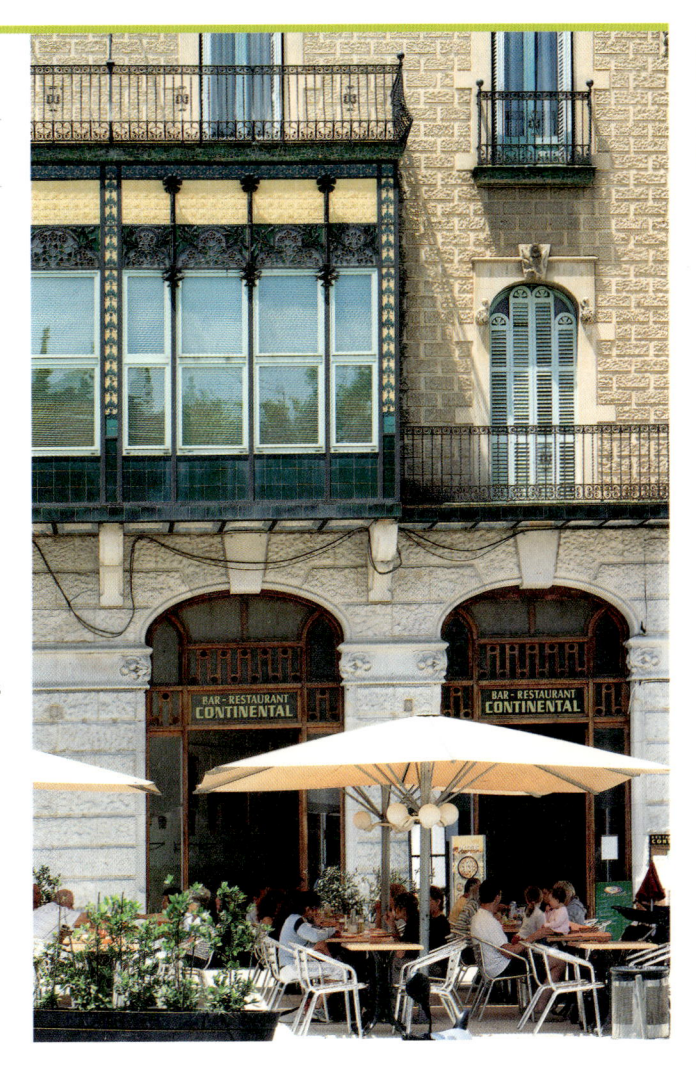

003

FIGUERES MUNICIPAL ABATTOIR
COUNTY HISTORICAL ARCHIVE

Josep Azemar i Pont
1907

Pl. de l'Escorxador - Figueres

SUBSEQUENT INTERVENTIONS:
Jordi Casadevall, 1985-1990. County Historical Archive.

004

MAS I ROGER HOUSE
PRIVATE DWELLING

Josep Azemar i Pont
1910

C/ Caamaño, 9 - Pl. de la Palmera
C/ Monturiol, 10 - Figueres

A programme for a private dwelling in the centre of Figueres giving onto a square and two side streets allowed Azemar to apply rigorously scientific construction criteria. The base is stone built and embraces the entire ground floor, perforated by semi-circular arches. The volume of the house is rendered. A railing runs the entire length of the façade overlooking the square, supported by two small built volumes that define a porch. The crown combines the slopes of the tiled roof with small towers at the corners, and each opening is framed by elements at the small scale that set it apart, according to its respective function and position.

005

GUILLAMET HOUSE
APARTMENT BUILDING

Emili Blanch
1935

C/ Ample, 14 - C/ Sant Rafael, 22 - C/ Santa Llúcia, 1
Figueres

In accordance with the ideological guidelines of Modernisme, Azemar brings an austere response to programmes for social buildings, where structural and ornamental criteria adopt different hierarchies to those applied to private housing. The abattoir, situated in a hitherto peripheral position in the town, comprises three brick-built volumes supported by wrought iron pillars, with a symmetrical arrangement that is reminiscent of the layout of a basilica. The volumes are left bare, and the channel-tiled roofs adopt two or four slopes. All the decoration is concentrated in the openings in the form of bevelled features, projecting reliefs and ceramic units. The openings of the central volume take the form of semi-circular arches, whereas those in the side volumes adopt abstract forms or arabesque patterns. Azemar follows the same order of hierarchies in all buildings for public institutions.

This four-storey building in the outer ring of the old town contains two dwellings per floor. The apartment on the inside of the plot occupies two bays running between two façades and the other, at the front, overlooks all three streets. Blanch highlights the upper volume of the dwellings, emphasizing the two street corners with great windows of three lights and addressing the three façades as plain surfaces with openings effected in them. Blanch applies a purist rhetoric to buildings in growing urban fabrics, where the only compositional element that stands out are the meticulous patterns of the ironwork railings.

DALÍ THEATRE AND MUSEUM
REMODELLING OF THE TEATRE PRINCIPAL AS A MUSEUM

Salvador Dalí, Joaquín Ros de Ramis, Alejandro Bonaterra
Emilio Pérez Piñero (geodesic dome)
1970-1974

Pl. Gala-Salvador Dalí - Figueres

SUBSEQUENT INTERVENTIONS:
Salvador Dalí, Oscar Tusquets, 1974. Mae West Room
Daniel Freixes, Vicente Miranda, Eulàlia González, 1995. New halls.

The Teatre Principal, built in 1849 by the architect Roca Bros, was practically destroyed when Francoist troops bombed Republicans fleeing to France. The idea of remodelling it as Dalí's personal museum was promoted by the then Mayor of Figueres, Ramon Guardiola, who convinced the Ministries of Tourism and Housing to support the project. The theatre-museum was designed not just to exhibit works of art, but also as an architectural recreation in which Dalí expressed his wild world in spatial terms. However, particular mention must be made of the fifth floor, which contains an exhibition of masterpieces from the painter's private collection: *Saint Paul* by El Greco; *The Doctor's Visit*, by Gérard Dou; *Portrait of Napoleon*, by Meissonier; the *Court of the Alhambra*, by Marià Fortuny; *Cemetery*, by Modest Urgell; *Suitcase*, by Marcel Duchamp, and a facsimile of Piranesi's *Prisons*, among others. In 1974, the architect Oscar Tusquets worked with Dalí on the Mae West Room, a scenographic montage that recreates the actress's face by means of an arrangement of clearly defined architectural elements.

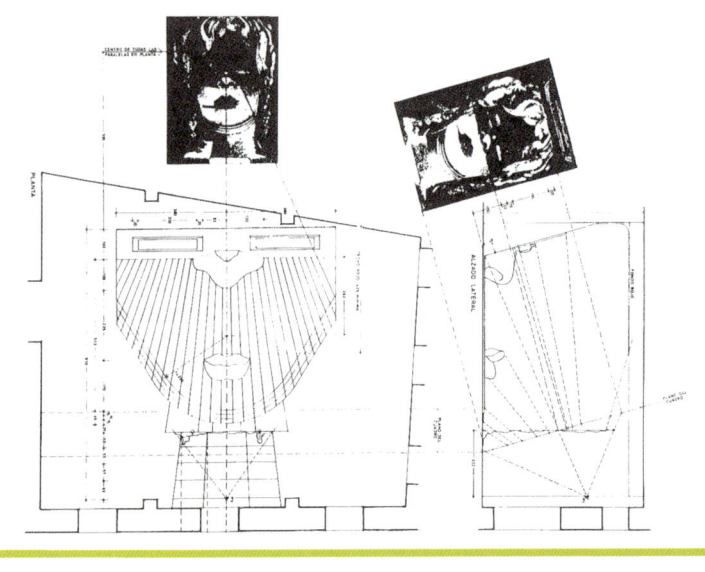

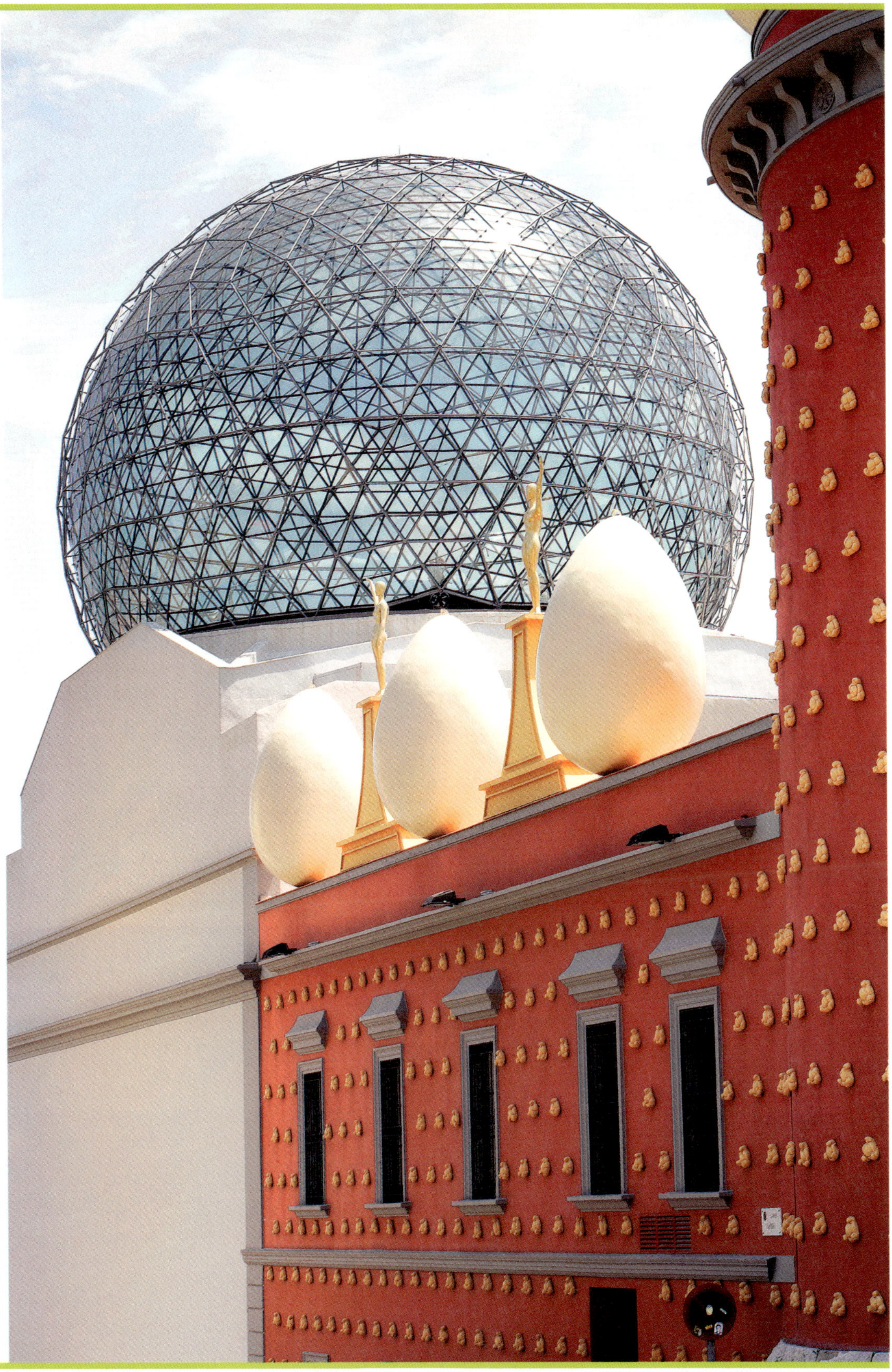

FGR

007

ROZES HOUSE
SINGLE-FAMILY DWELLING

José Antonio Coderch de Sentmenat, Manuel Valls
1961-1962

Av. Díaz Pacheco, 184 - Roses

The house is situated in a prime position: a foothold in the Gulf of Roses, with views of the sea on three sides. Coderch chose to terrace the layout from the entrance to the furthest point, following the downward slope of the rocky topography to give the house a lengthwise distribution. Two routes are organized around a patio beside the entrance: the first, facing south-east, contains the sequence of living room, dining room and kitchen; the second contains the garage and the servants' quarters. The two sequences meet at the point where the series of bedrooms begins, ending with the master bedroom. The house configures its orientation, making all the rooms east-facing and turning its rear façade to look westwards, though it is linked to the site by the direct contact between the terraces and the rocks, reaching almost down to the sea.

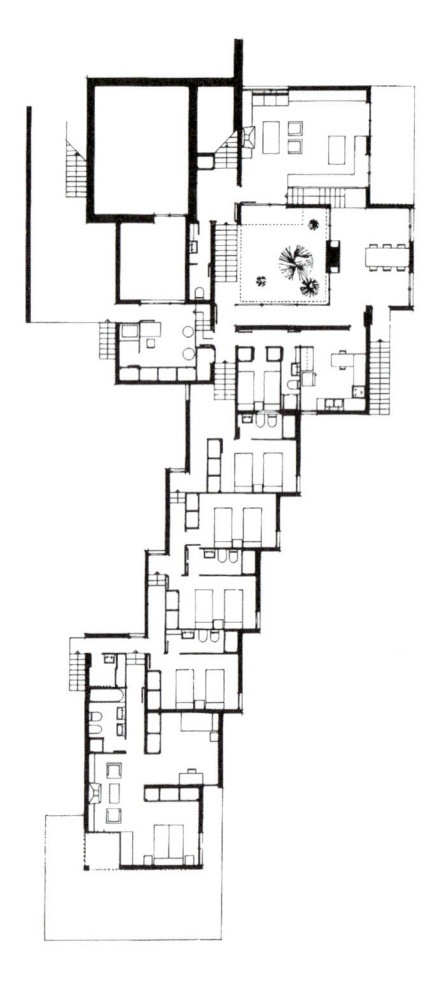

CLOS-RAHOLA HOUSE
SINGLE-FAMILY DWELLING

Víctor Rahola
1971-1974

Cala la Pelosa - Cap de Norfeu - Roses

The house stands on a large sloping site, where the presence of the Mediterranean melds with a Pyrenean foothill landscape. A series of independent volumes is scattered across the descending terrain. The garage leads via two runs of steps to a garden that brings visitors to the front door, which separates the living room from the rest of the house. The kitchen is connected to a rear court in which a single olive tree grows. The living room leads to a small volume on top of the house that holds the master bedroom. The children's bedrooms form a wing perpendicular to the coast, advancing towards the sea. The horizontal nature of the volumes is emphasized by the picture windows, protected by shutters. The house colonizes the plot by means of small terraces that blend in with the contour lines.

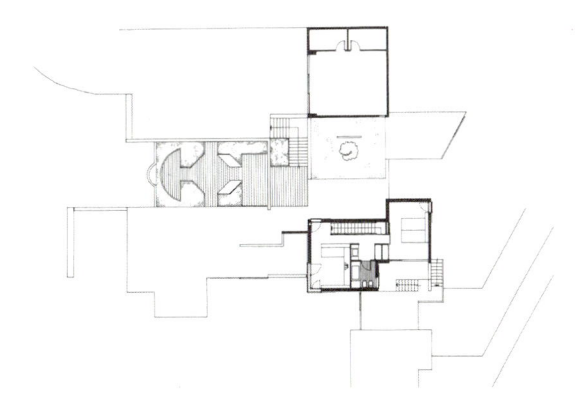

009

VILLAVECCHIA HOUSE
SINGLE-FAMILY DWELLING

Federico Correa, Alfons Milà
1955

Riba del Pixot - C/ Eduard Marquina, 7 - Cadaqués

010

SENILLOSA HOUSE
SINGLE-FAMILY DWELLING

José Antonio Coderch de Sentmenat, Manuel Valls
1955-1956

C/ Guillem Bruguera, 6 - C/ Eliseu Meifrén
Cadaqués

On this singular site with a square floor plan and limited dimensions, just one practicable façade and four floors, Coderch came up with an imaginative solution for a single-family dwelling with five bedrooms. The structure is a stone casing that acts as a retaining wall. The four levels are laid out in two bays: the larger holds the parking area (ground floor), the master bedroom (first floor), dining room (second floor) and living room (third floor). The smaller bay houses a single bedroom on each floor. The stairway communicates the streets below and above through the entire dwelling.

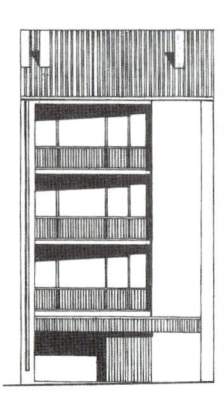

011

PÉREZ DEL PULGAR CHALET
SINGLE-FAMILY DWELLING

Francisco Juan Barba Corsini
1957-1958

Torre Zariquiey area - Cadaqués

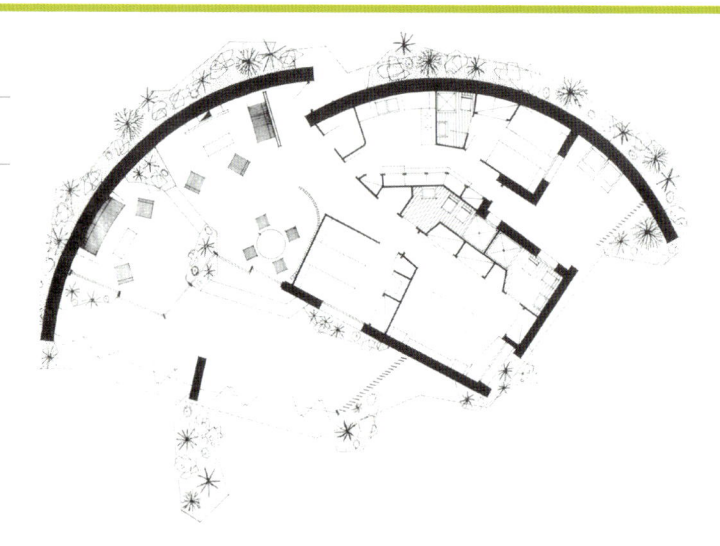

This house represents the desire to overcome the contradictions between local construction procedures and the Modernista rhetoric that was so fashionable in the Cadaqués of the 1950s. The authors took as their reference traditional construction elements (brick walls, tiled roofs) and applied them imaginatively to the search for a truly genuine figurativeness. The house is divided crosswise into two bays that produce a clear interior organization. The living room forms a shady empty space on the third floor and offers a contrasting image to the rhetorical façade of the house to its left.

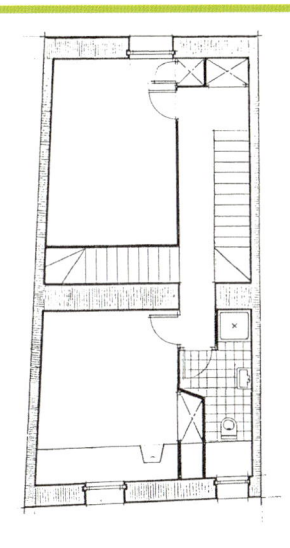

The floor plan of the house interprets two basic elements that shape the site: the north wind and the views of the two bays to the south. Two concave walls of Cadaqués stone support a concrete floor slab that serves for the whole house, leaving a small chink of light right around the perimeter. The living room is given pride of place with regard to the views, and a system of bare brick walls forms the facings of the bedrooms. The planimetric configuration prevents the house seeming entirely closed and creates a domestic atmosphere that shuns conventional notions of interior space.

MARY CALLERY HOUSE
REMODELLING AND EXTENSION OF AN EXISTING CONSTRUCTION

Peter Harnden, Lanfranco Bombelli
1961-1962

C/ Roses, 8 - Cadaqués

In 1961, the sculptor Mary Callery bought a small plot of land in the old part of Cadaqués, occupied by a two-storey construction, with three sides giving onto three narrow streets and a courtyard to the rear. The programme suggested by the client led Harnden and Bombelli to position the living room, kitchen and dining room on the ground floor, in direct contact with the courtyard. The living room is double height and communicates with an intermediate floor occupied by a bedroom and its bathroom. The first floor accommodates a second living room and another bedroom. The newly constructed top floor rises above its neighbours to offer views of the village and the bay, and contains the artist's bedroom and a large terrace. In this way, the architects addressed the issue of maintaining the privacy of the rear garden and raising the house above the old fabric of the village centre, while respecting its structural aspects.

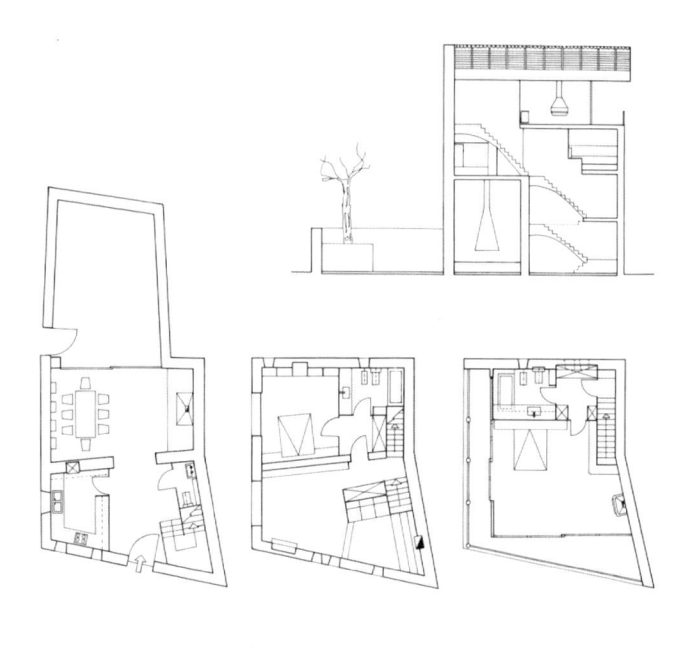

FASQUELLE HOUSE
SINGLE-FAMILY DWELLING

Peter Harnden, Lanfranco Bombelli
1968

Portlligat - Cadaqués

The house was built in response to a commission by a publisher who formed part of the small colony of North Americans to settle in Cadaqués in the 1960s, set apart from local life in a microcosm of their own, though physically present in the town. Harnden and Bombelli designed a house that clearly expressed the defining features of their client's culture, combining solutions borrowed from the North American domestic tradition with some traditional construction procedures characteristic of the place and the country. The house is organized by means of a system of parallel stone walls that are left bare on both the outside and the interior. These walls support a series of ridge roofs starting with a ridge beam supported by brick ledges with a bearing function. The ridge beam coincides with the principal axis of distribution, laying the house out crosswise to the wall system.

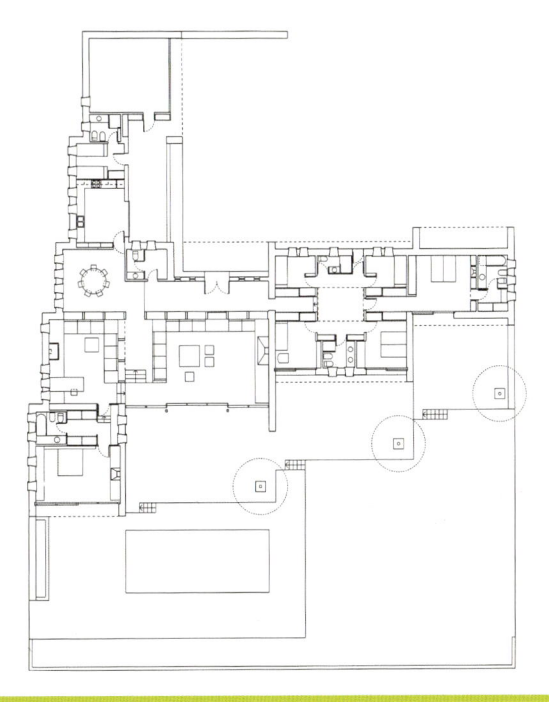

JOVER-SALA HOUSE
SINGLE-FAMILY DWELLING

Beth Galí, Màrius Quintana
1990-1992

C/ Llevant - Plot 5 - Les Figuerasses sector
El Port de la Selva

The composition of the house adopts a specific form in response to the conditioning factors of the place: a small terrain on the edge of a residential development and the village centre, with a 40-degree slope. Three walls faithfully follow the contour lines, forming two bays that organize the whole house: the living room, the kitchen and the dining room above, with great views of the monastery of Sant Pere de Roda, and the bedrooms on the lower floor, with direct access to the outside and the swimming pool. The house obeys the initial approach rhetorically at all points: the walls, in which openings are freely effected according to the demands of circulations, are separated from the alignment of the windows as required by the initial layout. Seen from a distance, the crown of the bearing walls emerges above the thick pinewood that surrounds the house and reproduces the lines of the pre-existing topography in architectural terms.

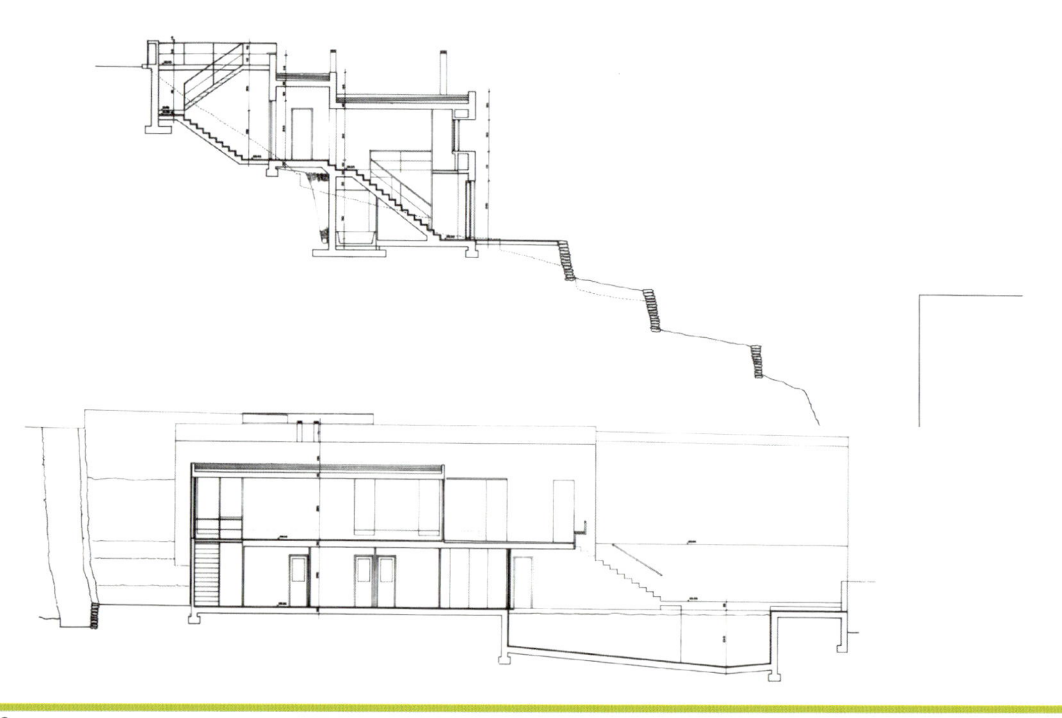

MARGARIDA FONTDEVILA HOUSE
SINGLE-FAMILY DWELLING

Ignasi de Solà-Morales, Javier López del Castillo
1997-1999

Carrer B – Plot 24 - Morasol residential development - El Port de la Selva

The house interprets a very simple programme for a single-family dwelling on a small plot near the sea, in a place characterized by old terraces originally built to grow vines and subsequently destroyed by the growth of a pine forest. The reference in the composition is provided by the sea views and protection from the north wind. From the starting point of a wall along the north-facing edge, the construction is defined by a further two walls that form a fan, generating areas of differing dimensions and heights. The first bay, larger and more open, houses the living room, the stairs to the first floor and a large terrace. The second, smaller and more closed, contains the kitchen and dining room. The front door is situated at the meeting point of the two bays. The upper floor repeats this symbiosis between dimension and use, with the master bedroom in the small bay and the children's bedrooms in the large one.

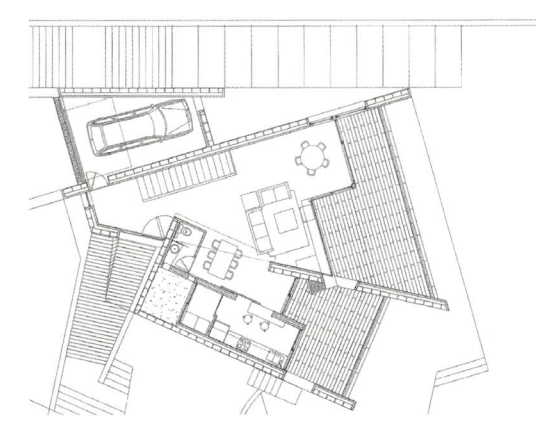

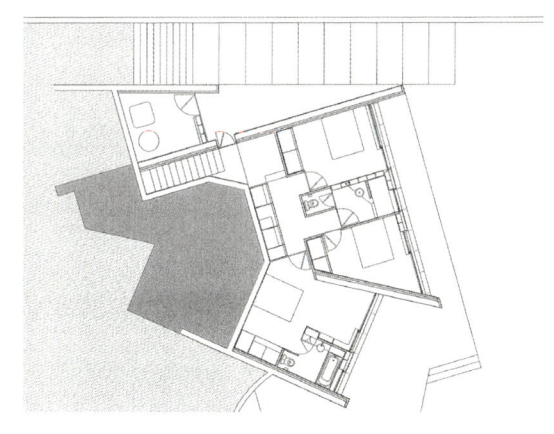

016

HEADQUARTERS OF THE UNIÓ MAÇANETENCA
COOPERATIVE BUILDING

Josep Azemar i Pont
1906

Pl. de la Vila, 6 - Maçanet de Cabrenys

This building is the headquarters of the livestock farmers' cooperative in a small Pyrenean village, very close to the French border. The building occupies a large site and rises above the neighbouring houses, presenting a large plane of frontage that Azemar arranged according to the criteria of construction rigour that characterized his training. The ground floor comprises three semicircular arches that reveal the construction process: a low stone base, dressed stone pilasters and the actual arches, comprising three courses of bare brick. Above them, a rendered stretch incorporates seven tall narrow windows and the inscription of the institution's name on a long strip that runs the length of all seven. The second floor comprises bare brick wall with three openings and a central balcony. At the crown, the cornices of the roof are interrupted by four merlons that return to the order of the ground floor.

017

AGULLANA SCHOOLS

Josep Azemar i Pont
1910

Ctra. de la Vajol, 4 - Agullana

The programme for a public building allowed Azemar to deploy all of his mastery in his recourse to the various orders that make up the construction. It comprises two volumes raised above street level, highlighting the stone base, made up of a system of steps and ramps leading to the ground floor. A small central volume interrupts the symmetry of the whole, as the main door is positioned on the right. The volumes of the classrooms are rendered, forming two differentiated strips. The two orders of windows point up this difference: those on the ground floor are broad with segmental arches, while the small narrow windows on the upper floor are flanked by the false crenellation of the crown. The small central volume breaks the lengthwise order of the building with a tympanum that marks the entrance to the institution and four large windows that rest directly on the base.

018

HOUSE AND STUDIO FOR A PHOTOGRAPHER

Carles Ferrater
1992-1993

Road from Llampaies to Camallera (GI-623)
Llampaies - Saus

019

BIO VILLA
SINGLE-FAMILY DWELLING

Enric Ruiz-Geli
2003-2004

C/ Sant Jordi, 24 - Montserrat residential development - Llers

The house is designed as a place to encourage events that transcend the commonplaces of domestic life and the demands of the typological legacy of architecture. It is a concrete surface with a C-shaped section that rises in a spiral, forming four sloping stretches along which the necessary elements are arranged to accommodate these activities. The ramps are supported by blind side walls and, with their single point of support, form large projections. The genesis of the house was determined by the operative logic of the computer programme used.

020

MARE DE DÉU DE LA SALUT SOCIAL HEALTH CENTRE
SISTERS OF CHARITY OF SAINT ANNE

Francesc Hereu, Joaquim Español
1995-1998

Ctra. de la Salut - Terrades

The house comprises various volumes fitted together in the style of rural constructions. The first, pre-existing block, a stone-built granary with a square floor plan, was turned into a living room. The bedroom volume is separated from the first, and a third, situated between the two, forms the entrance and accommodates the dining room and kitchen. Inserted behind these elements is the studio, with measurements stipulated by the client. The roof section includes an overhead opening for light and a window in the west side, which lets the warm evening light into the studio. The guest pavilion, a little wooden structure, stands on the opposite edge of the garden.

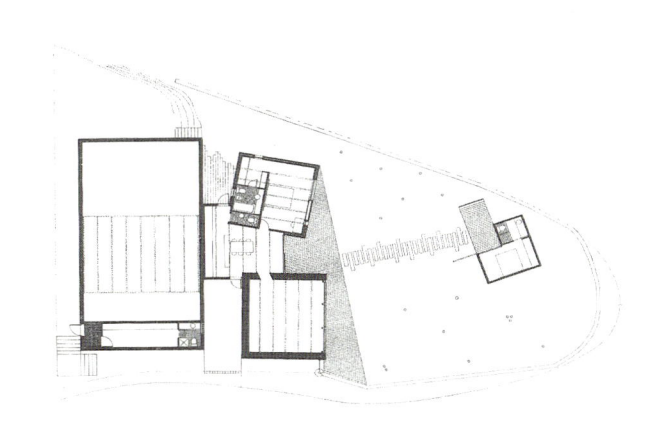

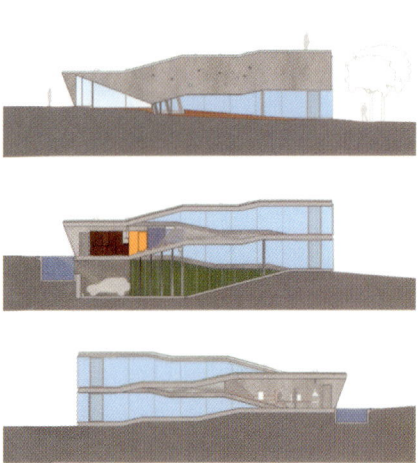

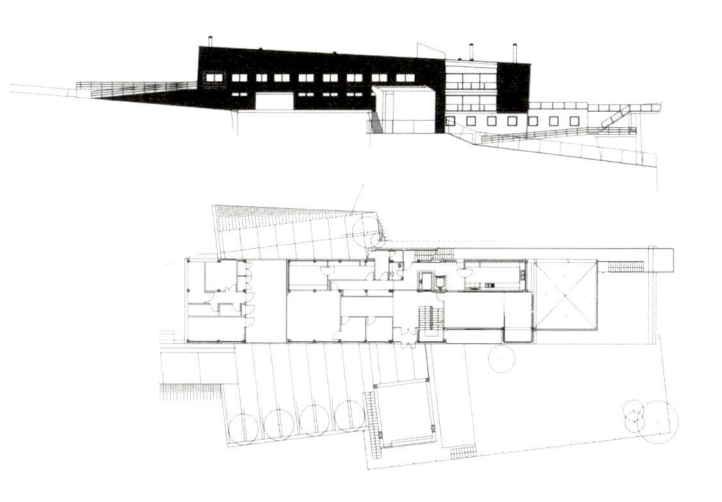

The building is located in a wooded area near the sanctuary of La Salut, on a steeply sloping plot that is very exposed to the elements. A linear building was designed following a line perpendicular to the contours, with the façade turned to face south-east to make sunlighting compatible with good views. The process of adapting the building to the slope produced three displaced levels that contain the three functional modules. The building emerges from the hillside like the prow of a ship to capture the sunlight and views. The terracing of the floors ensures their discreet engagement with the setting.

021

VILANOVA-CULLELL HOUSE
SINGLE-FAMILY DWELLING

Albert Illescas, Jeroni Moner
1972

Pg. Mossèn Constans, 217 - Banyoles

022

HOUSING BLOCK NO. 10 IN THE OLYMPIC VILLAGE

Josep Fuses, Joan Maria Viader
1990-1992

C/ Lluís Companys, 23-27 - Banyoles

The general project approach sought to avoid an overly urban configuration and apply a series of criteria to make the building blend into its natural surroundings.
The housing complex is divided into three blocks joined only on the second floor, which forms the cornice. The duplex apartments are located in the central block, with a perimeter similar to that of a leaf, at the ends of which there are passages to the courtyard inside the street block. The treatment of the façades also seeks to introduce variety and avoid repetition by combining natural sedimentary stone, white rendering and painted metal sheet.

023

CEIP PLA DE L'AMETLLER
INFANTS' AND PRIMARY SCHOOL

José Miguel Roldán, Mercè Berengué
2001-2002

C/ Formiga, 117 - Banyoles

The design for this house applies an L-shaped floor plan with a south-facing bisector to a traditional typology, a series of variants intended to transform the dwelling as seen from the street. The living room, housed in one of the wings, is separated from the rest of the house by a glazed corridor. The stairway leading to the first floor extends beyond the main footprint, like the children's bedroom, which projects over the ground floor. On the second floor, a small studio raises the top edge of the corner. The house presents a series of blind, bare brick volumes in an atypical interpretation of the sensibility that characterized the architecture of the period.

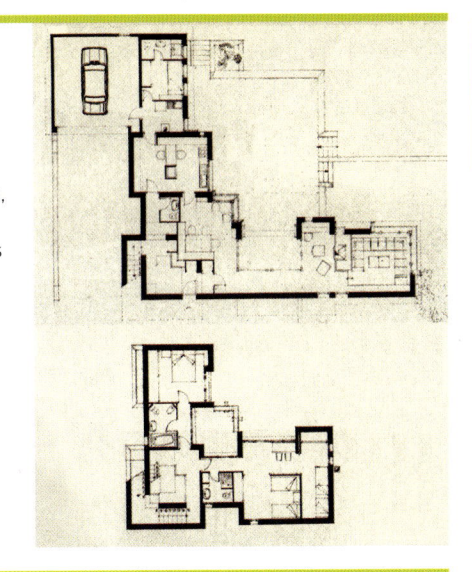

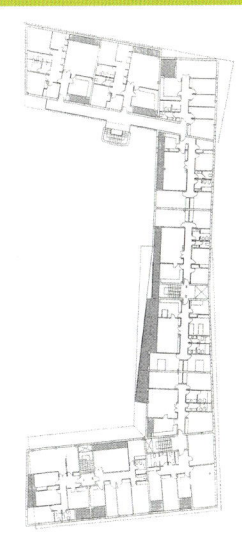

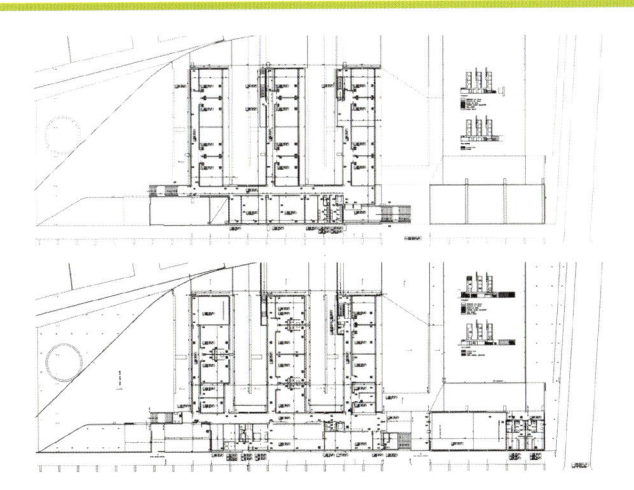

The school stands on a completely flat site to the south of Banyoles, furrowed by the sluices that regulate the water level of the town's lake. The project takes as its reference the park beside the plot and the character that the rural constructions give to the landscape. The communal activities are situated in an arm that turns its façade onto the park, from which the three two-storey classroom blocks are laid out. The entire organization respects the layout of the existing sluices and paths, and presents to the park a staggered façade reminiscent of the industrial constructions that are so frequent on local farmland.

Figueres 37

024

PESQUERA D'EN MALAGELADA
FISHING PAVILION
JUDGES POST

Jeroni Moner, Joaquim Figa, Josep Riera
1990-1991

Pg. Darder – Fishing pavilion no. 16
Banyoles Lake - Banyoles

025

ELS BANYS VELLS
BAR KIOSK

Josep Miàs
1995-1996

Pg. de Lluís Maria Vidal, 25
Banyoles Lake - Banyoles

026

BOAT RACE FINISHING LINE PAVILION

Josep Cargol, Ricard Turon
2001-2003

Finishing line area - Banyoles Lake - Banyoles

With the rowing competition of the 1992 Olympic Games in mind, the architects designed two lakeside constructions housing installations for the judges who were to monitor the starting line. The Pesquera d'en Malagelada, situated on a headland ideal for this purpose, occupies a triangular floor plan, and its bisector points towards the starting line. The metal structure supports a small terrace that projects out over the water. The architects took as their inspiration the 19th-century fishing pavilions, constructions that meet all kinds of needs as well as fishing and leisure activities.

The programme addresses the insertion of a bar-restaurant in a place characterized by natural elements: water and trees. The project invents a completely new artificial topography comprising successive sections and creates a new building that sets this specific spot apart. The kiosk is designed to house the activities of an open-air bar and restaurant, producing only very small enclosed spaces. The activities are arranged in orderly fashion in the various resulting spaces: the dynamism of the leisure activities in the urban façade and the contemplative spots overlooking the lake.

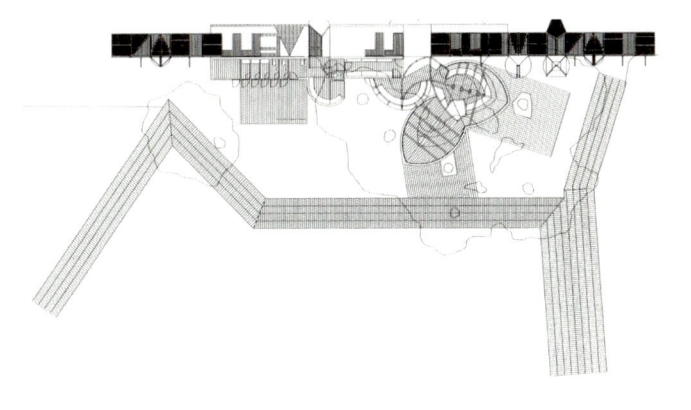

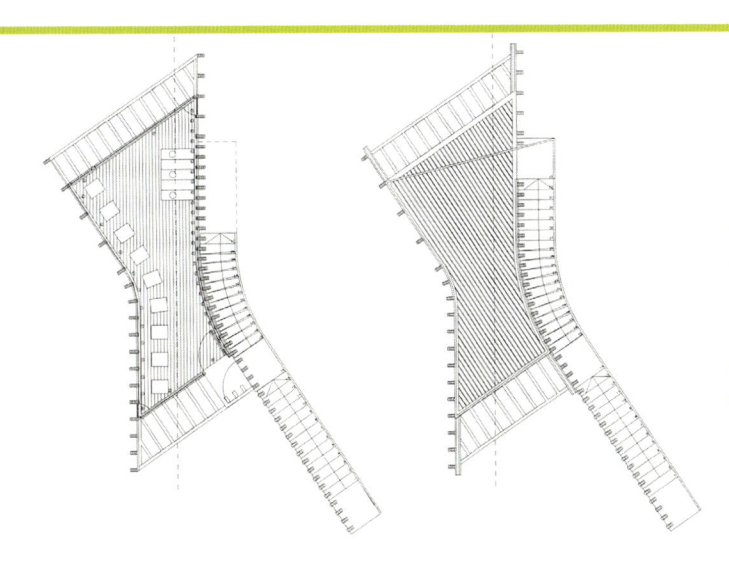

The project forms part of a more general landscape intervention to design the finishing line area of the regatta course for the World Rowing Championships and for subsequent permanent use. The observation deck is a vertical, transparent, lightweight timber structure anchored among the rushes in the water. The tower-observation deck, a construction raised up on concrete micropiles driven 15 metres into the bed of the lake, floats above the surface on 65 timber pillars, treated and laminated up to the seven-metre level. The new construction is like an updated fishing pavilion, incorporated into the lakeside landscape.

Vilopriu
Sant Julià de Ramis
Torroella de Montgrí
La Pera
Salt
Girona
Pals
Begur
Fornells de la Selva
Palafrugell
Mont-ras
Vall-llobrega
Palamós
Santa Cristina d'Aro
Sant Feliu de Guíxols
Tossa de Mar
Lloret de Mar
Blanes

GRN – The Girona Area

Territorial scope

The Girona Area is based around the *comarca* of Gironès and, to the east, covers almost all of Baix Empordà, as far as the Costa Brava. To the south, it makes a slight incursion into the county of Selva, in the form of a small strip along the Mediterranean. It therefore centres on the city of Girona and extends mostly eastwards. The only important municipality it includes to the west of Girona is Salt. To the south, this area enters the counties of Vallès Oriental and Maresme, and to the west it borders on Garrotxa and Osona, which, in this guide, are included in the inland areas.

Road structure

If you are driving from Barcelona, the AP-7 motorway leads directly to the city of Girona before continuing north to Figueres and the border crossing point at La Jonquera. If you are coming from France and cross the border at Portbou, take the N-260 to Figueres and pick up the motorway. There is no major road from Girona to Olot. The best option is to take the local GI-514 road to Banyoles, and then the GI-524 to Olot. Communication between Figueres and Olot is rather easier, as the N-260 from Portbou carries on to Olot after Figueres.

ROUTE 1 in this area covers the northern part of Baix Empordà, including the municipalities of this part of the Costa Brava. In Girona, take the N-II to Sant Julià de Ramis, and then pick up the C-66 county road to Palafrugell, via Flaçà and La Bisbal de l'Empordà. From Palafrugell it is very easy to reach Begur, Pals, Palamós, Mont-ras and Vall-llobrega. Heading north from La Bisbal de l'Empordà, you will find Vilopriu and Torroella de Montgrí. The coast road south from Palamós will take you to Santa Cristina d'Aro and Sant Feliu de Guíxols. Palafrugell and La Bisbal de l'Empordà are therefore the main towns of reference on this route.

ROUTE 2 has just one town, Salt, which is very close to Girona, on its west side, on the N-141 road.

ROUTE 3 leads directly southwards from Girona to Blanes via a series of local roads. Head for Fornells de la Selva, Cassà de la Selva and Llagostera on your way to Tossa de Mar, where you reach the coast and links to the coast road. From Tossa there is easy access to Lloret de Mar and Blanes along the coast road, heading south. The two main roads in this area are, then, the C-66, to the coast, and the C-65, which heads southwards.

This entire area is organized around the AP-7 motorway, which runs from La Jonquera south to Barcelona, and the C-65 and C-66 roads, which pick up the outlined routes. The N-II trunk road, running from Barcelona to Girona, was the main road before the motorway was built and may be necessary to get onto smaller roads that lead off the N-II rather than directly out of Girona.

Olot

Figueres

Vilopriu

Sant Julià de Ramis

La Pera

Torroella de Montgrí

Salt   Girona

Pals

Begur

Fornells de la Selva

Palafrugell

Mont-ras

Vall-llobrega

Palamós

Santa Cristina d'Aro

Sant Feliu de Guíxols

Tossa de Mar

Lloret de Mar
Blanes

Municipalities	Comarca	Surface area (municipality)	Population (2001)
GIRONA	el Gironès	39.1 km^2	74,879 inhabitants
ROUTE 1			
SANT JULIÀ DE RAMIS	Gironès	18.8 km^2	2,098 inhabitants
LA PERA	Baix Empordà	11.6 km^2	392 inhabitants
TORROELLA DE MONTGRÍ	Baix Empordà	65.9 km^2	8,244 inhabitants
VILOPRIU	Baix Empordà	17.0 km^2	152 inhabitants
PALS	Baix Empordà	25.8 km^2	2,046 inhabitants
BEGUR	Baix Empordà	20.7 km^2	3,459 inhabitants
PALAFRUGELL	Baix Empordà	26.9 km^2	18,322 inhabitants
MONT-RAS	Baix Empordà	12.3 km^2	1,676 inhabitants
VALL-LLOBREGA	Baix Empordà	5.5 km^2	438 inhabitants
PALAMÓS	Baix Empordà	14.0 km^2	14,842 inhabitants
SANTA CRISTINA D'ARO	Baix Empordà	67.6 km^2	2,873 inhabitants
SANT FELIU DE GUÍXOLS	Baix Empordà	16.2 km^2	17,994 inhabitants
ROUTE 2			
SALT	Gironès	6.6 km^2	21,238 inhabitants
ROUTE 3			
FORNELLS DE LA SELVA	Gironès	11.9 km^2	1,627 inhabitants
TOSSA DE MAR	la Selva	38.5 km^2	4,366 inhabitants
LLORET DE MAR	la Selva	48.7 km^2	20,239 inhabitants
BLANES	la Selva	17.7 km^2	30,693 inhabitants

TEIXIDOR FLOUR MILL
HEAD OFFICE OF *EL PUNT* NEWSPAPER

Rafael Masó
Phase 1: 1910-1911
Phase 2: 1915-1916
Phase 3: 1923-1924

C/ Santa Eugènia, 42 - Girona

SUBSEQUENT INTERVENTIONS:
Arcadi Pla, 1991-2000. Corporate headquarters of Hermes publishing company

This is a large industrial complex comprising two industrial buildings, a factory and a third office and housing building, joined by a bridge. The complex was extended in 1915-1916 by means of a small built volume beside the dwelling, after the purchase of an adjacent plot that the owner had initially intended to buy. In 1923-1924, a further extension was carried out in the form of two more industrial spaces beside the office building. The present-day façade is the result of these three phases. The original volume housing the offices and the dwelling is fantastic and extravagant in appearance as a result of the architect's references to a mound of flour, making this the building in which Masó came closest to the language employed by Gaudí. The volumes are broken down into planes in keeping with his experience in furniture design and construction. The warehouses, workshops and factory were demolished in 1991. This project is not particularly representative of Masó's body of work, a fact that accords all the more significance to this departure into the world of allegory, sensuality and breakdown that characterizes Modernisme, something that was not repeated in his career.

Girona 45

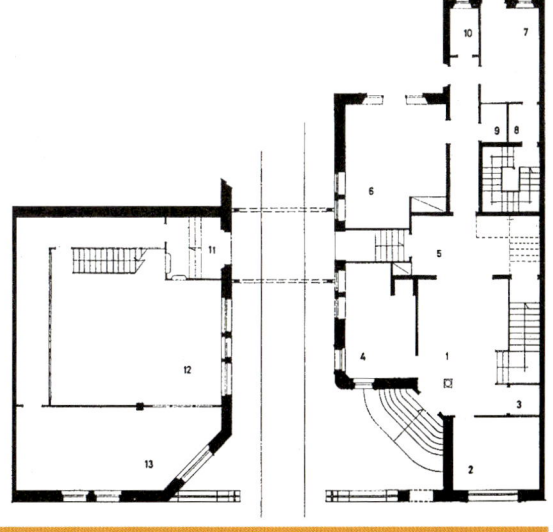

BATLLE HOUSE
REMODELLING OF A 19TH-CENTURY BUILDING

Rafael Masó
1909-1910

C/ Fontanilles, 2 - C/ Nou, 15 - Av. Sant Francesc, 16
Girona

Masó set out to transfigure the house by means of ornamental elements and turn it into a modern dwelling. His idea was to give the house an air of lightness, creating an outline and according it rationality. Many of the ornamental elements that Masó envisaged were not incorporated due to disagreements with the client, who considered the cost of the intervention to be excessive. Masó relinquished site management in 1910, and remodelling work was completed without his participation and without many of the elements he had designed. The building is an apartment block outside the old town of Girona, releasing Masó from commitment to tradition and enabling him to have recourse to forms of abstract ornamentation which he associated with the image of rationalism and modernity. Both the imprint of the Vienna Secession and, to a lesser degree, the influence of Gaudí are visible.

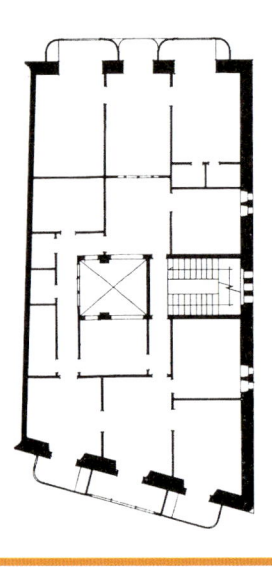

SALIETI HOUSE
RESTORATION AND REMODELLING OF A 14th-CENTURY TOWNHOUSE

Rafael Masó
1910-1911

C/ Ciutadans, 8 - Girona

The old Gothic townhouse had three storeys. The first floor is the *piano nobile* where the Salietis lived, and the second floor, which Masó remodelled in 1920 for the Aragó-Masó family, was rented out. The architect's intervention centred on the courtyard and the main stairway. The arches and capitals of the Gothic arcades are pre-existing elements that Masó incorporated into the project and which explain the nature of the intervention. More than a restoration project, this was a new construction that set out to evoke the world of Girona's Gothic townhouses. This departure point brought Masó back to certain approaches that he had hitherto abandoned, related to the historicist review of the English Gothic. He also intervened in the decoration of the *piano nobile*, introducing ceramic elements, paintings, wrought iron and carved stone. The house is currently in a very good state of repair, with the exception of certain features that have been removed due to the change of ownership.

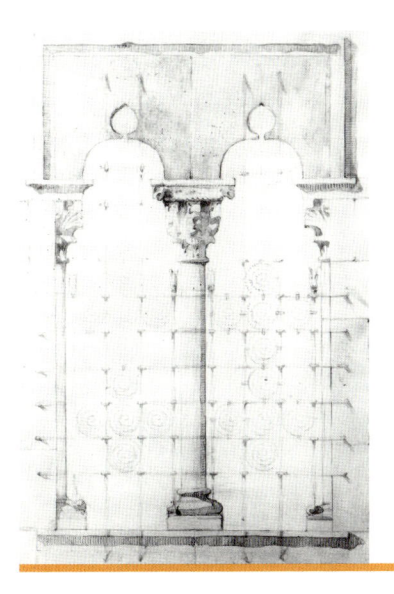

NORAT HOUSE
REMODELLING OF AN OLD HOUSE
IN THE RAVAL DISTRICT

Joan Roca i Pinet
1912-1913

Rambla de la Llibertat, 25 - Girona

Many buildings on the right bank of the river Onyar were remodelled in the late 19th and early 20th centuries. They were old constructions in the Raval area, protected by the curve of the riverfront, which in previous centuries had undergone all manner of military, governmental and fluvial incidents. Roca i Pinet's intervention focused on the façade of Norat house overlooking the Rambla, applying the possibilities of combination and the compositional resources that were showcased by Modernisme. The composition is based on the plain treatment of much of the façade, offset by the elaborate gallery on the *piano nobile*, with a railing that combines dressed stone and filigree wrought iron work, and the topmost element in the crown, comprising two lateral concavities and a smooth-lined central convexity. The overall plane is set in a framework of darker stone that confers unity on the composition and gives the façade its specific identity.

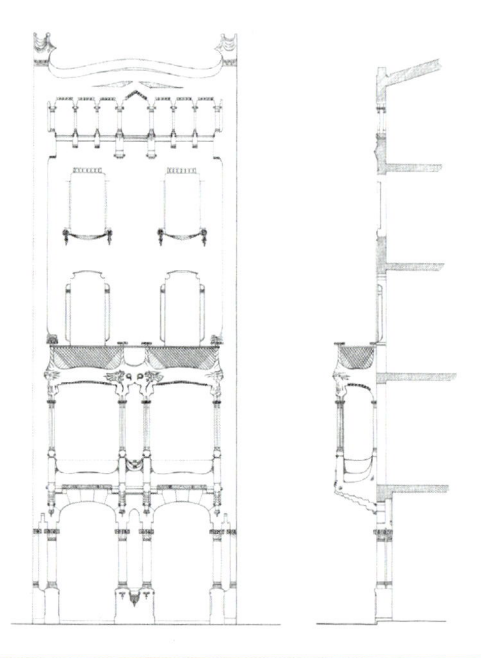

DALMAU HOUSE
PRIVATE DWELLING

Joan Roca i Pinet
1917-1918

C/ Portal Nou, 17-19 - Girona

Subsequent interventions:
Josep Maria Masramon, 1941. Remodelling
Francesc Hereu, Joaquim Español, 1989-1992. Remodelling

On a large plot of land in the old town, Roca i Pinet took as the basis for his interpretation of a single-family dwelling the references of rural constructions and local building techniques, influenced by the emerging ideas of the new sensibility of Modernisme. The house structure comprises adjoining volumes, the most representative composition being a capsular two-storey volume with a ridge roof and a gallery of semicircular arches. The construction of the corner, beneath the house's garden, is totally independent of this central volume and adopts its own axes of symmetry and composition, corresponding to a single-storey construction. The base of ashlar work unifies the various volumes, including the small construction at the rear of the garden and the wall that encloses the house, which adopts the characteristic stepped configuration of rural properties.

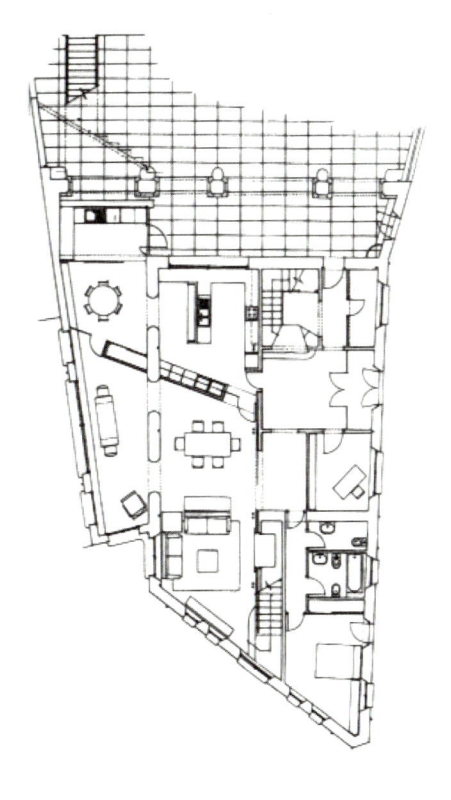

Girona

TEIXIDOR HOUSE
CASA DE LA PUNXA – COL·LEGI OFICIAL D'APARELLADORS I ARQUITECTES TÈCNICS DE GIRONA - COAATG

Rafael Masó
1918-1922

C/ Santa Eugènia, 19 - Girona

SUBSEQUENT INTERVENTIONS:
Jordi Bosch, Joan Tarrús, Santiago Vives, 1979-1982. Remodelling and restoration as the headquarters of the Girona Branch of the (COAATC).

This rental apartment house forms part of the Teixidor flourmill complex. Teixidor House marks another stage in Masó's search for modern forms in the framework of a collective architectural culture that was committed to both this endeavour and the political situation and events in Catalonia. Masó chose to simplify the treatment of the facades, at the same time taking a Gothic approach to the volumes, culminating in the corner tower, crowned by a sharp conical roof over an arrangement of attic windows that play an important role in the building. Masó relinquished more personal innovations in order to draw on a shared tradition, headed by Puig i Cadafalch, with recourse to historicism as a sign of architectural and political identity.

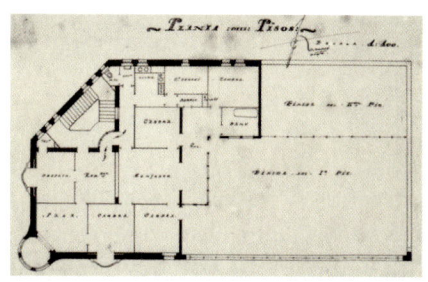

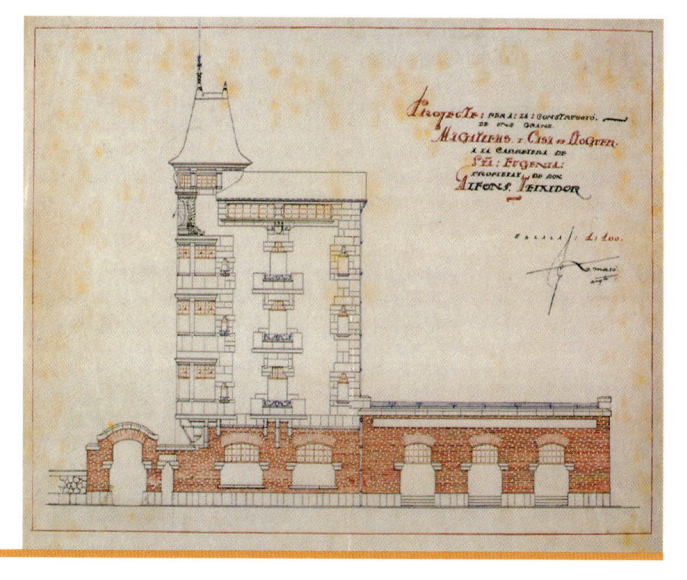

GISPERT SAÜCH HOUSE
PRIVATE DWELLING

Rafael Masó
1921-1923

C/ Álvarez de Castro, 9 - Av. Jaume I, 66 - Girona

This was a newly constructed three-storey building, with an open terrace roof. The ground floor was designed as storage space and the upper floors for housing. The house includes Masó's most genuine contributions to the consolidation of a characteristic modern architectural language. The volume of the building is chamfered at the corner, with large openings that separate the two stretches of wall. Masó chose smooth stucco for the façades, with a cadence marked out by windows set in very slender frames. An outstanding feature is the bare brick pilaster built against one of the façades, an apparently arbitrary element that helps to resolve the excessive simplicity of this stretch of wall. The roof is completely separated from the volume of the building and throws a deep shade that highlights the purist design of the whole.

034

IGNASI IGLESIAS SCHOOL
MONTJUÏC INFANTS' AND PRIMARY SCHOOL

Ricard Giralt
1930-1932

Pda. Montjuïc, 1 - Girona

035

BLANCH HOUSE
ARCHITECTS' HOUSE AND STUDIO

Emili Blanch
1931-1932

C/ Bernat Boadas, 6 - Girona

SUBSEQUENT INTERVENTIONS:
Emili Blanch, 1984. Remodelling
Miquel Ferrer, 1996. Restoration of the original

While this programme called for various parts and complex circulations, Blanch exploited the perfect pentagonal form of the site to make the house a symmetrical organism, facing the street corner and presenting a single image from a single viewpoint. The stairway communicating the three floors is positioned at the centre of the pentagon, with a passage at the rear and a small court behind it. The two corner balconies on the bedroom floor draw the three façades together into a trihedron that reconstructs the corner, giving it a unitary image in accordance with Blanch's interest in finding a suitable language for new urban housing.

036

TARRÚS HOUSE
SINGLE-FAMILY HOUSE

Josep Claret i Rubira
1935

C/ Rutlla, 137 - Girona

The school stands on a slope on the mountain of Montjuïc, with the first two floors built into the rock by means of a retaining wall. The open ground floor provides an arcade for games, and the first floor houses the dining room and communal spaces. The final two floors contain the classrooms for girls and boys, respectively. The volumetric study of the complex is oriented according to the circular balcony that commands views and the stairwell at the rear. The rationalist rhetoric extends to the oscillating sash windows, justified by good ventilation and lighting of the classrooms.

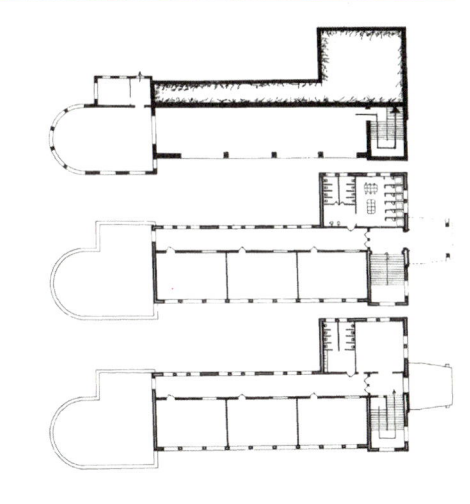

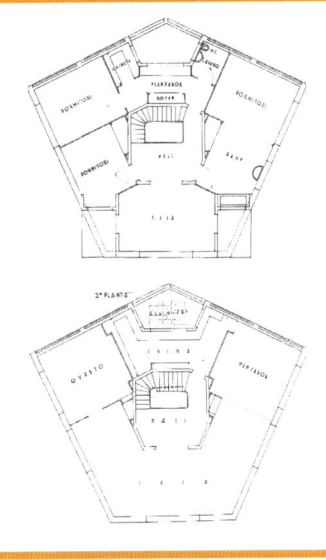

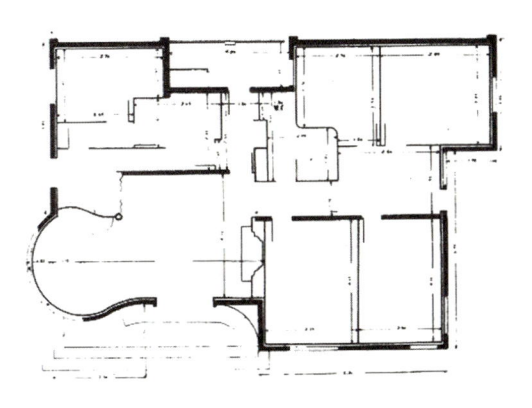

This small-scale house is built on a single floor, though the roof forms a walk-on terrace. Claret i Rubira created two separate parts: at the rear, the bedrooms are laid out according to a rigorous distribution. At the front, the versatility of circulation gives great dynamism to the series of spaces comprising the living room, dining room, utility room and kitchen. Various features, such as the railings, fences, borders and drainpipes, manifest a refined concern with style in a constant allusion to the early housing designs of Le Corbusier.

Girona

FORNÉ GARAGE

Joan M. de Ribot
1957

Ctra. de Barcelona, 39 - C/ Bisbe Lorenzana, 55
Girona

Ribot's interpretation of the site, a street corner on the outskirts of Girona, takes a rigorously rational approach that produces the structural and distributive solution. Vehicle entry is at the corner, via a helicoidal ramp supported by an octagonal system of pillars that are reflected in the façade by a quarter glass cylinder. The circular structural system penetrates as far as the second bay, finally merging with the straight lines of the pillars around the perimeter. The order of the structure is a faithful reflection of the order of vehicle circulation. The building is presented to the street as two lightweight glass volumes articulated by the reinforced cylinder at the corner. In this atypical programme, in a place without a specific identity, Ribot melds the arguments of rationalism and the sensibility of *Modernisme* in a building that is surprising in its historical context.

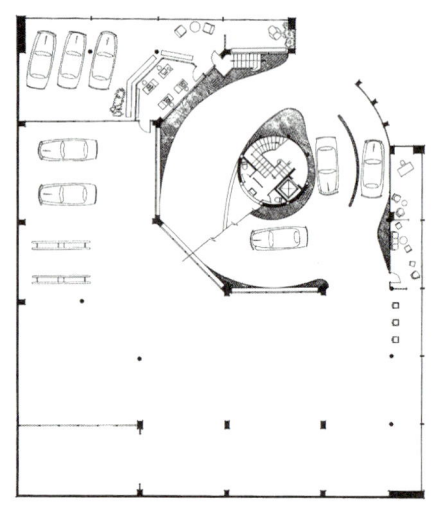

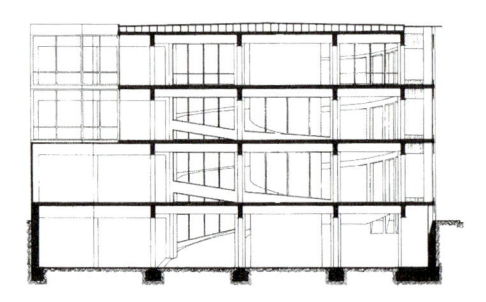

THE MARIST SCHOOL OF GIRONA

Joan M. de Ribot, Josep Maria Pla
1972

Av. Josep Tarradellas, 5 - Girona

The project echoes the pedagogical ideas of the 1970s, tending to promote interrelation within schools and develop more flexible, versatile spaces for education. The translation into architecture of this new sensibility coincided with the revision of the modern movement and the search for new forms of spatial configuration. The school repeats 50 m² modules that form trilobulate units. A hexagonal structure of metal uprights produces an open-plan space, implemented by a cast-in-situ concrete floor and technological innovation in the systems used to fit out the space. Also characteristic of this new architectural culture is the use of prefabricated elements and the application of concrete to non-structural elements. Ribot and Pla adopted this new way of understanding architecture as a source of solutions for the planning challenges presented by successive periods.

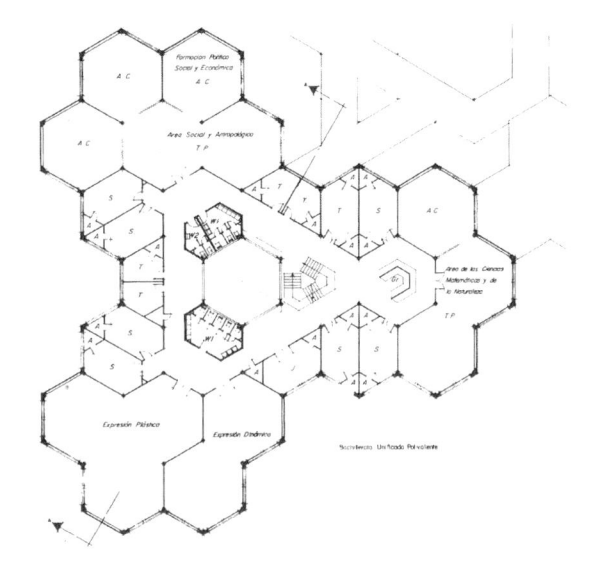

HOUSING BLOCK IN FONTAJAU

Josep Fuses, Joan M. Viader
1990-1994

C/ Can Sunyer, 11 - Girona

The building constitutes the edge of a residential fabric of row houses, on the other side of which lies a large space set aside for a future urban park, crossed by a stream. This specific location explains the choice of a higher built volume and the fact that the building adopts a marked orientation, reflected in the treatment of the façades and in the roof. It comprises three identical volumes with two dwellings per floor, in which the space comprising the living room, dining room and kitchen is organized between the two façades, while the bedrooms occupy another bay with two at the front and two at the rear. The fact that the building is freestanding contributes to the regularity and dimensioning of the layout. The top floor is a duplex penthouse with a façade treatment that is associated more with the roof than with the plane of the façade overlooking the park.

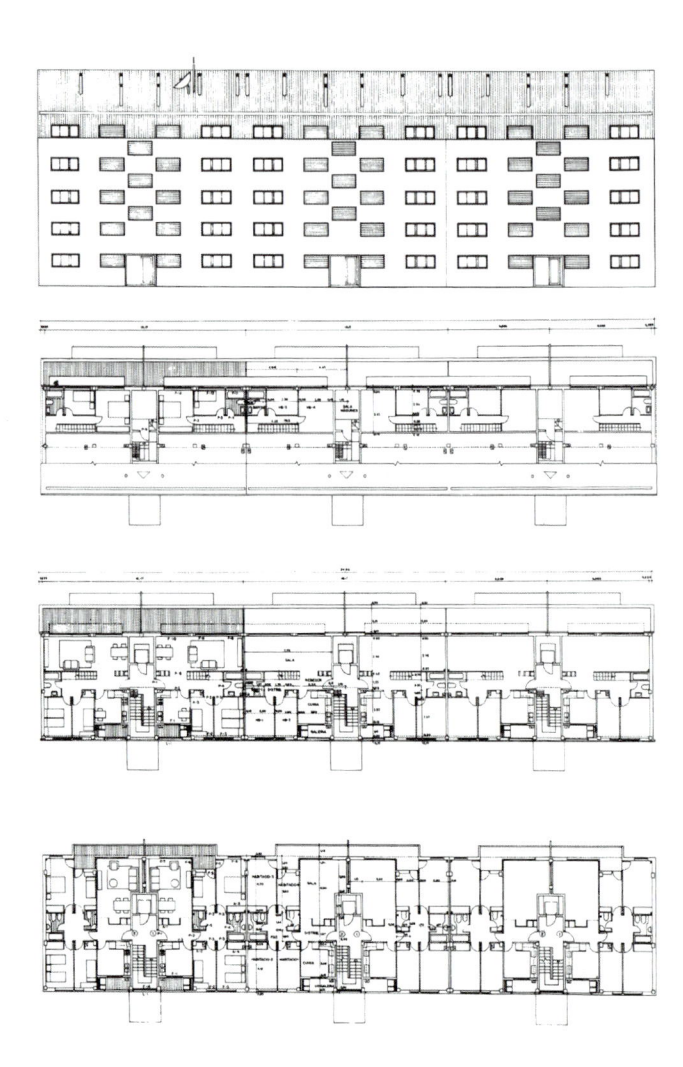

OFFICIAL SCHOOL OF LANGUAGES

Víctor Rahola
1991-1994

C/ Josep Viader i Moliner, 16 - Girona

The building, a freestanding block surrounded by a landscaped space stretching in all directions, jointly with the new school of hotel and catering, forms an education complex which, thanks to its dimensions, serves to revitalize what is essentially a residential area. A container measuring 80 metres long and 3 floors high houses repeated units such as the classrooms, seminar rooms, services and communication shafts. The library, events hall, bar and offices are individualized in three separate volumes which, from the outside, create an interplay of light and shade. The two parts of the building are joined by a central space that provides the function of an entrance hall. In terms of hierarchy, this is the most important space in the school, which, due to the regular comings and goings of students, takes on a role of centralization and interrelation.

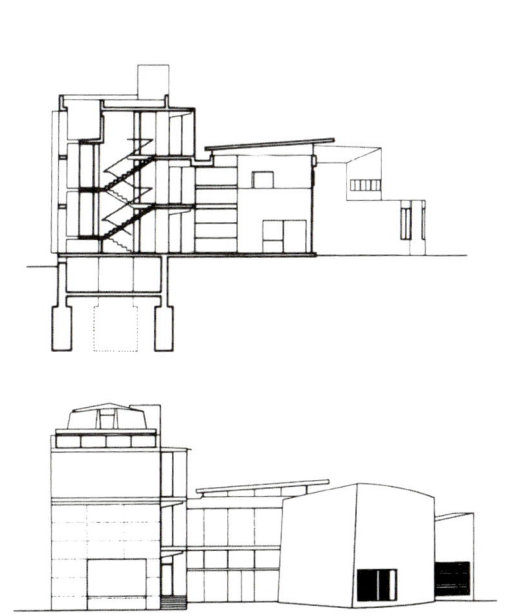

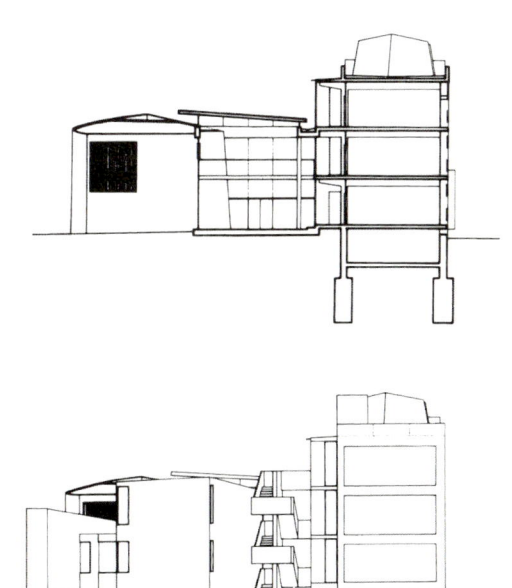

PLA-BARBERO HOUSE
SINGLE-FAMILY DWELLING

Arcadi Pla
1990-1993

C/ Serra de Bestracà, 4-6 - Girona

The configuration of the house arises from the relation with the site and its views and orientation. The mechanism underlying this adaptation is a basic layout comprising a 5.40 x 5.40-metre grid allowing subaxes of 3.60 and 1.80 metres. Each 1.80 x 1.80-metre module is subdivided into 30 centimetre-wide strips that reveal nine square modules of 50 x 50 centimetres. Rather than creating a rigid configuration, this model channels the growth and dimension of each part and generates a high level of mobility over the plot. The house materializes as a collection of numerous variations on this basic device.

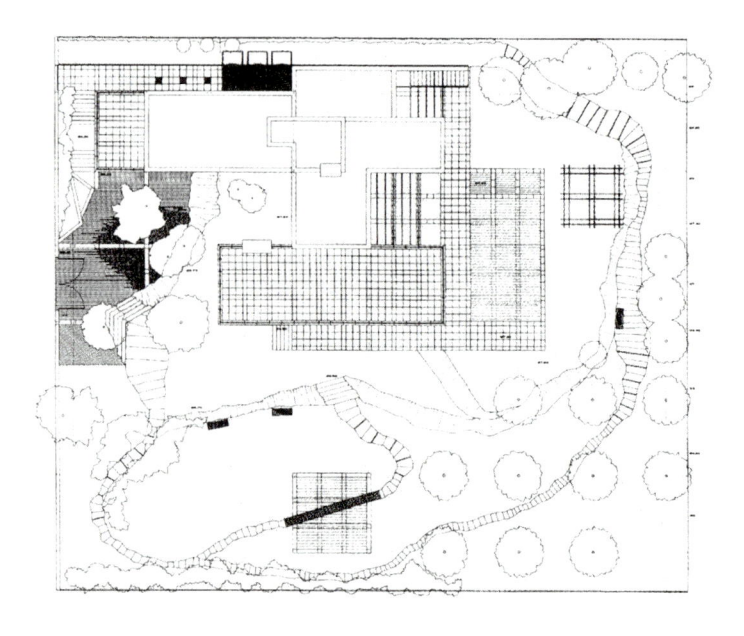

FIGUERES HOUSE
SINGLE-FAMILY DWELLING

Àlex Sibils
1995-1996

C/ Àngel, 5 - Girona

The intervention consisted in the construction of a single-family dwelling on the site of a ruined house in the old town of Girona. The dwelling takes the form of the superposition of various volumes grouped into three trapezoid floors around a central volume that extends and increases as it descends, to the point of engaging on the ground floor with the existing wall system. In this way it occupies the total perimeter of the property, enclosing a small inner courtyard with a well of historical value and creating a dispersed volume that is apparently constructed of layers, as happens with the old houses built in the historic centre.

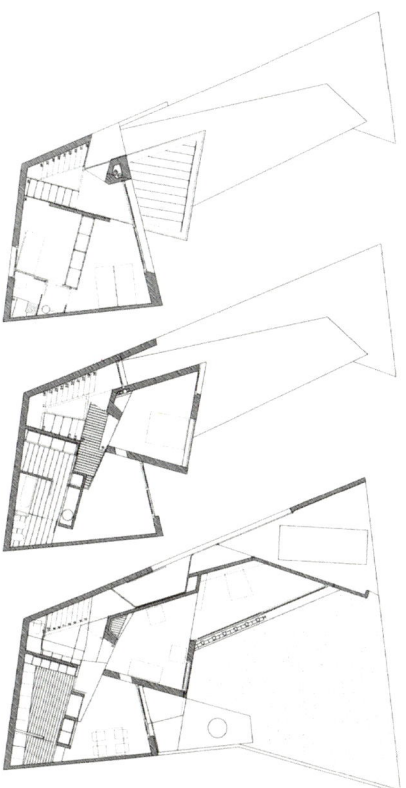

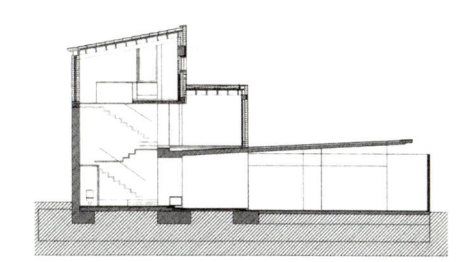

PALAU DE JUSTÍCIA
NEW LAW COURTS BUILDING

Esteve Bonell, Josep Maria Gil
1987-1992

Av. Ramon Folch, 1 - Girona

The new law courts building in Girona stands on a site near the river Onyar, on the other side from the old town and its monumental complex with the reference points of the cathedral and the church of Sant Feliu. On the other side, the Parc de la Devesa and the railway line mark the outer edge of the cityscape. The building solves the complex atomization of the programme by means of two wings laid out in an L-shape. The wing arranged along Avinguda Ramon Folch houses the magistrates' and institutional offices, and is organized around an inner atrium with straight-run stairs leading to the upper floors. The second wing contains the court rooms, all on the ground floor. The foyer is at the meeting point of the two wings and is connected to the atrium by a great stairway. The main façade adopts a concave alignment that highlights the building's function, as an extension of the classicistic façade of the Post Office.

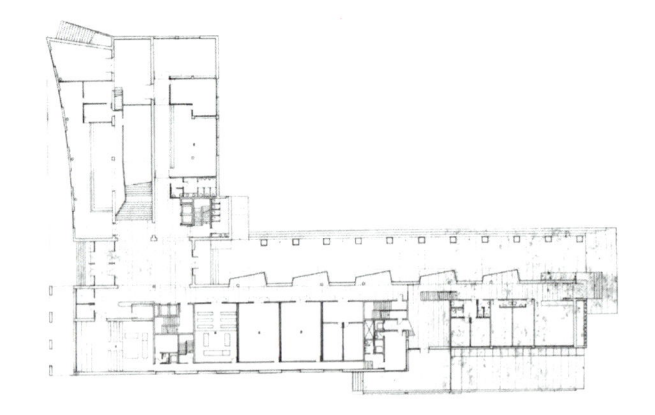

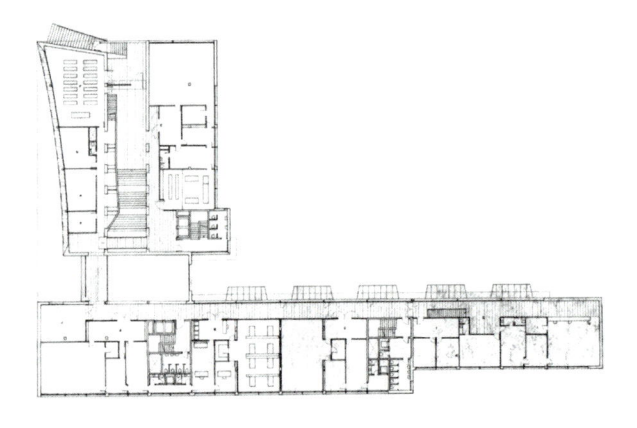

GIRONA-FONTAJAU MUNICIPAL SPORTS CENTRE

Esteve Bonell, Josep Maria Gil
1991-1993

C/ Josep Aguilera i Martí, 2 - Girona

The new sports centre is located in a new leisure area on the periphery of the city overlooking the Parc de la Devesa, on the other side of the river Onyar. The project takes on the role of organizing the future sector. The difference in level of the site led to the creation of two floors, the public upper level for spectators and the lower level exclusively for sportsmen and women. The ambivalence between the north-west and south-east façades suggested the creation of two entrances, though the main entrance overlooks the future sports facilities. The stands are laid out in a horseshoe shape, with capacity for 4350 spectators, in order to single out the front façade, where a stage can be erected. The exit steps are inserted at the sides and lead directly to the two sloping car parks that flank the building.

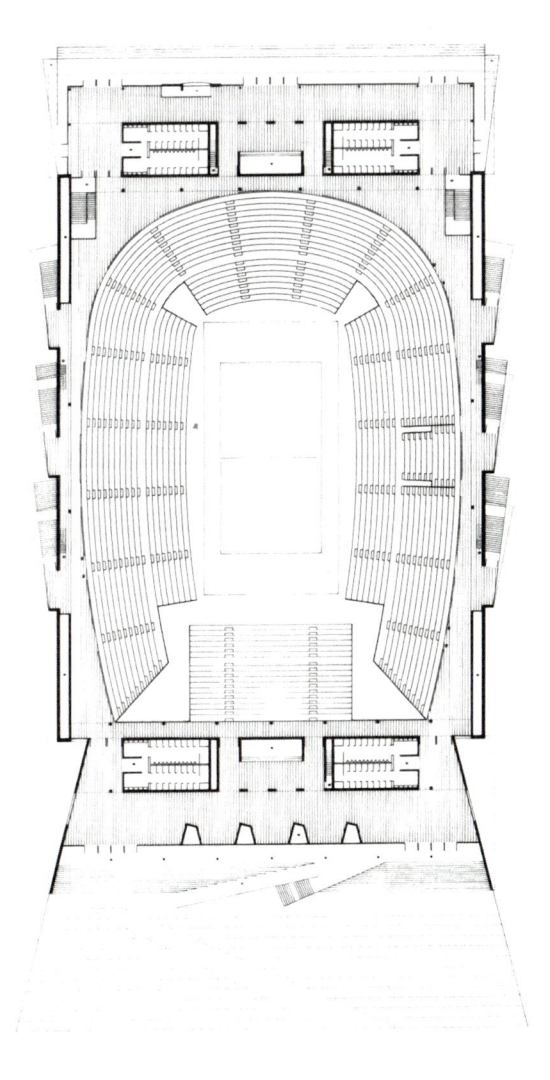

FACULTY OF ECONOMIC AND BUSINESS STUDIES
UNIVERSITY OF GIRONA

Arcadi Pla
1988-1993

Av. Lluís Santaló - Montilivi Campus
University of Girona - Girona

The building interprets the grid of the Montilivi campus, designed by the same architect, by means of a perfectly square central courtyard, in the same way that the block is generated by the campus. This courtyard channels all circulations and marks the starting point of the freer, more dynamic growth of the various parts of the faculty. The volume containing the seminar rooms and offices opens up onto a nearby wood, indicating the specific nature of its use in its exterior image. The courtyard remains open on one side and the lecture rooms are laid out around the two remaining sides. The pattern dictated by the grid of the campus and the inner courtyard is reflected in the ceilings and floorings of the interior spaces. The growth of the constructions around the courtyard is manifested not in the programme or its volume, but in a series of geometric layouts that deliberately activate the organic nature of the building.

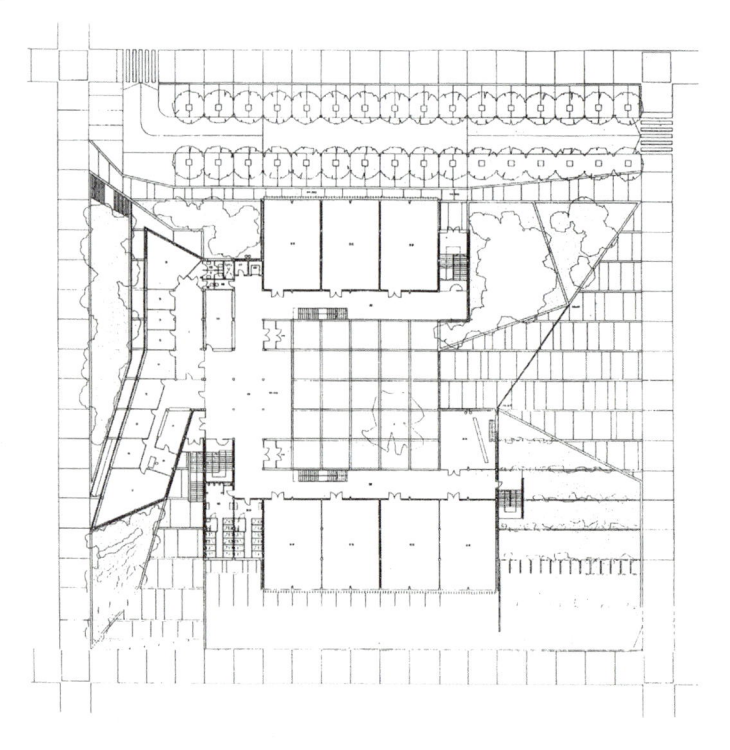

FACULTY OF EXPERIMENTAL SCIENCE
UNIVERSITY OF GIRONA

Josep Fuses, Joan M. Viader
1996-1997

Av. Lluís Santaló - Montilivi Campus – University of Girona - Girona

The building comprises two linear blocks, parallel to the contours of the site, which form an inner courtyard that respects the original slope of the plot. This courtyard communicates with the nearby woods, and the slope continues into the main lecture hall and the foyer of the faculty, interconnecting the interior and the exterior by means of these two spaces. The materials used reflect on the outside the functional parts of the building: inside, painted perforated-brick walls, visible installations and terrazzo throughout. On the outside, the volume housing the lecture rooms forms a two-storey socle treated with bare concrete. The entrance to the lecture rooms is via a black slate corridor volume. The shaft communicating the lecture rooms and the laboratories stands out for its cladding of the same black slate.

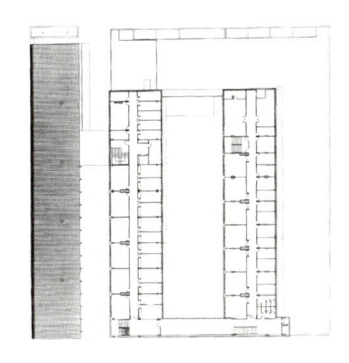

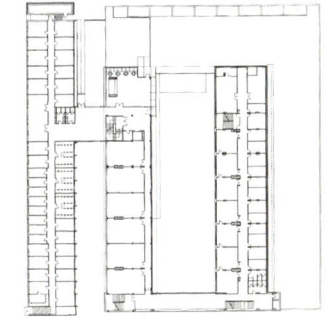

047

LAW FACULTY
UNIVERSITY OF GIRONA

Rafael Aranda, Carme Pigem, Ramon Vilalta
1997-1999

Av. Lluís Santaló - Montilivi Campus
University of Girona - Girona

048

WORKSHOP AND GREENHOUSE BUILDING
UNIVERSITY OF GIRONA

David Baena, Toni Casamor, Josep Maria Quera
2000-2002

Av. Lluís Santaló - Montilivi Campus
University of Girona - Girona

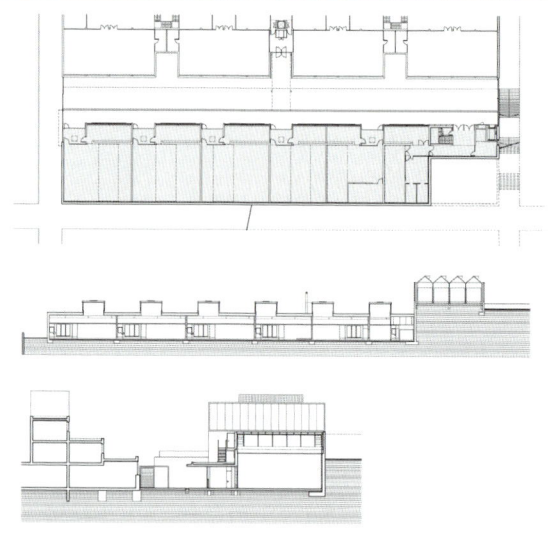

049

UNIVERSITY LIBRARY
UNIVERSITY OF GIRONA

Javier San José
Phase 1: 1998-2004
Phase 2: 2004-2007

Av. Lluís Santaló - Montilivi Campus
University of Girona - Girona

The project is a direct response to the urbanistic conditions of the place: the grid of the campus superposed on varied relief with a whole range of vegetation. An embankment on the two lower streets recreates an artificial horizontal plane with three volumes running its length, housing the lecture rooms and offices. All the spaces receive daylight from the spaces between the volumes, giving the building the appearance of a series of engaged blind surfaces. A three-storey volume marking the entrance at the least steep part of the embankment contains the communal activities.

This is an annexe to the Polytechnic School, built to accommodate two quite distinct uses: the workshops, on the ground floor, and the greenhouse, a small volume emerging from the roof. The solutions applied and the choice of materials used seek a uniformity that adapts to flexibility of use, allowing greater ease of maintenance and energy saving. High-insulating translucent glazing unifies the facings, with skylights in the roof arranged to provide overhead lighting in the working areas.

The building is situated beside a gully that separates it from a leafy wood, on the edge of the university campus. The configuration of the library is based on the concept of breaking down the volume that forms it to avoid presenting a contrasting image to the wood. It is divided into two lengthwise volumes, separated by a 10-metre space that filters daylight and draws it into the interior. The block beside the wood is treated in black, and the block on the street side is treated in white. A secondary stairway, leading directly to the first floor, reduces the height of the building and completes the desired breakdown.

Girona 65

APARTMENT BUILDING IN SANT PONÇ

Arcadi Pla
1996-1999

C/ Esport, 3-5 - Girona

The building stands on the left bank of the river Ter, near the northern exit from the city. The arrangement established by the Partial Planning Project has been replaced by an undulating volume inspired by the great beauty of the spot. This change also made it possible to adapt the types of dwelling to real market demands, on the basis of a 60-m^2 dwelling with two bedrooms, and establish variations in size at singular points in the floor plan. The fan-shaped layout opens the rooms to the best views. The fan-shape continues in the volume with an increasingly terraced layout. All the apartments look inwards, and the kitchens give onto the entrance hall, which is exterior and adopts the role of gallery. The stair- and lift-well forms the centre of an ascending spiral whose highest point coincides with the point with the best views and, consequently, the largest number of dwellings.

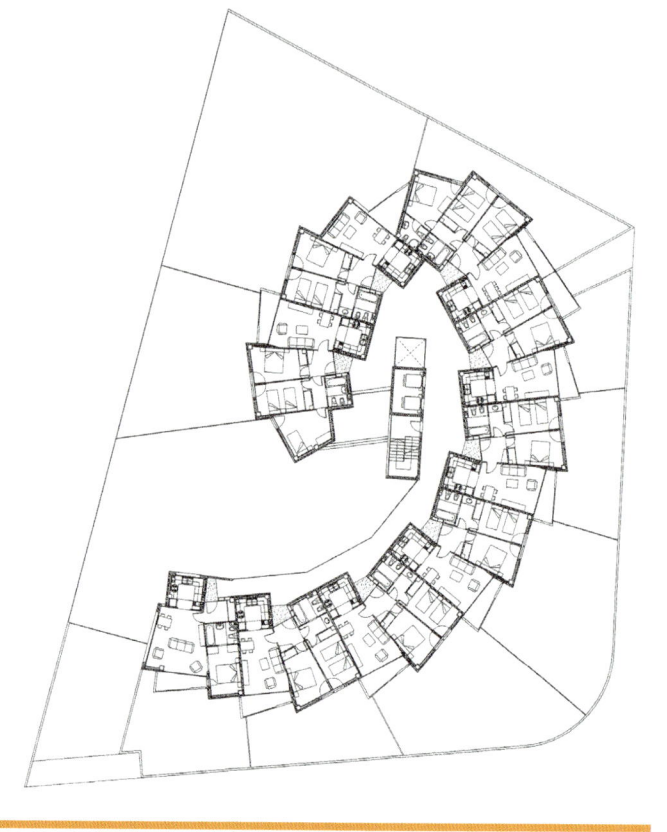

CAP MALUQUER SALVADOR
HEALTH CENTRE

Jaime Coll, Judith Leclerc
2001-2003

C/ Castell de Solterra, 11-17 - Girona

The project adopts a layout that seeks to address equally the corridor, waiting room, hall and surgery, the characteristic elements of a health centre. The rectangular ground floor is crossed by four corridors that divide the area into five equal bays. The elements of the programme are inserted into the strips, shunning the continuity of the corridors and implementing the flexibility of circulation. The inner courts become the key elements that give each area its identity and are reflected in the roof floor as the only fixed parts of the overall arrangement.

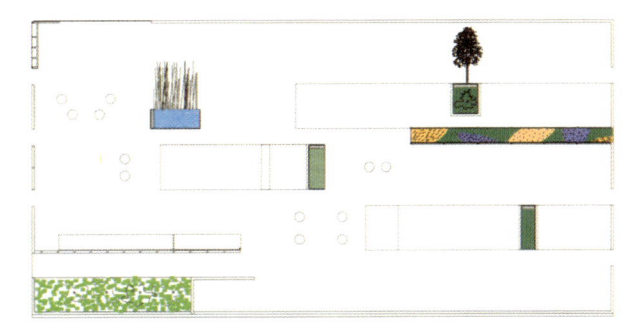

IES CARLES RAHOLA
SECONDARY SCHOOL

Enric Massip-Bosch
2003-2006

C/ Joan Miró i Ferrà, 10 - Fontajau - Girona

The site on which the school stands is located at the edge of the city beside a new residential area. The project concentrates all the functions in a compact elongated block that creates an almost non-existent street. The ground floor restores the horizontal to this long site that presents a difference in level of two metres between its two ends. The principal façade is determined by the variation of filters nuancing the entrance of daylight. The communal areas are all situated on the highest ground, connected to the playground by a terraced area for games.

ELS QUÍMICS
RESIDENTIAL COMPLEX

Eduard Gascón, Carles Martí Arís
Phase 1: 2001-2004
Phase 2: 2003-2006

C/ Migdia, 137-139 - C/ Marquès de Caldes de Montbui, 70-104 - Pujada de la Creu de Palau, 2-4
Girona

The project is the product of converting industrial into residential land in response to the rapid growth of the city of Girona in recent years. Initially, the project was commissioned to Aldo Rossi, who died three years after designing it, before it was built. Gascón and Martí Arís substantially reworked Rossi's project, changing the role of the pre-existing chimney to make it the element that draws together the tree-lined avenue and the central square. The new project sees the central square as part of a front overlooking the city, while the two squares to the sides, facing south, relate more to the scale of the housing. The treatment of the façades also responds to the different conceptions of the three squares.

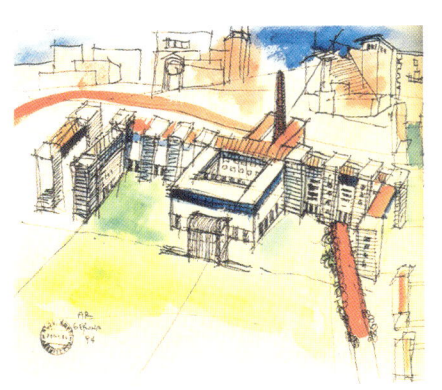

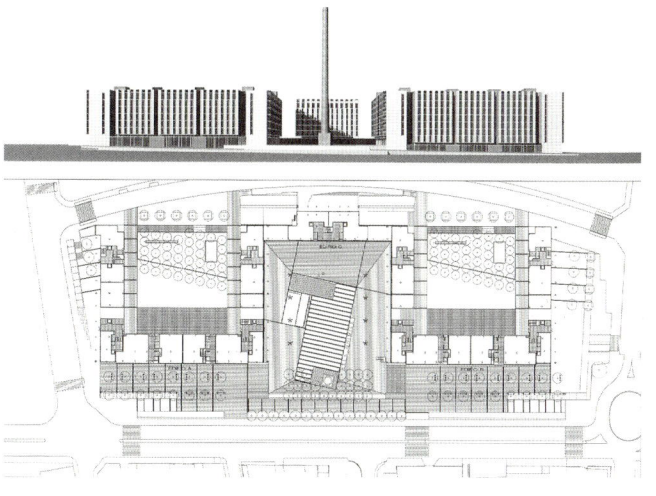

054

CEIP SANTA FE
INFANTS' AND PRIMARY SCHOOL

Jordi Ros
1986-1990

Pujada al Castell - Medinyà
Sant Julià de Ramis

GRN-1

055

JORDI CANTARELL HOUSE
SINGLE-FAMILY DWELLING
AND EXHIBITION GALLERY

Lluís Jubert, Eugènia Santacana
1996-1997

C/ Migjorn, 1 - Púbol - La Pera

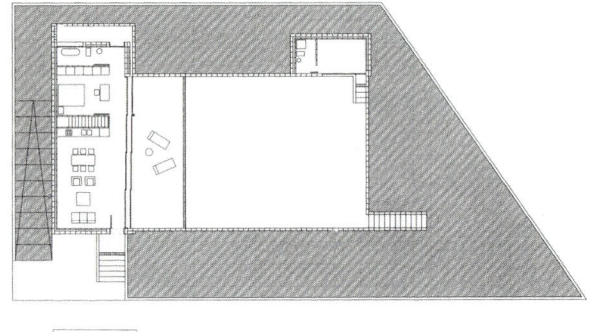

056

MONTGRÍ SPORTS PAVILION

Carles Ferrater, Jeroni Moner, Arcadi Pla
1982-1985

Rda. Pau Casals - Torroella de Montgrí

The site on which the school stands is bordered on the west by a narrow track that winds between the trees around a hill crowned by Medinyà castle. Part of this track is used as a pedestrian approach to the school. To the east, it is bordered by fields of crops that guarantee daylight as of early morning. To the north, the road to the cemetery provides vehicle access to the building. The slight prolongation of the difference in level above this road protects the school from the north wind. Its south-facing orientation offers views of the mountains in the distance, above the village rooftops.

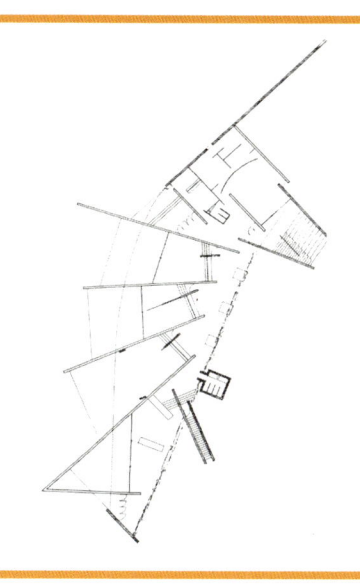

The project responds to the atypical nature of the programme and the client: a house with a gallery for a painter and furniture restorer. The house establishes a radical relation with its immediate surroundings by means of a courtyard-cum-garden sunk below the ground beyond, without affecting the views in the distance of Púbol castle. The house is topped by the gallery, a closed volume that is lit from overhead and ventilated via a small opening at either end. The house and the gallery have independent entrances via a stairway and a ramp, respectively. A single-flight staircase leads directly from the house to the gallery.

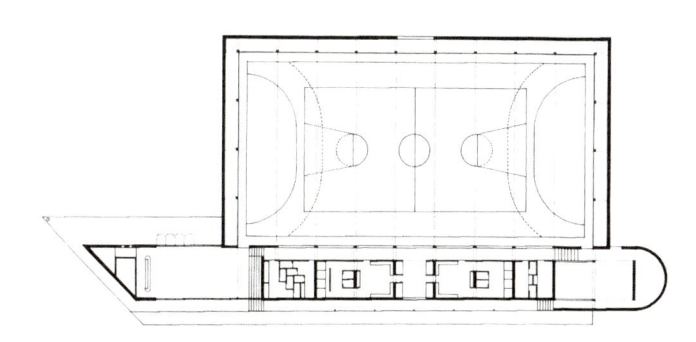

The project takes up the challenge of building a small sports pavilion on a slightly sloping site on the side of the Montgrí massif. The solution at once serves functional, constructional and landscape functions: the box of the sports courts is the only volume visible from a distance, and is clad with reinforced translucent glass. Direct contact with the site is provided by an arcade that surrounds the courts and establishes continuity with the stands via cascade steps. The lengthways volume housing the services, in contact with the ground, lays out an exterior route that leads, at the eastern edge of the building, to a viewpoint.

Girona

L'ESTARTIT YACHT CLUB

Carles Ferrater, Gerardo Rodríguez, Juan Díaz
1988-1991

Port of L'Estartit - L'Estartit
Torroella de Montgrí

The building occupies one of the corners of the wharf in the marina, set in a dock in the port of L'Estartit. It comprises two volumes brought together in an L-shape. A wall at the bisector of the corner acts at once as a separator and an element of union. The principal volume commands sea views through a great picture window and a small mezzanine that provides a raised vantage point. The lines of sight, studied one by one, set out to create a series of sequences leading from the seafront promenade, behind, to the horizon of the sea. The building acts as a delicate visual device that takes each of the surrounding elements into account.

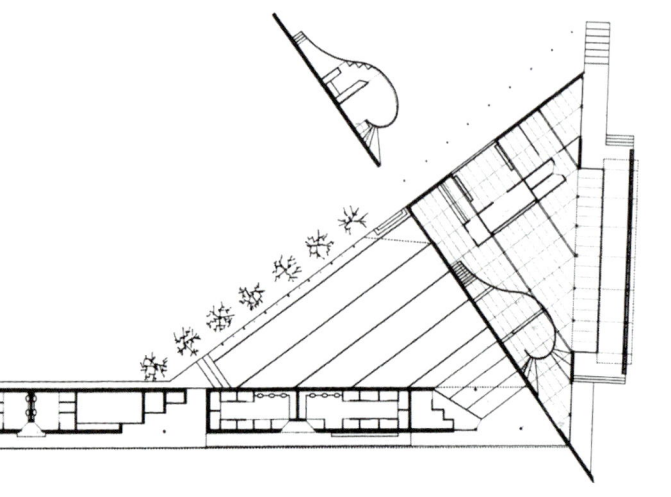

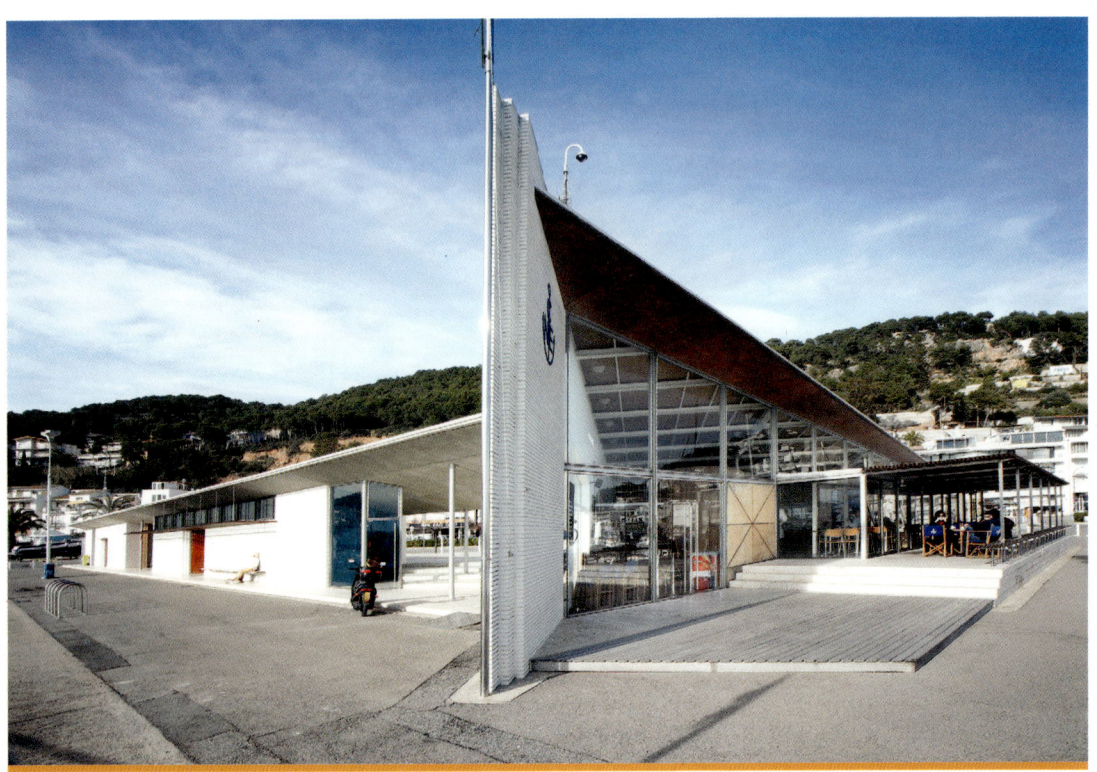

EL GUIX DE LA MEDA
SINGLE-FAMILY DWELLING

Carles Ferrater
1983-1984

C/ Cap de la Barra, 31 - L'Estartit
Torroella de Montgrí

The house is situated between two streets on very different levels, with the entrance on the higher street. As a result, the entrance terrace takes on a special role, with its view at the far end of the site of a very significant triangular rock. The programme is accommodated by distributing the different uses over the two narrow, elongated levels. The force of the section is expressed in the different materials used in the successive courses, from the rough stone at the bottom to the delicate brickwork at the entrance, crowned by a copper and glass triangle, a metaphor for the islet that is the inspiration for the whole house.

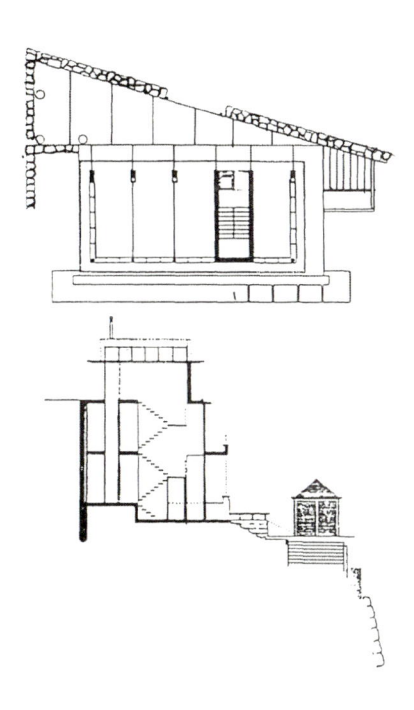

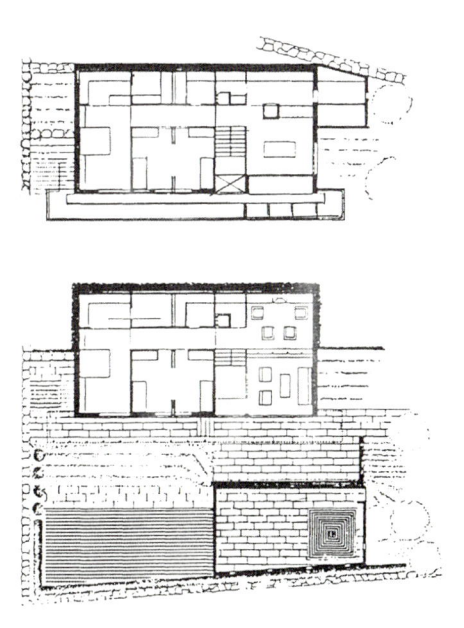

SINGLE-FAMILY DWELLING

Gustau Gili i Galfetti
2002-2005

Road from Gaüses de Dalt to Gaüses de Baix,
Gaüses - Vilopriu

GRN-1

Standing on a piece of set-aside between an area of grassland and a pine forest, the house deliberately adopts a long, narrow form to act as a filter between the landscapes to either side. The layout of the rooms obeys the order dictated by the structure and the variants it allows. The house opens up to both sides via long openings with sliding doors. The roof alternates the direction of its slopes along its length, creating a second entrance of light and offering fragmented, nuanced views of its surroundings.

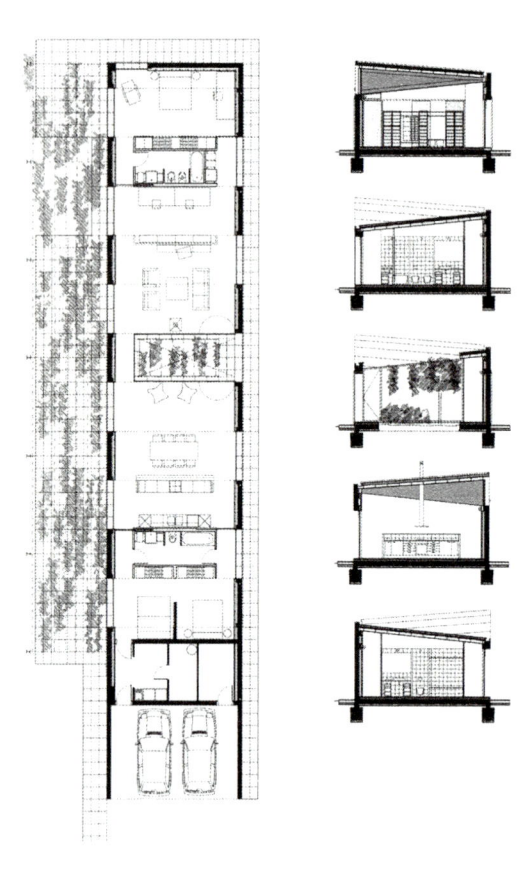

APARTMENT COMPLEX AT PALS GOLF COURSE

Oriol Bohigas, Josep Maria Martorell, David Mackay
1971-1973

Platja de Pals Golf Club - Pals

This elongated block is situated in a pinewood, following a mountain-sea orientation. It comprises two bays separated by an entrance passage. There are three types of apartment. The smallest are on the top floor, producing a terrace configuration and good views. Those on the ground floor connect directly with the exterior. The rigidness of the floor plan contrasts with the variety of the section, which seeks integration into the block's setting and draws attention to the individuality and specific character of each apartment. The façades have a pink rendering, picked out in white, and the arrises are highlighted by a ceramic trim.

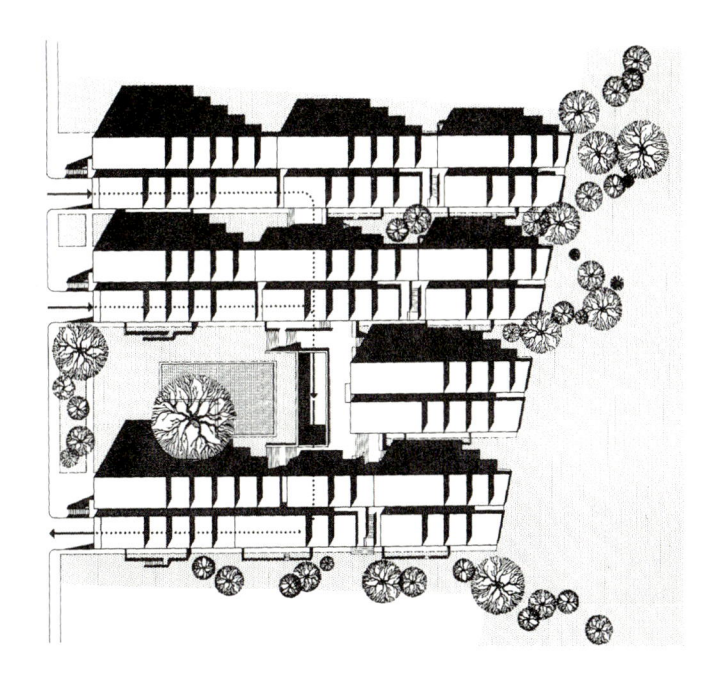

CANTARELL HOUSE
SINGLE-FAMILY DWELLING

Josep Pratmarsó
1962

Punta d'en Toni, 6 - Port des Pins - Sa Riera - Begur

The house is approached via a meadow at one end. A two-run stairway leads to a porch that overlooks the meadow without architectural references, comprising six modules of 4.30 metres square. To the left, a pond with a statue of a female figure points to the entrance. One side comprises a volume with the living room and master bedroom, separated by a small difference in level. To the right are the dining room, kitchen and service areas. At the rear, the staircase leads upstairs to the remaining bedrooms. The floor plan respects the squared modulation of the porch, though with a series of variants: the square may be divided in two or doubled up. The roof structure, ridge roofs in all cases, faithfully reflects the order of the bearing system. Pratmarsó created spatial effects of great intensity by means of very simple procedures combined with great skill.

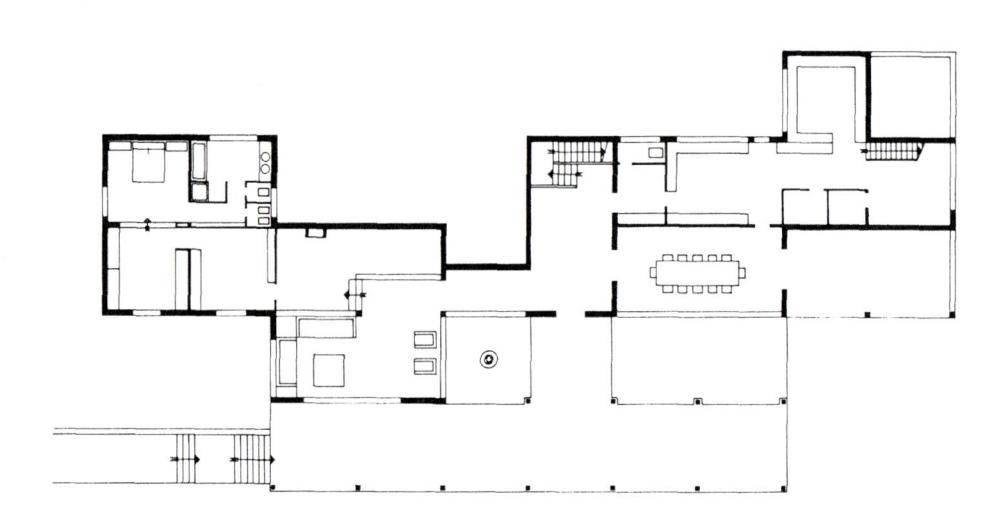

CRUYLLES HOUSE
SINGLE-FAMILY DWELLING

Antoni Bonet i Castellana, Josep Puig i Torné
1967-1968

Ctra. del Port d'Esclanyà, 5 - Aiguablava - Begur

The house stands overlooking a cove at the end of a valley bottom that opens up as it nears the sea. Bonet interprets the characteristics of the place by means of a trapezoidal geometry that affects the configuration of the facings, the vaults in the ceilings and even the flooring, likening the entire house to a vast composition of channel tiles. A spiral staircase leads down from a landscaped platform into the house. The family's bedrooms are located on an intermediate level, followed a few steps below by the living room, with its three large vaults. On a lower level stands a porch that acts as a summer dining room, connected to the rocks leading to the cove. On the upper platform, an inverted spherical roof over the guest bedrooms completes the composition. Bonet uses geometry to interpret the location and the complex constraints of a domestic programme.

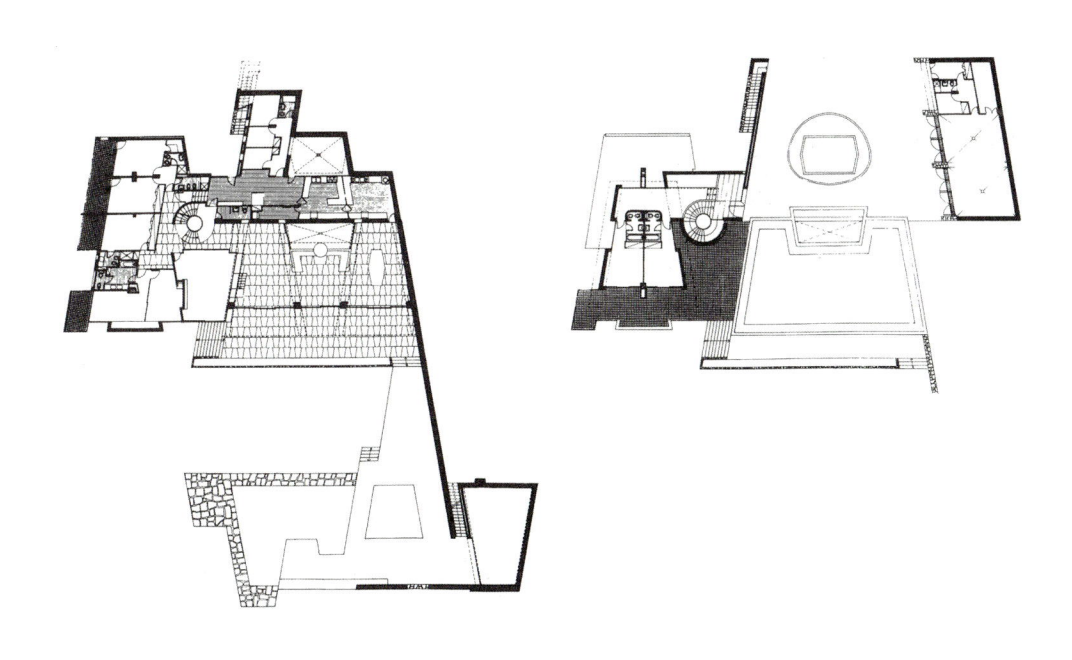

LLINÀS HOUSE
SINGLE-FAMILY DWELLING

Josep Llinàs
1978-1980

Road from Begur to Sa Tuna (GIV-6534), km 0.800
Begur

Situated on a small sloping plot beside the road, the house resolutely adopts the configuration of a cubic volume, the rear half of which is rendered while the other half presents a glazed front. A metal pergola in the west façade projects noticeably from the two edges of the volume, providing protection and regulating direct sunlight into the glazed box. This very small programme is laid out on two floors, with a stairway at an angle to the façade leading up to the entrance. Llinàs investigated new arrangements that transformed the image of the Mediterranean house and selected architectural elements taken directly from the modern tradition. The expression of the house shuns the breakdown of volumes and resources handed down by tradition, and the pergola independently highlights the predominant element in southern landscapes: the luminosity of the sun's rays and its influence on the equipping of spaces.

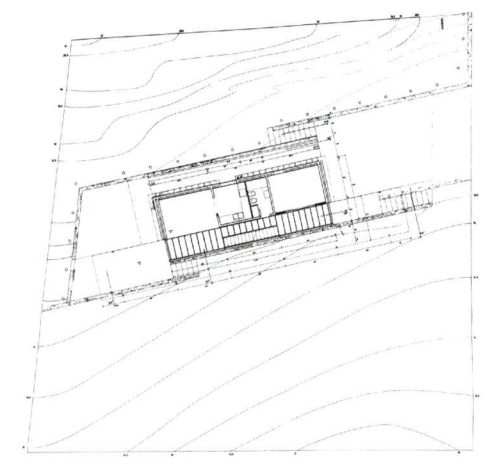

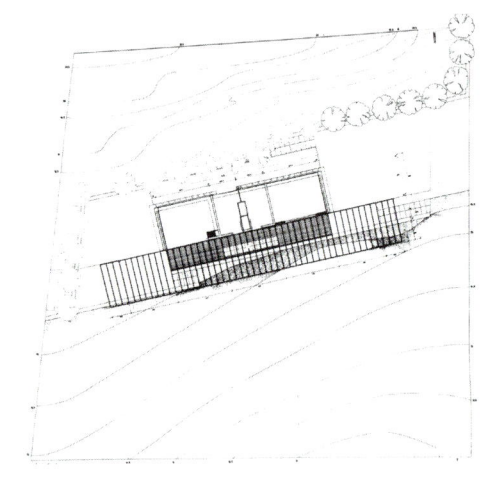

JORI-MISERACHS HOUSE
SINGLE-FAMILY DWELLING

Ignasi de Solà-Morales
1988-1990

C/ Port dels Orats, 9 - Aiguablava
Begur

The house stands on a regular rectangular plot of land sloping gently down to the sea and facing east. The departure point for the project is a line that crosses the site from one side to the other and establishes the secondary lines. This long glazed straight line becomes both the façade of the living room and the corridor leading to the bedrooms. The open space around the swimming pool and terrace calls for a second façade for the living room, defining the geometry that closes the house at the rear. The particular form of the house, apparently arbitrary, is the result of accepting the guideline of configuration suggested by the functional programme. The house presents an opaque image in all its façades, and the only open space that seems to generate activity is the private corner of the terrace and swimming pool.

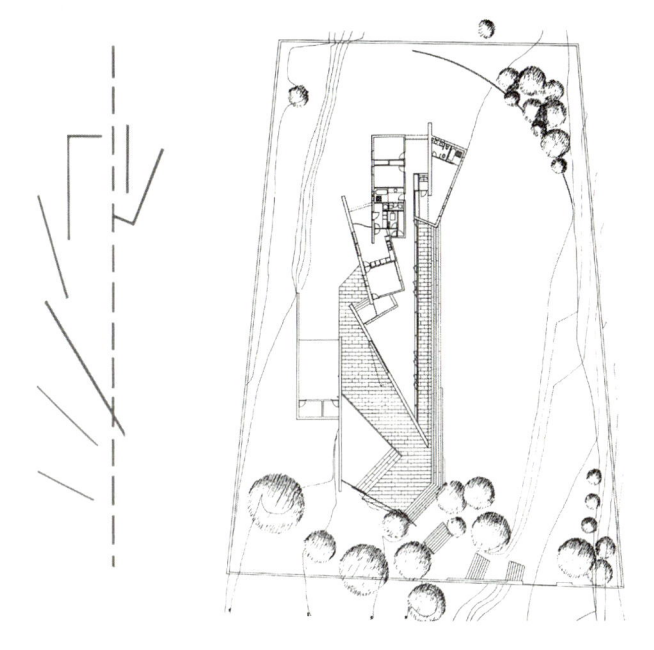

CASTANERA HOUSE
SINGLE-FAMILY DWELLING

Antoni Bonet i Castellana
1963-1964

C/ Golfet, 12 - Calella de Palafrugell

The house creates a platform of its own that dissociates it from the irregularities of the terrain. A large terrace with sea views incorporates various living areas: the inner lounge, on the same level; a courtyard with lines of sight over the lower level, where the bedrooms are situated; the stairway that leads down between this court and the living room; two large flowerbeds; the swimming pool and a large concrete pergola, at a height of 4.50 metres, resting on just three points. This great pergola on the terrace uses forceful architectural means to define a separate outdoor space, relegating the natural qualities of the place to the background.

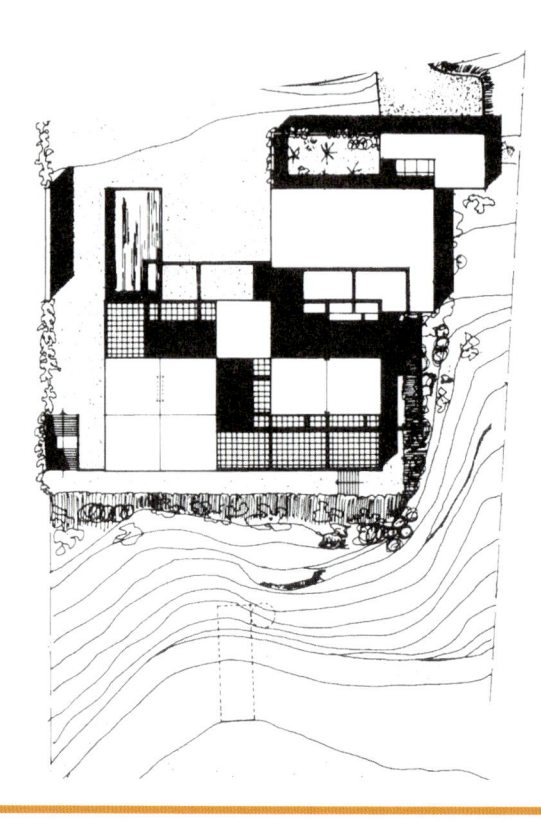

RAVENTÓS HOUSE
SINGLE-FAMILY DWELLING

Antoni Bonet i Castellana
1973-1974

C/ Golfet, 22 - Calella de Palafrugell

Bonet applied to Raventós house some of the criteria he discovered in other houses with similar locations, and invented new layouts using tried and tested elements. The house addresses the steep slope of the terrain by excavating a large chunk of ground in order to reduce the emerging volume to a minimum. The bedrooms are housed on the lower floor, tucked into the site, adapting the line of the retaining wall to the slightest peculiarities of the programme. On the upper floor, an array of trapezoid concrete vaults allows the domestic programme to develop freely. These vaults rest on large summers that free up the entire floor plan, producing visual communication throughout. The bedroom level moves further across the terrain to create a large terrace on the upper floor, enclosed by a stone wall that highlights the succession of volumes that make up the roof.

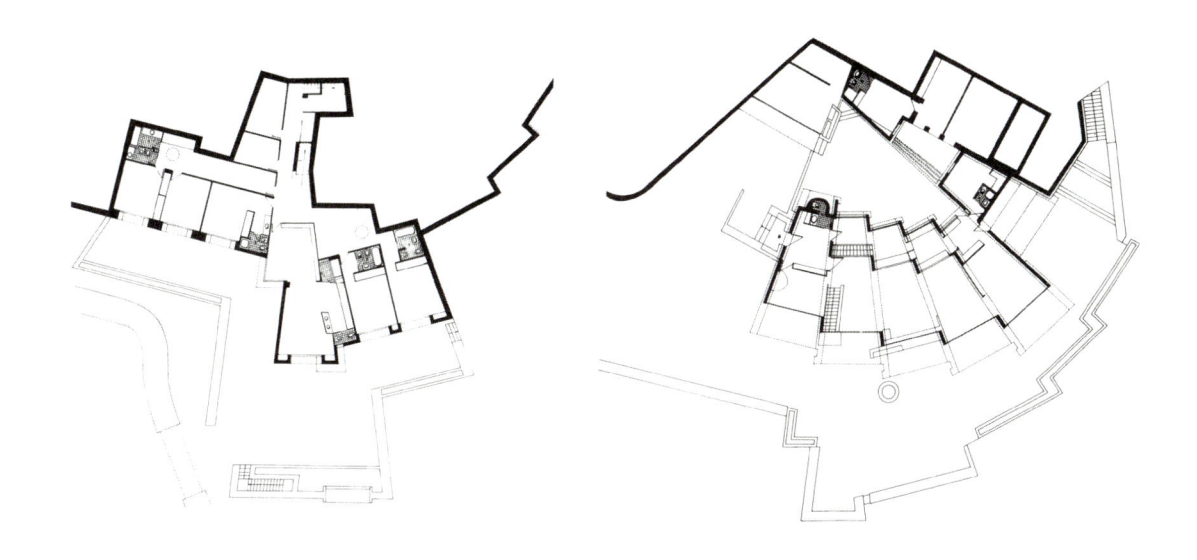

REGÀS HOUSE AND VANTAGE POINT
SINGLE-FAMILY DWELLING

Lluís Clotet, Oscar Tusquets
1970-1971

Mas Catalanet - Paratge Sobirà - Llofriu
Palafrugell

The site's prime position was occupied by a small farmhouse standing in ruins. This seemed to suggest that the best course of action was to demolish it and build a new house. Finally, it was decided to conserve the farmhouse to accommodate subsidiary functions. The new house is built against it, ensuring that its language does not mimic the old construction. The farmhouse is a tall building with well-defined edges and surfaces, and a tiled ridge roof. The extension is low, with a curved exterior profile and a flat landscaped roof. The strong north wind suggested creating an enclosed space to the south, where the swimming pool stands. The extension forms two sides to this courtyard, the old farmhouse one. The floor plan follows an orthogonal layout, opening like a stage curtain in its curved façade. The daytime area opens up southwards onto the courtyard through a porch and a completely glazed facing.

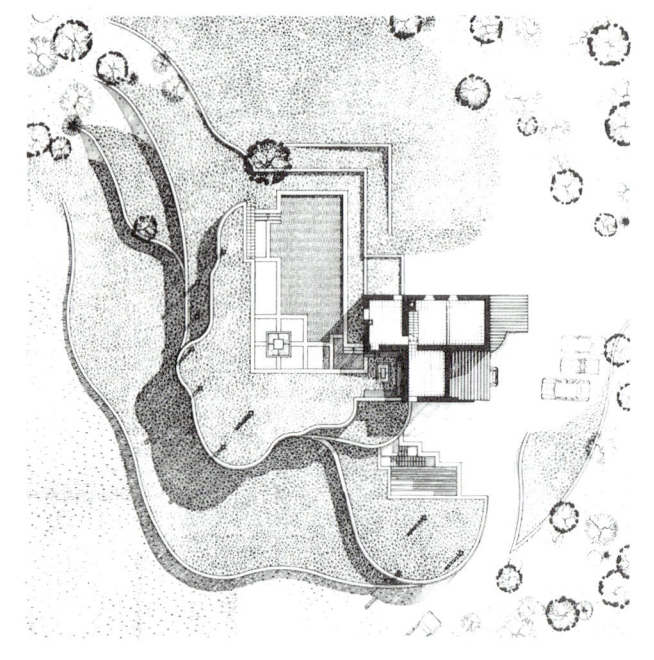

BOFILL HOUSE
SINGLE-FAMILY DWELLING

Ricard Bofill
1973

C/ de la Font, 20 - Mont-ras

Bofill built his parents' summer residence around an old ruined *masia* or farmhouse, distributing the different parts of the programme in independent pavilions. A large platform connected to the surrounding land by great stairways accommodates the swimming pool, which comprises the centre of the whole complex. The main L-shaped pavilion contains the living room, music room and master bedroom on the ground floor, and the library, games room and a second living room on the first floor, which is connected to the swimming pool by a stairway. A second pavilion beside the pool houses the dining room, which is the meeting place for the household. The remaining modules, 3 x 6 x 6 metres, contain the children's bedrooms and are built on the platform. The central platform generates a landscape of stairways and cypress trees that frees up life in the house from any kind of functional relation.

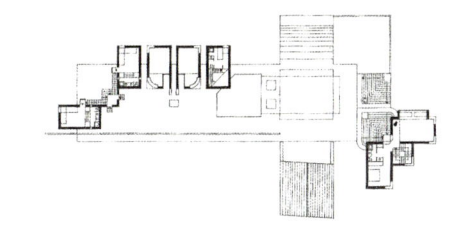

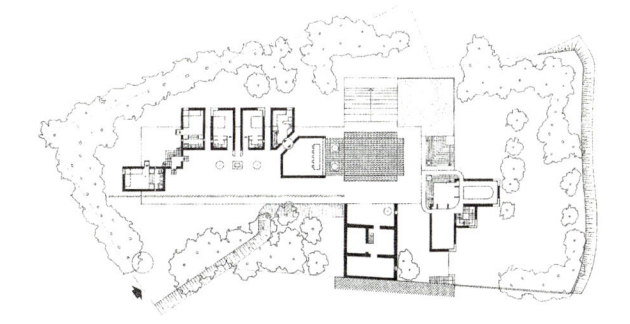

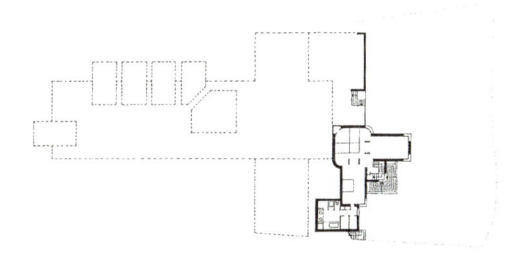

MAS VIDAL HOUSE
SINGLE-FAMILY DWELLING

Josep Pratmarsó
1958

C/ Raval de Baix - Vall-llobrega

The *mas* stands on the remains of a medieval structure comprising rough stone walls and a pointed-arch bridge. The ground floor accommodates secondary spaces: the tenant farmers' dwelling, a studio and service areas. The remainder forms a porch leading into the house, a brick masonry building that follows the layout of the lower walls. The upper volume adopts an L-shape of whitewashed walls and cut-out windows. The dining room forms a projecting volume, while the living room is concealed behind a large covered terrace. The house stands astride the old wall and a second bridge, parallel to the original. Pratmarsó engaged the new construction with the three dimensions of the old stone structure. Seen from a distance, the *mas* offers the image of an engagement of purist volumes that seem to float above the trees.

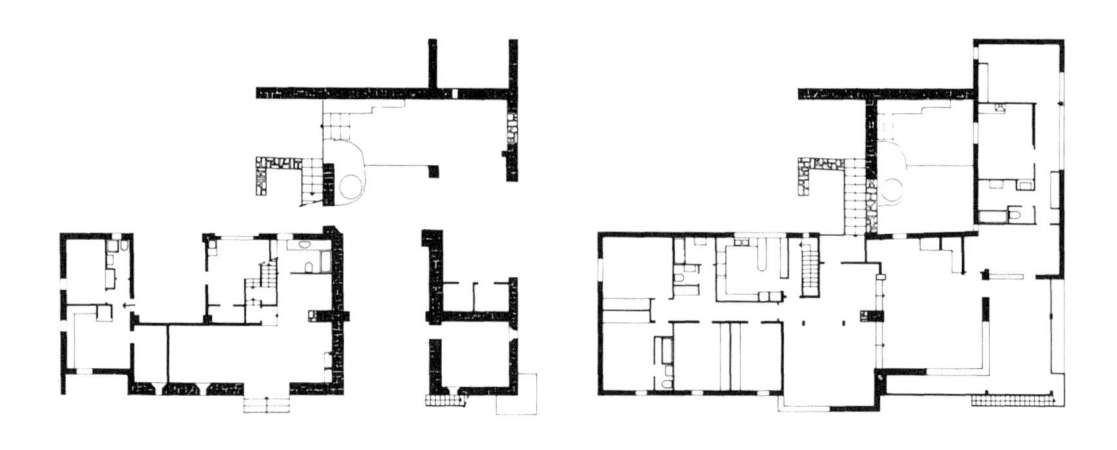

MAS GARBÀ HOUSE
SINGLE-FAMILY DWELLING

Josep Pratmarsó
1959

C/ Roca de Gria, 1 - Vall-llobrega

Situated on a gentle south-facing slope, the house reproduces the compositional criteria of traditional architecture, though highlighting the points in common with the best of modern architecture. The general approach separates two volumes: daytime spaces to the west and nighttime spaces to the east. The two volumes are connected by a glazed corridor containing the entrance. Each room adopts its own specific configuration according to its judicious distribution and orientation. Priority is given to the use of traditional materials such as roof tiles and masonry walls, though concrete linear elements are adopted where larger openings are required. Though the house is based firmly on the site, the foremost volume projects, making it the most visible from the entrance. The final perimeter of the house is the result not of the desire to mould its volume but of a rigorous observance of the priorities of distribution.

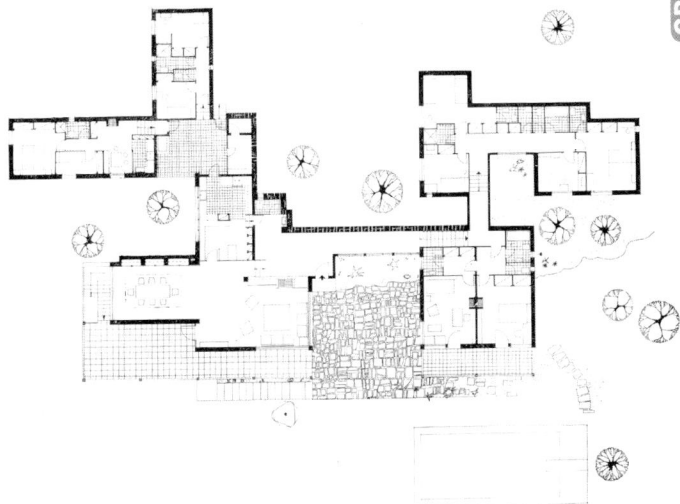

FOUR SINGLE-FAMILY ROW HOUSES

Lluís Nadal
1987-1989

C/ Josep Pla, 11 - Platja de la Fosca - Palamós

The programme of four dwellings for four siblings was the pretext for a very clear criterion of composition in a context marked by the inherent disorder of touristic colonization. The dwellings, standing on a corner site, are laid out successively to form a fan arrangement. The layout of the ground floors is determined by two typologically unusual elements: the small courtyard at the rear and the insertion of the stairs against the party wall, starting at the façade and leading to the centre of the upper floor. Access to the communal space at the rear is through a small door beside the washbasin, and the bedrooms open up onto the front façade via a terrace that is segregated from the general composition. The stairwells and large narrow eaves define the scope of each house. The complex stands on a slight embankment that isolates it from the street and raises its sights.

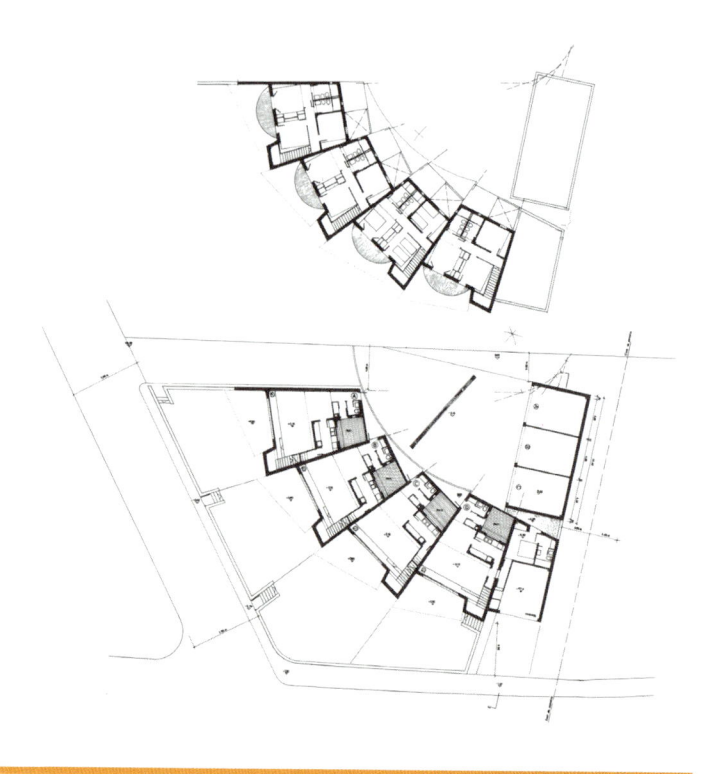

HOUSE AT LA FOSCA
SINGLE-FAMILY DWELLING

Jordi Garcés
2003

Pg. de la Fosca, 22 - Platja de la Fosca - Palamós

The particular configuration of the house responds to the unfavourable conditions of the site, which turns its largest side onto the street and its smallest towards the sea. Garcés adopted a compositional criterion of equal modules supported by elongated pilasters, a system that allows for free growth in width, depth and height. The house becomes a series of additional pieces that form a very powerful architectural infrastructure, enabling the highly versatile insertion of the more domestic areas. On the street side, the house adopts an urban appearance, with a façade that is flat yet modulated with irregular openings. The system of additions reaches the sea's edge with a large double-height porch that marks the furthest reach of the house. The exterior spaces are conceived of as part of the same system, with the capacity to accommodate very varied programmes and organizations.

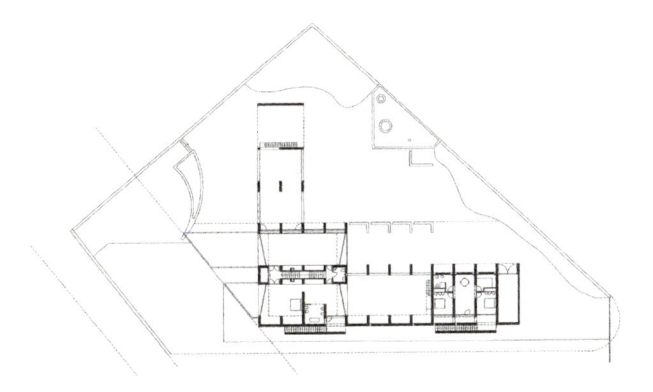

HOUSE AT THE GOLF CLUB
COSTA BRAVA GOLF CLUB

Lluís Clotet, Oscar Tusquets
1978-1979

Golf Costa Brava residential development - La Masia - Santa Cristina d'Aro

The treatment given to the urbanization of this golf club is unusual in this country. The grassy course extends with no fences into the gardens of the detached houses. The lawns continue into the clubhouse's garden, which is also planted with evergreen oak and pine like those covering the nearby mountainsides. A row of deciduous trees was introduced along the south-facing façade, two poplars and flowers were planted in the triangular courts, and two bay trees give the entrance a little added privacy. A gazebo at the far end of the plot, against the retaining wall, is overgrown with wisteria. The house and the swimming pool, with its annexe, are designed as a series of simple boxes built according to traditional means. These elements engage to adapt to the site and create open spaces that are protected from the wind and views from the street.

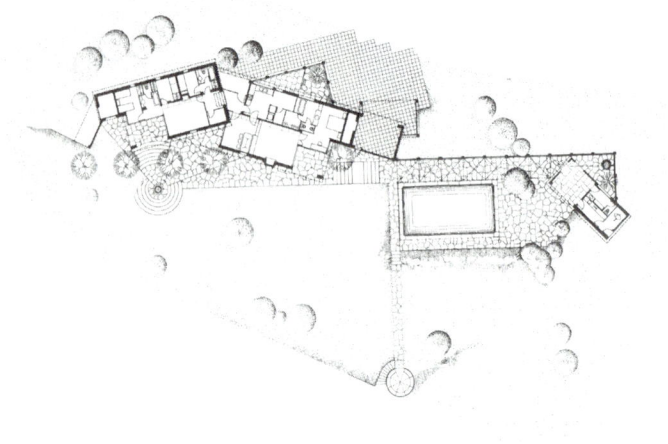

HOUSE-CUM-STUDY FOR THE CARTOONIST CESC

Esteve Bonell, Josep Maria Gil
1979-1982

Av. de l'Església - Santa Cristina d'Aro

This programme for a house-cum-studio for a cartoonist is set in the hills, in an undeveloped spot. The site is conditioned by a large granite rock that determines the arrangement of the volumes. The house is divided into two volumes separated from the rock, one to house the dwelling and the other for the studio. The space between the two volumes marks the entrance, and both are drawn back on the ground floor to show the way. The stairways of the two volumes, both comprising a single run, are situated at an angle to the rock. Entrance to the dwelling follows the withdrawn wall of the living room, around the rock. All the bedrooms are enclosed in a rigorously arranged unit, and the living room and studio are placed one to either side of the front path, configuring the complex articulation of the point where the two volumes come together.

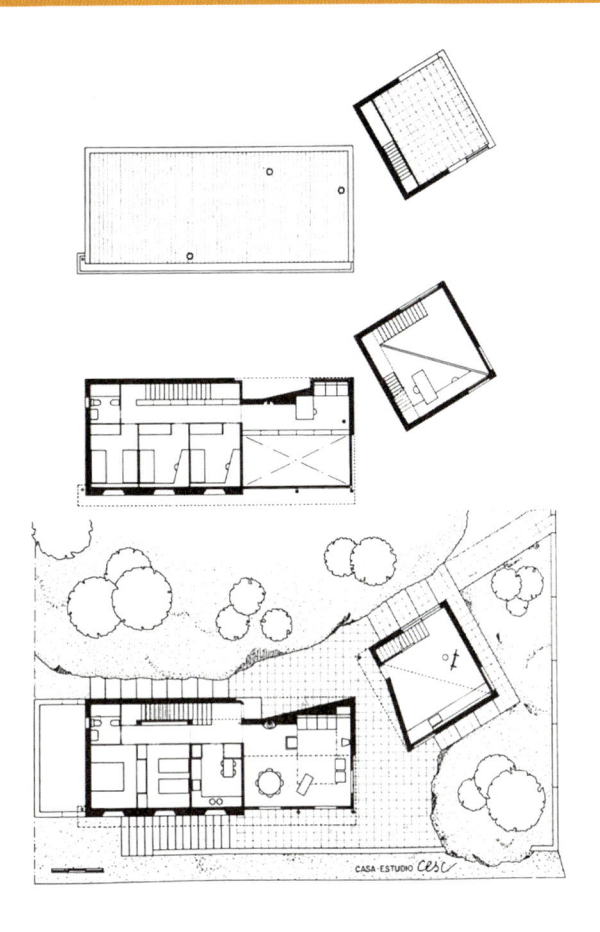

CENDRÓS HOUSE
MIXED-USE BUILDING

Manuel Ribas i Piera
1968

Rbla. Vidal, 1-5 - Pg. del Mar, 24 - Sant Feliu de Guíxols

The programme includes the use of the ground floor for shops, a rental apartment and the owners' home. The latter is a double-height dwelling on the top floor, leaving the mezzanine floor for the rental apartment. The limited dimensions of the site and the complex demands of the circulations called for a hierarchy of two stairwells and the setting aside of spaces such as the bedrooms of both dwellings and the ground-floor garage. The external configuration of the house reflects the nature of the programme, offering an unusual image among the surrounding buildings.

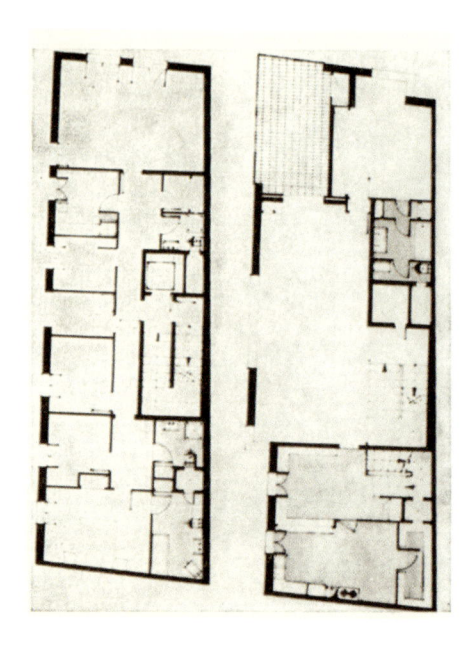

APARTMENT BUILDING

Ramon Muñoz, Robert Pallí, Rodrigo Prats, Antonio Sanmartín
1990-1992

C/ Gravina, 49-59 - C/ Fortuny, 26-36 - C/ Bourg de Peage, 25 - Sant Feliu de Guíxols

This project involved two independent interventions in a single street block with the aim of organizing the interior space and entrance to and good lighting of the ground-floor shops. The result is a passage between Carrer Bourg de Peage and Carrer Fortuny in the form of two large arabesque-shaped ramps that organize the inner courtyard. The transformation comprised an open, interwoven system of full and empty spaces that is reflected in all the façades, as the structural elements form cross-shaped groupings that restore the identity of each dwelling and extend the small interior spaces towards the street.

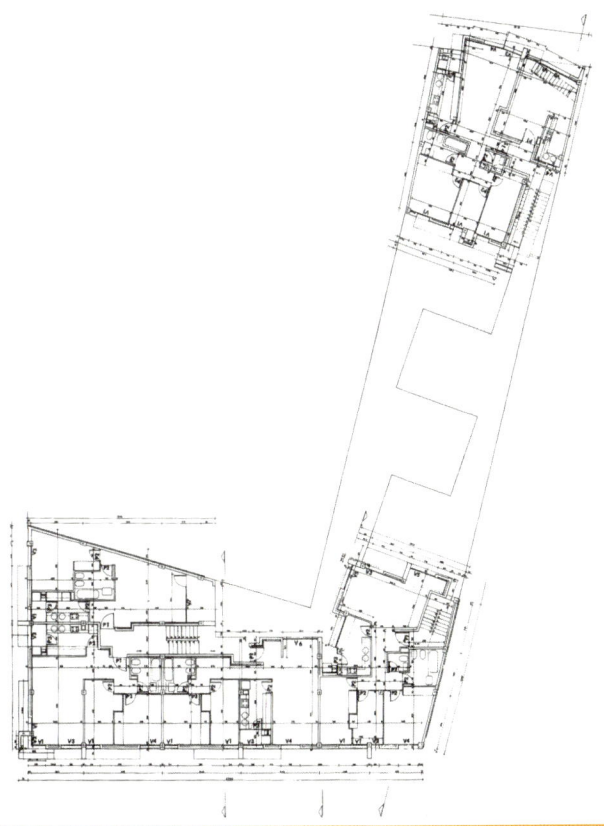

077

SALGOT HOUSE
SINGLE-FAMILY DWELLING

Jordi Garcés, Enric Sòria
1988-1989

Plots 6 and 8 - Vista Alegre development - St. Telm
Sant Feliu de Guíxols

078

COURTS BUILDING

Jordi Moliner, Josep Lluís Mateo
1990-1993

C/ Antoni Campmany, 15-21 - Sant Feliu de Guíxols

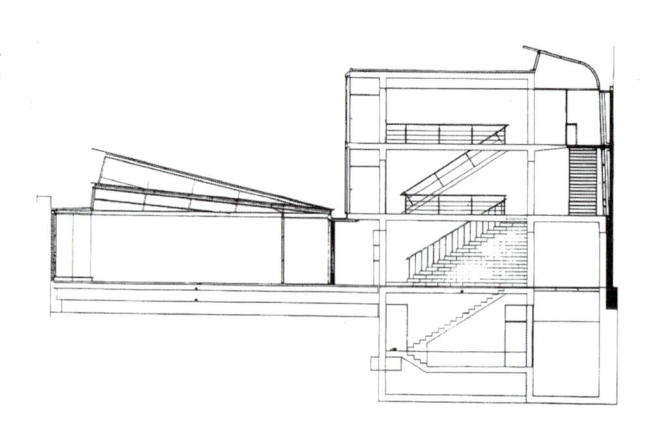

079

IES SANT FELIU
SECONDARY SCHOOL

Rafael Aranda, Carme Pigem, Ramon Vilalta
1997-2001

C/ Canigó, 41 - Sant Feliu de Guíxols

The house is situated on a raised platform with vistas over the sea. The overall configuration is governed by the long uninterrupted lines of vision that start at the opposite side. It is made up of two rectangular volumes, bevelled at the edge pointing out to sea. The single-storey rear volume houses the bedrooms. The front volume contains the daytime areas with a studio on the upper floor. This volume faces northwards in the form of a terrace that opens up to the horizon, filtered by a pergola that runs crosswise. The geometry of the circulations generates all the layouts, producing itineraries that either head towards or away from the sea.

The main reference of the project is the party wall left by the pre-existing construction, which stands independently of the new building. The roof of the main volume, parallel to the party wall, is pinched in at the rear and opens up to the other side of the site. This volume houses the courtrooms, and is smaller than the neighbouring buildings. The remainder of the programme is contained in volumes at the front with differing rooftops. This gives the building a front and a back that relate to the urban fabric and are indifferent to the street, where the composition can be seen in the section.

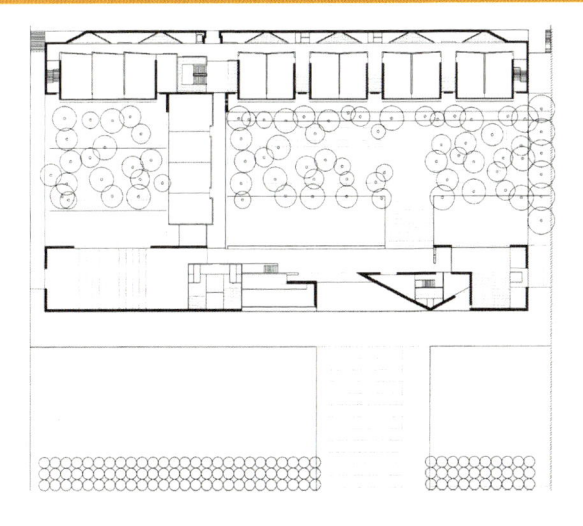

The project abandons any attempt to dialogue with pre-existing elements or act as a mechanism to transform the place. This totally decontextualized building manifests itself as a blind volume that conceals the heights and the expression of the programme. The floor plan is laid out in the form of two very long volumes, one for the classrooms and the other for communal spaces, offices and services. The lighting is resolved at all points by indirect openings in order to preserve the clean lines of the elevations. The windows highlight the exaggerated proportion of the building, which, in its extreme horizontality, alludes to a completely flat, isotropic base.

Girona

"ESCOLA DEL VEÏNAT"
INFANTS' AND PRIMARY SCHOOL

Oriol Bohigas, Josep Maria Martorell,
David Mackay, Albert Puigdomènech
1988-1991

C/ Enric Granados, 8 - Salt

The school comprises a one-storey circular space that turns around a small playground for the nursery school. Each classroom is communicated both with the playground and the tree-lined exterior. The classrooms have a ridge roof incorporating a transom for cross ventilation. The circular space is divided into two clearly differentiated parts, the primary and the nursery school. The slits left between the two parts channel entrance from the street and to the sports courts, situated in an annexed space. Two taller elements emerge from the complex: the circular tower of the library, beside the entrance, and the volume of the multipurpose hall, with a higher prismatic roof of corrugated sheet, painted a dark colour, like the rest of the roofs. The structure combines brick pilasters with concrete beams and supports, and adapts at all times to the specificities of the programme.

081

SANTA CATERINA GENERAL HOSPITAL

Manuel Brullet, Albert de Pineda, Alfonso de Luna, Albert Vitaller
1995-2005

C/ Doctor Castany, 90 - Martí i Julià Hospital Complex- Salt

The new hospital forms part of the Martí i Julià Hospital complex, originating with the presence of the old psychiatric sanatorium designed by Francesc Folguera and Emili Blanch in the 1930s. The hospital of Santa Caterina is situated on the south side of the complex, and its interior is occupied by a grid of single-storey pavilions generating courtyards that are invaded by vegetation. The hospital's implantation is low-rise and extensive, and comprises a bi-reticular grid superposed over a linear structure that stretches from east to west. The lines of circulations obey two parallel lines that follow the same orientation: one for staff and one for outpatients. Each functional unit is situated within this basic structure. The product is a hospital structure that allows for growth and modification, an open organization that is one of the main premisses of the design.

DIVÍ-BAENA HOUSE
SINGLE-FAMILY DWELLING

Josep Maria Birulés, Frederic Cabré, Pià Romans
1992-1993

C/ Eugeni d'Ors, 24 - Fornells de la Selva

This large north-facing plot was chosen for a correspondingly large domestic programme. The position of the house is determined by orientation and gradient, which suggested a position at the far end of the garden, acting as a retaining structure. The project showcases the north-facing views via a porch that looks out in two directions and is connected with the garden and the living room. The layout of the ground floor reflects the decision to define open-plan spaces articulated by their geometry. The living room is laid out independently, a square space that engages diagonally with the orthogonal layout of the rest of the house. While the general implantation forms an L-shape at a corner of the plot, the approach rejects the typological dwelling legacy and proposes an engagement of the various rooms based on a genuine interpretation of the specific conditions of place.

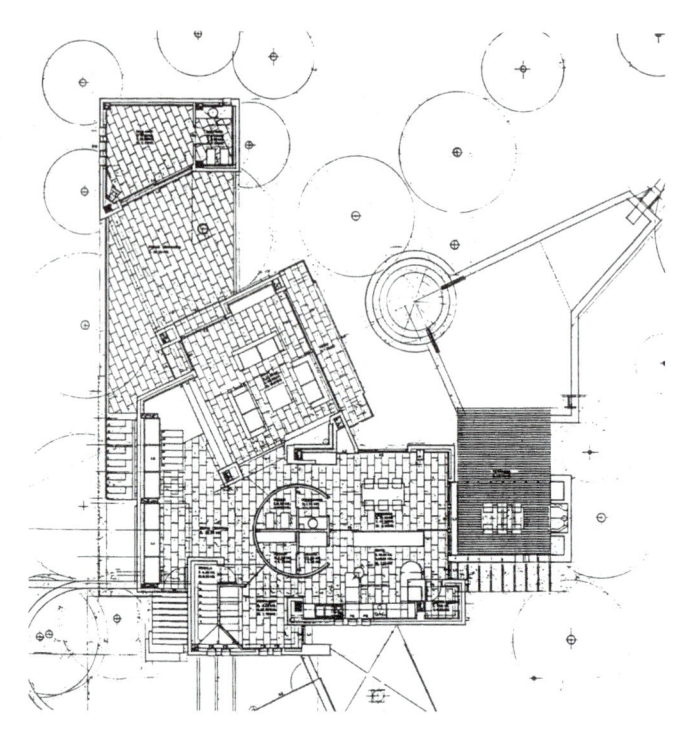

HOTEL SANT MARCH

Joan M. de Ribot
1955

Av. del Pelegrí, 2 - Tossa de Mar

The hotel adopts specific solutions for each part of the site, a plot with a very narrow façade that opens into the interior. The entrance stands back from the façade alignment, and a sloping false ceiling emphasizes the opening into the inner courtyard. Here, the rooms are laid out in a two-storey L-shape, and the entire ambience of the garden is determined by the composition of the façades. The terrace is protected by a series of vertical slats held in place by a brace. The railings are brightly painted panels. The whole is a rhythmic succession resting on a regular-coursed masonry base, finished off by the outline of the curved roofing tiles. Ribot reinvented the stylistic discourse of modern architecture in the context of the world of tourism, where the picturesque and the values of vernacular architecture were invading every town and village on the Costa Brava.

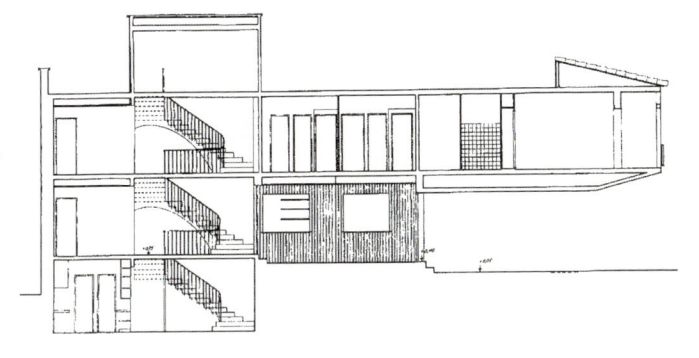

NICOLÁS VALENZUELA HOUSE
SINGLE-FAMILY DWELLING

Eva Jiménez, Xavier Llobet
2003-2007

C/ dels Satèl·lits, 38 - Lloret Residencial housing development - Lloret de Mar

PRESENT STATE:
In construction

The house relates to the site with the intention of freeing itself of functional constraint. The wall around the plot also acts as a retaining structure, folding to form the entrance to the garage on the semibasement floor. The ground floor comprises a volume that extends over the plot at one end and takes in the swimming pool at the other. The first floor runs crosswise to the ground floor, projecting out from the stairwell. Two picture windows in the longest facades look out over both sides of the site. This solution frees the site from functional requirements, as the only point of contact is the front door, in the volume containing the bedrooms. The house consists of a reinforced concrete structure, and the projecting upper volume comprises two Vierendeel girders running between the outer walls.

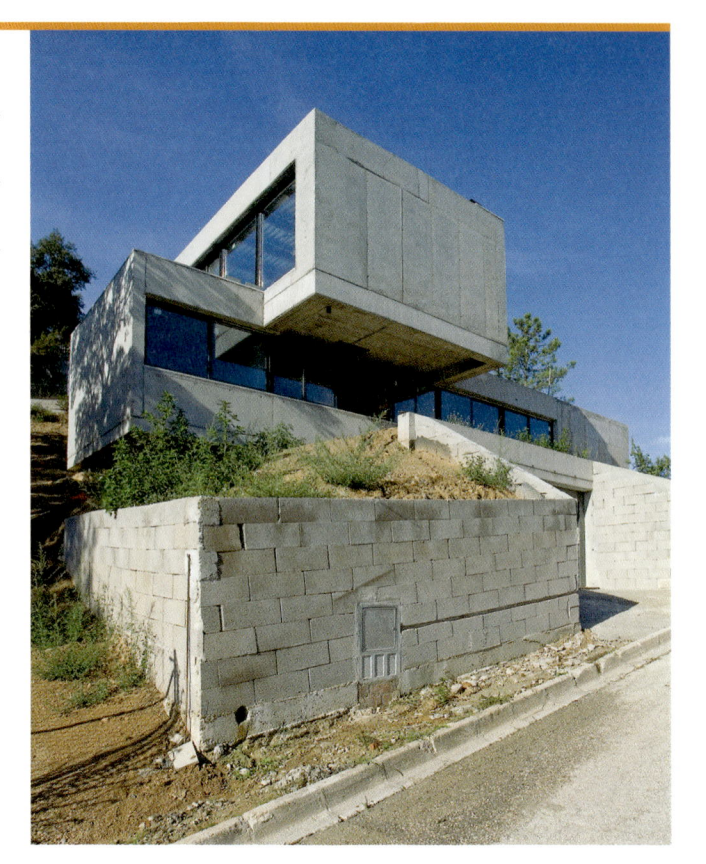

BLANES COUNTY LIBRARY
BLANES TOURIST OFFICE

Ramon Artigues, Ramon Sanabria
2001-2002

Pg. de Catalunya, 2 - Blanes

The design of the building reflects its suburban condition as an element with the potential to create a new focus of activity, away from the centre and near the seafront. The organism turns its back on the town, presenting an almost blind volume of three façades that form an acute angle containing the entrance. The ground floor constitutes a continuous itinerary from the entrance to the opposite façade, which opens up to the sea via a glazed wall that runs the height of the building, and is protected by a large awning that overlooks the Mediterranean. The ground floor is an open-plan space that continues the square created to the rear, with a landscaped courtyard that guarantees transparency between the front and the rear areas. This floor houses the tourist office and other small rooms, while the library proper is on the upper floor.

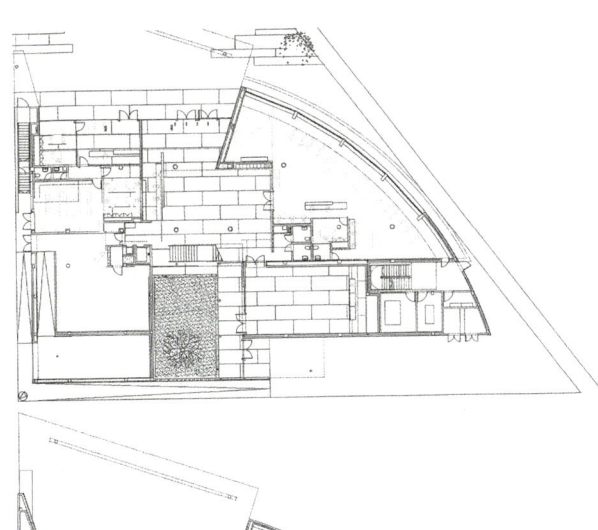

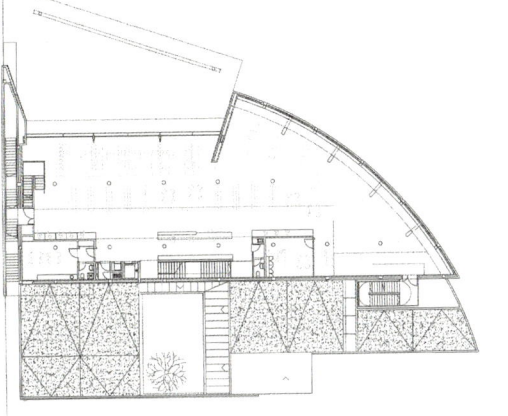

BCN – The Barcelona area

Territorial scope

The centre of the Barcelona area is the *comarca*, or county, of Barcelonès. To the northeast, following the line of the coast, it includes the whole *comarca* of Maresme, reaching its upper border. Heading inland, it takes in the *comarca* of Vallès Oriental, coinciding approximately with Route 2. Route 3 roughly covers Vallès Occidental. To the south, it encompasses the coastal strip of Baix Llobregat, descending as far as the *comarca* of Garraf. This area therefore follows the Barcelona coastline, heading northeast and southwest, with two incursions inland into the Vallès area. The counties of Bages, Anoia and Alt Penedès lie outside this area.

La Garriga
L'Ametlla del Vallès
Palafolls
Cardedeu
Llinars del Vallès
Canovelles
Castellar del Vallès
Granollers
Pineda de Mar
Matadepera
Palau-solità i Plegamans
Terrassa
Argentona
Caldes d'Estrac
Sabadell
Mollet del Vallès
Vilassar de Dalt
Mataró
La Llagosta
Premià de Dalt
Cerdanyola del Vallès
Vilassar de Mar
Santa Coloma de Gramenet
Sant Cugat del Vallès
Badalona
Sant Feliu de Llobregat
Sant Just Desvern
Barcelona
Santa Coloma de Cervelló
Esplugues de Llobregat
Sant Joan Despí
Cornellà de Llobregat
Sant Boi de Llobregat
L'Hospitalet de Llobregat
Viladecans
El Prat de Llobregat
Sant Pere de Ribes
Castelldefels
Sitges

Road structure

CITY

If you are driving from France, the fastest route is via La Jonquera, taking the AP-7 motorway that passes through Figueres and Girona. If you enter via Portbou, the best option is to take the N-260 to Figueres and then pick up the motorway. Heading southwards, the AP-7 takes you to Tarragona and Amposta. If you are travelling from Barcelona to Tortosa, the best route is to go first to Amposta and then follow a short stretch of the C-12. If you are going from Barcelona to Lleida, the A-2 motorway goes there direct via Igualada, Cervera and Mollerussa. On the south side of Barcelona, the A-2 motorway takes a major detour near Vilafranca del Penedès, the AP-2, which also enters Lleida from the south. If you are travelling to Madrid, the fastest route is via Lleida.

ROUTE 1 covers Maresme as far as the town of Palafolls, on the border of the county of Selva. All the municipalities featured are by the coast and are interlinked by the N-II coast road. There is also a motorway running parallel to the N-II with exits for all of the places listed, offering faster access: the C-32 motorway. It is therefore best to take this motorway and look out for the right turnoff. After Badalona, there are turnoffs to Premià de Dalt, Vilassar de Dalt, Vilassar de Mar, Mataró, Caldes d'Estrac, Canet de Mar, Pineda de Mar and Palafolls. The C-32 motorway goes as far as Palafolls, which is slightly inland.

ROUTE 2 takes the C-33 expressway direct to Mollet del Vallès, after passing through Santa Coloma de Gramenet. After Mollet, the route branches three ways, to Llinars del Vallès, Granollers and La Garriga. From Mollet, the AP-7 motorway to Girona takes you to Granollers and Llinars. For La Garriga, there is a turnoff at Granollers and the C-17 expressway goes via Canovelles and Ametlla del Vallès. For Cardedeu, the best route is via Llinars.

ROUTE 3 takes the C-58 motorway to Cerdanyola, Sabadell and Terrassa. For Sant Cugat del Vallès, take the Cerdanyola turnoff. From Sabadell, the C-55 goes to Palau-Solità i Plegamans, and take the B-154 for Castellar del Vallès. For Matadepera, the best route is via Terrassa, as it is a few kilometres to the north of this former textile town.

ROUTE 4 covers the inland stretch of the *comarca* of Baix Llobregat. Sant Just Desvern, Esplugues de Llobregat, Sant Joan Despí and Sant Feliu de Llobregat are all towns in Barcelona's metropolitan area of influence. The best route is the west exit along Diagonal, taking the B-23 motorway and heading inland out of Barcelona. Santa Coloma de Cervelló is a village on the other side of the river Llobregat, best reached via Cornellà and Sant Boi de Llobregat.

ROUTE 5 follows the coast southwest, covering the coastal area of Baix Llobregat and Garraf. Driving out of Barcelona via Hospitalet, the C-32 motorway continues to El Prat de Llobregat, Cornellà and then Gavà, Castelldefels, Sitges and Vilanova i la Geltrú. Viladecans is a little further inland, and the best route is from Cornellà. Sant Pere de Ribes is also a short distance from the coast, and is best reached from Sitges.

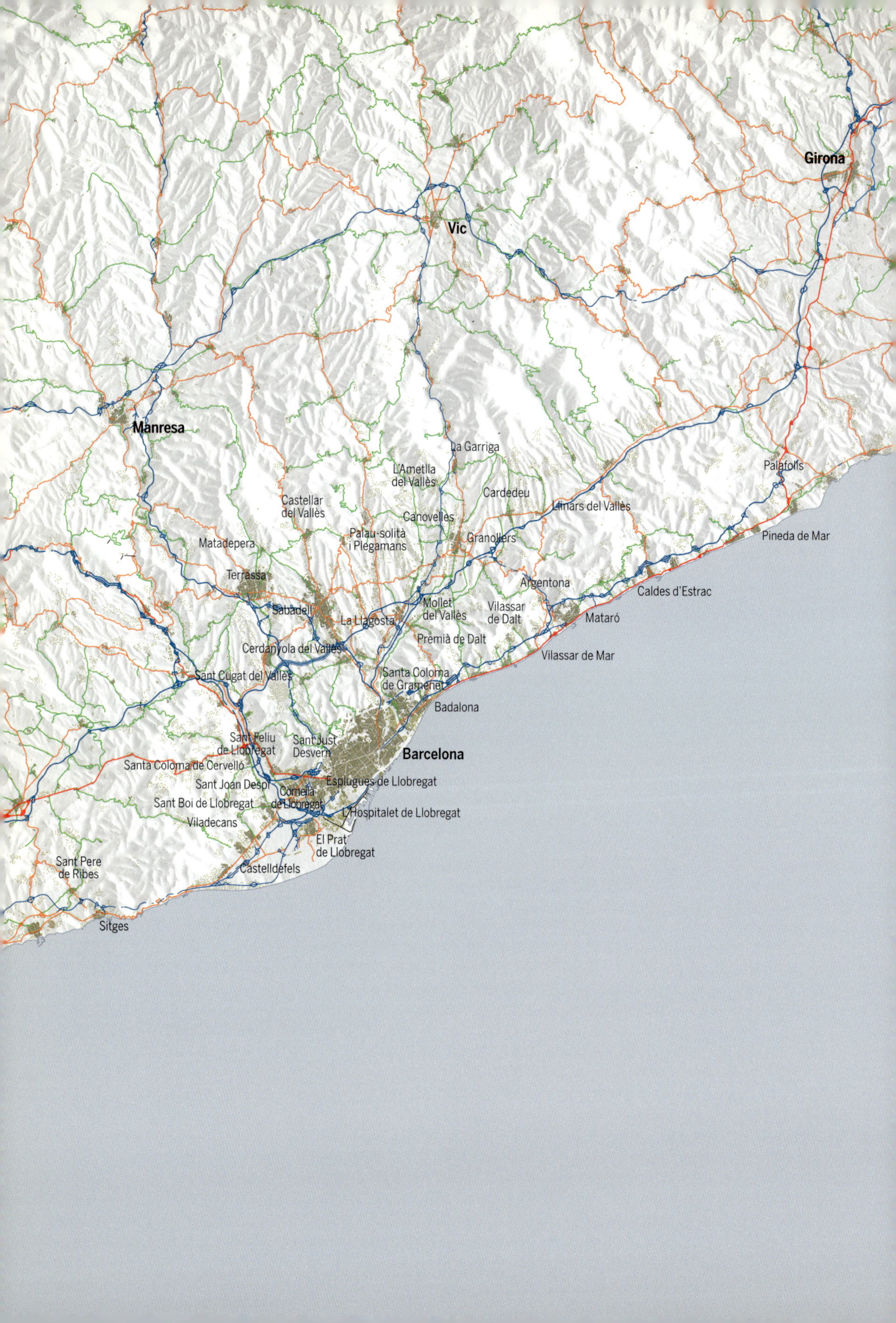

Municipalities	Comarca	Surface area (municipality)	Population (2001)
BARCELONA	Barcelonès	100.4 km^2	1,503,884 inhabitants
ROUTE 1			
BADALONA	Barcelonès	21.2 km^2	205,836 inhabitants
PREMIÀ DE DALT	Maresme	6.6 km^2	9,114 inhabitants
VILASSAR DE MAR	Maresme	4.01 km^2	17,369 inhabitants
VILASSAR DE DALT	Maresme	8.87 km^2	7,904 inhabitants
ARGENTONA	Maresme	25.4 km^2	9,896 inhabitants
MATARÓ	Maresme	22.5 km^2	106,358 inhabitants
CALDES D'ESTRAC	Maresme	0.9 km^2	1,974 inhabitants
PINEDA DE MAR	Maresme	10.8 km^2	21,074 inhabitants
PALAFOLLS	Maresme	16.5 km^2	5,917 inhabitants
ROUTE 2			
SANTA COLOMA DE GRAMENET	Barcelonès	7.0 km^2	112,992 inhabitants
LA LLAGOSTA	Vallès Oriental	3.0 km^2	12,042 inhabitants
MOLLET DEL VALLÈS	Vallès Oriental	10.8 km^2	47,270 inhabitants
CARDEDEU	Vallès Oriental	12.1 km^2	12,792 inhabitants
LLINARS DEL VALLÈS	Vallès Oriental	27.7 km^2	7,238 inhabitants
GRANOLLERS	Vallès Oriental	14.9 km^2	53,105 inhabitants
CANOVELLES	Vallès Oriental	6.7 km^2	12,912 inhabitants
L'AMETLLA DEL VALLÈS	Vallès Oriental	14.2 km^2	6,133 inhabitants
LA GARRIGA	Vallès Oriental	18.8 km^2	12,037 inhabitants
ROUTE 3			
CERDANYOLA DEL VALLÈS	Vallès Occidental	30.6 km^2	53,343 inhabitants
SANT CUGAT DEL VALLÈS	Vallès Occidental	48.2 km^2	60,265 inhabitants
SABADELL	Vallès Occidental	37.9 km^2	183,788 inhabitants
TERRASSA	Vallès Occidental	70.2 km^2	173,775 inhabitants
PALAU-SOLITÀ I PLEGAMANS	Vallès Occidental	14.9 km^2	11,384 inhabitants
CASTELLAR DEL VALLÈS	Vallès Occidental	44.9 km^2	18,255 inhabitants
MATADEPERA	Vallès Occidental	25.2 km^2	7,190 inhabitants
ROUTE 4			
ESPLUGUES DE LLOBREGAT	Baix Llobregat	4.6 km^2	45,127 inhabitants
SANT JUST DESVERN	Baix Llobregat	7.8 km^2	13,870 inhabitants
SANT JOAN DESPÍ	Baix Llobregat	6.2 km^2	28,772 inhabitants
SANT FELIU DE LLOBREGAT	Baix Llobregat	11.8 km^2	40,042 inhabitants
SANTA COLOMA DE CERVELLÓ	Baix Llobregat	7.5 km^2	5,557 inhabitants
ROUTE 5			
L'HOSPITALET DE LLOBREGAT	Barcelonès	12.4 km^2	239,019 inhabitants
EL PRAT DE LLOBREGAT	Baix Llobregat	31.2 km^2	61,818 inhabitants
CORNELLÀ DE LLOBREGAT	Baix Llobregat	7.0 km^2	79,979 inhabitants
SANT BOI DE LLOBREGAT	Baix Llobregat	21.5 km^2	78,738 inhabitants
VILADECANS	Baix Llobregat	20.4 km^2	56,841 inhabitants
CASTELLDEFELS	Baix Llobregat	12.9 km^2	46,428 inhabitants
SITGES	Garraf	43.9 km^2	19,893 inhabitants
SANT PERE DE RIBES	Garraf	40.8 km^2	23,134 inhabitants

CAFÉ-RESTAURANT OF THE 1888 WORLD FAIR
MUSEUM OF ZOOLOGY

Lluís Domènech i Montaner
1887-1888

Passeig Picasso
(Parc de la Ciutadella) - Barcelona

This building manifests a new series of architectural values in the framework of the first Great Exhibition. A large hall housing a café-restaurant occupies the ground floor. This rectangular box has double façades, allowing the building's outer image to be modelled independently of the interior requirements. The four corners are each emphasized by a tower with a different crown. The structure reflects a rigorous application of brickwork masonry and iron, the protagonists of the new architecture. The relation between ornamentation and structure is also clearly addressed: the crenels in the outer wall run right around the building accompanied by vitrified ceramic shields with hermetic inscriptions. This was the first flagship building of Modernisme, presenting features that other architects would later apply to more complex programmes.

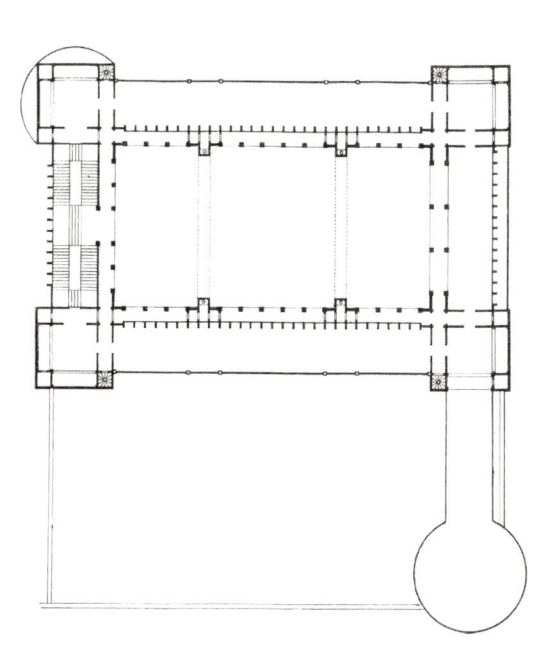

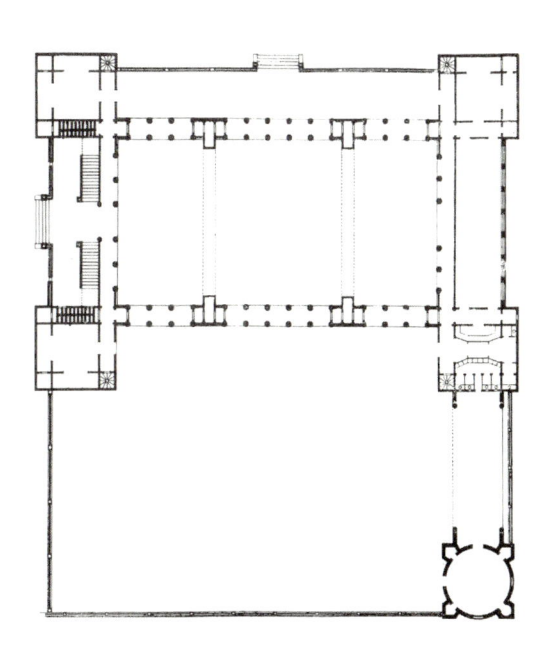

Barcelona 107

"ELS QUATRE GATS"
PERE AND FRANCESC MARTÍ I PUIG HOUSE

Josep Puig i Cadafalch
1895-1896

C/ Montsió, 3 bis - Barcelona

This was Puig i Cadafalch's first design in Barcelona after various works in Mataró and Argentona. It is a reinterpretation of the Gothic house: the ground floor houses Els Quatre Gats bar, a meeting point for the most cosmopolitan intellectual elite of Modernisme, the "lovers of the north", in the words of Opisso. The *piano nobile* contains the owner's private home, and the third and fourth floors hold rental apartments. Puig picked up his clients' northward-looking aspirations in a composition based on the Northern European Gothic style: brickwork masonry with profuse stone ornament, supported by seven large pointed arches and crowned by a gallery beneath the eaves, with sculptures by Josep Llimona and Eusebi Arnau, and ironwork by Manuel Ballarín. The galleries on the *piano nobile* and over the main doorway incorporate dense, flamboyant ornamentation. The house is a forceful representation of the sensibility of its owners.

PALAU GÜELL
NEWLY CONSTRUCTED TOWNHOUSE

Antoni Gaudí
1885-1889

C/ Nou de la Rambla, 3-5 - Barcelona

This was the principal townhouse of Baron Güell, built on the site of two apartment buildings at the cultural high point for the city that was the first Great Exhibition. The whole turns around a large central space on the *piano nobile* that rises above the roof and hosted all the cultural and social life. Gaudí created an unusual vertical order in which the four above-grade storeys are expressed in the façade by six different orders, also divided horizontally. Two catenary arches in the entrance channel access respectively to the coach houses, the stables and the great hall. This townhouse was designed as a unitary space experienced by means of the stairway, which makes its way around the great hall up to the bedrooms. It manifests Gaudí's respect for the typology of the medieval townhouse, though also infused with a sacralized sense of space.

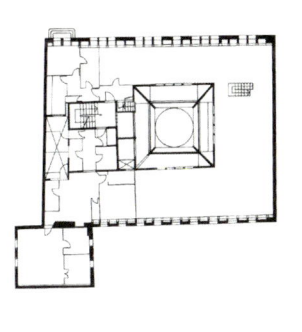

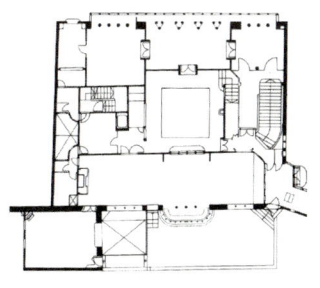

CALVET HOUSE
NEWLY CONSTRUCTED RENTAL APARTMENT BUILDING

Antoni Gaudí
1898-1904

C/ Casp, 48 - Barcelona

This is a bold interpretation of the characteristic rented apartment houses found in the Eixample district, in this case with two dwellings per floor and a façade marked by five openings. The street frontage, with its trilobate balconies, varied courses of ashlars and a crown of two baroque tympanums, contrasts with the rear façade, which incorporates strips of white sgraffiti in both galleries and balustrades of simplified lines. However, the street façade is full of small discreet symbols, such as mushrooms, a reference to the owner's interest in fungi, and the cypress tree, the symbol of hospitality, beneath the gallery. Gaudí also had recourse to the exception, with baroque references in the hallway and in the interiors of the dwellings, all different, not hesitating to employ pargeting, artificial stone or other arts of dissimulation to produce the aesthetic effects he desired.

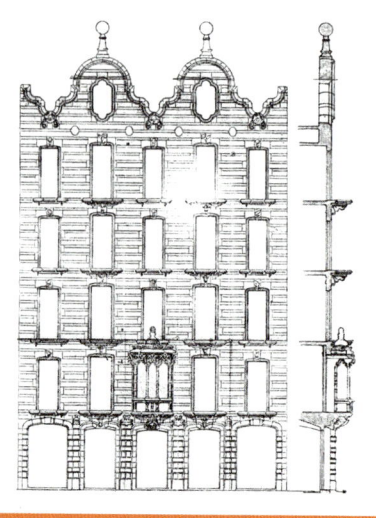

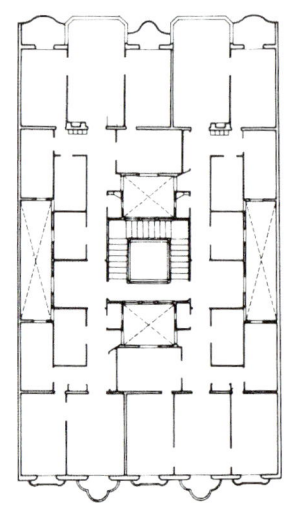

BATLLÓ HOUSE
REMODELLING OF A RENTAL
APARTMENT BUILDING

Antoni Gaudí
1904-1906

Pg. de Gràcia, 43 - Barcelona

Here, Gaudí was called on to completely transform the image of an existing house. He was given free rein to incorporate new structural ideas, references to nature, all manner of symbolism and abstract ornamentation. Another floor was added, giving the façade an asymmetrical crown that took into account the presence of the neighbouring Amatller House. The *piano nobile* incorporates naturalism in the actual bearing structure, and the attics introduce the parabolic arches that he had previously designed. The collaboration of Josep Maria Jujol lent greater freedom to the work with different materials and the intensity of effects. The two façades, forward and rear, ripple like curtains. This might be considered Gaudí's first mature work, in which he achieved a surprising synthesis of the structural materiality of the building and the dreamlike nature of the references that are found throughout.

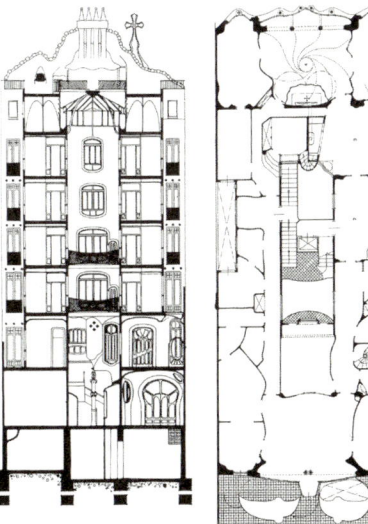

ANTONI AMATLLER HOUSE
REMODELLING OF A 19TH-CENTURY HOUSE

Josep Puig i Cadafalch
1898-1900

Pg. de Gràcia, 41 - Barcelona

The first phase of the project consisted in the refurbishment of an old rental apartment house, a habitual procedure in the late 19th-century Eixample. The second phase consisted in designing a photographer's studio on the top floor to justify a particular solution in the crown that did not comply with construction bylaws. The result is one of the most refreshing interpretations of northern Gothic architecture: the gallery with porticoes is transferred to the third floor, but is subtly echoed in the ground-floor shop windows; the symmetry is rigorously respected in the top half of the façade, but the composition is freer in contact with the street. The entire plane of the façade is ornamented with repetitive abstract motifs topped by the tiered outline of the crown, concealing a ridge roof. This building probably represents Puig i Cadafalch's boldest exploration of the freedom of composition that characterized the emerging modern sensibility.

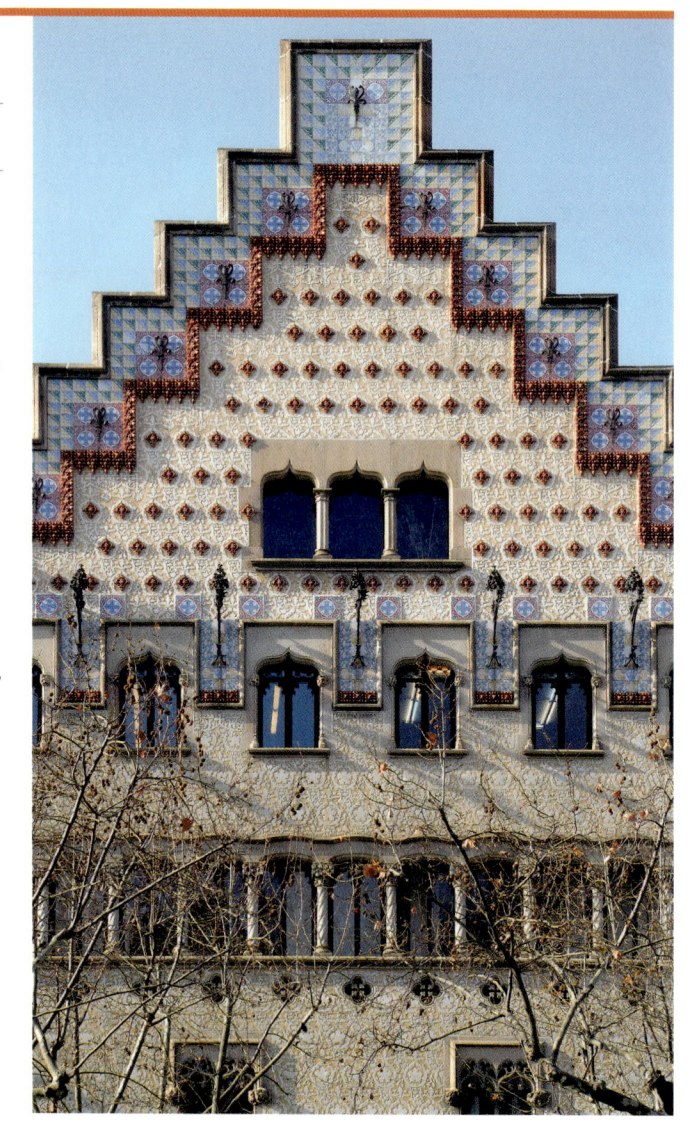

LLEÓ MORERA HOUSE
NEWLY CONSTRUCTED TOWNHOUSE

Lluís Domènech i Montaner
1903-1905

Pg. de Gràcia, 35 - Barcelona

SUBSEQUENT INTERVENTIONS:
Raimon Duran i Reynals, 1943. First remodelling work.
Carles Bassó, Oscar Tusquets, 1986-1988. Restoration of the façade and remodelling of the ground floor.

Domènech i Montaner's original project was for the remodelling of a façade but ultimately became a newly constructed building. This is the model Modernista dwelling designed to house the owners on the *piano nobile* with two or three rental floors. Domènech placed all the emphasis on avoiding repetition in the vertical orders by means of varied stonework that defines the house's tremendously diverse appearance. The architect highlighted the corner and gave a balanced treatment to the side façades, of different widths. The *piano nobile* is given a formal treatment, while the two upper floors, with their great circular windows and extended balcony, seek to ennoble the façade as a whole. Lleó Morera house exemplified the Modernista ideal of the rental house that presents itself to the city with a forcefully singular image.

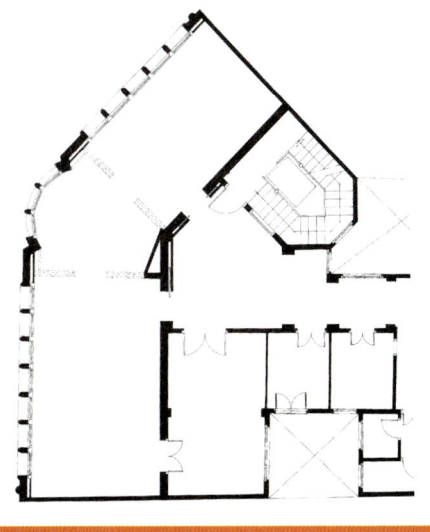

MONTANER I SIMON PUBLISHING HOUSE
FUNDACIÓ ANTONI TÀPIES

Lluís Domènech i Montaner
1881-1884

C/ Aragó, 255 - Barcelona

SUBSEQUENT INTERVENTIONS:
Roser Amadó, Lluís Domènech i Girbau, 1987-1990. Adaptations to fit out the publishing house premises for the Antoni Tàpies Foundation.

The building applies the procedures of industrial architecture to a programme with a high degree of fragmentation. The workshops are situated on a semibasement floor that reaches the far end of the site. The entrance is highlighted by an octagonal dome that provides overhead lighting and visual connection with the office mezzanine. The second section houses the archives, in a U-shape around a central skylight. The building is a structure of cast-iron pillars and girders arranged to produce clearly differentiated sectors and a brickwork façade with six large windows. The pattern of the façade adopts the filigree motifs characteristic of Islamic architecture, one of the principal referents of the time. The layout of the openings generates numerous vertical lines of sight and creates effects of light and space that foreshadow the concerns of modern architecture.

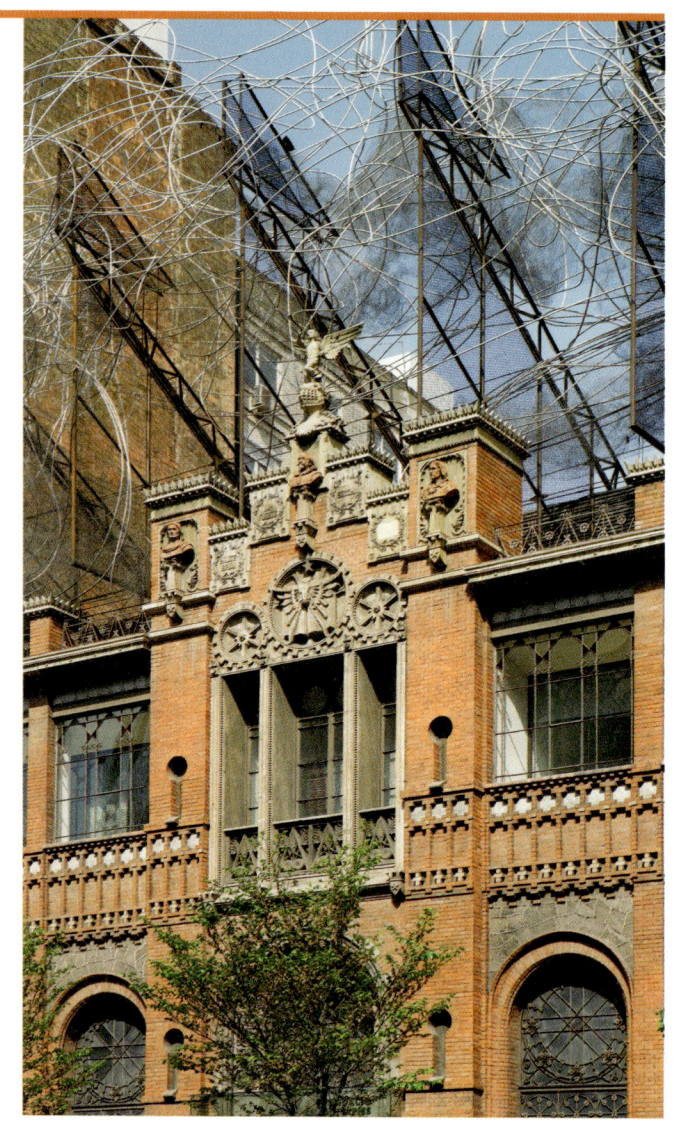

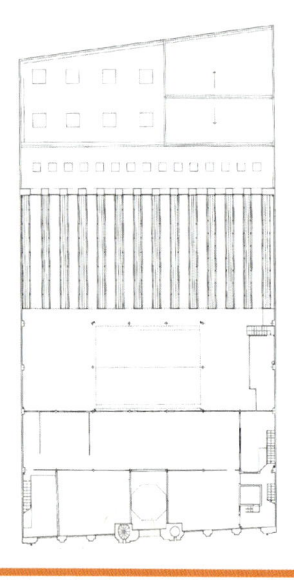

CASIMIR CASARAMONA TEXTILE MILL
CAIXAFÒRUM ARTS CENTRE
FUNDACIÓ LA CAIXA, 1998

Josep Puig i Cadafalch
1909-1911

Av. Marquès de Comillas, 6-8 - Barcelona

SUBSEQUENT INTERVENTIONS:
Arata Isozaki, Roberto Luna, 1998-2002
New acces to hall and basement floor

The Casaramona Mill, on a site on the outskirts of the city of the time, had to be built quickly due to a fire at the old factory in Carrer de la Riereta. The layout takes the form of three buildings for yarns, warehouses and fabrics, respectively, separated by two interior streets in accordance with the large site dimensions. The structure comprises brick vaults supported by iron porticoes, with traditional Catalan brick-built roofs resting on the vaults. The volumes at the four corners are taller, the stairwells emerge even higher and, at the centre, two towers (clock tower and water tower) form a vertical reference in keeping with the crenellated profile of all the façades. Using austere means and repetitive elements, Puig i Cadafalch produced a very attractive exterior image for the building, using the façade to express structural elements such as the ends of the vaults and the series of buttresses.

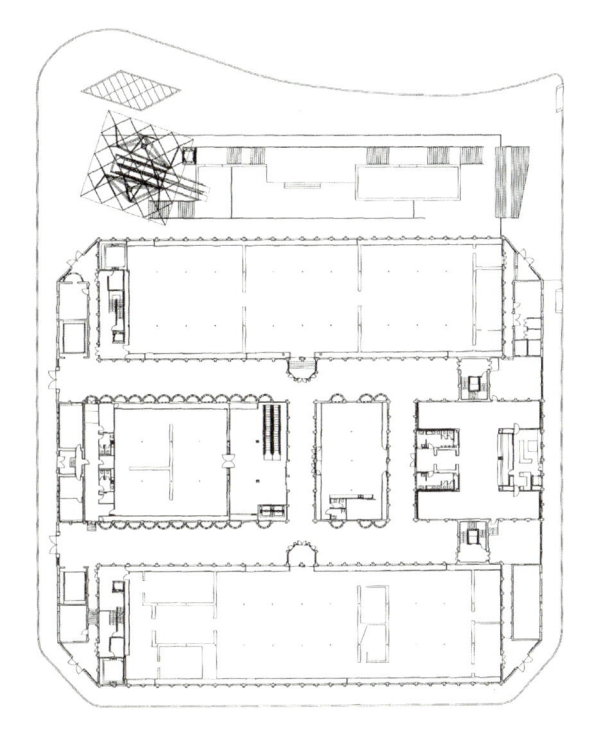

MILÀ HOUSE, "LA PEDRERA" (THE QUARRY)
FUNDACIÓ CAIXA DE CATALUNYA, 1996

Antoni Gaudí
1906-1910

Pg. de Gràcia, 92 - C/ Provença, 261-265
Barcelona

SUBSEQUENT INTERVENTIONS:
Francisco Juan Barba Corsini, 1953-1955.
New apartments in the attic.
Josep Emili Hernández-Cros, Rafael Vila, 1988-1996.
Restoration of the façade and improvements to the first floor for use as a cultural venue.

This was Gaudí's last civil project, with the emphasis on experimentation with structure and the implementation of bold solutions that represented a breakaway from traditional procedures. The side walls were built using calcareous stone from El Garraf combined with metal elements, and are scaled and configured according to the casuistry of their specific positions. The floors comprise metal girders laid out irregularly in accordance with the floor plan. The street façades merge with the perimetric pillars in a monolithic, self-supporting system. Gaudí set out to dissociate form from its material content and seek a synthesis between abstraction and the evocation of natural elements. This led him to convert the building into a great monument to the Blessed Virgin Mary, who was to have crowned the house, thereby turning it into a mere pedestal. The assistance of a naval engineer and the forms suggested in the roof reveal Gaudí as a forerunner of modern architecture, interested in breaking free from the regular courses of masonry, orders or the weight of construction materials. La Pedrera is an unfinished work that resolves each challenge of space and construction by means of completely new and, sometimes, incomprehensible solutions.

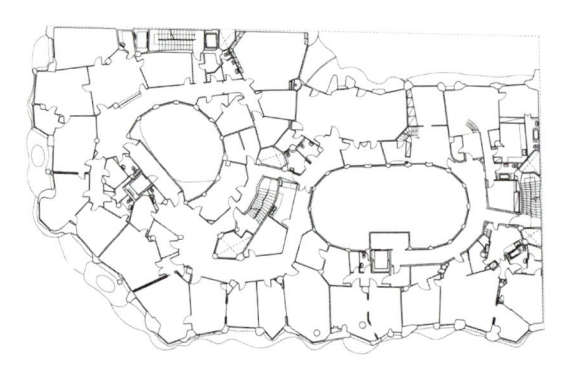

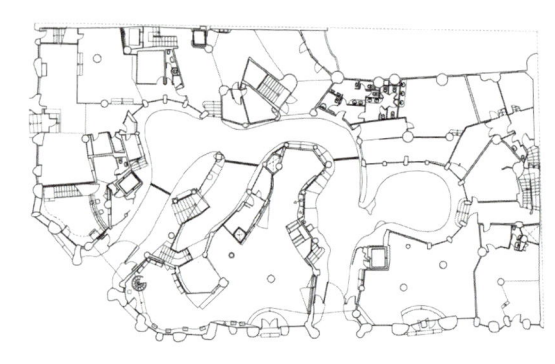

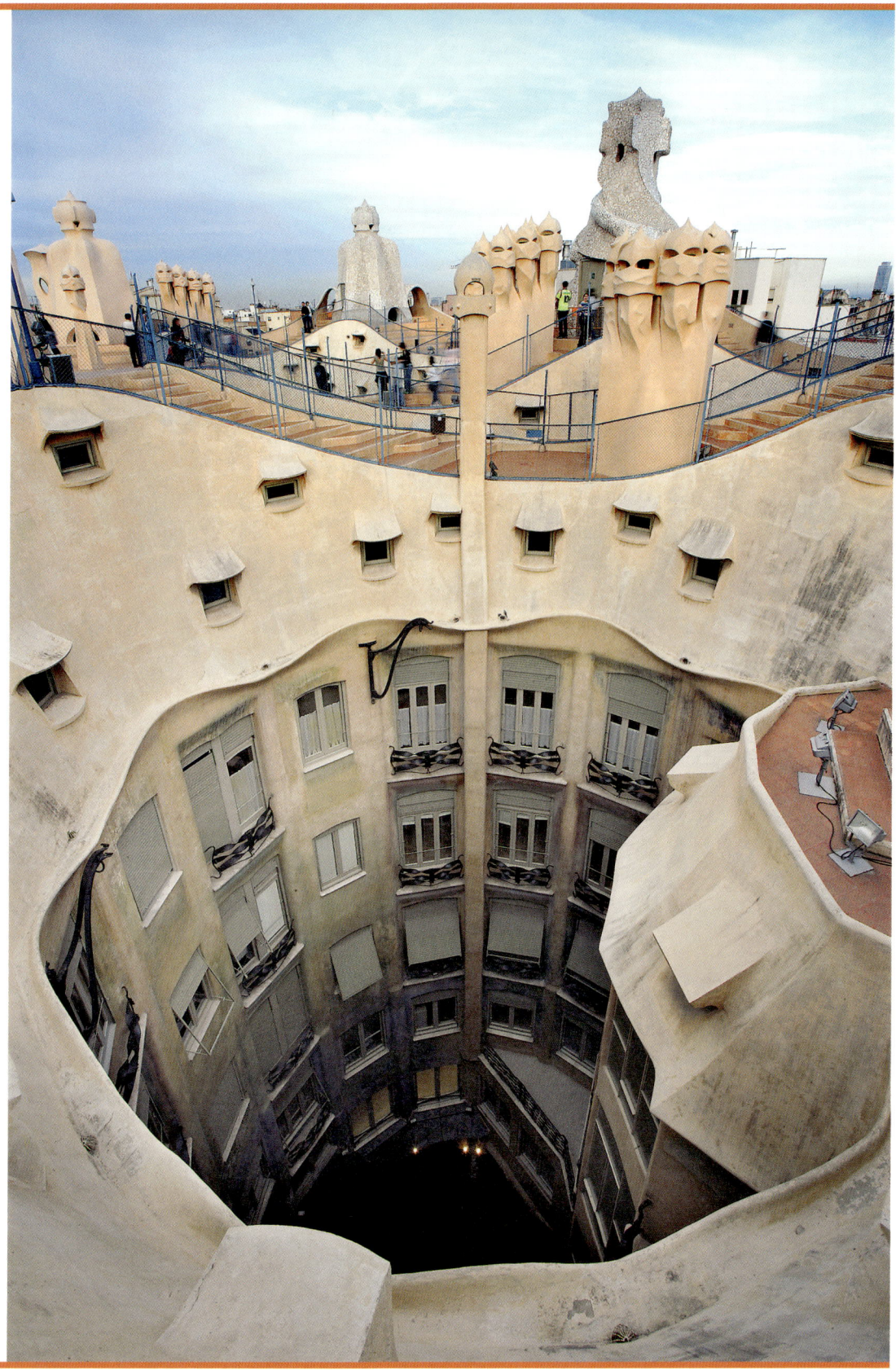

Barcelona

EXPIATORY TEMPLE OF THE SAGRADA FAMÍLIA
CRYPT, APSE, FAÇADE OF THE NATIVITY AND PARISH SCHOOLS

Antoni Gaudí
1882-1926

C/ de la Marina, 253 - Barcelona

SUBSEQUENT INTERVENTIONS:
Domènec Sugrañes i Gras, 1927-1935. Supervision of the works. • Lluís Bonet Garí (+1993), Isidre Puig Boada (+1987), Francesc de Paula Cardoner (+1997). Continuation of the works. • Josep Maria Subirachs (from 1987). Sculptural elements.

This was Gaudí's most ambitious project, which he began at the age of 31 and continued to work on until his death. The idea was to construct a great temple where the faithful from all over Catalonia could go to expiate their sins. Gaudí took a neo-Gothic floor plan by Francesc de Paula del Villar and gradually converted it into an organism in which the symbology of Biblical texts corresponds perfectly with a closed geometric and structural system: the 12 apostles are distributed in groups of four at the three portals, Christ is situated in the large central vault, surrounded by the four Evangelists, etc. Gaudí finished work on the façade of the Nativity, in the conviction that the temple would be completed for subsequent generations. The Sagrada Família is the pinnacle of Gaudí's achievements in his fervent search for pointed forms and establishes a bridge between Gothic and modern that drew the admiration of masters such as Wright and Le Corbusier.

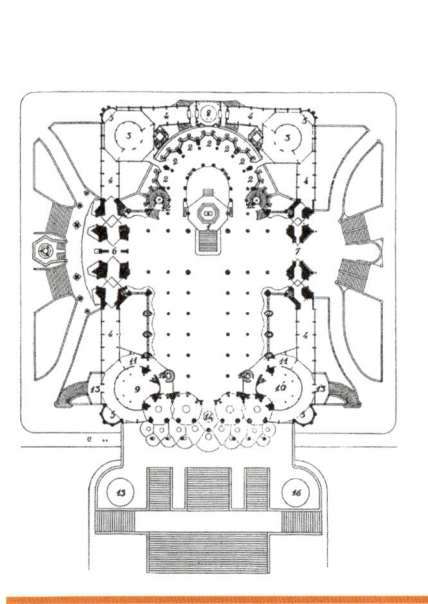

Barcelona

HOSPITAL DE LA SANTA CREU I SANT PAU

Lluís Domènech i Montaner
1902-1911

Av. Sant Antoni Maria Claret, 167-171 - Barcelona

SUBSEQUENT INTERVENTIONS:
Víctor Argentí, Antoni González Moreno-Navarro, Josep Lluís González Moreno-Navarro, 1979-1980. Restoration of the La Mercè Pavilion and adaptations to provide care services.
Esteve Bonell, Josep Maria Gil, 1998-2009. New Hospital de la Santa Creu i Sant Pau (under construction).

The project is the result of a merger between the Hospital de Sant Pau and the Gothic complex of the Hospital de la Santa Creu, creating one of the features with greatest urbanistic repercussions for the city. The hospital occupies nine street blocks of Cerdà's Eixample, bordering on Avinguda Gaudí to one side and the Sagrada Família to the other. Domènech i Montaner employed the same pavilion organization he used for the Pere Mata Institute, though creating a concentrated basement structure that avoids the functional dispersion of the pavilions, much criticized by experts in hospital construction at the time. It comprises 46 pavilions laid out around an axis running diagonally through the street block. Domènech thereby presented an open, innovative take on the model street block of the Cerdà grid. The structure of the pavilions comprises modular elements supporting brick vaults, allowing the wall system to adapt to the functionality of each pavilion. The axis formed by Avinguda Gaudí represents a unique monumental complex, at the ends of which stand two almost antithetical conceptions to the meaning of the new architecture and its function in the context of the social needs of the time.

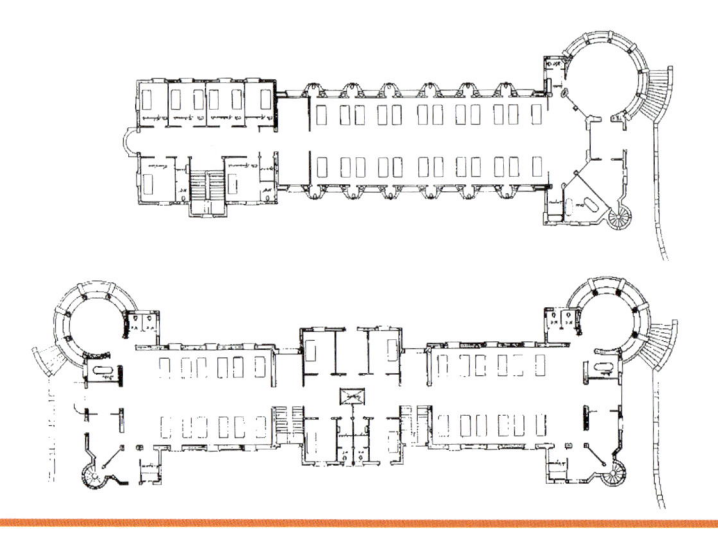

Barcelona

098

VICENS HOUSE
PRIVATE DWELLING

Antoni Gaudí
1878-1885

C/ Carolines, 18-24 - Barcelona

SUBSEQUENT INTERVENTIONS:
Joan B. Serra i Martínez, 1927.

099

GÜELL ESTATE
GATEHOUSE, ENTRANCE AND STABLES

Antoni Gaudí
1884-1887

Av. Pedralbes, 7-15 - Barcelona

These are the only remaining constructions of Gaudí's work on the estate of Baron Güell, which reached as far as Pedralbes Palace. The entrance is flanked by constructions of rammed earth and lime, and the large stables are roofed by a series of barrel vaults with skylights, supported by brick-built parabolic arches. On the outside, the abstract ornamentation is combined with iron features that refer to the symbology of Jacint Verdaguer's poem, "L'Atlàntida": the dragon cannot prevent Hercules snatching a branch of the tree of golden apples that crowns the great brick pilaster on which the gate turns.

100

MACARI GOLFERICHS HOUSE
PRIVATE DWELLING
FUNDACIÓ PI I SUNYER, 1988

Joan Rubió i Bellver
1900-1901

Gran Via de les Corts Catalanes, 491 - Barcelona

SUBSEQUENT INTERVENTIONS:

This was Gaudí's first commission on completing his studies. The house comprises two low-ceilinged floors accommodating the *piano nobile* and the bedrooms, and attics with much higher ceilings beneath a roof with differing slopes. The treatment of the masonry combines bare stone and brick in patterns organized in horizontal courses, and vertical ceramic elements, arranged in a chessboard layout and including the galleries at the corners and their supports. The house was designed as a great optical device in relation to the garden and the various oblique views from the street.

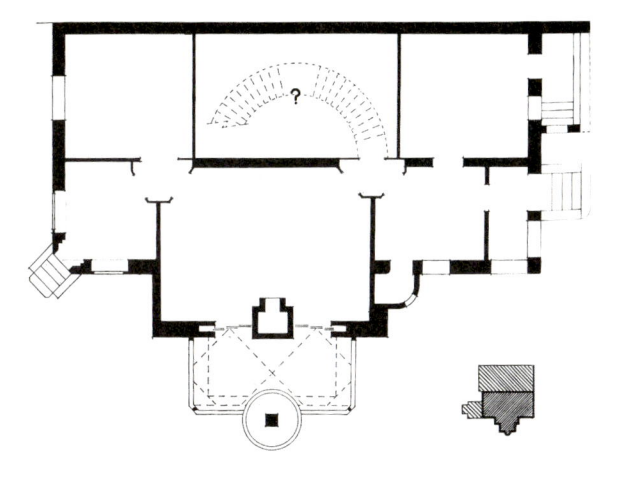

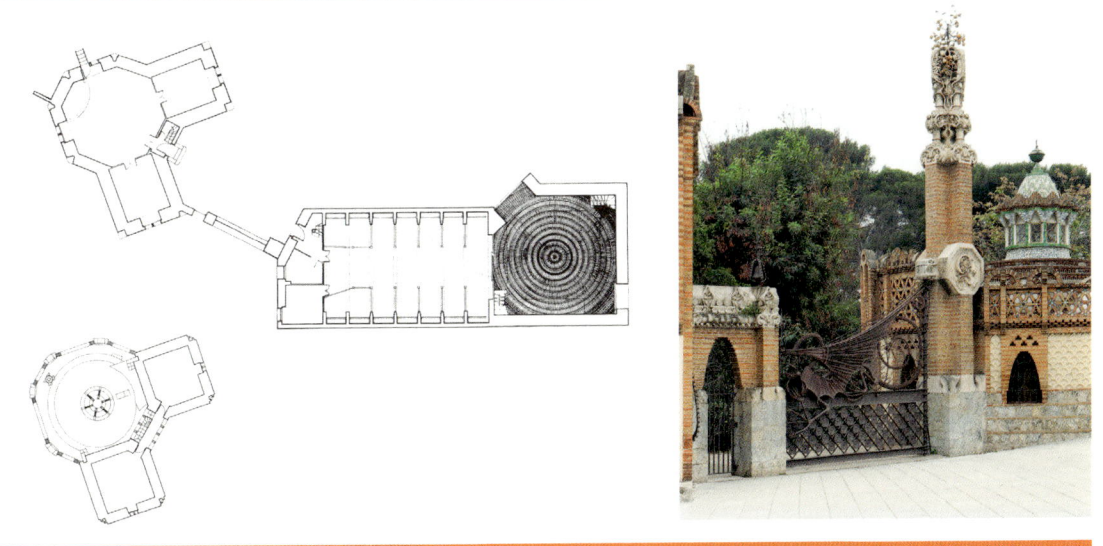

Macari Golferichs, a capricious civil engineer, timber merchant and collector, apparently made his fortune in the Americas, like other bourgeois of the time. On his return, he decided to buy land in the Eixample and have a residence built for him in the Modernista style. With this work, Rubió began his search for an architectural style of his own. The structural and construction value of the Gothic forms is tried and tested in an authentic process of research, as we see in the materials used, the construction technique and the ceramic ornamentation.

PALAU DE LA MÚSICA CATALANA

Lluís Domènech i Montaner
1905-1908

C/ Sant Francesc de Paula, 2 - Barcelona

SUBSEQUENT INTERVENTIONS:
Carles Díaz, Oscar Tusquets, 1983.
First refurbishment and extension.
Carles Díaz, Oscar Tusquets, 2001.
Second extension.

The project for the Palau de la Música was associated with the construction of Via Laietana, in which Domènech i Montaner was closely involved, and the foundation of the Orfeó Català, in 1891, by the composer Lluís Millet. The Palau stands at the corner of two narrow streets, and the emphasis of the overall project is on drawing the limited daylight into every corner of the interior, by means of numerous polychrome screens that create a dreamlike atmosphere. The large auditorium is on the first floor, with entrance via a great stairway that divides the building in two, setting aside the ground floor for administrative functions. Domènech decided to bring the same profusion to the façades in both streets despite their different hierarchical positions, in a demonstration of his skill in addressing unfavourable displacements. The bare brickwork, the stone carved into musical allegories and the coloured glass screens make the building seem to glow in the daylight, which makes its way into the concert hall. His attention to functional aspects of the programme reveals a modern Domènech who saw ornamentation as the necessary culmination of a work of architecture.

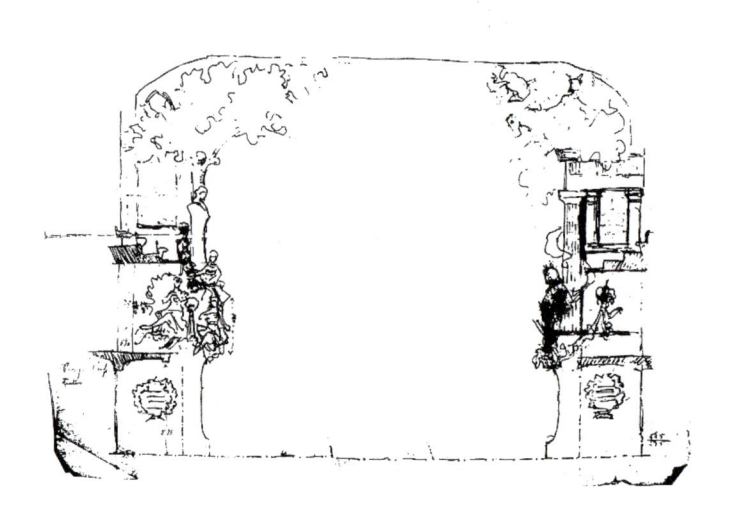

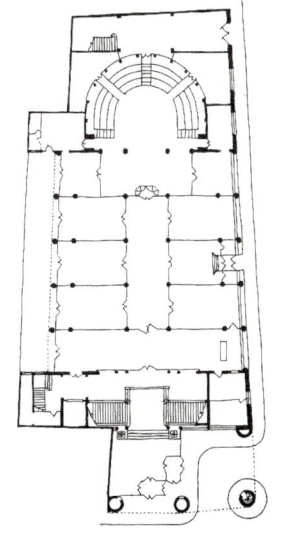

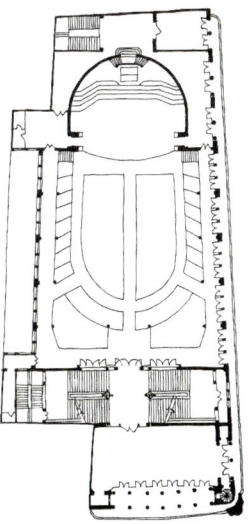

Barcelona

SCHOOL, ORIGINALLY A TERESIAN CONVENT

Antoni Gaudí
1888-1890

C/ Ganduxer, 95-105 - Barcelona

The building adopts an arrangement of three lengthwise bays, the central of which becomes a complex mechanism for lighting the interior, making the whole resemble a cloister. Conditioned by budgetary limitations, Gaudí chose to introduce a very narrow parabolic arch, repeated numerous times, to resolve both the central corridors and the openings in the façade. The central courtyards, staggered to let light pass along indirect routes, provide muted lighting on the ground floor. Worthy of particular mention is the simplicity of the window design: inside, the divisions between the panes adopt abstract forms, devoid of symbolism. The basic window opening in the façade consists of a rectangular blind, set into the masonry and covering the actual opening, which adopts the parabolic arch form.

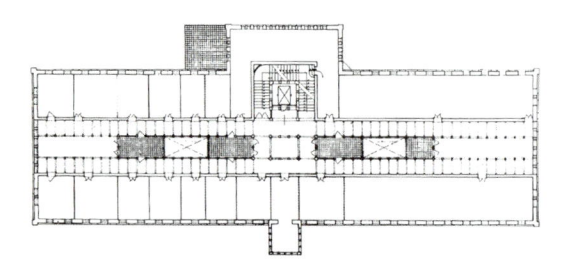

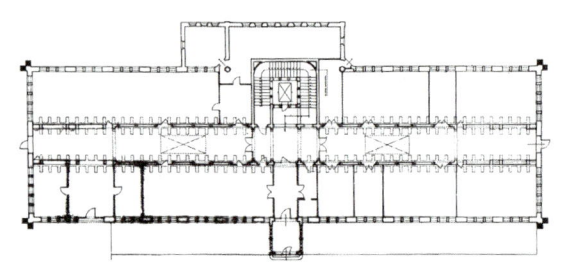

TALLERS MANYACH
JOSEP MARIA JUJOL STATE SCHOOL

Josep Maria Jujol
1916-1922

C/ Riera de Sant Miquel, 39 - Barcelona

SUBSEQUENT INTERVENTIONS:
Jaume Bach, Gabriel Mora, 1984-1987
Josep Maria Jujol Public-Sector School

In order to roof this large space, Jujol adopted the characteristic procedures of modern architecture but without recourse to their analytical basis and calculations, addressing the structure's stability by means of empirical and intuitive means. The building comprises a grid of remarkably slender pillars, supporting lattice girders perpendicular to the street. These girders are laid out on two levels to span tied vaults, arranged in a saw-tooth arrangement, made up of three layers of thin brick. The first vault to be built collapsed when the centring was removed, prompting Jujol to increase the curve of the vault and reinforce the tie system. To guarantee the overall stability of the work, Jujol employed large brick pinnacles that are clearly visible in the roof. This grants the structure stability despite the slenderness of the pillars and the minimum safety margin in the foundations.

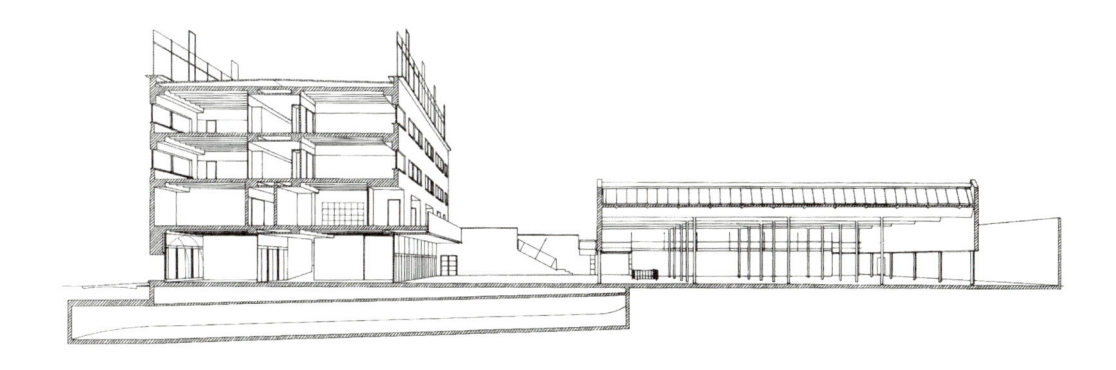

"BELLESGUARD"
(FAIR COUNTENANCE)
FIGUERES HOUSE

Antoni Gaudí
1900-1909

C/ Bellesguard, 16-20 - Barcelona

Gaudí was asked to design this house by the widow of Jaume Figueres, on a plot of land steeped in history that hold the remains of a former residence of King Martí the Humane, that Bernat Metge christened "Bellesguard", or Fair Countenance. The ground floor, raised slightly above grade, contains the stately bedrooms, beneath the *piano nobile*. A first series of attics house the servants' quarters and a second, directly beneath the roof, emerges above, presenting continuous openings. In the jambs and tympanums of the windows and in other ornaments Gaudí experimented with mouldings set with small stones. The ceilings of the *piano nobile* and the upper attics are supported by very slender arches, made lighter by latticework. Gaudí sought a structural function based on elements of small dimensions in an allusion to the femininity of his client, also referred to in the epigraph over the entrance: "Ave Maria Puríssima sens pecat fou concebuda" (Hail Mary, conceived without sin).

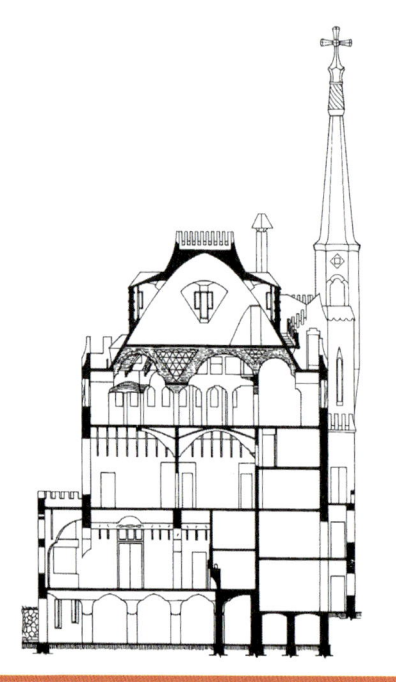

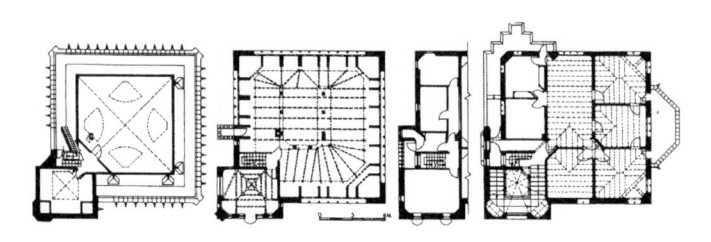

QUERALT HOUSE
SINGLE-FAMILY DWELLING

Josep Maria Jujol
1916-1917

C/ Pineda, 1 - Barcelona

In 1913, Jujol was commissioned to design a second family home on the land of Sansalvador house, which was given the name of Queralt as a tribute to the patron of Berga, the family's hometown. The very simple interior features a series of minor details that structure the exterior configuration, such as the hexagonal windows, the simple yet elegant wrought-iron work and, most of all, the chamfered window in the south-facing corner, comprising a gallery on the first floor and a triangular balcony on the floor above. The wall separating the estate from the street is built of unworked stone that contrasts with the simple lines of the iron garden gate. Jujol used the difference in ground level to create an aerodynamic image that gives the street the best views. The design of the gates and the vegetation surrounding the house complement the austere treatment of the side façades.

PLANELLS HOUSE
APARTMENT BUILDING

Josep Maria Jujol
1923-1924

Av. Diagonal, 332 - Barcelona

The building is the result of a succession of different programmes, all proposed by the contractor, Eveli Planells. The first proposal consisted in a single-family dwelling, where Jujol recreates the forms of La Pedrera to turn the building into a plinth for a large-scale statue of the Blessed Virgin Mary. The second commission was also for a single-family dwelling, in this case for a doctor, but the contractor finally decided to sell part of the plot and build an apartment building on the rest. A duplex system is employed to offset the plot's small surface area and increase the dwellings by a third. Jujol's project incorporated a penthouse for Planells' brother, with a strip of galleries in the façade supporting a dome decorated with the Marian anagram. The building that was ultimately constructed, up to the second floor, is more in keeping with the rhetoric of emerging rationalism than with the forms handed down by Modernisme.

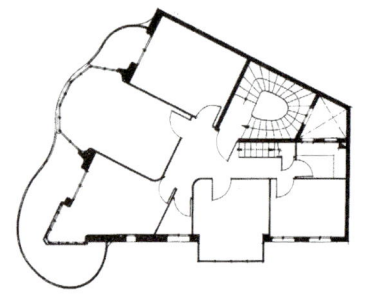

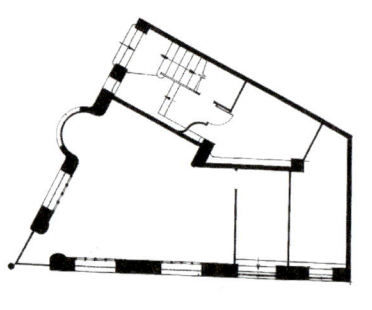

SANT JORDI TOWNHOUSE

Francesc Folguera
1929-1931

C/ Pau Claris, 81 - C/ Casp, 24-26 - Barcelona

The building is a clear exponent of the influence of purist central European architecture on the sensibilities of some Noucentista architects. It is divided into three parts: the ground floor and first four storeys are used for business purposes; the next two storeys house rental apartments and the top two floors form a duplex, where the owner lives, overlooking the interior of the street block. This represents a transgression in the usual order of Eixample buildings, where the *piano nobile* is reserved for the owner. The façade organizes the building's edges and vertical orders by means of a single window module positioned in different ways, marking the change of use from the fourth floor upwards. The use of a metal structure and its excellent implementation denote the intention of associating this architecture with a rigorous application of construction procedures.

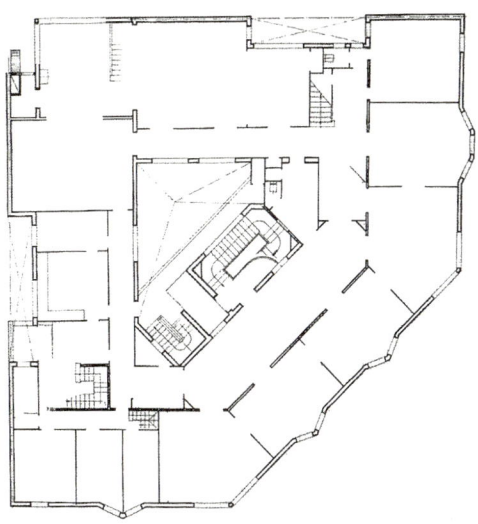

MASANA HOUSE
APARTMENT BUILDING

Ramon Reventós
1928

C/ Lleida, 7-11 - C/ Olivera, 78
C/ Tamarit, 70 - Barcelona

Reventós reflected the hygienist, rationalist ideas at the centre of architectural debate about social housing in central Europe in the 1920s. In Masana House, he situated the stairways against the façade, where they emerge from the plane to draw light and fresh air into these spaces. He also suppressed closed interior courtyards, instead drawing the street block courtyard into the building. The exterior demonstrates a clear mastery of pure forms and their organization, with an initial order on the ground floor marked by a slight cornice, and the brick masonry crown of the façade. For the same client Reventós also designed the neighbouring building in Carrer Tamarit, establishing a U-shaped layout around a courtyard that is directly connected to the inner court. The bevelled and glazed volumes of the stairway contrast with the two types of windows in the dwellings, fitted with blinds and without borders.

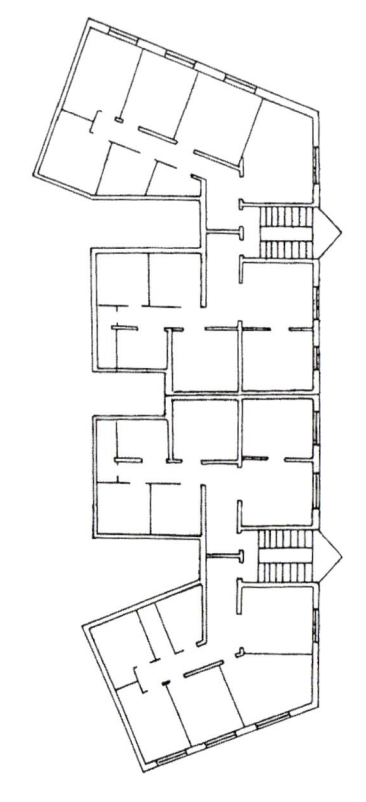

APARTMENT BUILDING

Carles Martínez
1932

Via Augusta, 12 - Barcelona

Martínez designed a floor plan containing three dwellings on an irregular corner plot with façades giving onto a main street and a small square. The position of the stairway and the lifts, overlooking the inner courtyard and forming a virtual bisector, marks the layout of the dwellings, with two on one side and a third dwelling on the other. Almost all the rooms give onto the façade, except the service areas and kitchens, for which small courts were equipped. This series of specific engagements is translated in the exterior of the building by a marked will to expressionism, centring on the predominant view from Via Augusta. The second and third floors form a corner gallery, while the first floor forms a covered balcony, repeated on the fourth floor. The building withdraws slightly as it rises, becoming simpler and presenting smooth volumes marked horizontally by the strips of windows.

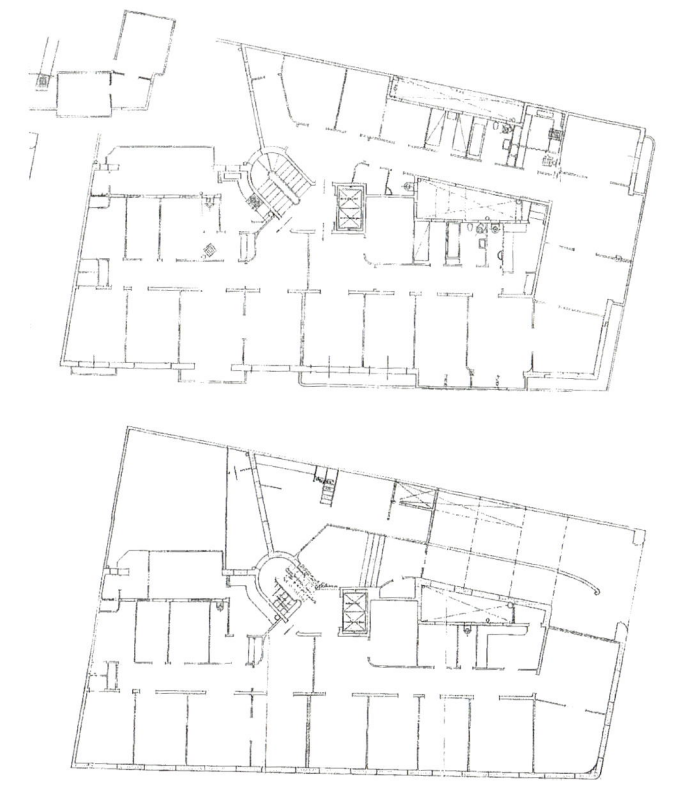

CASA BLOC (HOUSING BLOCK)
DEVELOPMENT OF 200 SOCIAL HOUSING UNITS

Josep Lluís Sert, Josep Torres i Clavé,
Joan Baptista Subirana
1932-1936

Pg. Torras i Bages, 91-105 - Barcelona

SUBSEQUENT INTERVENTIONS:
First phase: Jaume Sanmartí, Raimon Torres, 1987-1997. Restoration and alterations to fit out the building as an apartment block.
Second phase: Víctor Seguí, 1999.

This is a recreation of the dwellings *à redent* proposed by Le Corbusier in 1922 for an urban fabric of luxury homes with a density of 300 inhabitants per hectare. The GATCPAC project, offering social housing, also lays out the site in a north-south direction, making all the dwellings face south and east. Entry to the dwellings is via a long covered corridor on the north and west sides. The long, narrow blocks comprise a two-bayed metal structure. The lower floor has a covered terrace extending out from the living room. On the top floor, each pair of bays has three bedrooms, making the central bedroom balanced. The resulting density is 1,140 inhabitants per hectare, far lower than that of the traditional urban fabrics of closed housing blocks.

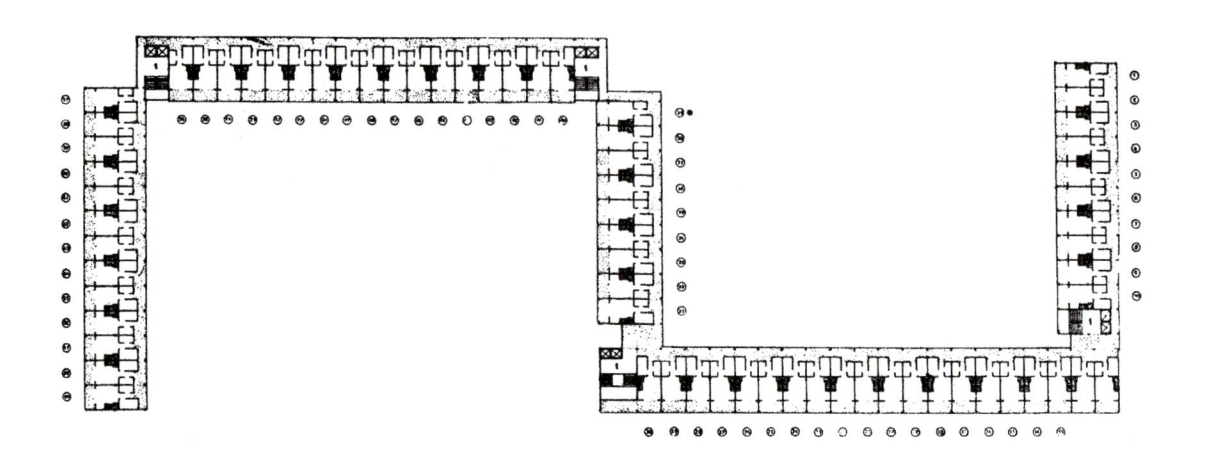

TUBERCULOSIS CLINIC
DR. LLUÍS SAYÉ HEALTH CENTRE

Josep Lluís Sert, Josep Torres i Clavé,
Joan Baptista Subirana
1934-1938

Ptge. Sant Bernat, 10 - Barcelona

SUBSEQUENT INTERVENTIONS:
Mario Corea, Edgardo Mannino, Francisco Gallardo-Bravo, 1993. Remodelling and rehabilitation as a health centre.

The building, originally constructed to meet the needs of a major health problem, pays no heed to the street alignment, instead adopting two parallel volumes running from east to west and joined to form an L-shape. Entrance to the complex is via a semi-public garden that leads directly to the two volumes. The block on the northern side contains the surgeries, laboratories and records. The volume at the rear of the site houses the lecture room and the library on the upper floors. The layout of all the spaces, the system of circulations and the treatment of the façades represent a rigorous response to the programme and the sun's movement within the constrictions of the site. It is a model of the application of rationalist concepts into a context that is ignored and implicitly criticized by the strict functionalism of the building.

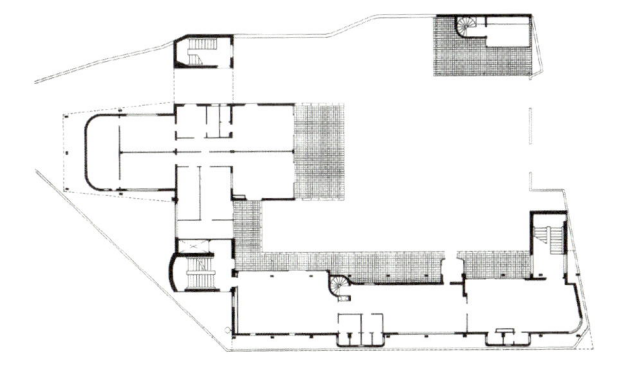

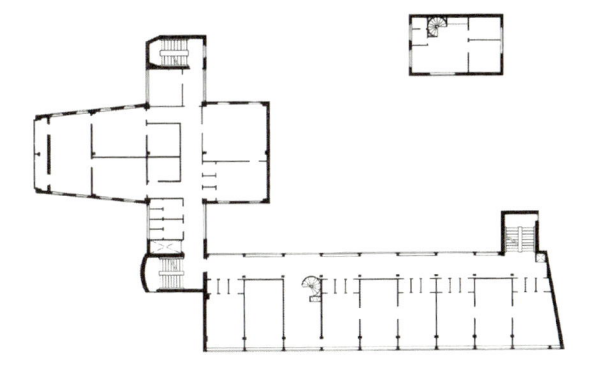

112

BUILDING WITH SIX DUPLEX APARTMENTS

Josep Lluís Sert
1930-1931

C/ Muntaner, 342-348 - Barcelona

113

APARTMENT BUILDING

Germán Rodríguez Arias
1930-1931

Via Augusta, 61 - Barcelona

In accordance with the premisses of the GATEPAC, Rodríguez Arias designed these apartments with ample surface areas and high standards of comfort at a very low cost, thanks to the construction procedures employed. The mixed structure comprises brick with iron supports to create large spaces independently of the layout of the bearing system. The ceilings are built using small vaults. The floors are tiled and the doors and windows adopt the standardized models designed by the GATEPAC. The building has central heating and all the kitchen and bathroom fittings employ the most innovative technology of the time.

114

BARANGÉ HOUSE
SINGLE-FAMILY DWELLING

Ricardo de Churruca
1931-1935

Pl. Mons, 4 - Barcelona

This is a personal interpretation of the concept of housing handed down by Le Corbusier. The dwellings are laid out on two floors, with independent entrances. On both floors, a small central hall leads into all the rooms. Downstairs is the living room, dining room, kitchen, one bedroom and service areas. Upstairs are the other bedrooms, plus a gallery that encircles the living room and closes on the small balcony at the corner. The duplex apartment organization is reflected in the façade, modifying the conventional scale and proposing a more dignified image of urban housing.

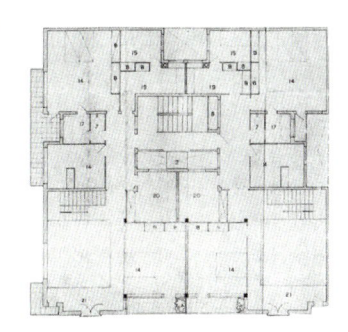

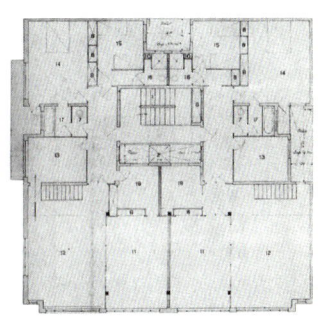

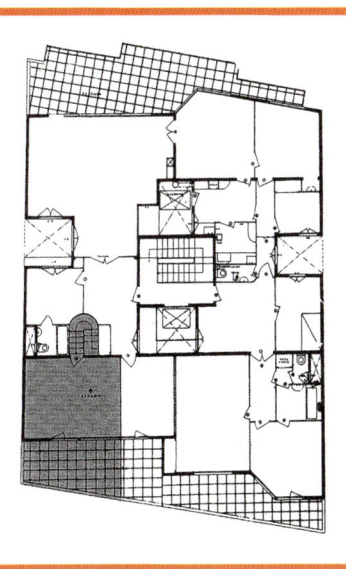

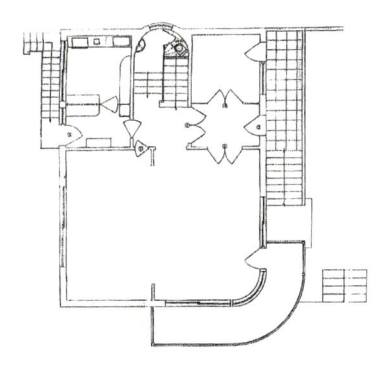

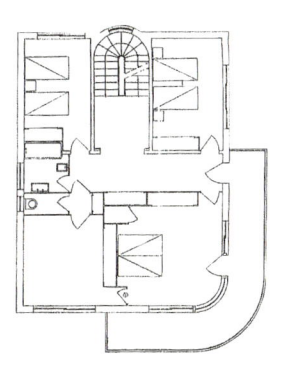

Churruca brings the best rationalist rhetoric to an unusual site: a small square situated on Vallcarca bridge, with one façade plunging down to the street that passes beneath. The detached house assumes the radically flat character of the side façade, while the main façade is divided in two by a series of elements that give depth to the garden: a gallery, curving eaves at the corner and a second stretch of eaves separated from the main plane. Churruca's formal work on a corner intensifies the interest of the object from every point of view.

Barcelona 137

115

BUILDING OF 40 APARTMENTS
ASTORIA CINEMA

Germán Rodríguez Arias
1933-1934

C/ París, 193-199 - Barcelona

116

APARTMENT BUILDING

Sixt Illescas
1934-1935

C/ Pàdua, 96 - Barcelona

The typical floor plan accommodates three dwellings per landing, though as many communal services as possible are housed on the ground floor and special treatment has been given to the top two floors. The dwellings on the fifth floor have a terrace garden on their roofs, reached by stairs from the dining room. The top floor is occupied by four studios, each with its own terrace garden. The building represents an experiment with new construction procedures, the purpose of which was to reduce the thickness of the flat roof and allow self-supporting slabs in the stairways.

117

APARTMENT BUILDING

Raimon Duran i Reynals
1933-1935

C/ Camp d'en Vidal, 16
C/ Aribau, 243 - Barcelona

The building comprises six dwellings per floor, of which three overlook the street, Carrer París, and the others give onto the inner courtyard of the street block. The dwellings on the top floor are duplexes, with exterior stairways in addition to the interior ones to communicate the two levels. The bearing structure addresses the fact that the ground floor houses a cinema and takes the form of metal supports with a minimum section. The layout of the dwellings reflects the contradictions between the GATEPAC's aspirations as regards housing and the permissiveness of municipal bylaws with regard to land use.

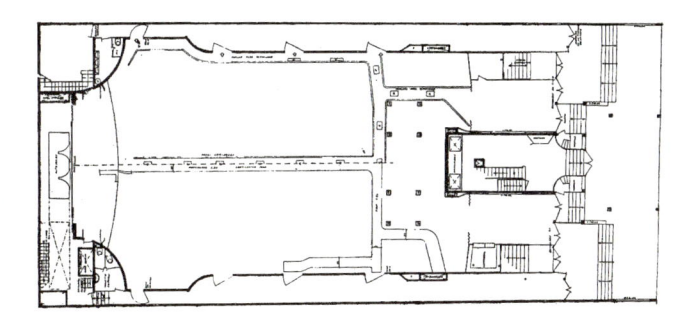

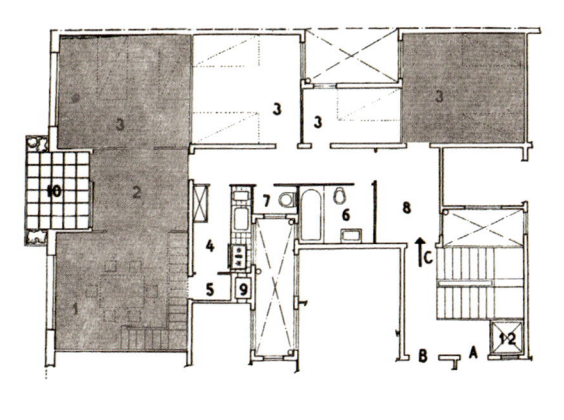

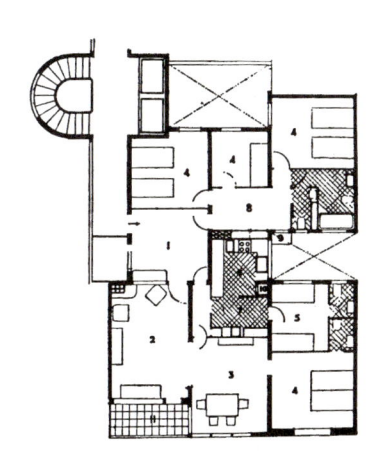

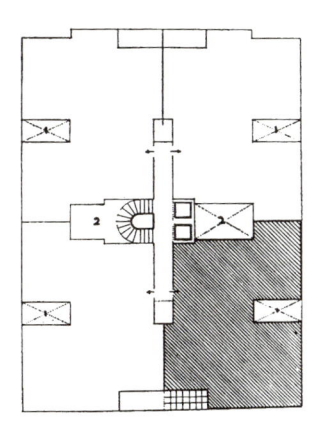

The building seeks to rationalize the traditional houses in the Eixample as regards the excessive space occupied by corridors. On this 22 x 28 metre site with façades on two streets, each floor contains four dwellings, forming a double axis of symmetry. The vertical communications are positioned at the centre, so that the landing provides direct access to the heart of each dwelling. The apartments are laid out in three bays, formed by bearing walls that situate the living and dining rooms in the façade, and the bedrooms next to the party wall. Lighting is provided by two inner courts of minimum dimensions.

Barcelona

APARTMENT BUILDING

Francesc Mitjans
1941-1943

C/ Amigó, 76 - Barcelona

This is a meticulous essay from Mitjans' academic phase, incorporating numerous discoveries that were later to become characteristic of his work. The typical floor plan adjudicates the rear space to bedrooms and the front bay to daytime spaces, directly linked to a large balcony running right across the façade. The interior layout shuns the use of corridors and implements a circular route around the kitchen, with small spaces of transition between different uses. The treatment of the hall is a masterly combination of elements from the past with markedly modern concepts, beyond acknowledgement of any particular historical style.

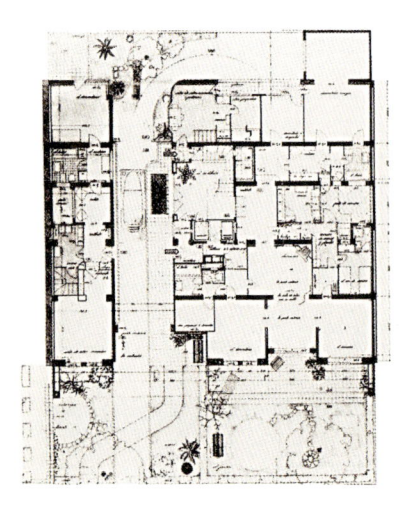

"CASA DE LA MARINA"
APARTMENT BUILDING FOR THE INSTITUTO SOCIAL DE LA MARINA

José Antonio Coderch de Sentmenat, Manuel Valls
1951-1955

Pg. Joan de Borbó, 43 - Barcelona

The site stands at the end of one of the long street blocks in La Barceloneta. The programme stipulated two dwellings per floor, each with three double bedrooms. Coderch elected to use stone and brick bearing walls for the structure. The geometry respects the parallel line to the party wall but twists freely across the site and also implicates the bearing elements. The result is an introverted dwelling with a large dose of rusticity and drama thanks to the slant of the walls, the texture of the materials and the filtered daylight.

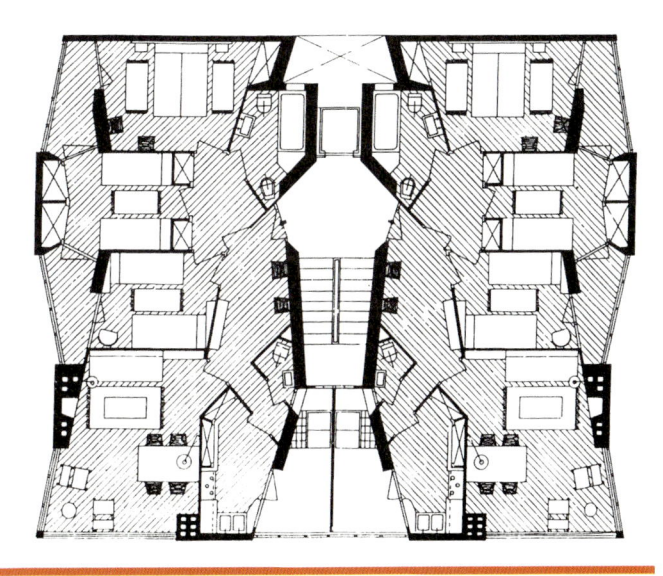

HOTEL PARK

Antoni de Moragas
1950-1953

Av. Marquès de l'Argentera, 11 - Barcelona

The project responds to a programme for a small hotel situated opposite the Estació de França railway station. The solution takes different approaches to the part of the building overlooking the narrow streets and the part looking onto the broad avenue. The result is the combination of two totally different volumes. The volume overlooking the avenue is the widest, with a glazed facing and pillars and summers that are left on view. The rear volume is a wall structure housing individual rooms. The stairway concentrates all the vertical dynamism in a continuous railing that rises in a spiral to the top floor.

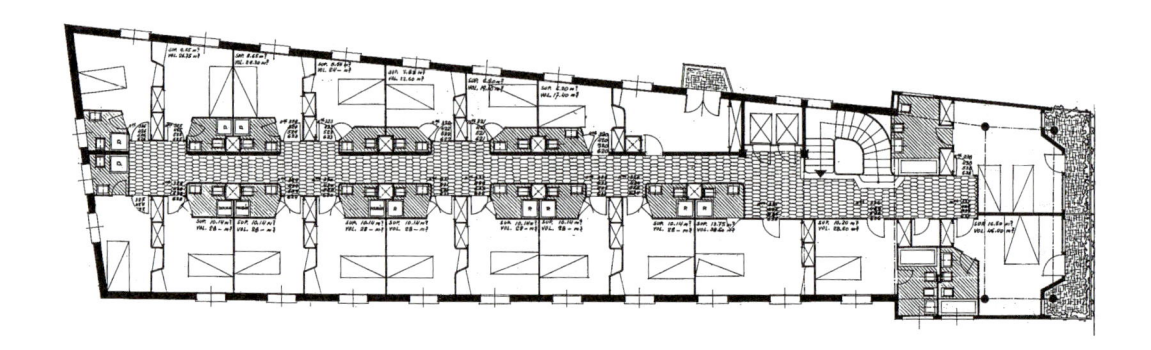

HOUSING FOR "LA MAQUINISTA" WORKERS' COOPERATIVE

José Antonio Coderch de Sentmenat, Manuel Valls
1951-1953

Pl. del Llagut, 1-11 - Barcelona

In the imposing urban fabric of La Barceloneta, the project proposes a concentration of the built sector in order to free up a large area of public space in the form of a central square, decreasing the density of occupation. The dwellings are grouped in modules of three, totally exterior, with a minimum occupation of the façade thanks to the solution chosen for the layout. The use of the oblique allows all the living rooms to overlook the central space. This space is organized by the bevels of the façade surfaces, combined with the successive projection of the eaves that appear between the stretches of wall. The exterior façade around the perimeter houses just the smaller bedrooms. This façade is laid out to optimize diagonal lines of sight, avoiding excessively narrow streets. The project was drafted by Coderch and Valls in 1951, though they were not responsible for site management.

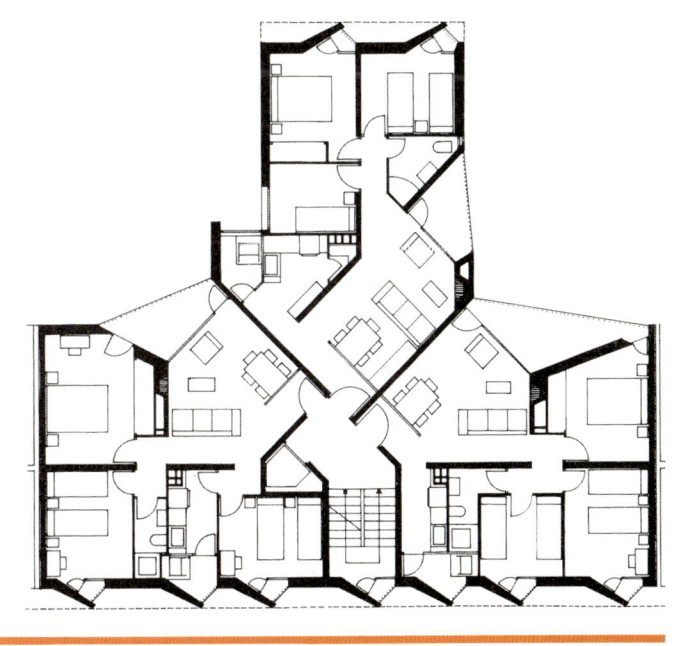

GUSTAVO GILI PUBLISHING HOUSE

Francesc Bassó, Joaquim Gili
1954-1961

C/ Rosselló, 87-89 - Barcelona

SUBSEQUENT INTERVENTIONS:
Gustau Gili Galfetti, 1998.
Apartment block on Carrer Rosselló.

The new head office of Gustavo Gili publishing house occupies the inner courtyard of a street block in the Eixample, filled in other cases with low-level volumes used for garages, storehouses and similar functions. In response to a highly atomized programme that needs to provide various functions, the building is divided into three clearly differentiated volumes. The central unit houses the commercial and technical offices. This volume overlooks the front garden, which leads into a double-height foyer, the only space with obvious formal and architectural connotations. The block on the left houses the management office and its annexed spaces. The volume on the right is for storage and packaging, and is clearly separated by the other two. The structure forms a grid independent of the facings and adopts a different module in each of the volumes, which are given different roof solutions.

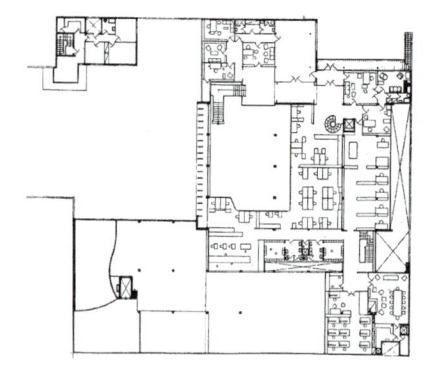

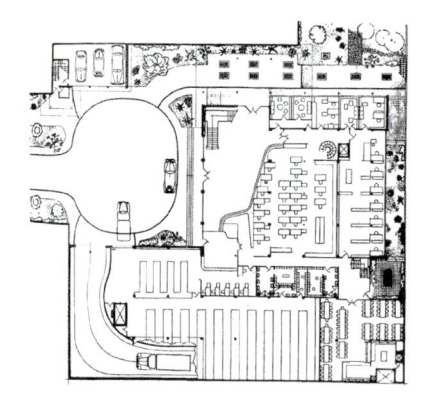

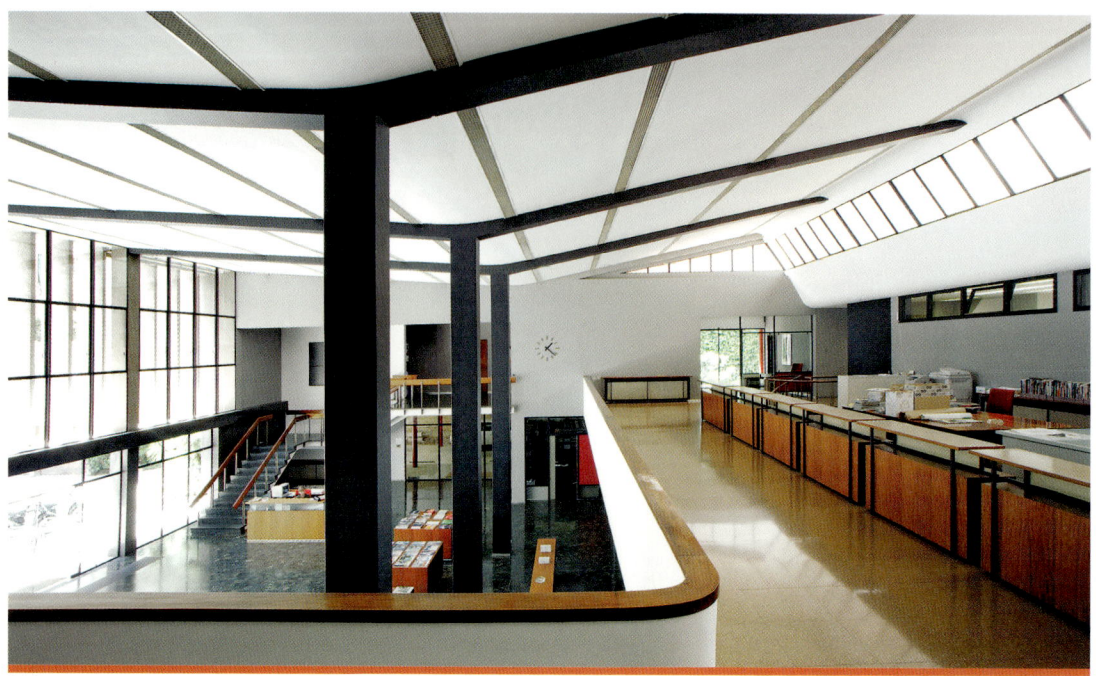

COL·LEGI D'ARQUITECTES DE CATALUNYA · COAC

Xavier Busquets
1958-1962

Plaça Nova, 5 - Barcelona

This project was chosen as the winner of a competition that addressed the challenge of constructing a building with modern technologies in the context of Ciutat Vella, the old town, near the cathedral and the Roman town wall. The winning solution makes a marked differentiation between a low-rise volume that follows the street alignment and an independently laid out high-rise tower with a rectangular floor plan. The low-rise volume houses the events hall and is directly linked to the foyer via a mezzanine floor inserted above the ground-floor gallery. This produces a building with four levels (semibasement, ground floor, mezzanine and events hall), giving representative functions to the building that communicates with the street, while the tower rises up like a series of independent trays with its vertical communications shaft (containing lifts and stairs) situated at the rear of the site.

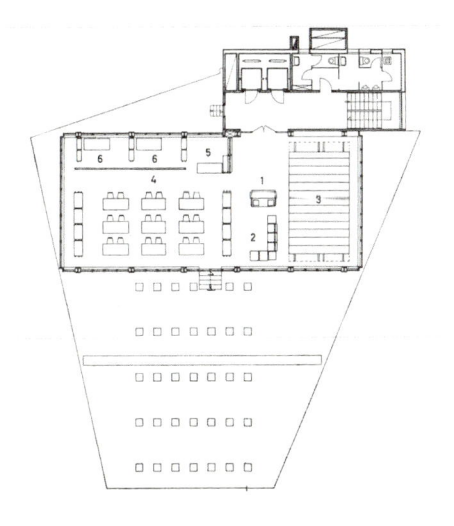

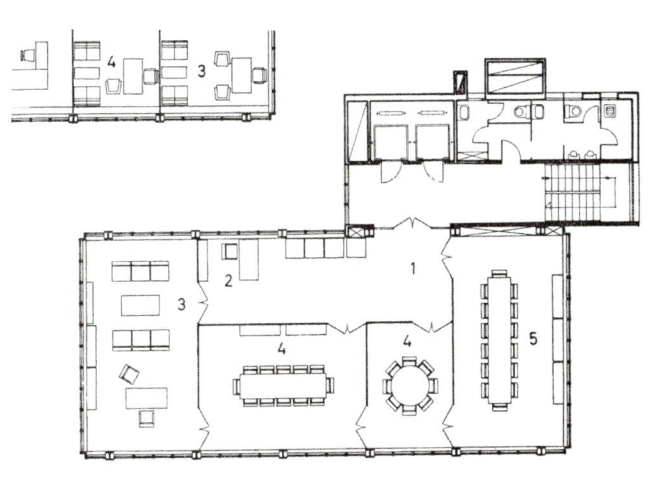

LAW FACULTY

Guillermo Giráldez, Pedro López Iñigo,
Xavier Subías
1958-1959

Av. Diagonal, 684 - Barcelona

SUBSEQUENT INTERVENTIONS:
Josep Llinàs, 1998. Annexed building.

The configuration of the building adopts criteria of clarity and economy in accordance with the short timeline imposed to draft and construct the project. Discrimination between the teaching and representative functions is reflected in the two-volume composition. The two-floor lecture room building is parallel to Avinguda Diagonal, with three light shafts along the central strip. The volume that houses the administrative and study functions stands five floors high with a perpendicular layout. The ground floor, which contains lecture rooms along the rear side, communicates the two volumes in a single circulation space. The overall structure of the building, of laminated steel, forms a regular module of 6.20 x 3.84 metres, doubled when a larger surface area is needed. The building applies criteria of construction economy, bringing up to date the guidelines applied in Catalonia by the first generation of modern architects.

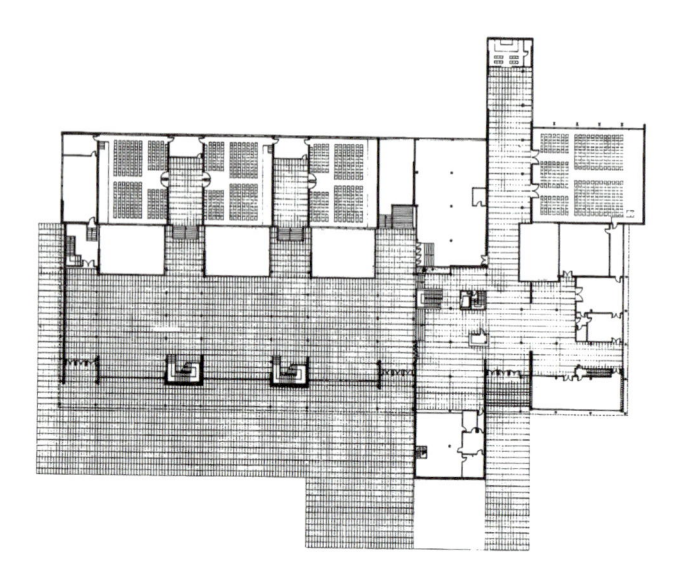

UNIVERSITY SCHOOL OF BUSINESS STUDIES
SCHOOL OF COMMERCE

Javier Carvajal, Rafael García de Castro
1955-1961

Av. Diagonal, 694 - Barcelona

The project addresses the introduction of a large university faculty in the framework of urban development created by Avinguda Diagonal and the emergence of the architectural modernity that characterized the period. The programme is laid out in accordance with the structural constraints. The large lecture rooms and conference hall are housed on the ground floor to avoid the need for mechanical means of displacement. These spaces receive overhead lighting through spherical skylights. The smaller rooms are accommodated in a longitudinal five-floor block, with a regular modulated structure: a 12-metre space between façades and modules of three metres crosswise, generating a series of repeated windows. The large footprint of the ground floor is offset by a series of light shafts situated between the lecture rooms and the corridors that organize all the circulations in a ring configuration.

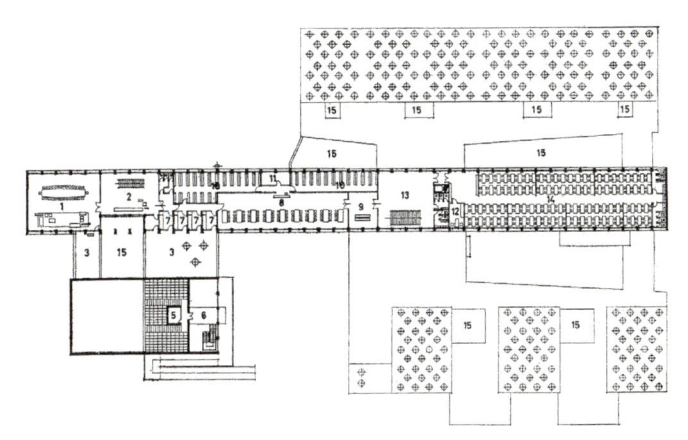

CAMP NOU
FC BARCELONA STADIUM

Francesc Mitjans, Josep Soteras,
Lorenzo García-Barbón
1954-1957

C/ Arístides Maillol, 12-18 - Barcelona

SUBSEQUENT INTERVENTIONS:
Francesc Mitjans, Josep Soteras, Juan Pablo Mitjans, Francesc Cavaller, Antoni Bergnes, 1982. First extension.

The project responds to the need to accommodate an ever-increasing number of spectators for a constantly growing football club with an ever-higher social profile. The design criteria were based on a critical analysis of the world's foremost football stadiums. The pitch is below grade in order to reduce the ascent to the highest stands. The stands follow the lines of four shallow curves to guarantee the maximum proximity of spectators to the pitch. In section, the stadium is organized in the form of three stacked tiers, producing the maximum vertical occupation. The first tier rests directly on the site. The second houses the VIP stand and the only covered seats. The third tier holds general seating and increases in height opposite the VIP stand. Evacuation is organized by the combination of numerous vertical communication shafts that are interrelated by open passages. The Camp Nou applies criteria of rationality to a programme for a large-capacity stadium in which the spectators are the true protagonists.

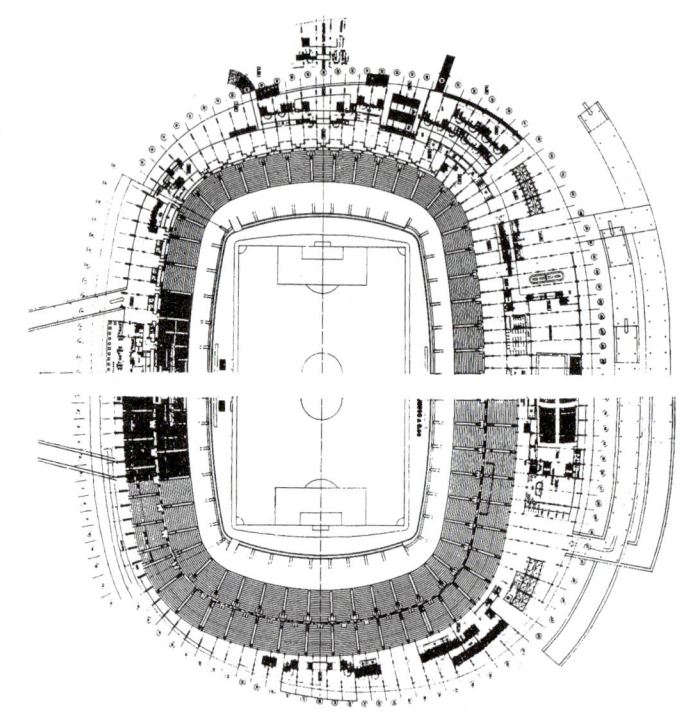

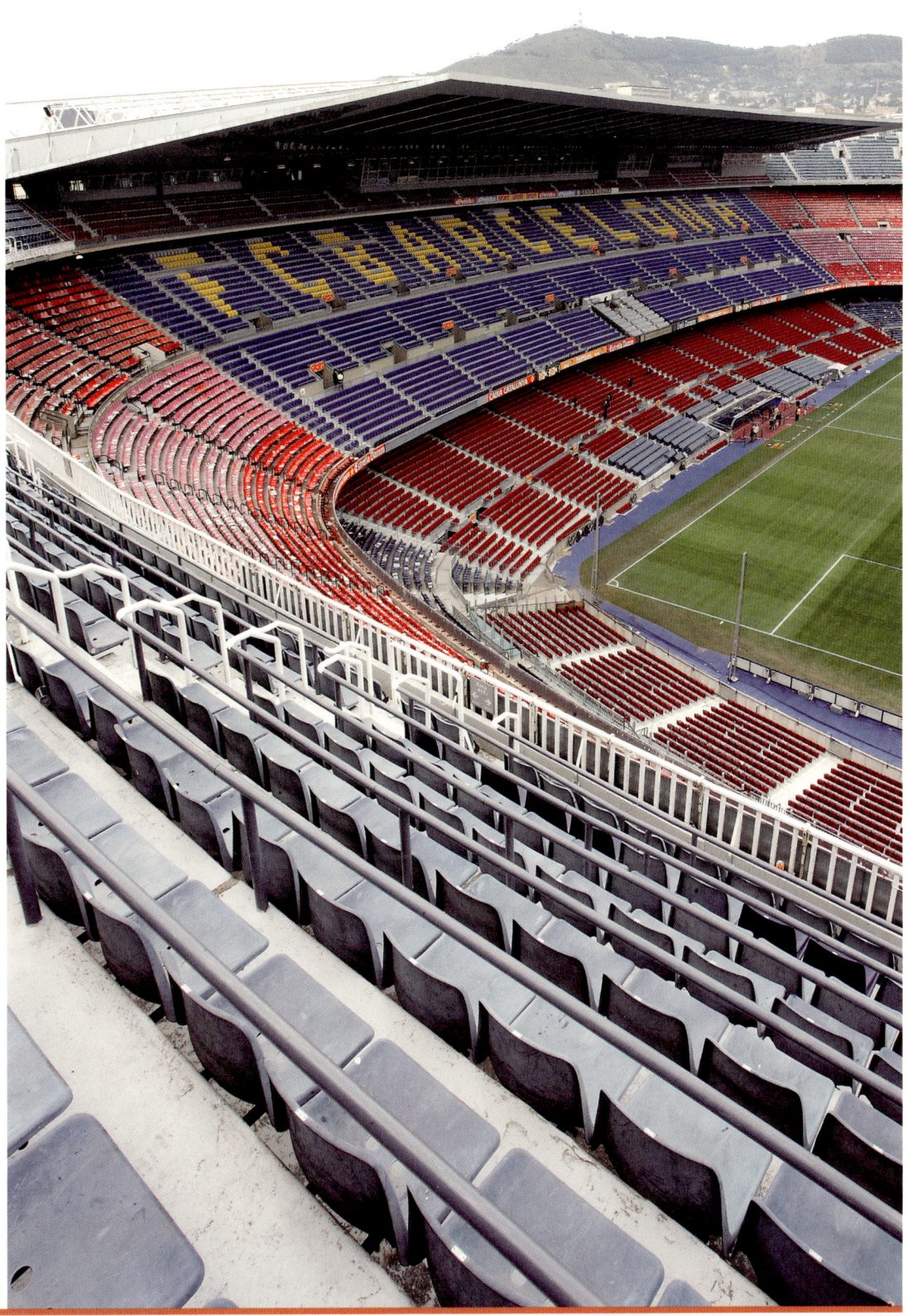

Barcelona 149

MERIDIANA GREYHOUND STADIUM

Antoni Bonet i Castellana, Josep Puig i Torné
1962-1963

C/ Concepción Arenal, 165 - Barcelona

The programme for a greyhound-racing track produced an unusual building with its own constraints. Bonet designed a large construction in the shape of an orange segment under a single roof structure. The model support element is a single steel pillar positioned at the centre, supporting a main beam that projects to either side. The resulting imbalance is compensated by the weight of the sunshade that filters the southern light, attached by ties to pillars that offset the weight. The fragile, fluctuating roof comprises braces to support prefabricated sheet elements that are firmly attached by a tie at each end. Beneath this great domed surface is the platform for spectators, with access to the betting counters and the stands. Beneath the platform are the kennels and service areas.

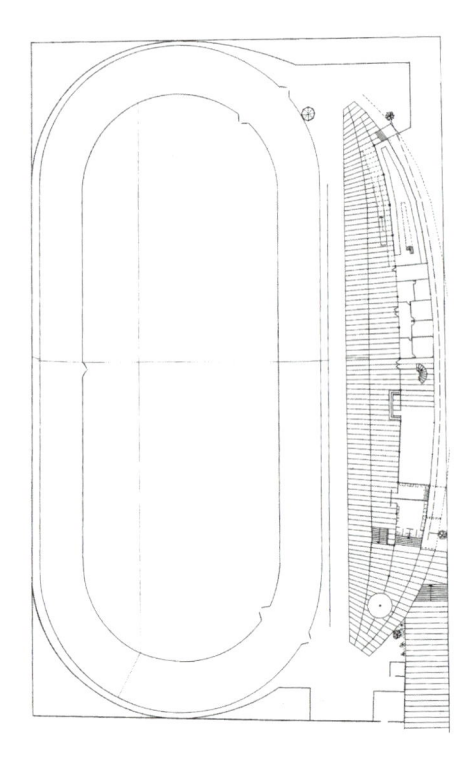

HORTA MUNICIPAL CYCLE TRACK

Esteve Bonell, Francesc Rius
1983-1984

Pg. Vall d'Hebron, 185-201 - Barcelona

The project undertakes the challenge of meeting a series of programmatic requirements that seem simple, though they are marked by urban implications that question the suitability of the proposal. The new cycle track stands on a plot with no specific character of its own, edged by the Llars Mundet residence, the Labyrinth gardens, a natural valley bottom and Passeig de la Vall d'Hebron, an avenue that marks the frontier between the built city and the start of non-urban land. The form and dimensions of the track are determined by strictly technical factors. The main project decision was to enclose the place within a circular portico that brings the same criterion to the site's various irregularities, at the same time foreseeing the possibility of covering the track over with a dome. The portico is 4 metres thick, housing spectator services and leaving space for a possible extension of the stands, TV cameras and so on.

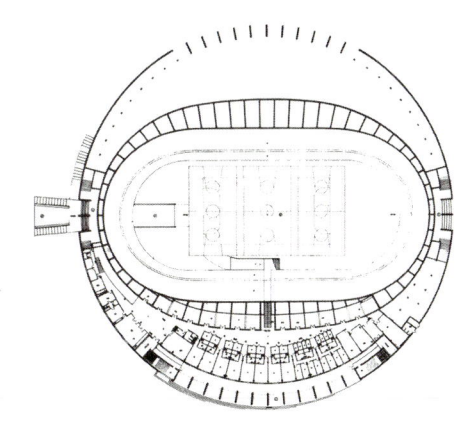

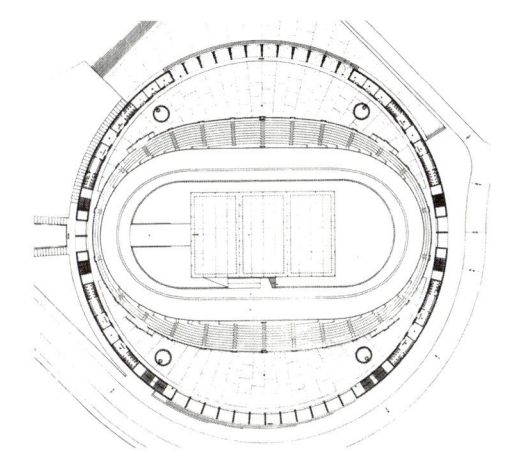

129

PALLARS HOUSING BLOCK
BUILDING OF 130 SOCIAL DWELLINGS

Oriol Bohigas, Josep Maria Martorell
1958-1959

C/ Pallars, 299-317 - Barcelona

130

MITRE BUILDING
BLOCK OF 298 APARTAMENTS

Francisco Juan Barba Corsini
1960-1964

Rda. General Mitre, 1-13 - Barcelona

In the early 1960s, the area in which this building stands was being developed. The block is aligned along the street to the rear, drawn back from Ronda del General Mitre. It comprises seven independent buildings housing 298 dwellings. Apart from those at the end wall, the apartments, all rental accommodation, comprise 46 square metres. The model apartment was designed for a family with up to three young children. The block concept is the legacy of certain modern movement ideas, though in this case produced by a private developer.

131

SEIDA BUILDING
BLOCK OF 96 DWELLINGS

Francesc Mitjans
1959-1967

Av. de Sarrià, 130-152

The building represents an attempt to rationalize social housing, taking the Cerdà street block as a reference. The model block contains four dwellings, with a small light well at the centre to serve the bedrooms. Each block is clearly separated from its neighbour by a space containing the stairway and utility spaces. The basic dwelling comprises two bays, one for the bedrooms and the other for the kitchen and bathroom. The building as a whole, GF+5, presents a cadenced façade created by the differentiation of volumes. The project simultaneously addresses all working scales: from basic living standards to control of the urban form.

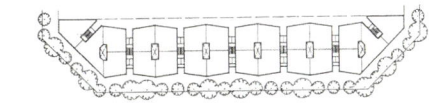

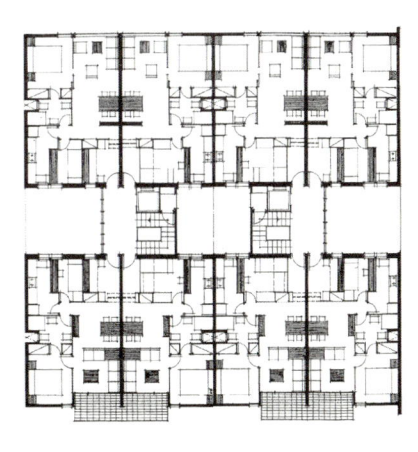

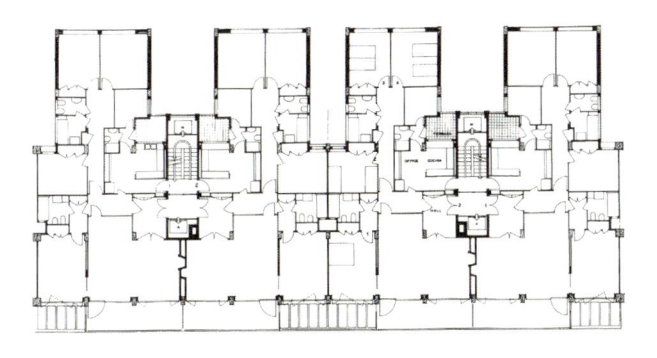

This is a real-estate operation to offset the use of this block as a car storage warehouse. The project presents a block of 12 T-modules that prevent the need for inner courtyards and turn the complex to overlook Avinguda de Sarrià. This very long façade is regulated by the inclusion of vertical latticework to filter low sunrays and an alternating layout of terraces that makes it more dynamic. The block as a whole represents the rigorous application of the logical principles of concrete structures.

Barcelona

26-DWELLING APARTMENT BUILDING

José Antonio Coderch de Sentmenat, Manuel Valls
1957-1961

c/ Johann Sebastian Bach, 7 - Barcelona

The building responds to a programme of four dwellings per floor of 200 square metres, in an urban area of tower blocks separated by a minimum distance. Coderch focused on a study of the housing unit to produce a building with two axes of symmetry. The two façades the block presents to the street and the back garden are the same, as are the two side façades. Within the layout of the dwelling, all the main rooms, including bedrooms and bathrooms, are placed next to the outer walls, leaving the kitchen and service areas in contact with a central court. The main and the service routes are clearly separated, only crossing in the hall at the entrance. The dining and living rooms have a gallery that combines sliding windows, canopies and fixed blinds in a lighting and ventilation mechanism superposed on the structure.

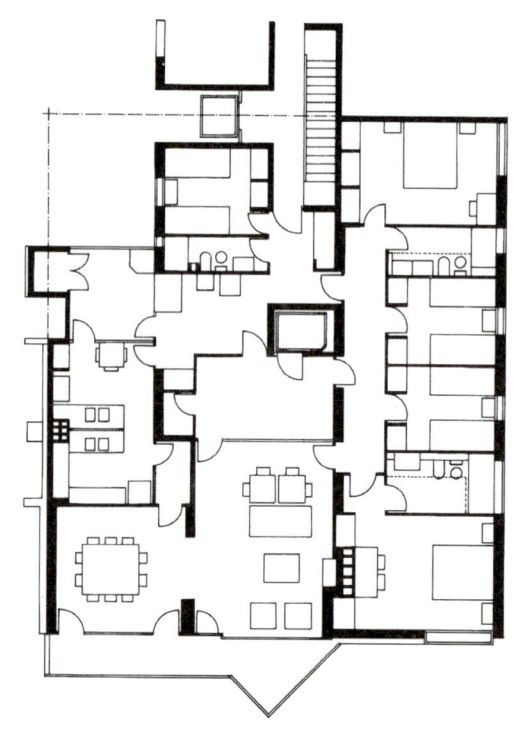

APARTMENT BUILDING

Emili Bofill, Ricard Bofill
1962-1963

C/ Johann Sebastian Bach, 28 - Barcelona

The special conditions of the site produced a layout that ignores the characteristic typological repertory for apartments in an urban context. The only façade on the street faces north. To the south, there is only a very small connecting space leading to the inner courtyard, and it is situated on a corner. Bofill chose to insert the living rooms on the street side and turn the bedroom volumes to overlook the inner courtyard, creating a space that guarantees good lighting and ventilation of the rear part of the dwellings. The two bedroom wings are staggered to seek the best orientation, and the master bedroom stands at the end, in the best position. The spaces left between the two volumes are occupied by the kitchens, with an opening into the courtyard, and the bathrooms, against the party walls. The façade overlooking the street combines brick latticework with wooden blinds, arranged asymmetrically at the openings of the living rooms.

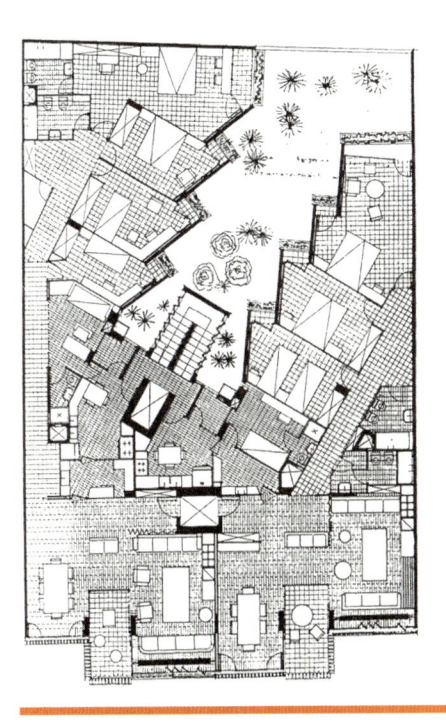

134

APARTMENT BUILDING

Emili Bofill, Ricard Bofill
1962-1963

C/ Johann Sebastian Bach, 2-4
C/ Francesc Pérez-Cabrero, 6 - Barcelona

135

APARTMENT BUILDING

Emili Bofill, Ricard Bofill
1962-1965

C/ Nicaragua, 97-99 - Barcelona

This is a programme for social protection dwellings on a north-facing corner site. The distribution frees up a large courtyard to the rear, ensuring light and ventilation for the bedrooms in the side dwellings. The entire central dwelling overlooks the street, though it presents almost blind walls to the corner and opens up at a slant to the east and west. The building offers the image of brick screens that fan out towards the two favourable orientations, from where the views are more permeable. A singular dwelling on three levels gives way to the withdrawn volumes of the roof.

136

APARTMENT BUILDING

Manuel de Solà-Morales i Rosselló,
Manuel de Solà-Morales i Rubió
1964-1967

C/ Muntaner, 271 - C/ Avenir, 35-37 - Barcelona

The building houses a programme of 12 free-market and 21 social dwellings and a penthouse, a one-off design drawn back from the façade. Bofill takes as his reference the traditional construction of brick masonry to adapt to the circular perimeter of the square, giving it a defining role. The two hierarchies of dwellings are reflected in the façade and, like the autochthonous modernist tradition, they showcase small-scale elements (drainpipes, gargoyles, chimney pots, railings) to give expressiveness to the building, seen as a delicate fabric of brick masonry with ironwork features that acquire a sculptural quality.

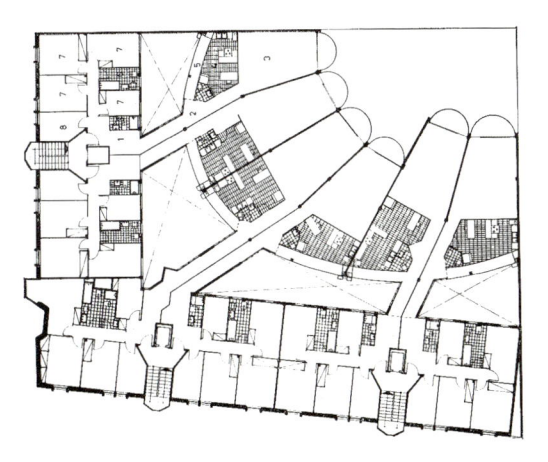

The layout of the dwellings adopts a solution that transcends traditional time-honoured typologies. All the dwellings turn their façades onto the inner courtyard of the street block, which offers the best sunlighting conditions for the living rooms. The bedrooms form a separate volume, aligned with the two streets and connected to the interior volume by long corridors. The two volumes are separated by an open court that runs from one side of the building to the other. The corridors play an important role in the layout of the dwellings, as they are well lit and create a greater sensation of openness in the residual centre space.

Barcelona

137

BUILDING OF 121 SOCIAL DWELLINGS

Oriol Bohigas, Josep Maria Martorell, David Mackay
1959-1965

Av. Meridiana, 312-318 - Barcelona

138

APARTMENT BUILDING

Antoni de Moragas, Francesc de Riba i Salas
1966-1968

Via Augusta, 128-132 - C/ Brusi, 37-45
C/ Sant Elies, 11-19 - Barcelona

On a large site overlooking three very different streets, Moragas designed a housing programme in the form of three blocks separated by a semiprivate space. The three blocks are very compact and are ventilated by a system of minimal courtyards. This allows a layout of the apartments according to a general model that allows numerous variations. The emphasis on quality in the hallways, the recourse to coloured ornamentation and the vividness of the bare materials demonstrate the determination to interpret communal housing by respecting the human scale in all aspects of urban life.

139

LA VINYA HOUSING COMPLEX
BLOCK OF 288 SOCIAL DWELLINGS

Lluís Nadal, Vicenç Bonet, Pere Puigdefàbregas
1966-1968

C/ Alts Forns, 85-87 - C/ Ferrocarrils Catalans, 71-85 - Barcelona

The building follows a north-south axis, distributing the dwellings along the sides and producing four spacious courtyards to ventilate the homes on the inside façades. A structural system of concrete walls accommodates four dwellings per landing, and each dwelling is laid out in two bays: the smaller contains the kitchen, dining room and living room, and the larger contains the bedrooms. A system of variants for the openings means that the windows turn to face south, modelling the great plane of façade like a varied, three-dimensional fabric in which tiles combine with the concrete of the bands and dihedrons that support the bay windows.

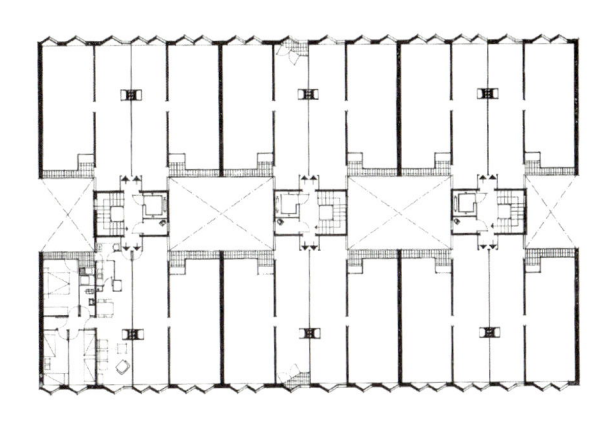

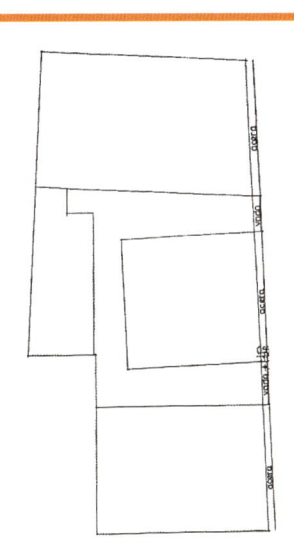

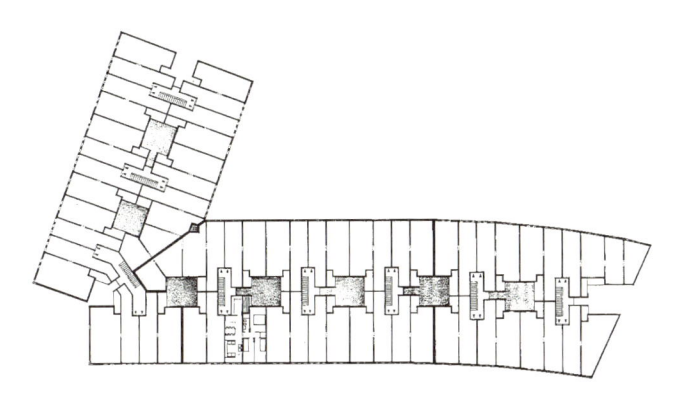

The guidelines of the project are determined by a determination to keep to the initial budget. A single housing type is repeated throughout the complex, with variations in the end walls and at the corner between the two blocks. The window overlooking the street is the same in all cases: the brick bearing wall resting on a pyramidal base, with the brightly-coloured window frame on the inside, connected to a metal protection element painted in the same colour. The result is a smooth façade, greatly enhanced by this feature. The concrete porch on the ground floor creates low ribbed vaults that are reduced to a linear profile.

Barcelona

HISPANO-OLIVETTI OFFICES

Ludovico Belgiojoso, Enrico Peressutti,
Ernesto N. Rogers
1960-1964

Rda. Universitat, 18 - Barcelona

The building takes on the challenge of inserting an office programme into a site set in 19th-century urban fabric that was consolidated shortly before the demolition of the town walls. Its frontage onto Ronda de la Universitat, which faces north, comprises a glazed wall supported by a metal facing in an unusual response to municipal bylaws on projecting volumes, with a successive staggering towards the centre. The south-facing rear façade incorporates a sunshading element to filter solar radiation. The structure is optimized by a double central row of pillars that allows the creation of open-plan space throughout much of the floor. A 0.90 x 0.90-metre grid uses dismountable screens to implement a flexible distribution of the programme on each floor. On the double-height ground floor, the pillars are given a more careful treatment, as they are on view in this display area.

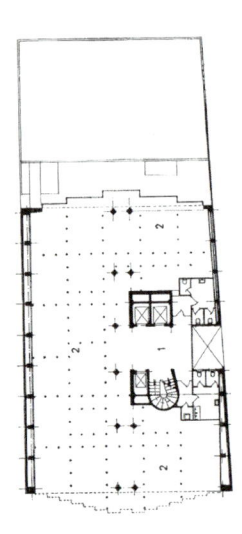

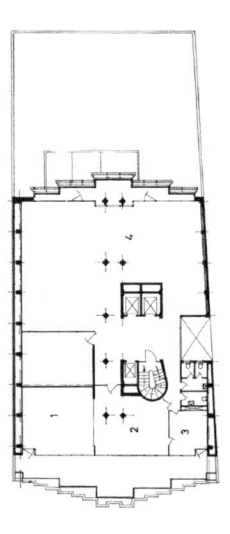

141

BANCA CATALANA
BANCO DE BILBAO - VIZCAYA / ARGENTARIA (BBVA)

Josep Maria Fargas, Enric Tous
1965-1968

Pg. de Gràcia, 84 - Barcelona

The project won first prize in an invitation competition organized by Banca Catalana, and it was undoubtedly the façade solution that won the casting vote. As a representative building on one of the city's foremost avenues, its image is necessarily conditioned by the context of the surrounding architecture and the requirements of the bank. Comprising a combination of glazing and paraboloid plastic elements, the façade presents a strictly two-dimensional plane that reflects all the aesthetic potential required of it. Tous and Fargas innovated with the façade design, constructing it of parts that are assembled in a mechanism that encloses the building like the streamlining of a car. They subsequently applied the same criterion to other office buildings, with numerous variations. The structural solution is also interesting; it is reduced to two spans requiring a single row of columns, revealing the great framework of girders that supports the various floors.

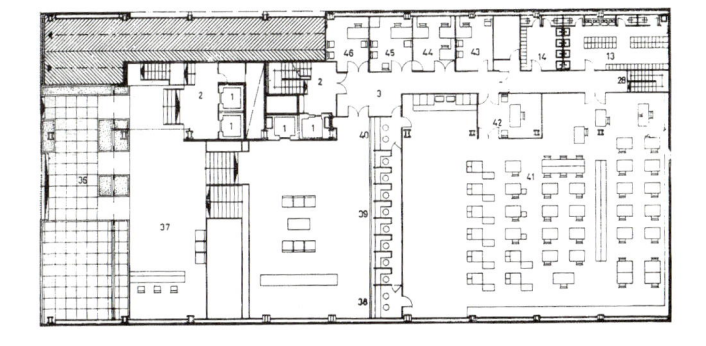

TÀPIES HOUSE
STUDIO-HOUSE OF THE PAINTER
ANTONI TÀPIES

José Antonio Coderch de Sentmenat, Manuel Valls
1960-1963

C/ Saragossa, 57 - Barcelona

On a long narrow site on the edge of the district of Gràcia, Coderch designed a house in which the length and the vertical dimension are balanced by a series of fixed elements that break with the spatial continuity: a covered courtyard to either side of the site, and two stairways running crosswise. The ground floor forms a discontinuous sequence that leads from the entrance atrium to the double-height studio at the far end. The first floor contains the daytime areas and the second floor houses the bedrooms. The library forms a weightless separate volume, withdrawn from the line of the street. The house is a mechanism that comprises a vertical and horizontal façade of white-painted wooden slats that harness the scant available light, which once inside is absorbed by walls that reveal the dark tones of the brickwork.

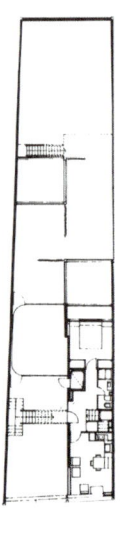

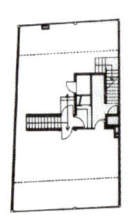

OFFICES AND PRINT SHOPS OF *EL NOTICIERO UNIVERSAL*
GOODBAR "NOTI" RESTAURANT

Josep Maria Sostres
1963-1965

C/ Roger de Llúria, 35 - Barcelona

The first brief for the extension of the headquarters of *El Noticiero Universal* involved raising a lower volume on the same site as the present building. In the final solution of the extension, occupying an entire built volume between party walls with its own façade, Sostres took as his reference the early houses built in the Eixample, with very flat façades and horizontal continuity in the fenestration. The façade of *El Noticiero Universal* is a smooth plane in which the vertical order of the openings follows the lines of the neighbouring building to the north, also part of the newspaper's premises. In this façade, Sostres combined purist solutions with rigorous reflection on the most essential features of Eixample architecture, returning to its origins and linking the urban planning spirit of Cerdà with the new freedom of distribution offered by modern architecture.

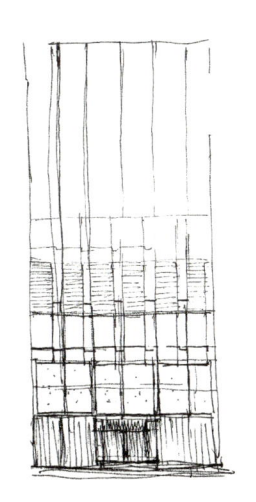

BANCO ATLÁNTICO
BANC DE SABADELL
HIGH-RISE OFFICE BUILDING

Francesc Mitjans, Santiago Balcells
1965-1969

C/ Balmes, 168-170 - Barcelona

Mitjans designed the tower's outline by taking as his inspiration the Pirelli building in Turin, after meeting its designer, Giò Ponti. That said, the structural solution is completely new: four metal pillars situated at the centre of gravity of the floor plan produce a totally open-plan space and contain all the installations. The four side screens are also bearing elements, and all the support elements are expressed on the outside by white marble cladding. The two vertical communication shafts are situated at the ends to facilitate evacuation in the event of fire. The tower is linked to the fabric of the Eixample by means of a low-rise volume, and plunges 20 metres below grade to provide car parking. This is a solution for a mid-rise office block that makes its mark on the surrounding urban landscape.

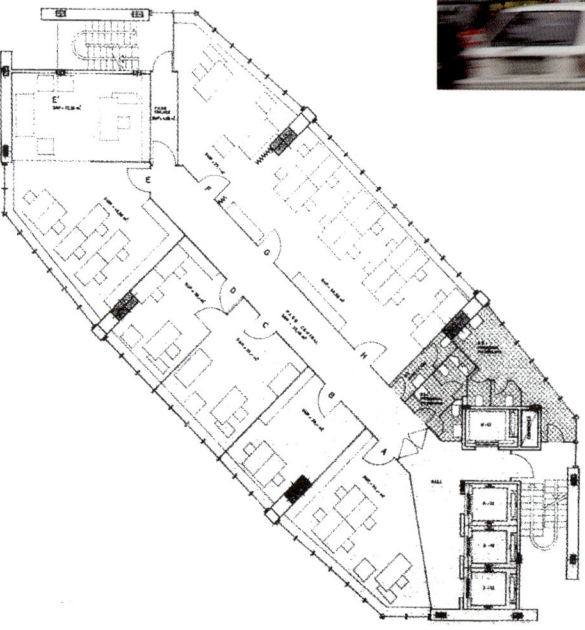

TRADE BUILDINGS
COMPLEX OF FOUR HIGH-RISE OFFICE BUILDINGS

José Antonio Coderch de Sentmenat, Manuel Valls
1965-1969

Av. Carles III, 84-98 - Barcelona

In a peripheral area of Barcelona with large freestanding constructions, Coderch clearly differentiates the world of the ground floor and the emerging high-rise volumes. In response to a large-scale tertiary programme, he designed an organism comprising four quatrefoil buildings with very gentle curves and reverse curves. Three of the towers share the first two floors, with a perimeter that embraces them in a great unifying base. The modulation of the curtain-wall is very narrow to allow for the turns, and the modules follow the perimeter in a saw-tooth arrangement. The vertical communication shafts, at the centre of each tower, are set between four great concrete pillars, complemented by series of equidistant metal pillars. The image presented by the towers expresses the mobility of a city sector marked out by major streets and freestanding buildings.

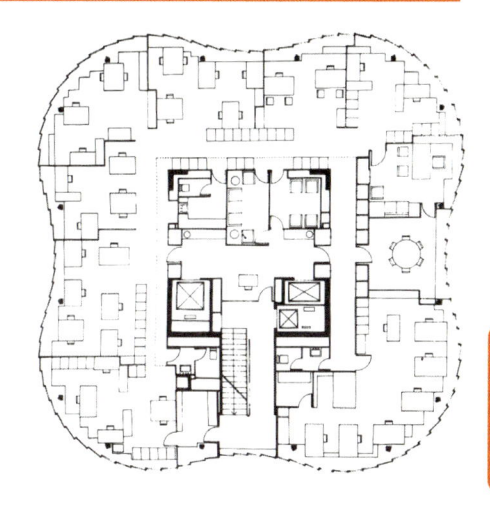

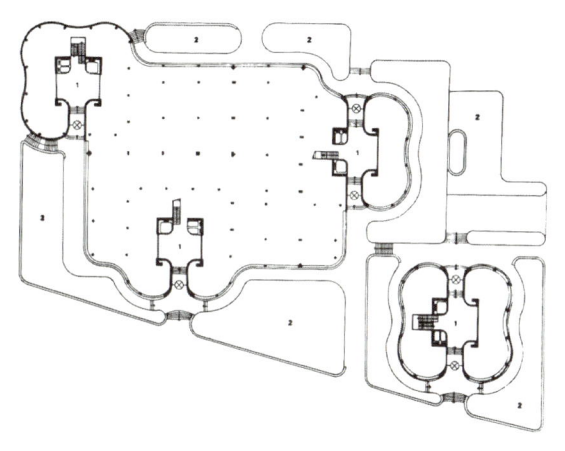

TORRE ATALAYA
HIGH-RISE APARTMENT BUILDING

Federico Correa, Alfons Milà,
José Luis Sanz Magallón
1966-1971

Av. Diagonal, 523 - Barcelona

This tower block was part of the first generation of high-rises to be built in Barcelona in the early 1970s. The idea was to incorporate a new scale of building into a few strategic points in the city. In this case, the original commission consisted in the site management of a completed project that had been turned down by the City Council. Correa and Milà effected a change starting on the 17th floor, decreasing the number of dwellings per floor from four to two and thereby generating an innovative order in the distribution of heights. The entire building is modulated according to a 1 x 1-metre grid that determines both the prefabricated elements in the façade and the small-scale features: parapets, lintels, etc. The top floor is occupied by a restaurant that forms the cornice of the whole building, thereby inverting the interpretation of the lines of North American skyscrapers.

MONITOR BUILDING
HOUSING BLOCK

Federico Correa, Alfons Milà
1968-1970

Av. Diagonal, 672 - Barcelona

The building adapts to an arrangement of this stretch of Diagonal designed by the architect Xavier Subias, though forcing a series of alterations. The plan envisaged a freestanding building with a perfectly square floor plan and a flat roof. The built project draws back the corners, housing the dining rooms and living rooms, and applies a similar system right round the building's perimeter. The programme recommends two dwellings of 200 square metres per floor, ideal for the market in this area, though the top floor was designed to accommodate just one, a top-floor villa, with a continuous balcony around the edge. Finally, the pretext of housing installations made it possible to adopt the solution of a multi-faceted slope to the roof. The compositional freedom of all the walls in the block arises from relations at the time with certain Italian architects, specifically Ignazio Gardella.

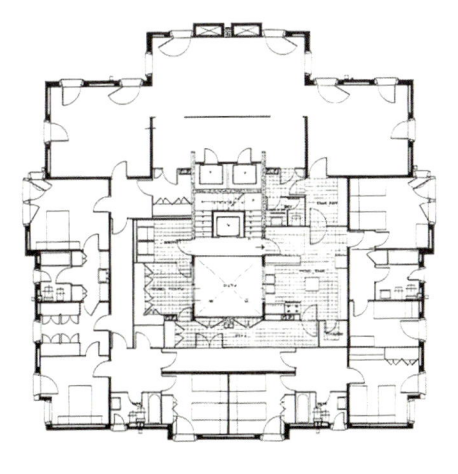

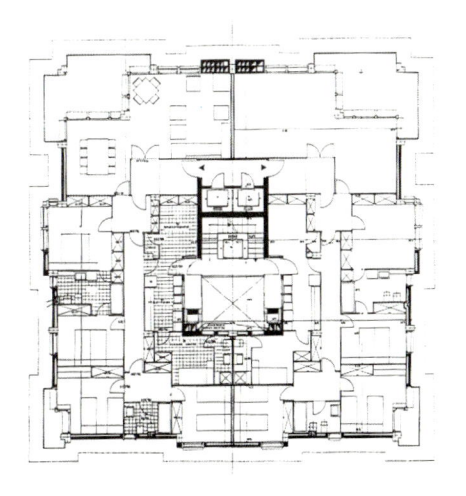

BANCO URQUIJO HOUSING COMPLEX

José Antonio Coderch de Sentmenat, Manuel Valls
1968-1973

C/ Raset, 21-29 - C/ Modolell, 29-31 - C/ Freixa, 22-30 - C/ Vico, 12-18 - Barcelona

The project for a residential complex within the city fabric allowed Coderch to define his conception of urban housing. The apartments are grouped in twos in three-storey blocks and form a series of six blocks arranged according to a symmetrical double axis. The ground floors absorb the difference in level of 5.5 metres between Carrer Raset and Carrer Freixa, avoid presenting shops in the façade and accommodate offices away from the street. The semi-public space left between the six blocks forms a single architectural landscape, characterized by the brick cladding, the vertical wooden blinds and the combination of bays with profuse vegetation. The dwelling extrapolates the staggered floor plan of Coderch's previous single-family dwellings. Thanks to a structure of metal uprights and waffle slabs, the perimeter of the floors can be foreshortened and the facings distributed independently of structural requirements.

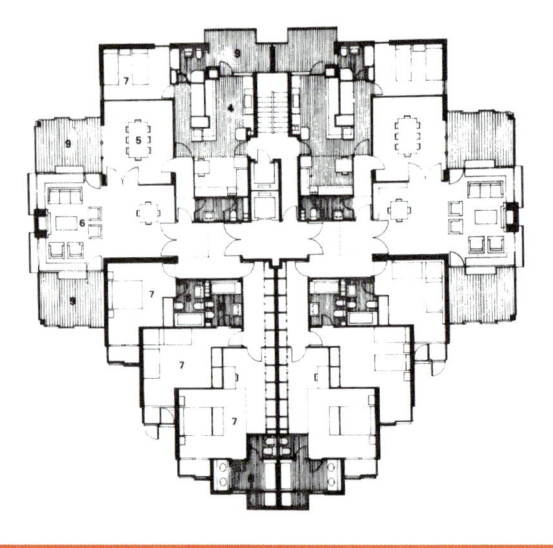

149

LES ESCALES PARK
RESIDENTIAL COMPLEX

Josep Lluís Sert
1967-1973

C/ Sor Eulalia de Anzizu, 46 - Barcelona

The project was carried out in two phases, as it became necessary to dispense with a series of blocks that had been designed initially and compensate for the available building levels on a smaller site. The complex is made up of the repeated addition of a single unit comprising two duplex apartments. Each unit has a blind wall to either side, allowing for the addition of neighbouring units. The façades facing the sun house the living rooms, laid out in an L-shape and fronted by a large covered terrace. The north-facing façades hold the kitchens, dining rooms and utility galleries. A staircase in the side wall leads upstairs to the bedrooms and is accompanied in some cases by an empty space above the living room. The combination of symmetry with mass housing and the system of additional units reflects an interpretation of the rationalist concepts that characterized the 1960s.

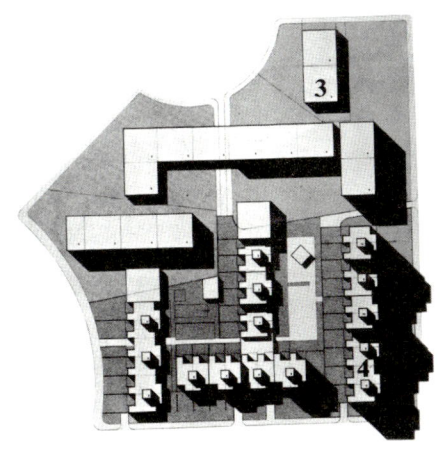

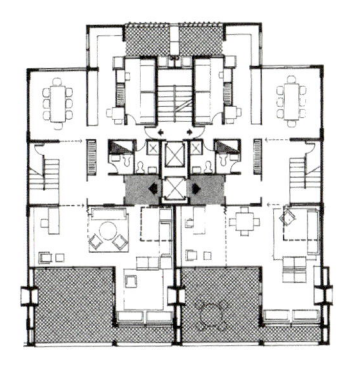

FRÉGOLI APARTMENT BUILDING

Esteve Bonell
1972-1975

C/ Madrazo, 54-56 - Barcelona

The building occupies a very long, narrow corner plot, with little potential for creating spacious apartments. Bonell drew on a model from the rationalist tradition: a duplex apartment with some double-height spaces. The layout of the dwellings along the strip produced different housing types: on the party wall side, two symmetrical dwellings have a mezzanine containing two bedrooms. In the centre, the stairs are outside, occupying the entire width of the site and leading to two dwellings that are asymmetrical but mimic the mezzanines of the previous modules. The corner dwelling has a specific configuration, modifying the layout of the mezzanine and the entrance stairway. The complexity of the series of dwellings is reflected in the façade, with the interruption of the volumes of galleries and the vertical continuity of the balconies.

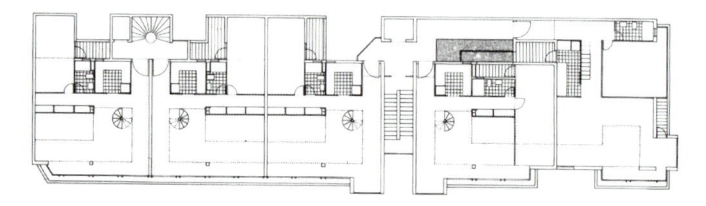

CAN BRUIXA APARTMENT BUILDING

Gabriel Mora, Helio Piñón, Albert Viaplana
1974-1976

C/ Galileu, 281-285 - Barcelona

The building responds to the need to accommodate six dwellings per floor on a north-facing corner site, with scant contact with the courtyard at the centre of the street block. It lays out five apartments in a fan arrangement, leaving the remaining space for the sixth dwelling, which adopts an atypical configuration. In this way, all the apartments are guaranteed a minimum space in the façade. The inner courtyards follow the lines of the fan-shape, as does the bearing structure, comprising rectangular-section pillars that enclose the smallest bays. On the first floor, each pair of pillars joins to form a single one, producing bays more suitable for office use. The entire rear party wall is freed up for the entrance stairways, and the entrance halls are lit via the inner courtyard. The façade forms a double skin that filters contact with the street and allows an arrangement of the openings that is independent of internal requirements.

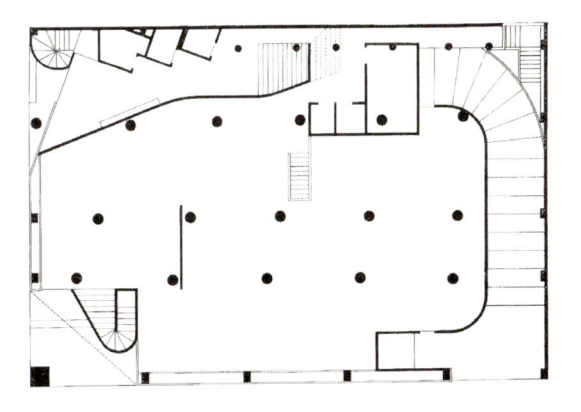

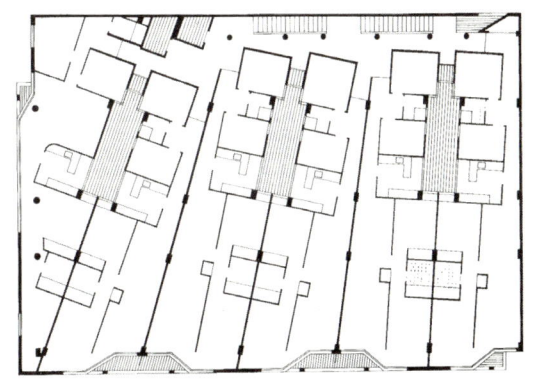

FUNDACIÓ JOAN MIRÓ
CENTRE OF CONTEMPORARY ART STUDIES

Josep Lluís Sert
1972-1975

Av. Miramar, 1 (Parc de Montjuïc) - Barcelona

SUBSEQUENT INTERVENTIONS :
Jaume Freixa, 1987. First extension.
Jaume Freixa, 2000-2001. Second extension.

This is the foremost exponent of Sert's work in Barcelona during his American period. The museum space is conceived as a circular route around a courtyard, linking together various rather small spaces and clearly distinguishing their functions. The route goes back on itself to create the longest itinerary and invites visitors to view the works at their leisure. The specific lighting of each area combines overhead, general and filtered resources and the light provided by the glazed facings, offering a degree of visual contact with the surrounding garden. A further two courts, to the north and east, create interrelation between the Foundation and the panoramic cityscape. The roof is also treated as an exhibition space. The entire wall system comprises concrete screens that leave on view the joins between the prefabricated bearing and facing elements. The conception of the museum space places all the emphasis on the relation between a certain type of work and the architectural setting, a synthesis between art and architecture that was one of the greatest ambitions of a whole generation of modern architects.

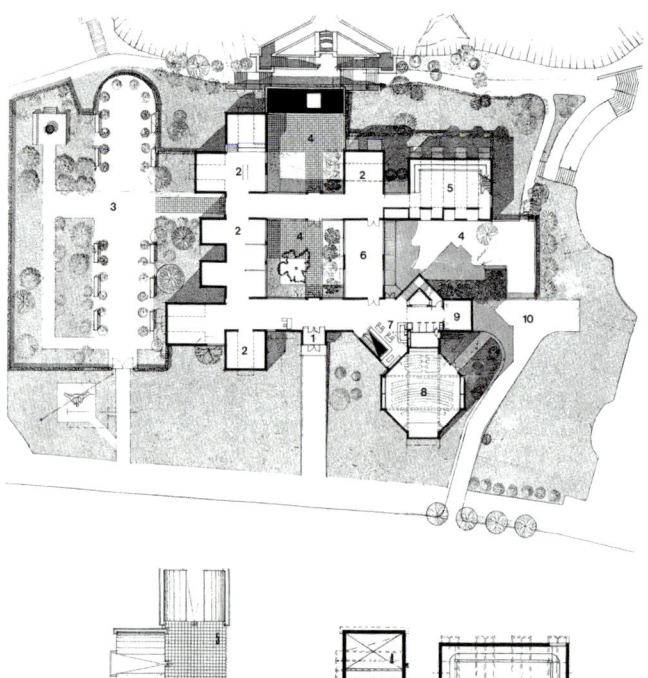

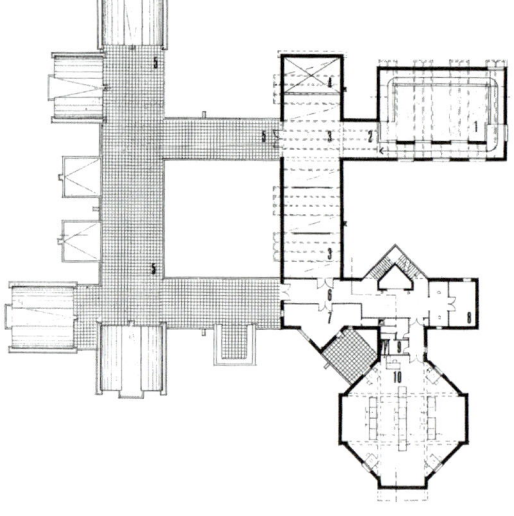

El que vols que digui... Jo ja sóc mort.
Douglas Gordon
24 març
4 juny 2006
Fundació Joan Miró

THAU SCHOOL
INFANT, PRIMARY AND SECONDARY SCHOOL

Oriol Bohigas, Josep Maria Martorell, David Mackay
1972-1975

Ctra. d'Esplugues, 49-53 - Barcelona

The building comprises two distinct volumes, situated at two different levels on a sloping site. The lower volume houses infant and primary classrooms on three floors, leaving the ground floor free for the pre-school spaces to open out directly into the playground. The upper volume, two floors above the first, houses secondary education. The classrooms occupy the sunny façades (south-east and south-west), while the north-east and north-west façades contain the stairways connecting the various floors in glazed volumes, differentiated from the main body of the building. The whole is laid out around a series of terraces for the entire school's outdoor activities. The general plan is governed by the economy and rationality of the structural solution and by careful attention to teaching conditions and interrelations between the different parts of the brief.

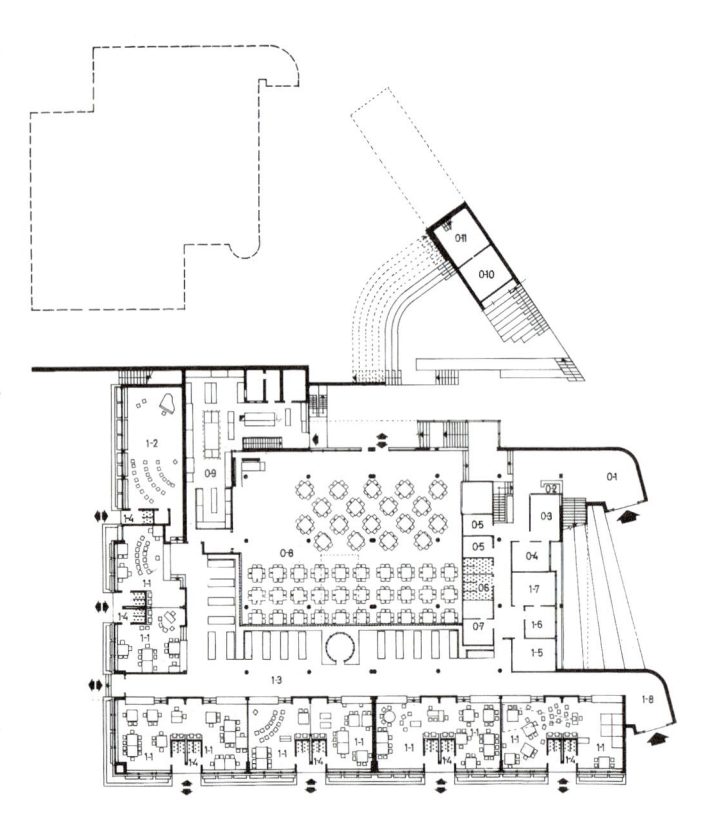

INSTITUT FRANCÈS DE BARCELONA / FRENCH INSTITUTE IN BARCELONA

José Antonio Coderch de Sentmenat, Manuel Valls
1972-1975

C/ Moià, 8 - Barcelona

This is a clear exponent of Coderch's conception of urban architecture, in this case applied to an education and cultural building. The site is occupied throughout by two basement floors and a ground floor, and the remaining eight floors form a clean-lined prism, drawn back from the street and standing apart from the neighbouring constructions. The image of this prism from different viewpoints in the street suggested that the building design should concentrate on the skin. Reinforced concrete pillars are absorbed into the thickness of the skin, and the very slender openings in the exterior plane accentuate the smooth impression of the brick cladding and draw a filtered, generalized light into the interior. The result is a large, smooth volume that adopts its urban role and manifests itself as a fragment of the city that addresses both its position and the open spaces it generates.

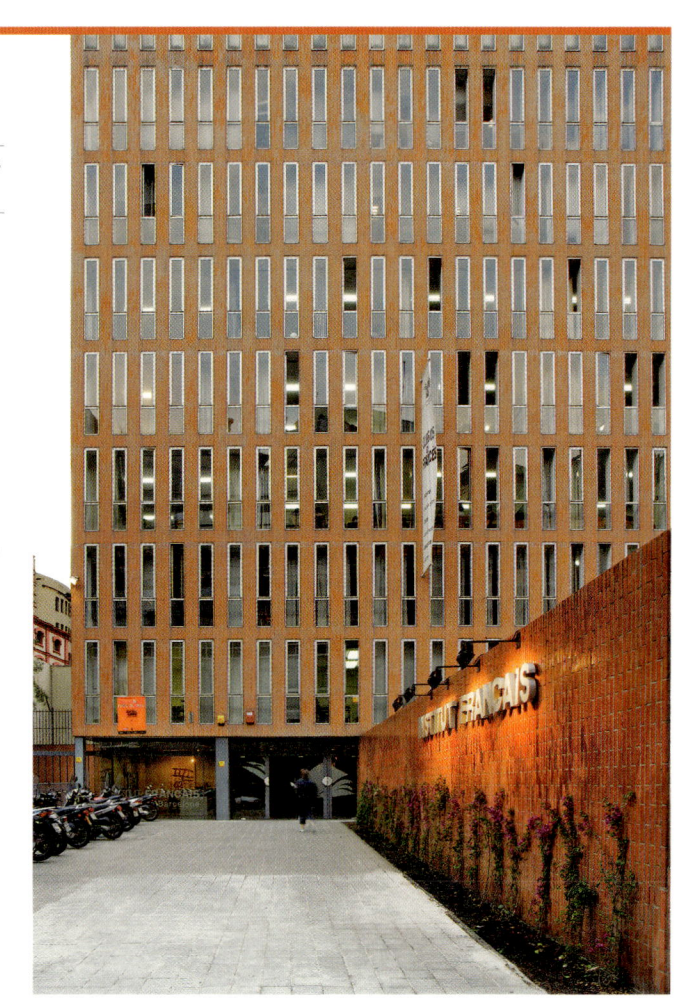

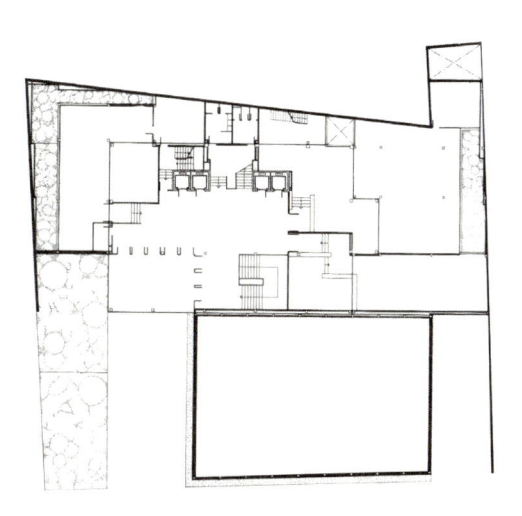

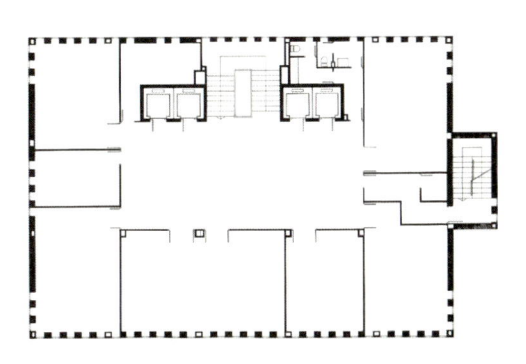

CEIP LA TAXONERA
INFANTS' AND PRIMARY SCHOOL

Emili Donato, Uwe Geest
1978-1982

C/ Farnés, 60 - Barcelona

The district of La Taxonera lies on the north-facing slope of the mountain of El Carmel, its growth reflecting an absence of urban planning or clearly recognisable typological features, on one of the remaining tracts of the city to be subject to unregulated development. The building seeks to recover the constants of the architectural discipline as an instrument of intervention in the context. The plot of land, on the former site of the Camí dels Plàtans track, receives the imprint of an architectural geometry associated with the school's programme: a triangle forms the entrance and communal rooms, and a rectangular brings together the classrooms in twos, interrelated by a courtyard that filters contact with the exterior. Beneath this courtyard, a porch measuring 100 metres by 16 restores the layout of the former Camí dels Plàtans as an itinerary within the overall pedestrian network.

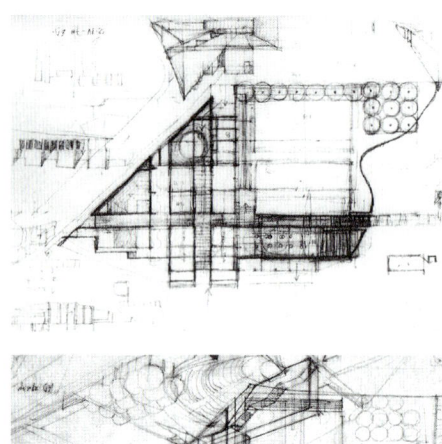

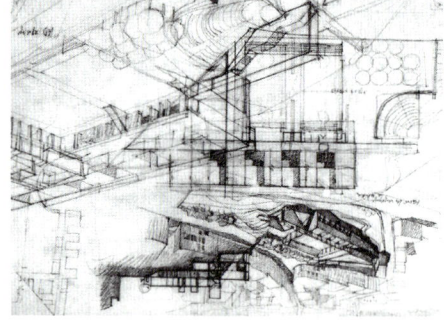

HORTA GERIATRIC HOME

Emili Donato, Miguel Jiménez, Ramon Martí
1988-1992

C/ Josep Sangenís, 75 - Barcelona

This old people's home is in the district of La Taxonera, a few metres above the infants' and primary school designed a few years previously by the same architect. Familiarity with the district and the morphological relation with the existing school led Donato to take the reference of the north-facing slope of the mountain to generate an expressive interplay of geometries in response to the slope's contour lines. The building opens up in a convex arc to create a south-facing public space, a venue for open-air activities for the residents. This reverse curve superposed on the original topography allows the construction to receive natural lighting through its sides. The platform is linked to the open landscape by means of a porch in one stretch, the other stretch being reserved for private rooms. The circle set in the volume clearly separates the two parts of the programme and lays out the main entrance, leading to the lower levels of the building.

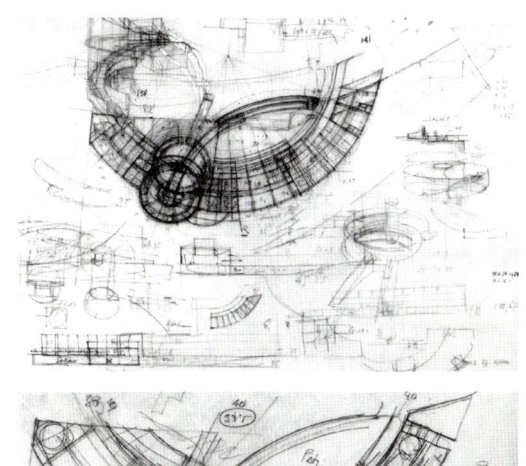

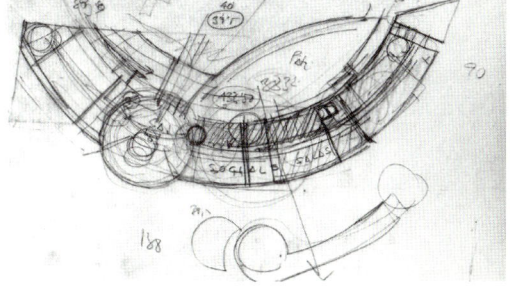

BARÓ DE VIVER HOUSING BLOCK
SOCIAL HOUSING COMPLEX

Emili Donato, Miguel Jiménez, Ramon Martí
1985-1988

Pg. Santa Coloma, 94-112 - Pl. Baró de Viver, 1-15
C/ Campins, 5-19 - Barcelona

The existing building is part of a larger project intended to replace the district of "cheap housing" constructed there for the 1929 Great Exhibition. The renovation of the district involved the construction of a large hall completed by two concave volumes, plus a third space running crosswise at the intermediate point. The idea was to put an end to the area's urban isolation by means of a large block of housing that generates its own public space, indifferent to the morphological diversity of the rest of the city. The dwellings are built three to a landing in order to avoid the need for inner courtyards and allow all of them to overlook the central hall space. The cross section makes up the difference in level between Passeig de Santa Coloma and the street below by means of an intermediate platform that provides a base for the stairways and lifts, beneath which are spaces to accommodate car parking and shops.

JOAN GÜELL BUILDING
MULTIFUNCTIONAL COMPLEX

Josep Lluís Mateo, Jaume Arderiu,
Josep Maria Crespo
1989-1993

C/ Joan Güell, 213 - C/ Joaquim Molins, 5
C/ Les Corts, 22-38 - Barcelona

The building obeys the urban planning regulations of the 1950s, comprising linear blocks with commercial spaces in the inner courtyards. It is situated in an area that combines recent typologies (tower blocks and offices) with remnants of relatively traditional urban fabric, and the singular presence of the Trade building and the solid opaque volume of El Corte Inglés department store. The project approach brings a varied programme to this specific context, including housing, offices and an apartment hotel, as well as five basement floors for car parking. The bearing structure, determined by the car park, establishes the order of the entire building and the situation of the various parts of the programme. The dwellings in the end wall are set apart, with a terrace-cum-room that enjoys the best position in the complex. The surface areas devoted to offices are given an open floor plan, with all the services concentrated in the innermost sector.

BARCELONA PAVILION
RECONSTRUCTION OF THE GERMANY PAVILION OF THE 1929 GREAT EXHIBITION

Ignasi de Solà-Morales, Cristian Cirici, Fernando Ramos
1981-1986

Av. Marquès de Comillas - Barcelona

Original: Ludwig Mies van der Rohe, 1929

The original proposal for the reconstruction of the Barcelona Pavilion was formulated to Mies van der Rohe by Grup R, who received an enthusiastic response from the architect, though the idea then languished due to lack of interest on the part of the administration. A second proposal was made by Joan Bassegoda i Nonell in 1964, and in 1974 Professor Fernando Ramos organized a seminar to thoroughly map the building in the absence of an original project. The definitive proposal came about in 1981, when scholars and historians had acquired a relatively comprehensive knowledge of archive materials in Barcelona, Berlin, New York and Chicago. Along with a series of working hypotheses and analyses of the remains found on site, this knowledge guaranteed a rigorous reconstruction, based on the original building as opposed to the new drawings made by Mies van der Rohe himself for Werner Blaser. The reconstruction departs from the original as regards the waterproofing of the roof, the water collection system and security. The building is now the headquarters of the Mies van der Rohe Foundation and functions as a venue for small events.

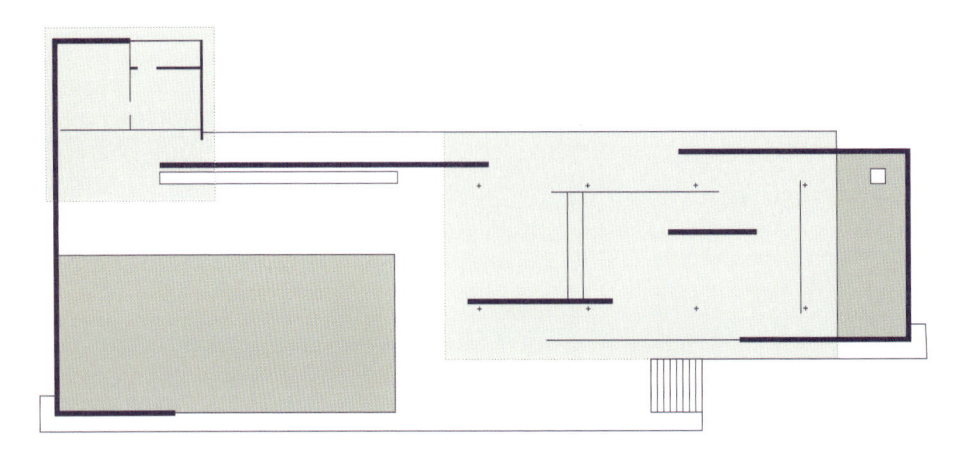

Barcelona 181

MONTJUÏC TELECOMMUNICATIONS TOWER

Santiago Calatrava
1989-1992

Pg. Minici Natal (Montjuïc Olympic Ring)
Barcelona

A slanting concrete shaft, with the centre of gravity at the base coinciding with the vertical of its own weight, is supported by three points over a circular platform of stone-clad reinforced concrete, with access via a 30-metre arc. The platform is enclosed by a sheet-metal door that is opened and closed by a hydraulic motor. When activated, it rotates through 90 degrees, suggesting an eyelid, a feature with which Calatrava has experimented in other works. The tower stands 130 metres high and is crowned by a semicircular element that houses the technical installations and a vertical spar, a javelin suspended in the air. The slant of the shaft coincides with the angle of the summer solstice in Barcelona, so that the shadow it projects onto the circular platform serves as a sundial.

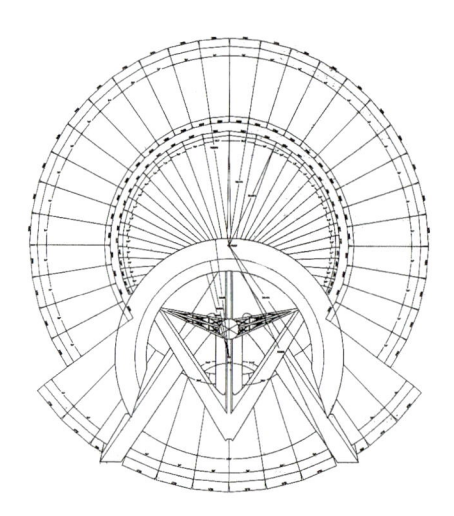

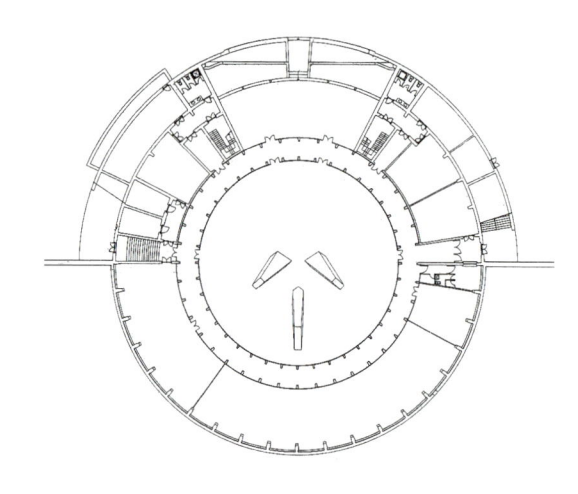

COLLSEROLA COMMUNICATIONS TOWER

Norman Foster
1989-1992

Turó de Vilana (Tibidabo) - Barcelona

Foster addresses this programme for a communications tower by applying the very latest technological innovations in order to obtain the greatest height, the minimum diameter and, as a result, the maximum slenderness. Situated 440 metres above sea level, the tower stands 288 metres high, and the viewing platform is 135 metres above ground level. A single concrete bearing element, just 4.50 metres in diameter, supports the volume of the equipment decks. The stability of the structure relies on a system of nine steel cables, in groups of three, which are braced to prevent oscillation. The top cables supporting the antenna are copper fibre, which does not conduct electricity. To meet the same requirements using more conventional means would have called for a shaft 25 metres in diameter. Its position and characteristic outline have made the tower one of the city's icons.

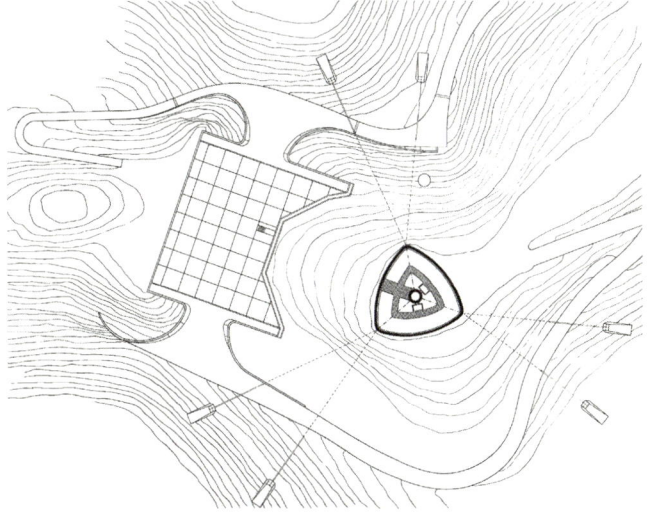

PALAU SANT JORDI STADIUM
SPORTS PAVILION, 1992 OLYMPIC GAMES

Arata Isozaki
1985-1990

Pg. Minici Natal (Montjuïc Olympic Ring)
Barcelona

The definitive project is the result of a series of successive transformations caused by a change of site and various interpretations of the programme. The original site, Montjuïc dumpsite, presented a compact solution to minimize the problem of the foundations. The change of location enabled the extension of the floor plan with a new 200-metre covered athletics track. It also saw a change in the roof solution, which was originally to be made of corrugated sheeting. The new roof consists of a central vault measuring 136 x 110 metres, which was assembled on the ground and jacked up to a height of 45 metres using the Pantadome system. It comprises a space grid made up of 4000 cylindrical tubes and 500 spherical nodes into which the tubes are inserted. The compact volume was maintained by eliminating the warm-up room. The third important innovation is the air-conditioning system. A system of pumps and heat exchangers was implemented to obtain calories, while the cooling system harnesses the wind outside and mobilizes cool air by means of a system of conduits to produce a similar effect to that of a breeze.

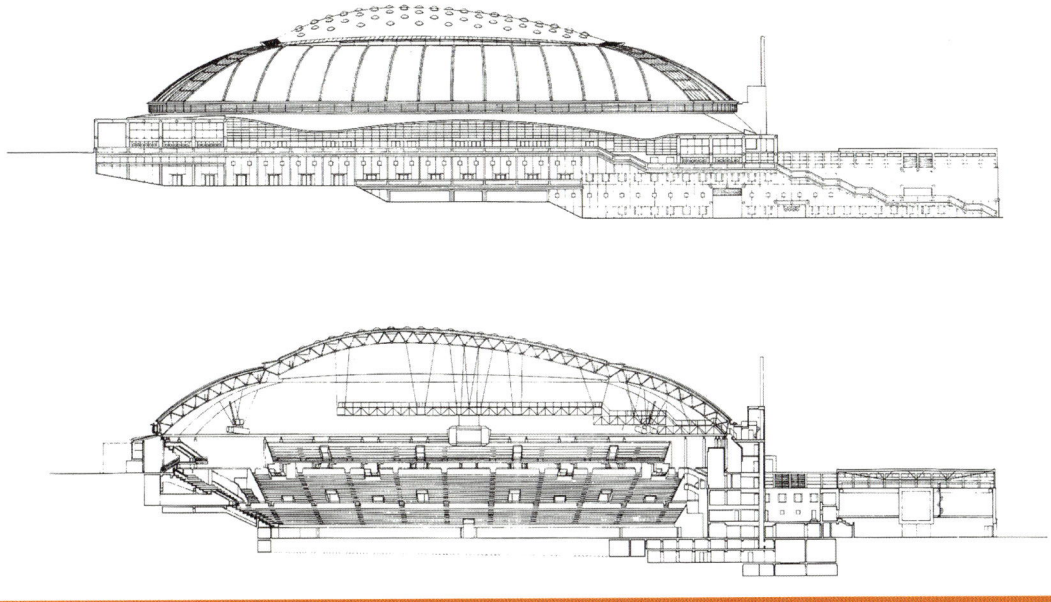

Barcelona

REGIONAL METEOROLOGICAL CENTRE OF CATALONIA
HEADQUARTERS OF THE DELEGATION OF THE MINISTRY OF PUBLIC WORKS AND PLANNING

Álvaro Siza Vieira
1990-1992

C/ Arquitecte Sert, 1 - Barcelona

The building responds to a programme of mixed uses that does not require spaces with a particular architectural quality. Siza addresses the multiple references of the context by means of a building with a circular, indifferent configuration that brings its own logic to its shape. It is laid out around a narrow central space that runs the height of the building, establishing two functional bays separated by a corridor. The intermediate bay adopts an octagonal form, and its 16 component pillars determine the position of the facings, allowing very flexible variations. The resulting cylinder is bevelled on two of its sides, offering a remote allusion to the layout of the coastal ring road. Up to the third floor, the structure comprises bare concrete walls, while the two top floors are clad with white stone. Direct admission to the ground floor is by means of eight equidistant doorways, giving the overall organism a high degree of abstraction.

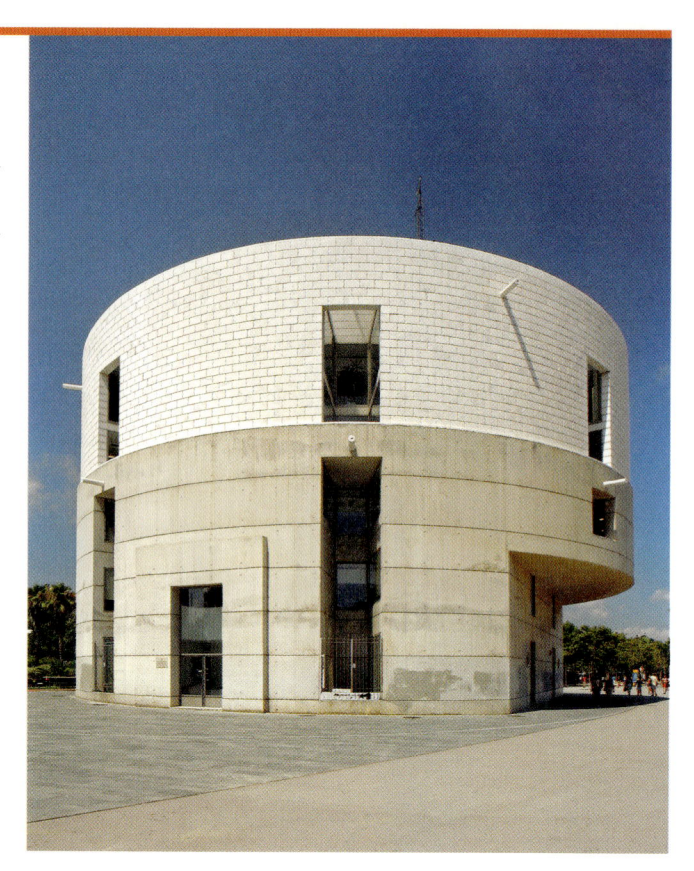

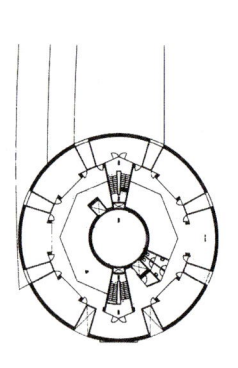

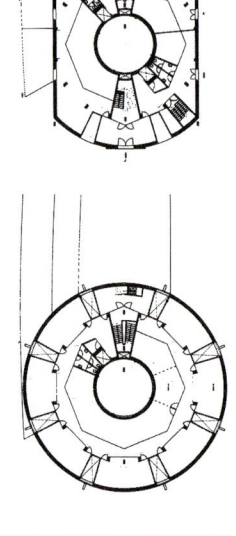

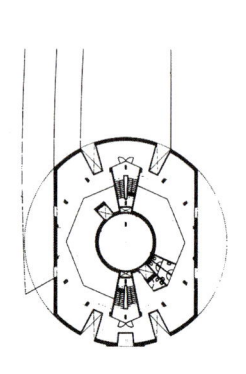

NOVA ICÀRIA MUNICIPAL PAVILION
SPORTS CENTRE AND LIBRARY

Franc Fernández, Moisés Gallego
1990-1994

Av. Icària, 167 - Barcelona

On a corner site in Barcelona's Eixample, the programme called for the inclusion of sports courts, a cultural amenity and a gymnasium, with the possibility of all three uses functioning independently at once. The building adapts to the bevelled street corner, against which it aligns the sports courts, forming a central box that provides the guidelines for the overall volume, with its staggered roof and the smaller volumes to the sides. The building reaches its maximum height at the corner, slopes down towards the centre of the street block and implements low fences at the sides to protect the remaining gardens and the rear volume of the library. This is an interpretation of the typical Eixample corner that makes up for the absence of openings with a delicate articulation of volumes. The gymnasium is suspended from the roof, guaranteeing natural lighting and freeing up space in the floor plan for the rest of the programme.

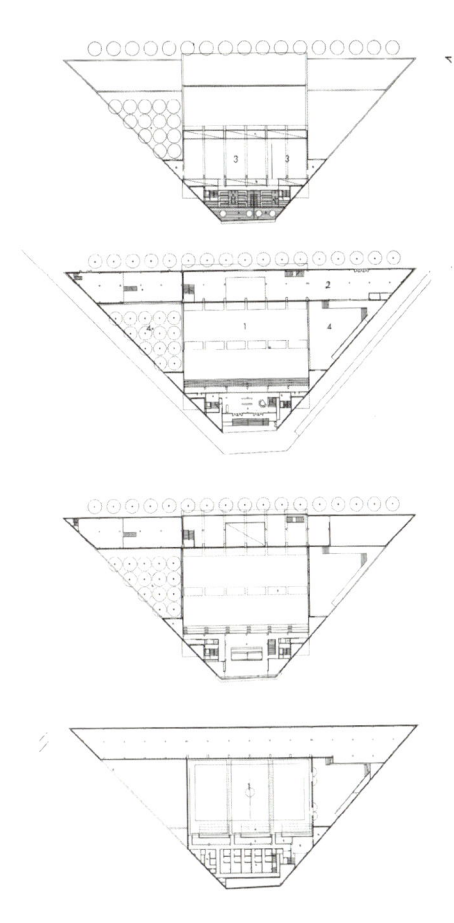

APARTMENT BLOCK
IN THE OLYMPIC VILLAGE

Albert Viaplana, Helio Piñón, Ricard Mercadé
1989-1992

C/ Arquitecte Sert, 18-20 - Av. Icària, 174-184 - Av. Bogatell, 1-3 - C/ Frederic Mompou, 6
(Vila Olímpica) - Barcelona

This housing complex occupies an irregular street block, truncated by the diagonal layout of Avinguda del Bogatell. The main built volume maintains the continuity of the façade of Carrer Arquitecte Sert and Avinguda d'Icària, and presents its chamfered corner as a screen that disguises the separation between two independent buildings. Two smaller volumes, representing the same housing typology, restore the diagonal layout of Avinguda del Bogatell. The block that fronts onto Avinguda d'Icària stands back from the street to maintain the strict orthogonal layout, while a staggered series of terraces restores the line of the avenue. Both the arrangement of the blocks and the treatment of the façades reveal the irregular form of the street block by means of an adaptive mechanism that seeks autonomy in the layout of the dwellings. The openings to the street highlight this departure of the blocks from the street layout.

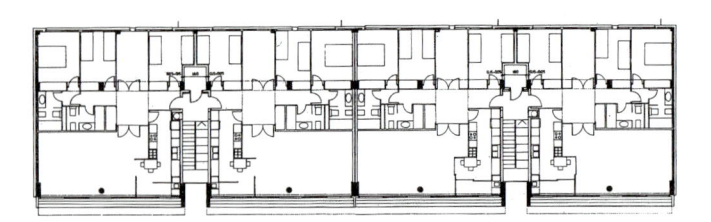

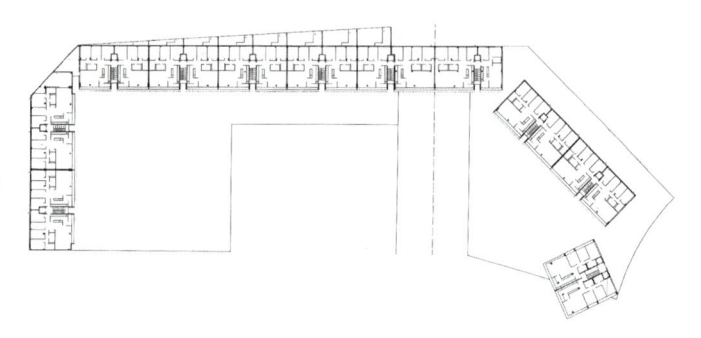

TIRANT LO BLANC HOUSING COMPLEX

José Antonio Martínez Lapeña, Elías Torres
1989-1992

Pl. Tirant lo Blanc, 1-9 - C/ Salvador Espriu, 89-91
(Vila Olímpica) - Barcelona

The layout of the blocks is the result of a substantial modification of the crescent established by the Development Plan. The principal block is turned around and distorted in order to offer the best sea views. The isolated block gives the square a partially closed quality, leaving a slit that offers views northwards. The main block is the result of piecing together a basic module and applying numerous variations on it. The stairs lead to two apartments per floor, with their living rooms overlooking the sea and forming a slight bevel. The addition of these bevels creates an overall façade that is a series of strata, including the adjustable leaves of the blinds. The entrance doorways are situated at the foot of each bevel, forming a slight canopy over the door. Entrance to all the stairways is via a raised terrace that runs from one end of the block to the other, whereas the rear façade is reserved exclusively for vehicles.

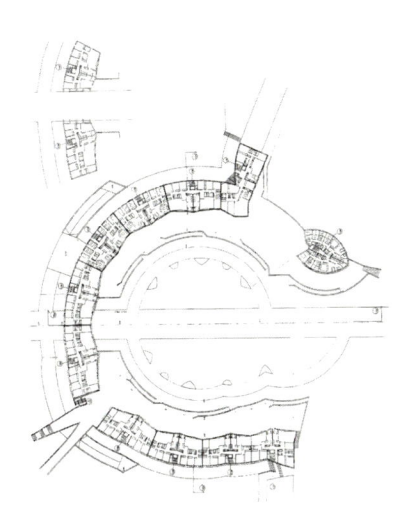

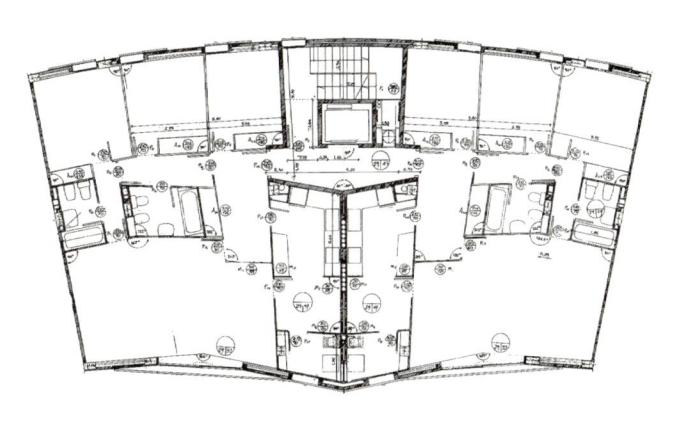

SWIMMING POOLS AT THE SANT SEBASTIÀ BATHS

José Antonio Martínez Lapeña, Elías Torres
1988-1995

Pl. del Mar, 1 - Barcelona

The programme for a new project envisaged two areas: an indoor pool and a family pool in the open air, with a terrace-cum-solarium and boat storage space. The covered pool building is divided into three floors. The ground floor houses the main entrance, inspection tank, reception, administration and a gymnasium. On the second floor are the swimming pool, changing rooms and control area. The third floor comprises spectator stands and an open-air fronton court. Structurally the building comprises grey reinforced concrete walls with exterior treatment, a fast-assembly material that stands up to environmental aggression. The canopies, eaves and projections are protected by copper sheet. A single lengthwise opening creates a visual relation between the freshwater surface and the sea.

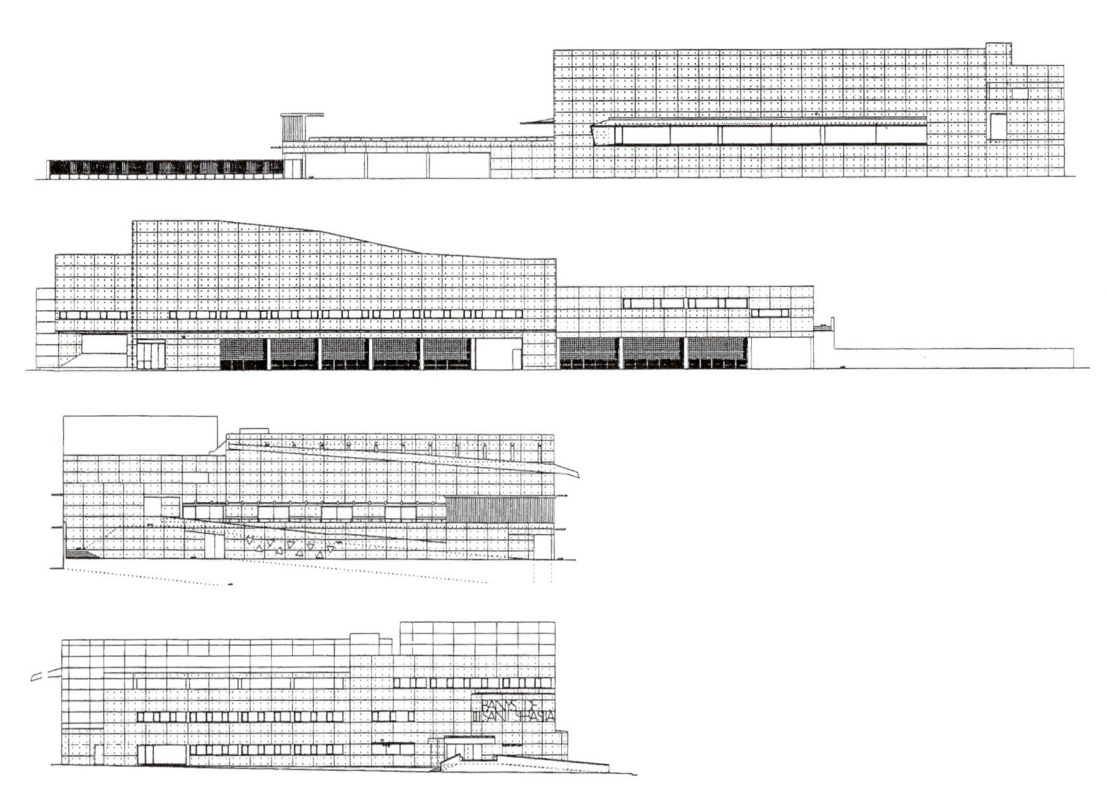

NEW MARKET IN LA BARCELONETA
REMODELLING AND EXTENSION
OF THE OLD MARKET

Josep Miàs
2002-2007

Pl. Poeta Boscà - Barcelona

The old market required remodelling when it became obsolete from a programmatic point of view. The new market incorporates a catering school, a space for offices and some restaurants, plus two floors for car parking and the urbanization of two new public squares on its main façades. The remodelling project suspends the new features of the programme from the roof, forming a series of variable sections that use the original structure. As a result, the life of the old market can continue independently of the new additions. The entrances in the squares to either side are also modified to encourage the recreational activities that take place there. The result of the intervention is a series of volumes added around the edge of the old structure, generating a new image and reflecting their part in the space and activities that continue as before.

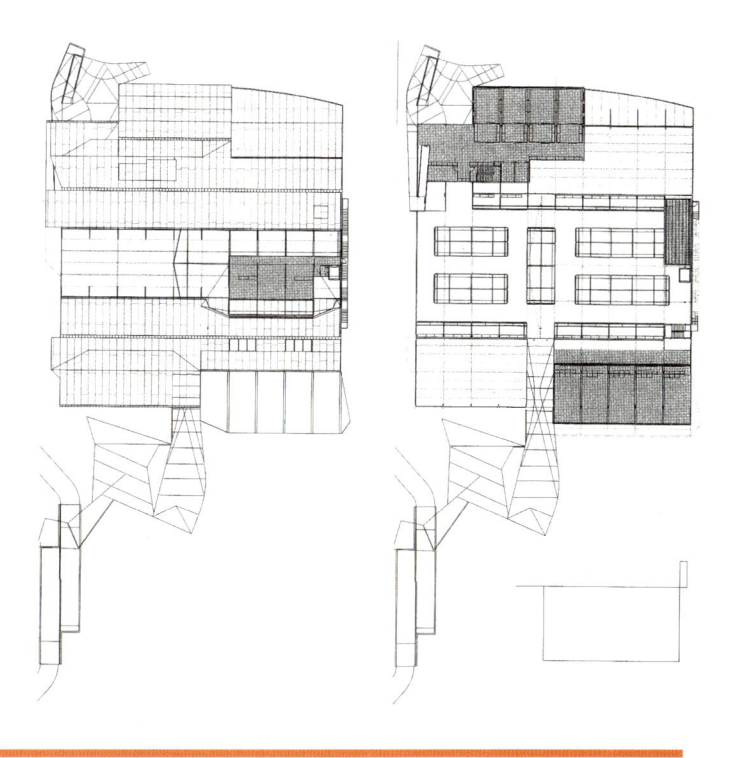

L'ILLA DIAGONAL
MULTIPURPOSE BUILDING

Rafael Moneo, Manuel de Solà-Morales i Rubió
1986-1993

Av. Diagonal, 545-575 - Barcelona

The building is the result of a unitary operation on a street block in a prime position, presenting 300 metres of façade to Avinguda Diagonal, one of the city's major streets. The morphological response of Moneo and Solà-Morales is based on respect for the traditional Eixample street block, at the same time adopting the discontinuous nature of the more open constructions in the area. The building breaks with the scale of its dimension by fragmenting the volumes and creating diagonal lines of sight, at the same time ensuring unity by means of the repetitive openings and the stone cladding of the façade. The complex adapts its perimeter to the streets that delimit it and relinquishes the straight-lined grid. The result is a metaphor of the city condensed into a single building, the volume of which is a reflection of the irregularities produced in a building when introduced into an urban continuum.

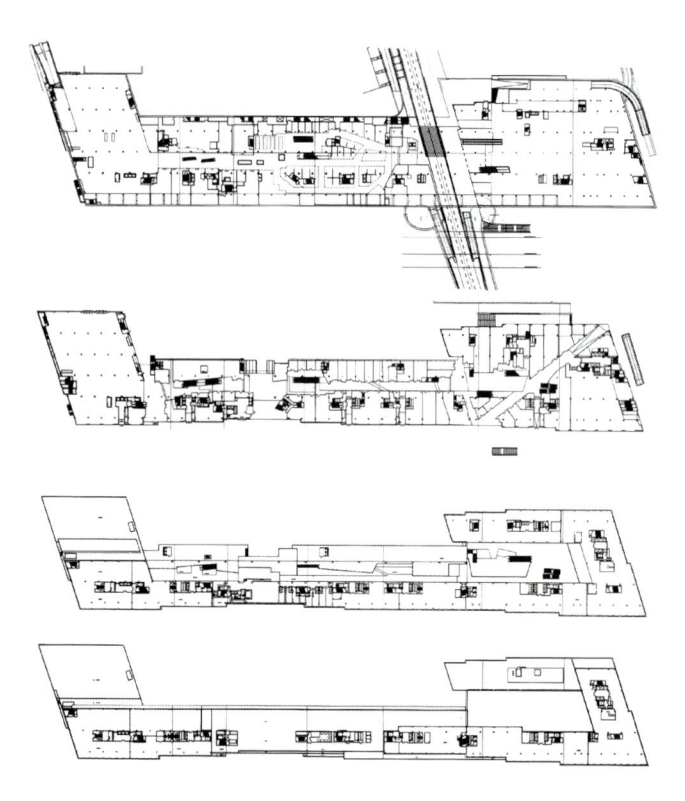

CATALAN CONGRESS CENTRE

Carles Ferrater, Josep Maria Cartañà
1996-2000

Av. Diagonal, 661 - Barcelona

Despite being the product of private development, the project reflects on the place and the programme as though it were a public amenity. The university area is interpreted as city periphery with urban aspirations, marked by the presence of various faculties and sports amenities. The place is interpreted as a context that is packed with references, to which the building responds with a series of built volumes that aspire to unity. The planimetry is organized in three main bays separated by two lengthwise streets connecting the higher grade of the Diagonal with the gardens to the rear. The white concrete of the entire façade unites the different-sized volumes, and the openings adapt to a very strict repertory in order to create stylistic coherence. The building promotes the urban nature of the area and respects the continuity of existing uses.

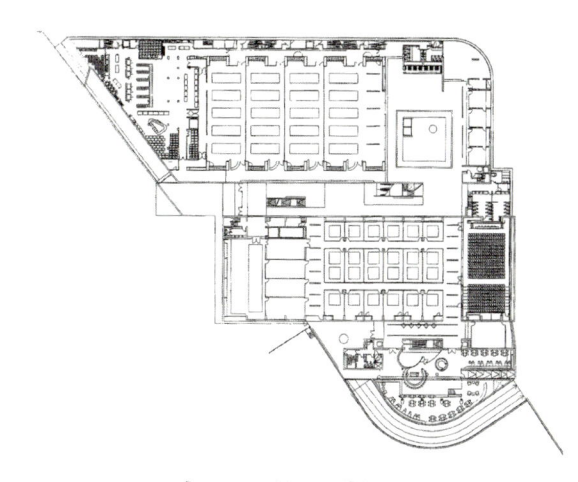

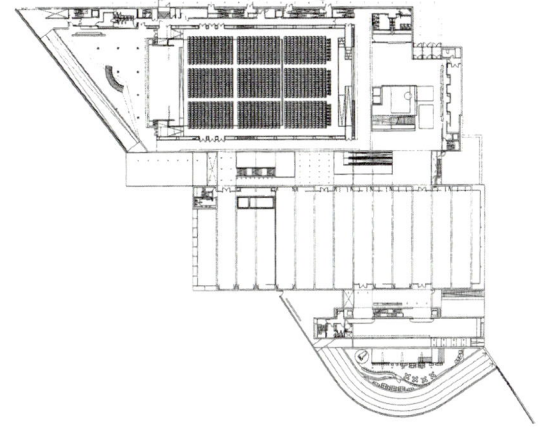

CENTRE DE CULTURA CONTEMPORÀNIA DE BARCELONA CCCB
REMODELLING AND EXTENSION OF THE OLD CASA DE LA CARITAT ALMSHOUSE

Albert Viaplana, Helio Piñón
1990-1993

C/ Montalegre, 5 - Barcelona

The aim of this project was to convert the former Casa de la Caritat almshouse into a metropolitan cultural amenity, respecting the old building and incorporating a programme that comprises a new foyer, two exhibition galleries and a system of ramps connecting all the floors. Viaplana decided to build a new volume on the unoccupied side of the almshouse and turn the basement floor beneath the Pati de les Dones courtyard into a new foyer. The way in leads under the courtyard along a ramp, into the foyer and on to the ramps that ascend the façade of the new building. This intervention gives the courtyard a new functional nature and character, closed in on one side by a great glass screen. At the point where the screen reaches the top of the pre-existing building, it bends in over the courtyard, suggesting a covering gesture, while, with its reflections, it hints at the urban landscape spreading away beyond the courtyard.

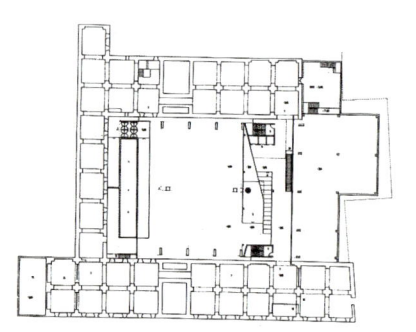

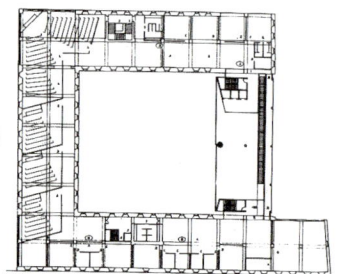

MUSEU D'ART CONTEMPORANI DE BARCELONA · MACBA

Richard Meier
1988-1995

Pl. dels Àngels, 1 - Barcelona

The museum forms part of a strategy to reclassify the Raval district by introducing new municipal institutional buildings. This is a newly created museum, without a pre-established collection, so it is the urban morphology that dictates the main lines of the project. Meier occupied a former street block to the rear of the Casa de la Caritat almshouse, thereby giving the Plaça dels Àngels a completely new character. The building responds subtly to the elements around it. The sinuous volume containing the small specialized exhibition rooms determines the line of sight from Carrer dels Àngels. Entrance is via a great fissure reminiscent of the narrow streets of the Raval. The building scrupulously respects the height of the area's built fabric and adapts rigorously to the depth of the Casa de la Caritat. It is a formally exuberant organism, ready to house highly flexible, undetermined ways of exhibiting works of art.

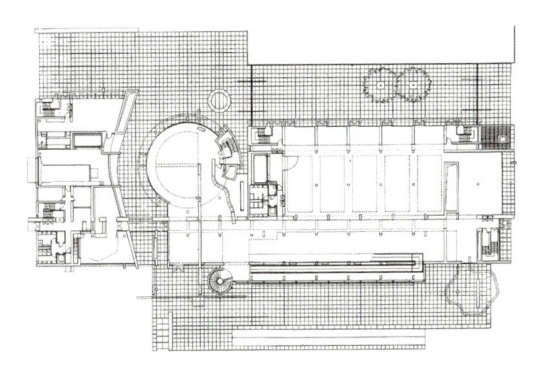

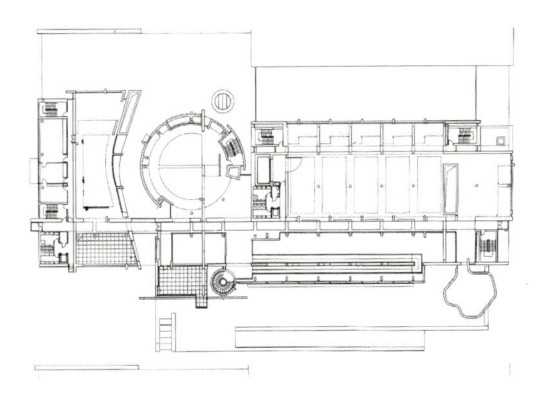

BARCELONA AUDITORIUM

Rafael Moneo
1988-1998

C/ Lepant, 150 - Barcelona

The auditorium is situated on a plot of land on the edge of the Eixample produced by the union of two street blocks, a habitual occurrence in this urban fabric. The building responds to its location by means of a compact volume, marking out a configuration of the overall area that other buildings will subsequently complete. The project defines a concrete grid that is the correlate of its urban form, while the concert hall, in the interior, responds meticulously to its function. The seats adopt a biased layout to produce a foreshortened view of the musicians, quite distinct from the visuals required in the theatre. The two main halls, for concerts and rehearsals, are separated by an exterior space that stages the social aspect of the musical events, beneath a great glazed lantern decorated by the artist Pablo Palazuelos.

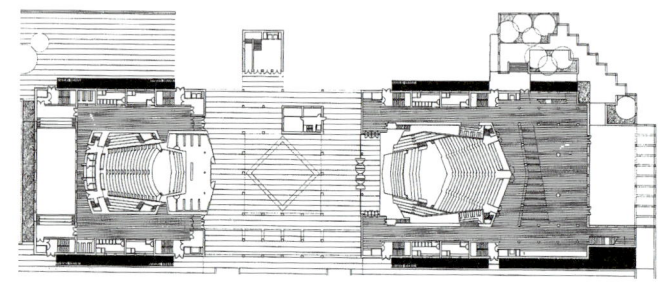

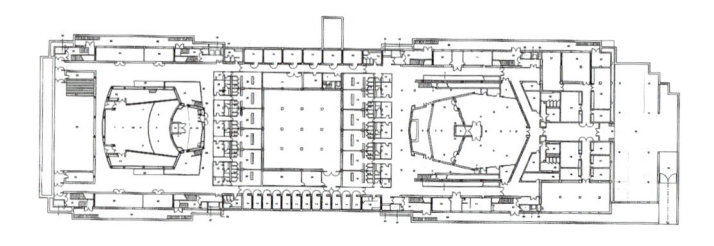

GRAN TEATRE DEL LICEU OPERA HOUSE
RECONSTRUCTION, REMODELLING AND EXTENSION OF THE OLD OPERA HOUSE

Ignasi de Solà-Morales i Rubió,
Lluís Dilmé, Xavier Fabré
1990-1998

La Rambla, 51-59 - Barcelona

ORIGINAL: Miquel Garriga i Roca, 1862

FIRST RECONSTRUCTION:
Josep Oriol Mestres, 1844-1848

The new building came about in response to the desire to conserve the memory of one of the city's most emblematic institutions after the fire that took place in 1994, destroying the entire opera house except some small areas: the Salon of Mirrors, the foyer on the Rambla, the entrance porch and the main stairway. The new project involved a faithful reconstruction of the theatre, adopting modern technological and compositional criteria to give it the necessary infrastructures and services for present-day functioning. New construction occupies 70 per cent of the present building. The new roof contains the fly tower and the auditorium in a single volume, marking the original orientation of the opera house on the site in accordance with the criterion of respecting the original project.

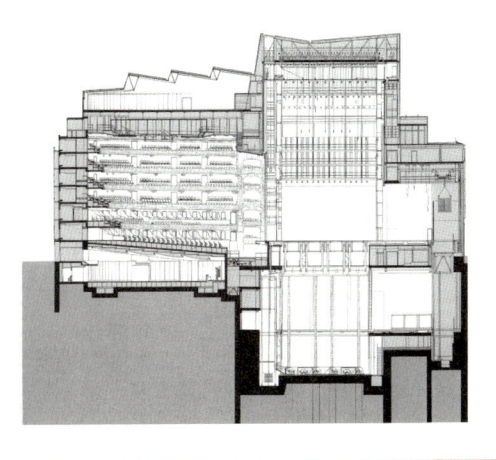

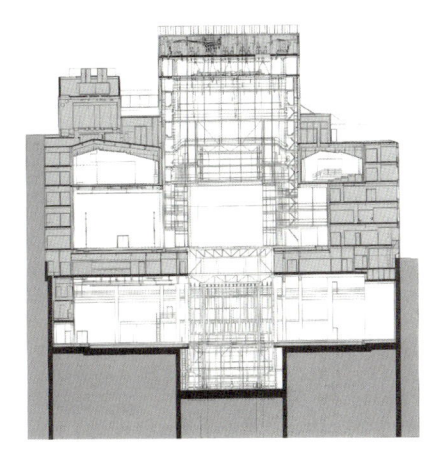

APARTMENT BUILDING

Josep Llinàs
1989-1994

C/ Carme, 55 - Barcelona

The chosen approach addresses the project's influence on the public space, particularly its effect on Carrer Roig, a very narrow street without ventilation or daylight. The building comprises three independent volumes built against the plot's party walls, freeing up a space in the façade that connects directly with the slits and small corners left between the three blocks. Each block has its own stairway but all share a single entrance on the ground floor, and the stairways divide on the first floor. The definition of all three pays careful attention to the spatial relations between the horizontal planes: the street and the building, the public and the domestic spaces, spaces of transition. The project reflects on the value of street alignment in the Ciutat Vella district, an undefined line, a strip of tolerance between diverse peoples, the borderline of a dynamic of infringement and legality.

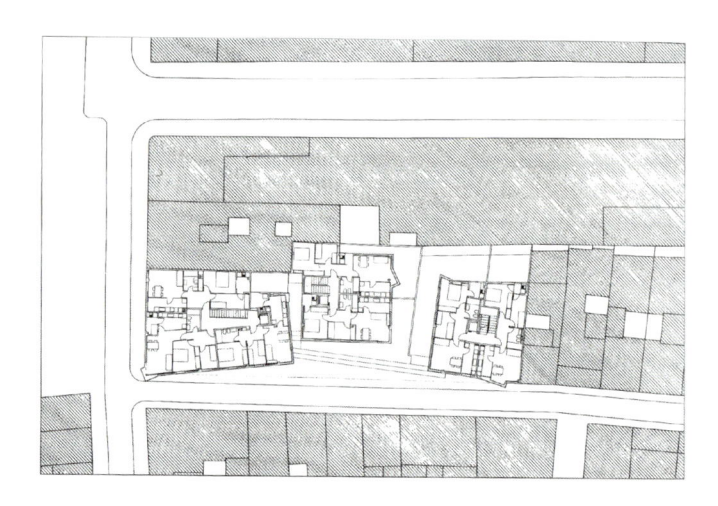

VILA DE GRÀCIA PUBLIC LIBRARY

Josep Llinàs, Joan Vera
2000-2002

C/ Torrent de l'Olla, 104 - Barcelona

In terms of communications, the junction of Carrer del Torrent de l'Olla and Travessera de Gràcia is one of the foremost points of connection between the district of Gràcia and the rest of the city. This gives the library a representative role that does not correspond to the characteristically small dimensions of a plot in the urban fabric of the area, making it an unusual choice of use for a site that would normally be given over to housing. The building's configuration expresses the conflict between the site and the new programme occupying it. The habitual column of apartments is swollen by gradation, expressing the activities that take place inside the building. The street façade does not substantially affect the organization of the building; it has recourse to a series of specific elements that grant the skin thickness, while an emergency pillar does the work that the wall has ceased to do.

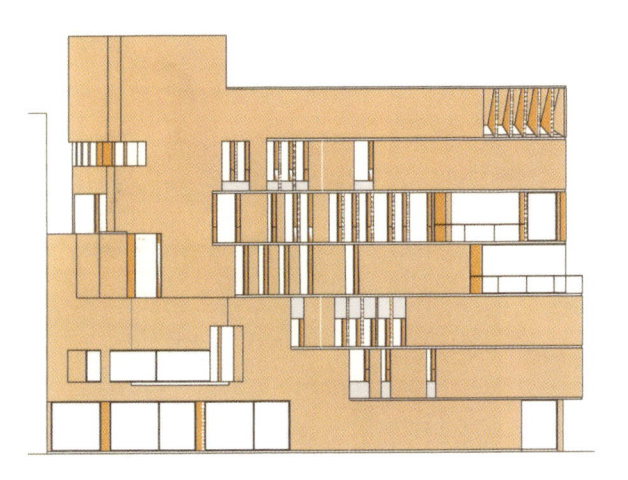

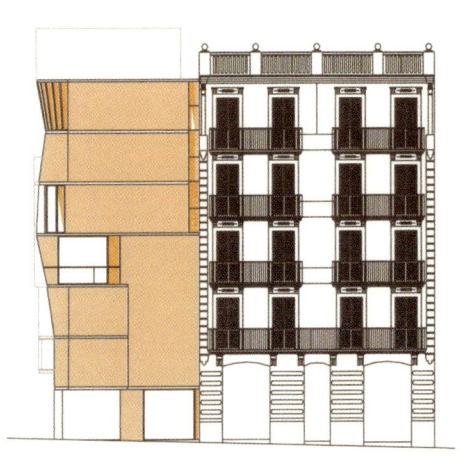

HOUSE IN LA CLOTA
REMODELLING AND EXTENSION OF TWO EXISTING HOUSES

Enric Miralles, Benedetta Tagliabue
1998-1999

Ptge. Feliu, 15-17 (District of La Clota) - Barcelona

The district of La Clota, near the Vall d'Hebron, is one of the few places in Barcelona where there are still market gardens and low, two-storey farm buildings. The project involved remodelling and joining two such buildings to form a single dwelling. The existing spaces were very small, so openings were made in various rooms to allow daylight in. The structure of the existing constructions was maintained, though the structural floor of one of the two was removed to create a double-height library, and a new façade was built onto the garden to extend the house. The resulting dwelling combines the pre-existing elements and the new features, concealing all traces of intervention by means of simulation in the new walls or the finish. The new construction procedures mimic the techniques formerly used, and some structural elements are left bare, such as the timber cross beams revealed in the library.

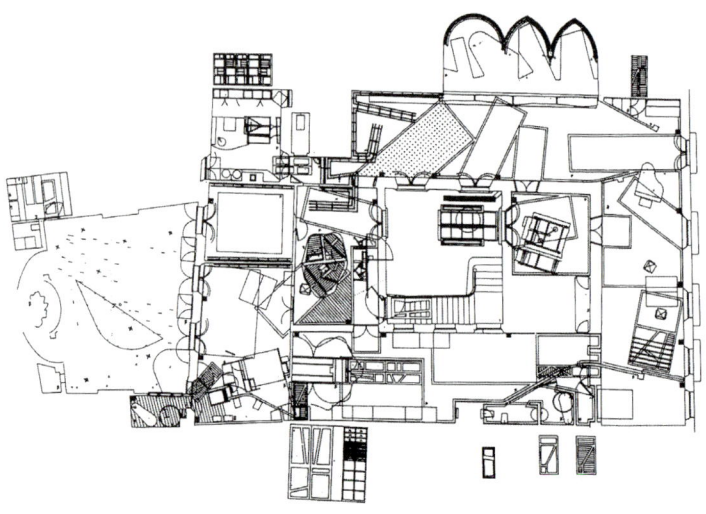

NEW MARKET OF SANTA CATERINA
REMODELLING AND REHABILITATION
OF THE OLD MARKET

Enric Miralles, Benedetta Tagliabue
1998-2003

Av. Francesc Cambó, 16 - Barcelona

The site of the market of Santa Caterina is the result of the superposition of numerous historical strata, starting in the Bronze Age, with a necropolis of which some remains still exist. The 19th century saw the construction of the first market on the ruins of a convent, and the latest intervention seeks to remedy the structural and organizational shortcomings of that market. The project was addressed as the superposition of new over old according to a conception that sought to establish continuity with this series of historical superpositions. The number of stalls was reduced, creating lines of force on the inside that generate new connections between the surrounding streets. The new roof, based on a structural principle of stable fragility, is superposed on the old perimeter, making it a point of reference for the neighbouring houses.

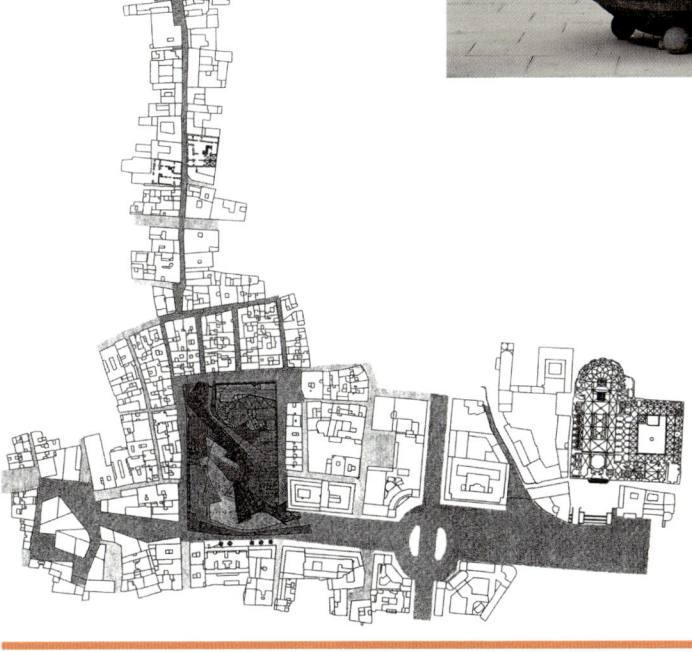

BARCELONA INTERNATIONAL CONVENTION CENTRE
FÒRUM 2004

Josep Lluís Mateo
2000-2004

Rambla de Prim, 1-17 - Barcelona

The building is the result of an intervention in a housing block in the Forum 2004 sector, where no specific definition had been established for the uses, programmes and clients. The block is divided into a series of strips allowing maximum availability for future interventions. The part furthest away from the sea is occupied by a hotel and an office building, with the CCIB building in the foreground, providing a plinth for the towers to its rear. The convention centre is a great metal structure covered with uneven undulating cladding that provides the roof and determines the wall facings. All the bearing elements are concealed behind this uneven plane. Mateo explores the possibilities of bar structures in the roofs and facings. The spaces contained inside are open plan and very flexible. Only the foyer is given the distinguishing feature of an intervention by the artist Cristina Iglesias.

FORUM BUILDING
FORUM 2004

Jacques Herzog, Pierre de Meuron
2001-2004

Rambla de Prim, 2-4 - Barcelona

This was the main building that housed the Forum of Cultures held in 2004. It forms part of an operation to recover obsolete industrial land to create an area of new centrality for cultural and leisure activities. The building adopts a long, low configuration on three floors that respects the level of the Plaça del Fòrum, the large esplanade for open-air events. The entrance level is a prolongation of the square over which a great triangular prism is supported, perforated by numerous light shafts and providing protection for participants. On the first floor is an auditorium, the central venue for debates, with seating for 3200 people. The upper level comprises a triangular steel megastructure supported by concrete columns and contains the exhibition area. The building adopts a triangular floor plan, the remnant of the plot left between Diagonal, Rambla de Prim and the coastal ring road.

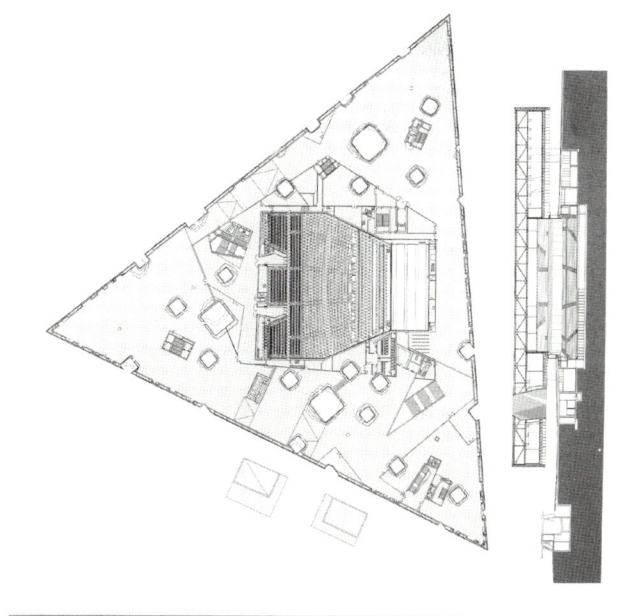

AGBAR TOWER
HEAD OFFICES OF BARCELONA WATER BOARD

Jean Nouvel
2000-2005

Av. Diagonal, 209-211 - Barcelona

In an area with few urbanistic conditioning factors, pending subsequent interventions, the building is designed as a small high-rise with 35 storeys, standing 142 metres high. Its form simulates a jet of water under constant pressure, an image that is reinforced by the crater at its base, with a surface of water interposed between the tower's interior and exterior. The office programme occupies the first 18 floors, completed by a further four floors under grade that occupy the entire site. On the first basement, an auditorium emerges to the exterior in the form of a small hill. The six remaining floors contain management offices. The tower as a whole has three equidistant installations floors. The loads are transferred via the perimeter and the central shaft, freeing up all the floors of columns. The façade completely dematerializes the outer cylinder by means of the lighting mechanism, which has become one of the city's main channels of news and publicity.

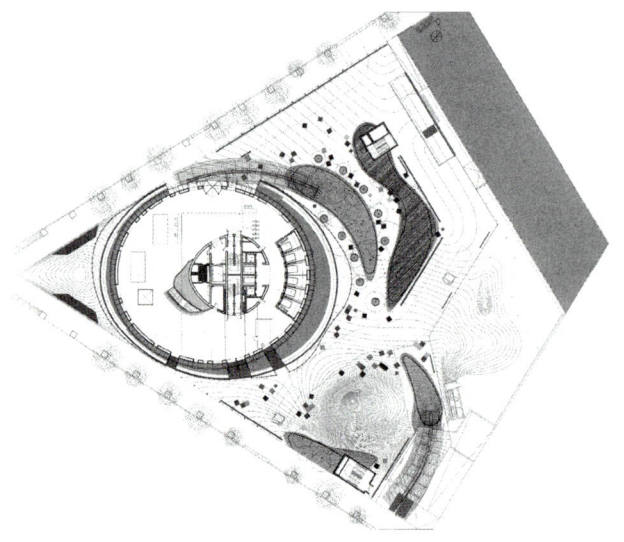

APARTMENT BUILDING IN DIAGONAL MAR

Lluís Clotet, Ignacio Paricio
2001-2005

C/ Selva de Mar, 2 - Parc de Diagonal Mar
Barcelona

The building is located on a large irregular site left by the construction of Diagonal Mar Park. It was subject to very strict planning regulations that left little room for manoeuvre. Clotet and Paricio decided to forego the compositional approach and adapt faithfully to urban planning strictures with a series of volumes that are subject to the repetition of a single element in the façade. This repetitive element is aluminium elements and panelling, forming an opaque facing over the pillars. The panelling is mounted on frames comprising a framework of galvanized tube (120 x 40 mm) anchored to the structural floor. The blinds are adjustable aluminium slat structures on extruded aluminium frames mounted on a double rail of the same material. Clotet and Paricio shift the concern with composition to systematic construction details and create an organism that acquires its scale and dimensions from the activity of the users.

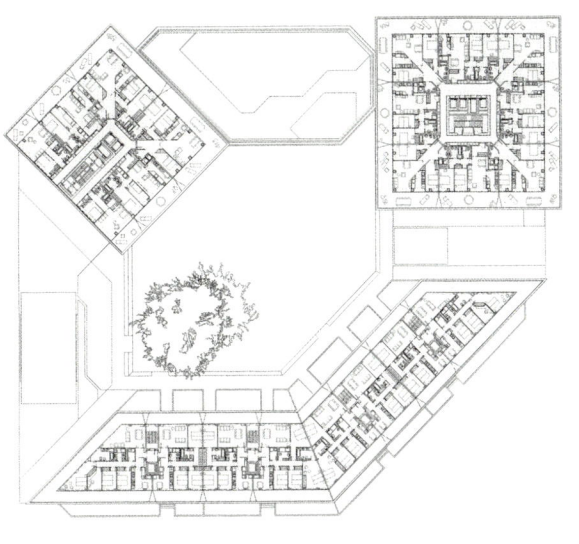

GAS COMPANY TOWER
HEAD OFFICE OF GAS NATURAL

Enric Miralles, Benedetta Tagliabue
1999-2006

Pg. Marítim de la Barceloneta, 15
(Parc de la Barceloneta) - Barcelona

The building recovers land formerly belonging to the Companyia del Gas, converted into a park dominated by its new head office. The new tower block is broken down into four quite different volumes in an attempt to address its singularity and establish a dialogue with the elements around it: the city ring road to one side and the low-rise housing on the other. These four volumes are each identified by a name: the *tower* is the tallest volume, an H-shape formed by the union of two more narrow volumes of different heights. The *corbel* is a volume built against the tower whose lower surface marks the entrance to the building. The *aircraft carrier* is a long but shallow projecting volume that horizontally reinstates the stairs of the tower and is turned, like the *corbel*, to face the entrance. The fourth volume is the *cascade*, a volume that stays near the ground, with a staggered façade that responds to the scale of the surrounding buildings. The four volumes are arranged according to a single idea, and the glass facing of each part picks up the shadows of its neighbour in an interplay of transparencies and reflections that generates an unreal, dematerialized image.

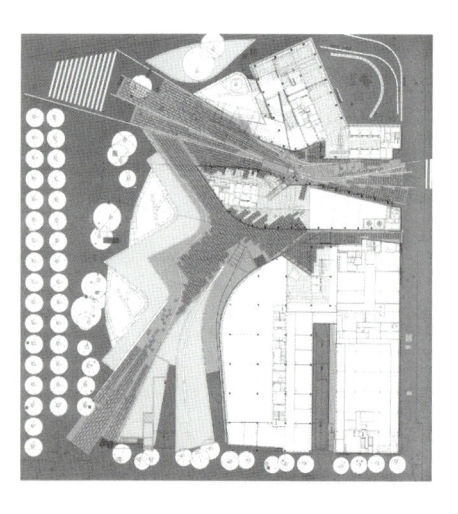

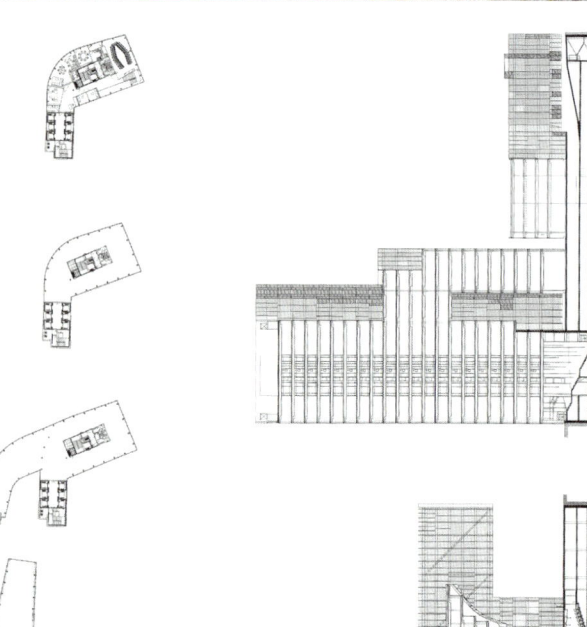

Barcelona

FORT PIENC STREET BLOCK
MARKET, CIVIC CENTRE, LIBRARY, NURSERY SCHOOL, HOME FOR THE ELDERLY

Josep Llinàs
2001-2003

C/ Ribes, 12-18 (Pl. Fort Pienc)
C/ Sardenya, 101-147 - Barcelona

The programme called for the inclusion of a series of very varied activities in a street block in the Eixample, truncated by the junction with Carrer Ribes and some existing constructions that did not obey the site's construction criterion. The project sets out to reconstruct the limits of the block and give it its own specific typology. The result is a new square beside Carrer Ribes that serves as an entrance and a point of reference for the civic centre. The square leads into the market, the library, the nursery school and the civic centre which all find their place in the street block without losing their point of connection with the square. The student hall of residence and the home for the elderly form a separate volume with its entrance on Carrer Sardenya, though it also folds back on itself to partake in the space generated by the square. The order of Carrer Ribes and the new square establishes clear criteria for the location of each part.

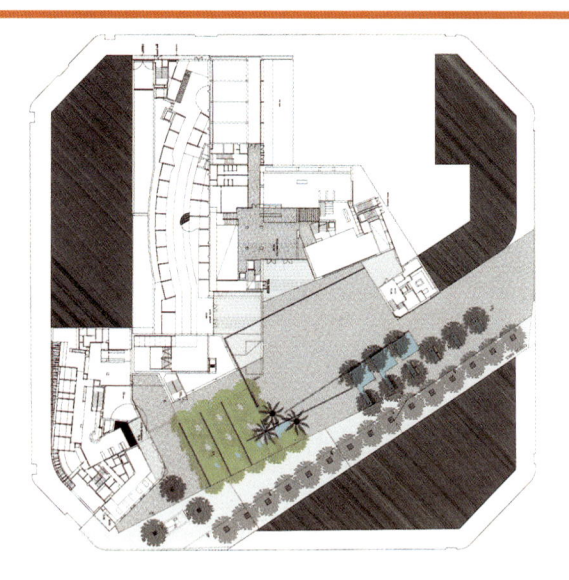

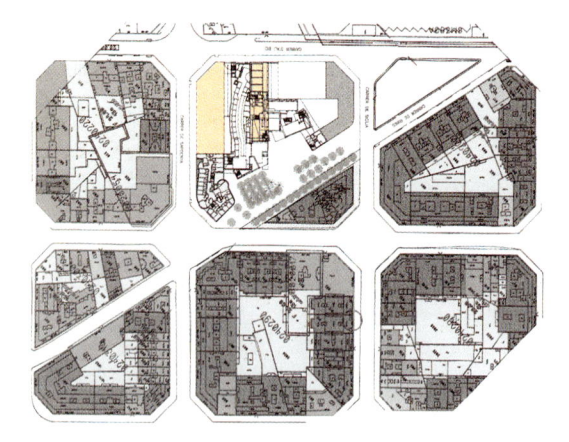

JAUME FUSTER PUBLIC LIBRARY

Josep Llinàs, Joan Vera
2001-2005

Pl. Lesseps, 20-22 - Barcelona

The project suggests a complex form in response to a place marked by a variety of urban interferences. The choice of this form is based on two considerations. The first is the character assumed by the main façade as a backdrop to the site on which the building stands. This façade has to be seen as an addition to the large rear façades of the buildings with access via Avinguda de la República Argentina. Secondly, the project takes into account the changes in use and concept wrought in this part of the city, represented by the connection of the green corridor with Plaça Lesseps. In the first case, the aim is to make the volume of the library merge into the buildings behind it. This materialises in the floor plan, in the laying out of a rhomboid geometry that completes the morphology begun by the buildings behind. As a result, the library addresses the scale and character of Plaça Lesseps as one piece more in the urban fabric that lies behind it.

ENRIC PAVILLARD HOUSE
SINGLE-FAMILY DWELLING

Joan Amigó i Barriga
1906

Av. Martí Pujol, 23-25 - Badalona

Joan Amigó was one of a second generation of Modernista architects, along with Raspall, Jujol and Masó. In Pavillard house, Modernisme makes its presence felt more in the detail than in the general conception. The house presents three façades to the street and adopts a symmetrical scheme in its planimetric configuration, though the vertical organization is bolder. The two top floors form a single volume that rises far above that of the ground floor, addressed with great simplicity and devoid of ornamentation. A wrought-iron and glass gallery links up with a balcony that runs around the three stretches of façade, with a highly elaborate wrought-iron railing. The facings of the upper volume are rendered with stucco to imitate ashlar masonry, combined with panels ornamented with naturalist motifs. This interpretation of the *piano nobile* incorporates Secessionist ornamental solutions, also presenting a very free solution in the general volumetric arrangement.

ENRIC MIR HOUSE
SINGLE-FAMILY DWELLING

Joan Amigó i Barriga
1908

Av. Martí Pujol, 45-47 - Badalona

The house is a judicious reflection of the sensibility of a generation of architects who saw Modernisme independently of its political and social connotations, an approach that offered unexplored possibilities for the arrangement of façades and the use of ornamental repertory. The house presents a single plane of façade, with a base that is differentiated by colour and a crown that implements the utmost in expressive resources. The ornamental repertory reflects the influence of Mackintosh, with cylindrical pinnacles and abstract ornamentation, the ridge cap of the roof that forms two gently rounded slopes, and the galleries on the top floor. The façade is divided into two asymmetrical stretches, highlighted by openings and balconies that are marked by rows of railings. The façade's graphic arrangement is emphasized by its position between party walls and its scant height.

MR-1 HOUSES
TWIN DWELLINGS

Miguel Donada, Josep Maria Massot,
Alfons Soldevila
1971

Av. dels Castanyers, 14
Mas Ram residential development - Badalona

This is an economical construction built with uneconomical materials, which are exploited to the utmost. It comprises two juxtaposed parallelepiped modules, with a base of 4 x 16 metres and respective heights of 8 and 9 metres, which enclose a volume of over 500 cubic metres per module. A non-specialized labour force was able to rapidly construct the dwellings thanks to the simplicity of the envelope and the openings. Each envelope adopts quite different and highly mobile interior solutions according to the specific requirements. Maintenance is much lower than usual.

IES LA LLAUNA
SECONDARY SCHOOL
REHABILITATION OF THE FORMER
LA LLAUNA FACTORY (1906-1919)

Enric Miralles, Carme Pinós
1984-1986

C/ Sagunt, 11 - Badalona

The project addresses the rehabilitation of a three-storey factory as a secondary school. The building has three lengthwise bays, all of the same width. The columns on the ground and first floors are concrete, and those on the second floor are cast-iron pillars. The ceilings are brick-built vaults supported by open-web girders. The entire intervention is based on respect for the pre-existing structure; some elements are removed and others added to organize the programme and the circulations, and establish a clear spatial and functional hierarchy between the three floors.

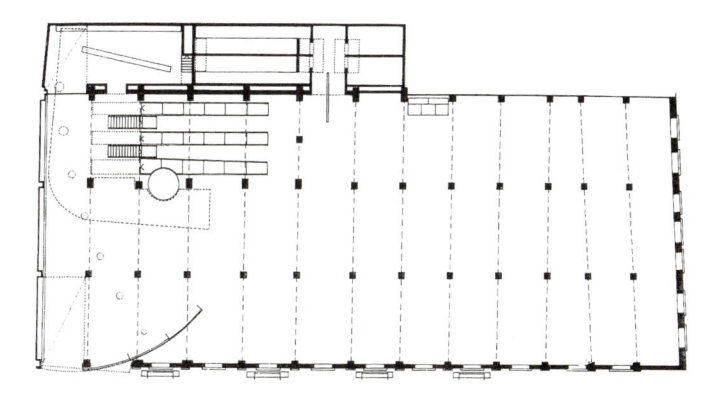

BADALONA BASKETBALL STADIUM

Esteve Bonell, Francesc Rius
1987-1991

Av. Alfons XIII - Badalona

The project approach addresses the fact that this is a sports centre for competition level basketball and is therefore linked to one of the town's most popular and representative features. The various problems generated by its dimensions and importance are addressed independently, though brought together in a fairly simple organism. The layout of the stands adopts an elliptical form: four interwoven arcs, two large and two small. Exterior circulation is resolved by means of a large main entrance that overlooks the town, along the urban axis to which it marks an end, and ten perimetric exits, accessible from the intermediate level. The roof comprises six symmetrical main beams, arranged in twos and braced by a central tie. The building has capacity for 12,500 spectators and measures 150 x 120 metres at its largest points.

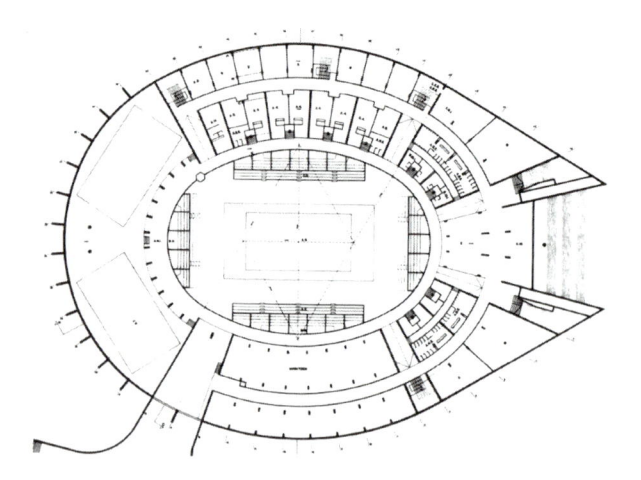

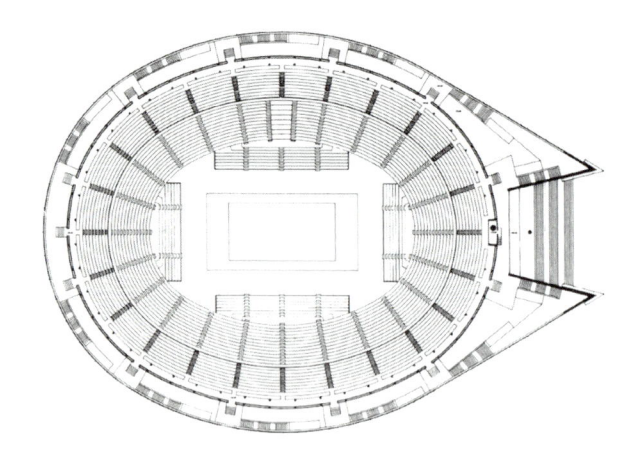

191

CEMETERY OF SANT PERE

Albert Viaplana, Helio Piñón
1984

Ctra. de la Conreria (Barcelona - Mollet) - Camí del Xiprer - Badalona

The project extends Badalona's cemetery over the undeveloped mountainside, creating a geometrical order that develops a series of routes around the slope. The recessed tombs are grouped in a series of cubes, all of the same dimensions, which mark out the implantation of the graveyard across the plot. A second scale of groupings is formed by a series of right-angled triangles built one overlapping the last, which adapt to the rising slope. The project is the result of the intersection of these two formal patterns with the topography of the site. The arrangement of the triangles favours the regularity of the cubes along the itinerary, at the same time offering views of the town at the end of the steps that make up the difference in levels. Ultimately, the image of the cemetery is defined by its slope, which establishes the level of each group of cubes and leaves the topography intact after the intervention.

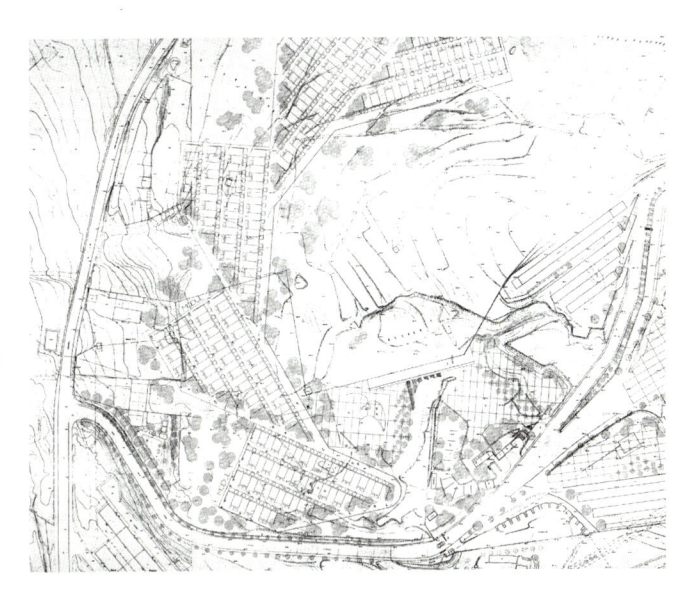

HOUSE B
SINGLE-FAMILY DWELLING

Alfred Arribas
1997-2003

Camí de la Font
La Caritat residential development
Premià de Dalt

The plot has a definite slope that conditions the layout of the house. The first line of pine trees, parallel to the approach, is left untouched, and the house adapts to the topography of different levels by means of a series of folds that follow the contour lines. The house comprises a single space where the vertical planes with their changes of direction extend or compress a horizontal itinerary that generates the various rooms. Vertically, narrow runs of steps trip along the retaining walls, slide along the planes of the façade or rest on perforations in the floor slabs to join the different levels. An elongated slab with an irregular perimeter houses the main floor, raised up on sloping piles that simulate the irregular verticality of tree trunks in the wood. A final, half-open lower level houses the more recreational activities.

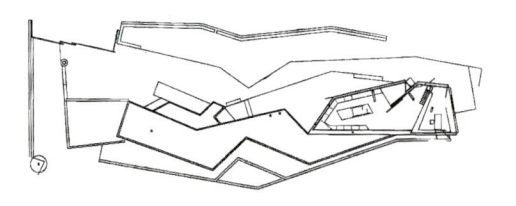

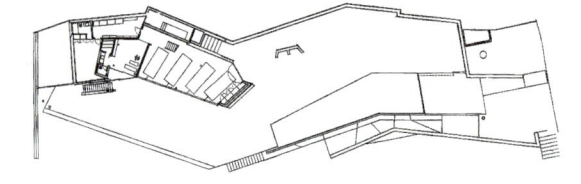

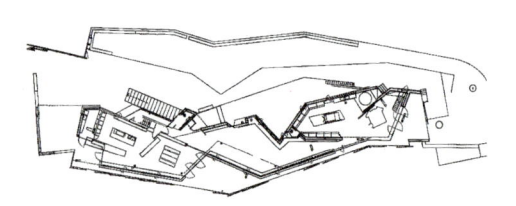

CEIP VAIXELL BURRIACH
IES VILATZARA
INFANTS' AND PRIMARY SCHOOL
SECONDARY SCHOOL

Manuel Brullet, Alfonso de Luna
1990-1993

Av. Arquitecte Eduard Ferrés, 81 - Vilassar de Mar

The project is for a primary and a secondary school within a trapezoid street block of housing covering 5000 square metres in the new town extension of Vilassar de Mar, laid out on former farmland. Although the two schools are included on a single plot, they are independently functioning organisms that are related by the simple juxtaposition of their respective social areas. Both are laid out in the form of pavilions that are interconnected by outdoor corridors, which may or may not be covered. The variety of outdoor spaces (cloisters, courtyards, squares, gardens, porches, landscaped roofs) defines the character of each building. The project is structured around the arrangement of these exterior spaces which engage with the built elements by means of alternating roofs.

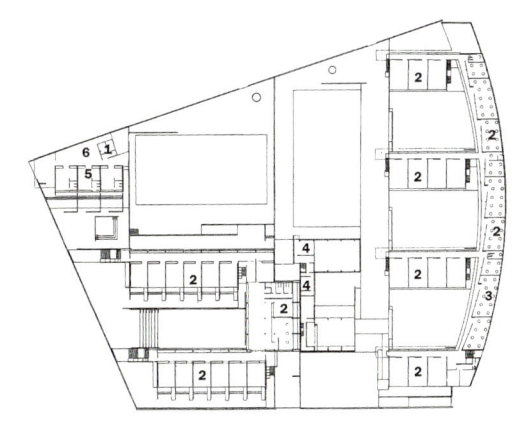

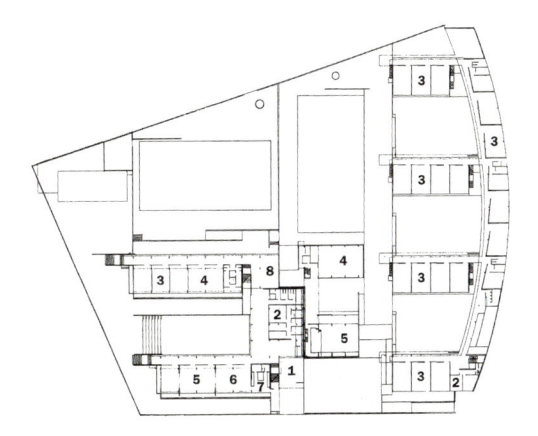

JOAQUIM COLL I REGÀS HOUSE
REMODELLING OF A HOUSE – HEADQUARTERS OF THE FUNDACIÓ LAYETANA

Josep Puig i Cadafalch
1896-1897

C/ Argentona, 55-57 - Mataró

ORIGINAL: Rafael Guastavino, 1880-1881

The plans for the project are signed by Antoni Maria Gallissà, due not to a problem of incompatibility, since by 1896 Puig i Cadafalch was no longer town architect, but to the architect's poor relations with Mataró Council. The house skilfully combines a wide range of ornamental genres, such as sculpture, glasswork, sgraffiti and ceramics. Stone is used not just to frame the openings but also to incorporate the carvings of the artist Arnau, who sculpted two main figures. One is in the tympanum over the door, representing a girl holding a spindle, an allusion to the owner's textile business; the second, the habitual figure of Saint George, is at the foot of one of the arches. The rest of the façade is decorated with sgraffiti, around a gallery that stands out for its Nordic references. The terraced crown foreshadows the silhouette of Barcelona's Amatller House.

197

PUIG I CADAFALCH HOUSING BLOCK

Lluís Clotet, Oscar Tusquets
1970-1975

C/ Joan Maragall, 2-12 - Mataró

The project aims to make the most of the advantages of the block as a housing complex in terms of economy and construction rationality. The ground floor leaves an open inner space that is related to an avenue on the other side of the street and leads to the stairways. The block respects the alignment of the four streets that delimit it, and the internal distribution of the typical floor plan overcomes the contradictions produced by the irregularity of layout. On the penthouse floor, the corridor leading to the dwellings is moved to give the apartments a large façade onto the street. As a result, the exterior façades are neutral planes that do not differentiate the dwellings, whereas the inner courtyard recreates a place for interrelation and mobility induced by the vertical circulations and the volumetric activity of the roofs.

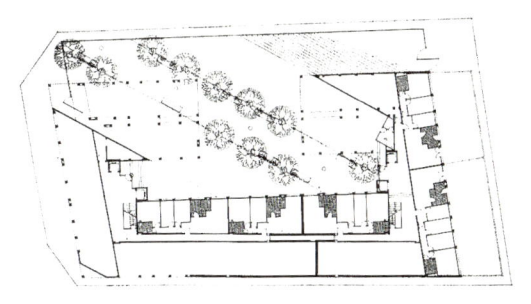

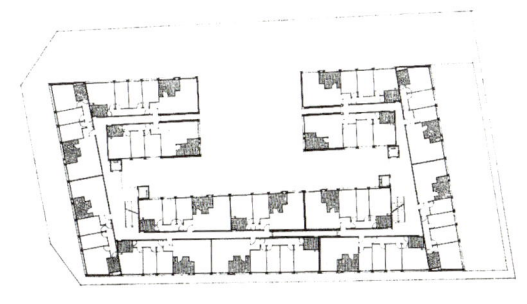

UGALDE HOUSE
SINGLE-FAMILY DWELLING

José Antonio Coderch de Sentmenat, Manuel Valls
1951-1953

C/ Torrenova, 16 - Caldes d'Estrac

On a south-facing hillside, Coderch chose a point emerging between two slopes on which to position the house, offering the broadest possible panoramic view. The principal layout is defined by the topography, with a retaining wall at the rear and a platform with a circular profile. The lines of the walls are determined by the different angles of vision of carefully framed vistas: the four openings of the living room, the separation of the guest wing and the porch beneath the master bedroom. Entrance from the street is accompanied by a dwarf wall that links up with the general wall system. The living room, dining room and hallway are situated on the level of the platform. The hall on the upper floor is situated on an intermediate level, acting as a balcony over the living room. The master bedroom is on the same level. On the next level up are another bedroom and a spacious study looking westwards towards the entrance. The project is very free in the design of the floor plan and section, and pays meticulous attention to the different views, identifying life in the house with the combined effect of the vistas and the house itself.

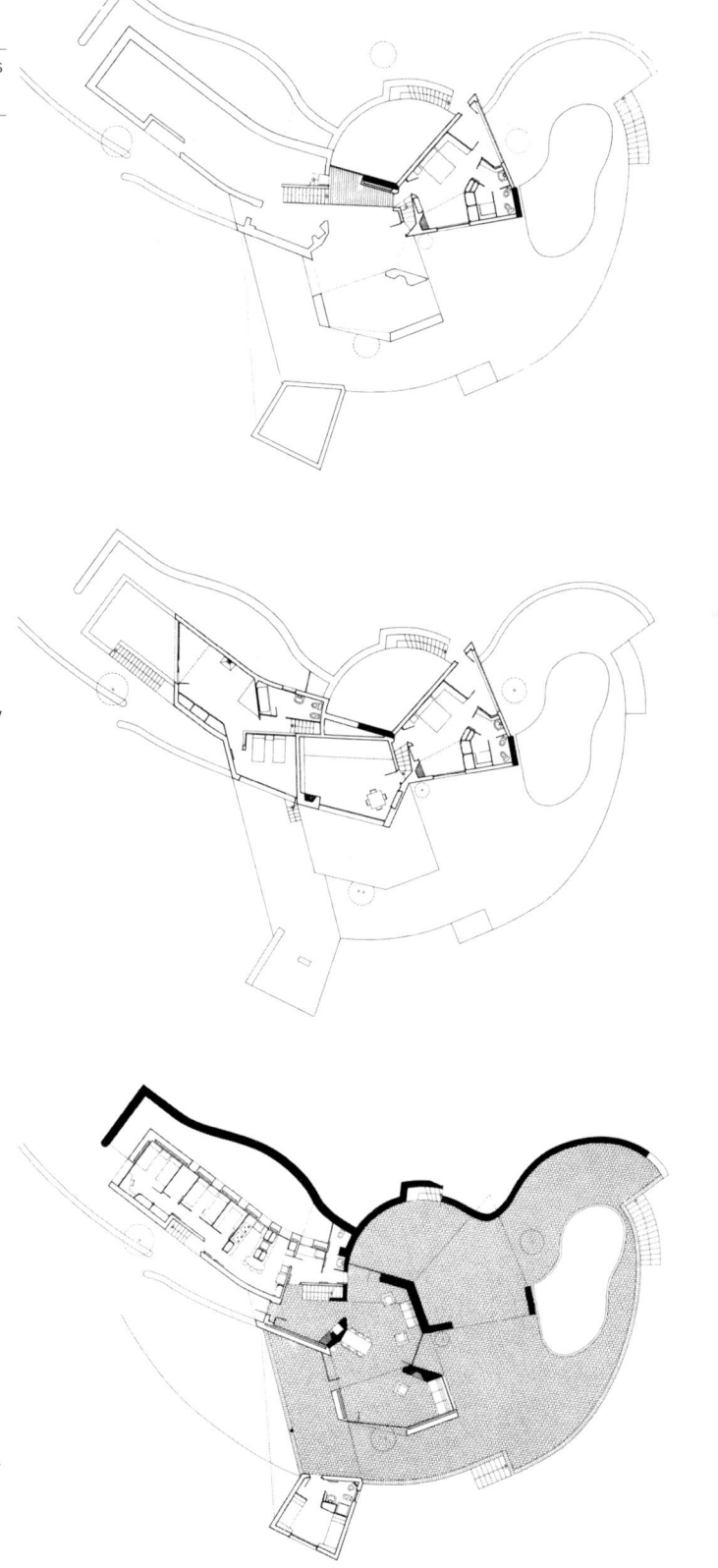

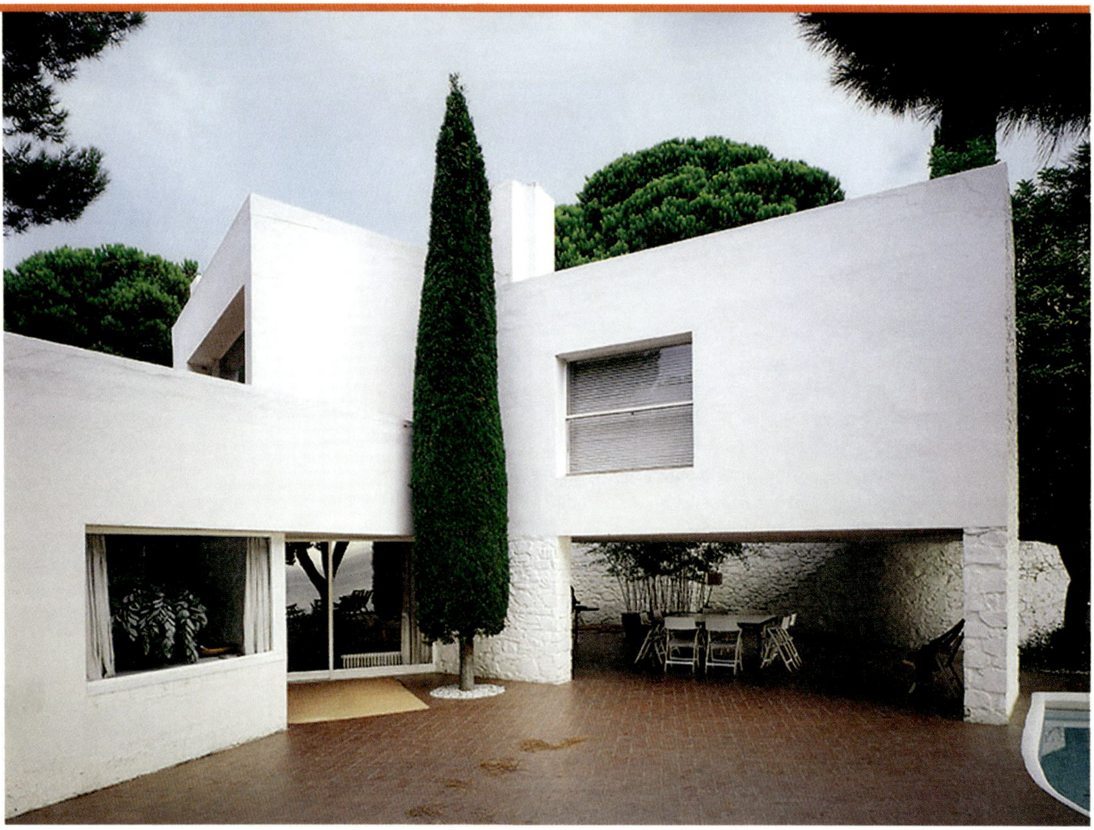

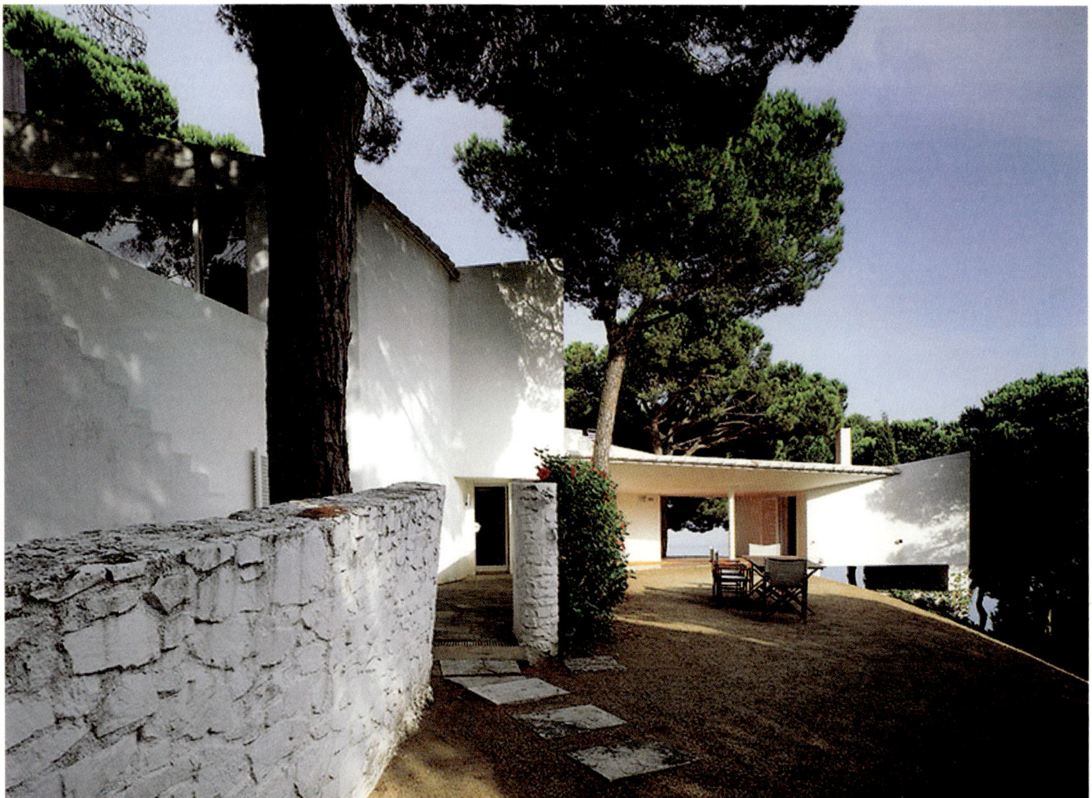

ESCOLA SANT JORDI
INFANTS' AND PRIMARY SCHOOL

Oriol Bohigas, Josep Maria Martorell, David Mackay
1967-1969

C/ Jacint Verdaguer, 15 - Pineda de Mar

The project responds to an experimental education programme in which personalized activities are accorded particular importance. The school is laid out around a double-height central space for the development of expression, and the various communal spaces on the ground floor are reached via routes that shun the row layout with the aim of giving each working area its own identity. The first floor holds the actual classrooms, though the circulation spaces are also understood as places for working and learning. The roof floor holds the sports courts, and the terraces and various routes, including two steel bridges formed by tiered seating, provide the functions required for recreation. The structure comprises a waffle slab that can be cut back at any point, supported by steel columns that go unnoticed in the facings.

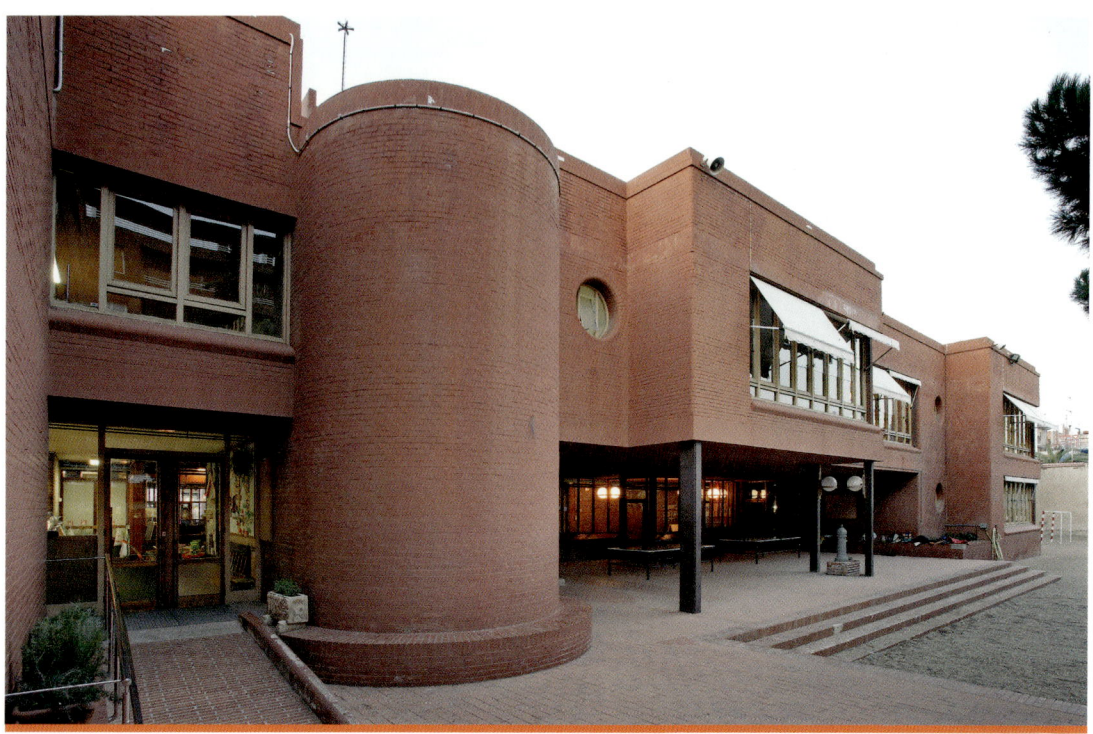

EL PALAUET STADIUM
MUNICIPAL SPORTS PAVILION

Arata Isozaki
1990-1996

Ribera de la Burgada - C/ Ramon Turró - Palafolls

On a practically flat site with a trapezoid floor plan, Isozaki traced a circle of 66 metres in diameter, in which he marked out a square. The circle was therefore divided into two equal parts: an open-air enclosure and the actual pavilion. The rectangular garden on the outside corresponds to the sports court within. In the roof, Isozaki picked up the original idea of the Palau Sant Jordi stadium: an undulating plane supported exclusively at the outer edge. This is a form that combines a flat vault around the perimeter with a half-dome at the centre. The complex surface was addressed using a space grid resting horizontally on the perimeter of the covered area and, in the vertical plane formed by the diameter of the circle, a glazed wall that absorbs the metal bars of an open-web girder. The roof plane folds to form three north-facing points, leaving slits through which daylight enters the pavilion.

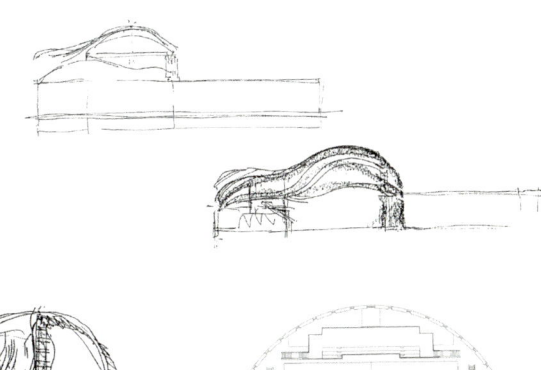

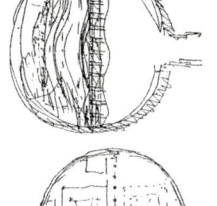

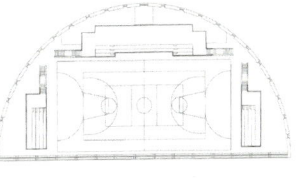

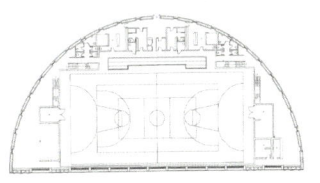

Barcelona

IES LA BASTIDA
SECONDARY SCHOOL

Eduard Bru, Josep Lluís Mateo
1981-1983

C/ Santa Eulàlia - Santa Coloma de Gramenet

The building is the product of a critical reading of the urban periphery as seen in the 1980s, as a series of fragmented tracts lacking in cohesion. The project provides a monumental response in the form of an elongated volume that imposes a clear geometry on the place. The school is situated near a street that leads out of the town, and articulates the programme and the volumetric composition around it. The curved layout of the street and the straight line of the classroom building determine the overall implantation. The classroom building forms a bridge over the street, the site of the entrance to the whole complex. The ground floor is built as far as the line of the street, whereas the basement floor, where the workshops are situated, covers the entire surface area marked out by the street and the building's frontage. The school is organized along the road that connects it with the urban nucleus and responds forcefully to the topography, its volume becoming less dense as it rises towards the roof.

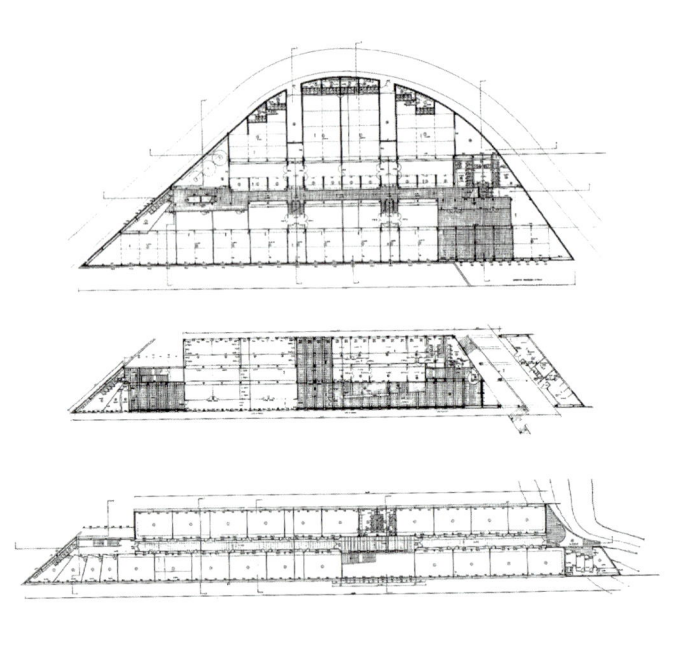

LA LLAGOSTA MUNICIPAL CEMETERY

Conxita Balcells, Santiago Vives
1997-2001

Camí de Can Donadeu - La Llagosta

The built part corresponds to the first phase of a larger project that envisages a capacity of 400 recessed tombs and 110 columbaria. The project configuration responds to a phase-by-phase intervention. The built phase consists in an enclosed rectangular precinct, accessible only via a sliding wooden door. At the entrance is a courtyard leading to the chapel and to two paths that divide the area into three strips of different widths. The recessed tombs are arranged along these strips in various positions, each in relation to a small courtyard. The cemetery turns its back on views and monumentality, instead emphasising meditation and the human scale, and the identity of each specific corner. The exterior spaces are shaded by vegetation and horizontal slabs that cover the paths to create a system of more intimate areas that serve just three rows of tombs.

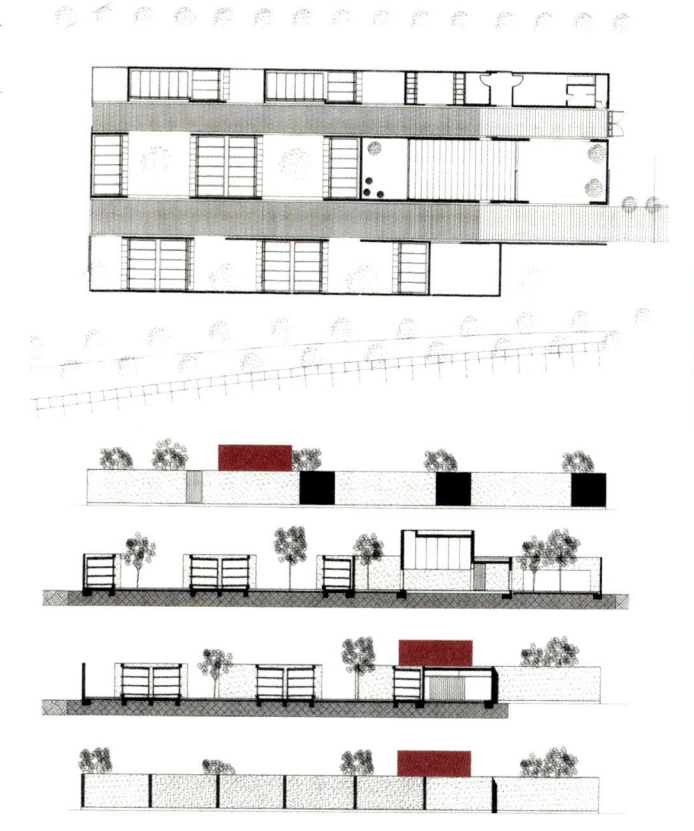

SHOOTING RANGE
INSTALLATIONS FOR THE OLYMPIC SHOOTING COMPETITION, BARCELONA '92

Esteve Terradas, Robert Terradas
1990-1992

Ctra. N-152, km 20 - Mollet del Vallès

The shooting range is situated in an area that also includes the School of Police, designed in the 1980s by the same architects. The two areas are clearly distinguished and separated by a watercourse. The different buildings are organized like a campus, far from the traditional image of police institutions. The complex is an open enclosure framed by the surrounding countryside. The classroom buildings and the sports hall are laid out parallel to the N-152 road that edges the site on one side. These buildings are interrelated by a boulevard that also leads to the swimming pool and athletics track. The different galleries that make up the shooting installations are marked out by the distance between the shooter and the target. A large rectangular platform provides an abstract support for the galleries, whose different characteristics and dimensions are established by specific regulations.

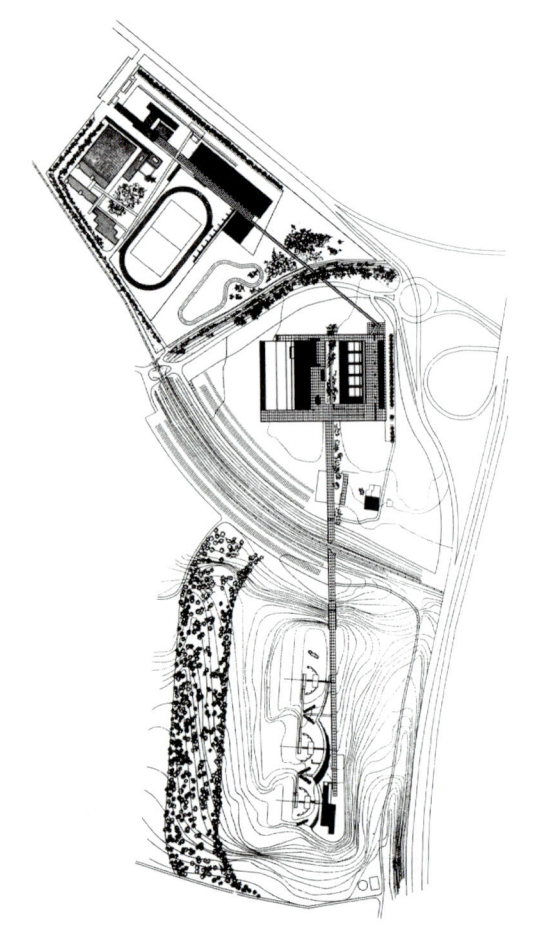

CAN BORRELL HOUSING BLOCK
GALLECS TOWN EXTENSION

Oriol Bohigas, Josep Maria Martorell, David Mackay
1983-1987

C/ Gallecs, 50 - Av. Rivoli, 22 - C/ Salvador Espriu, 1-5 - Ptge. Mestre Vinyas, 1-9 - District of Can Borrell - Mollet del Vallès

This 200-apartment social housing complex is accommodated in a street block in the new town extension of Mollet, a 100 x 100 metre grid, with the four façades facing the points of the compass. The project applies a different solution to each face according to the orientation and urban nature of each street. The blocks to the south and west comprise two floors of duplex apartments. Access to the bottom floor is from the interior of the street block and to the top floor via a raised corridor that emerges out of square at the corner. On the east side the block is doubled, with vertical access from the interior passage and one-floor dwellings that give onto both sides. The northern block also contains single-floor apartments, with access from the inner courtyard. The complex highlights the south and west façades of the street block, the only ones to contain shops, and reiterates the aim of making the courtyard a public space by means of the routes running through it.

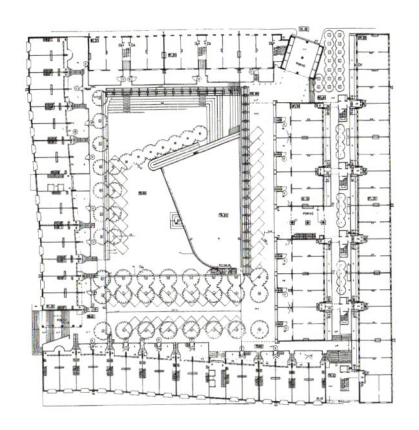

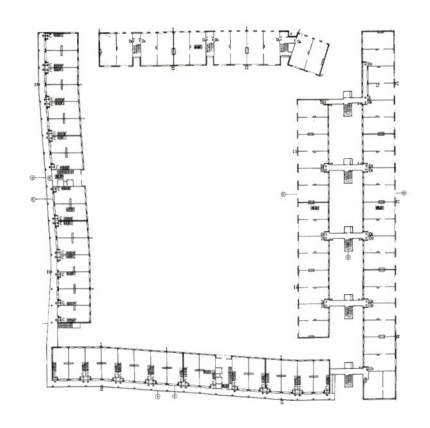

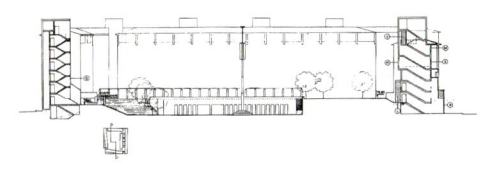

PENINA HOUSE
SINGLE-FAMILY DWELLING

Lluís Clotet, Oscar Tusquets
1968-1969

Av. Adolfo Agustí, 46 - Cardedeu

The project sets out to reconcile the client's need for nature and peace and quiet with the characteristics of a triangular site, the product of a previous plot division. The house adopts the triangle's geometry in its general layout and in the smallest details, and opens out in the form of three arms that free up the surface area of the garden and create two courtyards with quite different uses. The house turns away from the street, and all its openings overlook the inner courtyards. The courtyard outside the parents' bedroom serves the bedroom itself, the living room and the games room. The two children's bedrooms overlook the second courtyard. The kitchen, with its small service court, is the only element that communicates with the exterior, at the vertex of the triangle. Clotet and Tusquets have recourse to the contradictory aspects of the architecture to come up with unusual solutions associated with atypical lifestyles.

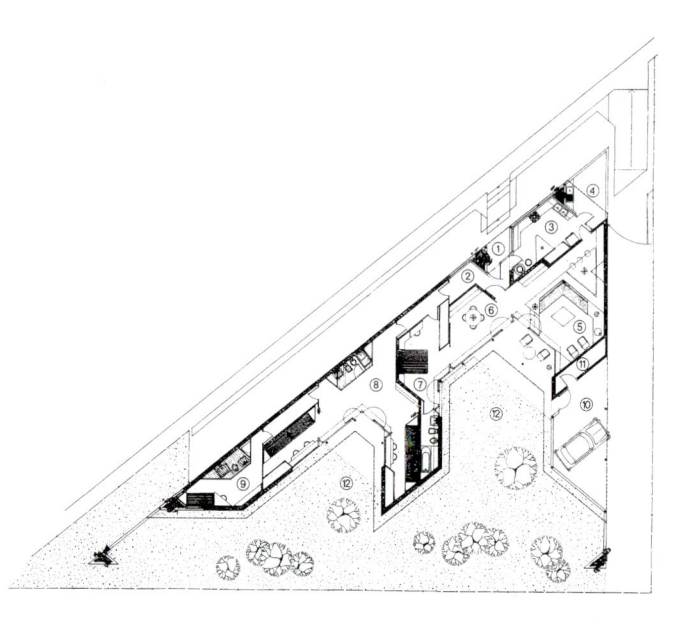

SINGLE-FAMILY DWELLING

Jaume Valor, Fidela Frutos, Josep Maria Sanmartín
1994-1995

C/ del Cirerer, 7 - Llinars del Vallès

The construction of this house includes prefabricated industrialized methods due to their low cost and short assembly times. It consists of a semi-basement floor with retaining walls built of concrete mixed on site, above which a metal structure of pillars and girders supports the structural floors, slabs of pre-stressed concrete measuring 9 x 2.4 metres. The material qualities of the sheet facings produce a south-facing volume that is apparently closed in on the other sides, where the street and entrance are situated. The openings are protected by perforated sheet of the same characteristics, producing a twofold perception by night and day. The solar energy collector wall is integrated into the building. It comprises a cavity with a polycarbonate outer facing and a black-painted iron sheet interior with thermal insulation.

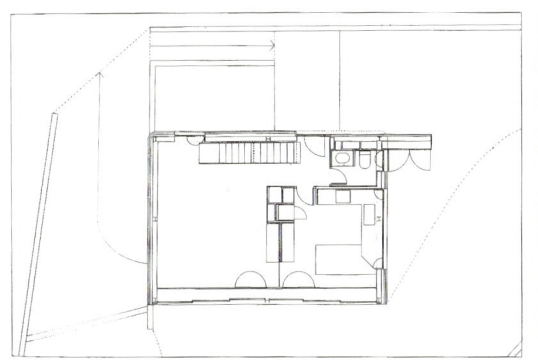

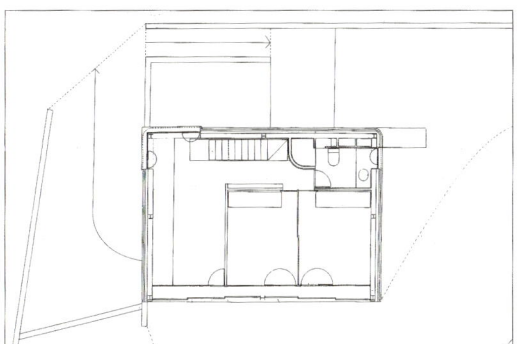

GRANOLLERS MUSEUM

Andreu Bosch, Josep Maria Botey, Lluís Cuspinera
1971-1976

C/ Anselm Clavé, 40-42 - Granollers

The building houses the programme for a recently established town museum on a site between party walls in the high street that leads into and out of town. The situation of the various galleries (permanent and temporary exhibitions, restoration, conferences) called for the insertion into the plot of a grid of concrete pillars, divided in three on each side to leave a small bay on the façade side and a large space inside. This structure frees the party walls and the façade of their bearing functions and allows the insertion of a specialized programme onto each of the six floors. The stairs and lifts stand outside this grid on the remaining part of the site. The level of the floor slabs is separated from the street by entrance to a mezzanine floor, allowing the conference room to be located in the semibasement.

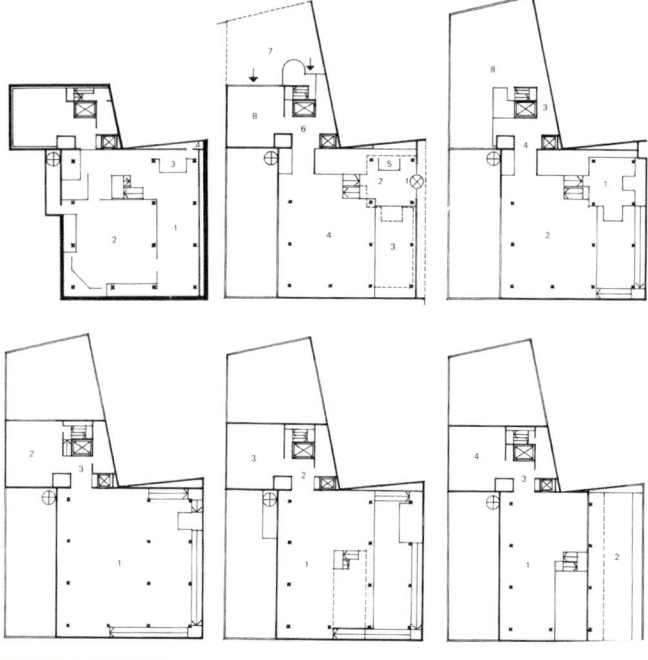

CEIP FERRER I GUÀRDIA
INFANTS' AND PRIMARY SCHOOL

Jordi Badia
2003-2006

C/ Roger de Flor, 123 - Granollers

The school is divided into two parts: the classrooms and a lower volume that houses the dining room and gymnasium. The classroom sector comprises a long narrow block between party walls, aligned with Carrer Roger de Flor. This volume is closed on the street side and opens up to the interior via courtyards that provide natural lighting, forming a series of three-storey empty volumes for the children's recreational use. A linear stairway communicates these three floors and constructs the interior space, joining the three floors into a single volume that receives light filtered through cadenced vertical openings. The façade highlights the opacity of this volume, while the ground floor is displaced to extend the pavement and make space for an independent entrance to the infants' school. The main entrance is via the main courtyard, through a porch that joins the classroom block with the services, at the same time dividing the courtyard naturally between the areas intended respectively for the infants' and the primary school.

209

170-APARTMENT SOCIAL HOUSING DEVELOPMENT

Lluís Cantallops, José Antonio Martínez Lapeña, Elías Torres, Miguel Usandizaga
1977-1980

C/ Molí de la Sal, 90-94 - C/ Setcases, 1-67
C/ Molló, 1-69, 2-12 - Joan Miró district
Canovelles

210

SERRAS HOUSE
SINGLE-FAMILY DWELLING AND PRIVATE MUSEUM

Oriol Bohigas, Josep Maria Martorell, David Mackay
1977-1981

C/ Bellmunt, 4 - Bellulla residential development
Canovelles

This house stands on a steeply sloping site between two streets. The extensive brief covers 620 m^2 and includes a small antique car museum. The project produces two separate volumes, formed by a metal structure that supports the floor slabs and creates a structure that contains the interior and exterior spaces. The level containing the bedrooms and the museum takes the form of a plinth. The front door is on the upper floor, where the two volumes unite to form the large living room area. The project explores a formal order that combines the cubic image of the house, the logic of movement, the independence of the living room's facings from the structure and close adaptation to the gradient of the site. Beginning at the entrance, the house can be read as a great stairway comprising various runs that lead in orderly fashion to each part of the brief before continuing to the lower level with the swimming pool.

211

PUIG HOUSE
SINGLE-FAMILY DWELLING

Gabriel Mora, Helio Piñón, Albert Viaplana
1972-1973

C/ Sant Sebastià, 22 - L'Ametlla del Vallès

This housing development was built in two phases, corresponding to two complexes situated on independent sites with different typologies. All the dwellings are built using tunnel formwork with a three-metre span. In one of the complexes, the apartments occupy three horizontal modules, whereas the other is occupied by three vertical modules. Entrance to the apartments is via semi-public passages perpendicular to the tunnels, leading to the apartments on the floors above, with four dwellings per landing. The dimension of the interior passages turns them into landscaped streets with small squares, likening the complex to an urban layout superposed on an uneven plot of land.

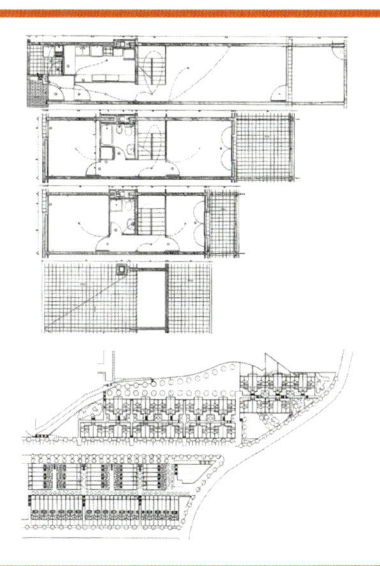

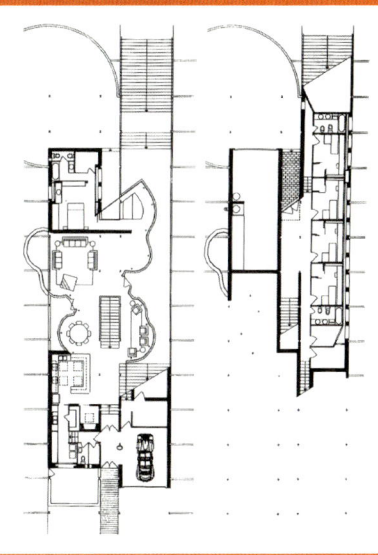

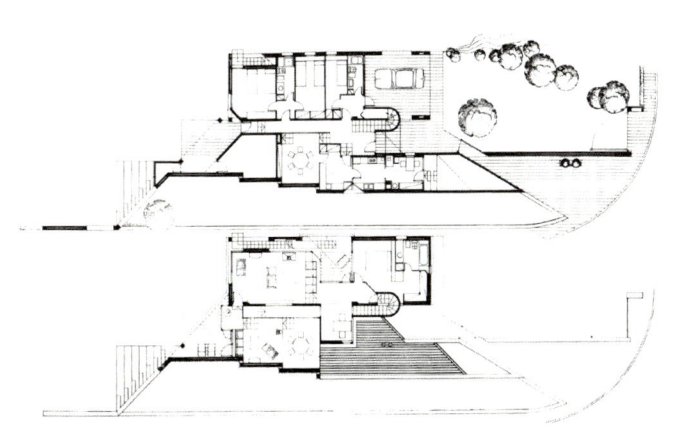

BCN-2

The house addresses the specific programme for a mother and son, responding rigorously to their requirements in the arrangement of each room and the definition of its particular use. The overall spaces are integrated by means of a straight-run stairway situated along the lengthwise axis, leading to small spaces that are separated by differences in level. A second hierarchy of stairs allows each occupant to adopt different routes. The roofs faithfully follow the interior slopes of rising movement, and the walls in the façade extend to the limits of the site, enclosing the plot and leaving just a slit for pedestrian entry.

Barcelona

212

IRIS HOUSE
CECÍLIA REIG HOUSE

Manuel Joaquim Raspall
1910-1911

El Passeig, 1 - La Garriga

213

"LA BOMBONERA"
CECÍLIA REIG HOUSE

Manuel Joaquim Raspall
1910-1911

El Passeig, 3 - La Garriga

"La Bombonera", the sweet box, stands on a small plot of land with a single façade overlooking the avenue, a fact that prompted Raspall to make the most of small-scale elements and combine the house's small dimensions with an unreal, dematerialized image. Raspall picked out the white of the rendered walls with the green of the doors and windows, and the dark blue of the sgraffiti work with its filigree decoration. The house adopts the same configuration as Raspall's other holiday homes, with a stairway topped by a tall tower. The front door is marked by a wrought-iron lamp that is unique in Raspall's work, later repeated in the house built in 1914 by Manuel Maresma.

214

JULI BARBEY HOUSE
SINGLE-FAMILY HOLIDAY HOME

Manuel Joaquim Raspall
1910-1911

C/ Manuel Joaquim Raspall, 1 - El Passeig, 5
La Garriga

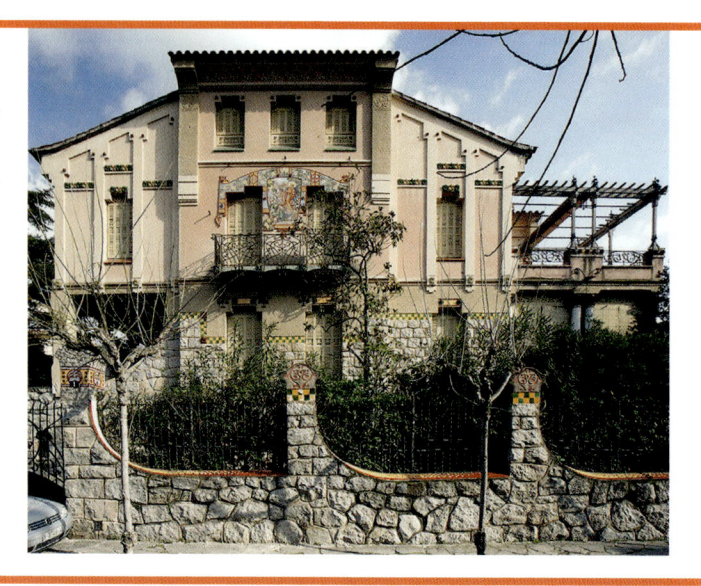

Built during the same period as the rest of the "Raspall block", Iris house is light and immaterial in appearance thanks to the chromatic treatment of white, cream and yellow tones given to the façades. It follows the typology of the other holiday homes designed by Raspall, its vertical continuity reflected by the tall tower. Here, Raspall concentrated on the small-scale elements, like the balcony vaults, clad with *trencadís* tile pieces, or the grilles of the railings with their filigree lines. The stone base extends to the foot of the fence, aspiring to clad all the surfaces and generating an unreal, dreamlike image.

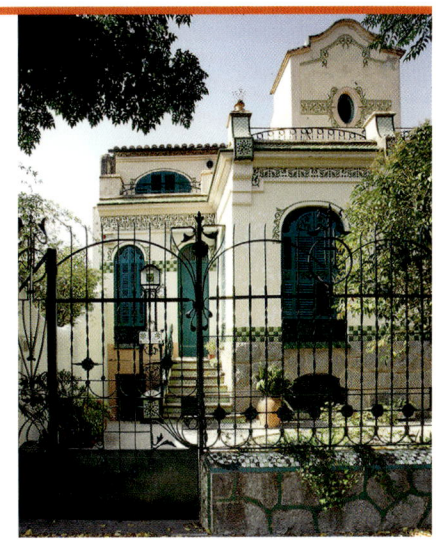

This was a newly constructed holiday home, comprising a ground floor, two upper storeys and rooftop spaces. Each floor is organized around a distribution space that is connected to the other floors by a stairway that reflects and unifies the ascending movement of the house. The stone base rises to a considerable height, and the overall building is crowned by a ceramic strip that frames the different sectors as it converges on them. The roofs follow the ascending movement of the volumes towards the central part. Over and above the ornamentation, the house is an example of the research carried out by Modernisme into the volumetric and spatial conception of construction.

Barcelona 237

215

JIMÉNEZ DE PARGA HOUSE
SINGLE-FAMILY DWELLING

Gabriel Mora, Helio Piñón, Albert Viaplana
1974

Ctra. de la Garriga a l'Ametlla del Vallès (BP-1432)
Can Busquets - Estate 7 - Plot 7 - La Garriga

216

CH HOUSE
SINGLE-FAMILY DWELLING

Jordi Badia, Mercè Sangenís
2001-2002

C/ Les Alzines, 21 - La Garriga

On this long, narrow site with entrances on two streets, the house is conceived as an object, a box placed on the grass, very hermetic on its long sides due to the proximity of the neighbours, and completely open on its short sides, where the garden is broader. The interior is laid out around a courtyard that separates lesser-used areas from the rest of the house, designed as a single space that flows around two light-coloured wooden pieces of furniture. The exceptional views suggested that the house should be raised up at a point that is manifested in the façade, giving the living room a diagonal section.

217

LLORET HOUSE
SINGLE-FAMILY DWELLING

Tonet Sunyer
2001

C/ Guinardó, 33 - La Garriga

The house is located on a large property between the towns of La Garriga and L'Ametlla del Vallès. The project responds to the isotropic, indifferent nature of the place by means of an extensive implantation guided by a random geometry that marks out each area. The living room and dining room on the ground floor and the master bedroom above present a clear façade plane overlooking the swimming pool. The children's and guest bedrooms form a separate volume to the rear. Open space makes its way into the heart of the house where the stairway communicates the two floors.

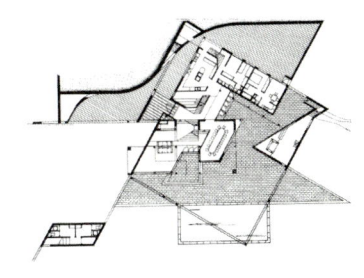

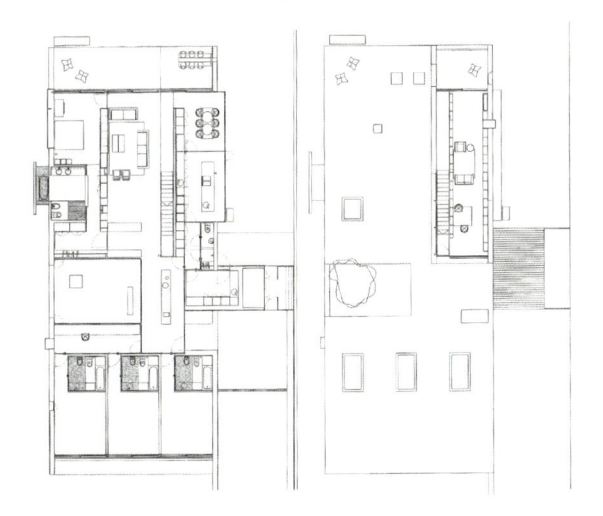

The house is situated on a large plot of land, limited on its east side by the railway line. It is arranged perpendicular to the street to enable entrance at an angle, thereby protecting the garden area. Entrance to the house is at the centre, and the different uses are laid out to either side. All the ground floor spaces communicate directly with the garden, and a pavilion housing an indoor swimming pool closes in the house and protects it from the railway track. The pavilion has an outdoor entrance, so that the well-protected garden organizes all the itineraries.

APARTMENT COMPLEX

Lluís Clotet, Oscar Tusquets
1976-1979

C/ Jaume Mimó i Llobet, 14-16
Cerdanyola del Vallès

The project is a throwback to the apartments designed in Carrer Mozart in Sant Cugat. Each apartment is laid out around a central area that allows its use as a single space or a series of independent rooms. In this case, the dwelling is divided into two blocks that leave a semi-public space at the centre, so that the block overlooking the street follows the curve of the alignment, giving it an urban dimension. In addition, the possibility of building to a greater height made it possible to include studios on the top floor. The entrance to the apartments is via the ground floor, with a metal gallery leading to the studios. This means that the central space can be enjoyed by all levels. The outer edges of both blocks are lined by private gardens connected to the apartments. The studios have their own spacious terrace, which can be used as a garden.

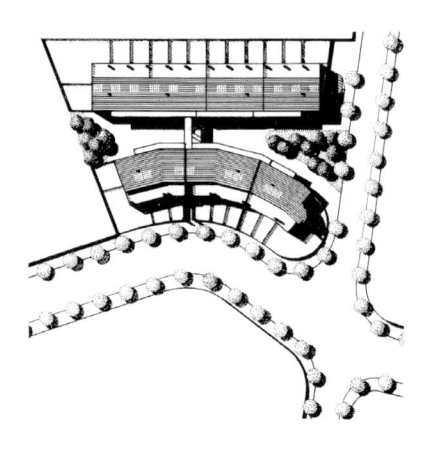

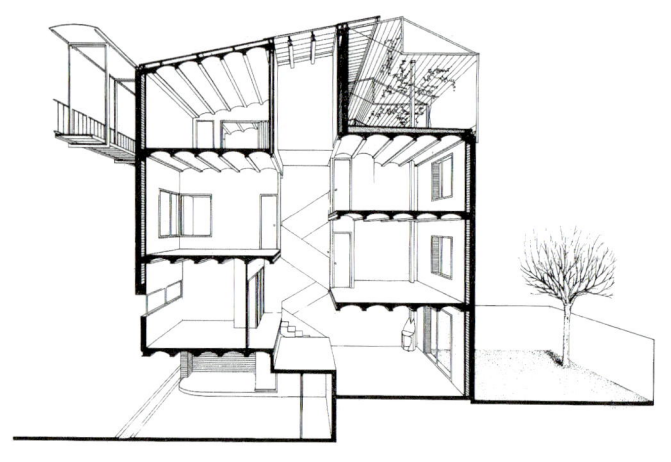

M&M HOUSES
TWO DWELLINGS FOR THREE ARCHAEOLOGISTS

José Miguel Roldán, Mercè Berengué
1999-2001

C/ Mercè Rodoreda, 11-11b - Bellaterra
Cerdanyola del Vallès

The idea for the project arose from the specific nature of the commission: two dwellings with different programmes sharing a single wooded, sloping site. The two houses obey a single set of general rules that are independent of the particularity of each programme. The datum plane is emphasized, marking the difference between the uses accommodated below and above: below, car parking, workshops and water deposits, with entrances at the ends of the plot; above, each programme is deployed independently over two levels. The common element is the central wooded strip shared by the two houses via their facing porches. M1 house is for a couple and their small child. M2 house is for a teacher who spends long periods away from home and rents out part of the house to other teachers. The materials and layout of the windows deliberately evoke the archetypal iconography of the domestic world.

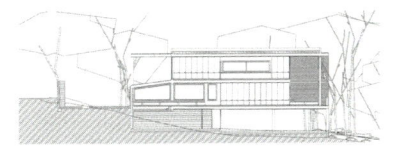

CENTRAL SPORTS SERVICES BUILDING
UNIVERSITAT AUTÒNOMA DE BARCELONA

Josep Lluís Mateo, Ferran Cardeñas
1987-1993

Bellaterra Campus - Universitat Autònoma de Barcelona - Cerdanyola del Vallès

The building is the result of the idea of creating a bridge over a watercourse that marks the configuration of the campus, thereby interrelating the two sides where the sports courts are situated. The programme comprises miscellaneous activities associated with sport and leisure: changing rooms, bar, gymnasium, offices, events hall, etc. The dimensions of the building are much smaller than those of the other constructions on this historic campus. This is the reason for its implantation and form, which set out to highlight the lightness of the scale of work. The building is linked to the topography and the landscape, taking the form of an infrastructural tube reminiscent of images of industrial facilities superposed gracefully over the landscape.

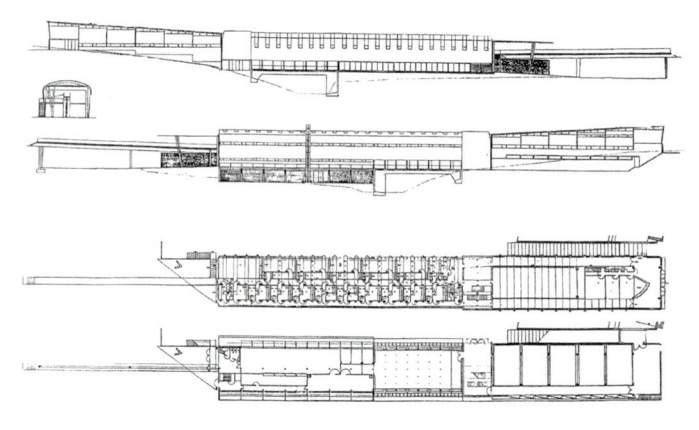

FACULTY OF TRANSLATION AND INTERPRETATION
UNIVERSITAT AUTÒNOMA DE BARCELONA

Jordi Bosch, Joan Tarrús, Santiago Vives
1995-1998

Bellaterra Campus - Universitat Autònoma de Barcelona - Cerdanyola del Vallès

The building echoes the scant references presented by a place with as little urbanization as the Humanities campus: a square to the north, a strong slope to the south, and the railway line that provides access to the whole campus. The programme is clearly separated into two volumes that are configured in accordance with these references: the office building takes the form of a prow shape overlooking the gully and the railway track, while the lecture room building adopts a terraced section that also gives it a specific orientation. In this way, the complex seems to start out from the square and be suspended over the slope. The north-facing façade unifies the two volumes by means of a mesh lattice that responds to the consolidated nature of the square. Between the two volumes, a landscaped courtyard houses the entrance and organizes the circulations that unify the complex. The programme is deployed independently of morphological considerations.

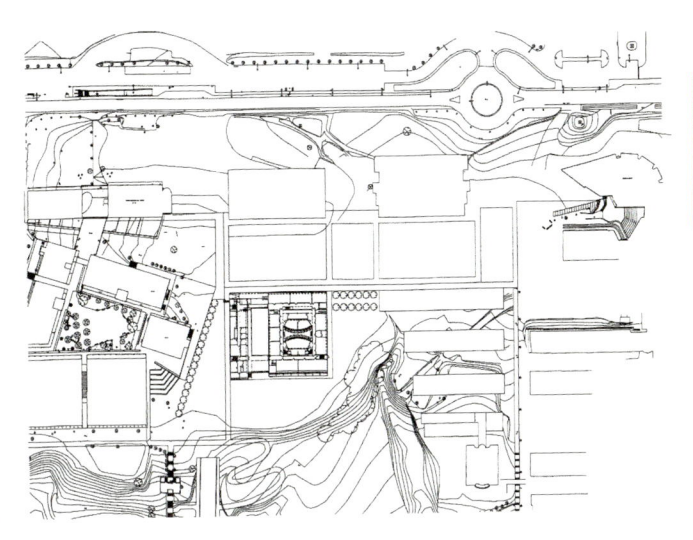

LUQUE HOUSE
SINGLE-FAMILY DWELLING

José Antonio Coderch de Sentmenat, Manuel Valls
1964-1966

Av. Canadà, 35 - Sant Cugat del Vallès

Coderch addresses the gentle slope of the site by creating a difference of levels within the house. At the top are the entrance and a space for car parking, and a group of two bedrooms and the master bedroom with its studio. At the bottom there are a further two bedrooms, the daytime spaces and the kitchen and service wing. The bedrooms on the north side follow the bay layout and the staggered section. Each different use of the house has its own façade, clearly separated from the others by the prolongation of the walls. Facing north-east, the house seeks light through a crosswise axis running from the car-parking space to the living room, passing through its principal element, an interior courtyard that receives light from the south. This courtyard becomes a central nucleus that organizes all circulations, making life in the house turn around its luminosity.

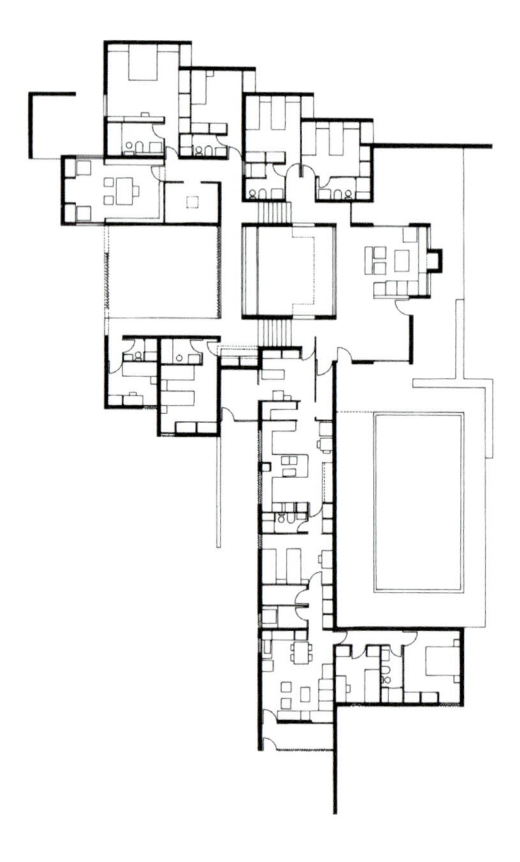

ROGNONI HOUSE
DWELLING FOR A BROTHER AND SISTER

Lluís Clotet, Oscar Tusquets
1976-1978

Passeig de l'Havana, 59 - Sant Cugat del Vallès

The dwelling combines apartments for a brother and a sister, plus a communal area to entertain guests. Building regulations dictated that the garden should occupy the northern part of the plot. The main rooms, communicated with the garden, receive sunlight through small openings and large windows in the opposite façade, which is well oriented despite its proximity to neighbouring constructions. The sister, who lives in the house nearest the street, moves around in a wheelchair. For greater ease of movement, her two rooms are very large and communicate on a single level. The brother's house is laid out on various floors, due to the lack of available land. The façade has a sand-coloured rendering and is seen as a sheet with holes practised in it for windows. It is completely covered by ivy, as is the pergola that protects cars and the entrance to the house.

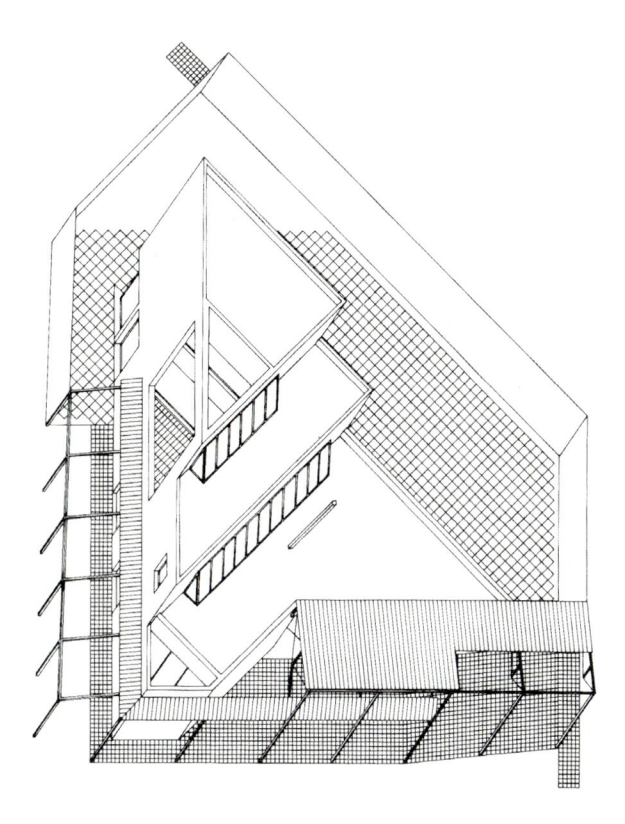

MARTÍ L'HUMÀ STREET BLOCK
145-APARTMENT HOUSING COMPLEX

Oriol Bohigas, Josep Maria Martorell, David Mackay
1974-1979

C/ Martí l'Humà, 1-9 - Av. Barberà, 290-300
C/ Doctor Roges, 2-4 - C/ Cerdanyola, 1-3
Sabadell

The project sets out to establish a closer relation between the dwelling and the public space in an urban context. The street block forms part of an old industrial belt that has gradually been incorporated into the town's residential fabric, calling for major renovation of the buildings. In this case, the part of the street block requiring renovation forms an L-shape that covers almost all of it. The project creates two housing blocks separated by an interior street that functions as a semi-public space, associated with both the dwellings and the general street network. The outer block, which overlooks the two largest streets, contains four levels of apartments on eight floors, while the inner block holds two levels of housing on four floors. The resulting complex forms a south-facing arc, producing good lighting and ventilation for all the dwellings without recourse to courtyards. The ground floor of the tallest block is reserved for shops, whereas that of the lowest incorporates some private gardens. The first-floor apartments are entered directly from the street, while access to the upper floors is via north-facing corridors above the two main streets.

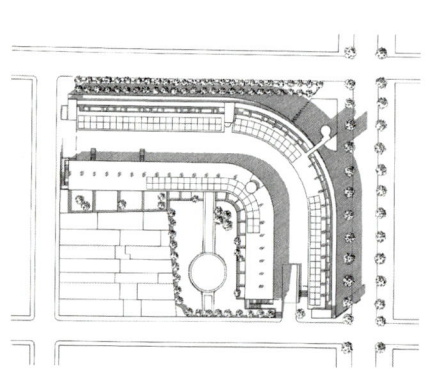

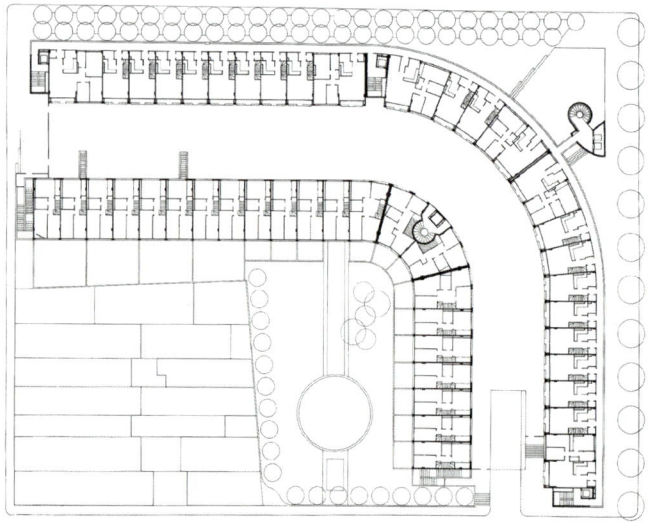

CAN BACIANA
2 APARTMENT BLOCKS

Felip Pich-Aguilera
Phase 1: 1995-1997
Phase 2: 1999-2000

Pl. Aurora Bertrana, 14A-14D, 16 - Sabadell

The new buildings emerged as the result of a process of urban restructuring on the site occupied by the former Baciana factory. The new constructions and the resulting spaces come into their own in a changing fabric. The building erected in phase one, rather than an oval screen, is the sum of four freestanding concrete towers suspended in the air by panels, between which the residents gain access. This generates an ambiguous contrast between marked solidness and a certain volatility. The glass and sheet-steel elements disappear behind the solid masses of concrete, built of the largest possible industrialized panels. The dwellings respond to the versatility, spaciousness, precision and security that characterize new lifestyles and new sensibilities.

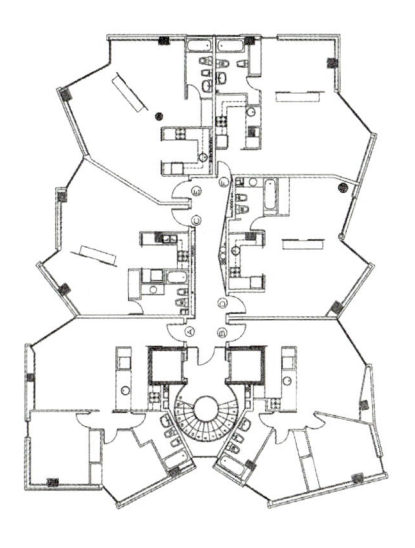

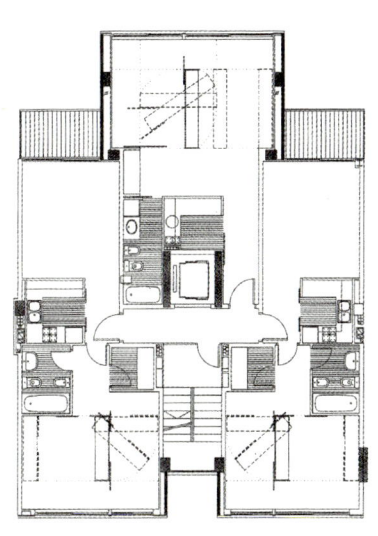

MILLENNIUM TOWER
HIGH-RISE OFFICE BLOCK

Enric Batlle, Joan Roig, Juan Manuel Sanahuja, Ricardo Sanahuja
1999-2002

Av. Francesc Macià, 62 - Sabadell

Millennium Tower is associated with the creation of the Macià axis which was the driving force of Sabadell's economic growth beginning in the 1980s. It stands on a site near Parc Catalunya, surrounded by heterogeneous urban fabrics, where single-family dwellings combine with buildings on a variety of scales. The tower block organizes its surroundings and rises up as a referent which is the first to emerge above the bell tower of the church. Planning regulations envisaged a square floor plan, but the built project adopts a slightly rectangular configuration, with rounded edges for greater slenderness when seen front on. The vertical communications shaft is slightly off centre to accommodate up to four businesses on each floor with no need for corridors. The interior commands a 360-degree panoramic view of the old town, the expanding town and the future town.

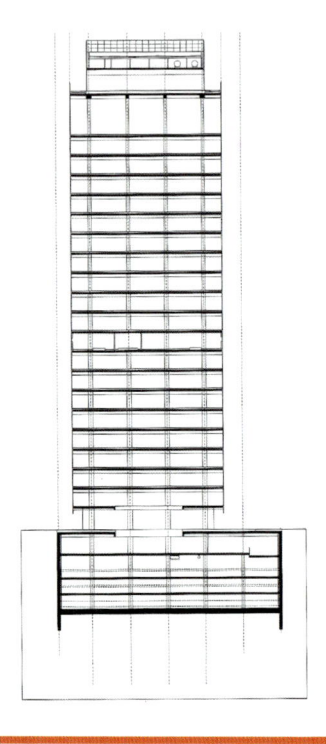

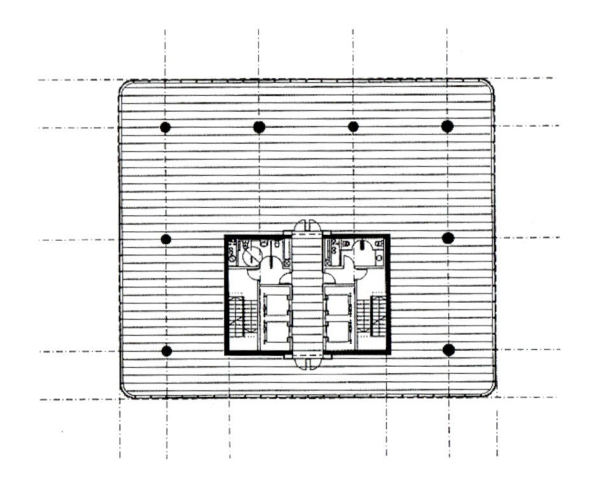

VAPOR SAMPERE APARTMENT AND OFFICE BUILDING

Rafael Moneo, José Antonio Martínez Lapeña, Elías Torres
2001-2005

C/ Tres Creus, 88-104
C/ Sallarès i Pla, 3 - Sabadell

The project completes a street block occupied by the remains of the Vapor Sampere, one of the town's principal exponents of early 20th century industrial architecture. The volume of the building and the treatment of the facades are determined by the different conditions of the setting. The highest point is at the street corner of Tres Creus and Sallarès i Pla, and the lowest in Carrer Turull. On the south side, commanding the best views of the textile mill, the building opens up with a staggered diagonal that turns the interior space into a semi-public enclosure. The exterior façade combines the arrangement of bare brick masonry, windows and the skylights of the stairwells to prevent monotony. With the volumetric treatment and the skin defined, the living rooms are arranged on the south side, fitted with moving wooden blinds to filter the sunlight and enable the use of the exterior galleries almost all year round.

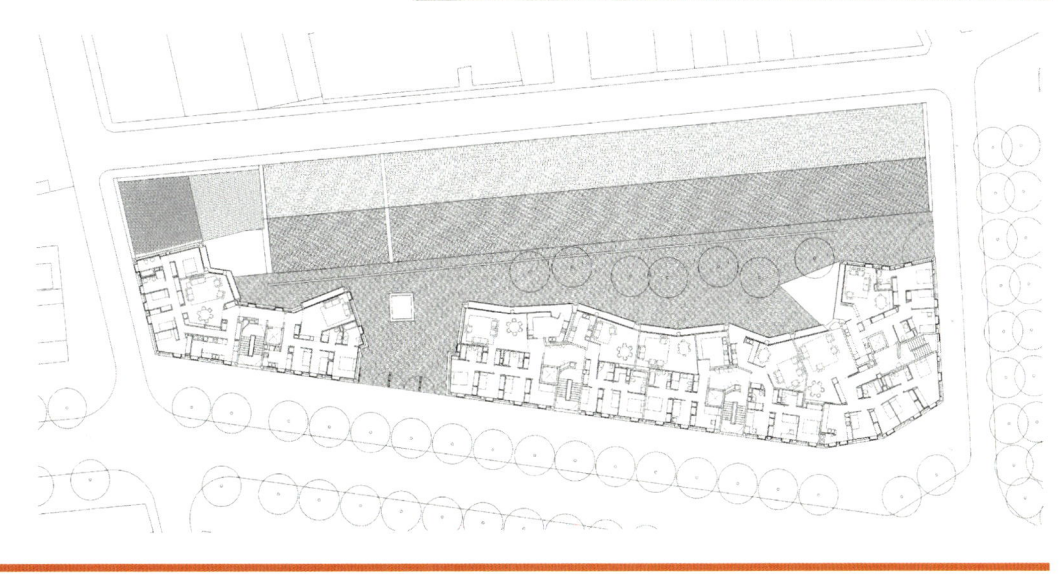

AYMERICH, AMAT I JOVER FACTORY
MUSEUM OF SCIENCE AND TECHNOLOGY

Lluís Muncunill
1907-1908

Rambla d'Egara, 254-270 - Terrassa

SUBSEQUENT INTERVENTIONS:
Carles Buxadé, Joan Margarit, 1985-1996. Works to fit out the building as the Catalan Museum of Science and Technology.

Of all the industrial buildings designed by Muncunill in Terrassa, the Aymerich, Amat i Jover factory is the most important due to its dimensions and the construction procedures employed. It occupies a surface area of 15,000 square metres, of which 12,000 are occupied by the large machinery floor. This is a large space comprising seven volumes arranged around cast-iron columns, covered by brick-built vaults and ties. The hall is lit through north-facing openings that form a saw-tooth arrangement. Each vault has a circular generatrix and an arbitrary directrix. The directrix rests on two sections of the hall and is situated over two arches, one segmental and one elliptical. The generatrix draws out a very shallow arch. The vault has two layers to facilitate insulation. Each vault comprises three layers of flat brick, separated by slim brick partitions that leave an air cavity of 15 centimetres. The vaults are subjected by ties with a diameter of 30 millimetres. The resulting structure provides homogeneous lighting throughout the hall.

MASIA FREIXA
MUNICIPAL CONSERVATORY

Lluís Muncunill
1907-1910

Pl. Josep Freixa i Argemí - Terrassa

The "masia" is the result of remodelling and rehabilitating an existing industrial building. In 1907, the Freixa i Sans company decided to construct a new building for alpaca manufacture. Muncunill conserved the old factory structure in its entirety, over which he superposed new elements. The original walls support brick-built vaults with ties and brick partitions. The walls are given an inner facing into which doors and windows were inserted. Further interventions served to substantially modify the visual effect of the building. The walls were rendered in white. The great gallery was built in the south-facing side, comprising a succession of eight parabolic arches over a broad pavement of undulating shapes. Each sector is roofed by a small dome in proportion to those over the central sector. A great arch closes the gallery on its west side, roofed by a dome that stands out above the others. Subsequently, a further two floors were added to accommodate a kitchen and service spaces.

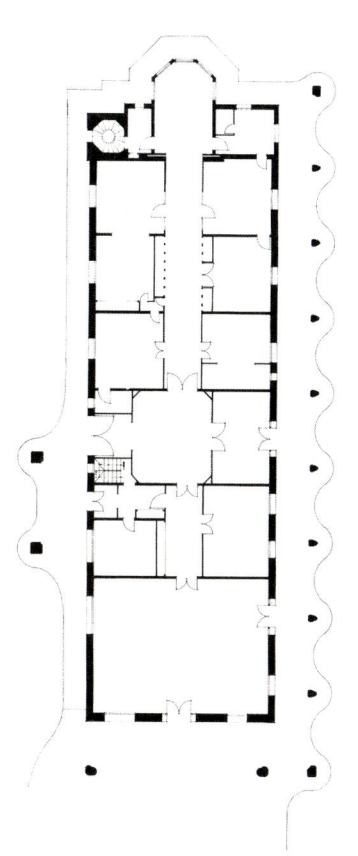

TERRASSA CENTRAL LIBRARY

Josep Llinàs
1995-1998

C/ Sant Gaietà, 94 - Terrassa

The library is situated in one of the town's areas of expansion, where the presence of old textile mills and small family dwellings is giving way to new architectures. The complex comprises two quite different volumes, arranged at a slant. The space between the two accommodates the main entrance. The larger volume houses the book stacks, on a level with the ground floor, and the lower level contains the children's library and warehouse. The ground floor of the small volume is given over to a press reading room, and the lower level holds an events hall and the foyer, which communicates with a patio along the south side. The two volumes are defined by their cross section, designed to provide the whole interior with uniform lighting and comprising large curved vaults that evoke the town's industrial past.

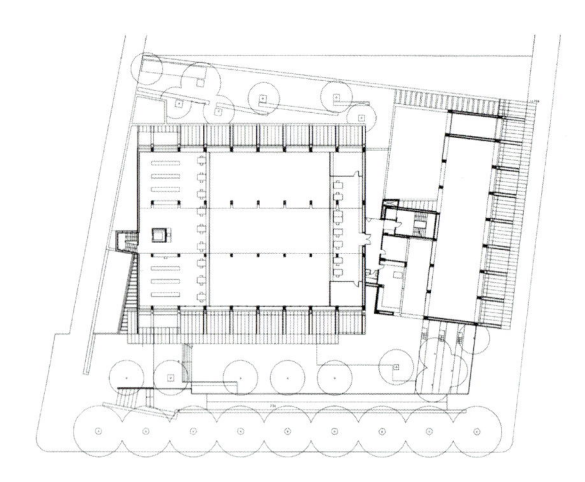

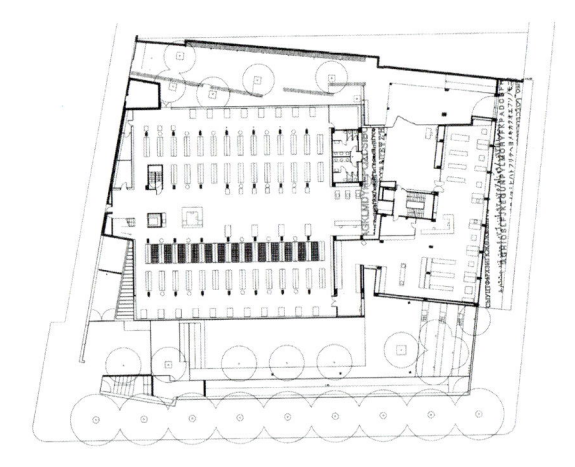

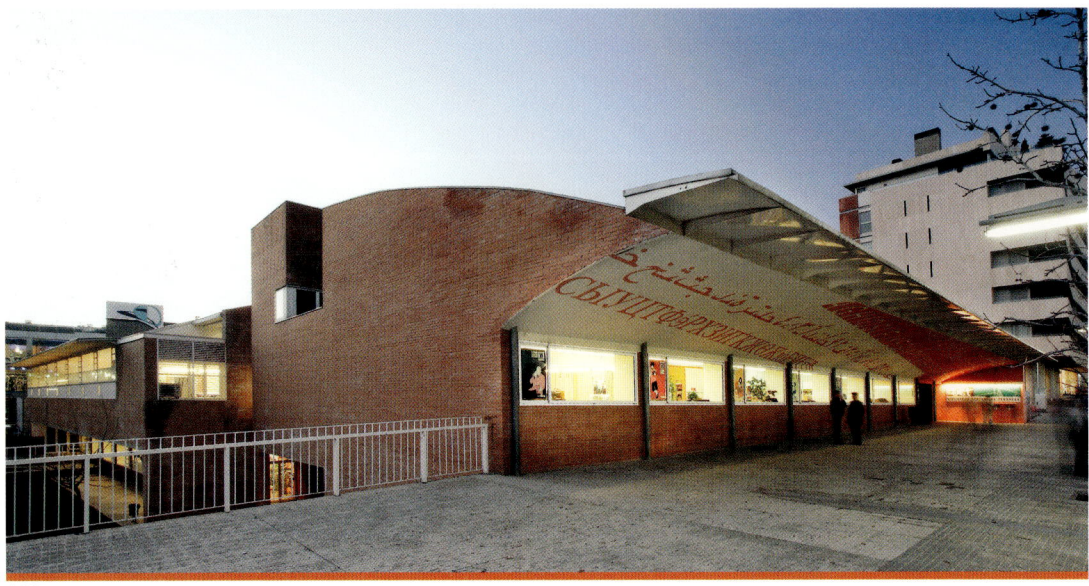

LES PALMERES
HOUSING COMPLEX

Josep Lluís Mateo
1994-1998

Av. Béjar, 222-232 - Ctra. de Matadepera, 295-315 - Pg. Lluís Muncunill, 45-57 - Pl. de Montserrat Alavedra - Terrassa

Standing beside a large avenue that separates an empty urban space from the developed town, the building takes the form of a single curved volume, 280 metres long. The complex comprises one long building with two small constructions at the end that serve to manifest the scale and the unitary dimensions of the linear block. The main building is divided in two: a large, semibasement socle over which slides a narrower volume containing the dwellings. The treatment of the surfaces increases this intensity. In the convex part, the galvanized steel and glass base supports a red-brick strip with systematically arranged perforations. The concave part also expresses standardization by means of great stone blocks measuring 3 x 1.5 metres. The mission of this panelling is to fragment the overall impression, transforming the hard concrete into a fabric more appropriate for the daytime areas it encloses.

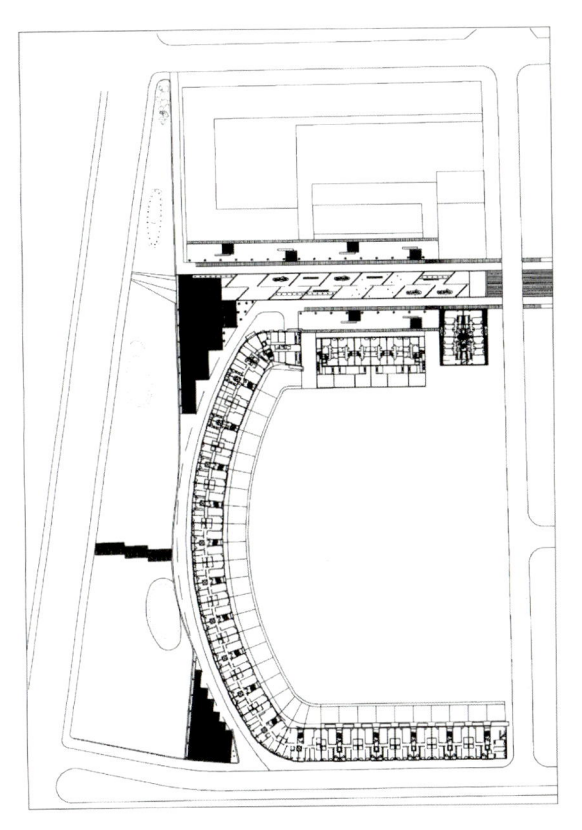

TERRASSA MUNICIPAL FUNERAL SERVICES

Jordi Badia
2001-2002

Ctra. N-150 - Funeral complex - Terrassa

The building consists of an elementary white prism placed gently on the site, opening to the outside via a porch that runs the whole width of the façade. The topography of the site is slightly sloping, so the building, which keeps to the horizontal, does not touch the ground. This arrangement summarizes the symbolism underlying the project: the levitating position of the prism and the large opening of the porch are references to a conception of earth as a journey, a starting point—a conception that replaces "here lies" with "this is the point of departure". The programme is organized around a courtyard with water that separates and distributes the three main sectors: the vigil rooms, the chapel and the cafeteria. Passage from one space to another is necessarily via the courtyard, which acts as a decompression chamber. The conception of each interior space combines artificial light, natural light and views of the sky, graduating the light and dark of each space according to its use.

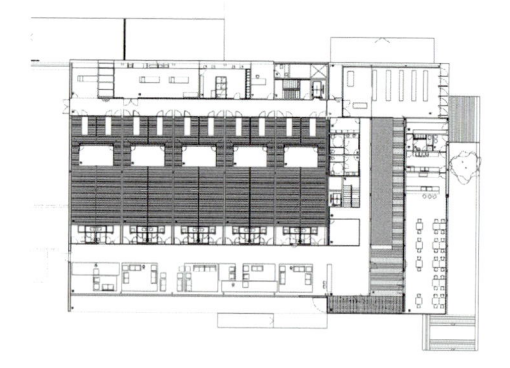

S-T HOUSE
SINGLE-FAMILY DWELLING

Iñaki Alday, Margarita Jover
1999-2001

C/ Múrcia, 46 - Terrassa

The house is situated in an outlying district characterized by a landscape of courtyards, empty tracts and exposed party walls. The site is 13.50 metres wide, twice the usual measurement in the area, allowing the construction of two bays. The project moves the usual programme for a dwelling to the first floor in order to maintain the link between the bedrooms and the outdoor space. One of the bays is located on the inside of the site, creating new courtyards on the façade side. The roof comprises two copper strips that undulate from façade to façade, forming an enclosure and freeing up the attic as a large continuous space. The result is a dwelling that is full of openings and corners, where at least two routes lead to each space, which has its own area of expansion. The house shares the garden with another two homes, and the south-facing façade overlooks the house across the street, six metres away.

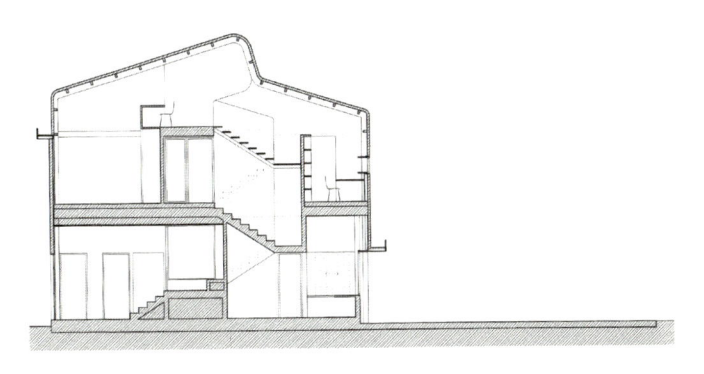

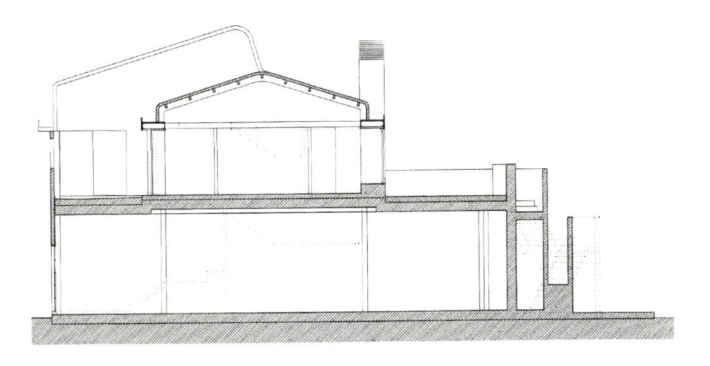

234

CEIP PALAU
INFANTS' AND PRIMARY SCHOOL

Conxita Balcells, Santiago Vives
1999-2001

C/ Arquitecte Falguera, 37 - Palau-solità i Plegamans

235

CAP CASTELLAR
HEALTH CENTRE

Carles Muro, Charmaine Lay, Quim Rosell
1995-1999

C/ Ripollet, 30 - Castellar del Vallès

The health centre adapts strictly to the outlines dictated by building regulations and interprets the programme by dividing it into two parts, one to either side of the entrance. The part occupied by the health-care areas is organized around a basic unit, comprising a surgery, nursing bay, waiting room and courtyard. Two units together form a single area, which can be identified by the colour of its courtyards. The roof reflects the layout of the floor plan, indicating the entrance of air and light. On the other side of the entrance, the remainder of the programme adopts a compact form, occupying two floors.

236

6 SINGLE-FAMILY DWELLINGS

Alfons Soldevila, Josep Ignasi de Llorens
1977-1979

C/ Poeta Maragall, 27-35
La Muntanyeta residential development
Matadepera

The school is situated in a low-density residential area, not far from farmland, and characterized by the complete absence of urban qualification. The nature of the programme recommended planning the entire school on a single floor to create direct relations with outdoor spaces and avoid the need to go up and down stairs. The school is laid out in the form of two crossing arms, organized by orthogonal corridors, with some gentle ramps that adapt to the slight gradient of the site. The classrooms are arranged in the volume parallel to the street into which the crosswise volume is inserted, containing the more singular areas of the programme. The roof system is laid out from one space to the next, a slope marking each element in the programme. Seen from the street, the school presents an ordered cadence of built volumes that provides a counterpoint to the disorder of the single-family dwellings across the street.

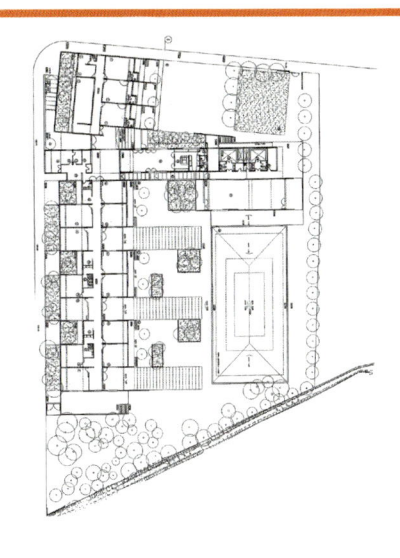

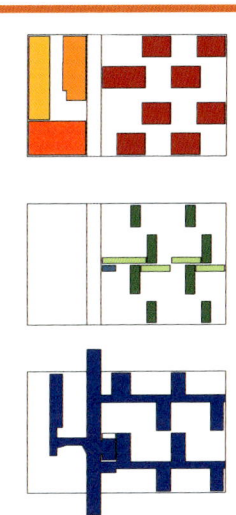

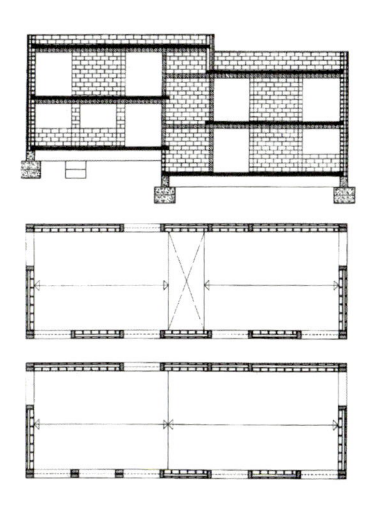

The six houses respond to a clear and simple construction procedure, in which each element acts independently, giving it great flexibility. The structures are bare concrete-block walls with unconcealed installations situated in the exterior facings. The basis of their simplicity is the modulation of the concrete block, the volumetric approach, the distribution of the dwellings and the independence of treatment given to the various elements. The stairwells, structural floors, roof, partition walls, door and window frames, installations and finishes are practically independent, facilitating the task of the construction workers, simplifying repairs and allowing the users great flexibility. The bare blocks and their modulation call for the rigorous implementation of all the elements. The tolerances are very small, the engagements call for great attention and the elements are very few. The result of this simplicity of construction is not a cheap product but sheer quality.

Barcelona 257

MMI HOUSE
SINGLE-FAMILY DWELLING (MORATIEL HOUSE)

Josep Maria Sostres
1955-1957

C/ Apel·les Mestres, 19 - Esplugues de Llobregat

This is Sostres' best critical interpretation of the masters of the modern movement who had such an influence on him. The brief is laid out on a single floor, raised slightly above grade, with the different rooms laid out for optimum sunlighting. The combination of various types of bearing elements and facings, inspired by his interest in Terragni and other Italian Rationalists, tends to dematerialize the house, incorporating transparency for a more intense experience of the space. Seen from the street, the dichromatism of the two planes, the slit of the entrance and the two stair towers emerging in the roof, the study and the stairwell, reflect a revision of the old icon that is Villa Savoye: an almost foursquare house with a raised walk-on roof and a small inner courtyard that completes the organization of the space and helps to create a more complex domestic atmosphere than the old international-style interiors.

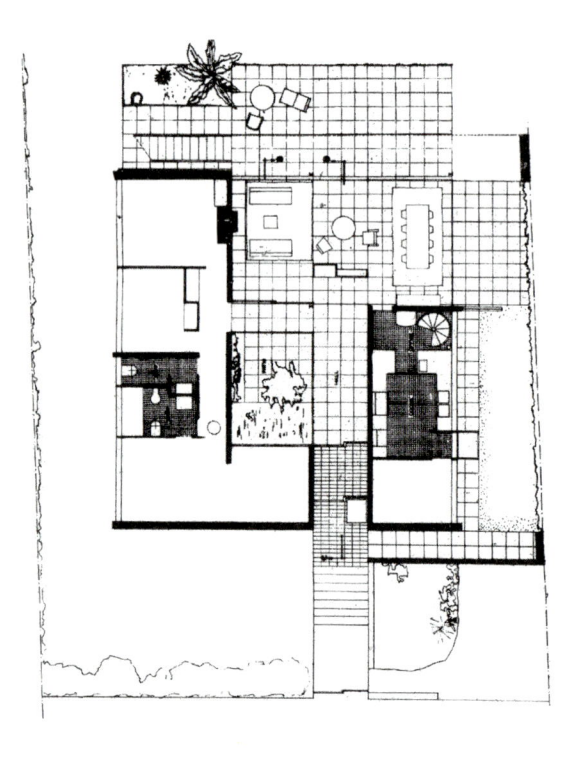

IRANZO HOUSE
SINGLE-FAMILY DWELLING

Josep Maria Sostres
1955-1956

C/ Apel·les Mestres, 8-10 - Esplugues de Llobregat

This extensive, generous brief is interpreted by the decision to establish a strict correspondence between each of the parts of the house and its structural and volumetric resolution, thereby forcing the articulation of the different volumes. The result is a combination of volumes and openings that form a series of tense rhythms with no repeated elements. Sostres gives new life to compositional outlines proposed by the modern movement: the location of the entire brief on the first floor is a reference to Le Corbusier, while the strictly equitable use-form-structure approach is inspired by the most rigid Bauhaus principles. However, the result is more than a mere exercise in historicism: by interpreting ideas and procedures rather than stereotypical forms, Sostres regenerates the vitality of the house as a complex system of rooms in which the projecting volume of the living room plays a dominant role.

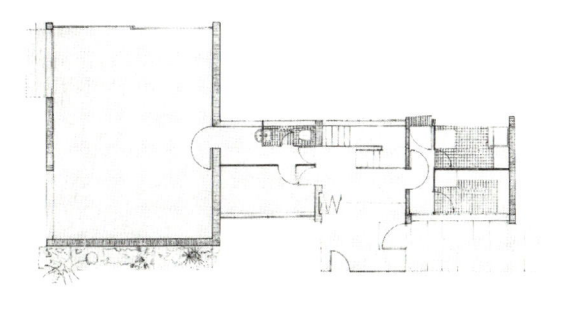

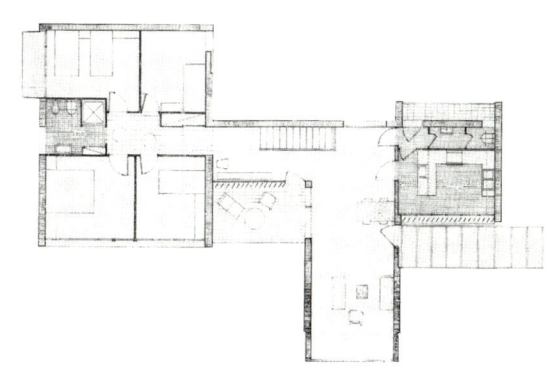

WALDEN 7
RESIDENTIAL COMPLEX

Ricard Bofill
1970-1975

Av. Indústria - Sant Just Desvern

With a lower budget than usual for social housing and a series of atypical financing instruments, Ricard Bofill and the Taller d'Arquitectura managed to produce a housing complex based on a critique of the existing city that proposes lifestyle as well as architectural alternatives. The development comprises 18 tower blocks that curve as they rise and eventually touch the neighbouring towers, leaving at the centre large, interconnected empty spaces that encourage relations between the different dwellings. The outside of the complex presents walls clad in red brick with very small openings. The inner courtyards, conversely, are addressed with very lively colours. The housing units practise numerous variations on the square module, which can be duplicated or form groups of four, establishing new possibilities of interrelation between the inhabitants of each unit.

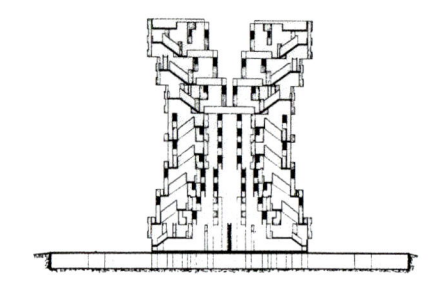

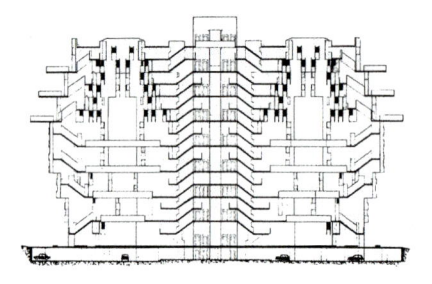

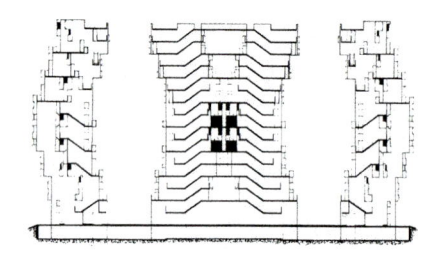

LA BONAIGUA SPORTS COMPLEX
REMODELLING AND EXTENSION OF SPORTS INSTALLATIONS

Jaime Coll, Judith Leclerc
1997-2001

Pg. de la Muntanya - Sant Just Desvern

The project addressed intervention on a sports complex built in 1976, with a swimming pool that was added 10 years later. The pre-existing complex presented serious problems of circulation and communications, both internally and in relation to the elements around it. The initial proposal was to construct a sports pavilion beside the existing installations, but the definitive intervention addressed all the elements of the old facility, with the addition of new elements of architecture and the restoration of others that had become functionally obsolete. A new building was constructed that acts like a transport interchanger. The intervention took into account two basic considerations: the relations between the new sports complex and its immediate surroundings, and the articulation and coherence of the various functional components.

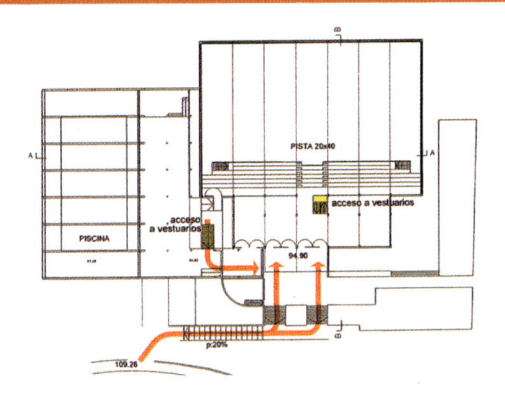

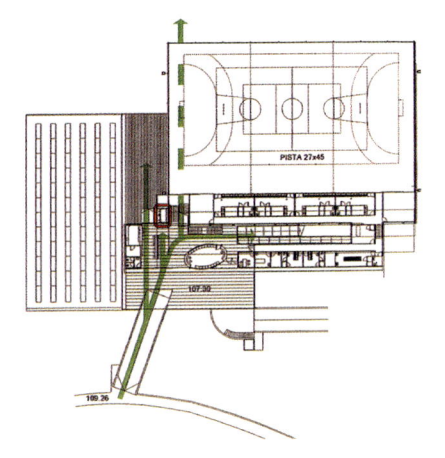

GIBERT HOUSE
TORRE DE LA CREU, TORRE DELS OUS

Josep Maria Jujol
1913-1916

Pg. Canalies, 12 - Sant Joan Despí

This is a project for two semidetached dwellings for the architect's aunt. Jujol created an organism comprising five cylindrical volumes. The three larger volumes have their crowns at the same level, whereas the two smaller ones emerge at different heights, containing the stairways of the two houses. Another two cylinders stand out on the roof terrace, containing stairs to the penthouses and lookout points. Each cylinder is roofed by a dome clad with fragments of glass from the glass factory in nearby Cornellà. In the main façade, another small cylinder provides a porch, with openings formed by two parabolic arches. Jujol created a unitary organism that only had to be divided by a straight line to form the two dwellings. Iron elements are used to mark singular features: the start of the stairway, the galleries of the dining room or the lookout points on the roof terrace.

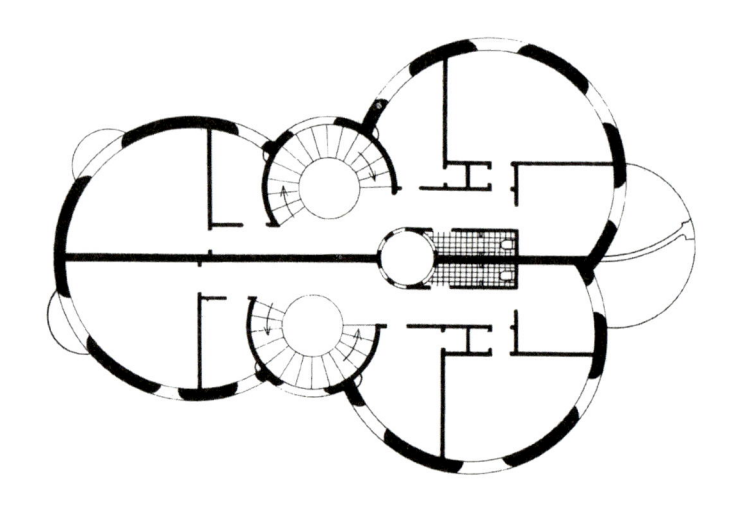

CAN NEGRE
BARCELONA BRANCH OF
THE COL·LEGI D'ARQUITECTES DE CATALUNYA
BAIX LLOBREGAT HEAD OFFICE

Josep Maria Jujol
1915-1930

Pl. Catalunya - Sant Joan Despí

Jujol approached the remodelling of a baroque farmhouse with the intention of changing the aesthetic parameters that were so important to Modernista culture as it entered the 20th century. The principal interventions in the interior were to the chapel and the stairway. Jujol maintained both the existing wall system and the arrangement of openings. He placed all the emphasis on the transfiguration of the main façade, summarized in a single project drawing that reflects his intentions. Further courses, all different, of flat tile were added to the undulating cornice. The two side windows on the first floor were converted into two symmetrical galleries, flanking a new central gallery that evokes the form of a carriage in delicate ironwork, and an unusual system of glazed openings. The plane of the façade is divided into polychrome patches that seek to unify the resulting dissymmetry.

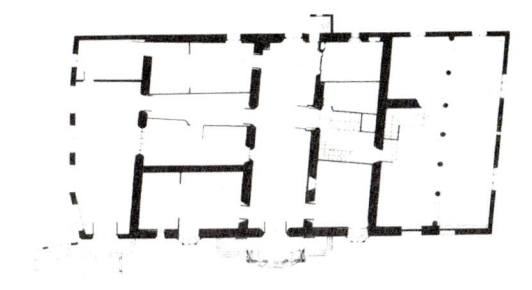

LA SALUT HOUSING BLOCK

Oriol Bohigas, Josep Maria Martorell, David Mackay
1969-1973

C/ Falguera, 94-102 - C/ Prolongació de Falguera, 1-15 - C/ Sant Josep, 74-84 - Pça. Falguera, 3-5
Barri de la Falguera - Sant Feliu de Llobregat

This was the first project by the MBM practice to occupy an entire street block, with a programme for social housing run on a cooperative basis. The block presents an irregular footprint as a result of the tangent marked by the torrent of La Salut. The project rigorously maintains the exterior alignment of the four streets and creates an inner square reached from two opposite corners. The individual blocks comprise a double bay with a courtyard that also houses the vertical communication shafts, leading off the square along a series of arches. The overall configuration highlights the semi-public nature of the system of spaces within the street block, which are addressed as a network of irregular itineraries on different levels. The apartments in the inner blocks and the shops on the ground floor turn their façades onto this inner system of spaces that is markedly urban due to the treatment of the volumes and the facades.

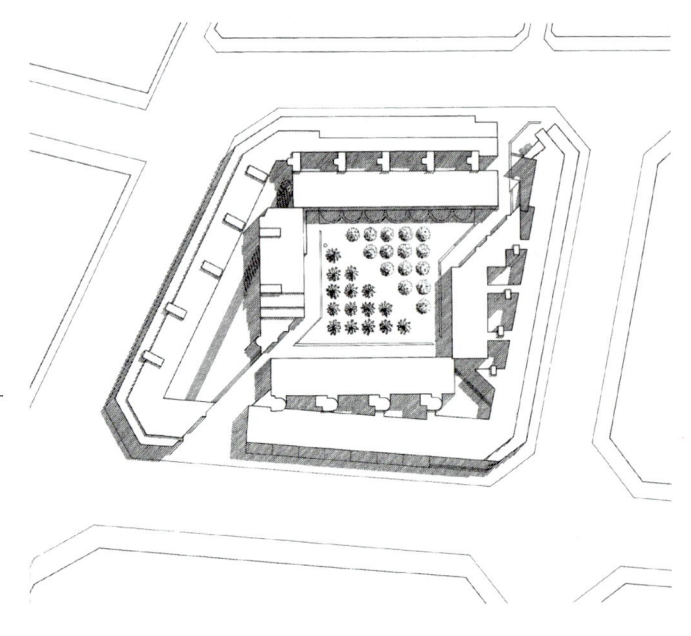

MONTSERRAT ROIG PUBLIC LIBRARY

Albert Viaplana, Helio Piñón, Ricard Mercadé
1990-1993

C/ Verge de Montserrat, 3 - Sant Feliu de Llobregat

The library is situated in a sloping park beside the railway line and laid out according to an interpretation of the altimetry of the place that does not interfere with the park's continuity. Entrance to the building is on the highest ground, through a porch formed by the two upper floors. Above the porch, a 45-degree slit opens the two floors to face north through a great window, offering views right across the park. In the street along its side, the two floors begin the formation of a lengthwise vault, independent of the structural supports, which generates a porch with its concavity. On the opposite side, the reading rooms turn their windows onto the park. In this way, the building adopts an orientation in relation to the point that generates it. The book stacks are accommodated beneath the square in front of the library, which also takes as its reference the higher ground of the park.

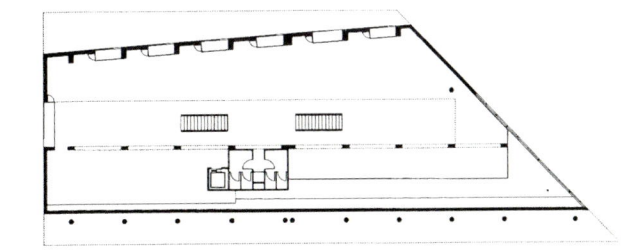

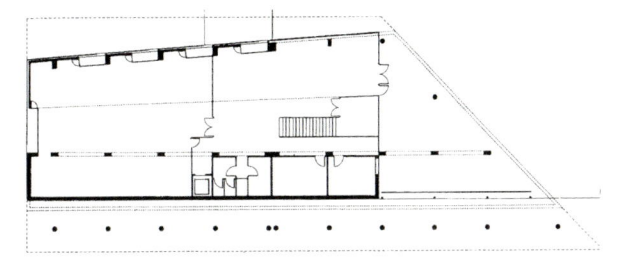

CHURCH CRYPT AT COLÒNIA GÜELL

Antoni Gaudí
1898-1914

C/ Reixach - Colònia Güell
Santa Coloma de Cerelló

SUBSEQUENT INTERVENTIONS:
Antoni González Moreno-Navarro,
José Luis González, Albert Casals, 1999-2002.
Restoration and new roof.

Gaudí worked on this project for 10 years, with building work only beginning in 1908. It was a veritable laboratory set in nature, where Gaudí tried out the discoveries he made at La Pedrera, La Sagrada Família and Parc Güell. The crypt consists of a basaltic rock structure of sloping pillars, with monolithic shafts, constructed to support the church that was to be built on them. The ceiling is a complex system of slender catenary arches of thin brick that obey a very irregular geometry, informed by numerous allusions to the animal and plant kingdoms. The darker first courses of the walls are succeeded by courses that are reddish in tone, and the church was to continue with tones of green and finally blue, imitating the chromatic order of the surrounding woods. Gaudí worked with models of catenaries to trace the vaults that were to complete the construction, though the crypt is the result of on-site work using all kinds of found and recycled materials, such as the grilles at the windows and left-over bricks. On all the surfaces, Gaudí stamped numerous religious and Catalan nationalist symbols, such as the four cardinal virtues represented in the mosaic above the entrance.

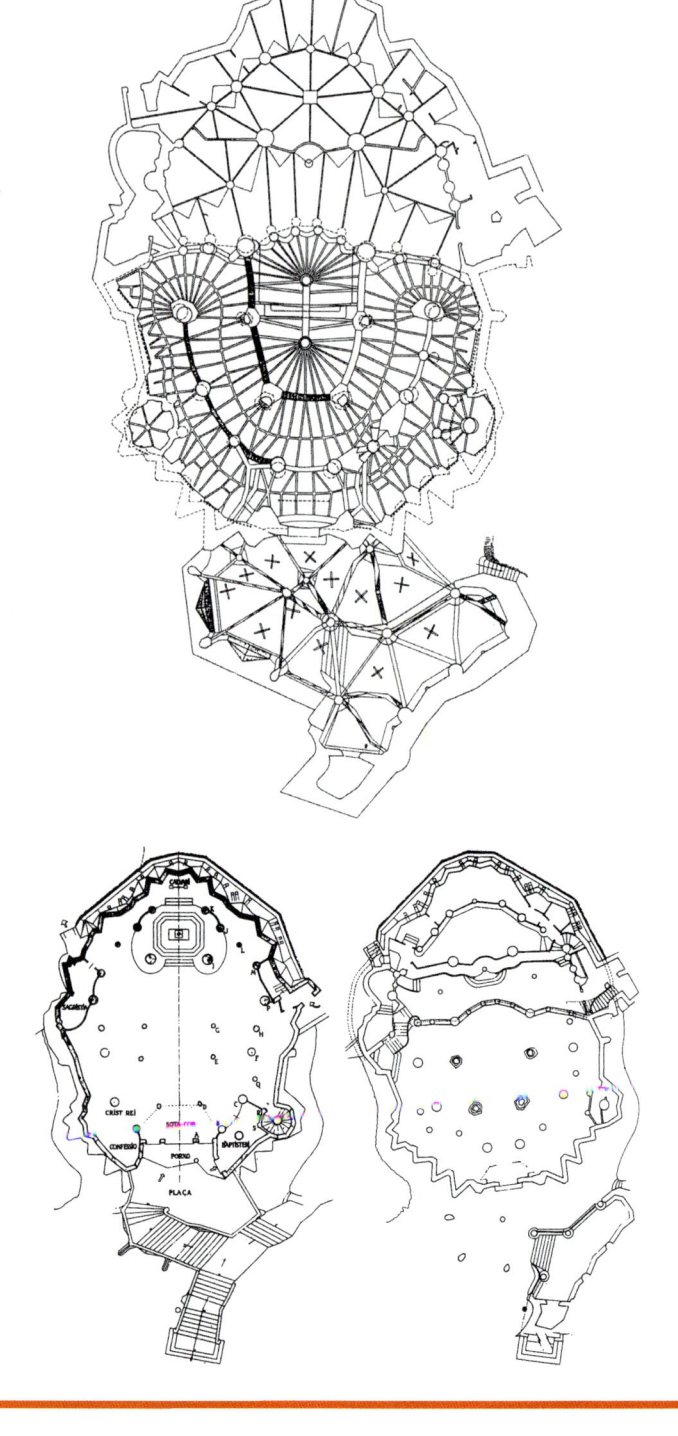

Barcelona

PONS HOUSE
HIGH-RISE HOUSING BLOCK

Ramon Puig i Gairalt
1931-1933

Ctra. de Collblanc, 43 - L'Hospitalet de Llobregat

Situated at the junction of a major thoroughfare and a narrow street, the building responds to the need to solve the problems of urban congestion of the time. The tower block adopts a long narrow floor plan that follows Carrer Progrés, giving particular importance to the corner of this street with Carrer Collblanc. The floors decrease in size as the building rises; the first six have four dwellings per floor, the next four have three, the next have two and the final floors just one. The long narrow form of the floor plan makes it possible to give all the apartments two minimum courtyards in their central parts, though for reasons of space Puig i Gairalt had recourse to diagonal layouts in order to avoid, as far as possible, losing space to corridors. The building partakes of both the rhetoric of Noucentisme and the social agenda that characterized the following generation of architects.

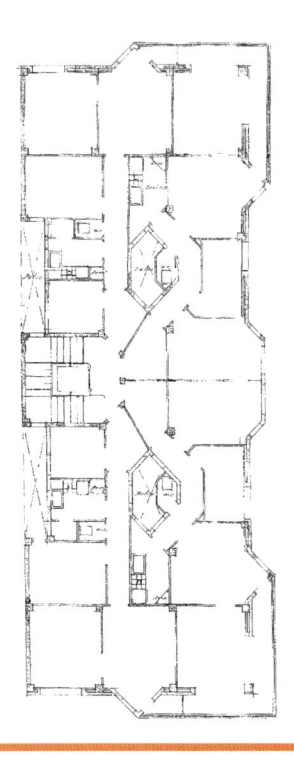

HESPERIA TOWER
HOTEL, CONVENTION HALL, AUDITORIUM AND METROPOLITAN SPORTS CENTRE

Richard Rogers, Lluís Alonso, Sergi Balaguer
1999-2006

Av. Mare de Déu de Bellvitge, 1 - L'Hospitalet de Llobregat

The building stands on the edge of the Bellvitge estate, beside Gran Via de les Corts Catalanes, in a location that gives it the role of a driving force in the area's urbanistic renovation. Its position perpendicular to the motorway prevents it being a visual obstacle to the apartments in Bellvitge and creates a new urban façade on the avenue that it also generates. This represents the suppression of a historical scar, giving rise to the disappearance of the condition of the motorway as a physical boundary. The programme is distributed between the high-rise building that is the hotel and a great long plinth that houses the congress centre and sports club. The point of union of these two volumes is a glazed atrium that stands six floors high. The tower clearly separates all the structural and communication elements of the functional areas, creating open-plan spaces given over to hotel rooms.

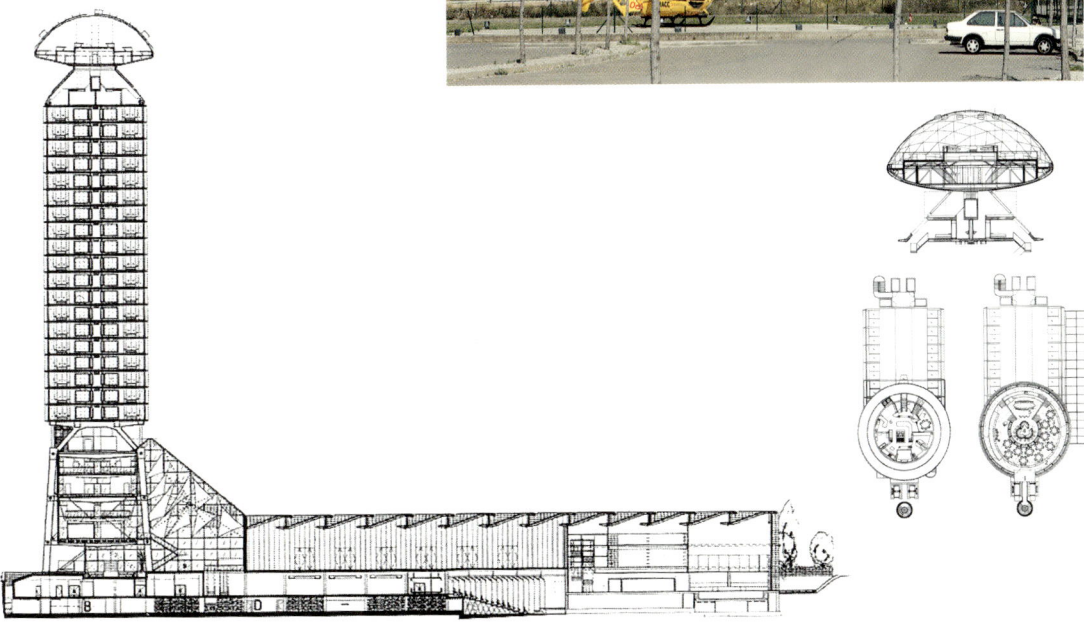

LA RICARDA VILLA
SINGLE-FAMILY DWELLING

Antoni Bonet i Castellana
1953-1962

Camí de l'Albufera - El Prat de Llobregat

The house occupies a large site covered by a pine grove, near the sea. Bonet interpreted the place as an isotropic territory, marked out by an 8.80 x 8.80-metre grid that exactly follows the orientation of the sun. Each domestic function coincides with the modules of this grid, roofed by brick vaults that are supported by square-sectioned metal pillars. This renders the facings completely independent of the roof, producing circulations, exterior spaces, furnishing and minor details that are understood as infinite variations on the initial grid.

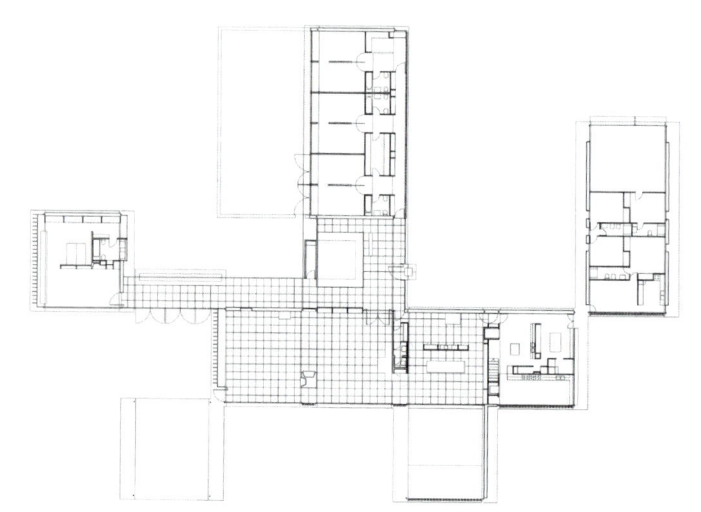

EL PRAT ROYAL GOLF CLUB
SERVICE PAVILION

Robert Terradas i Via, José Antonio Coderch de Sentmenat, Manuel Valls
1954

Camí de la Volateria, Zona Camp de Golf nº 1
El Prat de Llobregat

The pavilion turns its back to the golf course and faces south-west, forming a two-winged volume that accommodates two sets of quite different functions. At the meeting point of the two wings is a large, transparent space that turns to look out of the opposite façade, with the club house, bar and dining room. To the north, the service staff wing has its own patio onto which it looks out. The second wing extends south, housing the offices and changing rooms. The pavilion responds to the characteristic landscape qualities of a golf course, comprising a single-storey construction, glazed from floor to ceiling throughout most of the façade, and unified by a large flat roof that forms eaves around most of its perimeter. The result is a series of spaces directly related to the outside and clearly delimited beneath the tops of the trees.

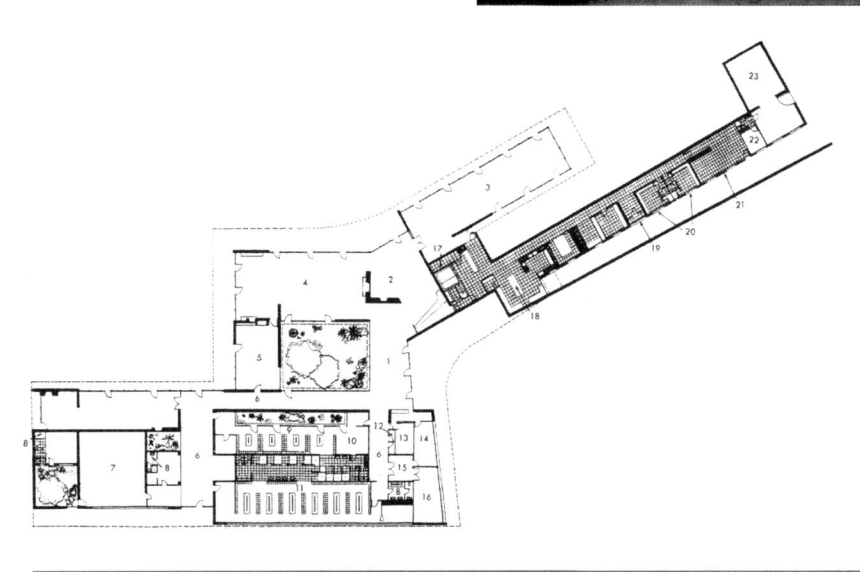

EL LLOBREGAT SPORTS PARK
RIBERA-SERRALLO SPORTS FACILITIES

Álvaro Siza Vieira
2002-2006

Av. del Baix Llobregat - Cornellà de Llobregat

This sports complex is designed as a long winding itinerary that starts with two ramps or sloping public squares and ends by the swimming pool, a space of great sacrality. The squares lead on to the sports courts and the linear block containing the gymnasiums. This allows the pavilion to function independently of the other parts, while the corridor of the linear block organizes the whole complex. The next step is the indoor pool. It owes its form to the Roman *caldarium*, with a slightly curving dome perforated by 62 circular openings that give the interior a diffuse, dreamlike light. The pool extends outdoors to create an open-air bathing area surrounded by grass and enclosed by a curved wall that folds to create shade. Siza conceived of the sports park as a many-faceted experience of light and shadow, "a tribute to the quality of life in Cornellà".

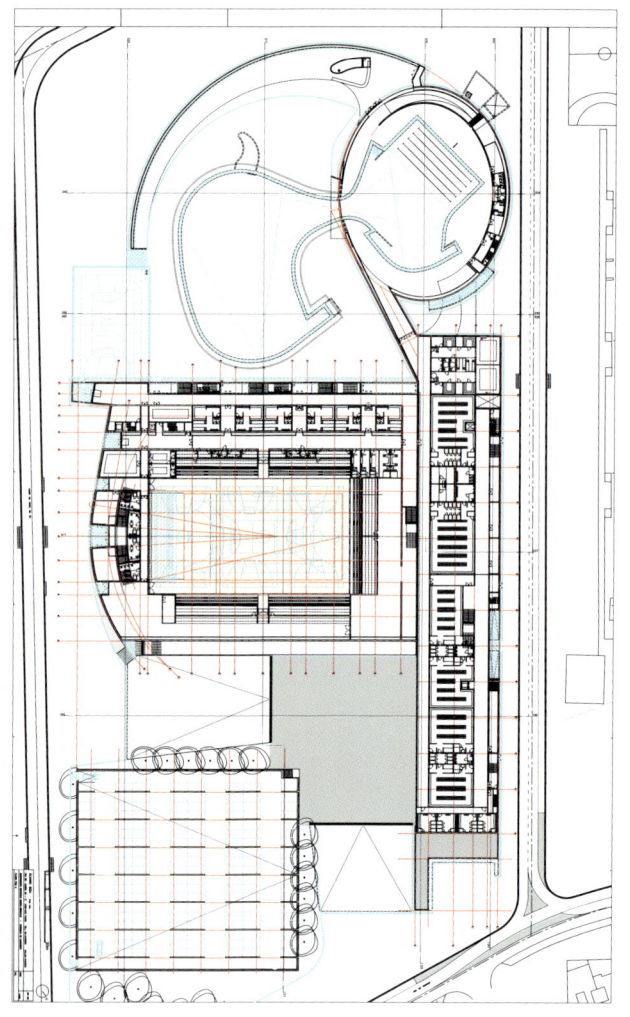

251

L'OLIVERA CIVIC CENTRE AND SPORTS FACILITY

Moisés Gallego
1995-1998

Pl. Montserrat Roig, 1 - Sant Boi de Llobregat

In the northwest of Sant Boi, a tongue of green creates a funnel-shaped empty space, closed in at its widest end by the rear façades of a row of buildings. The site offers the possibility of creating a backdrop that did not previously exist. The new building is generated by a uniform plane of few lines, related to the large scale imposed by the exterior space. The programme suggests the organization of a single envelope enclosing three buildings: a social club, a cultural and social building, and a sports facility. The three parts of the programme are contained in a single enclosure, forming three juxtaposed volumes, and the façade acts as a unifying element. In this way, once the mechanisms of interrelation are established each part of the programme can function independently. The result is a large, uniform container linked to the scale and the urban demands of the site.

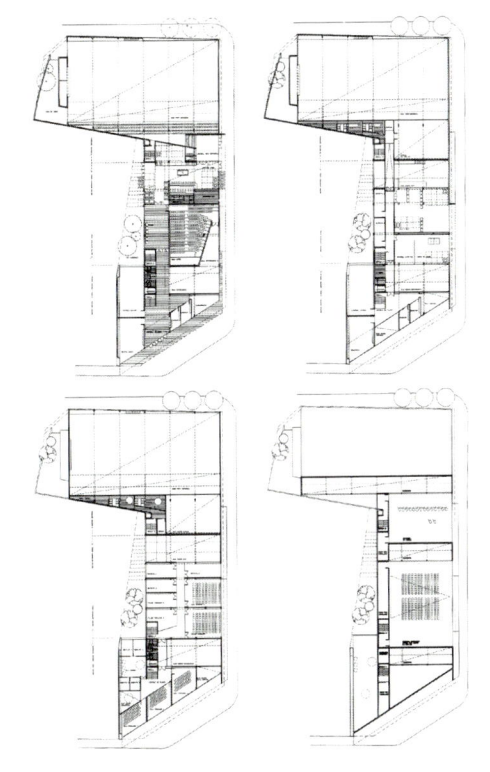

252

EL BOLET (THE MUSHROOM)
SINGLE-FAMILY DWELLING

Blai Pérez
1992-1997

C/ Hortènsies, 6-8 - Alba Rosa residential development - Viladecans

253

CAMY-NESTLÉ FACTORY BRIDGE

Enric Miralles
1991-1994

Ctra. de la Llobatona, 18 - Centre industrial area Viladecans

The programme called for the construction of a bridge to connect two buildings in the same factory, separated by a street on the industrial estate. The bridge facilitates worker movement and the construction of two conveyor belts for packaged material, electricity cables and installations for the cold processes. The structural section groups together the various loads and offers a specific solution for each, allowing for the displacement caused by variations in weight. The footbridge comprises a section of post-stressed concrete supporting a system of prefabricated elements that allow light to shine in.

254

CEIP LLUÍS VIVES
INFANTS' AND PRIMARY SCHOOL

Carme Pinós
2003-2007

Pg. del Ferrocarril, 266 - Castelldefels

The project accords the building an emerging position on the highest level of the site, and the descent from one floor to the next forms steps down to the lowest point. In section, each floor projects less and, in floor plan, the various volumes curl around to embrace the plot, producing an exterior enclosed space between the house and the natural slope of the terrain. This arrangement produces flat surfaces on an apparently inaccessible plot and creates a long façade with views, along which all the rooms in the house are laid out.

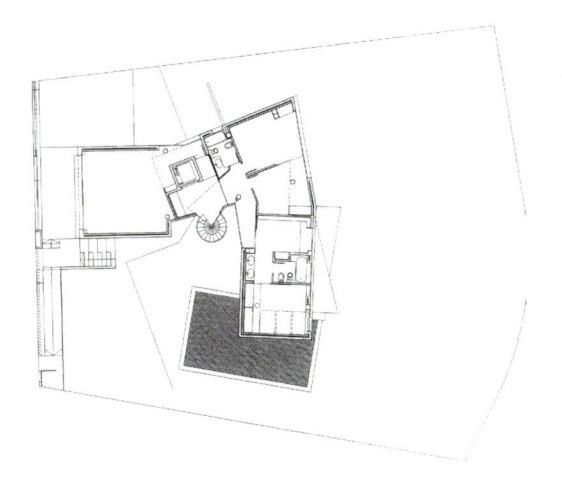

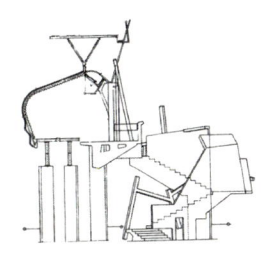

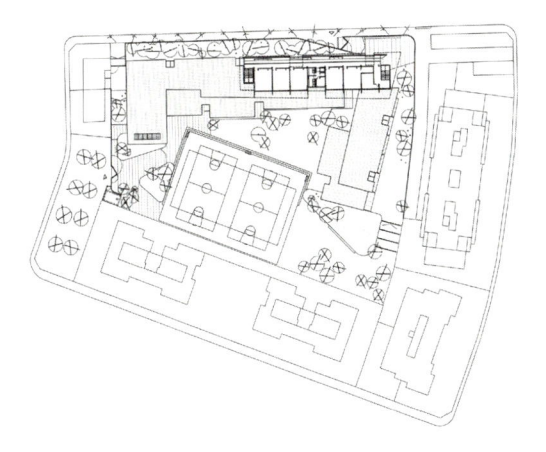

The general project approach addresses two site characteristics: the intermittent noise of passing trains and exposure to surrounding homes. The L-shaped building is situated at an appropriate distance from the housing and parallel to the railway line, closing in the plot and organizing a south-facing playground. This protects the play area from the noise of trains and ensures its visual privacy. The ground floor of one wing is used for communal activities. The ground floor of the other accommodates the youngest children, who have their own outdoor space, and the classrooms are on the upper floor, overlooking the school grounds and turning their back on the train tracks.

Barcelona

GÜELL WINE CELLAR IN GARRAF
GAUDÍ GARRAF RESTAURANT

Francesc Berenguer, Antoni Gaudí
1895-1900

Ctra. de les Costes (C-246), Km. 25,000
El Garraf (Sitges)

This is a small construction built to store the wines produced on Eusebi Güell's estate in Garraf. The construction comprises three orders of parabolic arches, decreasing in size as they rise together to form a very steep ridge roof. The wine cellar stands beside the road, beside a large drop. It is built of rough-hewn masonry with blocks of stones at the corners, and supported boldly by a few points, such as the entrance to the chapel on the level above. Though it has always been attributed to Francesc Berenguer, Gaudí's intervention is evident in some smaller-scale details, such as the chimneys, the front door and the latticework. The intermediate level, the administrator's house, is built at the level of the road and the entranceway, at the point where the slope of the roof rises gently to form a pagoda-like outline.

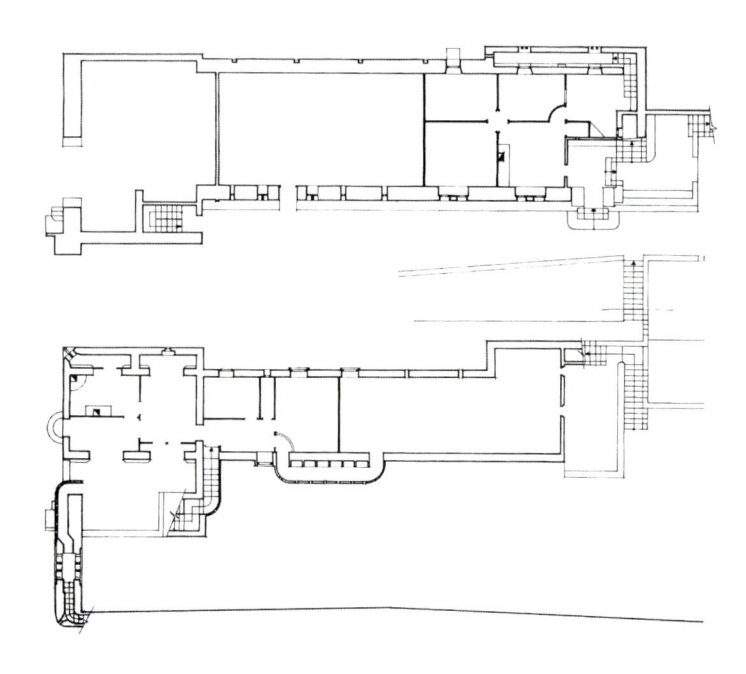

CASABÓ HOUSE
SINGLE-FAMILY DWELLING

Francesc Mitjans
1934-1935

Pg. Marítim, 64-65 - Sitges

Mitjans designed the house in his student days, before the civil war, mainly influenced by GATCPAC ideas. Like other architects of the time, he started out from a neoclassical design with brickwork masonry, which he altered with absolute freedom according to the brief and his interpretation of the place. The dwelling is raised a floor to create vistas of the sea. Entrance is at a tangent across the terrace, outside the living room, in the south-facing façade. The west wing houses the bedrooms and is raised slightly above the rest of the house. The east wing contains just the kitchen and the servants' quarters, freeing up space for large terraces that form a roof over the drive. Five cylindrical pillars protect the front terrace on the west side and configure the view of the house from the street.

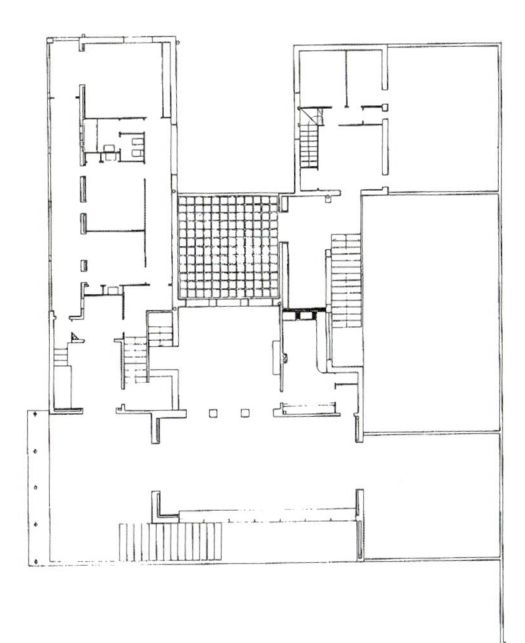

CATASÚS HOUSE
SINGLE-FAMILY DWELLING

José Antonio Coderch de Sentmenat, Manuel Valls
1956-1958

C/ Josep Carner, 32 - C/ Pintor Casas, 5
District of El Vinyet - Sitges

The neighbourhood of El Vinyet has a practically flat topography, in which Coderch chose to create a system of domestic spaces that look no further than the plot's large garden, with absolutely no reference to the exterior. The house takes the form of a single storey, forming an L-shape that embraces the garden. One arm of the L holds the bedrooms, and the other contains the living and dining rooms. The entrance is behind the bedroom volume, concealed by the garden, and leads to a third arm that holds the kitchen and service areas. All the openings overlooking the plot can be opened, leading straight out into the garden, or closed by shutters the height of the house's brickwork. The result is a series of areas laid out on one level around the garden that unifies the principal areas of domestic life, while the entrance and services remain concealed at the rear and generate their own exterior spaces.

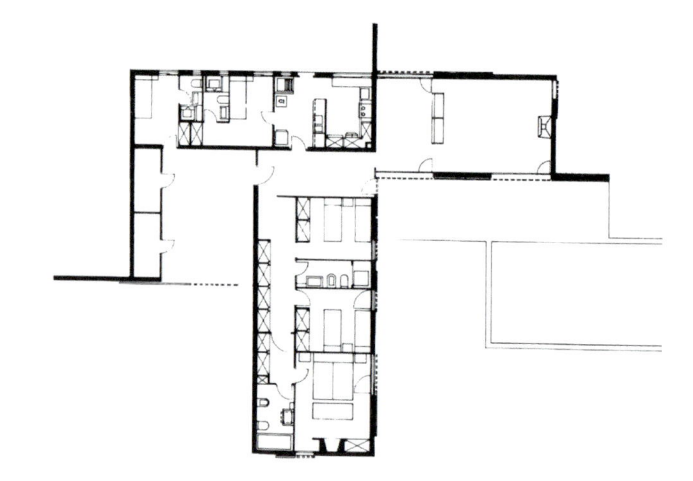

GILI HOUSE
SINGLE-FAMILY DWELLING

José Antonio Coderch de Sentmenat, Manuel Valls
1965-1966

C/ Salvador Casacuberta - C/ Torres Quevedo
District of El Vinyet - Sitges

The peculiarity of the programme prompted Coderch to essay a completely new layout on a plot adjacent to that of Catasús House, built 10 years previously. The entrance leads into a hallway connected to a courtyard that provides light to the central areas and is conceived as a semi-covered conservatory. A small porch then leads into the garden and to the bedroom wing via a second, totally independent hallway. The living room turns its back on the car-parking area and adopts a rather closed configuration, though it faces south to overlook the garden. The dining room is accorded particular importance by its position on the visual axis running right through the house, from the bedrooms to the opposite façade, with a second semi-covered court. Coderch gave the house an L-shape with a large central axis, in which the situation of each room is conditioned by its intrinsic configuration and the position it occupies in the general system of circulation.

KAFKA'S CASTLE
DEVELOPMENT OF 112 HOLIDAY HOMES

Ricard Bofill
1966-1968

Pg. Pujadas, 1 - Vallpineda residential development
Sant Pere de Ribes

This project approach finds its origins in the influence that the Archigram group had in the 1960s on members of the Taller d'Arquitectura. It sets out to mark a clear separation between the order of the circulations and the order of the dwellings, and to design a series of vertically rising cubes that connect with the network of circulations without structural constraints. The stairwells comprise brick bearing walls that extend to support half of each unit, while the other half rests on a metal pillar situated at a corner. Each cube contains a space—living-dining room or bathroom and bedroom—separated by a difference in level. The law of vertical growth follows the guidelines of a mathematic equation. The idea was to adapt the architecture to rather unconventional leisure activities, associated with a dramatic conception of the characteristic lifestyles of that decade.

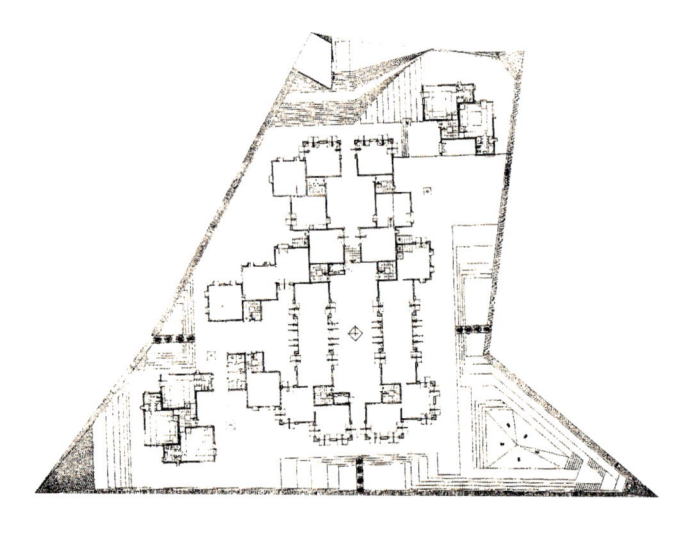

IES ALEXANDRE GALÍ
SECONDARY SCHOOL

Pere Joan Ravetllat, Carme Ribas
1992-1994

C/ Miquel Servet - District of Roquetes
Sant Pere de Ribes

The project comprises a main four-storey building that houses most of the programme and another on the opposite edge of the site that contains the gymnasium. The two buildings and the ramp that connects them delimit the sports courts. The absence of obvious alignments according to which to organize construction and the irregularity of the perimeters suggest a solution that generates its own geometry to define the different spaces, leaving the rest of the site, to its very edges, as a playground. The main building comprises an outer ring-shaped concrete structure that contains the classrooms and a central volume with a metal structure and glass-block walls housing the tutors' rooms, entrances and the assembly hall, a large covered courtyard situated below grade.

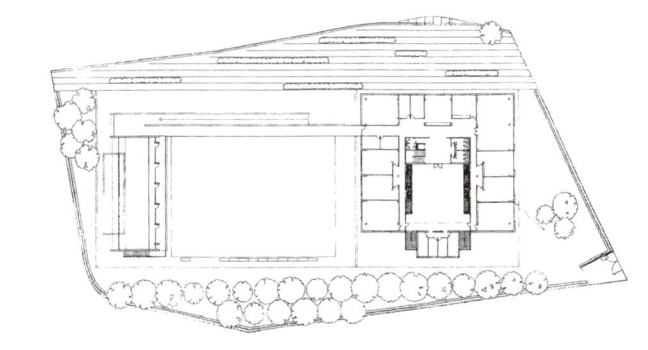

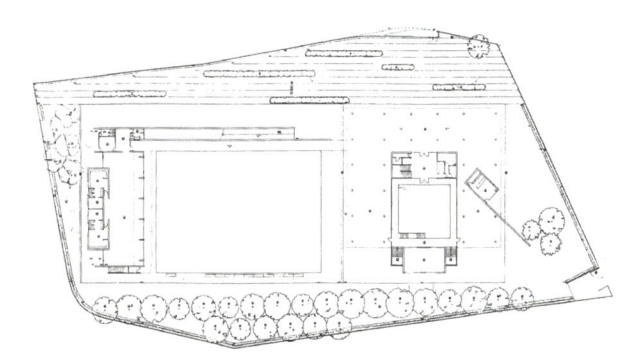

TGN – The Tarragona Area

Territorial scope

The Tarragona area centres on the *comarca* or county of Tarragonès. To the northeast, towards Barcelona, it encompasses the counties of Baix Penedès and Alt Penedès, firstly following the coast and then moving inland to the border of the county of Anoia. To the southwest, towards Tortosa, it takes in the coastal strip of Baix Camp, as far as the borders of Ribera d'Ebre and Baix Ebre, which form part of the Amposta area. Moving inland, it includes Alt Camp and the inland part of Baix Camp. The area therefore coincides roughly with these five counties. The only municipality outside this sector is Sarral, further inland, which is in the county of Conca de Barberà.

Sant Sadurní d'Anoia
Vilafranca del Penedès
L'Arboç
Montferri
Nulles
El Vendrell
Calafell
La Secuita
Alforja
Castellvell del Camp
Els Pallaresos
Creixell
Reus
Altafulla
Torredembarra
Vila-seca
Tarragona
Salou
Cambrils
L'Hospitalet de l'Infant

Road structure

If you are driving from Barcelona, take the AP-7 or C-32 motorways that meet at El Vendrell. The AP-7 motorway continues southwest to Tortosa, connecting the northeast and southwest extremes of Catalonia, from La Jonquera to Ulldecona and Alcanar, on the border with Castellón. If you are driving from Tarragona to Lleida, the best route is the AP-7 to El Vendrell and the AP-2 to Lleida. The AP-2 continues to Madrid. To get to Valencia, take the AP-7 southwest through Castellón and on to Valencia. The major references are the AP-7 motorway, which crosses Catalonia from northeast to southwest, and the AP-2 motorway, starting at El Vendrell and heading inland to Lleida and Madrid.

ROUTE 1
Route 1 of this area follows the coastline northeast and then heads inland into the county of Alt Penedès. The AP-7 motorway will take you to El Vendrell, via Altafulla, Torredembarra, Creixell and Calafell. The same motorway heads inland to Sant Sadurní d'Anoia, via L'Arboç and Vilafranca del Penedès. L'Arboç is a few kilometres away from the motorway, along a turnoff to the right.

ROUTE 2
Route 2 starts out from Tarragona and heads north along the N-240. Various turnoffs will take you to Pallaresos, La Secuita, Nulles and Montferri, along small local roads. To get to Sarral, first go to Valls and then head north along two local roads, the C-37 and the TP-2311. This route comprises a series of small scattered places, all joined by the N-240.

ROUTE 3
Route 3 centres mainly on Reus, a town close to Tarragona that is very important for its architecture. The easiest route from Tarragona to Reus is the T-11 expressway. When you reach Reus, take the C-14 to Alcover. Another small local road, the TP-7049, leads out of Reus to Castellvell del Camp. Heading west, the N-420 takes you to Les Borges del Camp, when the C-242 turnoff on the right leads to Alforja. The focal point of this route is Reus, which serves as a reference for all destinations.

ROUTE 4
Route 4 follows the coastline southwest, in the same direction as the AP-7 motorway. However, the towns of Vila-seca, Salou and Cambrils are very close to Tarragona, making the best route the old N-340 national road, which keeps closer to the coast, whereas the motorway lies further inland and heads straight for Amposta. To get to L'Hospitalet de l'Infant, which is quite a lot further, you can take either the AP-7 motorway or the N-340 road.

Manresa
Sant Sadurní d'Anoia
Vilafranca del Penedès
L'Arboç
Alforja
Montferri
Nulles
Castellvell del Camp
La Secuita
El Vendrell
Calafell
Els Pallaresos
Creixell
Reus
Altafulla
Torredembarra
Vila-seca
Tarragona
Salou
Cambrils
L'Hospitalet de l'Infant

Municipalities	Comarca	Surface area (municipality)	Population (2001)
TARRAGONA	Tarragonès	64.6 km^2	113,129 inhabitants
ROUTE 1			
ALTAFULLA	Tarragonès	7.0 km^2	3,293 inhabitants
TORREDEMBARRA	Tarragonès	8.7 km^2	11,187 inhabitants
CREIXELL	Tarragonès	10.5 km^2	2,086 inhabitants
EL VENDRELL	Baix Penedès	36.8 km^2	23,744 inhabitants
CALAFELL	Baix Penedès	20.4 km^2	13,503 inhabitants
L'ARBOÇ	Baix Penedès	14.1 km^2	3,715 inhabitants
VILAFRANCA DEL PENEDÈS	Alt Penedès	19.7 km^2	31,248 inhabitants
SANT SADURNÍ D'ANOIA	Alt Penedès	19.0 km^2	9,843 inhabitants
ROUTE 2			
ELS PALLARESOS	Tarragonès	5.1 km^2	2,701 inhabitants
LA SECUITA	Tarragonès	17.8 km^2	1,153 inhabitants
NULLES	Alt Camp	10.6 km^2	359 inhabitants
MONTFERRI	Alt Camp	19.2 km^2	159 inhabitants
ROUTE 3			
REUS	Baix Camp	52.8 km^2	89,006 inhabitants
CASTELLVELL DEL CAMP	Baix Camp	5.2 km^2	1,537 inhabitants
ALFORJA	Baix Camp	38.2 km^2	1,344 inhabitants
ROUTE 4			
VILA-SECA	Tarragonès	21.7 km^2	13,353 inhabitants
SALOU	Tarragonès	15.1 km^2	14,164 inhabitants
CAMBRILS	Baix Camp	35.3 km^2	21,000 inhabitants
VANDELLÒS & L'HOSPITALET DE L'INFANT	Baix Camp	102.7 km^2	4,373 inhabitants

METROPOL THEATRE
FORMER THEATRE OF THE PATRONAT OBRER

Josep Maria Jujol
1908-1910

Rambla Nova, 46 - Tarragona

SUBSEQUENT INTERVENTIONS: Josep Llinàs, 1992-1995. Restoration and refurbishment.

The Patronat Obrer de Tarragona owned two buildings in Carrer d'Armanyà until it decided to purchase the building at number 46 Rambla Nova in order to have a theatre with an entrance on the city's main avenue. Jujol had to overcome the difference in level of the new entrance on the Rambla, 2.50 metres above the garden, and insert a particularly small space, the new theatre, measuring 17 x 20 metres. He solved the first problem by situating the theatre entrance on the first floor and the second by using as a stage the building constructed by Salas in Carrer d'Armanyà. Rather than aiming to build an Italian-style theatre, Jujol designed the Teatre Metropol as an open space to host the scientific and literary activities held at an *ateneu*. He used iron to create a sensation of lightness. The theatre hall is covered by three main beams with a span of 13 metres, spaced four metres apart and supported by three slender pillars, eight metres tall with a section of 26 centimetres. The result is a continuous space from the entrance to the garden at the rear. The passage built against the party wall also comprises a lightweight metal structure that supports seven small ribbed vaults.

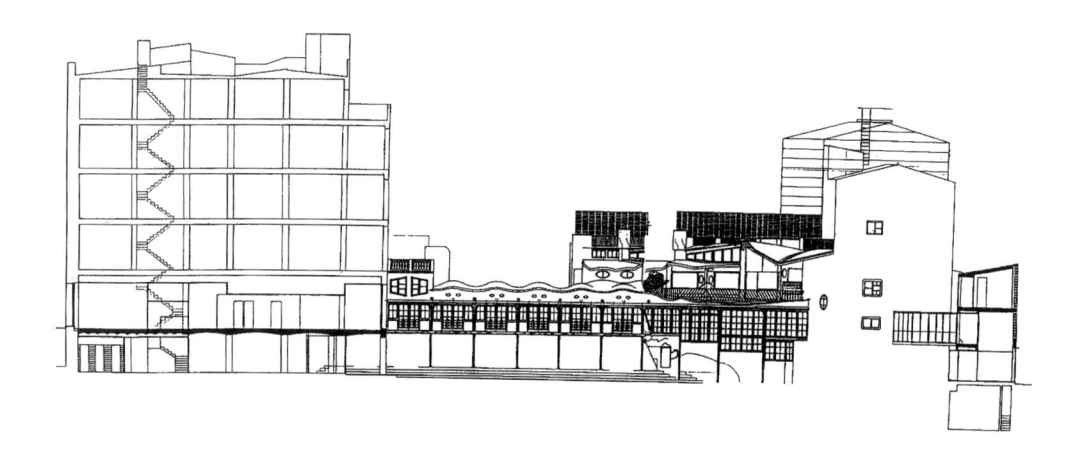

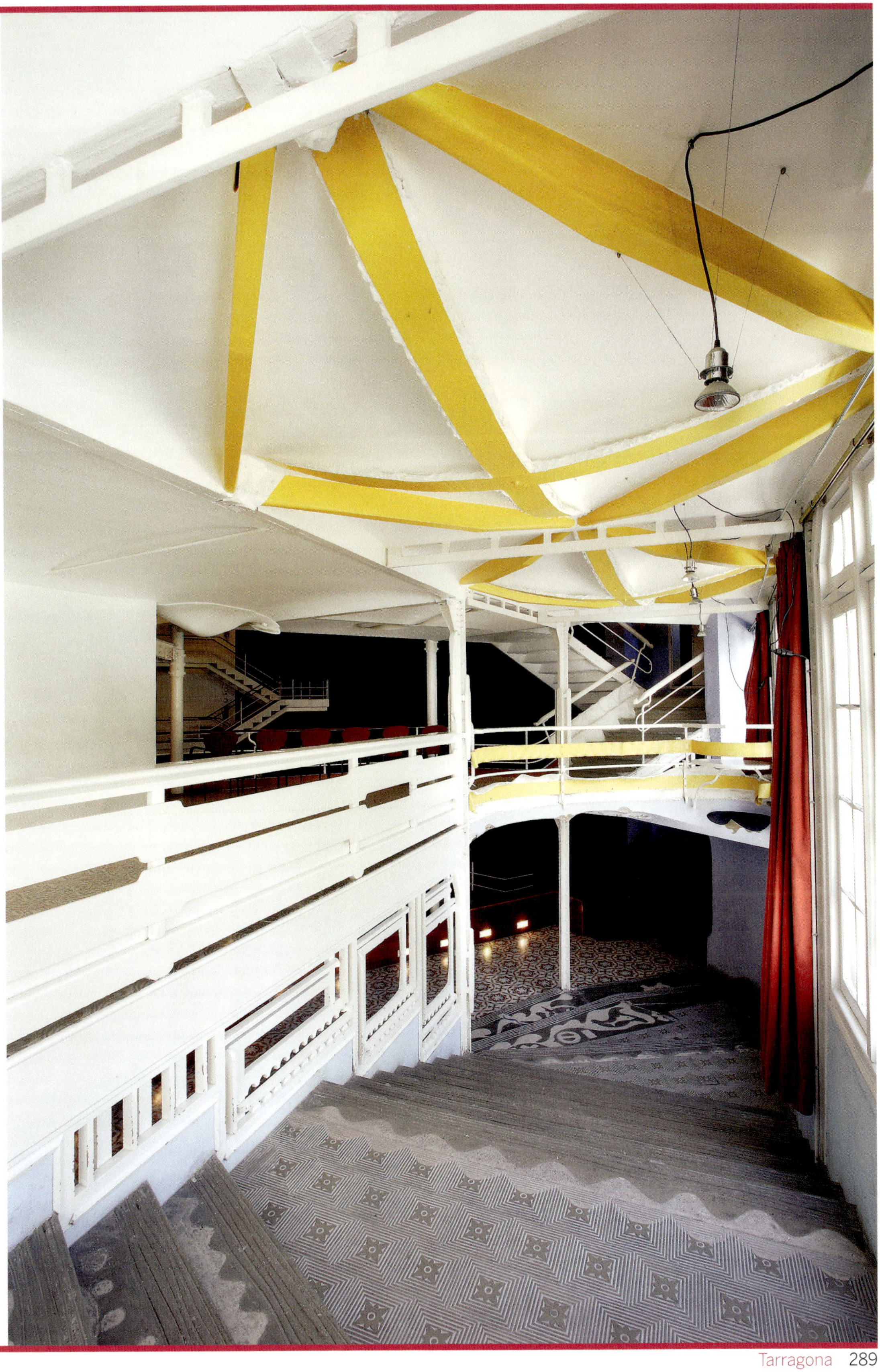

TGN

262

MUNICIPAL ABATTOIR
VICE-CHANCELLOR'S OFFICE, ROVIRA I VIRGILI UNIVERSITY

Josep Maria Pujol de Barberà
1895-1902

C/ Escorxador - Tarragona

263

TARRAGONA CENTRAL MARKET

Josep Maria Pujol de Barberà
1911-1915

Pl. Corsini - Tarragona

Tarragona's central market was originally built in an unoccupied area of its new town. It covers 2400 square metres and occupies a single floor. The central aisle is covered by a great fibre-cement vault. The corners and centres of the façades are highlighted by great openings that draw in daylight through the blinds. The structure, left bare on the inside, comprises wrought-iron columns and metal centring. Pujol de Barberà's design applies the creativeness that characterized the new trends of Modernisme, though also marked by the historicist restraint of his condition as restorer.

264

XIMENIS HOUSE
INSTITUTE OF INTERIOR DECORATORS AND DESIGNERS

Josep Maria Jujol
1914

Via Imperi Romà, 17 - Tarragona

SUBSEQUENT INTERVENTIONS:
Cinto Hom, Armand Fernández, 1989-1993. Restoration of the façade and rehabilitation of the penthouse floor.

The building is situated in the city's old town, beside the Roman wall. It comprises a main U-shaped volume with two side constructions of two floors. The structure combines bare brick masonry and rubblework, an austere formula that reflects the incipient trademark of Modernisme. Daylight is drawn into the building through vertical elongated windows protected by blinds. The building responds to a concept of civilian architecture that is characteristic of the origins of modernity, concentrating all the stylistic aspirations in the filigree patterns of bare brick that highlight the arches of the openings and the crown of the façades, giving the complex a marked relief.

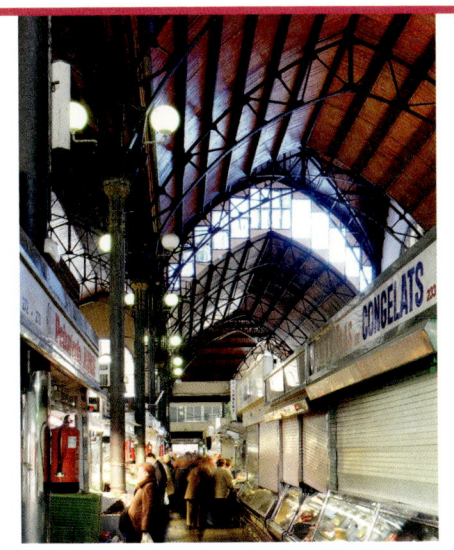

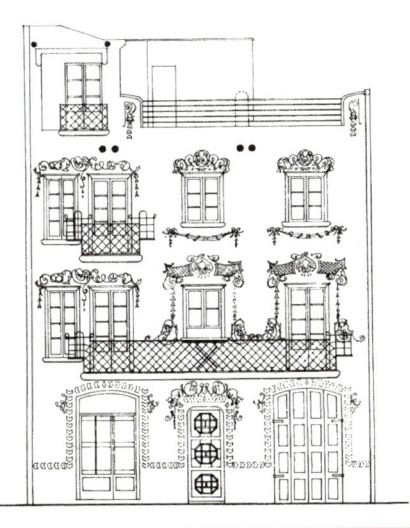

Ximenis House forms part of a row of buildings that extends the layout of a demolished stretch of the Roman wall, overlooking a large city park. Here, Jujol once again applied the effects of wrought-ironwork on plain and simple surfaces. The openings follow an irregular horizontal order, and the borders are rounded, decorated with sgraffiti of baroque inspiration. They are fronted by railings of black mesh which even forms little seats with backs at either end, projecting well-defined shadows onto the plane of the façade.

MALÉ HOUSE
REMODELLING OF TWO EXISTING HOUSES

Josep Maria Monravà
1930

Rambla Vella, 15 - C/ Portalet, 8 - Tarragona

This project approach finds its origins in the influence that the Archigram group had in the 1960s on members of the Taller d'Arquitectura. It sets out to mark a clear separation between the order of the circulations and the order of the dwellings, and to design a series of vertically rising cubes that connect with the network of circulations without structural constraints. The stairwells comprise brick bearing walls that extend to support half of each unit, while the other half rests on a metal pillar situated at a corner. Each cube contains a space—living-dining room or bathroom and bedroom—separated by a difference in level. The law of vertical growth follows the guidelines of a mathematical equation. The idea was to adapt the architecture to rather unconventional leisure activities, associated with a dramatic conception of the characteristic lifestyles of that decade.

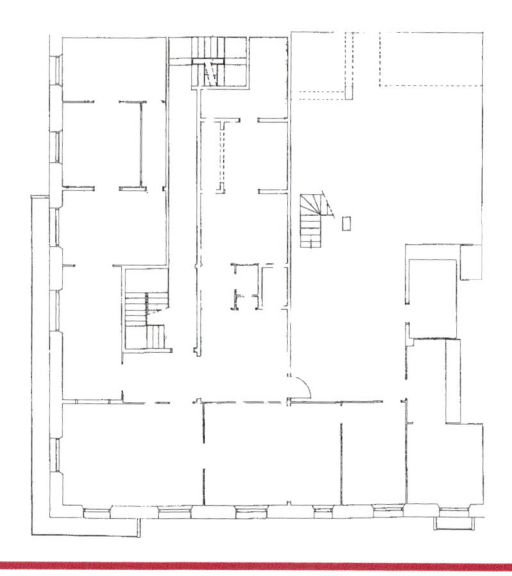

CASA BLOC APARTMENT BUILDING
DWELLINGS FOR REST AND JOY

Josep Maria Monravà
1940-1945

C/ Marquès de Guad-El-Jelú, 1-10 - Tarragona

This was a project for the Obra Sindical del Hogar, the institution responsible for social housing under the Francoist regime. It is a linear apartment block stretching from one street to the next, following an arc with its centre in the recently urbanized Plaça Imperial Tarraco. The building therefore determined the future urban growth of this sector along a radial layout. Monravà brought an austere approach to the construction and compositional rhetoric of rationalism in order to satisfy a programme based on low-cost construction. The block organizes a total of 74 apartments in twos, distributed on three floors, and the ground floor forms a large arcade that makes up the difference in level between the two streets. The living rooms project in galleries that mark a vertical cadence the entire length of the block, offset by the horizontal continuity of the balconies, skilfully interrupted on the two top floors.

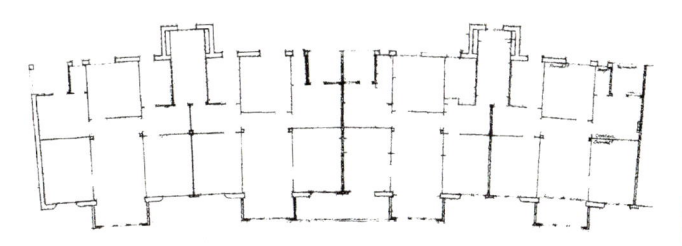

INSTITUT POLITÈCNIC
SCHOOL OF INDUSTRIAL PROFESSIONALS

Josep Maria Monravà
1931

Ptge. Soler i Morey - Tarragona

This building is an example of the best exponents of rationalism in the field of institutional architecture. Situated between the Casa Bloc apartment building and the future Civil Government headquarters, it interprets the radial layout of urban growth in a way that affects the overall organization of the building. It is a U-shaped organism in which all the rooms are laid out around the drawing hall. An intermediate bay accommodates the services and a series of four courtyards. The classrooms, in the façade, are reflected by long windows running the whole length of the building. Monravà highlighted the coherence between the distribution and the functionality of the programme.

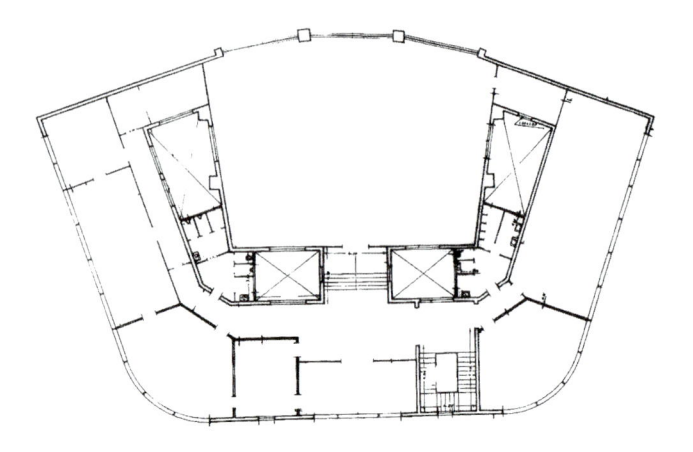

VERGE DEL CARME APARTMENT COMPLEX
2 HOUSING BLOCKS FOR THE INSTITUTO SOCIAL DE LA MARINA

Joan Zaragoza i Albí, José Antonio Coderch de Sentmenat
1949

C/ Salou, 6-12 - C/ Lepant, 1-7 - Tarragona

Coderch was called upon to modify a government project, thanks to his association with the Instituto Social de la Marina. His intervention consisted in a formal, functional, constructional simplification. The dwellings form two perfectly regular, curvilinear, parallel blocks, with each apartment extending between the two façades. The dividing bay runs lengthwise. One sector contains the living room and main bedroom; the other houses the other bedrooms, the kitchen and the stairs. Coderch introduced a slant into the dividing wall that separates the stairs from the kitchens, optimizing the functioning of the stairs and saving space in the kitchen. The blocks form completely flat façades, interrupted only by the openings, giving the slightly curved line of the whole its great expressivity.

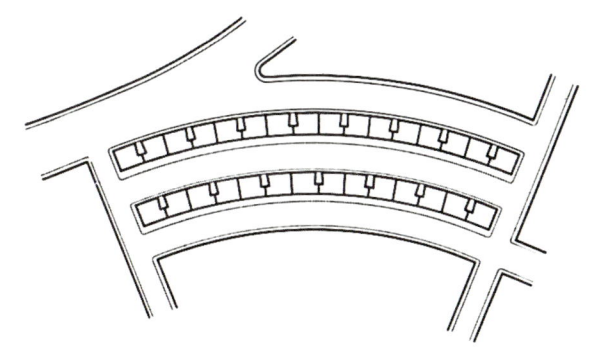

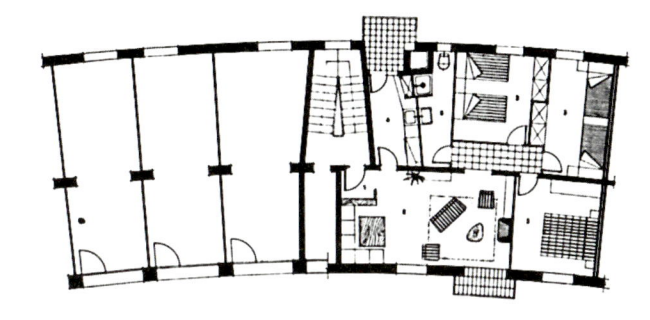

UNIVERSITAT LABORAL DE TARRAGONA / TARRAGONA LABOUR UNIVERSITY
EDUCATION COMPLEX

Antonio de la Vega, Manuel Sierra, Luis Peral
1952-1956

Salou expressway (C-31B)
Education Complex - Tarragona

The labour university project was the initiative of the then Minister of Labour, José Antonio Girón de Velasco, which aimed to "train, in addition to technically more able workers, men who were ready for anything, who were skilled in all the trials of intelligence, trained for the battles of the spirit...". The first was in Gijón, quickly followed by those in Seville and Tarragona. For the site of the latter, two properties were chosen, Mas de la Pineda and Mas de Palau, a total of 150 hectares situated three kilometres from Tarragona. The resulting construction is the product of the evolution of three proposals, based on the clear separation of functions within a general organization reminiscent of an urban enclave. The definitive version is divided into three parts, each commissioned to one of the three architects: the bedrooms and the dining hall joined by underground corridors, the lecture rooms and the workshops. This arrangement in distinct areas corresponded to the idea of spreading out the complex and obliging students to cover certain distances between their activities, as though they were in an urban location.

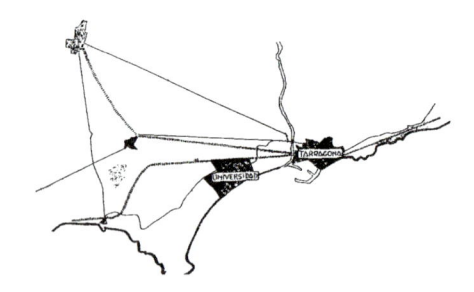

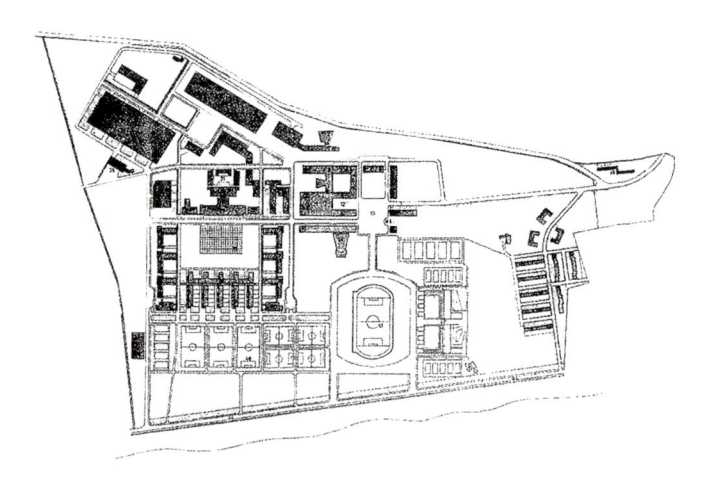

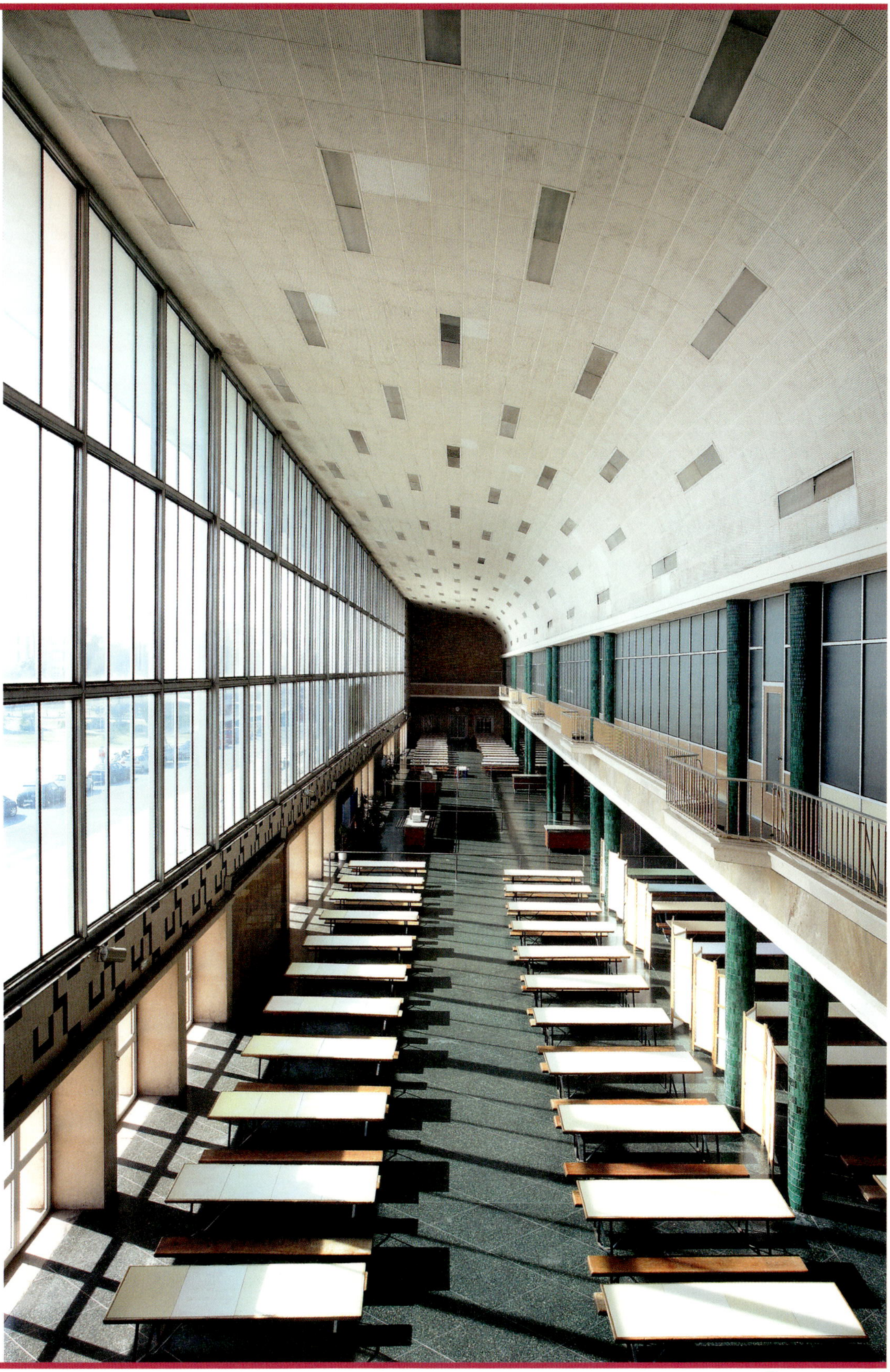

HEADQUARTERS OF THE CIVIL GOVERNMENT IN TARRAGONA
GOVERNMENT SUBOFFICE

Alejandro de la Sota
1954-1957

Pl. Imperial Tarraco, 3 - Tarragona

SUBSEQUENT INTERVENTIONS:
Alejandro de la Sota, Josep Llinàs, 1987. Restoration.

The project won a competition organized in 1956 by the Directorate General of Architecture. The solution proposed by De la Sota substantially modified the configuration of the buildings intended for administrative and representative functions, normally laid out over two floors. The building stands in a prime position, overlooking the Plaça Imperial Tarraco, with its back to the area of new urban growth defined by the construction of Casa Bloc housing apartment, by Josep Maria Monravà, and with the radius of the square as a basic geometry providing the guidelines for growth. The Civil Government building makes a clear distinction between the ground and first floors and the higher storeys. The project produces a reliable interpretation of the complex constraints of a highly atomized programme channelled by very limiting circulations. As many as three stairways emerge from the ground floor to offer three different itineraries. The upper volume presents three monumental balconies that employ a modern, euphemistic language to symbolize the three authorities: executive, legislative and judicial. The curve of the square is reflected in two subtle, insignificant points: the alignment of four pillars on the ground floor and the facing of the rear of the lower volume.

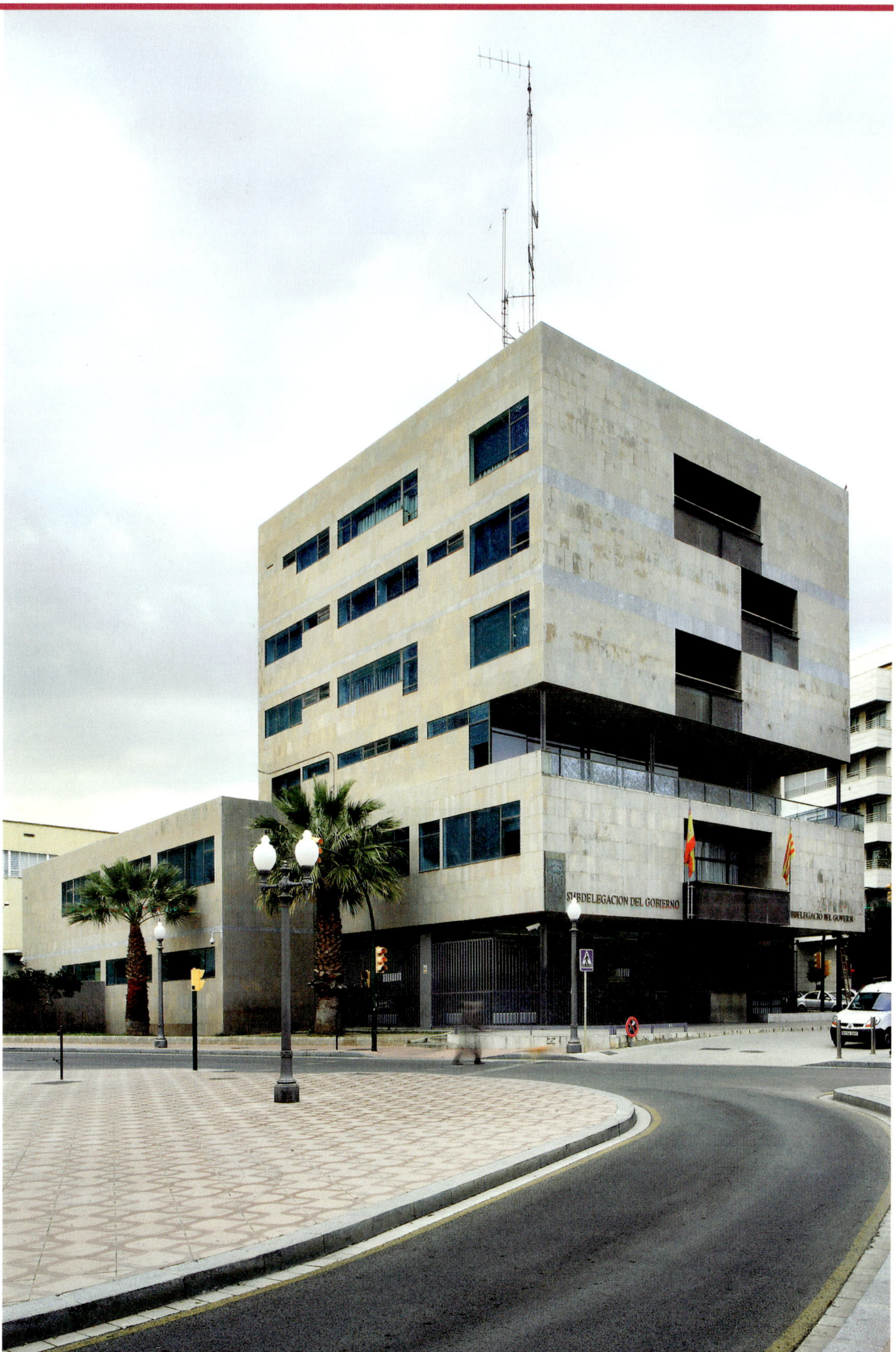

TGN

YXART HOUSE
COMPLEX OF 2 APARTMENT BLOCKS

Lluís Nadal, Vicenç Bonet, Pere Puigdefàbregas
1966-1969

Pg. de Sant Antoni, 16 - Tarragona

The initial proposal consisted of three apartment blocks with more or less square floor plans, of different heights and at different angles, which were to play an important role in completing the image of the city coastline as seen from a distance and various points. The two resulting blocks share a single entrance on Passeig de Sant Antoni, one halfway up and the other at roof level. The floor plan of the two blocks differs: the taller, to the west, has two dwellings per floor with a single inner courtyard on the north side. The other block has four south-facing dwellings, with a courtyard at the centre that serves all of them. The general implantation and the design of the elements at the small scale are designed to give continuity to a seafront image that retains its harmony thanks to the typological regularity and the variety of constructions that have comprised it over the years.

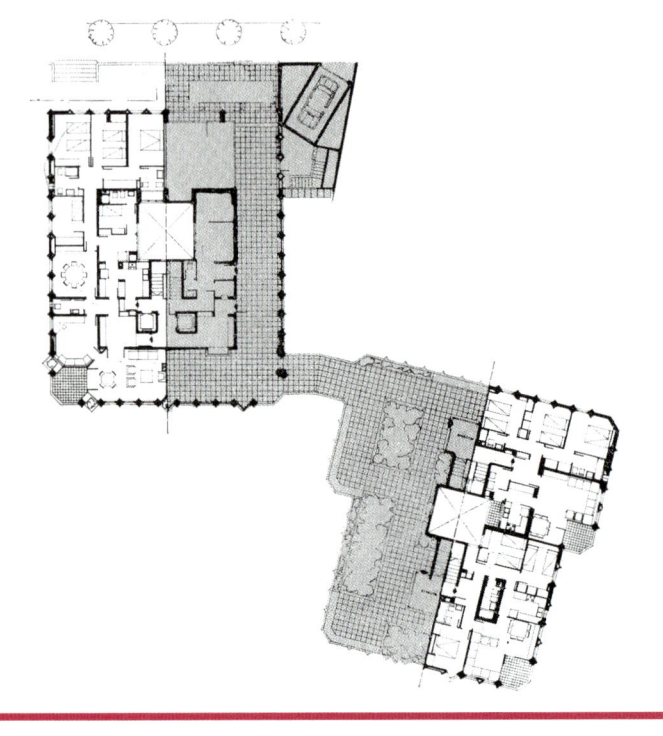

CAN GASSET
APARTMENT BUILDING

Jaume Bach, Gabriel Mora
1984-1987

C/ Santiyan, 7-9 - Tarragona

The building completes a street block occupied by a Neo-Classical townhouse, which it takes as a reference for its general layout. The new building respects the axis of symmetry of the old townhouse, with a single entrance at the centre leading into a courtyard to the rear that organizes interrelations and circulation. Built against the party wall of the old building is a low two-storey volume, containing two dwellings per floor, with direct access from the courtyard. The main block, separate from the townhouse, adopts a castle configuration with taller volumes at the corners. Entrance to the stairwells of the dwellings is via the courtyard. The living rooms and kitchens overlook the interior façade and highlight the importance of the courtyard to the interrelation of the entire building. The complex closes in the street block with the forceful reference of the monument on the other side of the party wall, which determines the strict regularity of the layout.

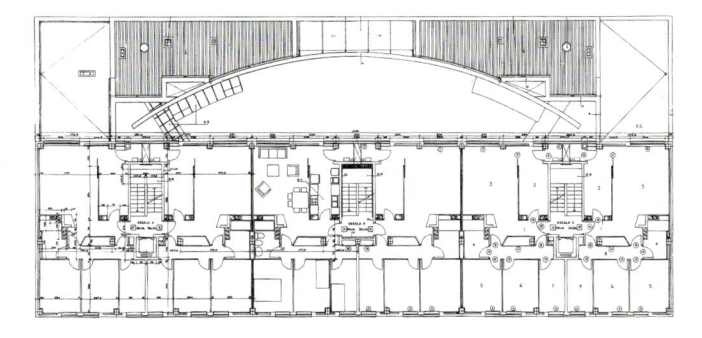

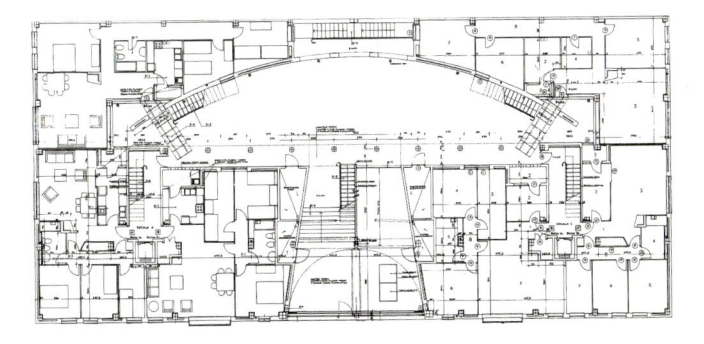

273

HEADQUARTERS OF THE TARRAGONA BRANCH OF THE COL·LEGI D'ARQUITECTES DE CATALUNYA · COAC

Rafael Moneo
1983-1992

C/ Sant Llorenç, 22 - Tarragona

274

NEW HEADQUARTERS OF THE REIAL CLUB NÀUTIC DE TARRAGONA
(TARRAGONA YACHT CLUB)

David Baena, Toni Casamor, Josep Maria Quera, Carles Casamor
1995-1997

Marina - Tarragona

The building stands on a platform in the port with its back to the city, between a seafront street and the open sea. The project takes as its reference the artificial nature of the location and proposes a volumetric layout that represents an altimetric modification of the base plane. The programme is distributed between the new pedestal and two cubic volumes seen as protuberances from the platform. The roof is an inverted U-shape, a bridge that envelopes all the constructions and adopts the representative function of the new building. The roof is displaced in relation to the built volume, generating a portal onto the avenue for pedestrians entering the club. A wooden terrace built against the rear façade acts as a bridge between the interior and exterior platforms. The original platform, the plinth, the built volumes and the roof form a system of superpositions that generates a new topography ready to accommodate the programme.

275

SANT SALVADOR SPORTS COMPLEX
SPORTS HALL AND CHANGING ROOMS OF THE ANNEXED SWIMMING POOL

Moisés Gallego, Pau Pérez, Anton Banús
1998-2002

C/ Estadium - Tarragona

The area in which the complex is set is a fragment of garden city, with single-family dwellings on small plots. The immediate surroundings comprise a large sports complex characterized by open spaces. The design of the hall responds to the difficulty of inserting a large parallelepiped volume without upsetting the existing balance. The building is drawn back from the line of the façade, seeking a similar implantation to that of the neighbouring houses. It is also sunk 3.30 metres into the ground, producing a semi-basement court. This minimizes the impact of this box on the landscape. The final height of the volume is little more than that of its neighbours. Two concrete walls enclose the shorter sides, and the metal trusses supporting the roof rest on the longer sides, which are glazed, with horizontal aluminium slats to filter the sun's rays.

The building is situated on a site that contains the remains of the structures of two old houses, Canon Canals house and the Archdeacon's house. Moneo chose to prioritize the programmatic and urban demands of the new institution, maintaining the street alignments and leaving a garden, through which admittance is gained, in front of the new building. As a result, the building was constructed over the remains of the Archdeacon's house, which determine the design and layout of the basement floor. The archaeological remains are thereby conserved and respected, being interpreted as living elements that participate in the design of the new building, providing its support and marking out the dimensions of the elements in the new programme.

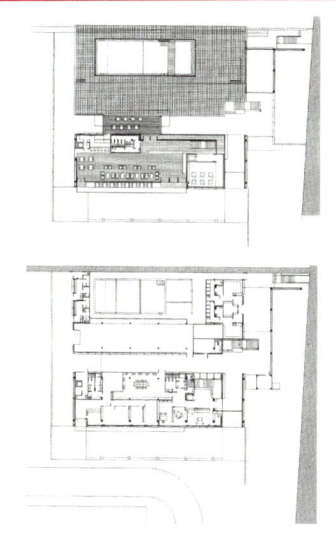

Tarragona

SCHOOL OF CHEMICAL ENGINEERING
ROVIRA I VIRGILI UNIVERSITY

Manuel Brullet, Alfonso de Luna
1997-2001

Av. Països Catalans, 26 - Sescelades campus
Rovira i Virgili University- Tarragona

The functional programme of a university faculty adapts perfectly to the arrangement of the general campus landscape and the considered balance between the private and the public sphere, the latter represented by a large central square. The new building largely determines the campus' new frontage on the city. This new university zone is organized around large built packets, responsible for the image of the streets and footpaths on campus. These large containers create different interiors for communal use, such as squares and courtyards of various sizes. These interior spaces generate the programme's organizational structure. The new buildings reproduce the typological bases of the constructions existing previously on campus and are laid out around the outer streets, leaving the central square free to be completed by the new library.

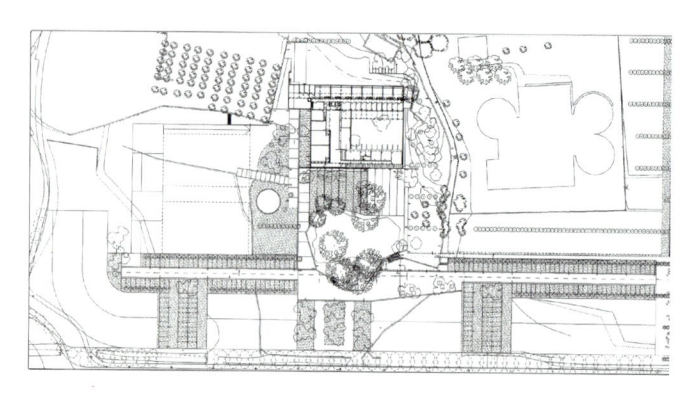

UNIVERSITY LIBRARY
ROVIRA I VIRGILI UNIVERSITY

José Antonio Martínez Lapeña, Elías Torres
1999-2003

Av. Països Catalans, 26 - Sescelades campus
Rovira i Virgili University- Tarragona

This building completes a block in the Sescelades campus which is already consolidated by the presence of existing faculties. To avoid creating a formal interference amid these pre-existing elements, it adopts the form of a small prism, entered on the intermediate level. This floor makes up the difference in levels between the different heights of the faces of the prism, with entrance via a stairway and a ramp that are the only elements situated outside the prism. The ramp starts in the street and is supported by L-shaped concrete elements. The stairway is protected by a concrete roof and emerges from the prism in a sculptural, representative role. The study and computer rooms occupy the foyer and lower levels, whereas the double-height reading room is situated on the upper floor. The bearing structure allows great flexibility in the distribution of uses.

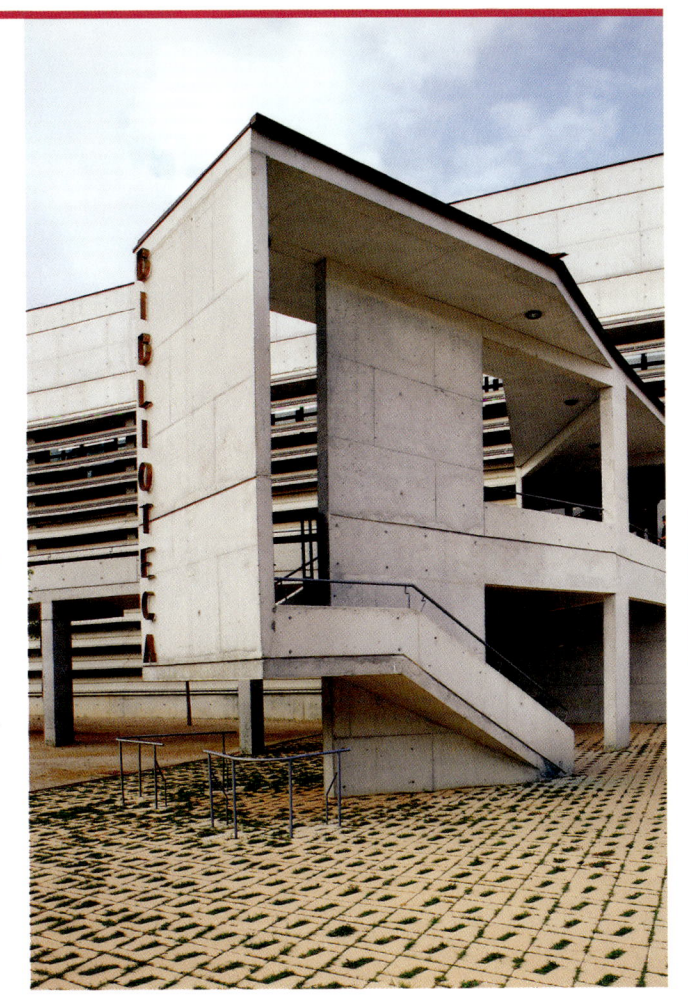

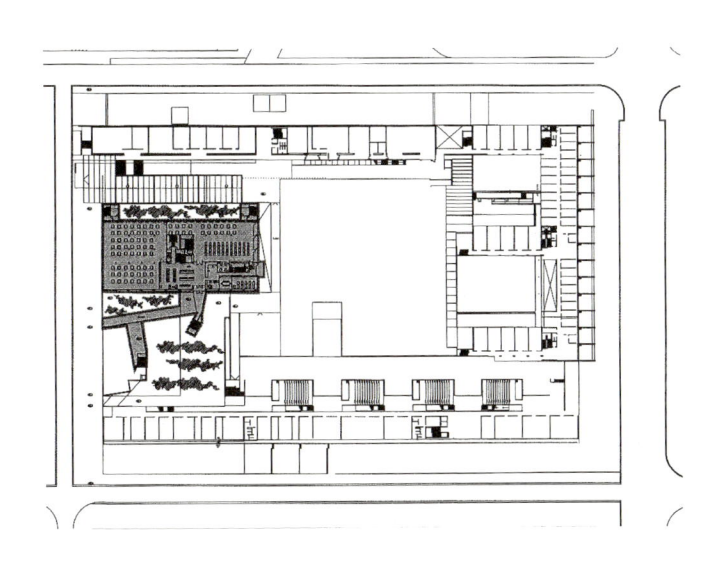

FERRÁNDIZ HOUSE
HOLIDAY HOME

Rafael de Cáceres
1970-1971

Camí de l'Ermita de Sant Antoni - Altafulla

This is a holiday home for a client who does not live in Catalonia. The house takes the form of two pavilions arranged parallel to either side of a courtyard, which acts as a hallway and an outdoor domestic space. One of the pavilions houses daytime activities and the other the bedrooms. The house picks up certain traditional elements of Mediterranean construction, such as the courtyard and terrace, though it is also based on a central axis, marked by the courtyard and the spillway of the lake. The construction procedures used are taken from local tradition and are conditioned by the contractor's inexperience.

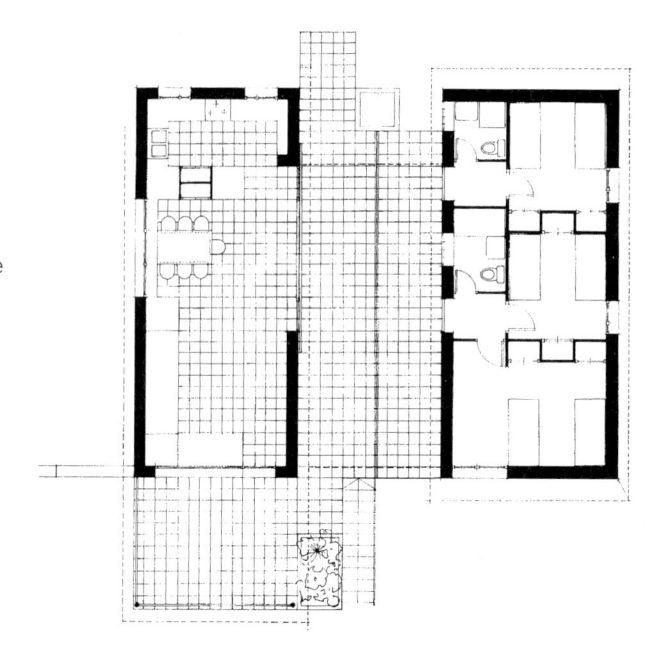

CEIP LA PORTALADA
INFANTS' AND PRIMARY SCHOOL

Pau Pérez, Jordi Bergadà
1987-1991

Pl. Portalada - Altafulla

The site, situated on the edge of the village of Altafulla, forms a triangle with one side overlooking the sea and the national trunk road along the coast. The school fills the plot of land and is laid out around three courtyards: the first is open to the south, with views of the sea from the classrooms. The second is a playground with a sports court and faces northwest. The third is a shady inner courtyard, full of plants, which provides ventilation and light for the central communal areas, offices and staff rooms. The school is built of concrete screen walls and slabs for the roof, which begins to slope and rise where it engages with the classrooms.

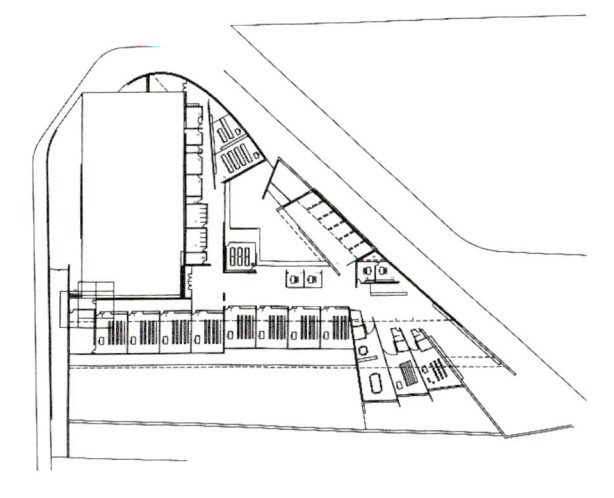

COMPLEX OF FOUR MOTELS

Josep Maria Sostres
1954-1957

C/ Aragó, 11 - Torredembarra

The whole is made up of four identical elements repeated in a staggered arrangement. This solution allows prime adaptation to the irregularity of the plot and offers more possibilities for the design of each dwelling. Each motel adopts a T-shape and adjoins its neighbour by means of the minimum surface area. The entrance is at the meeting point of the two arms of the T, where there is a stairway leading upstairs, rationalizing circulation. The volume housing the two children's bedrooms, positioned crosswise, covers a more retired porch, a place for outdoor activities. The arm leading towards the sea houses a first-floor study suspended over the living room. After his experience with Agustí House, here Sostres concerned himself with the economy of structure and materials, with order in the geometry and legibility of volumes and facings, with a view to generating a mass-produced housing model.

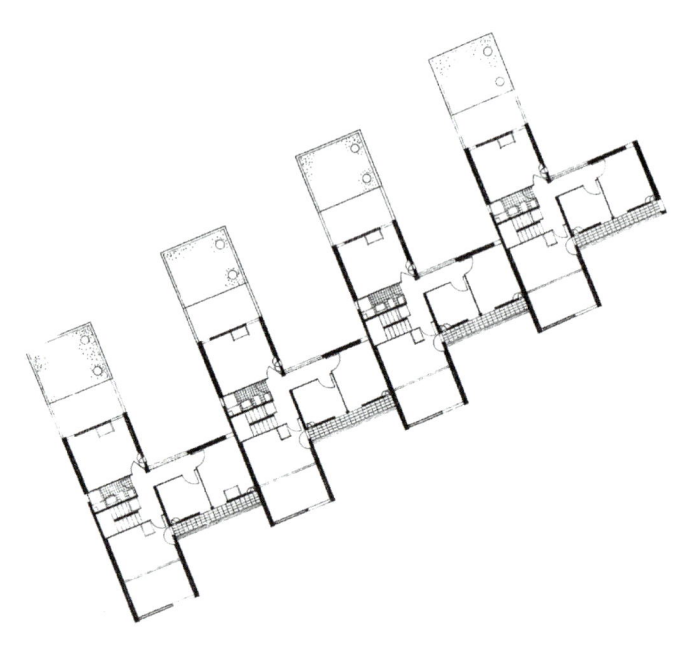

IES TORREDEMBARRA
SECONDARY SCHOOL

Josep Llinàs
1994-1995

Av. Sant Jordi, 62-64 - Torredembarra

The school stands atop a hill on the outskirts of the town, with good views in all directions. The building responds to these conditions and is designed as a foursquare volume around a large courtyard. This layout ensures a judicious relationship between the corridors and the classrooms. The school appropriates the qualities of its location, enclosing part of its surroundings in a courtyard, thereby gaining in ventilation and sunlighting. While the compactness of the volume distinguishes the school from the houses around it, a single-storey volume near the entrance prevents it appearing monolithic. The horizontal line of the building plays with the background of the sky, introducing a series of emerging and cut-out volumes around the top. The project makes good use of the coherence established here between the location and the proposed programme.

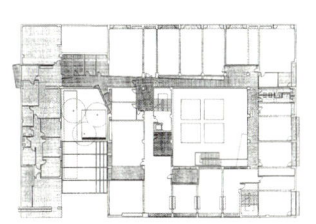

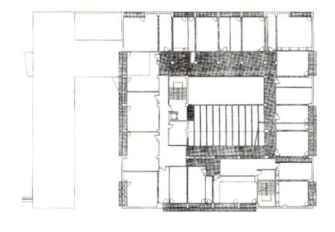

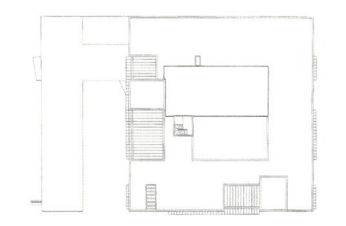

L'ESTEL DE MAR NURSERY
PRE-SCHOOL CENTRE

Manel Bailo, Rosa Rull
1998-2000

C/ Onze de Setembre, 4 - Creixell

The conception of the building and the design of the various elements respond to the specific condition of the centre's users: small children. It is a box suspended above the ground, directly related to the sandy ground beneath. Entrance is via a long ramp that penetrates inside the building and descends to the level of the garden with the sand bank, a second hollow inside the first. The openings occupy all the sides of the box and generate an isotropic notion of the space, in which the interior relates to all the elements in the natural surroundings, tending to remove traditional guidelines of orientation. The interior is experienced as a lightweight unitary space, in which the reference of the sky counterbalances that of the sandy ground. The interior is subdivided by means of cupboards associated with the faces of the container: the openings, the entrance, the plane of the ceiling, the earth.

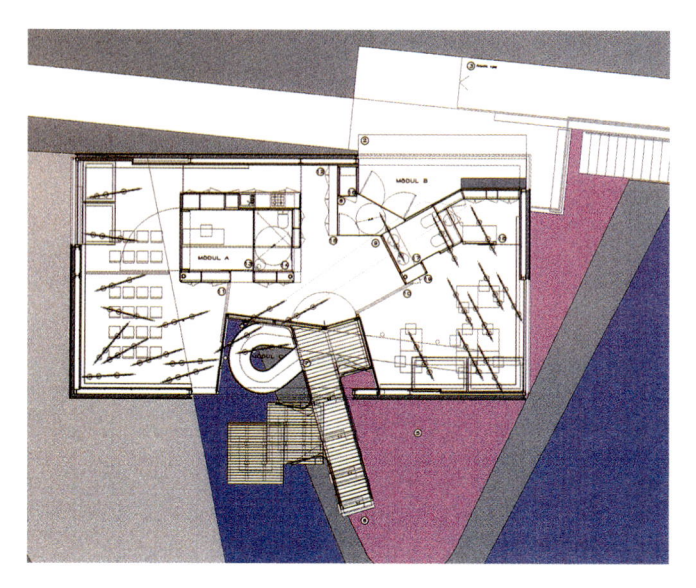

HORTAL HOUSE
SINGLE-FAMILY DWELLING

Vicente Guallart
2001-2003

C/ Santa Isabel, 72 - Nirvana 2 residential development
Coma-ruga (El Vendrell)

Situated on a steep site overlooking the sea, the house prioritizes a clear view of the horizon, to a distance of three kilometres. Its configuration is reminiscent of a periscope; the top floor emerges from the site in search of views of the Mediterranean. Different parts of the house offer a variety of images and materials, suggesting unfinished construction and modifying the imaginary of traditional domestic architecture. Entrance is from the street to the rear on the intermediate floor. From this point, the house rises, leaving the lower floor on a semibasement set into the hillside. The entrance floor contains the kitchen, dining room and living rooms, as well as the master bedroom. The upper floor comprises three bedrooms and a multiuse space, all communicated by a gallery. The façades seek out elements of their surroundings, responding differently on each front.

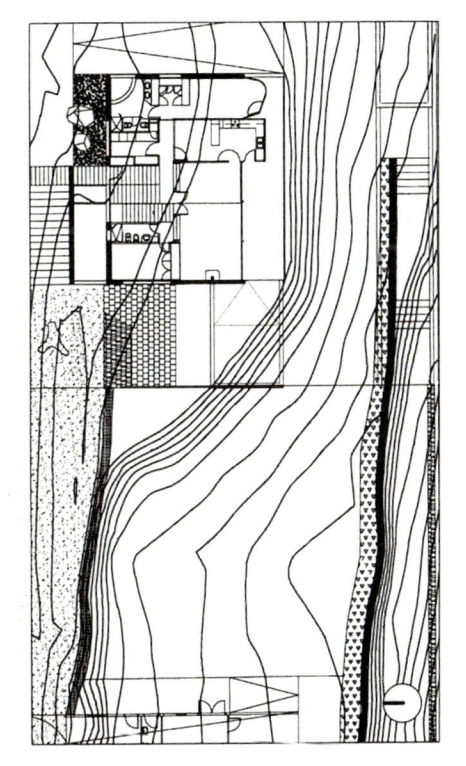

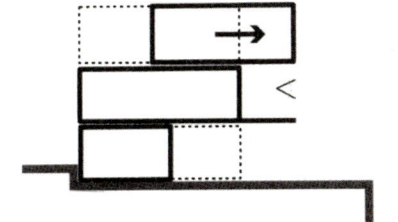

GARCIA HOUSE
SINGLE-FAMILY DWELLING

José Antonio Martínez Lapeña, Elías Torres
1968-1970

Av. de França, 27-29 - Segur de Calafell (Calafell)

Situated on a small, steeply sloping plot of land, the house adopts a formal configuration that is independent of the programme, subsequently adapting to it by means of a series of irregularities that depart from the original approach. A central linear stairway, with runs of just a few steps, ascends the slope and stops at three foyers that lead into the rooms to either side. At the start, two parking spaces form a perfectly symmetrical volume; the first foyer leads into the south-facing living room and the kitchen opposite. The second stopping place leads to the sleeping area, with four symmetrically arranged bedrooms, two to either side, separated by bathrooms. The volume of the bedrooms forms a compact box, though its windows, which open above the rooms below, break with the symmetry in search of a south-facing orientation.

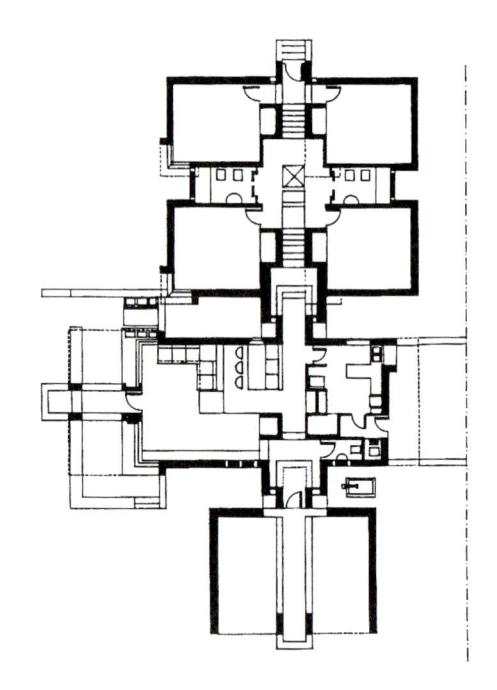

IES L'ARBOÇ
SECONDARY SCHOOL

Emili Donato, Miguel Jiménez
1993-2000

C/ Pompeu Fabra - L'Arboç

L'Arboç is a small municipality in El Penedès, situated on a hillside surrounded by almond and olive trees and vines, near a valley through which the Via Augusta Roman road passed. The village has some late 19th-century residences, as well as pre-Roman and medieval ruins. Donato picked up the monumental theme of the village when designing this school building. Situated to the north of the village on undeveloped land, the building stands on the northern side of the plot, beside the railway line. The playground, on the village side, soon acquired the quality of a public square. The school organizes all of its spaces around a large central area with a great skylight running lengthwise above it, giving the hallway a marked sacrality. The building looks rather like a civic cathedral, both in its typological layout and its presence in the place.

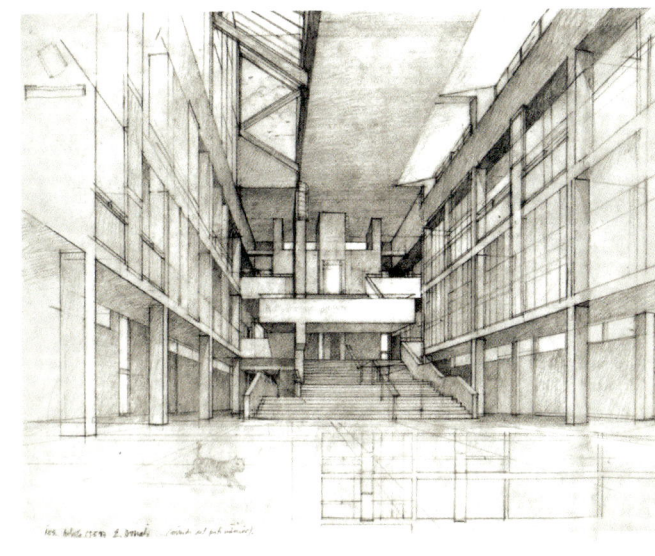

OFFICE AND APARTMENT BUILDING

Josep Llinàs
1988-1990

Av. Tarragona, 35 - Vilafranca del Penedès

The building responds to a series of highly specific conditions of location and programme. It is a long, narrow plot of land that presents an exaggeratedly vertical façade onto a large avenue, with another, more intensely occupied façade overlooking a long, narrow crossroad. The programme required two floors of offices for the owner's use, and a duplex apartment on the top two floors. The entire building was encompassed beneath a semicircular roof in order to reduce the verticality of the façade onto Avinguda Tarragona. The façade on the narrow street adopts the role of main frontage and relates to the building opposite by means of the replica of three small balconies on the fourth floor. The windows on the bias at the corner organize the meeting of the two façades. The building adopts its form by breaking down the pre-existing conditions, then recomposing itself as a unitary volume in keeping with everyday experience of the place.

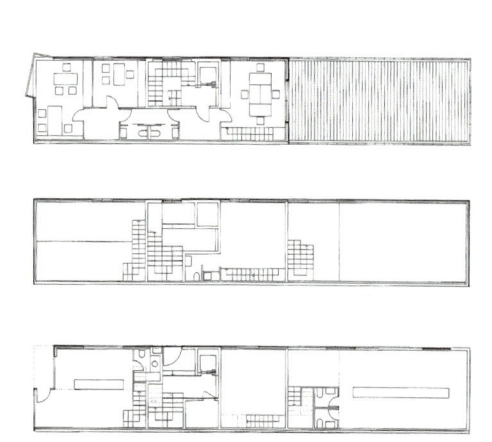

287

COVERED SPORTS COURT

Esteve Aymerich, Ton Salvadó
1995-1997

Sport facilities - Vilafranca del Penedès

The project responds to the need for a covered sports court beside an existing sports centre. The structure consists of a single bar that rises from the ground, curves to form the roof, rests on the old building and projects above it. The surface of the new roof consists of galvanized sheet supported by circular-section tubes. In this way, despite not touching the ground, the roof provides the function of a façade, folding and forming a channel to collect rainwater that drains into a gravel container. The order of the supports in the new roof breaks away from those of the existing pavilion, establishing a line of displacement that highlights the new construction's independence. The final solution provides transparency of lines of sight at ground level, at the same time recreating the atmosphere of an indoor court.

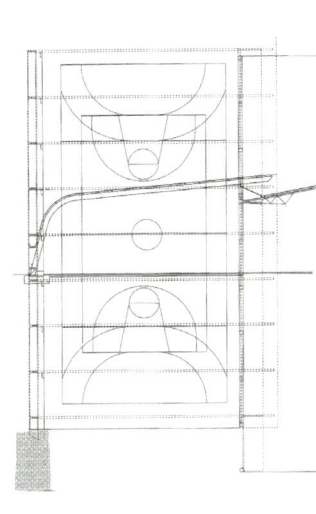

CODORNIU WINERY
WINE CELLAR, PORCH FOR PRESSES AND DISPATCH PAVILION

Josep Puig i Cadafalch
1904

Av. Codorniu - Sant Sadurní d'Anoia

The complex is an austere fabric of industrial constructions where Puig i Cadafalch set out to prove the relevance of the construction procedures of the past to modern needs and programmes. The large cellar employs semicircular arches with six brick courses, supporting segmental vaults that reach to the façade, combined with slightly pointed arches. The dispatch pavilion is based on a large inverted catenary built solely of brick, subjected by brick structural elements and stone facing. Puig i Cadafalch used the forms created by the support elements to compose the side and end façades in such a way that they would express this support, at the same time introducing other strictly ornamental elements, such as the fretted outline of the openings, the brick lattices, the series of buttresses and the stone pinnacles.

RAVENTÓS BLANC WINERY

Jaume Bach, Gabriel Mora
1985-1988

Pl. del Roure - Sant Sadurní d'Anoia

The new complex for the production of cava is situated on a large estate, opposite the old Codorniu cellars designed by Josep Puig i Cadafalch. The project seeks out views of the mountain of Montserrat and the presence of a hundred-year-old oak tree, the symbol of the firm. The complex is laid out around two courtyards, one circular and the other rectangular, which together form a floor plan shaped like a sickle, the tool used in farming work. The circular courtyard leads into the corporate buildings, and the other is the hub of the wine-production business, with the cellars and offices organized around it. The cellars are roofed by a system of tied dihedra allowing the uniform entry of light, reminiscent of turn-of-the-century industrial roofing systems. The roofs are covered with flat tiles, and the projections are clad with stoneware.

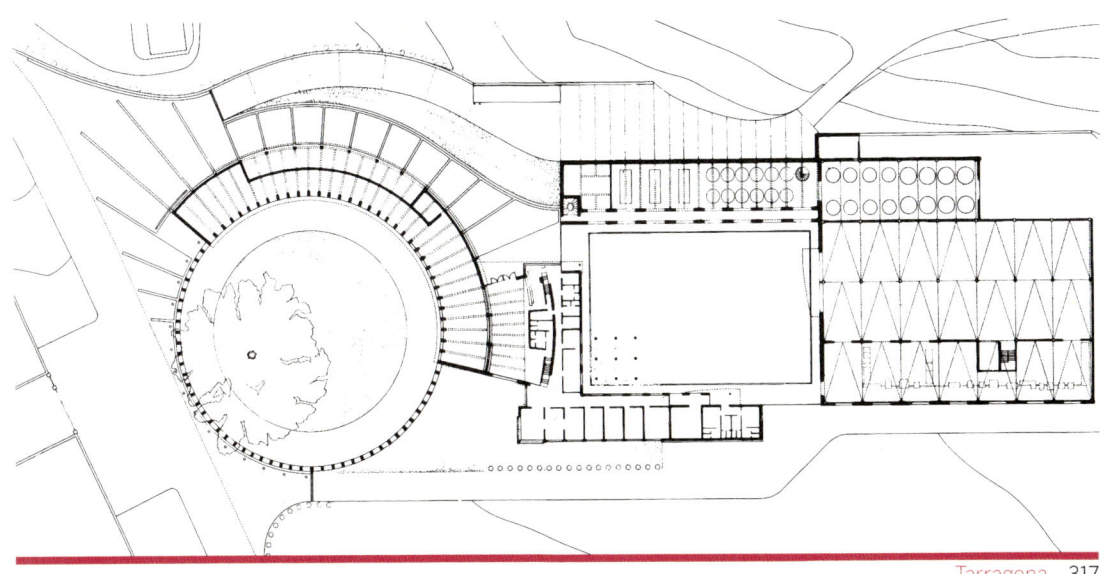

MAS BOFARULL
REMODELLING AND EXTENSION OF AN OLD FARMHOUSE

Josep Maria Jujol
1914-1931

C/ Barcelona, 11-13 - Els Pallaresos

The work on Mas Bofarull marked the start of a series of interventions by Jujol in the small village of Els Pallaresos, including Fortuny House (or Ca l'Andreu), between 1920 and 1944. The Bofarull sisters contracted Jujol to give the old farmhouse "an air of distinction", a common request at the time, when many Modernista architects were involved in similar commissions. Jujol carried out two main structural interventions: the extension of the main staircase as far as the pyramidal tower, presided over by a weathervane in the form of an angel, whose face was created from the mask of a human face, and the addition of a bay at the front of the house to create a gallery of ribbed arches supported by a large segmental arch on the ground floor. The numerous details included had the effect of indefinitely extending the intervention, which was never officially completed.

CHURCH OF SANT BARTOMEU IN VISTABELLA

Josep Maria Jujol
1918-1924

Pl. de Josep Gaspé i Blanc - Vistabella
(La Secuita)

Vistabella was originally a three-house hamlet that gradually grew as a result of vine-growing and stock-keeping activities. By the start of the 20th century, it was equipped with a school, and when the moment came to build a church, it was commissioned to Josep Maria Jujol. In order to explain the project, Jujol used the reference of Byzantine Christian architecture. The church comprises a square supported by four pillars, the springs for all the arches that form the terraced rise of vaults. The projections of the arches form square and triangular figures, and the groins of the vaults are smooth surfaces, providing an ideal space for mural paintings. The structure is built using solid pieces of dressed local limestone with the predominance of two dimensions, laid in similar fashion to brick courses. The church has a double roof: the interior layer comprises vaults and the exterior covering is built of layers of tiles.

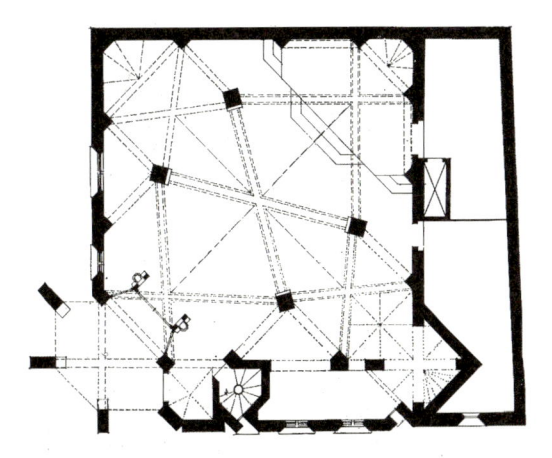

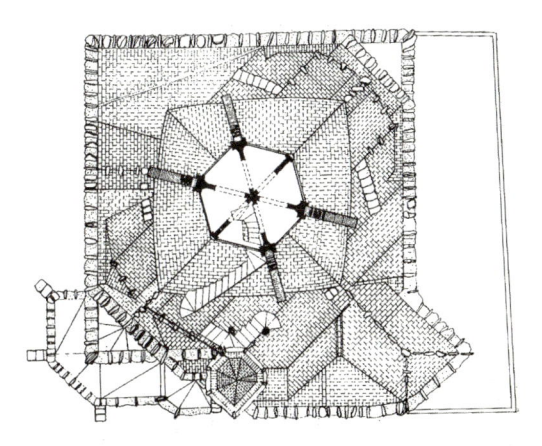

COOPERATIVE CELLAR OF THE SINDICAT AGRÍCOLA DE SANT ISIDRE

Cèsar Martinell
1918-1919

C/ Estació - Nulles

The interruptions in the construction of the cellar in Rocafort de Queralt convinced Martinell of the need to use only local materials and procedures. On the basis of the Rocafort project, however, the Sant Isidre Farmers' Cooperative commissioned him to design a cellar with capacity for 13,000 hectolitres. Martinell sought to comply by using the same constructional practice: the result was a double warehouse measuring 21 x 28 metres, constructed in a single process, though without the dividing wall adopted in Rocafort, where the first two warehouses had been built at different times. The Nulles project has a more open-plan interior, allowing greater ease of movement above the vats. The vats are laid out in four rows: two central rows, each of six vats, and two side rows of seven vats, separated from the others by wide passages.

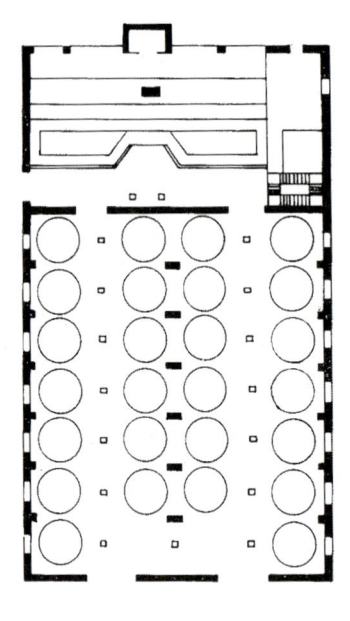

SANCTUARY OF THE BLESSED VIRGIN OF MONTSERRAT

Josep Maria Jujol
1926-1930

Camí del Correlot - Montferri

SUBSEQUENT INTERVENTIONS:
Bassegoda, Jané, Tomlow, 1999. Restoration of the original work and finishing of the building.

This is a project to construct a sanctuary to the Blessed Virgin of Montserrat using limited economic, technical and human resources. Jujol decided to use local stone, Portland cement and sand to construct, on site, prefabricated elements for both the structure and the great windows. The arches, walls and vaults were built using units measuring 10 x 15 x 30 centimetres and rubblework. The windows were constructed using prefabricated units put together on site and designed by Jujol himself to form hexagonal figures when put together. The general structure comprises a series of parabolic arches that spring from very slight pillars. The general system is based on a triangulated floor plan that forms a perimeter divided into 24 segments of different sizes. In total there are 42 pillars, topped by 33 vaults that are a reference to the forms of the mountain of Montserrat.

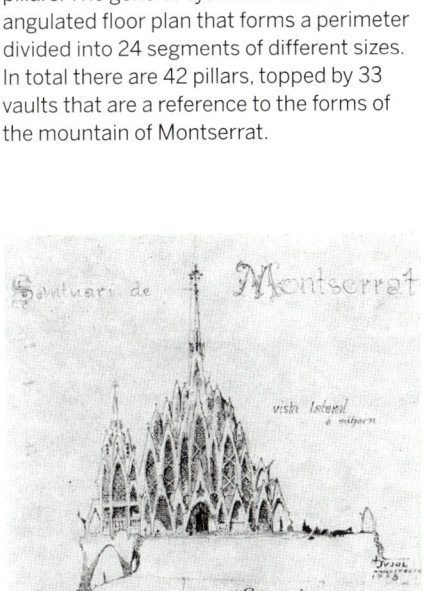

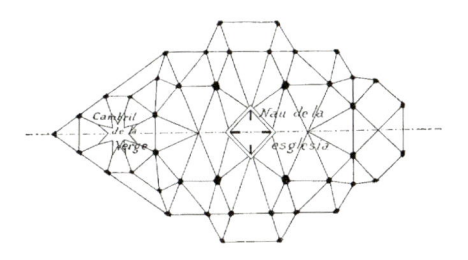

NAVÀS HOUSE
SINGLE-FAMILY DWELLING

Lluís Domènech i Montaner
1901-1907

Pl. del Mercadal, 7 - Reus

The house was commissioned by Joaquim Navàs, an important fabric merchant who was also a founder member of the company that developed the Pere Mata Institute. Navàs wanted a highly representative building to house his business and residence. The house stands on a square, on the corner with a narrow street, which allowed Domènech to play with the corner solution. The ground floor establishes continuity with the arches around the square, which do not continue into the side street. The column at the corner generates an ascending composition that culminates in a slender tower on the roof that was destroyed by bombing in 1938.

Tarragona

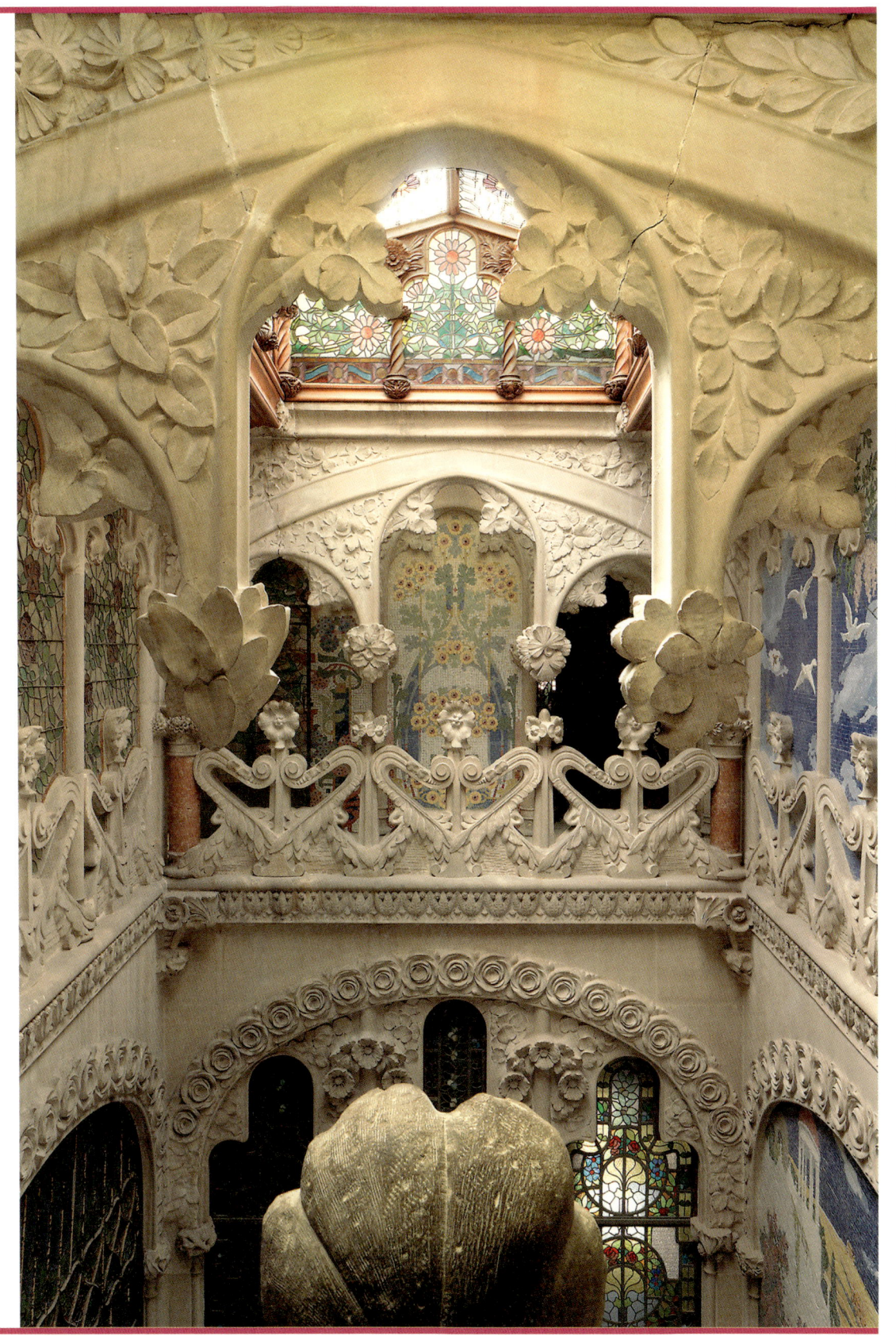

RULL HOUSE
SINGLE-FAMILY DWELLING

Lluís Domènech i Montaner
1900-1901

C/ Sant Joan, 27 - Reus

This was Domènech i Montaner's first project in Reus after undertaking work on the Pere Mata Institute. The house is a box that is profusely organized in three façades: one virtually symmetrical with the exception of the corner column and the balcony on the *piano nobile*, overlooking the street; the rear façade that generates a regular symmetry based on different elements, and the balcony that has become a light iron railing, with supports that link up with the openings on the ground floor. The use of architectural elements to organize the volumes is a clear precedent of the compositional procedures of modern architecture.

GASULL HOUSE
APARTMENT BUILDING

Lluís Domènech i Montaner
1911-1912

C/ Sant Joan, 29 - Reus

Domènech i Montaner designed Gasull House ten years later than Rull House, when the more radical sensibility of Modernisme had given way to the refined, austere tastes of the new trend of Noucentisme. Domènech had to combine a residential building covering 882 square metres, housing 8-metre high apartments, with the 1000 square metres of the olive oil and dried fruit warehouse connecting two streets, Carrer de Sant Elies and Carrer de Sardà i Cailà. Gasull House retains certain reminiscences of the greater capriciousness of Modernisme in the sgraffiti and mosaics deployed in its decoration, though the general lines tend more to the classical, devoid of floral motifs, stained glass and carved stone.

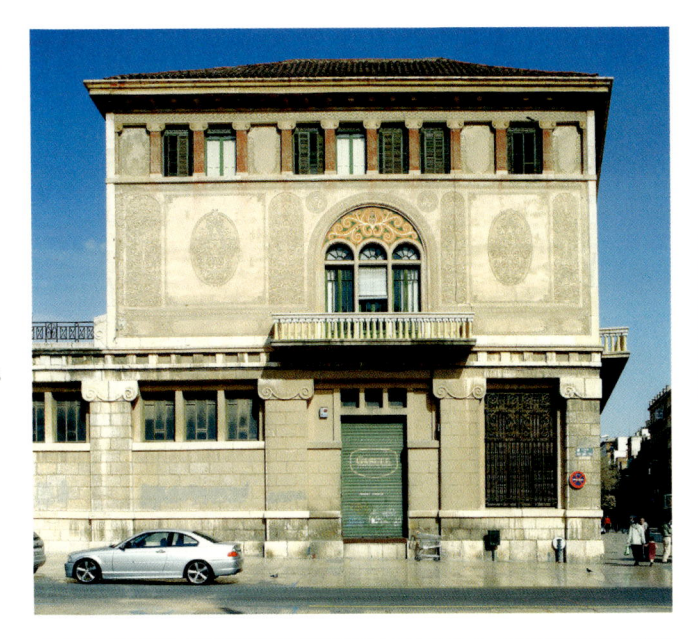

PERE MATA INSTITUTE
PSYCHIATRIC SANATORIUM

Lluís Domènech i Montaner
1897-1919

Ctra. de l'Institut Pere Mata, 1 - Reus

SUBSEQUENT INTERVENTIONS:
Pere Benavent de Barberà, 1950s, pavilions
Jaume Argilaga, 1970s, pavilions
Joan Figuerola, 1993, rehabilitation

The Pere Mata Institute was the result of an initiative to adapt health care for the mentally ill to the new therapeutic procedures emerging at the time. Domènech i Montaner came into contact with the Reus Mental Institution Society in the person of its president, Pau Font de Rubinat, a fellow member of the Unió Catalanista. In the Institute, Domènech essayed the criteria of hospital architecture that he was to develop a few years later in the Hospital de la Santa Creu i Sant Pau in Barcelona. He proposed a system of pavilions laid out in a large garden, so that each pavilion could house various patients according to the type of illness, social class or sex. All the pavilions are built of bare brick with polygonal stone bases, and all the roofs are ridge roofs with channel tiles. The door and window openings are framed with roughly dressed limestone. In some cases, blue and white ceramic is used to decorate the façades. There are 11 pavilions arranged around a central pavilion with more abundant decoration, which houses the general services. Domènech based his project on detailed knowledge of therapeutic praxis and the patients' needs.

Tarragona 327

298

LAGUNA HOUSE
APARTMENT BUILDING

Pere Caselles i Tarrats
1904

C/ Monterols, 15 - Reus

299

GRAU HOUSE
APARTMENT BUILDING

Pere Caselles i Tarrats
1910-1911

C/ Sant Joan, 32 - Reus

Caselles organized the façade of Grau House according to the symmetrical arrangement of openings, two on each floor and one round window at the centre of the top floor. The framing of the windows combines the geometry of the circle with the straight lines of the doorjambs. These borders concentrate the ornamental intensity, with plant motifs such as laurel leaves, an allusion to the name of the builder's owner, Baron Llorach. The framed stretch of wall in the façade is stuccoed to imitate stone masonry, whereas the ground floor is built entirely of natural stone.

300

SERRA VILLA
REMODELLING AND EXTENSION
OF AN OLD DWELLING

Joan Rubió i Bellver
1911

Road to Castellvell (TP-7049), 20 - Reus

The building's scant width allowed Caselles to intensify the combination of ceramic tiles and employ a whole range of ornamental techniques. The first and second floor façades comprise bare masonry up as far as the impost, above a ground-floor level of turquoise glazed ceramic. The brickwork is topped by a surface of *trencadís*, and the third floor façade is clad with profusely decorated ceramic tiles. The windows are different on each level and are set in stone frames that mark out the various ornamental fields and finish at roof level in four pinnacles supporting a railing of twisted bars.

The building is the result of extending a dwelling built a few years previously by an English wine merchant. The features remaining from the original are the tower-mirador and the front-most volume of the building, to which Rubió added the rear volume. The façades of the added volume combine the use of bare brick with polygonal fields of stone masonry. The roof of the dining room, also designed by Rubió, rests on four subarches that spring from four marble columns. The corners formed by the union of the arches produce a grouping of three vaults, a pattern that is repeated three times to fill the domed space.

Tarragona 329

HOUSE FOR DOCTOR DOMÈNECH
SINGLE-FAMILY DWELLING
AND DOCTOR'S SURGERY

Josep Simó i Bofarull
1930

C/ Frederic Soler, 55 - Reus

The house is both a surgery and home to a Reus doctor, a defender of hygienist ideas and sport. It stands in a garden city that Doctor Domènech himself promoted in the area around the Reus Esportiu sports centre. The project for the house was commissioned to his friend Josep Simó as an architect specializing in health issues who qualified in Paris. Each area of the house corresponds to a specific volume and height, the tallest of which accommodates the stairway. Despite their different heights, the walk-on roofs generate an interplay of itineraries. The surfaces of the façade combine rendering, bare brick and recesses, and each of the volumes is crowned by an order of perpendicular bricks. Simó combined a great sense of movement with the possibilities of a purist approach to the interplay of volumes. The house was remodelling in the years following the Civil War by the Reus architect Antoni Sardà.

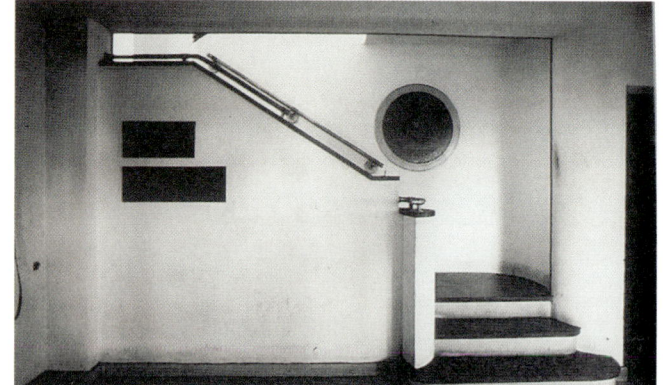

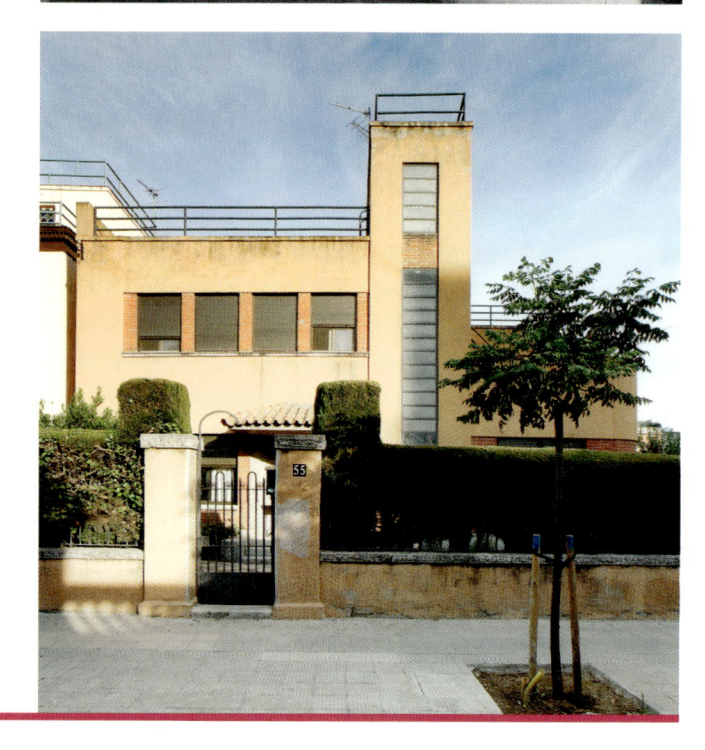

HIPÒLIT MONTSENY HOUSE
APARTMENT BUILDING

Antoni Sardà i Moltó
1934-1935

C/ Colom, 1 - Reus

Sardà designed several apartment buildings in the new town extension of Reus, applying different variations to the corner solution that was so highly prized by rationalist architects. Hipòlit Montseny house has just one apartment per floor, with a distribution denoting hierarchies of domestic spaces that are highly innovative in many respects. The living room, in the cylinder on the corner, is designed to include a great dining room. The gallery is adopted as the prime façade solution for the two master bedrooms, while the remaining bedrooms are somewhat deficient in terms of surface area and ventilation. Particular value is attached to the study: the house has two, one with a balcony of its own that defines the narrow façade. The windows are divided into shuttered lights and are protected by roller blinds. The building's crown comprises the only ceramic element visible in the façade, a course of bricks laid perpendicular.

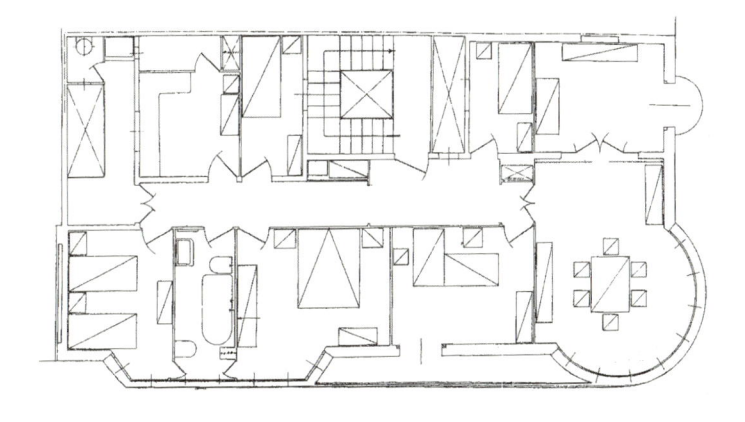

REUS CENTRAL MARKET

Antoni Sardà i Moltó
1934-1949

C/ Josep Sardà i Cailà - Reus

Sardà designed the first project for the Mercat Central in 1934, when he was Reus municipal architect, but the existing building responds to a project dated 1943 and was constructed in 1949. The market obeys the typology of a basilical configuration, a large central space with two lower side aisles supported by piers and metal soffits. The symmetrical arrangement of the market is reflected in the exterior by a purist interplay of volumes that seeks to downplay the building's large dimensions. The volumes at the corners are lower than the main façade, but taller than the sides. The central façade is withdrawn and floats above the shadow of the entrance, adopting a cadence of four long vertical openings. Sardà employed the technique of stepped volumes to give the building a more complex image and a monumental presence.

GAUDÍ DISTRICT
SOCIAL HOUSING COMPLEX

Ricard Bofill
1964-1968

Av. Comerç - Av. Saragossa - Pg. de la Boca de la Mina - Reus

The project was designed in response to a council commission to build a social housing complex on the outskirts of Reus. Bofill presents a positive interpretation of the communal life of this small industrial locality, reproducing in this new district an amalgam of shops, supermarkets, bars, leisure amenities and housing. The district is made up of eight-floor blocks, the result of combining a limited number of two-, three- and four-bedroom apartments. The combination of the different types of dwellings produces a variety of floor plans, all giving onto four façades, sometimes juxtaposing two towers in a single block and sometimes with a variation in height between floors. All the blocks are joined by four levels of passages that allow horizontal movement without having to descend to street level. The success of the development led to the design of the second and third phases.

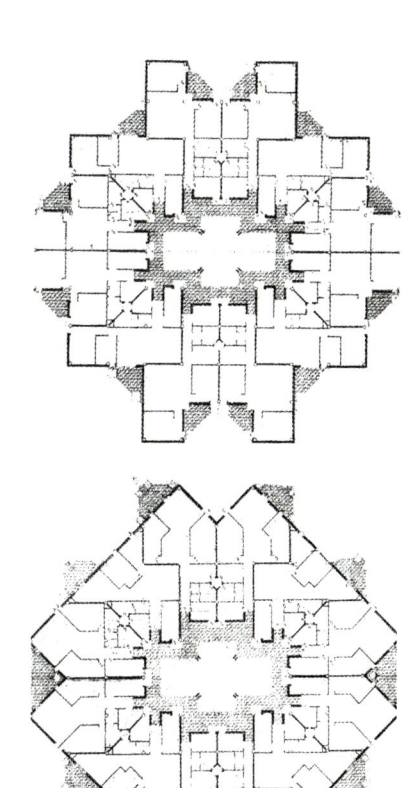

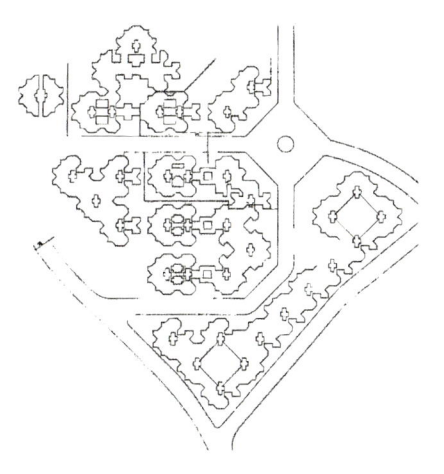

FACULTY OF ECONOMICS AND BUSINESS STUDIES
ROVIRA I VIRGILI UNIVERSITY

Pau Pérez, Anton Pàmies, Anton Banús
1994-1996

Av. Universitat, 1 - Bellisens campus
Rovira i Virgili University - Reus

The building stands on a rectangular platform on which are arranged the different volumes, of varying depths and heights, in accordance with the requirements of the various parts of the programme. Arranged on the platform are two volumes, one for lecture rooms and the other for seminar rooms. The floor plan is divided into three large bays, each with a different height and use. The central, lowest bay houses the library and the auditorium, with a span of 18 metres. The volume on the east side contains the lecture rooms, with a span of 10 metres. The façade of this volume is withdrawn due to a variation in the dimensions of the lecture rooms. The volume to the west houses the seminar rooms, with a span of six metres. The passage around the centrally positioned library leads to four stairways arranged at the corners of the building. This approach enables each part of the programme to be sized with no limitations imposed by structure or the demands of a general layout. Industrial prefabrication processes were used to ensure greater speed of construction.

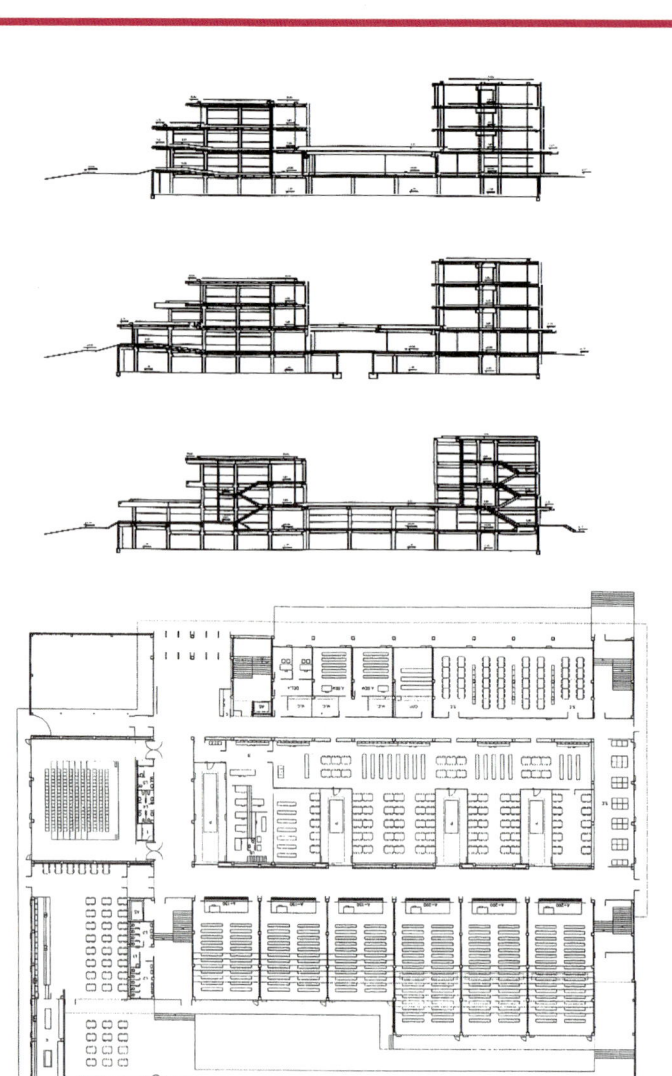

Tarragona 335

MAITE VILLA
SINGLE-FAMILY DWELLING

Mamen Domingo, Ernest Ferré
1998-2000

Av. dels Pins, 21 - El Pinar residential development
Reus

The dwelling is situated in a residential complex of principal dwellings and was designed for two residents. It occupies a single floor, raised considerably above grade. A double ramp connects the main floor, an intermediate floor and the roof, which acts both as a solarium and a vantage point, offering views of the sea in the distance at Salou and the skyline of the city of Reus. The house receives natural light via a skylight measuring 1 x 5 metres, which leads out onto the roof. The openings on the ground floor respond to some of the significant elements in the immediate environs: an advertising hoarding, a nearby wood and an unpleasant building. The dwelling therefore turns its back on the street and the mistral, and extends spatially and visually upwards, proposing life in this house as an ascending flow, a direction that is extended to the technical elements and the air conditioning conduits.

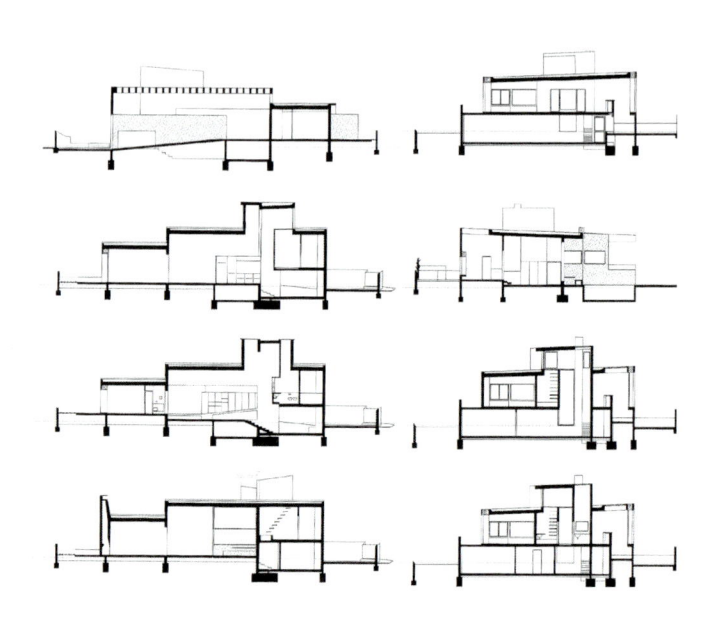

REUS CEMETERY CREMATORIUM

Pau Pérez, Anton Banús
2001-2003

Av. de la Pau - Reus cemetery - Reus

The new crematory building forms part of a larger-scale plan to transform Reus cemetery into an urban park, involving the reorganization of the road system, the incorporation of car parking areas, stands of trees and new funeral services: a morgue, the crematories and the multipurpose halls. The construction contains a hall and crematorium furnace, and is built of concrete screen walls that run the whole height of the building. These screens incorporate metal bars to support the intermediate structural floors of honeycomb slab. The exterior and interior facings, flooring and dividing walls are all timber. The central element is the chapel, a tall building, with artificial lighting at an intermediate level and a completely glazed rear facing, with natural light filtered by wooden slats.

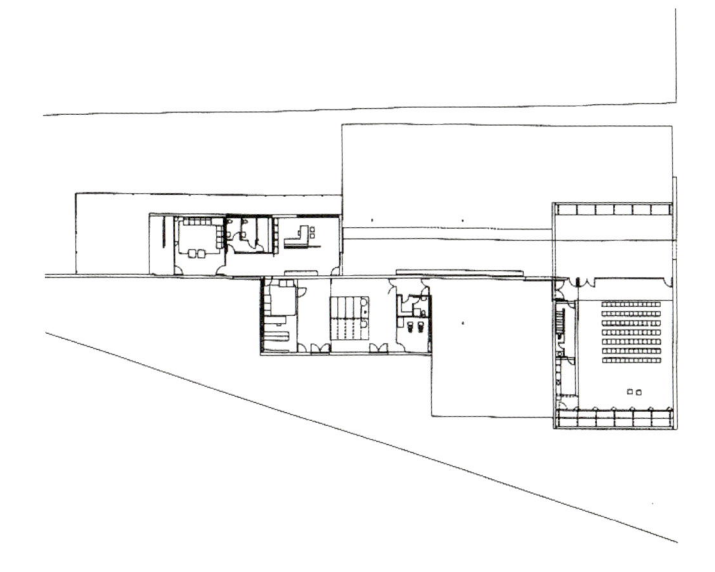

SÍLVIA VILLA
SINGLE-FAMILY DWELLING

Mamen Domingo, Ernest Ferré
1997-2000

Road to Almoster
(TP-7049) - Castellvell del Camp

The house is situated on the northern edge of its plot, protected from the north wind by a continuous concrete wall. This wall provides the departure point for the conception of the house as it advances southwards, creating more private spaces and views and generating courtyards that organize the interior layout. The whole programme is concentrated in an elongated volume of 6 x 22 metres, laid out in an east-west direction. The horizontal slabs are perforated at certain points to generate vertical spaces, in some cases very small. The vertical planes are also perforated freely, allowing great flexibility in the size and the position of the openings.

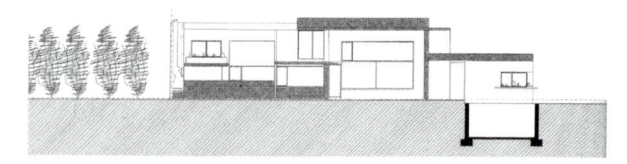

SERRA HOUSE
SINGLE-FAMILY DWELLING

Emili Donato, Uwe Geest
1986

Av. Catalunya, 47-49 - Alforja

This is a dwelling for a rural family, in which the interpretation of the programme reflects the customs and lifestyle of its inhabitants. The daytime area is broken down into two living rooms, one for family life and everyday activities, and another, more representative space for formal occasions. A studio on the roof level leads to a series of terraces overlooking life in the street. The ground floor is raised 1.60 metres above grade to allow the garden more privacy and prevent it shading the main rooms of the house.

VILA-SECA SCHOOL
SECONDARY SCHOOL

Jordi Sardà, Jordi Bergadà
1995-1997

Av. Alcalde Pere Molas - Vila-seca de Solcina

The layout of the building on the site seeks to control the shape and the nature of the open spaces in order to optimize their use and incorporate them into the shaping of the landscape. The ground floor is designed to embrace various of the open spaces, practically enclosing the school grounds on all four sides. The spaces produced where the façade is drawn back from the street are seen as parts of the general organization of the grounds. Several doorways communicate the interior courtyard and the street in order to encourage the independent functioning of the different parts of the programme. The three upper floors house both the regular and the special classrooms. On these three floors, each opening has a projection and sun-shading elements that filter the effects of the sun and protect the facings from rain and seepage.

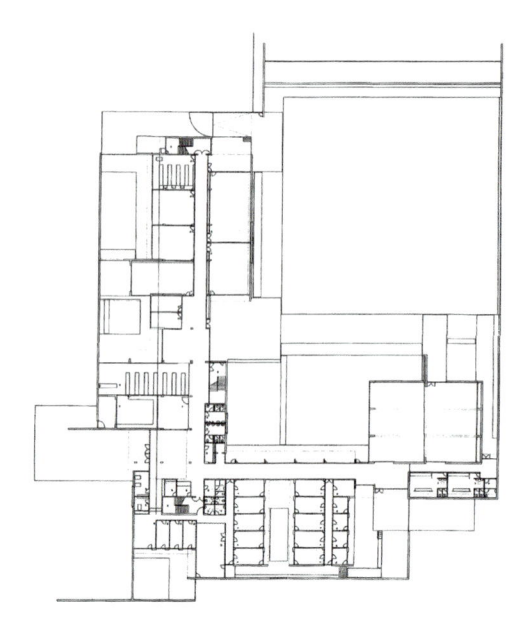

VILA-SECA TOWN HALL
EXTENSION OF AN EXISTING BUILDING

Josep Llinàs
1994-1997

Pl. de l'Església, 26 - Vila-seca de Solcina

The history of the project begins with the impossibility of competing with the position in the square of the church. The first project drafted by Llinàs involved emptying the centre of the plot, creating a new outdoor public space associated with the square and the new town hall building. In the face of the opposition generated by this solution, the definitive project conserves the façade and converts the planned open space into a service area for the new building. This courtyard adopts a complex configuration left over from the original idea. Finally, the main body of the project consisted in work on the old façade. New construction work gradually replaced the original fabric. Meticulous work with the colours of the stone in the façade creates the illusion of a taller building, though it is actually wider than the original.

VILA-SECA MUNICIPAL FUNERAL SERVICES

Mamen Domingo, Ernest Ferré
2001-2003

Av. de la Vila del Comú - Alba industrial estate
Vila-seca de Solcina

The site on which the funeral services stand is heavily conditioned by industrial constructions and the presence of the cemetery. The services comprise a landscaped area of 2200 square metres and a building with a surface area of 600 square metres. The site's frontage on the street is a 125-metre green fence that contrasts with the factory setting. On the eastern side is a garden crossed by an irregular winding path that cannot be trodden, a symbol of the path we will all walk one day. It is a plantation of small bushes and shrubs that accompany the upward sloping entrance. This path culminates in a large concrete gateway formed by two inverted L-shapes, suggesting the wings of a welcoming angel. The project combines symbolism and the reality of spatial experiences to produce a highly spiritual representation of death.

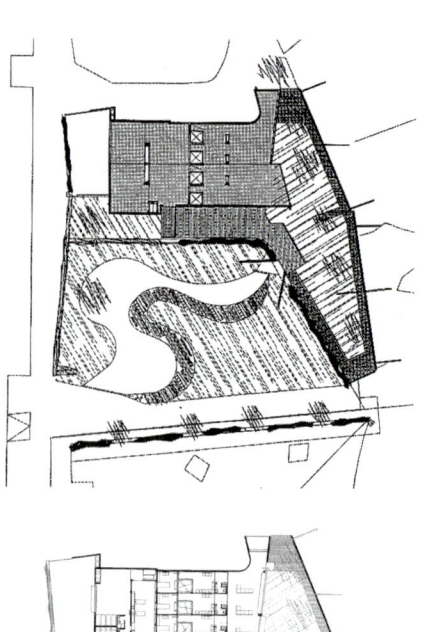

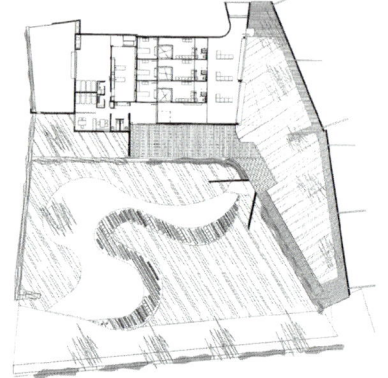

JOSEP CARRERAS AUDITORIUM
MUNICIPAL CONSERVATORY

Pau Pérez, Anton Banús
1996-2002

Pl. Frederic Mompou, 1 - Vila-seca de Solcina

The building is located at one end of a small park. It is a compact volume with a ground floor that occupies the whole site, with the exception of the four courtyards made in it. The conservatory and auditorium can function independently. The basement floor houses the installations, changing rooms and percussion rooms. On the ground floor are the classrooms and communal spaces of the conservatory, and two concert halls with respective capacities for 400 and 100 people, plus a foyer and bar. The first floor accommodates the conservatory's practice rooms and the auditorium's second foyer. The spaces designed for listening to music are constructed to float inside the general bearing structure, comprising reinforced concrete screens and slabs, and metal pillars. The interior finishes are of light-coloured materials: white marble and maple wood.

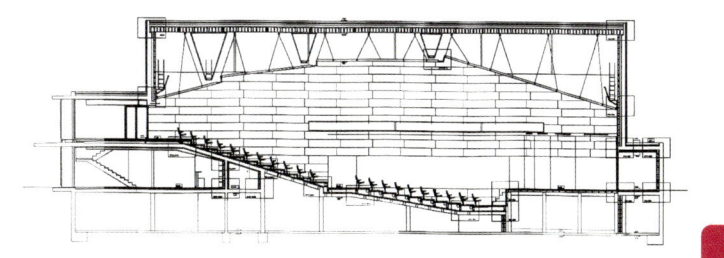

XIPRE APARTMENTS

Antoni Bonet i Castellana, Josep Puig i Torné
1960-1962

Punta del Cavall - Cap de Salou - Salou

On a plot of land with a rugged, variable topography, Bonet superposed 12 bays, each 5 metres wide, running in a strict north-south line as a guideline for the adaptation of the apartments to the gradient. The modules that make up the dwellings are gradually terraced and create leaps of one floor, adapting to the topography without levelled areas or embankments. This arrangement unifies repeated construction elements, such as door and window frames and railings, which are identifiable within the changing image of the complex. The apartments move through the bays to seek the best situation, and each unit occupies two bays and two floors. As in other projects of this period, Bonet worked on mechanisms that allowed him to combine the laws of nature with a geometric criterion, and the result is a unitary complex within which are generated a great many particular forms and situations.

RUBIÓ HOUSE
SINGLE-FAMILY HOUSE

Antoni Bonet Castellana, Josep Puig i Torné
1960-1962

Cala Crancs, 38 - Cap de Salou - Salou

Situated on a rocky promontory overlooking the sea, the house adapts to the irregularity of the site by means of numerous 45-degree angles and a combination of materials that include bare masonry, whitewashed walls and glazed surfaces. The living room looks out squarely onto the landscape, while the terraces form the acute angles. The bedrooms are situated beneath the main terrace, so that the whole house forms a large organism over two levels. The dihedron that completes the upper terrace and the rocky platforms leading down to the beach represent an overall transformation of the place.

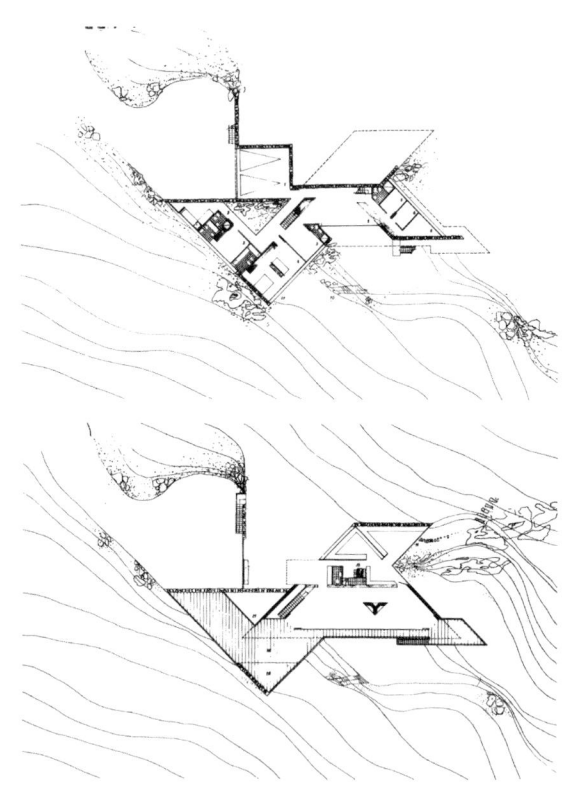

SALOU MUNICIPAL SPORTS CENTRE

Esteve Bonell, Josep Maria Gil, Francesc Rius
1986-1991

C/ Milà, 5 - Salou

The sports centre is set in a rectangular site in the north of the town. The narrow façade overlooks a newly created square between the town hall and a school. The new construction is designed as a small pavilion that presents its frontage to the square, which also contains the entrance, a glazed opening that occupies almost its entire width. On the opposite side is a small gymnasium that can be used for theatre. The stands, to either side, accommodate up to 800 spectators. The visual impact of the box is lessened by its division into three orders: the stands, the main beams that span the roof crosswise, and the skylights, divided into three volumes. Entrance from the square leads into the foyer via stairways and gently sloping ramps, and around the perimeter of this raised level to enter the stands and the gymnasium with its stage at the far end.

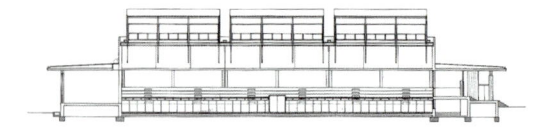

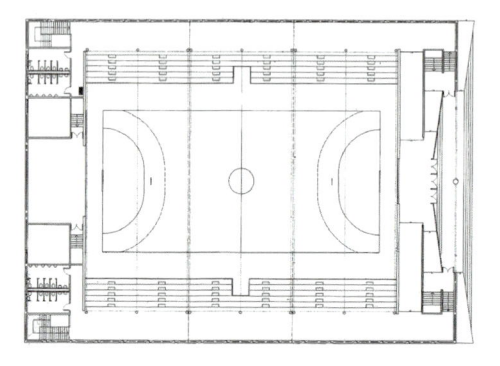

SALOU MUNICIPAL LIBRARY

Pau Pérez
1988-1992

C/ Ponent, 16 - Salou

This programme for a small municipal library was produced by using architectural elements put forward by the memory of the place: the huge pine forest that used to cover the municipality and the little holiday home that previously stood on the site. The new library's structure adopts the form of a cast-in-situ concrete slab that folds in all directions, forming even the roof and side facings. The slab is supported by metal props at those points where it is not self-supporting. The openings in the folds determine the entrance of light into the interior, and the other facings are enclosed by glass and timber. The versatility of this procedure gives each area a high degree of freedom. The hall merges into the surrounding pinewoods, and the newspaper library presents sloping walls to an inner courtyard onto which it opens via a ground-level opening. The overall effect is that of a cloth covering a series of sacral spaces.

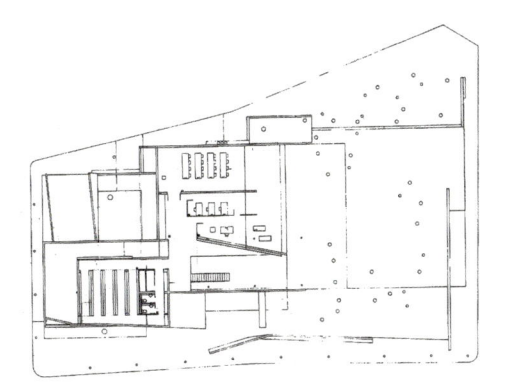

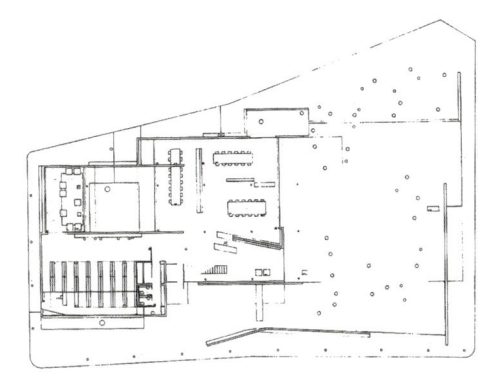

IES SCHOOL OF CATERING AND TOURISM
SECONDARY SCHOOL

Víctor Rahola
1986-1988

C/ L'Estel - Cambrils

It was the location that provided the departure point for the project: sea views, a nearby beach and, opposite, the skyline of the town of Cambrils. The complex programme was addressed in two phases, the first for the second cycle of vocational training. This phase involved two volumes: a square ground-floor volume containing the kitchens and restaurants, and a two-storey volume, superposed on the first, housing the hotel management and school programme. Phase two centred on the first-cycle programme, housed in a three-floor prismatic volume and a single-storey annexe. Entrance to the first building is at the side, via a freestanding large walled structure. The garden is divided into two areas: the one by the entrance is more functional, paved with concrete slabs and gravel. The second, at the front, is more natural, with landscaped terraces and embankments in contact with the beach and sea views.

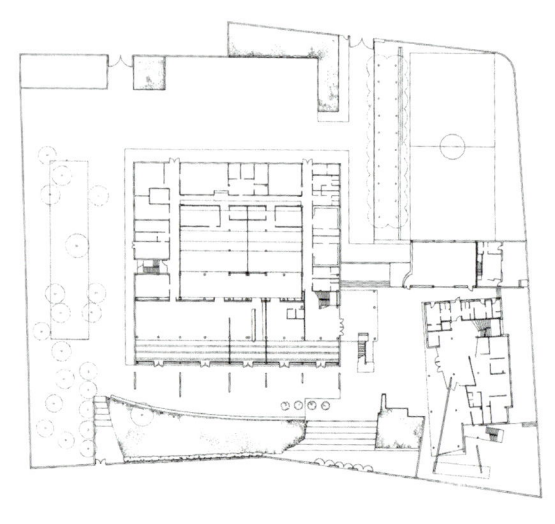

SAVALL HOUSE
SINGLE-FAMILY DWELLING

Tonet Sunyer
1998-1999

C/ Consolat de Mar, 5 - Cambrils

The project is constrained by the responsibility of constructing a seafront façade that conditions the image of the place and involves very strict bylaws for new building work. The long, narrow site (4.30 x 13 metres) accommodates a single-family dwelling, with the added limitation of occupation of the ground floor by a restaurant with a working terrace. The dwelling is laid out on three floors plus a covered rooftop. The position of the stairs, inserted against one of the party walls, creates greater ease of interior distribution. The roof, with its regulatory red channel tiles, is concealed from the façade by the empty space of a terrace, since municipal regulations also forbid projections. The metal structure, which had to be concealed, is clad with a teak beam infill. Large single-paned picture windows make up for the building's scant width.

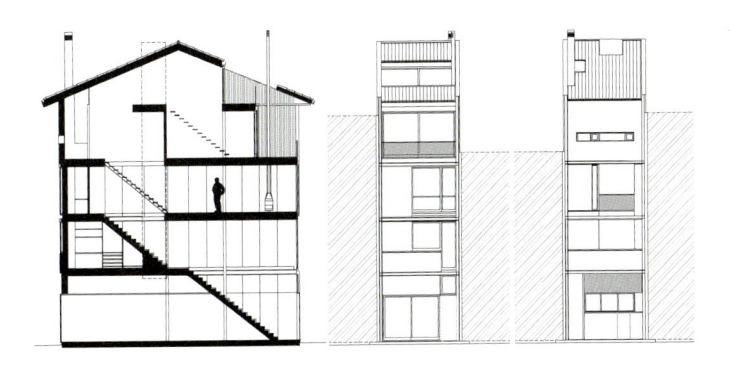

POBLAT HIFRENSA
RESIDENTIAL COMPLEX AND FACILITIES FOR WORKERS AT VANDELLÓS NUCLEAR POWER PLANT

Antoni Bonet i Castellana, Josep Puig i Torné
1967-1975

Via Augusta - C/ Ramon Berenguer IV - Via fèrria
L'Hospitalet de l'Infant

The project responds to a programme to house workers at Vandellós nuclear power plant in a development near the power station, designed by Bonet Castellana. The site slopes gently down towards the sea and groves of olive, carob, fig and pine trees. The commission stipulated that the constructions should respect the landscape and be concealed by the vegetation. The central area includes four buildings: a residence for unmarried workers, a club with a small health centre, a school and nursery, and a supermarket. The north sector contains an area for 280 dwellings and a space for communal use. The pedestrian layout comprises two squares joined by a broad avenue, and is complemented by secondary paths that rationally interconnect all sectors. At the entrance are the gatehouse, the telephone switchboard and the weather station, each roofed by a reinforced concrete dome clad with yellow pieces of tile, or *trencadís*, and supported by slender metal pillars. The residence was designed so that the workers and their families could live normal lives, both individually and collectively.

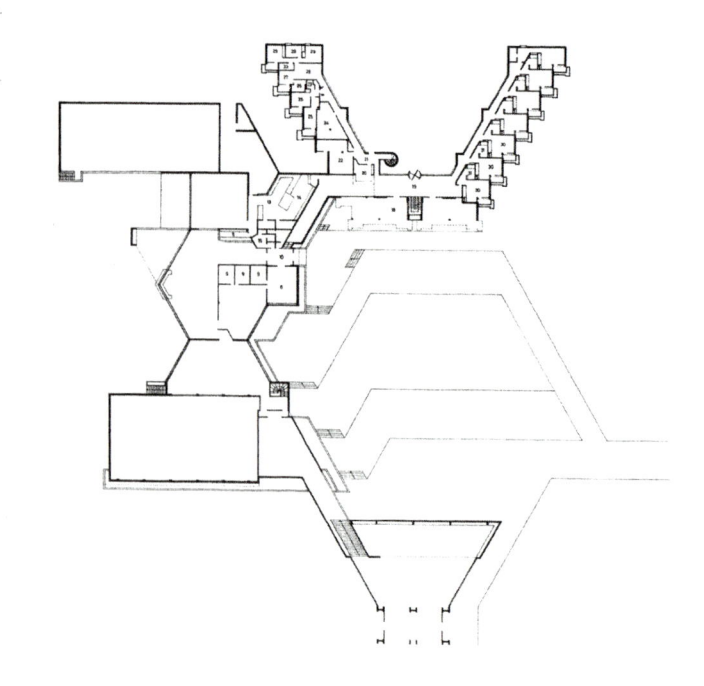

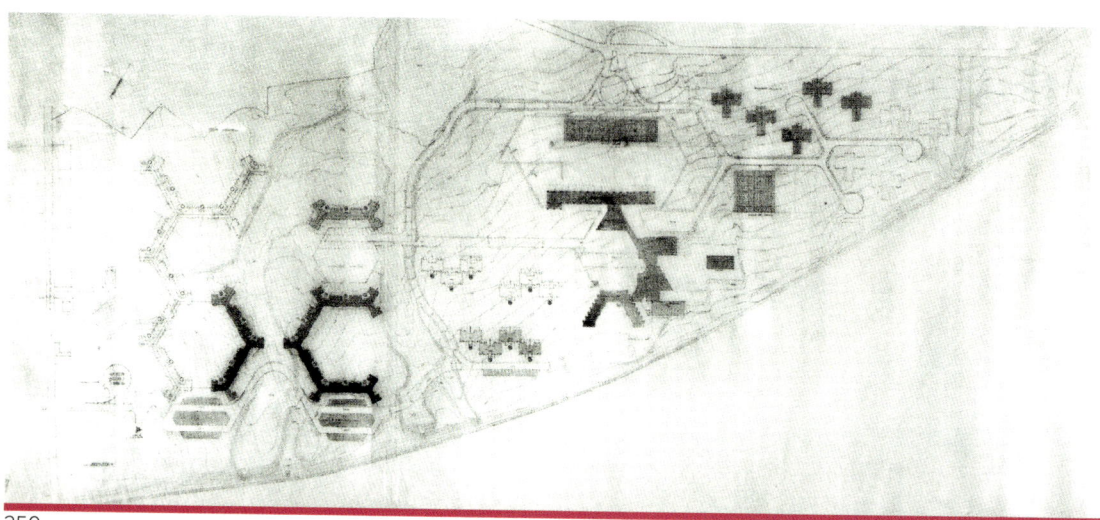

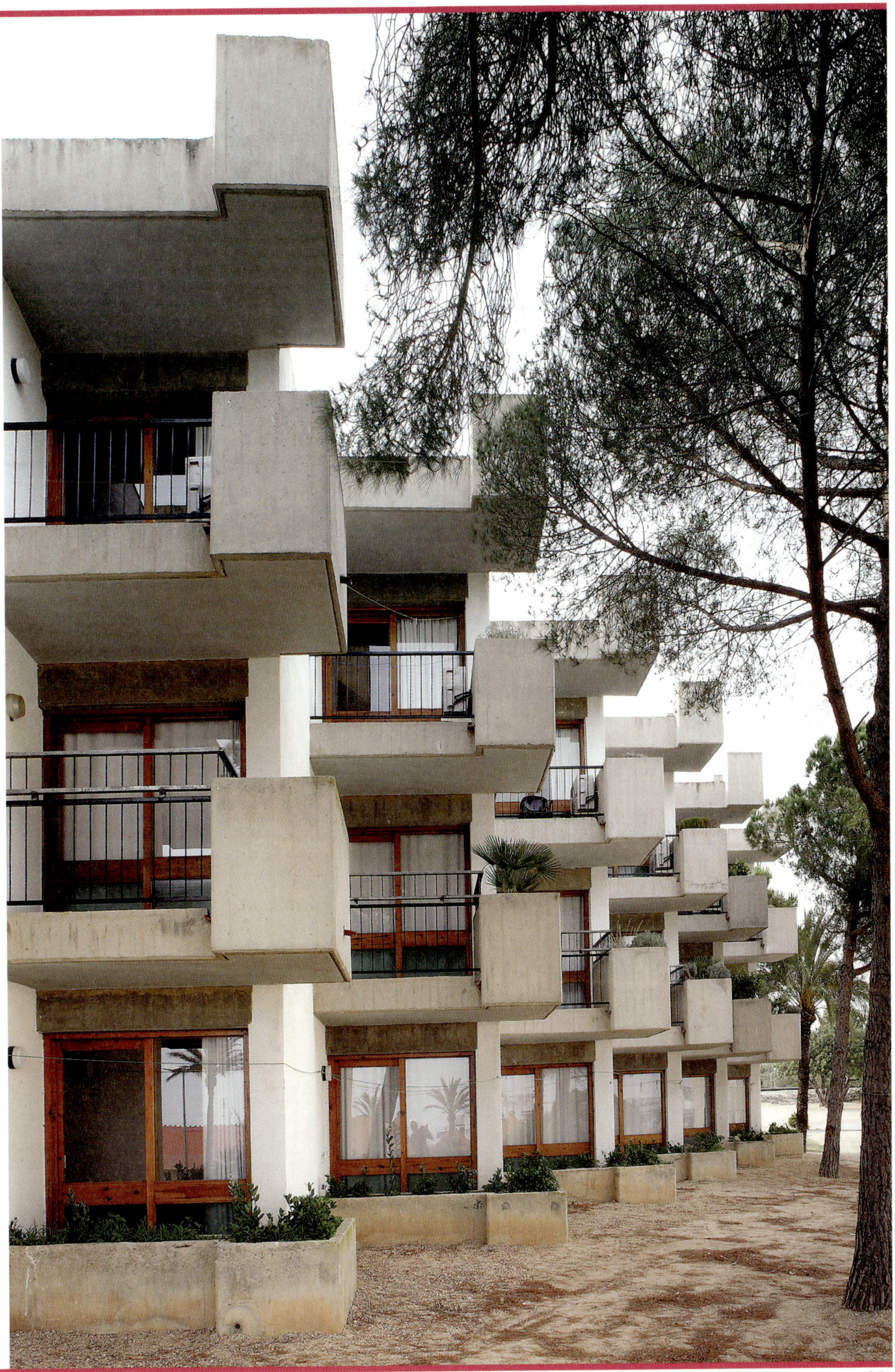

TGN-4

La Fatarella
Móra d'Ebre
Gandesa
El Pinell
de Brai
L'Ametlla de Mar
Tortosa
Deltebre
Amposta
La Sénia
Alcanar

TTS - The Tortosa Area

Territorial scope

This area covers all the *comarques* around the river Ebre delta. Tortosa is in the county of Baix Ebre, to the north are Ribera d'Ebre and Terra Alta, and, to the south, Montsià, the final *comarca* in Catalonia before Castellón. Despite the large surface area of these four counties, the population density is very low, and there are few towns of any considerable size. The Tortosa area is the last of the five that make up the coastal strip included in this guide: Figueres, Girona, Barcelona, Tarragona and Tortosa.

Road structure

Heading south from Tarragona, the AP-7 motorway arrives at Amposta, one of the largest towns in the county of Montsià. Tortosa is just a few kilometres to the north of Amposta, on the C-12 road. The same road continues north to Lleida. To get to Valencia from Tortosa, first go to Amposta and pick up the AP-7 motorway heading southwest. To get to Madrid, head first for Lleida, and there pick up the AP-2 motorway.

ROUTE 1
Route 1 sets out from Tortosa and covers the coastal part of this area, spreading out in four branches around the delta. Take the C-12 to Amposta and then pick up the AP-7 motorway northeast to L'Ametlla de Mar. A local road, the TV-3454, leads from Amposta towards the sea and Deltebre. Also starting in Amposta, the N-340 heads south to Alcanar. Amposta is therefore the focal point of this area, providing a reference for all destinations.

ROUTE 2
Route 2 covers the inland sector of this area. Heading north from Tortosa, the C-12 takes you to Móra d'Ebre, branching off to the left, on the way, to El Pinell de Brai and Gandesa via the C-43. To get to La Fatarella, go to Gandesa and take two local roads, the TV-7231 and the TV-7333. An alternative route is via Móra d'Ebre, taking the N-420 and then a turning to the right, the TV-7321 local road. The best route to La Sénia, to the southwest, is to take the T-331 out of Tortosa and then pick up the TP-3311.

Lleida

La Fatarella

Móra d'Ebre

Gandesa

El Pinell de Brai

Tarragona

L'Ametlla de Mar

Tortosa

Deltebre

Amposta

La Sénia

Alcanar

Municipalities	Comarca	Surface area (municipality)	Population (2001)
TORTOSA	Baix Ebre	218.5 km^2	28,933 inhabitants
ROUTE 1			
L'AMETLLA DE MAR	Baix Ebre	66.9 km^2	5,015 inhabitants
DELTEBRE	Baix Ebre	107.5 km^2	10,478 inhabitants
AMPOSTA	Montsià	138.3 km^2	16,865 inhabitants
ALCANAR	Montsià	47.1 km^2	8,032 inhabitants
ROUTE 2			
MÓRA D'EBRE	Ribera d'Ebre	45.1 km^2	4,612 inhabitants
EL PINELL DE BRAI	Terra Alta	57.0 km^2	1,099 inhabitants
GANDESA	Terra Alta	71.2 km^2	2,641 inhabitants
LA FATARELLA	Terra Alta	56.5 km^2	1,201 inhabitants
LA SÉNIA	Montsià	108.4 km^2	5,365 inhabitants

321

TORTOSA MUNICIPAL ABATTOIR

Pau Monguió i Segura
1905-1908

Rambla Felip Pedrell, 5 - Tortosa

322

GREGO HOUSE
FONTANET HOUSE – APARTMENT BUILDING

Pau Monguió i Segura
1906-1911

Pl. Nostra Senyora de la Cinta, 6 - Tortosa

The original project was drafted by Pau Monguió, though the plans are signed by Pere Caselles. The architect Ezequiel Porcel later removed a storey from Monguió's project before starting construction. The house looks out onto a square and a street through two non-perpendicular façades. The first floor is clad with ashlars and the others are rendered and decorated with sgraffiti. The door leading to the dwellings has an oval frame. The first and second floors are occupied by a long balcony with seven openings, supported by large corbels. At the Carrer de la Rosa end, there is a gallery on the first floor, and on the corner of Carrer Portal a glazed timber gallery encompasses all three floors.

323

PIÑANA HOUSE
PRIVATE RESIDENCE

Pau Monguió i Segura
1914

Av. de la Generalitat, 105 - Tortosa

The abattoir is situated between Rambla Felip Pedrell and the river Ebre, on land reclaimed from the river in the late 19th century, near the neighbourhood of Remolins. It comprises an arched structure to raise the reclaimed land to the surrounding level. The abattoir was built on this base. It is a rectangular enclosure containing various pavilions of the same shape and size, interconnected by courtyards. The façades combine rendering with brick and tile cladding. The openings, semicircular arches or caliphate in inspiration, are concentrated in the secondary walls. The main volume runs parallel to the river and is framed at either end by rectangular towers with openings in the form of semicircular or stilted arches.

This is a private two-storey house in the new town extension of Tortosa, on a plot of land between party walls. The ground floor, built for a shop, is given a plain treatment, and all the emphasis is given to stylizing the first floor, which contains the dwelling. Monguió used three parabolic arches to frame the great openings, divided into three windows with a rose window above each, the one in the central position being the largest. At the bottom of each opening is a railed balcony that extends the composition to ground level. The arches are clad with white and blue tiles. Monguió exploited the typological singularity of the building to experiment with a composition that shuns traditional construction orders.

MANGRANÉ HOUSES
4 SINGLE-FAMILY DWELLINGS

Emili Donato
1965-1966

Sector 1-C, plot 32 - Calafat Residential development
L'Ametlla de Mar

The project presents the origins of Donato's research into the distribution of the dwelling, which continued throughout his career. These four single-storey houses are laid out in the form of a swastika around the water deposit at the centre. Each house adopts an L-shape layout with its living room at the centre and the bedroom wings at the end of each arm. Each house has its own semiprivate area, and the general orientation of the complex allows for good sunlighting. The wall system comprises three orders: a masonry base, corresponding to the enclosure walls; an intermediate strip of dark-coloured rendering—the actual house—and a white rendering for elements emerging from the roof. The Mangrané houses foreshadow many of the architect's design features, as well as presenting specific solutions that were not repeated.

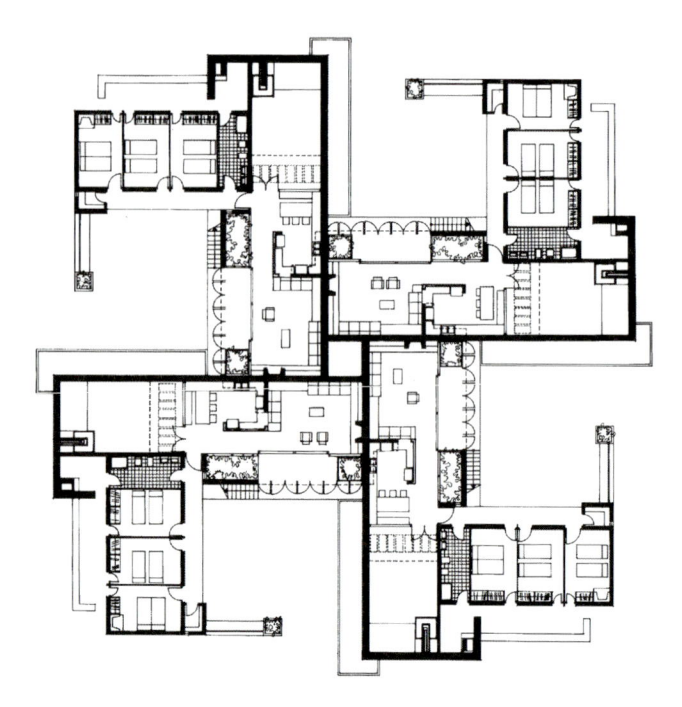

DOCTOR ARGANY HOUSES
TWO SINGLE-FAMILY DWELLINGS

Ramon Maria Puig i Andreu
1975-1977

Quarta Avinguda, 81-A - Sant Jordi d'Alfama
Residential development - L'Ametlla de Mar

The original project envisaged two houses for two quite different families, friends who decided to spend their holidays together, though the houses now belong to a single owner. They are situated on twin plots, each covering 500 square metres, which are joined to enable them to share outdoor space. The two houses are symmetrical, though one slants at a diagonal to avoid a tree. On the ground floor, a side porch leads directly into the garage, the kitchen and the courtyard in front of the living room. A central stairway, lit from above, leads to the bedroom level. All the walls and partitions are built of brick, which is rendered and painted on the outside. Indoors, it is just painted, not plastered. The wall separating the houses from the street joins the sites and the front door.

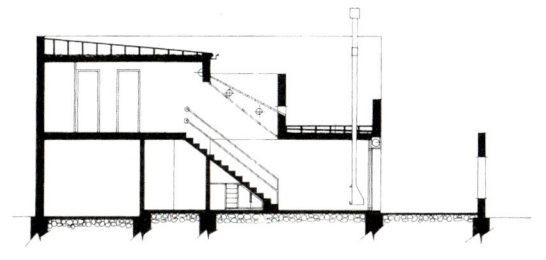

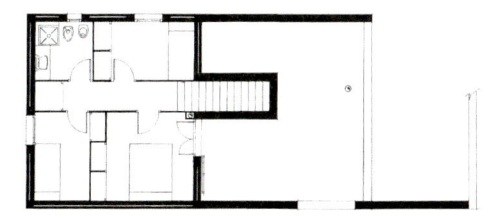

326

CEIP RIUMAR
INFANTS' AND PRIMARY SCHOOL

Manuel Ruisánchez, Xavier Vendrell
1994-1996

C/ Ignasi, 26 - Deltebre

327

IES RAMON BERENGUER IV
SECONDARY SCHOOL

Oriol Bohigas, Josep Maria Martorell, Francesc Bassó, Joaquim Gili
1955-1957

C/ Músic Sunyer, 1-37 - Amposta

The original project was for a Labour Institute, commissioned by the Ministry of Education as part of a development programme undertaken after the war. The building is organized in the form of a large H-shape that produces an entrance courtyard with a smaller court to the rear. The two side wings flanking the entrance court contain classrooms, and the rear part contains communal spaces. The floor plan is organized according to a layout of axial corridors that lead to each part of the programme. The classroom roofs adopt one of two types, according to their position: either saw-toothed, the slope with a circular directrix, or a tiled ridge roof with two different slopes, with a low volume running the length of it and openings in the side facings. The complex is an exercise in the application of some of the principles of the modern movement before the architects carried out a revision in the following decade.

328

HOUSE FOR A PHOTOGRAPHER IN THE EBRE DELTA

Carles Ferrater, Carlos Escura
2003-2006

Pg. del Mar - Les Cases d'Alcanar (Alcanar)

The urban fabric surrounding the school comprises small scattered constructions, producing a landscape characterized by interstitial spaces and labyrinthine vistas. The layout of the school respects these features as a value, attempting to leave pre-existing elements unchanged. It comprises a series of independent single-storey pavilions, connected in some cases by lightweight roofs. All the spaces are located on the same level, facilitating their interrelation. The volumes built alongside the street respond to apparently capricious alignments that are actually produced by the buildings opposite.

The house is located amid a landscape of long strips of farmland perpendicular to the coastline, with buildings situated at the rear of the plots. The house respects the original morphology and takes its place at the far end of one of these plots, broken down into three volumes that respect the dimensions of the neighbouring buildings. The first contains the bedroom, the second the living room and kitchen, and the third the studio. All three volumes are irregular in floor plan and section, and dialogue with a second, inaccessible level, where there are works of art and bookshelves. The small interior space where the three volumes converge becomes a place for passing, for sitting, for views and interrelation. A platform 70 centimetres above the ground, in case of flooding, is the sole element that unifies the house, made up of constantly changing lines of sight in all directions.

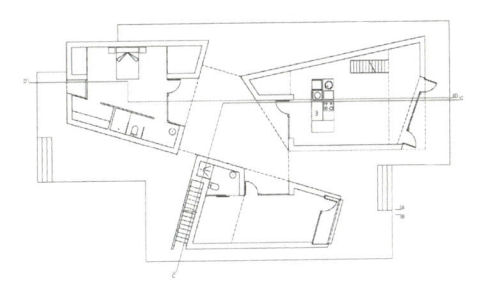

Tortosa

MÓRA D'EBRE COUNTY HOSPITAL

José Antonio Martínez Lapeña, Elías Torres
1982-1987

C/ Benet Messeguer, 2 - Móra d'Ebre

The hospital adopts an extensive low-rise configuration in response to the characteristics of the functional programme and the site. The east façade, overlooking the river Ebre, is given a fragmented treatment to avoid presenting a view of the hospital in its entirety. The Health Centre is inserted in the middle, interrupting the building's longest dimension and thereby concealing the continuous perception of its entire length. The hospitalization facilities face south and east, commanding the best views. The services (laundries, kitchens and boiler rooms) are accommodated in the north-facing façade, around a closed courtyard set apart from the general hospital itineraries. The other hospital services are located in a compact block with a west-facing façade overlooking a series of inner courtyards. The distribution of the various areas takes into account the various interrelations and connecting circulations. The whole building is constructed using local materials and traditional construction systems that do not require high levels of maintenance, ideal for a complex programme such as a hospital. The second floor has a higher ceiling than the others to incorporate the installations.

Tortosa 363

COOPERATIVE CELLAR OF THE FARMS COOPERATIVE AND OIL MILL

Cèsar Martinell
1919-1922

C/ del Pilonet, 10 - El Pinell de Brai

Martinell designed the cellar for the Sindicat Agrícola of El Pinell de Brai with all the enthusiasm of helping this cooperative to compete with the one in Gandesa that he was building at the same time. It comprises four warehouse spaces measuring 10 x 31.50 metres, one with two floors for an oil mill and the others as cellarage, with a capacity for 320 casks of oil and 22,000 hectolitres of wine. Martinell incorporated passages allowing operations from beneath the underground deposits. In the façade, the two central warehouses were joined together in a single higher volume, like in Falset. The arches of the interior were added at the insistence of the cooperative members, who had seen the brick-built Catalan vaults supported by arches used in Gandesa. Martinell decided to make the arches in El Pinell more spectacular, with bricks laid on edge and contoured bricks.

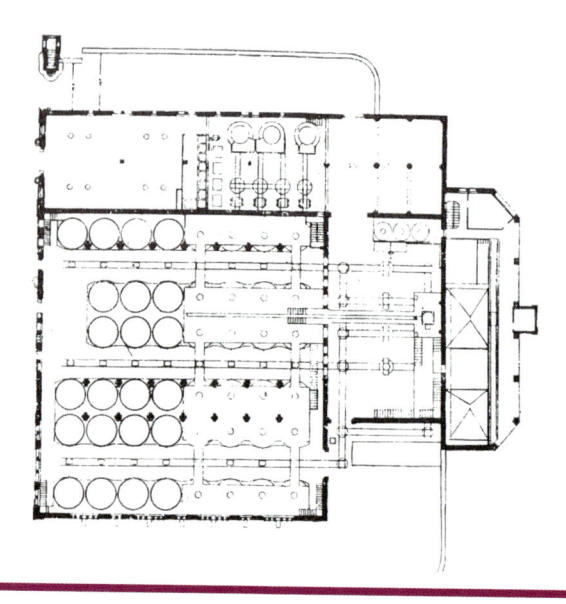

CELLAR OF GANDESA FARMS COOPERATIVE

Cèsar Martinell
1919-1920

Av. Catalunya, 28 - Gandesa

In Gandesa, Martinell was able to put into practice his structural innovations thanks to the willingness of the union members, who placed a site supervisor at his disposal, something that had not happened at the other cellars. Martinell went beyond the limitations represented by local procedures and was even able to use a type of sand that was not locally available. The roof comprises brickwork vaults with three layers of flat brick, supported by balanced arches. The vaults are arranged at different heights to allow daylight in. The Gandesa structure was the most criticized at the time, but it was also a major factor in the cooperative's economic growth; when work was completed, Martinell was asked to design another cellar on the other side of the road with a capacity of 17,000 hectolitres. The two constructions were designed to complement each other.

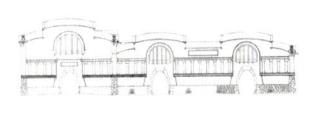

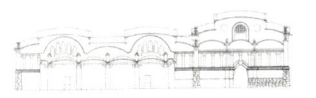

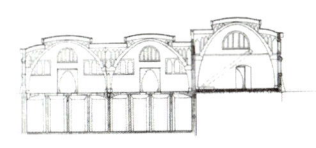

LA FATARELLA
ECOLOGICAL HOUSE - HOSTEL – SCHOOL OF THE RURAL ENVIRONMENT

Esteve Aymerich, Ton Salvadó, Joaquim Gascó
1993-1999

Camí de la Mare de Déu del Carme - La Fatarella

The conception of the hostel responds to the specific nature of the commission: a facility for use by anyone wishing to enjoy the rural environment. The building is constructed using local techniques and materials: dry-stone walls, stone-faced walls and vaults, ashlar pilasters, laminated stone walls; timber for the beams, rafters, joinery and floors, and tiles for the roof and claddings. The house also had to be energy-efficient: an inner courtyard generates shade and promotes cross ventilation, and pergolas with deciduous creepers regulate the sunlighting in winter and summer. The winter sun generates a greenhouse effect thanks to the house's large windows. The base of the construction adapts to the pre-existing terracing of the land, defining and completing three platforms that existed in the original topography.

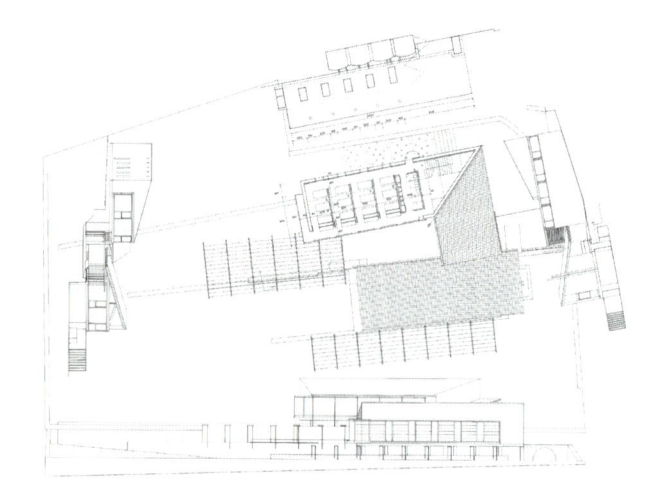

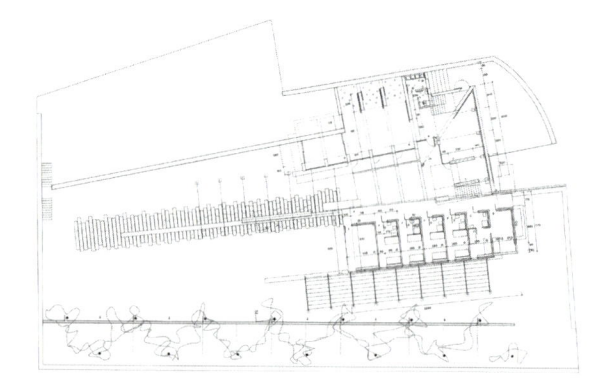

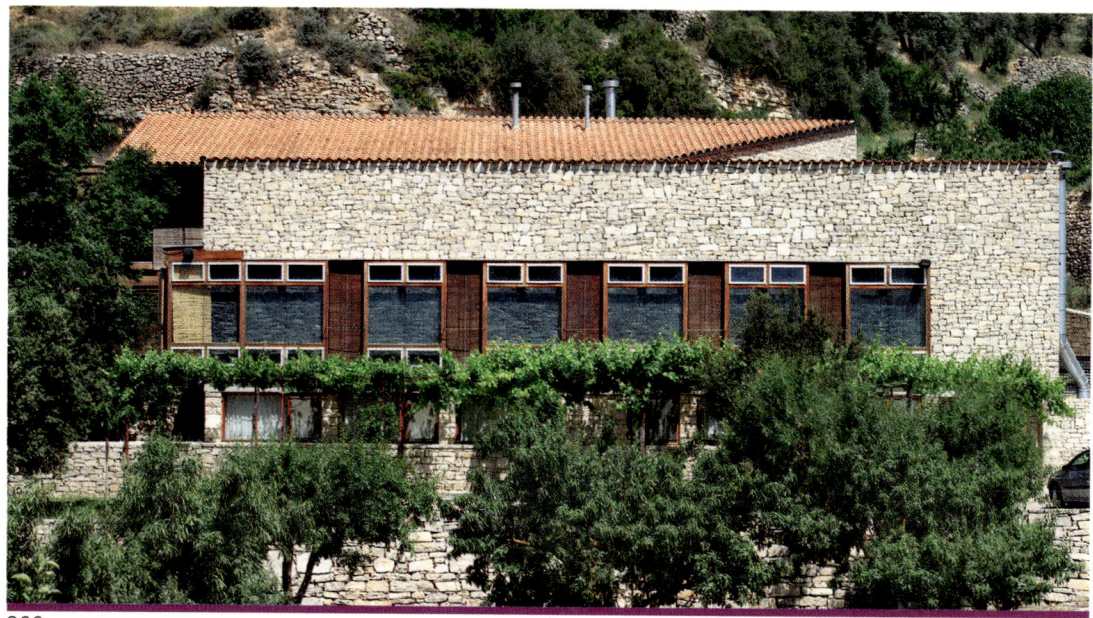

CAP LA SÉNIA
HEALTH CENTRE

Esteve Aymerich, Ton Salvadó, Gerard Puig
2001-2004

Pg. de la Clotada, 60 - La Sénia

The health centre is inserted into a small-grained sprawling urban fabric, its volume responding to these conditions. It comprises two volumes of different sizes, parallel to the high street and separated by a courtyard. The low volume is situated inside the street block in order to fit in with the neighbouring party walls. Entrance is via the courtyard, between the two volumes. The surgeries are situated on the two top floors of the taller volume. The on-call attention and health and personal education sectors are housed in the low volume. On-call activities are situated on the ground floor to facilitate functioning when the rest of the centre is closed. The central courtyard helps to create an internal microclimate and allows each use to be situated in a prime façade position. All the work areas are laid out on the north side, and the waiting areas are situated in the south-facing façades.

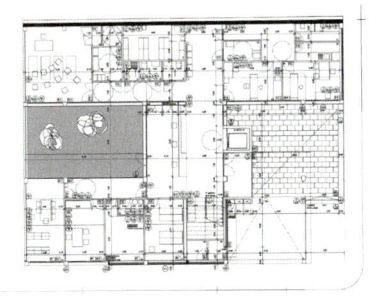

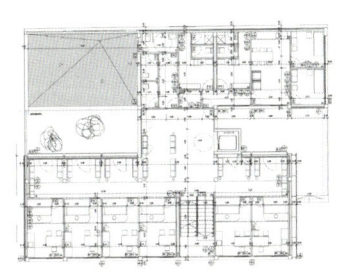

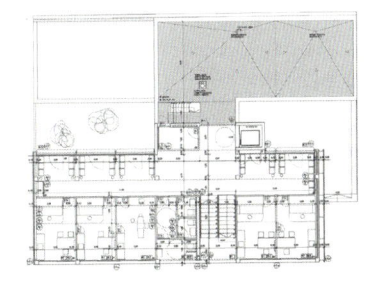

Montagut i Oix

Olot

Anglès

OLT – The Olot Area

Territorial scope

The Olot area covers a small surface area: it includes the *comarca* of Garrotxa and the inland part of the county of Selva. Its area of influence is only vaguely bounded by geographical borders with the western edge of the Figueres area and the eastern limits of the Vic area. The Olot area, the first of four inland areas, covers the sector left between the areas of influence of Figueres, on one side, and of Vic, on the other. It has just one route, crossing the capital of Garrotxa, Olot, from north to south, reaching as far as Montagut and Anglès.

Road structure

The N-260 runs from Portbou, through Figueres to Olot, where it ends. There is no direct route from Girona; the best option is to go to Banyoles, and take the GI-524 local road to Olot. If you are coming from Barcelona, the best route is to take the C-17 motorway to Vic and then pick up the C-153 to Olot. To get to Manresa and Lleida, you will necessarily go through Vic. The town of Vic is in all cases a point of reference on the way to Olot.

ROUTE 1
To get to Montagut, take the N-260 national road from Olot in the direction of Figueres and turn off to the north when you reach Castellfollit de la Roca. The same route includes the municipality of Anglès, to the south. The C-63 county road from Olot will take you directly to Anglès.

Montagut i Oix

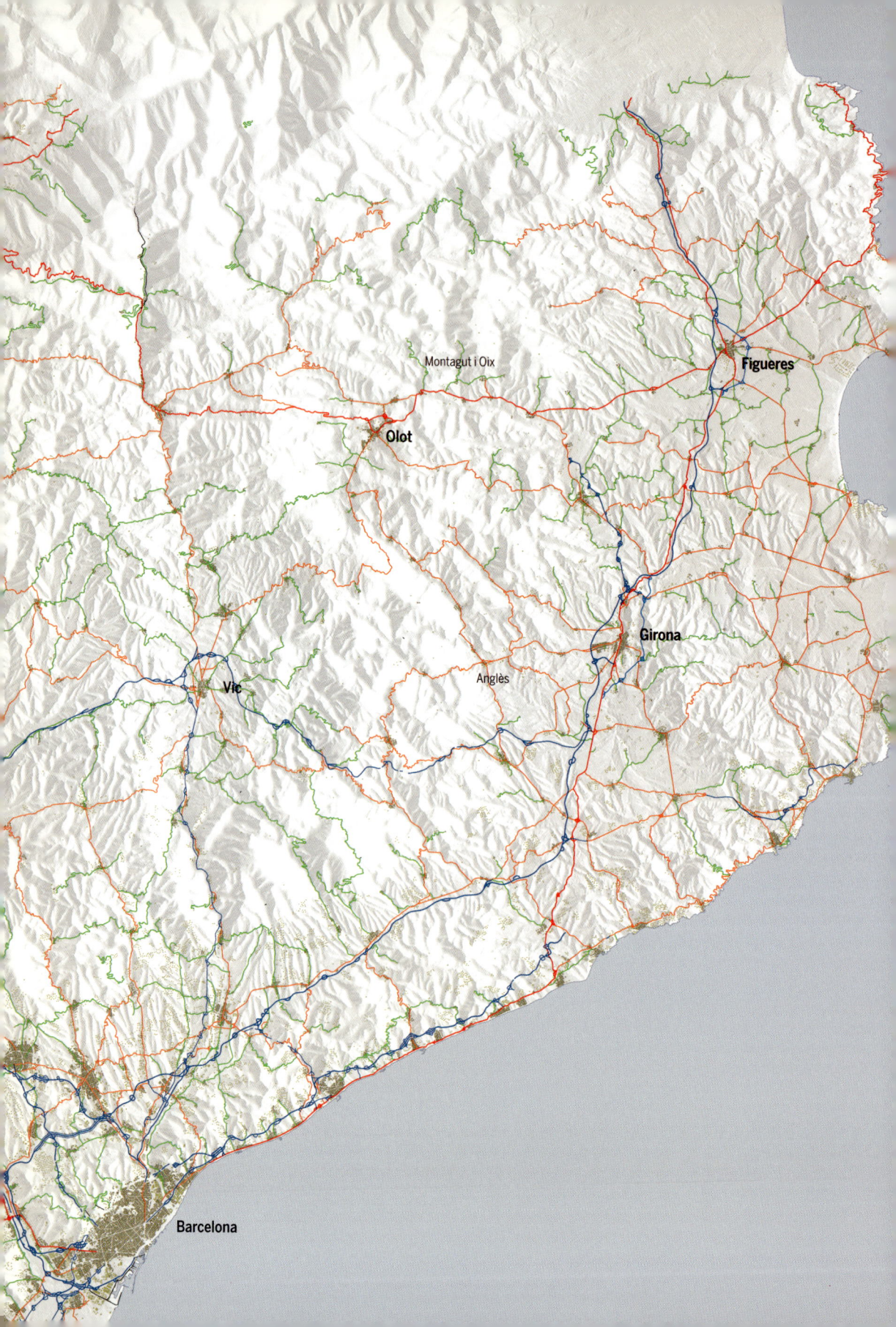

Olot

Figueres

Vic

Anglès

Girona

Barcelona

Municipalities	Comarca	Surface area (municipality)	Population (2001)
OLOT	Garrotxa	29.1 km²	28,060 inhabitants
ROUTE 1			
MONTAGUT & OIX	Garrotxa	93.8 km²	824 inhabitants
ANGLÈS	Selva	16.3 km²	4,739 inhabitants

SACREST FACTORY, "CAN JOANETES"
OLOT TOWN HALL

Joan Roca i Pinet
1927-1929

Pg. Bisbe Guillamet, 10 - Olot

SUBSEQUENT INTERVENTIONS:
Arcadi Pla, 1986-1990. Remodelling and rehabilitation as the new Town Hall.

The architecture of the Can Joanetes complex (or Sacrest Factory, or Subirà Factory) brings together the compositional elements of classical extraction that characterized the architecture culture of the 1920s. It comprises a main rectangular volume to the rear of which a series of lower volumes were added at a right angle. Joined by a square construction forming the axis, they produce a small central courtyard. In the original design by Joan Roca i Pinet, the whole was marked by symmetry, though only the main volume and one of the rear sheds were actually constructed. The rest of the constructions on the site were erected in more disorderly fashion and are of poorer quality than originally intended. The site measures 2600 square metres and is irregular in shape, with entrances via El Firalet and Carrer del Mirador. The rectangular volume stands back 5.5 metres from the line of the street and comprises three square stretches that are reflected in the composition of the main façade, with the axis of symmetry emphasized by a large visor and the pediment of the roof. The composition picks up some characteristic features of the traditional Catalan *masia* farmhouse. The original building was supported by industrial construction elements of the time: timber roof frames, laminated iron structures, etc. The central service volume was highlighted by its dual symmetry and the complex's main brick-built chimney.

Olot 373

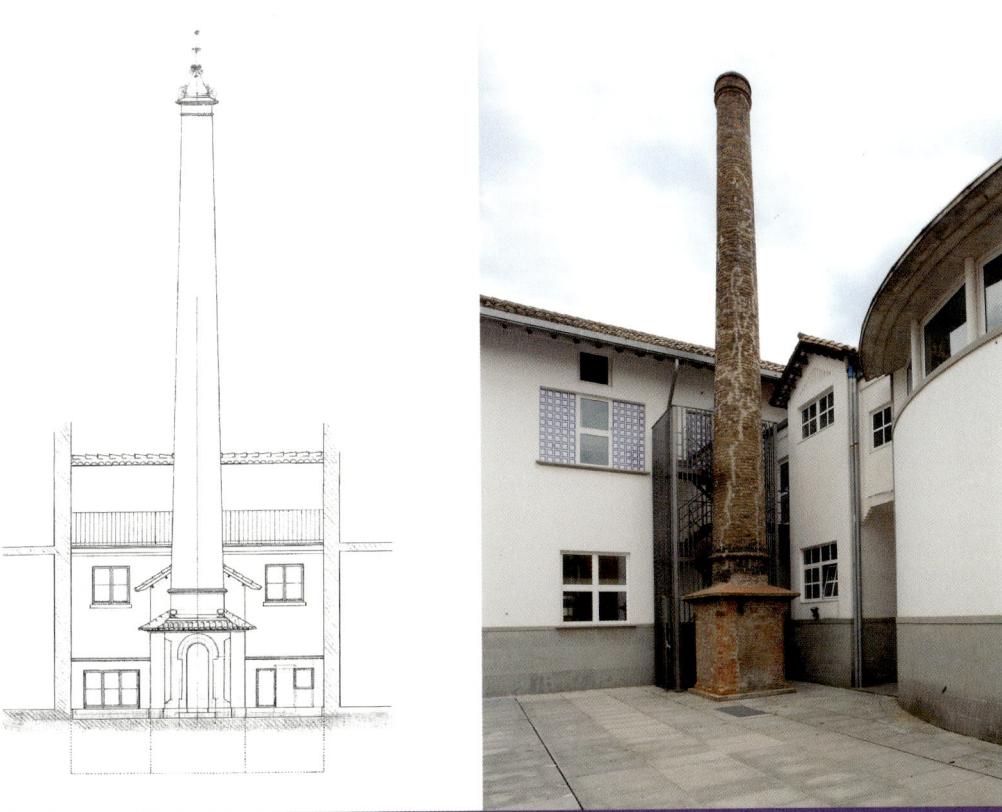

MASRAMON HOUSE
SINGLE-FAMILY DWELLING

Rafael Masó
1913-1914

C/ Vayreda, 6 - Olot

Masó proposed this model for a single-family dwelling in a garden city. For the first time, Masó had the opportunity to design a new construction for a young family, in which he could express his family ideal. The house comprises a main three-storey volume with a hip roof. Built against this volume is a single storey that is the entrance porch with a curved-section shed roof. A third volume, also three floors high, contains the staircase, with a curved ridge roof. The volumetric organization of the three volumes manifests a consolidated and controlled architectural language.

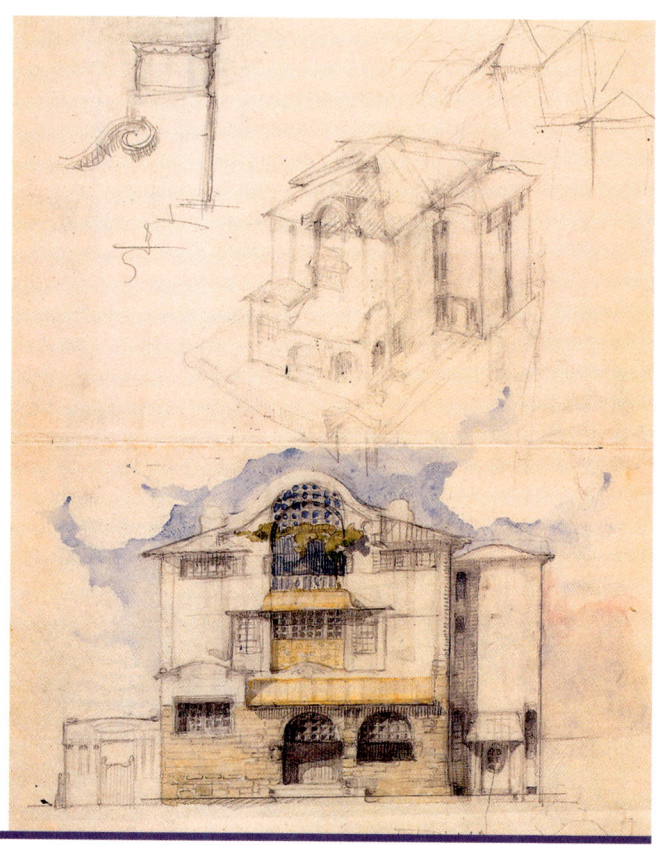

BASSOLS FACTORY

Joan Roca i Pinet
1916-1917

C/ Escultor Llimona, 1 - Olot

Roca i Pinet addressed the façade of an industrial building constructed between party walls with the instrumental baggage of domestic architecture, at the same time endeavouring to adapt to the characteristics of the programme. The great windows are located in the central part, divided into shutters, while those on the ground floor adopt curved borders and a central light that has a particular significance. The façade presents the classic gallery running beneath the eaves, displaying the metal supports. The mid-height base highlights the outlines of the ground-floor windows, and the basement openings have an ashlar base of their own.

337

SERRA HOUSE, "CASA DELS NASSOS"
APARTMENT BUILDING

Bartomeu Agustí
1931-1933

C/ Nou, 13 - Olot

338

AUBERT HOUSE, "EL CAFETÍN"
APARTMENT BUILDING

Joan Aubert i Camps
1936

C/ Sant Cristòfol, 3 - C/ Pont de la Salut, 2 - Olot

Aubert uses the building's corner situation to apply the best in rationalist rhetoric to the treatment of the built volume. The building has one dwelling per floor and, in the long façade, the architect created horizontal groupings of the windows of the kitchen, service areas and bedroom, reducing the surface area of voids in relation to full space. Concentrated at the corner are the openings of the living room, with its semicircular balcony and a window to either side. The ground floor and mezzanine form a great base to the building, from which it rises to the continuous eaves that unify the overall composition.

339

ARTUR SIMON FACTORY
DWELLINGS - OLOT CINEMAS
HEADQUARTERS OF TV OLOT

Joan Aubert i Camps
1940

C/ Josep Ayats, 10 - C/ Pou del Glaç, 6 - C/ Pere Lloses, 11 - Olot

Bartomeu Agustí (1905-1944) lived and worked in Olot all his life. Although he did not feature in the documents of the Associació d'Arquitectes de Catalunya until after his death, his limited built work is a faithful reflection of the guidelines of the rationalist movement. Serra House brings an intelligent solution to a residential programme on a street corner, positioning all the openings in the street façade and using a regular sequence of backward steps to address the irregularity of the plot. The resulting image of the building, seen from the corner, avoids presenting cut-off openings.

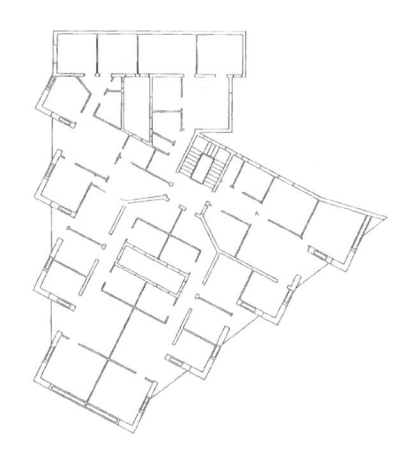

This is an example of the rationalism that prevailed during the years following the Civil War. This was originally an industrial building where electrical materials were manufactured. It comprises two storeys. The U-shaped floor plan has a focal point in the cylinder at the corner, where the openings extend double height: this is the point around which entrance to the building is organized. The factory presents innovations with regard to rationalist orthodoxy, such as the large openings divided into shutters or the flat façades organized around the structural columns. Aubert plays with elements from miscellaneous sources, such as the coffering and the singular outline of the canopy.

340

IES BOSC DE LA COMA
SECONDARY SCHOOL

José Antonio Martínez Lapeña, Elías Torres
1992-1995

C/ Toledo, 12 - Olot

SUBSEQUENT INTERVENTIONS:
José Antonio Martínez Lapeña,
Elías Torres, 2003-2004. Extension.

341

MARGARIDA HOUSE
SINGLE-FAMILY DWELLING

Rafael Aranda, Carme Pigem, Ramon Vilalta
1989-1993

C/ Sant Julià del Mont, 12 - Olot

The configuration of the house is determined by two pre-existing characteristics: the good orientation of the plot with regard to sun-lighting and the steeply sloping street, situated on the south side. The house takes the form of a cube with a terrace in front of it on a higher level, with the entrance from the street. An emerging volume welcomes those entering in a transitional movement, and on the other side are the garden and swimming pool, protected from the street. This volume leads into a vertical space that houses the stairs to the first floor, beside a double-height dining room at the heart of the house. The entire facing on the south side is designed as a moveable filter that allows numerous interplays of light, shade and transparency. The pergola that shades the façade on the ground floor also forms part of the facing. The house combines horizontal and vertical lines both in the floor plan and the elevation.

342

MIRADOR HOUSE
SINGLE-FAMILY DWELLING

Rafael Aranda, Carme Pigem, Ramon Vilalta
1997-1999

Road from Olot to Banyoles (GI-524), km 0,850
Olot

The school stands on the edge of the urban fabric of Olot, beside fields of crops, scattered constructions and a tree-covered hill. On one side, the site is bordered by an orthogonal edge, on the other by a winding track. The building is designed as an ordered structure of bare concrete and brickwork facings built over two levels to absorb the irregularity of the site. The classrooms on the upper level face south, and the staff rooms, library, assembly hall and gymnasium look northwards. The dining rooms and workshops are on the lower level, connected to the sports courts. The main entrance is located in the façade overlooking the only developed street. This is the building's centre of gravity and point of connection with the town. The project purposely seeks a sober finish that is obtained using limited materials and a uniform approach to the general organization.

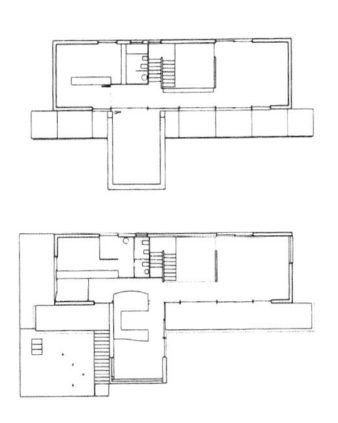

The house adopts as its central theme the magnificent landscape it overlooks. The architects inserted a conventional domestic programme into a symmetrical construction that stands open to views and is raised above grade over a basement with a glazed facing. The mirador feature is expressed in a configuration of two volumes, one to the fore and one to the rear, housing the kitchen, dining room and a gymnasium. The entrance hall is situated at the meeting point between the two volumes, with access via a great stairway at an angle to the house. The composition is based on symmetrical correspondences that do not adapt to the diversity of the programme: the living room, in the west, adopts the same configuration as the master bedroom, in the east; the entrance stairway has a replica in the stairs that descend to the basement. RCR Arquitectes explore formal regularity as a basis for investigation into potential new layouts of a domestic programme.

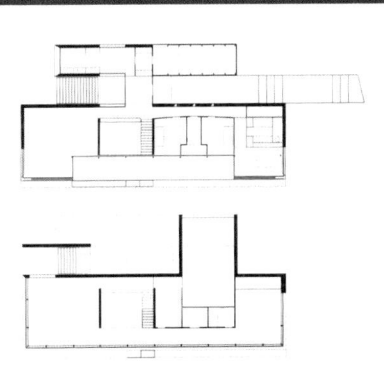

M-LIDIA HOUSE
SINGLE-FAMILY DWELLING

Rafael Aranda, Carme Pigem, Ramon Vilalta
2000-2003

C/ Sant Grau, 15 - La Cometa residential development - Montagut

On a small plot on the outskirts of the village, to which it is communicated by a track, RCR Arquitectes designed the house as a regular rectangle astride the track, which leads into the basement garage. The house, laid out on a single level, aspires to a high degree of formal regularity with its ABCBA layout, in which the Cs correspond to smaller bays, one of which contains the stairs leading up from the lower level. The house is a purist composition of three glazed volumes, clad with wire mesh, which accommodate the domestic programme in a transparent unitary space. The living-cum-dining room occupies the central volume, while the side volumes house the bedrooms of the parents and children, respectively. The other spaces, including the kitchen, bathrooms and study areas, are built against the far wall, forming a continuous cupboard that runs the entire length of the house.

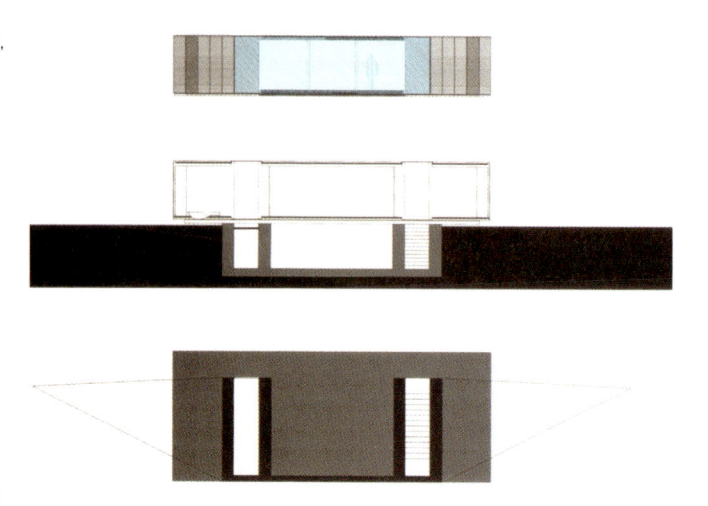

CENDRA HOUSE
REMODELLING AND EXTENSION OF A TOWNHOUSE

Rafael Masó
1913-1915

C/ Girona, 7-9 - Anglès

The extension of this townhouse comprises a series of volumes that make up the difference in level between the garden and the house, and reconstruct the rear façade. Masó recreated numerous elements of the house's architecture, such as the front door, outlined with abstract ornamentation and curvilinear vaults. These elements combine with others that seek to recover the imaginary of tradition, such as the white borders to the windows and the simple railings. Here, Masó began to combine bare brick, roofs with channel tiles, decorated and moulded facings and some surprisingly modern elements, such as the solution brought to the blinds. The house illustrates Masó capacity to be inspired by the sensibility of the Sezession or Mackintosh, combining it with solutions that manifest a desire to convey the values of tradition.

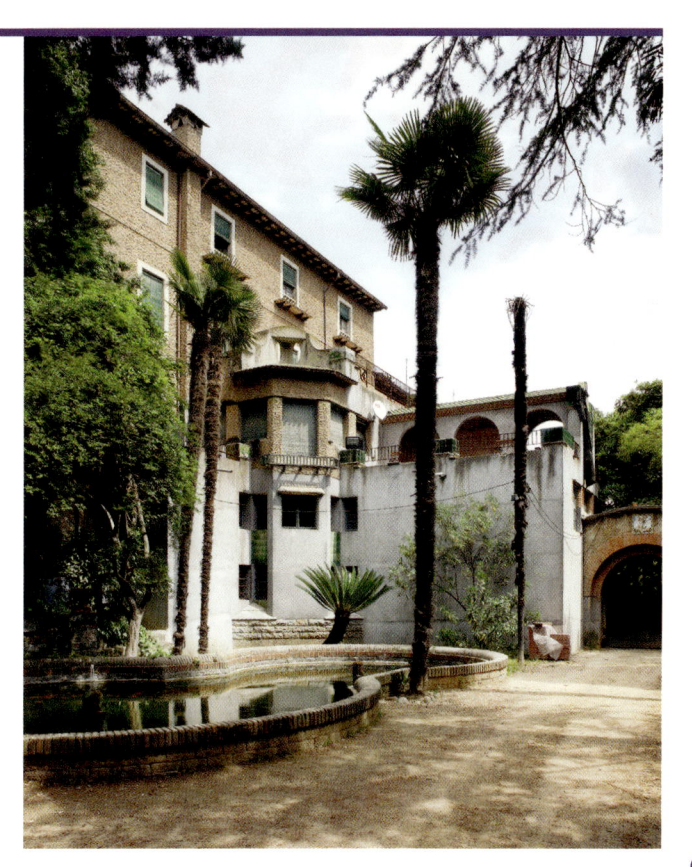

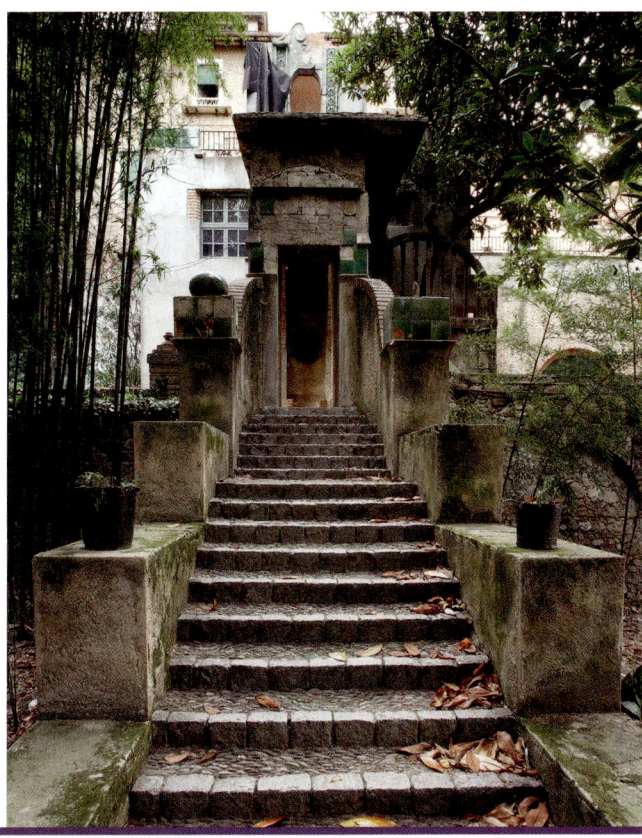

Ribes de Freser

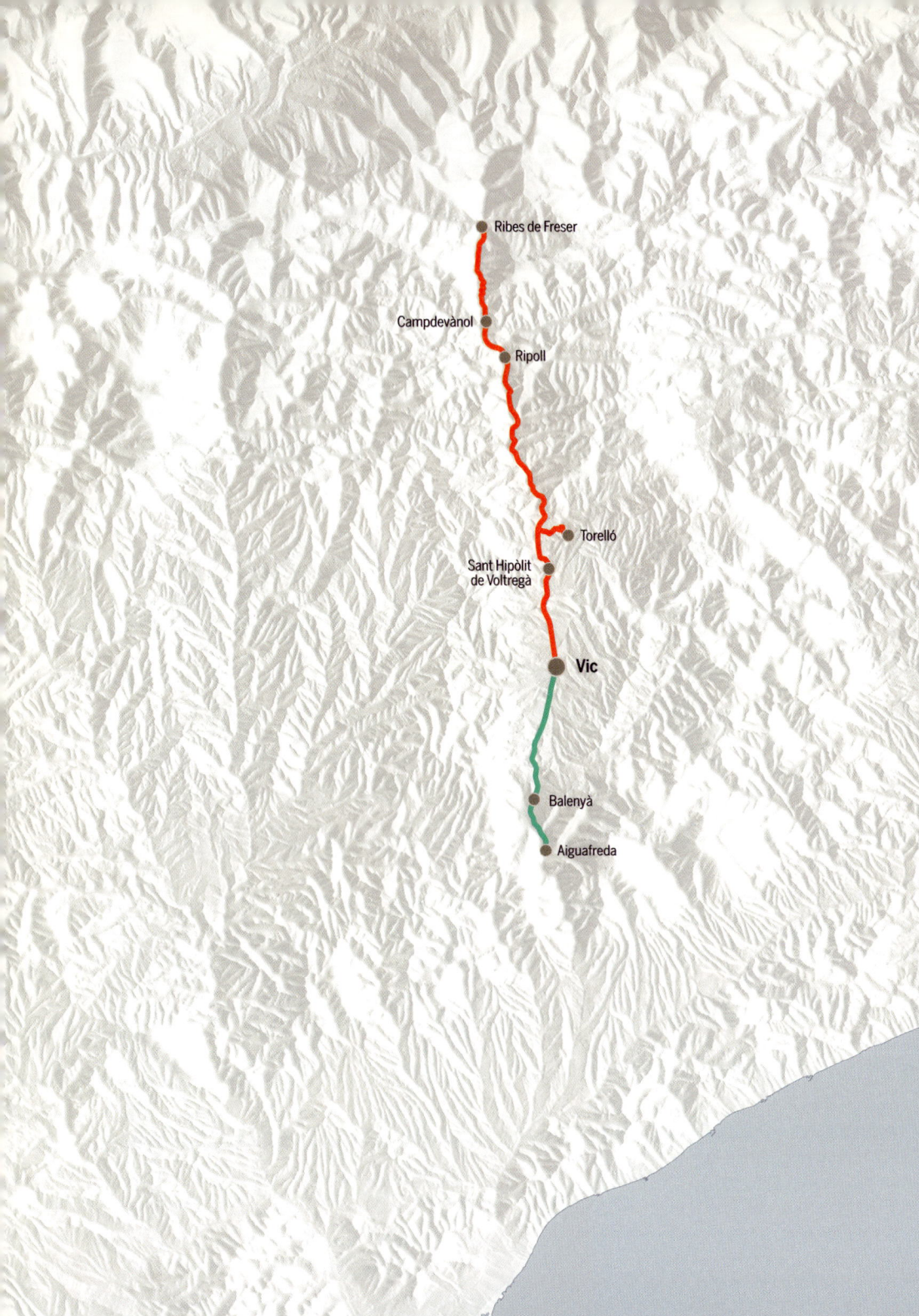

Campdevànol
Ripoll

Torelló
Sant Hipòlit
de Voltregà

Vic

Balenyà
Aiguafreda

VIC – The Vic Area

Territorial scope

The Vic area corresponds to the *comarques* of Osona and Ripollès, with a brief incursion into the *comarca* of Vallès Oriental to the south. This is the third area along the inland strip. To the east, it borders on Garrotxa and Selva, which correspond to the Olot area. To the west, it is edged by the counties of Bages and Berguedà, corresponding to the Manresa area. The area's central town is Vic, also the capital of Osona, from which one route heads north towards the county of Ripollès and another south, to Aiguafreda.

Road structure

The C-153 county road leads from Olot to Vic, taking a winding route over the Collsacabra range. To get to Vic from Figueres, you will also need to pass through Olot. From Vic to Manresa, take the C-25 county road, which offers a straighter route. Vic is well connected with Barcelona by the C-17 expressway that passes through Granollers and Hostalets de Balenyà. A network of county roads connects Vic to all the other main towns around it.

ROUTE 1
Route 1 starts out from Vic and heads north to Ribes de Freser. The C-17 county road will take you to Ripoll, where you can pick up the N-152 national road to Ribes de Freser, continuing to Puigcerdà. These two stretches will take you to Sant Hipòlit de Voltregà and Torelló before reaching Ripoll. On the way from Ripoll to Ribes de Freser you can stop off at Campdevànol. This route heads north in an almost straight line that dies out when it reaches the Pyrenees, leaving us at the foot of the Valley of Núria.

ROUTE 2
Route 2 also starts out from Vic and takes a straight line south to Aiguafreda. Here, the C-17 expressway to Barcelona will take you to Balenyà and Aiguafreda. You can also approach this area on your way from Barcelona, following Route 2 to Vic and then heading north to the Pyrenees along Route 1.

Ribes de Freser

Campdevànol
Ripoll
Olot
Vidrà
Torelló
Sant Hipòlit
de Voltregà
Vic

Balenyà
Aiguafreda

Manresa

Barcelona

Municipalities	*Comarca*	Surface area (municipality)	Population (2001)
VIC	Osona	30.6 km^2	32,703 inhabitants
ROUTE 1			
SANT HIPÒLIT DE VOLTREGÀ	Osona	0.9 km^2	3,047 inhabitants
TORELLÓ	Osona	13.5 km^2	12,286 inhabitants
RIPOLL	Ripollès	73.7 km^2	10,597 inhabitants
CAMPDEVÀNOL	Ripollès	32.6 km^2	3,378 inhabitants
RIBES DE FRESER	Ripollès	41.9 km^2	2,033 inhabitants
ROUTE 2			
BALENYÀ	Osona	17.4 km^2	3,213 inhabitants
AIGUAFREDA	Vallès Oriental	7.9 km^2	2,155 inhabitants

TOWN COURT

Pere Llimona, Xavier Ruiz Vallès
1967

C/ del Bisbe Morgades, 2 - Vic

The building interprets the varied, atomized programme for the town court by means of a metal structure that allows different distributions on each floor. The ground floor is a covered, open-plan space with an independent entrance to the Lawyers' Association inside the building. The openings on the various floors respond strictly to the requirements of the interior spaces. The building is manifested as a cube that fills in the corner between two streets in the new town extension, separated from its neighbours and structured like a series of trays ready to accommodate the diversity of the programme.

PUIG-PORRET APARTMENT BUILDING

Manuel Anglada
1971

C/ Verdaguer, 15-17 - Vic

Manel Anglada is the author of some of the most interesting apartment buildings constructed in the centre of Vic in the 1970s. The Puig-Porret building occupies a large site overlooking a street of some importància. The depth available for building and the width of the site led Anglada to design a building of ground floor plus five storeys in the north-facing frontage, with four dwellings per floor laid out around two stairways. The bedrooms are situated in the street façade, and the living rooms, kitchens and dining rooms are located on the opposite side, with good sunlighting conditions. Each dwelling has an octagonal gallery to optimize the amount of sunlight received in this façade. On the inside of the site is a lower three-floor volume, occupied by duplex apartments. Access from the street leads directly into the courtyard created between the two buildings. The façade overlooking the main street exploits the variety of projecting volumes and openings to avoid the monotony that could have been generated by the sheer size of the façade.

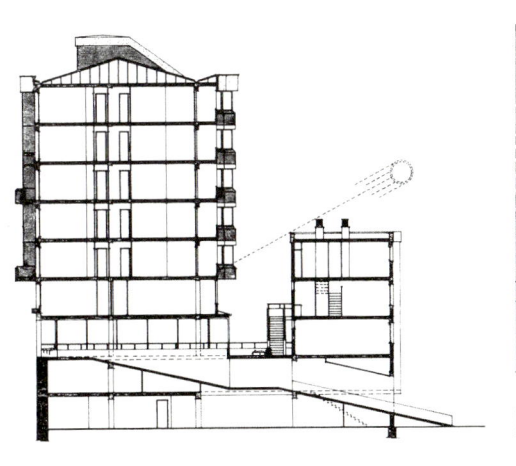

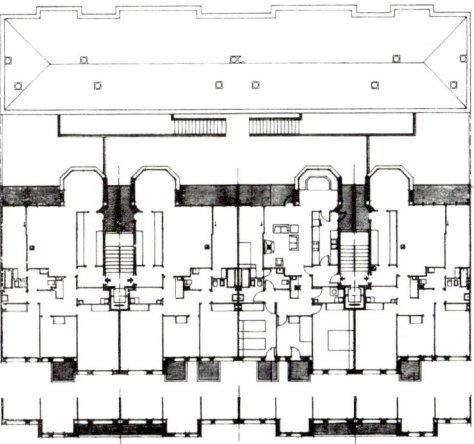

HEADQUARTERS OF THE OSONA BRANCH OF THE COL·LEGI D'ARQUITECTES DE CATALUNYA COAC

Dolors Ylla-Català, Joan Forgas
1993-1994

Pl. del Bisbe Oliva, 2 - Vic

The project establishes as its priority the configuration of the north side of the square, taking as a reference the buildings that surround it on the remaining sides: the cathedral, the old Episcopal Museum and a small apartment building. The site marks the corner of a street running crosswise and was previously occupied by a building, the wall of the Convent of the Servants of the Blessed Sacrament and the volume containing the convent cells. It was decided to demolish the old building and replace it with a new construction to complete the square and take on the representative role it required. The new building extends the wall of the side street and opens onto the square, generating the new façade. The choice of materials guarantees the status of the new construction in its monumental setting: stone cladding, stucco and timber lattices continue the construction procedures of the modern architecture tradition.

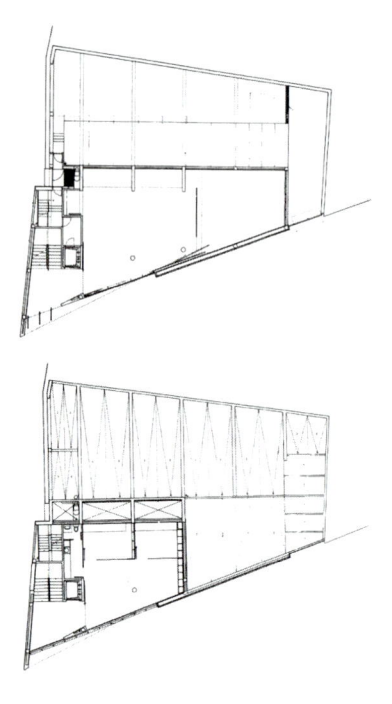

EPISCOPAL MUSEUM OF VIC

Federico Correa, Alfons Milà
1996-2002

Pl. del Bisbe Oliva, 3 - Vic

The project is based on a comprehensive knowledge of the holdings it houses, a closed collection, all of its exhibits, their dimensions and their artistic and historic value. The four-storey building adapts faithfully to the alignment of the narrow streets that delimit it, while the façade overlooking the square adopts a freer configuration. The arrangement of the openings, the roofing solution and the layout of the wall system establish a series of coincidences between the procedures and forms of modern architecture and the compositional logic of medieval constructions. The site's irregular shape lends itself to the arrangement of different elements. Vertical openings running the entire height of the building highlight views of monumental features of the town, seen from an interior where the lighting is controlled by mainly artificial means.

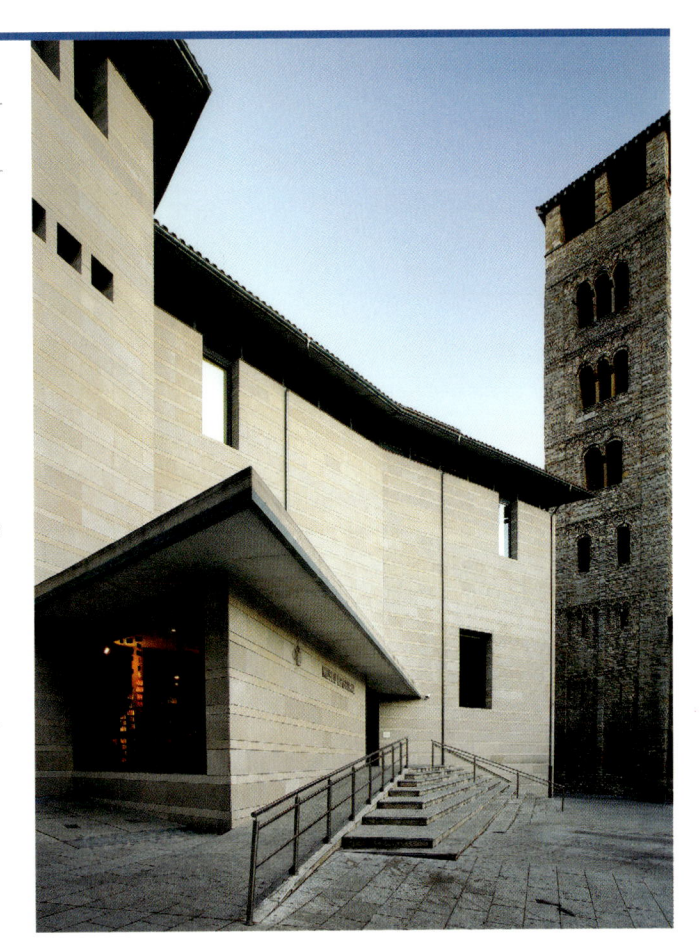

CAP SANT HIPÒLIT
HEALTH CENTRE

Albert Viaplana, Helio Piñón
1984-1986

C/ Vinya - Sant Hipòlit de Voltregà

The health centre stands on the edge of the municipality of Sant Hipòlit, on a site situated between the backs of the outlying houses and open countryside. The project responds to the peculiarity of the plot: it turns its back on the logic of the urban form and bases its formal elements on a diagrammatic reading of the programme. The health centre takes the form of an ellipsoid single-storey building, though the perimeter constructs the ellipse by means of a polygonal line. At the centre of the ellipse is the waiting room with an entrance at either end and direct access to the consultation rooms, which form a perimetric ring. The structure, comprising concrete pillars and main beams, faithfully follows this radial arrangement, even in the orientation of the pillars. The order of the openings highlights this indifference, as they start at ground level and their composition is dictated by sun-shading elements.

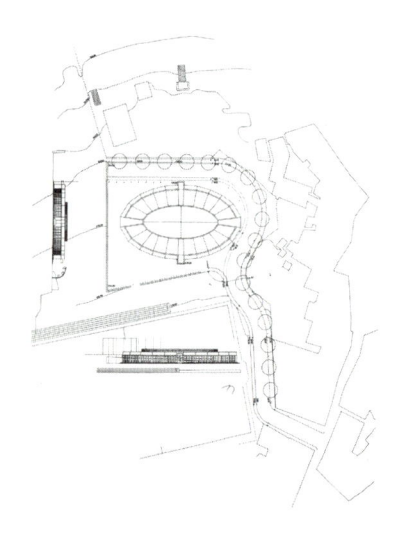

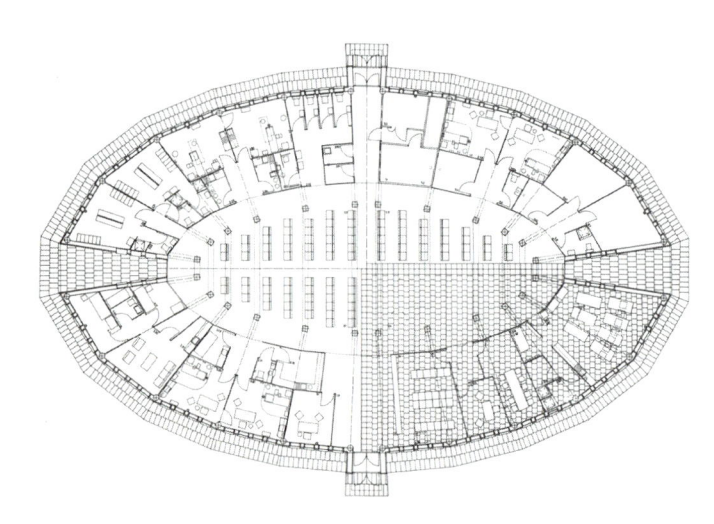

APARTMENT BUILDING

Josep Lluís Mateo
1992-1995

C/ Capsavila, 13-17 - Torelló

The building stands in a narrow, winding street in the old town of Torelló. The characteristics of the street prompt the building to relate actively and generously to make up for the shortcomings of the public space. The programme called for dwellings on the two top floors and public services on the ground floor. This twofold requirement brought about a juxtaposition of structural technologies. In the dwellings, brick walls form the bearing structure, while the ground floor rests on concrete pillars. By manipulating the resulting image, the building, which is solid at the top, seems to float over the street, thereby increasing the public domain. The apartment façade has deliberate recourse to the contextual commonplaces of long windows and balconies, distorting them without foregoing a stereotyped image that fosters communication.

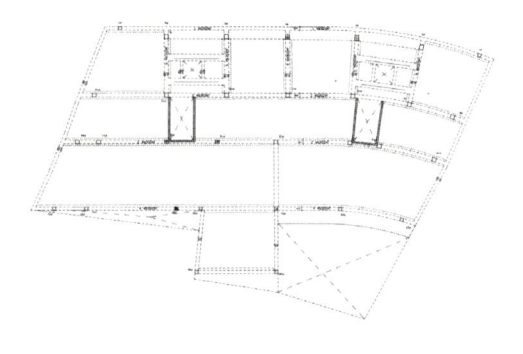

RETIREMENT HOME

Josep Lluís Mateo
1991-1994

C/ Girona, 9 - Campdevànol

In a mountainous landscape without urban references, the building takes the form of a block that highlights the straight line of the road running through the valley. The long side of the home, overlooking the road, gets the midday sun and commands good views. The north-facing rear of the building, overlooking the mountains, is like a retaining wall. The layout of the floors is also associated with this natural feature, at the same time forming a complex articulation of north-south, sun-shade, views-no views. The east façade, the first to be seen when arriving from the village, gives a fragmentary view of the depth of the building. The materials and construction follow the same logic: the south façade expresses the different dimensions of the rooms. The zinc projecting wall presents a lighter, mobile face. The north façade is built of concrete blocks, deployed using a technology that introduces horizontal openings.

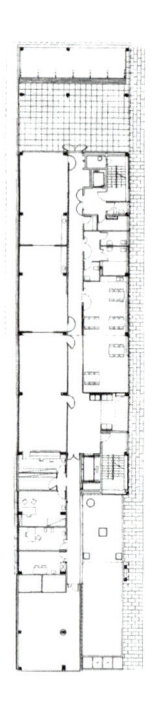

CHAPEL OF SANT MIQUEL DE LA ROQUETA
"LA CAPELLETA"

Joan Rubió i Bellver
1912

C/ Indústria, 1 - Ripoll

Rubió designed a small chapel dedicated to Sant Miquel de la Roqueta in the wake of his work on the baldaquin of the church at Ripoll monastery, marked by controversy. He decided to construct a small, modest Christian church using local natural stone. This chapel constituted a study for subsequent constructions. It is built of natural stone, as plain as when it came out of the quarry. In short, it complied with his theory of dry-stone construction. The chapel combines traditional forms of architecture with others clearly taken from Gaudí's imaginary, such as the arched portico and the amalgam of domed elements. The floor plan is a simple circle against which are built a main apse and four semicircular side chapels. The vaults of the chapels and the roof of the main aisle are also built of dry stone.

CAMPAÑÀ HOUSE

Josep Maria Sostres
1971-1974

Ventolà (Ribes de Freser)

The house is situated at an altitude of 1,400 metres on the outskirts of the village of Ventolà, on a steeply sloping site with 180-degree panoramic views. Two principal volumes separated by a smaller section that contains the entrance are situated on a lowered platform. An outdoor stairway linking the two volumes leads to the living space. The east volume with its square floor plan houses the daytime areas in a unitary space, in which the kitchen is not set apart. The west volume, containing the bedrooms, stands further forwards and rests directly on the platform. The shed roofs highlight the independence of each volume and, together with the openings and renderings, strengthen the tension between the two. Sostres employed characteristic procedures of modern architecture to recreate domestic life with the same intensity in a mountainous region.

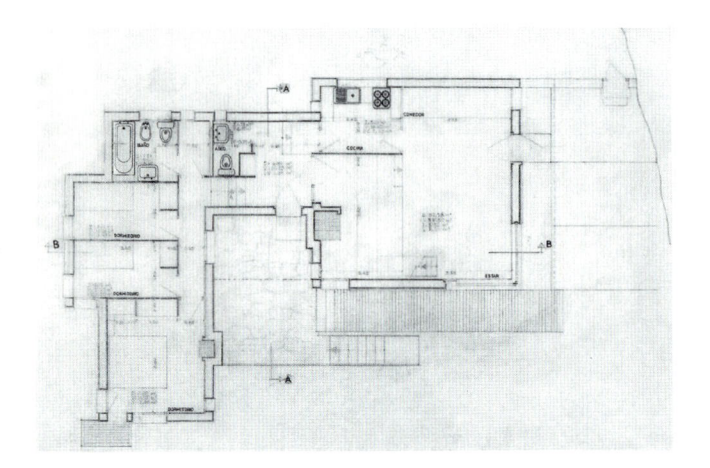

XAMPENY HOUSE

Josep Maria Sostres
1971-1974

Ventolà (Ribes de Freser)

Here Sostres applied a combination of procedures that tends to create great complexity in both the interior and the configuration of volumes. He employed two geometries at 45 degrees to create a space with a marked unitary character, in which each domestic function is judiciously positioned. A single ridge roof is superposed independently of the wall system, its limit established by intersection with the perimetric facings. Inside, its superposition over the various spaces produces a number of false ceilings, built according to the particularities of each room. The fireplace has a twofold distributive and structural function. Sostres created interferences between a variety of logics in order to combine complexity and random coincidences in a geometric mechanism based on a very direct interpretation of the programme that is free of formal prejudice.

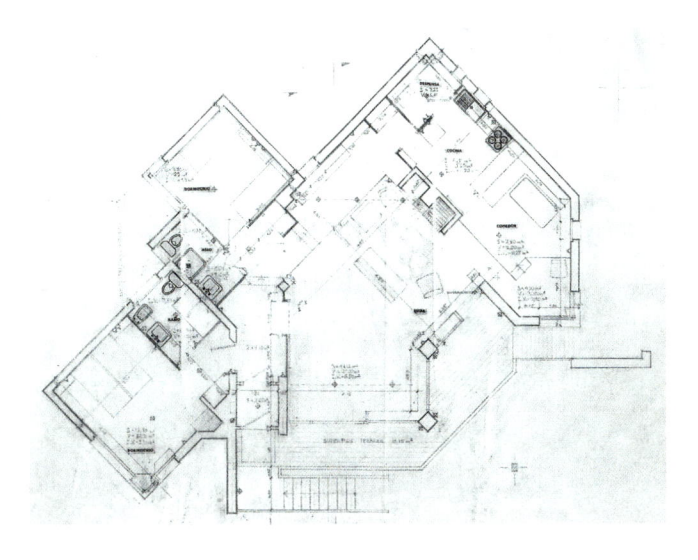

HOSTALETS DE BALENYÀ CIVIC CENTRE
BALENYÀ COUNCIL

Enric Miralles, Carme Pinós
1986-1993

C/ Pista, 2 - Els Hostalets de Balenyà
Balenyà

The programme was for the design of the characteristic spaces of a civic centre on a site on the outskirts of Hostalets de Balenyà. Miralles and Pinós designed a building that turns its back on the village and created a transparent façade that generates a public space of its own, on the other side of the street. The smaller spaces in the programme (workshops, classrooms, offices) are suspended on the upper floors, comprising a system of open-web girders that open in a fan arrangement with the height of one floor. This fan marks out the inner garden and the large empty space formed beneath it, an assembly hall for 300 persons. The programme is given a hierarchical interpretation that combines with the reading of the site, allowing the building to house programmes with a similar division. The stairs leading to the attic space embrace the building on both sides, inside and out.

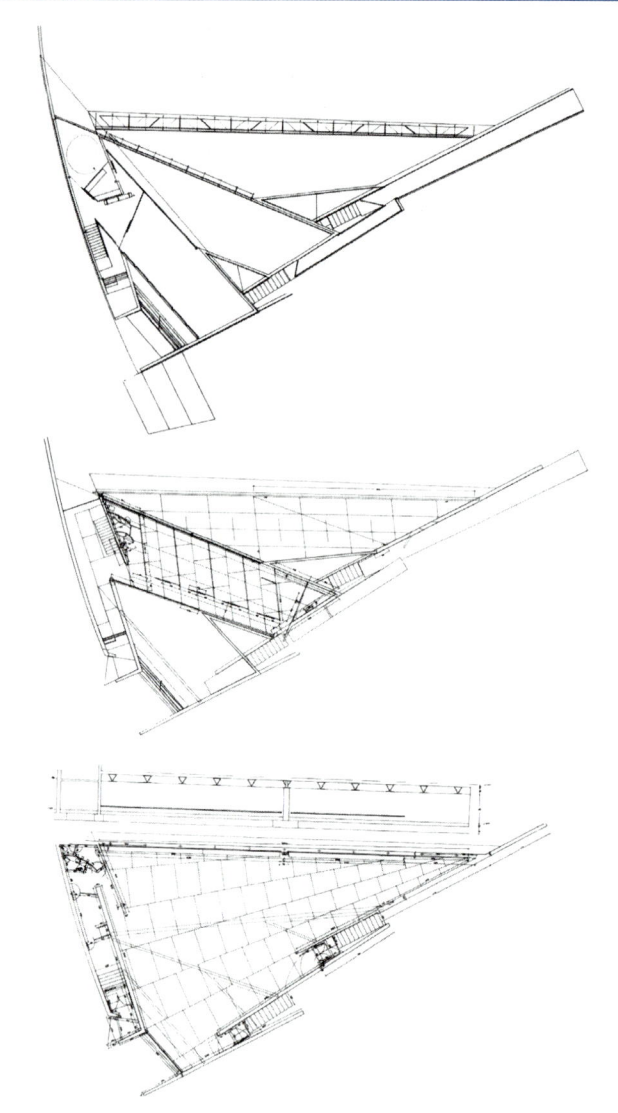

MARTÍN HOUSE
SINGLE-FAMILY DWELLING

Emili Donato, Uwe Geest
1972-1974

C/ Romaní - Serrabanda residential development
Aiguafreda

The house stands on a small, steeply sloping plot that commands splendid views of the wooded hillsides on the north side of the village of Aiguafreda. The dwelling lays out its programme very freely in the three dimensions, adapting to the slope and organizing the different rooms in a compact volume. The living room, kitchen and dining room are given a terraced layout over the ground floor that takes them up to the level of the small garden at the rear. An intermediate floor houses the master bedroom, and a third level contains the study. The scattered volumes of the house are brought together by a shed roof, a sloping plane that offers south-facing views from the street and the front door. The house comprises a single floor in some places and three levels at the highest points, allowing each part of the domestic programme to construct its own volume. An inner courtyard allows access right around the house via the garden. From the street, the porch, the semi-basement entrance and the door of the garage combine to comprise the house's outer image.

Castellar
de n'Hug
Guisona
Sant Fruitós
de Bages
Manresa
Cervera
Igualada

MNR - The Manresa Area

Territorial scope

The Manresa area centres around the *comarca* of Bages, on the inland edge of Catalonia. Although few buildings in this area are included in the guide, it has a very large surface. To the north, it takes in the whole Berguedà county, as far as Castellar de n'Hug, just before the county of Cerdanya. To the east, it borders on Vic, in the county of Osona. To the west, it includes the counties of Solsonès and Segarra, and to the south it makes a brief incursion into Anoia, the capital of which is the important town of Igualada. Along the west of this area are the counties that form part of the Lleida area, the final one in this inland strip. To the north it is bordered by the counties of the Pyrenean foothills and the Pyrenees themselves, which in this guide correspond to the area of La Seu d'Urgell.

Road structure

If you are driving from Vic to Manresa, take the C-25 road, which leads straight there. To reach Manresa from Lleida, the best route is the N-141 national road to Cervera where you pick up the A-2 motorway from Barcelona via Igualada. To drive from Barcelona directly to Manresa, the best option is the C-16 motorway, which leads out of the capital via the Vallvidrera tunnels. Manresa marks the halfway point of the C-16 motorway heading north to the tunnels of the Cadí mountain range, through the Pyrenees to Cerdanya, Puigcerdà and the south of France.

ROUTE 1
Route 1 follows the C-16 motorway northwards. Sant Fruitós de Bages is very close to Manresa, to the northeast, along the C-16. A turnoff to the left past Berga leads to Castellar de n'Hug, taking the B-402 local road that leads from La Pobla de Lillet.

ROUTE 2
Route 3 takes the N-141 westwards to Cervera, following the road to Lleida. From Cervera, the L-311 local road leads north via Guissona. This large flat area of land is crisscrossed by a whole network of county roads with no major road reference.

ROUTE 3
Route 3 leads southwest from Manresa to Igualada along the C-37 county road. Santa Margarida de Montbui is very close to Igualada, to the west along the C-241 county road.

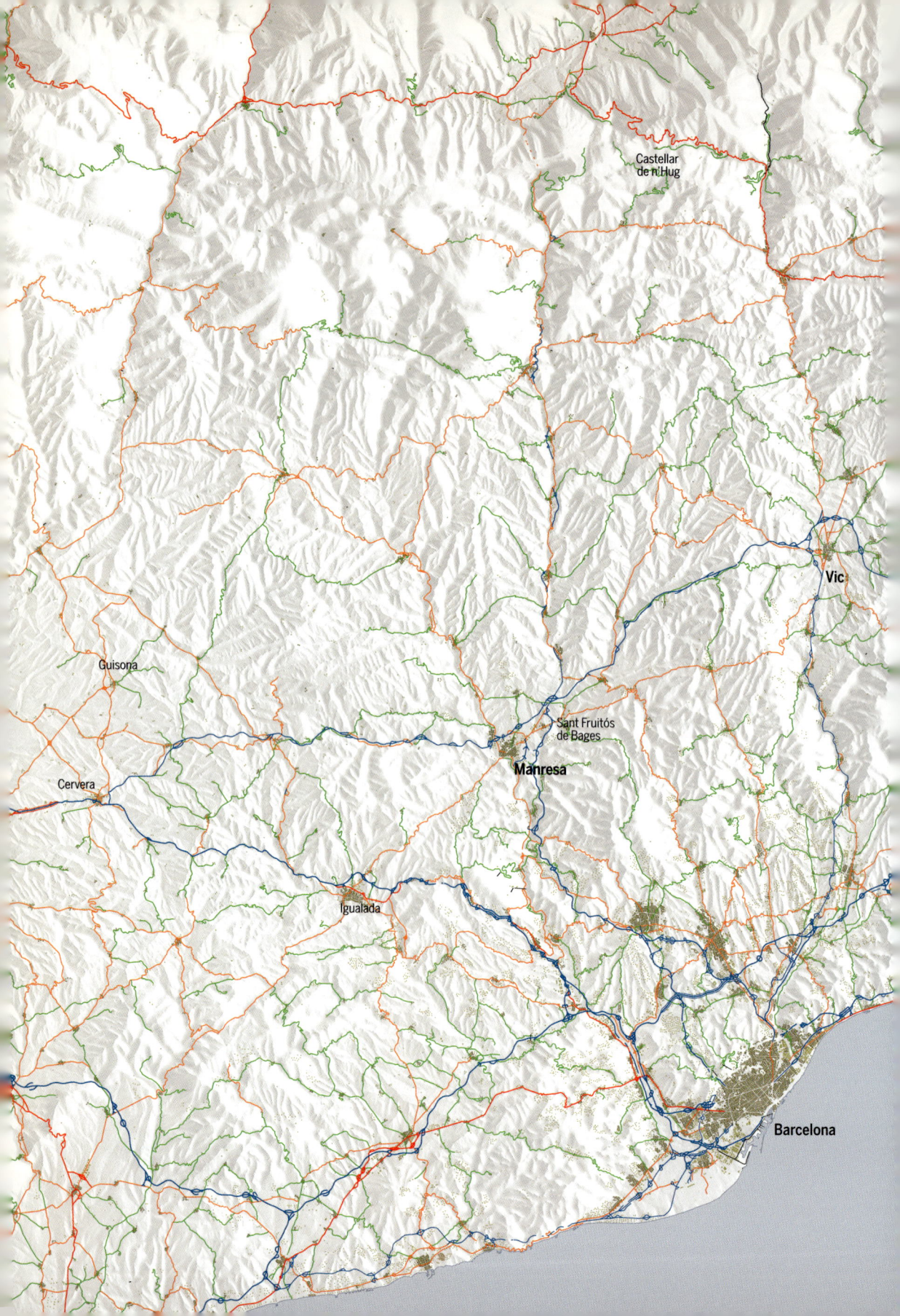

Castellar de n'Hug

Vic

Guisona

Sant Fruitós de Bages

Manresa

Cervera

Igualada

Barcelona

Municipalities	Comarca	Surface area (municipality)	Population (2001)
MANRESA	Bages	41.7 km^2	63,981 inhabitants
ROUTE 1			
SANT FRUITÓS DE BAGES	Bages	22.2 km^2	5,936 inhabitants
CASTELLAR DE N'HUG	Berguedà	47.1 km^2	170 inhabitants
ROUTE 2			
CERVERA	Segarra	55.2 km^2	7,917 inhabitants
GUISSONA	Segarra	18.1 km^2	3,581 inhabitants
ROUTE 3			
IGUALADA	Anoia	8.1 km^2	33,049 inhabitants

357

SANATORIUM OF SANT JOAN DE DÉU
HOSPITAL OF SANT JOAN DE DÉU

Germán Rodríguez Arias
1931

C/ Dr. Joan Soler - Manresa

358

RENAIXENÇA SCHOOL COMPLEX
SCHOOLS

Pere Armengou
1934

Pl. de la Independència, 1 - Manresa

359

DWELLINGS AROUND A SQUARE
TWO SOCIAL HOUSING BLOCKS

Enric Massip-Bosch, Joan Sabaté, Horacio Espeche
1996-2000 (phase 1)
2001-2002 (phase 2)

Phase 1:
C/ Santa Llúcia, 18-22 - Pl. de la Immaculada -
C/ Codinella, 11-15
Phase 2:
Via de Sant Ignasi, 1 - Pl. de la Immaculada
Manresa

The sanatorium was built for 35 rachitic, pre-tubercular children with Pott's disease, using the budget allocated for this purpose. It is situated in the highest part of the town, providing constant ventilation and splendid views all around. The floor plan follows a linear layout, interrupted by an obtuse angle, the bisector of which follows a strict north-south line, allowing sunlight into the gallery, the largest space. Part of the gallery receives the early morning sun, and the other part receives sunlight in the afternoon, guaranteeing maximum exposure to the sun for patients.

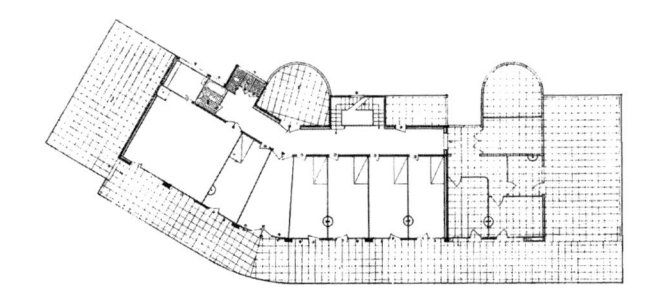

The project approach draws on the optimum conditions of the site: facing south-east, isolated, raised above the surrounding roads in a central location. The building stands to the rear of the plot, respecting the naturally terraced terrain, in order to create the most favourable sunlight conditions for the playground and the main façade. The main volume is divided into three bays, of which the front one, measuring 6.40 metres, houses the classrooms. Each classroom receives sunlight through two large windows with impermeable blinds. The second bay (3 metres) is occupied by the corridor, and the rear bay (4.75 metres) accommodates complementary spaces.

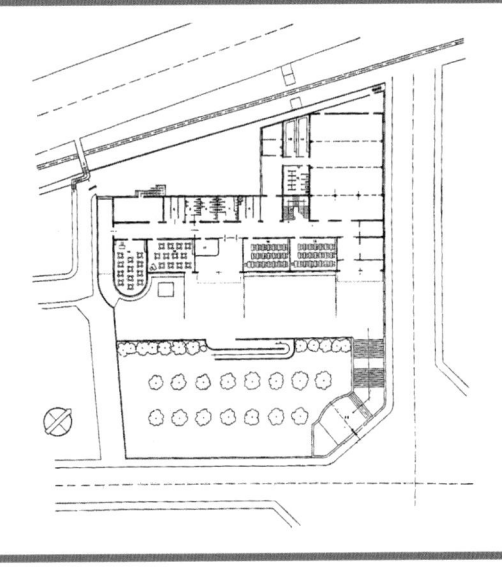

This is a unitary proposal for two separate blocks enclosing a square that are subject to the same urban planning conditions. The dwellings adopt present-day typologies, though the front and rear skins are configured in relation to the context: the outer limit of the town centre and, therefore, the façade of old Manresa. The rear façades pick up the traditional galleries, whereas those in the front, in keeping with prevailing legislation, adopt a succession of tall narrow windows that form a link, despite the difference in level, between the two blocks and the old houses to either side.

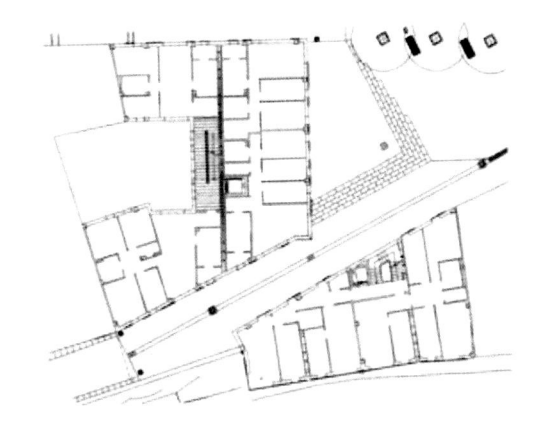

IES GERBERT D'AURILLAC
SECONDARY SCHOOL

Jordi Bosch, Joan Tarrús
1997-2000

Av. Lluís Companys - Sant Fruitós de Bages

The school occupies a plot on the edge of land for development, behind a ring road at the foot of a hill planned as an urban park. The building presents a forceful frontage, adjusting its volume to the curve of the road with a view to completing the urban context of the other side of the street. This very long, narrow arm comprises three different volumes for various uses, connected from one end to the other along the first floor. The classroom block forms a second arm that adapts to the topography of the site, separating the entrance from the playground and the sports courts. Entrance to the school is via a three-level porch at one end. It is implanted on the plot in such a way as to command views of the hill from inside the school, which forms a built limit between urban land and the park planned behind it.

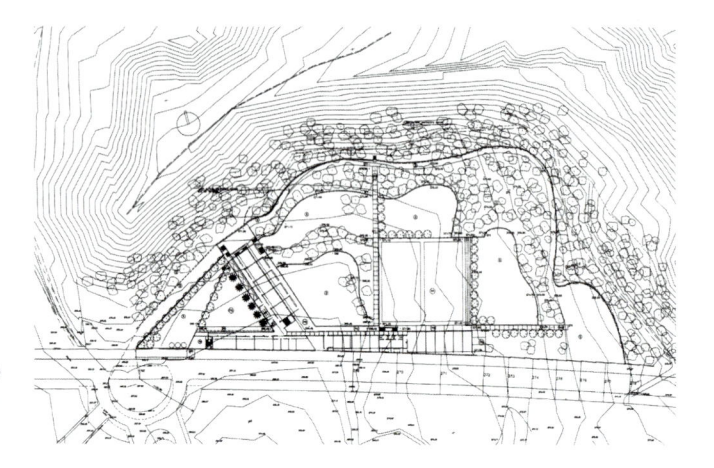

SINGLE-FAMILY DWELLING

Antoni Poch, Jordi Moliner
1998

C/ Bruc, 19 - Sant Fruitós de Bages

The house's bearing structure organizes and defines each of the spaces and uses of the plot as a whole. An orderly grid with bays of 4.5 metres determines the general areas of the house, both in the interior and outside. The ground floor adopts an E-shape, giving rise to courtyards between the wings that also address the issues of views and orientation. The upper floor follows a linear layout, superposed on the E-shape of the ground floor, creating terraces that overlook the courtyards below. These terraces are communicated by walkways that generate an interesting itinerary around the outside of the house. The result is the application of the domestic programme to a series of pre-established geometric and structural data.

ASLAND FACTORY
CEMENT MUSEUM (MNACTEC)

Rafael Guastavino
1901-1904

Paratge del Clot del Moro - Castellar de n'Hug

This was the first factory of Companyia Asland, set up in 1901 by the industrialist and patron Eusebi Güell. It started operations in 1903 and was the country's first factory to produce Portland cement. The complex was given a staggered or cascade arrangement on the right bank of the source of the river Llobregat. This arrangement facilitated the production process, thanks to its proximity to the source of extraction of the raw materials, allowing it to harness the hydraulic energy produced by the river. The factory functioned according to the principle of gravity. At the top, the marl and limestone were collected from quarries situated further up the hillside, and at the base the finished product was obtained. For the constructions, Guastavino used Catalan brick-built vaults and ties, with spans of 12 metres. A small narrow-gauge railway with 60-centimetre wide tracks connected the factory with the towns of Berga and Manresa. The factory closed down in 1975.

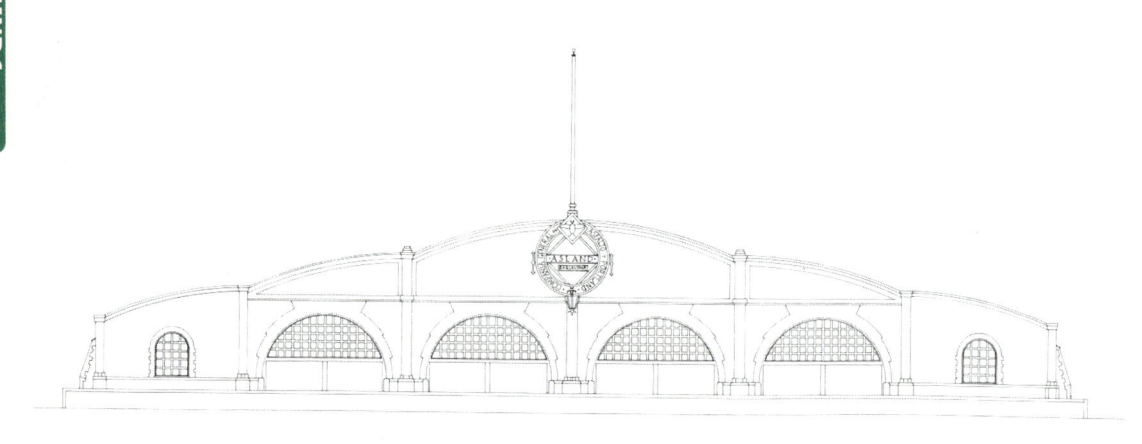

CABANÍ HOUSE
SINGLE-FAMILY DWELLING

Eduard Bru
1992-1994

Plot 2 - District of Cal Ros - Castellar de n'Hug

The principal values of the place are its location and the landscape. The lines of sight over the Pyrenean foothills and mountains follow the slope of the site. The house is set before the landscape, adapting to its incline. The front door is on the top floor, forming the entrance to a construction that comes to occupy two levels as it descends the slope. The lower floor is designed to house the cars and accommodate the library. It also organizes the outdoor space by imposing a series of geometries shared with the topography and the views, in the form of a series of descending terraces which communicate with the house. The top level stands firmly on the base created by the ground floor and, freed from contact with the ground, it seeks out relations with the landscape. The tension of the curve sloughs off the various layers that form the walls, producing habitable spaces.

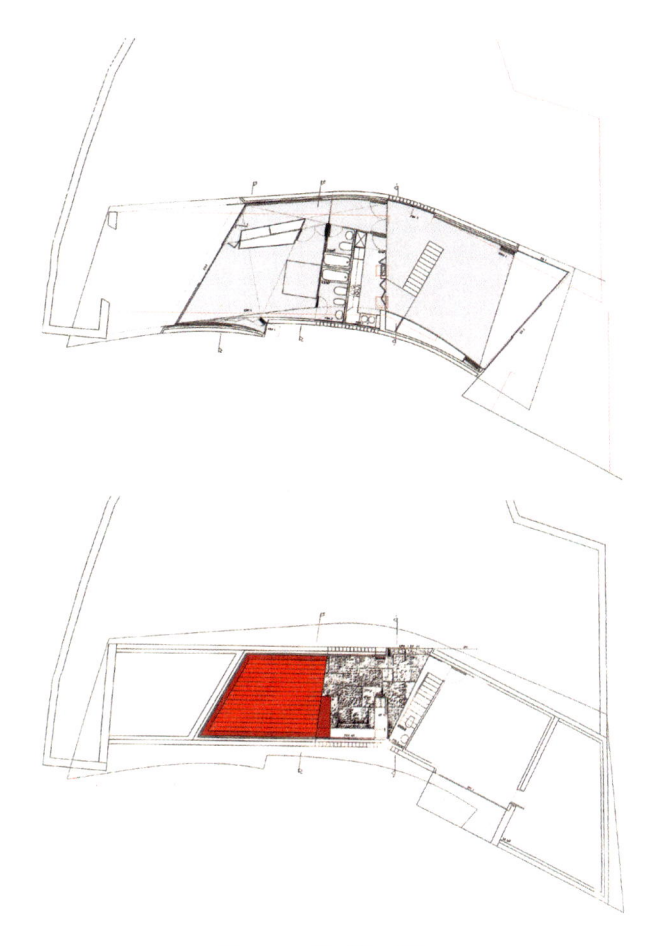

CERVERA FLOURMILL

Cèsar Martinell
1920-1922

Antic camí de Castellnou - Cervera

The task facing Martinell on this site was to design an architectural container to house the machinery needed for the mill flour, the plans for which were provided by the Swiss firm Maillart. Martinell designed a three-storey building with iron framework, timber flooring and walls built of local stone that was easy to square and engrave with exterior decoration. The programme included the construction of a raised water deposit built on brickwork vaults reinforced with two layers of brick, forming a tower with a semi-spherical dome at its centre.

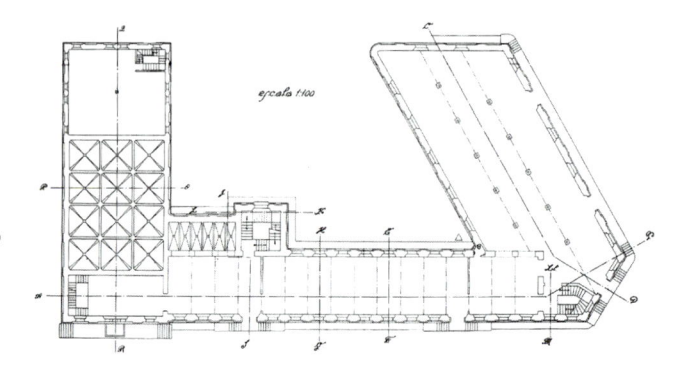

BLOCK OF 16 SOCIAL DWELLINGS AND DEVELOPMENT OF THE STREET BLOCK INTERIOR

Eva Prats, Ricardo Flores
2001-2004

C/ Sant Pol, 15-17 - Guissona

This building closes the perimeter of a street block of houses comprising different construction types in an area of new growth with no hierarchy of scale between public and private space. The project sets out to create a series of intermediate spaces of gradation between the dwellings, the street and the public square at the centre of the street block. The new building includes the design of entrances to the square via folds at the two ends and in the centre of the façade. Entrance to the dwellings, all south-facing, is via the central courtyard, making it a communal space for the residents of both blocks.

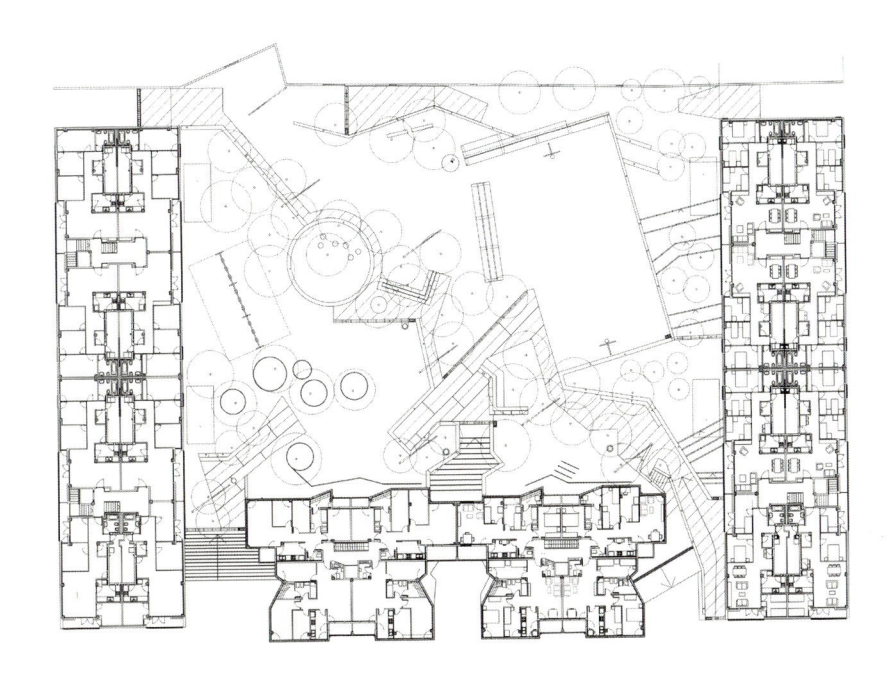

THE NEW CEMETERY, IGUALADA

Enric Miralles, Carme Pinós
1985-1991

Les Comes industrial estate - Igualada

The cemetery is designed as a park, as "the house of the living", a place to enjoy the sun and peace and quiet any day of the week. The configuration of the park has recourse to a promontory on the site to make a lengthwise loop and creates a zigzagging descent to a stream a few metres below. The overall project envisaged a zigzag of three sections, though just one was built in the first phase and the start of the second is merely suggested. The recessed tombs are arranged to either side of the path, forming intermediate terraces. Further paths branch off to the sides, leading to the terraces and generating a rising and falling movement with obvious allegorical connotations. All the recess tomb elements are built of prefabricated modules made of concrete, like the cladding of the retaining walls. As a result, at all points the dead are below ground level, and visitors descend to the lower level to reach the graves. The chapel is situated at the start of the itinerary, prompting a ritual that begins with the funeral and descends to each tomb. Enric Miralles is buried in one of the vaults bordering the square that marks the start of the second zigzag.

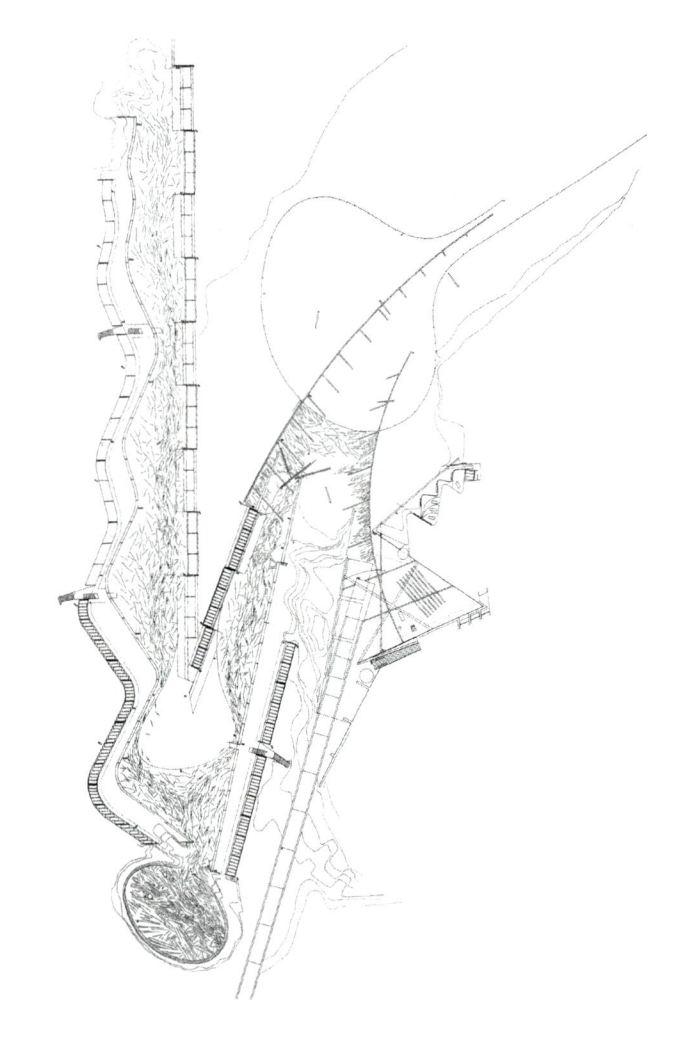

Manresa

HOTEL CIUTAT D'IGUALADA

Manuel Bailo, Rosa Rull
2003

Pg. Mossèn Verdaguer, 167 - Igualada

The hotel is situated on the corner formed by Passeig Mossèn Verdaguer and Avinguda Pau Casals, two of the town's main thoroughfares. The 1000 square metre site on which it stands was intended to close in a street block of residential buildings between party walls. The project approach is based on bringing an unconventional town planning approach to the completion of the street block, referring to the party wall context of the neighbouring streets as an element that classifies the urban space. Consequently, the new hotel does not fill up the available site, instead adopting a configuration in which its inner party walls, converted into structural elements, are revealed to view and constitute the image of the building and its internal organization. The possibility of making the party walls a visible part of the building also prompted their use as components in the interior space. The site is occupied by two narrower interlocking volumes that facilitate the application of this mechanism. As a result, the hotel rooms, on the top three floors, do not require specific treatment of the end walls, as in conventional hotel typologies.

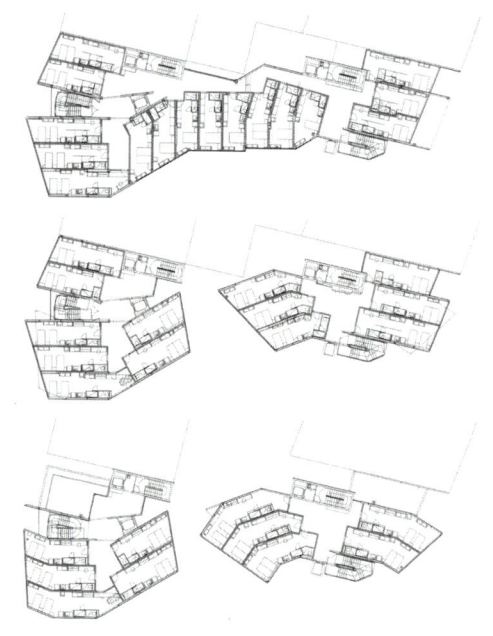

IGUALADA HOSPITAL

Emili Donato, Julio Alberto Pueyo, Miguel Jiménez
2002-2006

Av. Catalunya, 11 - Igualada

The new hospital adopts a low-rise, extensive layout which allows for greater flexibility of adaptation to future changes and restructuring required by the evolution of health-care technologies. This model also makes the most of the conditions of natural ventilation and lighting. The building is arranged according to the axis of Avinguda Montaner; on the basis of this directrix, it generates a rectangular grid that organizes the entire building and the internal layout of the site. The building is like a great two-storey base that accommodates the more dynamic and progressive services, while the more static traditional hospitalization facilities are housed at the top. The base forms an extensive volume that occupies the whole site, crisscrossed by a system of internal routes and a series of courtyards that guarantee natural ventilation. The two wings of hospitalization facilities are given a different roofing system, comprising a sheet-metal arc that reaches the end walls and gives this part of the building an identity of its own.

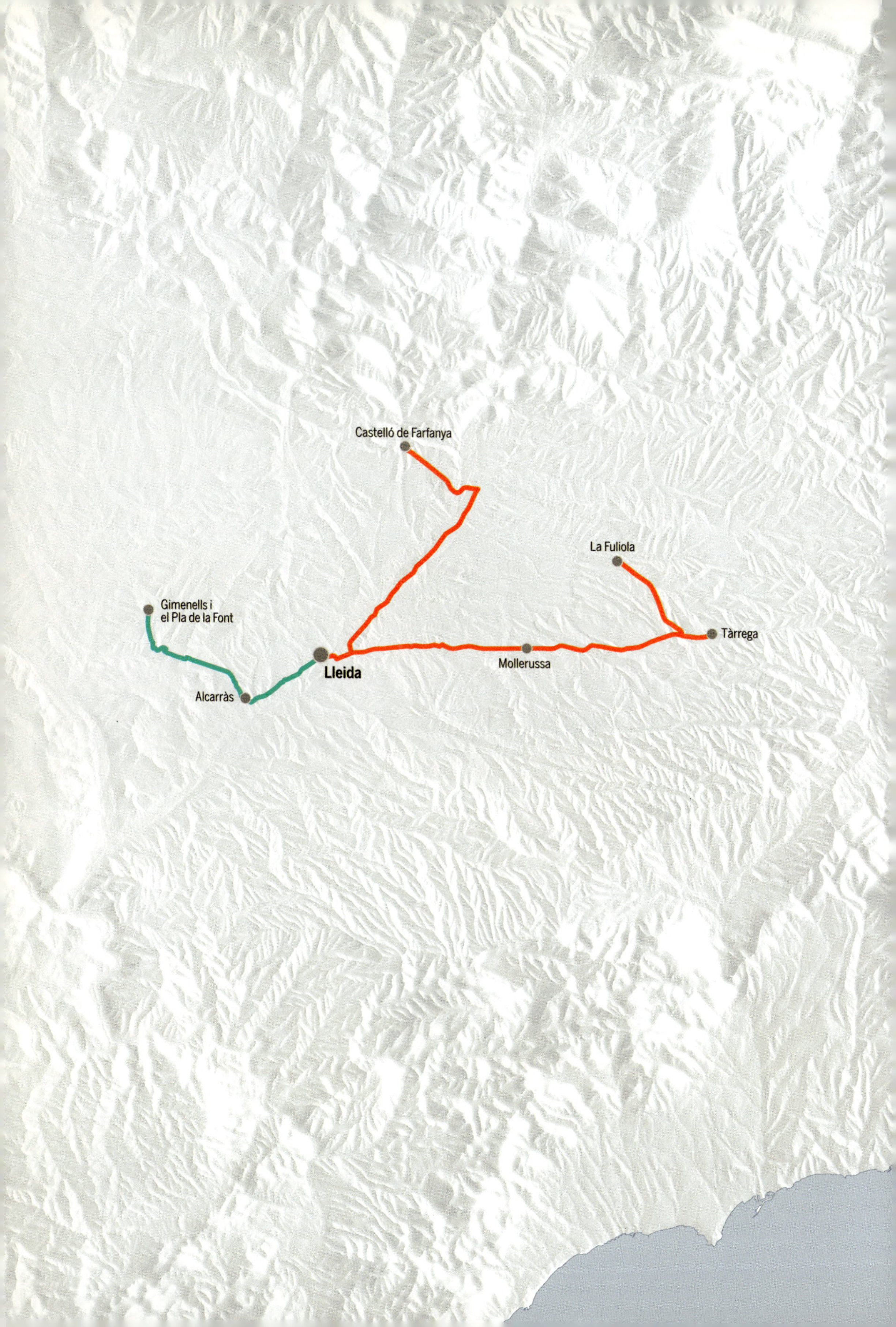
Castelló de Farfanya
La Fuliola
Gimenells i
el Pla de la Font
Tàrrega
Lleida
Mollerussa
Alcarràs

LLD – The Lleida Area

Territorial scope

The Lleida area covers a group of *comarques*, or counties, situated along the western strip of inland Catalonia. Lleida is the capital of the *comarca* of Segrià, on the border with Aragon. The area extends east to take in Pla d'Urgell and Urgell, and to the north it includes the southern half of the county of Noguera, as far as Castelló de Farfanya. This is a large high plain with a small population. It is bordered to the east by the counties of Segarra and Solsonès, which form the western part of the Manresa area. To the west it is bordered by Aragon, to the north by Pallars Jussà and Alt Urgell (the southern part of the area of La Seu d'Urgell in this guide) and to the south by Les Garrigues, Conca de Barberà and Priorat, three counties included in the north of the Tortosa area. This area is dotted with small scattered villages and towns, important for agriculture and crisscrossed by numerous county roads.

Road structure

If you are driving from Manresa to Lleida, the best option is to take the C-37 county road to Igualada and there pick up the A-2 motorway. An alternative route from Manresa is to take the N-141 to Cervera and then join the motorway. In either case, you need to take the A-2 motorway to Lleida. This motorway connects Barcelona directly with Lleida, as does the AP-2 motorway, via Vilafranca del Penedès. This latter, more recent motorway joins Lleida with Saragossa and Madrid. Tarragona and Lleida are also connected by the AP-2 motorway, which branches off northeast to Barcelona at El Vendrell or southwest to Tarragona.

ROUTE 1
Route 1 heads east out of Lleida, and has two branches. The A-2 motorway takes you to Mollerussa and Tàrrega. Before Tàrrega, a turnoff along the C-53 county road leads to La Fuliola. The second branch heads northeast out of Lleida, taking the C-13 county road to Balaguer. From Balaguer, the C-12, a completely flat, straight road, will take you to Castelló de Farfanya.

ROUTE 2
Heading southwest from Lleida, the N-II will take you to Alcarràs. The local L-800 road leads northwest from Alcarràs to Gimenells. This is Catalonia's westernmost municipality.

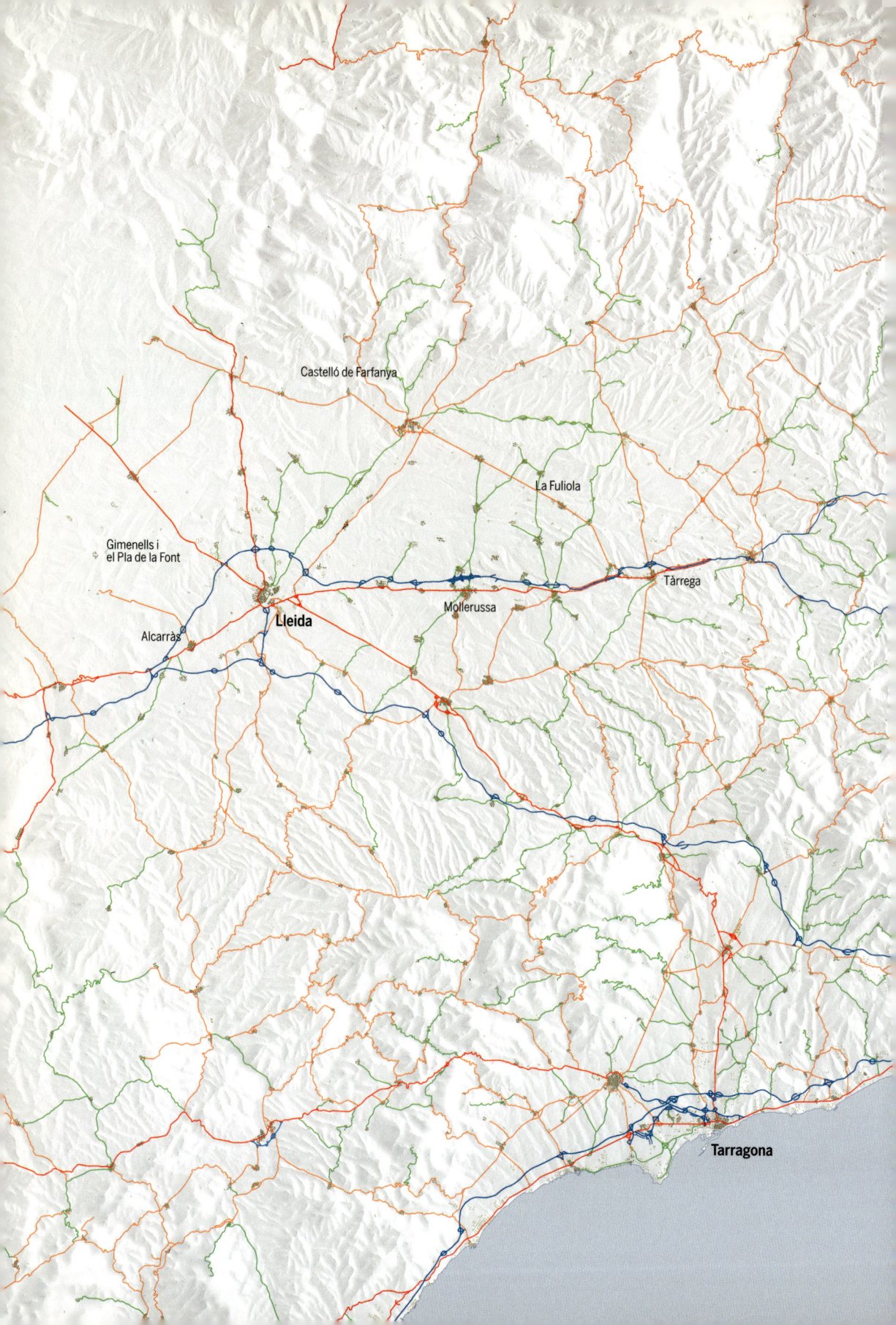

Castelló de Farfanya

La Fuliola

Gimenells i
el Pla de la Font

Tàrrega

Alcarràs

Mollerussa

Lleida

Tarragona

Municipalities	Comarca	Surface area (municipality)	Population (2001)
LLEIDA	Segrià	212.3 km^2	112,199 inhabitants
ROUTE 1			
MOLLERUSSA	Pla d'Urgell	7.1 km^2	10,004 inhabitants
TÀRREGA	Urgell	88.4 km^2	12,848 inhabitants
LA FULIOLA	Urgell	11.1 km^2	1,230 inhabitants
CASTELLÓ DE FARFANYA	Noguera	52.6 km^2	583 inhabitants
ROUTE 2			
ALCARRÀS	Segrià	114.3 km^2	4,788 inhabitants
GIMENELLS & EL PLA DE LA FONT	Segrià	55.8 km^2	1,066 inhabitants

HOTEL PAL·LAS
PAL·LAS BUILDING
COUNCIL PLANNING DEPARTMENT

Francesc de Paula Morera i Gatell
1900-1915

Pça. de la Paeria, 11 - Lleida

SUBSEQUENT INTERVENTIONS:
Lauri Sabater, Lluís Domènech i Girbau, Ramon Maria Puig i Andreu, 1972-1974. Banc Comtal.

Francesc de Paula Morera was the principal representative of Modernista architecture in the city of Lleida, though his buildings were concerned more with a very free handling of classical orders, far from the exuberance of the Modernisme associated with light and Mediterranean landscapes. He also designed Magí Llorens House (Carrer Cavallers, 1) and Melcior House (Plaça Sant Francesc, 2). Hotel Pal·las was originally an apartment building, Aunós House, later converted into a hotel. It has a double façade on Avinguda Blondel, overlooking the river Segre and the Plaça de la Paeria, the latter treated as a rear façade. The river frontage is characterized by a movement to lighten the structural elements by means of a gallery built with an order of slender pillars, doubled or tripled. The plane of the façade itself is restored only at the two extremes, and is overridden by a vertical order of large openings with blinds. The ground floor picks up the solid nature of the masonry fabric, highlighting the section of the supports and adopting a composition independent of the great gallery, which, in itself, forms the crown to the building by reducing its width and leaving two large openings of great lightness to finish off the overall effect.

RAVENTÓS RAÏMAT CELLARS
CHURCH AND WORKERS' HOUSING ESTATE

Joan Rubió i Bellver
1914-1925

Road to Huesca (N-240), km 15,00 - Raïmat
Lleida

In 1914, Manuel Raventós i Domènech, the well-known wine and cava producer, decided to create a housing estate in the Lleida countryside to accommodate the families who worked the land he had purchased. He commissioned Rubió i Bellver to design the church in the settlement and the cellars where the various wines would be made and stored. Rubió designed a residential area beside a wood belonging to the same estate. The cellars were built on the outskirts of the settlement. Particularly worthy of note is the loading bay, protected by a roof structure similar to the one designed by Gaudí for the schools at the Sagrada Família.

GOMÀ-PUJADAS HOUSE
APARTMENT BUILDING

Marià Gomà
1945-1947

Rambla d'Aragó, 5 - Lleida

Marià Gomà was one of the foremost exponents of a generació of academically trained architects who produced a large body of work in the years following the Civil War for institucions and civil architecture, and helped to gradually introduce modern architecture into the city of Lleida. The house in Rambla d'Aragó, built for himself and Antoni Pujadas, was the first project in which Gomà addressed the language of rationalism, though with a genuine, personal interpretation. The seven floor building presents a central gallery from the second floor up to the crown, rounded at either end, in which the windows turn, following the curve, to meet the plane of the façade. As a result, each dwelling has a side gallery made up of three stretches of window with their corresponding blinds. Gomà competed the simple façade with a finish that is staggered at either edge to make it stand out from the neighbouring façades, and with the vertical moulding that marks the axis of the building, comprising three projecting strips beneath the gallery that emerge slightly at the top.

MODEST ULIER HOUSE
APARTMENT BUILDING

Lluís Domènech i Torres
1955-1957

C/ Vila de Foix, 2-4 - Lleida

The project for Ulier House was subject to an unusual series of compositional demands due to its position next to two historic buildings of differing styles: the former Hospital de Santa Maria, dating from the 14th-15th centuries, and the new neoclassical cathedral, built in the second half of the 18th century. Domènech i Torres designed a skin for the façade based on a complex arrangement of the stone cladding. The ground floor is clad with reddish marble, and the four upper floors are artificial stone of a reddish earthy hue. The regulations governing the site prohibited projections or vantage points. The structure is built of reinforced concrete, and Domènech created a series of bevels at the engagement between the facing of the wall and the structural elements. The result was a façade with a very severe order of modulation and a colour scheme that made it blend harmoniously with the historic buildings. The building employs modern construction procedures to produce an image that shuns either rationalistic rhetoric or the manipulation of its academic legacy.

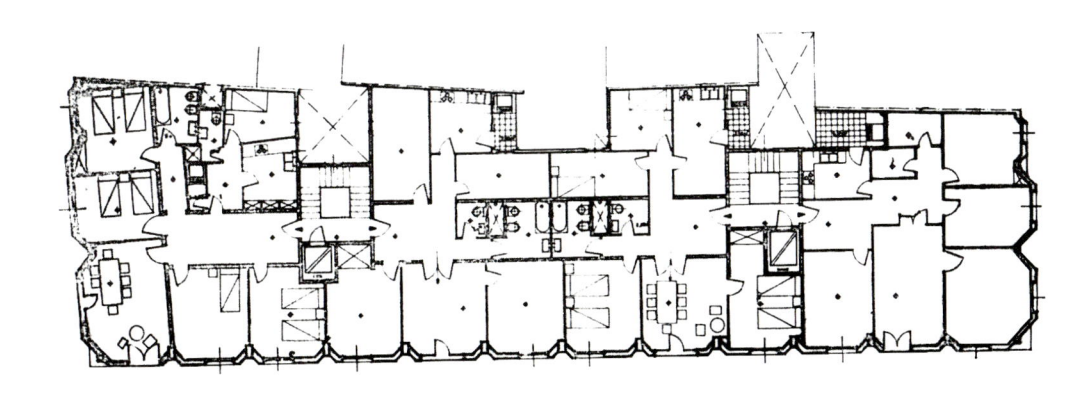

HOME OF THE LITTLE SISTERS OF THE POOR

Ramon Maria Puig i Andreu, Lluís Domènech i Girbau, Lauri Sabater, Jaume Sanmartí
1965-1968

Road to Vall d'Aran (N-230), Km. 5,500 - Lleida

SUBSEQUENT INTERVENTIONS:
Ramon Maria Puig i Andreu, 1978. Extension. Events hall and new dining rooms.

The programme stipulated by the religious order that owns the home envisaged the combination of uses required by a hospital and a home. It also imposed rigid divisions between men, women, married couples and the community. This necessary discrimination explains the complexity of the circulations, designed to avoid interference between the different groups. The project adopts a model bedroom cell which, also due to programme stipulations, required the three beds to be visually separated for reasons of privacy but within hearing distance (in the event of illness or a sudden attack, to enable the three users to assist each other). This model cell can be adapted to the different areas, and the entire internal structure of the project is based on the repetition of this element, following a 120-degree radial layout to turn the bedrooms to face east and south, and the services to the north and west. All the bedrooms enjoy the same conditions of orientation, and the circulations follow a layout of minimum interference. The building has a total of four floors. The ground floor contains the general services, and the remaining three accommodate the nursing station and the bedrooms. The largest spaces (chapel, living room, kitchen and oratory) are positioned outside the radial layout. The 1978 extension took the form of a freestanding rhomboid volume, also of bare brick, though with a different treatment and composition for the openings.

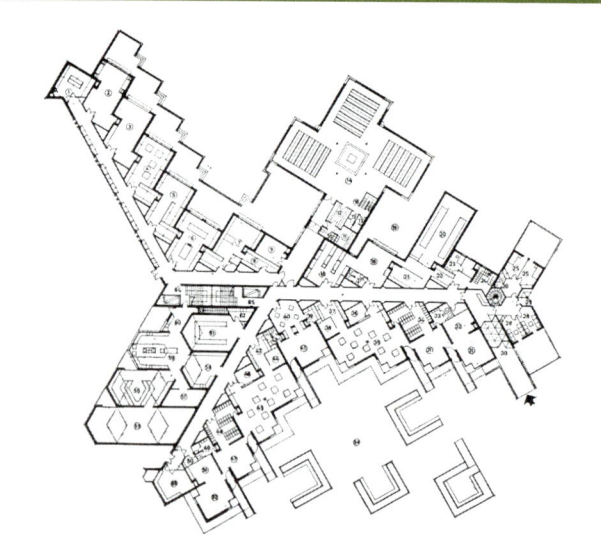

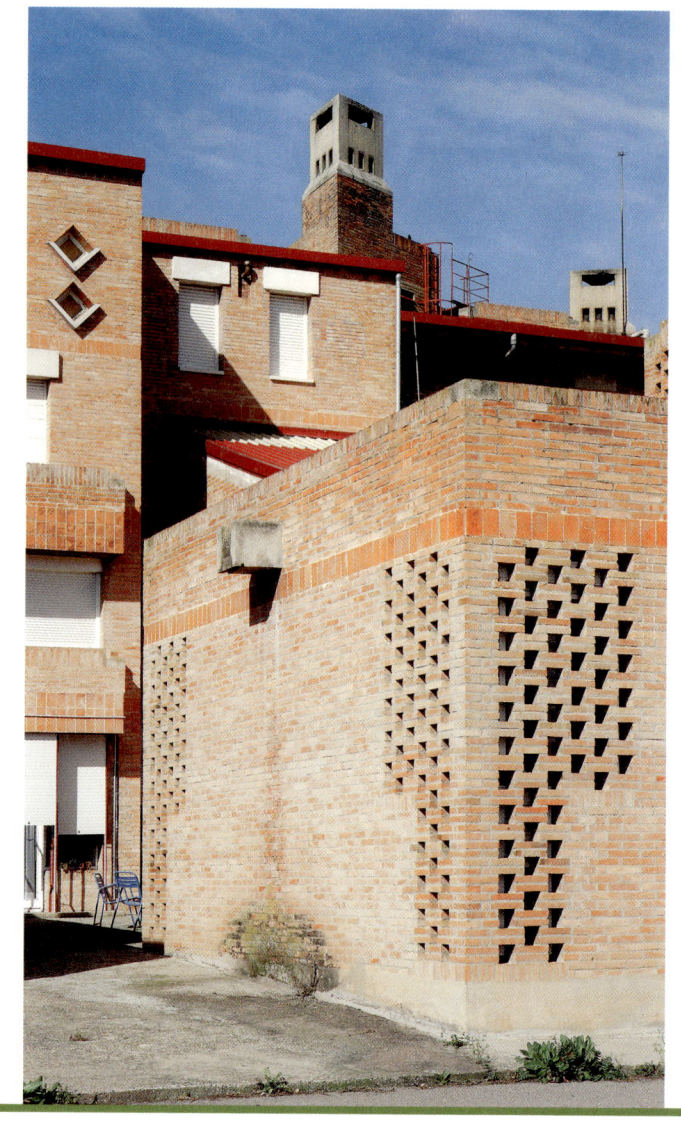

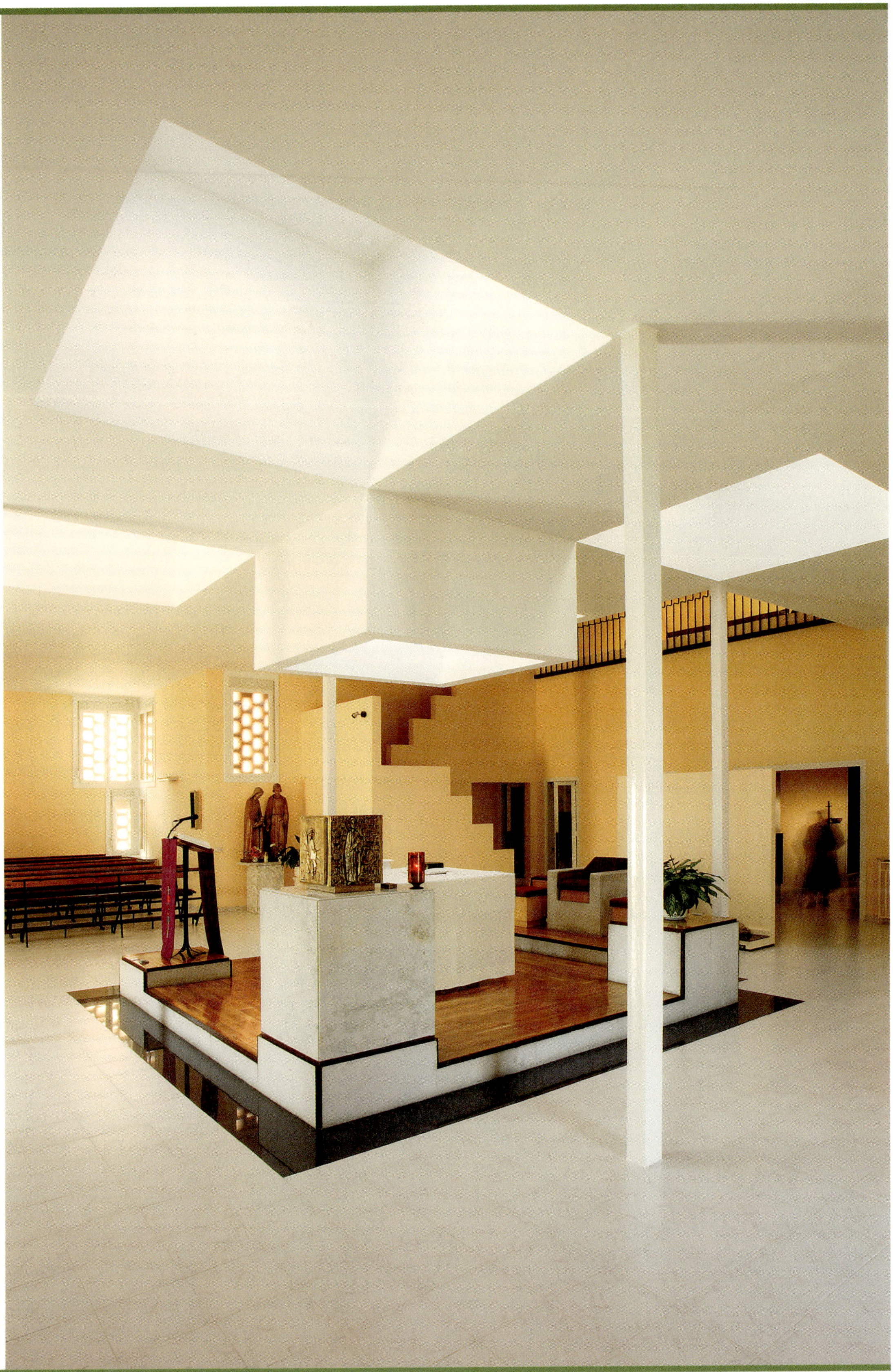

LLD

374

CASIMIR DRUDIS HOUSE
APARTMENT BUILDING

Marià Gomà
1968-1970

Av. Alcalde Rovira Roure, 34 - Lleida

375

SANTA MARIA MAGDALENA PARISH PREMISES

Ramon Maria Puig i Andreu, Lluís Domènech i Girbau, Lauri Sabater
1966-1970

C/ Ramon Llull, 10 - Lleida

The project addresses the extension of a suburban parish church to house the new rectory and spaces for work groups. The old church was unfinished, without the stone cladding originally envisaged, presenting a dry, bare masonry volume that reveals a church construction. The new building is situated on a remnant of land at the corner and creates a façade onto the side street, presenting the floating volume of the rectory and the blind rear of the new building to the right of the church façade. All the newly constructed volumes are clad with corrugated asbestos cement sheeting, and the windows are framed by two bare brick uprights. The general layout of volumes and the composition of the façades bear witness to the Italian influence that was so prevalent in the Catalan architecture of the 1970s.

376

CLUB RONDA BUILDING
COMPLEX OF 88 APARTMENTS

Antoni Sas, Ramon Maria Puig i Andreu, Lluís Domènech i Girbau, Lauri Sabater
1970-1974

Pg. de Ronda, 84 - Lleida

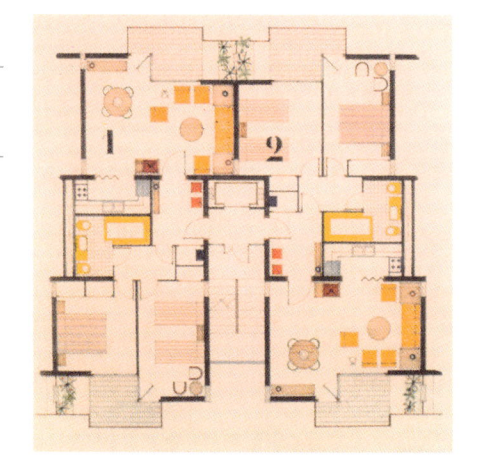

Drudis House represents Gomà's entry into the compositional procedures of modern architecture, particularly as regards the design of residential buildings in an urban context. Gomà used the thickness of the façade to create an isotropic composition formed by the balcony parapets, independently of the requirements imposed by the rooms in the façade. Distributed behind the weightless plane formed by the balconies are the empty spaces of the terraces, the tile-clad stretches of wall and the openings with blinds, all situated in the same plane as the final row of pillars, which are almost concealed. The clarity of the plane created by the smooth sheets of the balconies allows for great flexibility in the definition of closing elements, including the disorderly presence of the multicoloured awnings installed by the various occupants to provide shading.

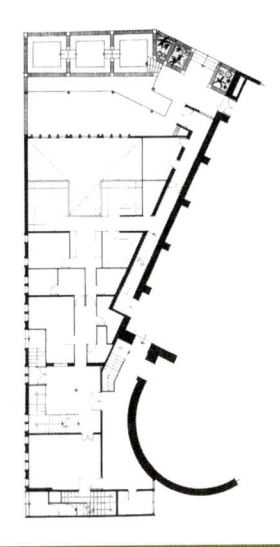

This was the first experience in Lleida of an apartment complex with joint organization of the restaurant, cleaning, chapel, dispensary, living rooms, etc. The complex has a single communal entrance, with a lobby that connects all the stairs. The communal services are situated on the penthouse floor. The module grouping the dwellings in twos is symmetrical, though its arrangement allows the living rooms to overlook the street or the courtyard at the centre of the street block. The façade is double. The interior part adapts to the irregularities in distribution of the floor plan, and the exterior displays a slatted metal facing that provides protection from the sun and street noise, at the same time creating a homogeneous surface at the scale of the overall building.

LAVEDA HOUSE
SINGLE-FAMILY HOUSE

Ramon Maria Puig i Andreu
1975-1978

Camí de Boixadors - Lleida

Designed at the same time as the houses in Sant Jordi d'Alfama, Laveda house occupies a plot of land covering 2600 square metres, larger than the figure that limits construction on country properties. The configuration of the house responds to the image of the Lleida fruit-growing region, reaching beyond the limits of the site. The house is organized into a series of horizontal bays that adapt to the function they are designed to provide. The ground floor extends lengthwise, whereas the upper floor, housing the bedrooms, adopts a more compact form. The result is a house with a ridge roof that reaches the ground on both sides. The porticoed bay at the front of the house stands independently of the interior distribution. The walls are built of white-painted concrete block, and the sheet metal of the roof is also white.

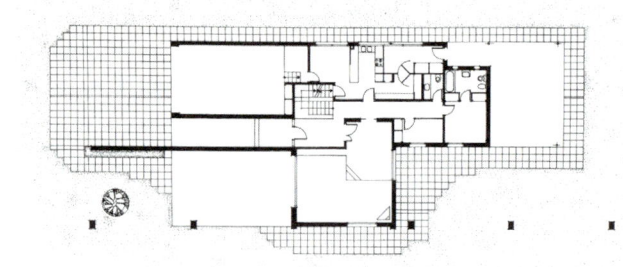

SOCIAL HOUSING COMPLEX WITH 56 APARTMENTS

Ramon Maria Puig i Andreu
1977-1980

C/ Sant Agustí, 2-4 - C/ Solsona, 5 - C/ Isern, 1 Av. Artesa, 62 - Lleida

The complex occupies an almost square street block of small dimensions: 42 x 45 metres. The project makes a departure from the closed street block arrangement proposed by the general plan, implementing two parallel blocks that leave an inner courtyard completely free at ground floor level, providing a communal space. The dwellings run between the two façades of each block, enjoying the spaces of the street and the inner courtyard. The south-facing end walls are given a different treatment as they house duplex apartments, giving way to an increase in the side facing, which becomes a façade of the first order. The choice of dwellings with three instead of four bedrooms allows for greater generosity of surface area, with the creation of a double circulatory layout in each dwelling. The outer façades of the blocks are opaque, built of bare brick with rather small openings, while the inner façades combine railings and reinforced glass to present a lightweight façade more in keeping with the nature of the courtyard.

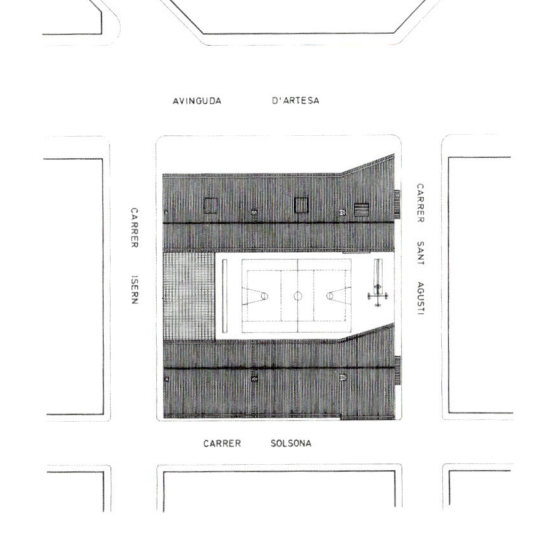

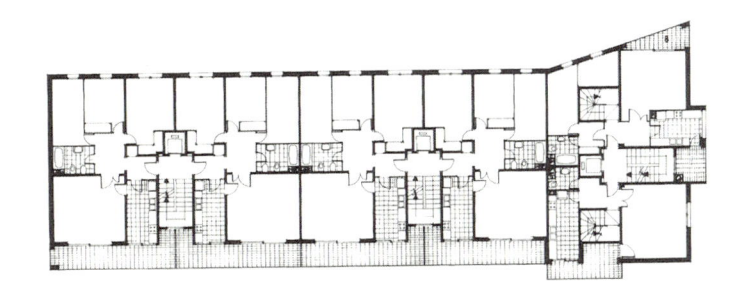

379

COL·LEGI D'APARELLADORS I ARQUITECTES TÈCNICS DE LLEIDA COAATL

Franc Fernández, Moisés Gallego
1981-1984

C/ Enric Granados, 5 - Lleida

380

LLEIDA PARK RESIDENTIAL COMPLEX

Miquel Espinet, Antoni Ubach
1983-1986

Av. Alcalde Rovira Roure, 163-165 - C/ Monestir de les Avellanes, 1-5 - Lleida

Following contextualist project mechanisms, the complex comprises various groupings of dwellings that blend into the landscape and form public spaces. The dwellings are organized in autonomous groups of four, within which each house is slightly displaced or turned away from its neighbours. The dwellings are laid out on four levels. The garage and entrance are on the lowest level. Access to the garden is via the first floor, at a slightly different level. The interior is organized around a stairway with a square base and a cylindrical volume. Entrance to the garage is via a communal space. The roof of the garage is landscaped, and the top floor also has a small, partially enclosed garden that faces north.

381

CEIP CERVANTES
INFANTS' AND PRIMARY SCHOOL

Roser Amadó, Lluís Domènech i Girbau
1990-1995

C/ Canyeret - Lleida

The building stands on the plot of land left by the construction of a street block of apartments, behind the rear façades of medium-rise apartment buildings. The project approach is based on a volumetric study that provides a suitable response to these difficult conditions. The programme for the new headquarters of the COAATC rests on a great socle raised above street level to accommodate the car park below. The ground floor holds the entrance foyer and the events hall, engaging with the edge of the site on two sides, leaving a small ventilation shaft. The two upper floors are built astride the entrance, making them open on all sides. The dislocation between the ground floor and the upper volumes produces the porch at the entrance, facing the great stairway that ascends the socle.

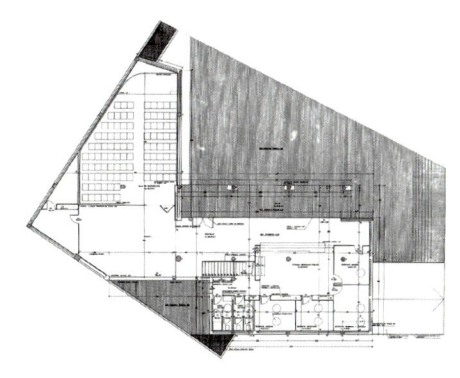

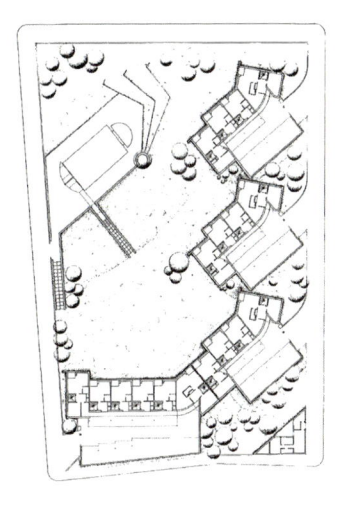

The school is situated on the west side of Carrer Canyeret on a steeply sloping site, at the point where the street merges into the fabric of the old town. Entrance is from above, through a large porch situated at the top part of the district of El Canyeret, offering a panoramic view of the city. The programme is laid out on three levels. Alongside the entrance there are three classrooms. On the intermediate level there are another four, with access to their own terrace. The lowest level, which communicates with a street, houses the assembly hall and cloakrooms, connected by a ramp and a tunnel to the sports complex on the other side of the street. The composition of the building is based on the form of the site and its orientation, seeking to adapt to the site and the existing wall system.

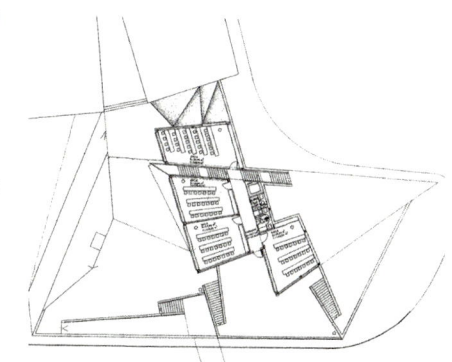

SCHOOL OF AGRICULTURISTS OF CATALONIA
REMODELLING AND EXTENSION OF EXISTING FARMING CONSTRUCTIONS

Miquel Espinet, Antoni Ubach
1982-1985

Av. Alcalde Rovira Roure, 191
Agronomist Campus - Lleida

The programme involved installing the new School of Agriculturists in existing constructions on an estate four kilometres outside the city, which needed to be extended by 3500 square metres to house the new functions. The project addresses the difficulty of combining the old and the new by applying a strategy to clearly distinguish the various existing constructions. The main building is visible against a continuous glazed background that reflects the landscape. The rest of the old constructions are concealed by the presence of the new volumes. The main façade, facing north, overlooks the estate's large tracts of fruit trees. A curtain wall encloses all the distribution circuits and a space of relation for the entire school. The south- and east-facing façades are bare brick with large openings. At all points, the project maintains a clear differentiation between the new part and the old, even in the programmatic distribution of uses. The contact spaces are treated as neutrally as possible, employing skylights, the colour white and large surfaces.

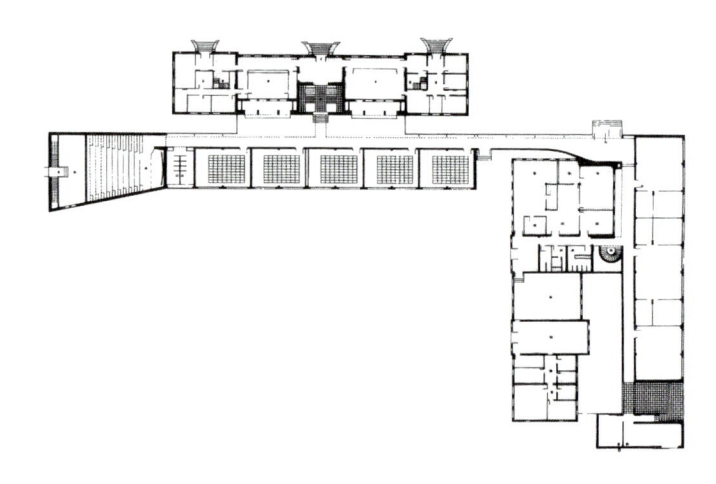

UNIVERSITY OF LLEIDA
REMODELLING OF THE OLD DIOCESAN SEMINARY

Miquel Espinet, Antoni Ubach,
Ramon Maria Puig i Andreu
1983-1992

Rambla d'Aragó, 37 - Lleida

The project addresses the remodelling and extension of the former Diocesan Seminary, a Beaux-Arts building in the neo-gothic style, to house the Vice-Chancellor's Office of the University of Lleida and four new faculties. The intervention starts with a reading of the old building and proposes continuity of composition using its basic features. The seminary building is laid out around two large courtyards, separated by the chapel. The chapel building is subdivided heightwise, and houses the cafeteria and the events hall. Along the same axis as this volume are located the great hall and the library. To the rear, after the demolition of a series of annexes built in the 1940s, the four new faculties were constructed in a comb arrangement directly connected to the cloisters, which continue to function as the main elements of distribution.

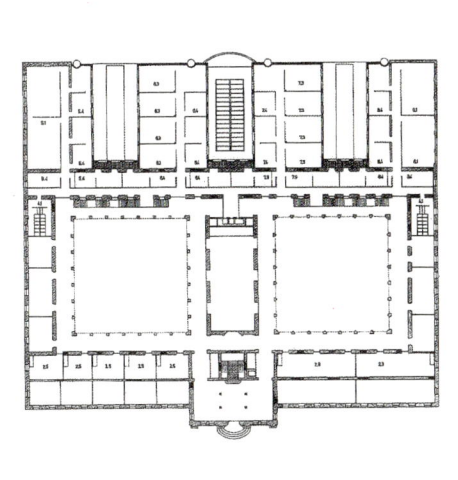

LAW COURTS AND COMMUNICATIONS TOWER

Roser Amadó, Lluís Domènech i Girbau
1984-1990

C/ Canyeret - Lleida

The building is the result of an overall planning intervention in the district of El Canyeret, in the framework of Lleida's Historic Centre Plan. The study detected a lack of connection between the old town, with its high street, Carrer Major, and the cathedral, the Seu Vella, due to the abandonment and decline in population of the hillside formerly occupied by this district. The project set out to revitalize the area and re-establish the connection between the old town and the cathedral. Geotechnical studies recommended creating a retaining wall across the hillside against which new constructions could be built, presenting fronts on two streets at different levels. This generated a lengthwise building, built against the screen, that conceals and presents a new façade. The connecting factor is a communications tower that provides access to three levels: at its foot, near Carrer Major; the street situated at the top of the screen and, finally, the old gate in the wall around the cathedral. The curved form of the screen makes it easily distinguishable from the traces of the Seu Vella wall, and is also the form that adapts best to the natural topography of the hillside.

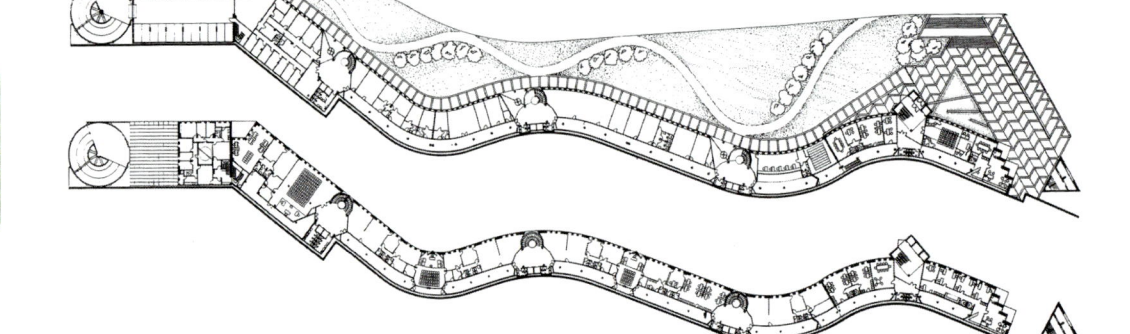

ENRIC GRANADOS MUNICIPAL AUDITORIUM
LLEIDA AUDITORIUM AND CONSERVATORY

Ramon Artigues, Ramon Sanabria
1983-1995

Pl. Mossèn Cinto Verdaguer - Lleida

The building is designed as a large container that stands on a square, which marks the entrance to the auditorium and the start of the urban fabric. The nucleus of the programme comprises two public halls for musical performances and a conservatory. A complex system of services and annexed spaces is organized around this central programme. The main hall occupies an empty space at the centre of the building, allowing the arrangement around it of smaller rooms and other services. This solution gives the four façades of the building an urban character. The most outstanding features are inserted next to the main façade, making it almost monumental in appearance when seen from the front but also at an angle from the side streets. The façades on these streets adopt a secondary role, subject to the volumetric regularity of the whole.

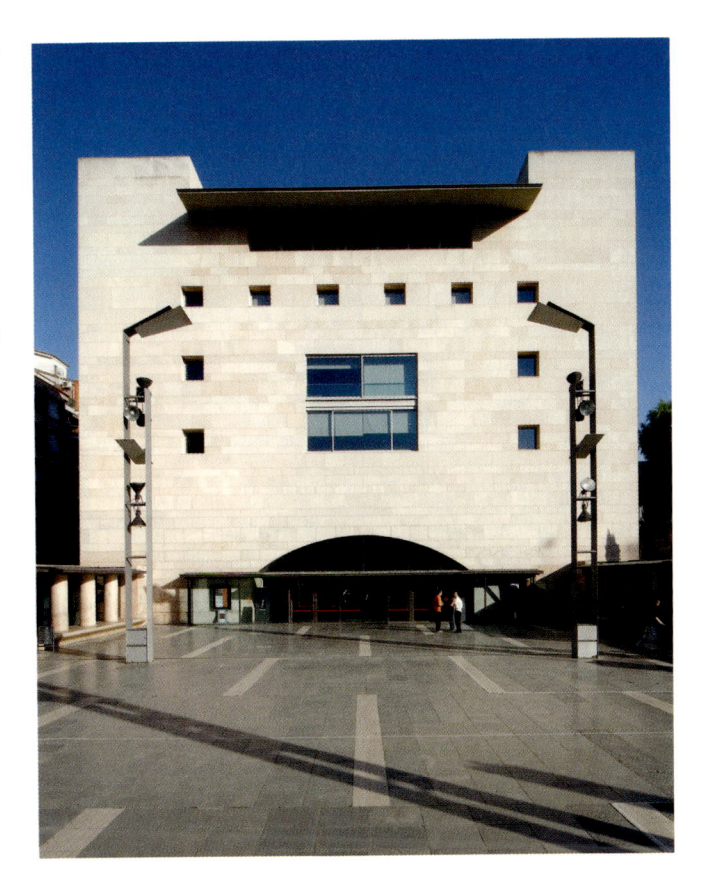

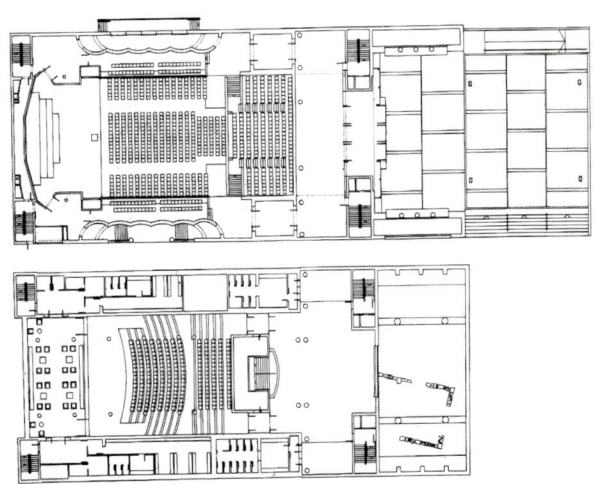

CAP PARDINYES
HEALTH CENTRE

Ramon Maria Puig i Andreu
1987-1991

C/ Alcalde Recasens - Lleida

The project interprets the standard health centre programme by means of a single-storey construction organized around a central axis running right through the centre and leading to the various departments. The entrance is halfway along the linear layout. As a result, throughout the building the various parts of the programme generate different volumes and dimensions that are reflected in the exterior image. The importance of the lengthwise axis is highlighted in the cross section, in which the roof skims the corridor to provide overhead lighting. Since this is a single-storey construction that does not need large spaces, its walls are built of white-painted concrete blocks. The exterior façades have no openings as such, instead presenting lattices built of the same material that allow sunlight to shine through in the winter and provide shading in the summer.

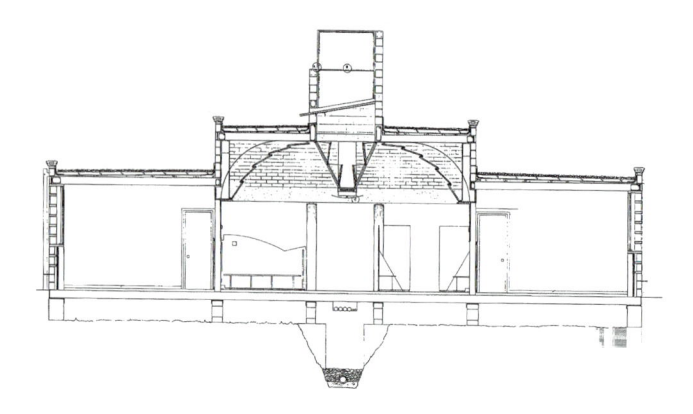

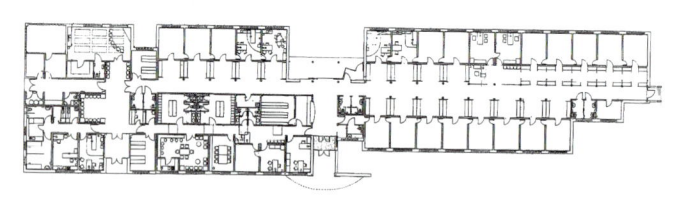

CAP CAPPONT
HEALTH CENTRE

Ramon Fité, Julio José Mejón
1999-2001

C/ Marquès de Leganés - Lleida

The building is situated on the city limits, on a strip of land adjacent to a series of high-rise apartment blocks that turn their great bare party walls to view. The project approach consists in closing in the block, making the most of its proximity to the street. The programme turns around the surgery spaces, housed in a white vitrified brick volume. The rest of the spaces protect the surgeries from the exterior space. The result is a volume with a stepped section that descends into the courtyard. This section is evident in the northeast façade. Seen from a distance, the aluminium of the façade provides the building with an element of attraction, set apart from the surrounding constructions. The reflection of the yellow tones of the opposite façade gives the interior a warm atmosphere.

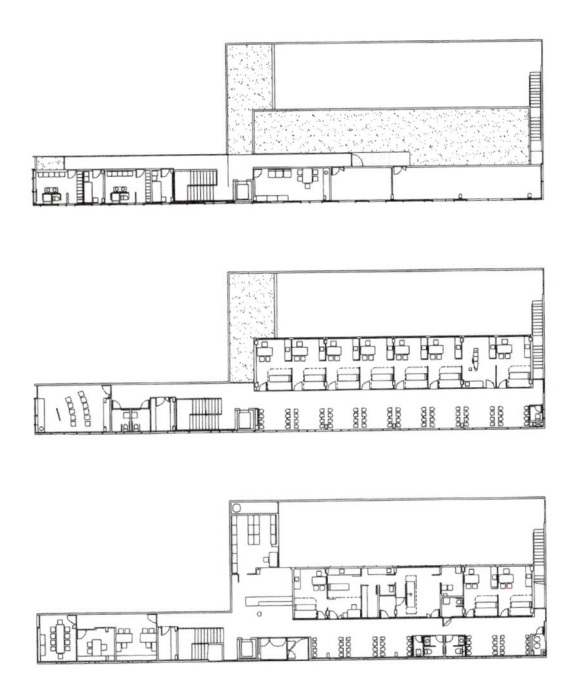

388

TORRE VICENS VOCATIONAL TRAINING INSTITUTE
SECONDARY SCHOOL

Ramon Maria Puig i Andreu, Carles Sáez
1986-1994

Av. Torre Vicens, 3 - Secà de Sant Pere - Lleida

389

OFFICIAL SCHOOL OF LANGUAGES

Ramon Artigues, Ramon Sanabria
1991-1996

C/ Corregidor Escofet, 53 - Lleida

The building adopts a lengthwise configuration parallel to the planned Rambla de Pardinyes. This layout makes it possible to accommodate the classroom programme along a corridor, with the vertical communication shaft forming a separate volume positioned at the centre. The assembly hall and library form two volumes of irregular geometry situated in the space that separates the building from the Rambla, and between the two volumes are the entrance way and a hall that unite the whole. The building aspires to construct an urban place that does not yet exist, where the ground floor has to take on the condition of a public space.

390

CEIP SANT JORDI
INFANTS' AND PRIMARY SCHOOL

Marta Gabàs, Anna Ribas
1993-1995

Partida de Montcada, 22 - Road to Vielha (N-230)
Lleida

The project takes as its departure point the premise of a two-phase construction. Phase one included the pre-school classrooms and the gymnasium, and phase two included all the other facilities. The volumes corresponding to the two phases had to be clearly distinguishable. The school is strictly regular in floor plan, whereas the section presents a complex combination of roofs to draw the southern light into the classrooms and northern light into the gymnasium. The side façades reflect the profiles created by the section. One of the sloping roofs is glazed and forms a porch that acts as the entrance between the school's two main volumes. The building comprises five bearing walls that generate four bays, allowing an orderly distribution of the various parts of the programme.

The nucleus of the school is laid out in two wings: the first houses the more fixed parts of the programme (offices, classrooms and tutors' rooms), and the second is set in the middle of the plot, housing the cafeteria and multi-purpose hall. The entrance, situated at the corner, is a large porch that runs the height of the building. This layout has three appendages: attached to the end of the main wing is the gymnasium; above the other wing is a corridor that leads to workshops and, via a series of ramps, to the library and laboratories. This corridor can be extended to accommodate further new parts of the programme that were not initially envisaged.

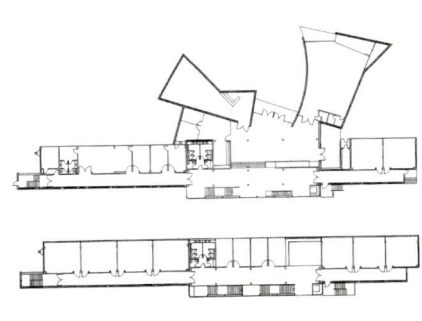

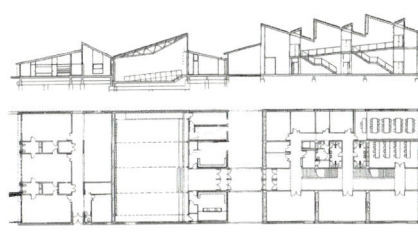

ARTS CENTRE OF THE ESTUDI GENERAL AND LIBRARY
UNIVERSITY OF LLEIDA

Kristian Gullichsen
1998-2004

C/ Jaume II, 67 - Cappont Campus
University of Lleida - Lleida

The Centre is situated on the corner of the Cappont campus nearest the network of roads into the city, beside the river Segre. Its location makes this building the gateway to the campus when approaching from the centre. An L-shaped unitary volume, set into the corner, forms the main entrance to the university campus. The approach road reaches as far as the great atrium, situated on the corner. The slit effected in this corner highlights the diagonal axis of the flows into and out of the campus. The building covers three storeys above street level, and a unified ground floor which, inside the campus, becomes a ground floor proper. Above this level, the building is divided into two independent volumes, joined by a single roof. The auditorium takes the form of an independent cylindrical volume that emerges from a pool in which it is reflected.

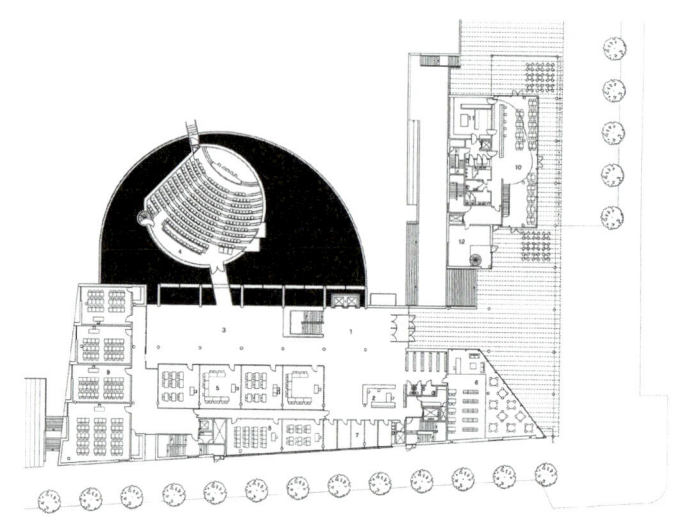

POLYTECHNIC UNIVERSITY SCHOOL OF INFORMATION TECHNOLOGY
UNIVERSITY OF LLEIDA

Miquel Espinet, Antoni Ubach
1993-1997

C/ Jaume II, 69 - Cappont Campus
University of Lleida - Lleida

The building comprises two volumes of markedly different conception that house the two main parts into which the programme is divided and respond individually to the urban conditions of Carrer Jaume II, in one case, and the campus interior, in the other. The volume aligned along the street assumes the urban condition of the various buildings that form this façade, constructing the street space by means of large buildings placed 25 metres apart, and creating a straight-lined avenue along the river. The inner volume, housing special workshops and classrooms, refers to the semi-rural nature of the origins of the place, with its curved roof and the presence of great windows. The two volumes are joined by a space of relation, a double-height glazed walkway. Entrance from the street is via a volume that adopts a specific geometry, independent of the rest of the building, which leads directly to the rear area. The building provides independent responses to the exterior and interior conditions of the campus, and uses this clear discrimination for a judicious organization of the programme.

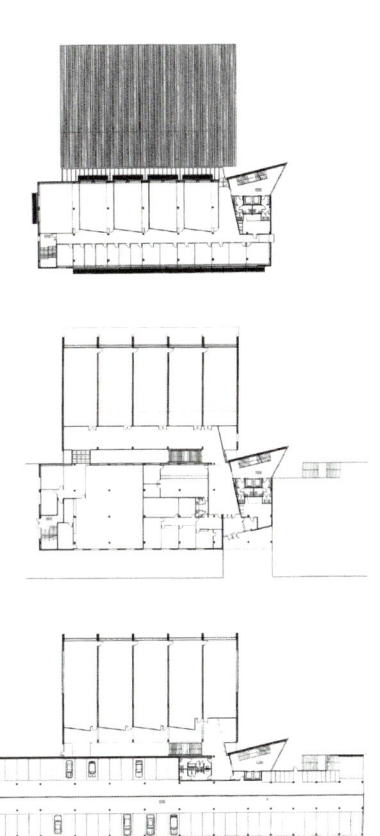

UNIVERSITY HALL OF RESIDENCE
UNIVERSITY OF LLEIDA

Ramon Artigues, Ramon Sanabria
1997-2000

C/ Jaume II, 75 - Cappont Campus
University of Lleida - Lleida

The hall of residence is situated on the north-west edge of the Cappont campus, at the end of a row of university buildings aligned along Carrer de Jaume II. The building adopts the form of an outstretched arm, with a central corridor lined on both sides by rooms. On the north side the circulation space opens up to shape the façade overlooking the river. The row of rooms in the west façade faithfully follows the gentle curve of the street without interruption. The bay overlooking the interior of the campus produces two openings that draw natural light into the circulation spaces and leave the best views for the rooms. In this way, the building represents a volumetric response to the conditions of its surroundings that is independent of each façade and gives the building its orientation and formal identity.

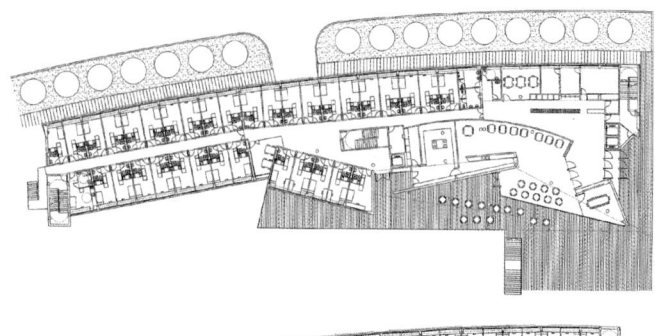

FACULTY OF EDUCATION SCIENCE
UNIVERSITY OF LLEIDA

Álvaro Siza Vieira
2003-2007

Av. Estudi General - Cappont Campus
University of Lleida - Lleida

PRESENT STATE: In construction

The building, situated on the north-east corner of the Cappont campus, adopts an L-shape which, on the ground floor, extends into a U. In this way it distances itself from the large volume of the university library and completes the north façade of the campus, creating a new public square that provides access and space for interrelation.
The great eaves of the building's west wing create a space of transition between the more urban Avinguda Estudi General and the garden on campus. The complex forms a non-orthogonal volume, as one of its sides overlooks the empty space between the library and the Polytechnic University School, providing a scenic backdrop to the intermediate space that can be seen from Avinguda de Jaume II. In this way the building finds its place in the façade of the campus that turns to face the city. The construction adopts a modulated structure that is open, if necessary, to orderly growth or a possible change of use in the future.

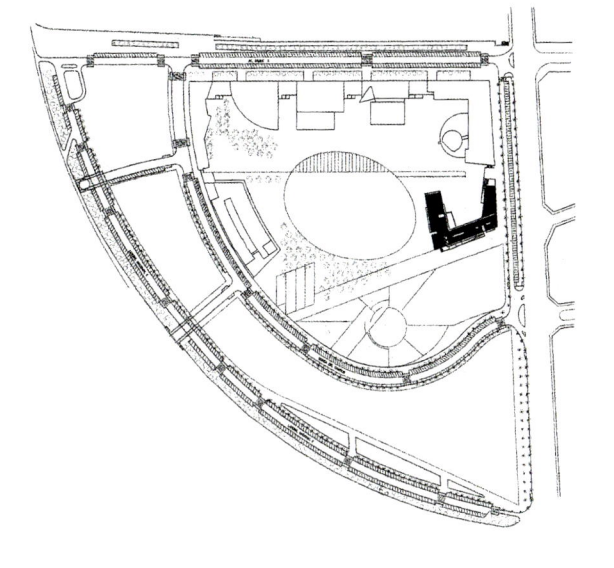

HEADQUARTERS OF THE LLEIDA BRANCH OF THE COL·LEGI D'ARQUITECTES DE CATALUNYA COAC

Francisco Burgos, Luis de Pereda
1993-1996

C/ Canyeret, 2 - Lleida

The building is made up of two quite different parts. The base adapts its form to the topography of the site. Its outline is stepped in the floor plan and section, with the exception of the small tower-mirador built against the party wall, which rises from the base. This part has large glazed openings, protected from solar radiation by a series of concrete projections that simulate a reconstruction of the contour lines. Resting on this base is a cubic prism that emerges above the surrounding buildings, like a watchtower looking out over the city, the river and the plain. On the lowest ground, a small square planted with trees reconstructs pre-existing pedestrian routes. The two parts of the building contain different functions of the programme. The lower floors house the public service areas, exhibitions, events hall and car park. The cubic volume contains the office and the library. The cladding materials serve to further highlight this duality.

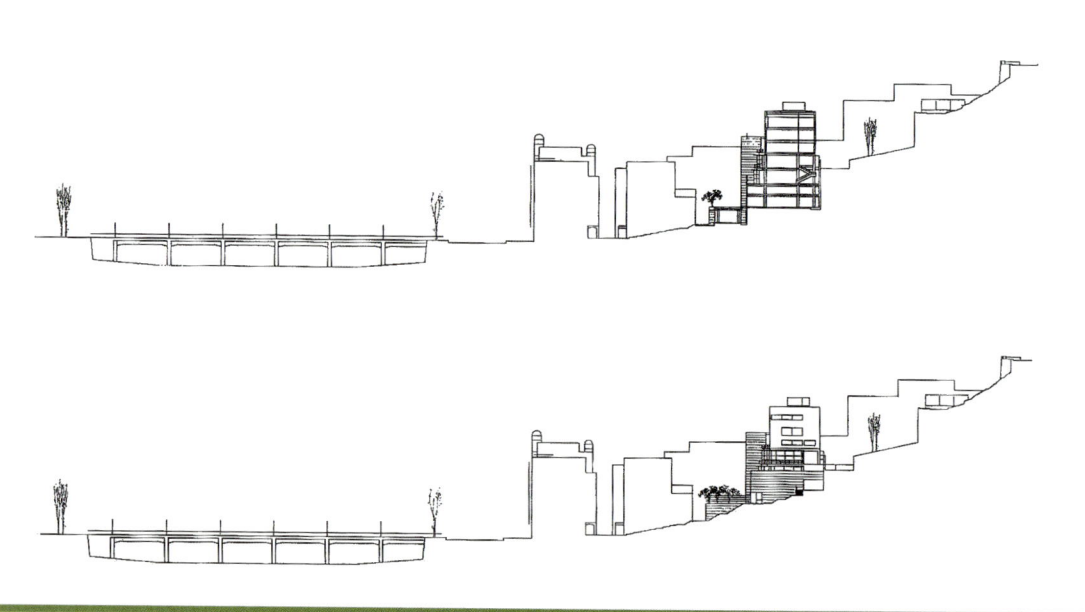

MONTULL HOUSE
SINGLE-FAMILY DWELLING

Ramon Fité, Julio José Mejón
2002-2003

C/ Castell de Formós, 4 - Lleida

The site is situated in the highest part of a residential development near the city, giving the house good orientation and seeking out views of the Seu Vella cathedral. The house consists of a lightweight metal volume standing on a concrete base. The upper volume houses the domestic programme and the base contains the garage. The floor plan adopts a U-shape, arranging the rooms around an inner courtyard. Thanks to its adjustable roof, the house is prepared for seasonal variations throughout the year. In construction terms it comprises prefabricated elements, dry assembled on site. For this reason, the floor plan responds to a schematic criterion of repeated spaces and concentrated wet areas. The adoption of dynamic structures used in truck cabs and refrigerated vehicles obeys a specific set of laws and methodology, allowing the introduction of innovative elements to transform traditional building procedures.

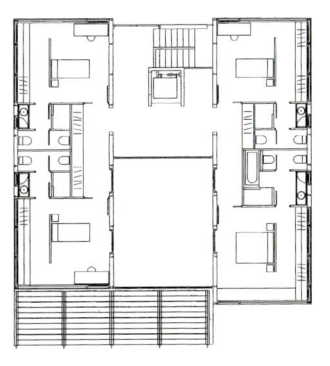

HOME FOR THE ELDERLY ON THE ESTATE OF THE HOUSE OF THE DUKE AND DUCHESS OF ALBA

Lluís M. Vidal i Arderiu
1991-1994

Plaça Major - Castelló de Farfanya

This intervention in an old building takes into account the urban structure of the village, a network of narrow streets that widen at certain points to form small squares. The new building is arranged behind the house of the Duke and Duchess of Alba, creating a new square that becomes an independent entrance to the events hall at the new home for the elderly. The configuration of its building is similar to that of the apse of the Church of Sant Miquel. The rear of the old building is left bare, conserving its current state. The new construction separates from the old walls at some points and, in others, it interlocks with the old structures, using a different, lighter material. The new addition thereby establishes continuity with the existing urban structure and uses its different language to distinguish the old from the new.

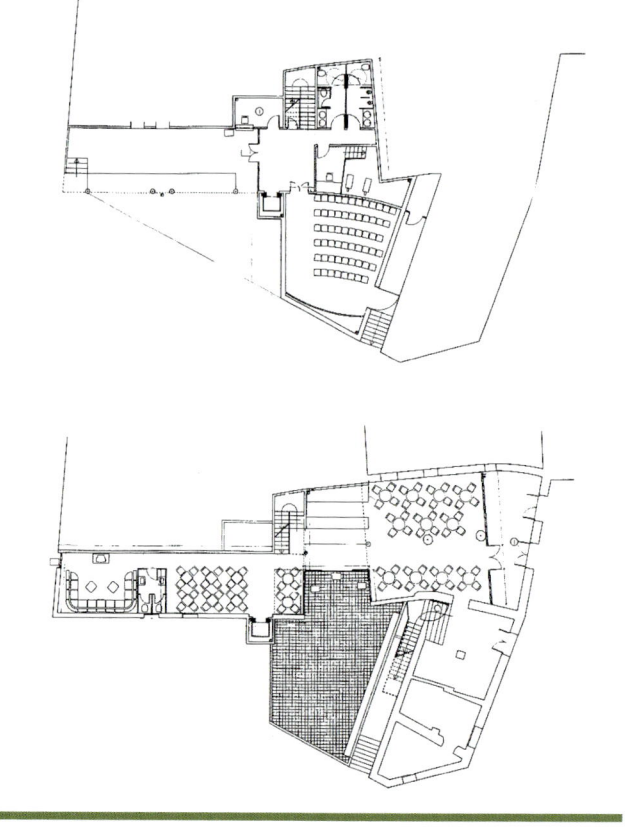

IES LA SERRA
SECONDARY SCHOOL

Carme Pinós
1998-2001

Road to Torregrossa (LV-2001)
La Serra - Mollerussa

The school is situated on farmland comprising fields of fruit trees and small constructions with ridge roofs. These elements suggest the use of repetition to generate the composition, along with the aim of concentrating construction to avoid occupying too much of the surface area. The building creates an interplay of sloping roofs at different heights, with three storeys along the central axis decreasing to one in the bays around the edge, thereby creating a repeated rhythm. The school is laid out in three volumes that form a Y-shape: one arm contains the gymnasium and sporting activities; the second houses the classrooms and the third the entrance and car parking. The classrooms are grouped around playgrounds that increase the compactness of the building and function as intermediate spaces between the exterior and the interior. The classrooms and laboratories face east; only the adjacent services and offices receive afternoon sun. The large central axis, lit from above, connects and relates the entire programme. It is an open, unitary space that provides a point of reference for pupils within the overall layout of the building.

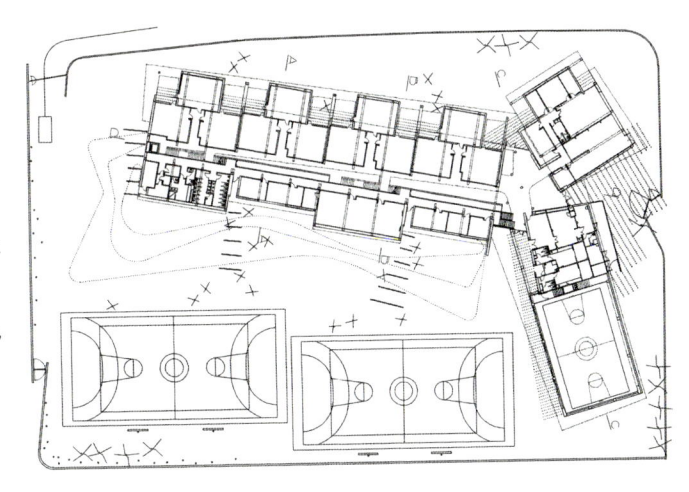

CEIP GUILLEM ISARN
INFANTS' AND PRIMARY SCHOOL

Maria Àngels Negre, Félix Solaguren-Beascoa
1991-1994

Av. Catalunya - La Fuliola

The school is situated on a trapezoid site surrounded by farmland, bordered to the north by a road and to the south by the old highroad. The location of the building is the result of a redistribution of land according to the guidelines of farmland division. It stands on an elongated site, reminiscent of its predecessors, freeing up space for the sports courts. The position of the building also leaves space to create a street that joins the road with the old highroad. The school is divided into two volumes that were given contrasting treatments. The first is opaque, built of local stone, and contains the gymnasium, the changing rooms and the main entrance. The second volume, of white-painted brick, contrasts with the weightiness of its stone neighbour, and the brick courses highlight its linear layout. The openings in the façade form a great rend that runs the length of the building, arranged to reflect the programme.

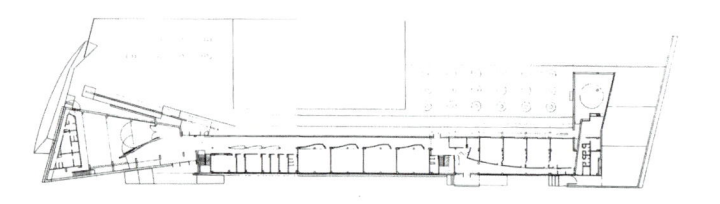

TÀRREGA MUNICIPAL SWIMMING POOLS

Moisés Gallego, Àlex Gallego
2002-2004

C/ Joan Brossa – Sports complex - Tàrrega

Tàrrega's sports complex forms a great esplanade to the south of the town, separated only by a watercourse. This affords the site good views and excellent accessibility. The development of the complex began with the construction of scattered amenities with no specific guiding criterion, so the new pool building sets out to create a reference for the future implantation of new installations. The new construction is laid out beside an existing pavilion, so the two volumes form an architectural unit and generate a joint effect on their surroundings. The building has two floors, with two pools on the ground floor and gymnasiums on the upper level. The foyer acquires particular importance, as it organizes independent itineraries around both installations.

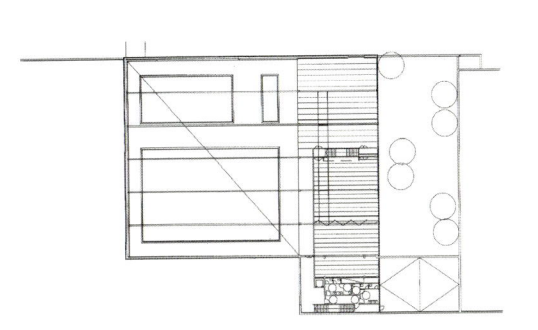

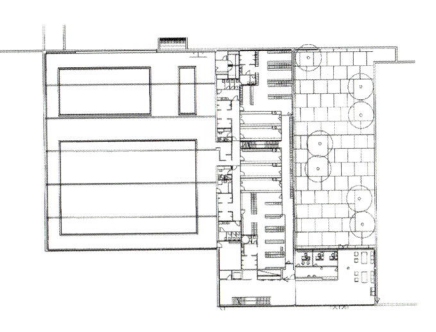

SINGLE-FAMILY DWELLING

Roser Amadó, Lluís Domènech i Girbau, Lauri Sabater
1972-1976

Road to Vallmanya (L-800) - Alcarràs

The house is situated at the brow of a high bank, characteristic of the local landscape. It consequently directs its volume towards the slope, emphasized by a large sloping roof at the rear that reaches the ground. The main parts of the domestic programme are situated in the front sector, near the bank. The living room and dining room occupy two levels, creating a large empty space at the centre around which the whole house gravitates. This floor is completed by a study on one side and the master bedroom on the other. A spiral staircase between the dining and living rooms leads to a walkway that communicates with the children's bedrooms to either side. The resulting T-shape focuses household life in the living room. Only the kitchen and the service spaces are set aside in a small side bay, apart from the rest of the house. To the rear, the sloping roof forms a porch over the swimming pool. The volume of the house and the organization of the domestic space present a direct correlation with this special location.

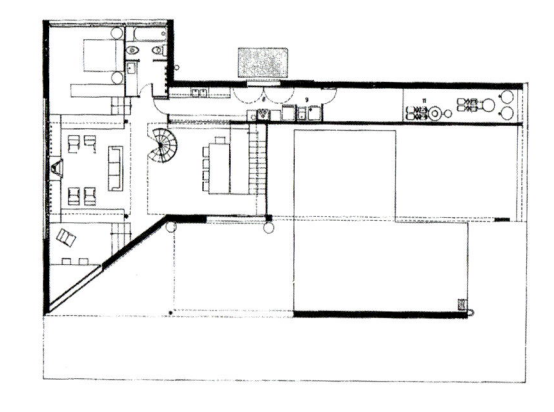

SIX DWELLINGS IN A FARMING COMMUNITY
DWELLINGS NOS 23-28

Lluís Domènech i Girbau, Ramon Maria Puig i Andreu, Lauri Sabater, Jaume Sanmartí
1965-1968

C/ Únic - Santa Maria de Gimenells (Gimenells)

This complex of six dwellings is situated amid farmland to provide homes for farm workers. The project studies the groupings of rural constructions, forming clusters of small volumes and shunning the disproportionate presence of large masses. These homes are grouped in twos, forming a T-shaped layout, leaving a partially sheltered space at the centre that functions as a space of interrelation and entrance to each dwelling. The two-storey constructions adopt bevelled corners to reduce the impact of the built volumes. The upper floors, housing the bedrooms, draw together each unit of two ground floors, leaving between them a covered passage leading to the respective gardens. The bevelled edges, the arrangement of the openings and the diffraction between the ground and first floors have the effect of breaking down the volumes and avoiding large stretches of wall. The complex forms a built nucleus at the scale of the landscape, in keeping with the agricultural work it serves.

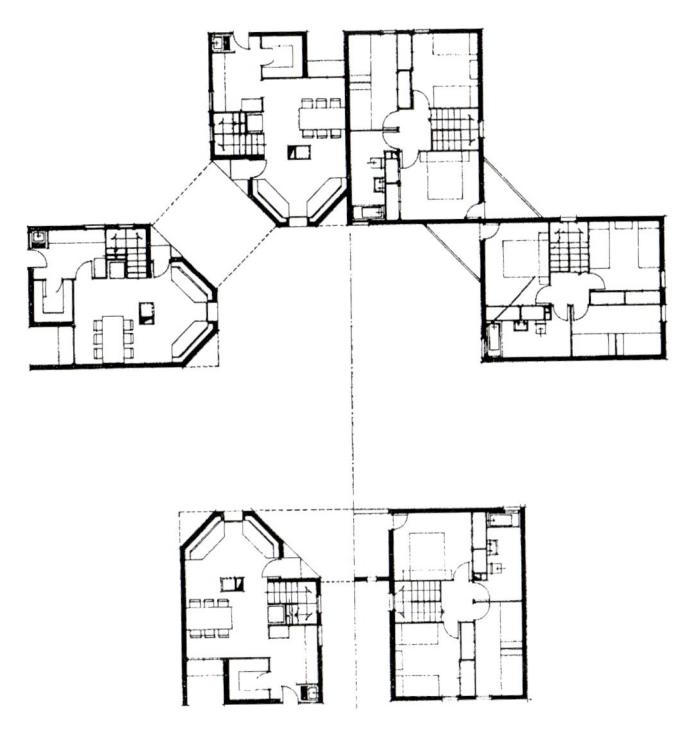

Naut Aran
Alt Àneu
El Pont de Suert
Sort
La Seu d'Urgell
El Pont de Bar
Lles de Cerdanya
Puigcerdà
Bellver de Cerdanya
Fontanals de Cerdanya
Ribera d'Urgellet
Oliana

SGL – The La Seu d'Urgell area

Territorial scope

This area covers the entire northern part of inland Catalonia: the Lleida Pyrenees and the Pyrenean foothills. It centres on the town of La Seu d'Urgell, in the *comarca* of Alt Urgell. To the east, it takes in the county of Cerdanya, as far as Puigcerdà. To the west, it includes the counties of Pallars Sobirà, Val d'Aran and Alta Ribagorça. The municipality of Sarroca de Bellera is situated in the northern part of the county of Pallars Jussà. This is the highest land in Catalonia, with relief rising as it progresses from southeast to northwest, to the Val d'Aran. It is dotted with small mountain municipalities, with a very low population density. The position of La Seu d'Urgell makes it a hub for the area, which is the largest in this guide but the least important in terms of architecture.

Road structure

THE TOWN

If you are coming from Lleida, La Seu d'Urgell is situated to the north along a series of county roads that pass through Balaguer and Artesa de Segre. The C-13 county road connects Lleida with Balaguer, the C-26 takes you from Balaguer to Artesa de Segre and the C-14 goes directly from Artesa de Segre to La Seu d'Urgell. If you are driving to La Seu d'Urgell from Barcelona, take the C-16 to Bellver de Cerdanya, where you can pick up the N-260 national trunk road heading west to La Seu d'Urgell. From La Seu, the N-145 heads north to Andorra, and the N-260 continues west, first to Sort, La Pobla de Segur and El Pont de Suert, and then on to the Pyrenees of Aragon.

ROUTE 1

Route 1 heads east to Cerdanya and the town of Puigcerdà. The N-260 national trunk road forms the axis of this route, passing through El Pont de Bar and Bellver de Cerdanya, with a turnoff to the north between these two villages that takes you to Lles de Cerdanya. When you are leaving Bellver de Cerdanya, a turnoff to the right will take you to Fontanals de Cerdanya, via Das and Alp. To visit these two latter villages, you will have to come off the N-260. The N-260 will also take you from Bellver to Puigcerdà. From here, you can head south towards the Cadí tunnels and Berga, a municipality that forms part of the next area, Manresa. From Puigcerdà, the N-152 road goes to Ribes de Freser and into the Vic area.

ROUTE 2

Route 2 takes the N-260 westwards to Sort. From here, the C-13 county road heads north to Alt Àneu. An alternative route from Sort is the N-260 to El Pont de Suert, via Sarroca de Bellera. Heading north from El Pont de Suert, the N-230 national trunk road goes to Vielha and then on to Naut Aran (or Salardú) along the C-28 county road.

ROUTE 3

Route 3 heads southwards to Artesa de Segre via Ribera d'Urgellet and Oliana. These two municipalities stand right next to the C-14 county road.

Naut Aran

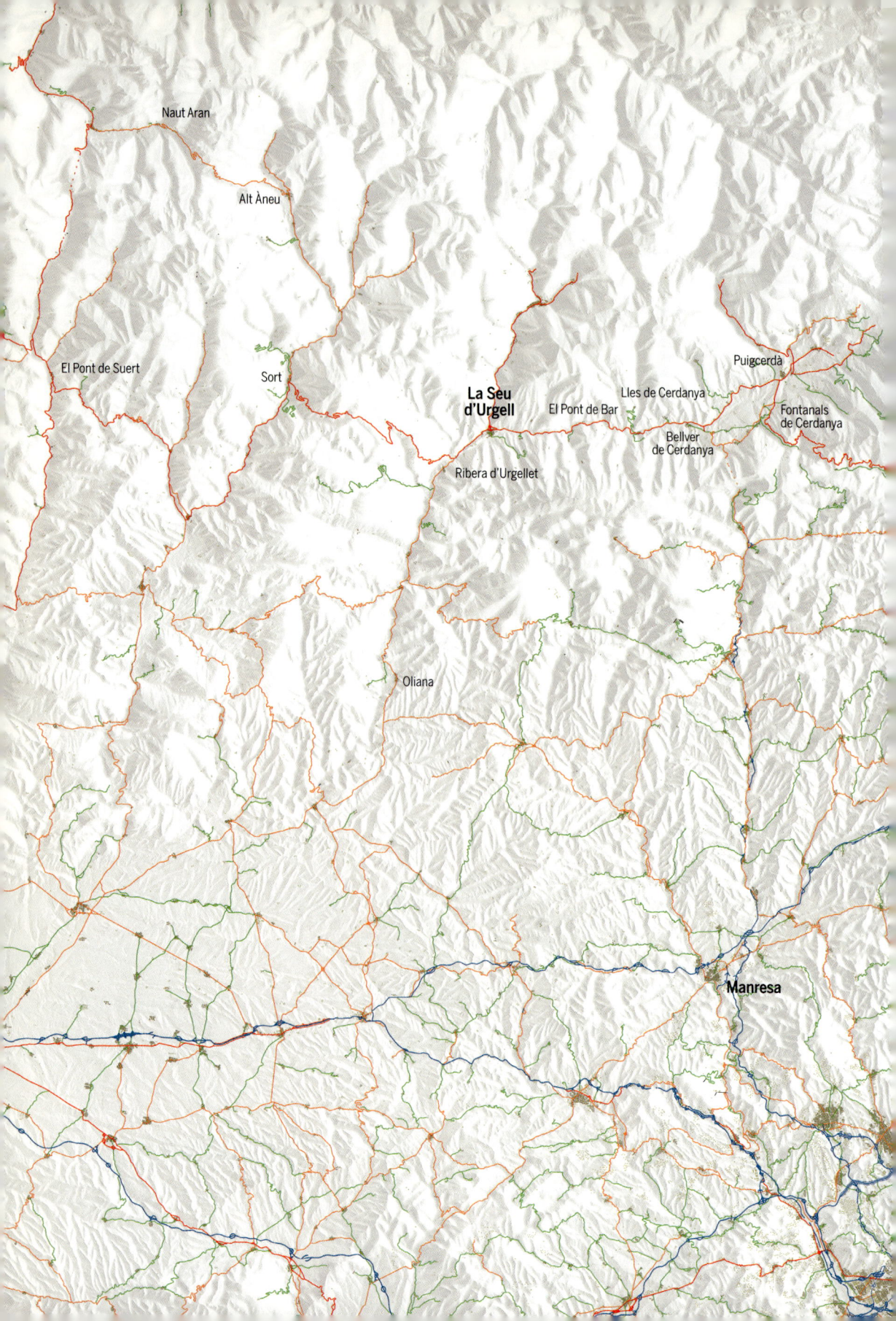

Alt Àneu

El Pont de Suert

Sort

Puigcerdà

La Seu d'Urgell

Lles de Cerdanya

El Pont de Bar

Fontanals de Cerdanya

Bellver de Cerdanya

Ribera d'Urgellet

Oliana

Manresa

Municipalities	Comarca	Surface area (municipality)	Population (2001)
LA SEU D'URGELL	Alt Urgell	15.4 km^2	10,887 inhabitants
ROUTE 1			
EL PONT DE BAR	Alt Urgell	42.6 km^2	159 inhabitants
LLES DE CERDANYA	Cerdanya	102.8 km^2	279 inhabitants
BELLVER DE CERDANYA	Cerdanya	98.1 km^2	1,614 inhabitants
FONTANALS DE CERDANYA	Cerdanya	28.7 km^2	406 inhabitants
PUIGCERDÀ	Cerdanya	18.9 km^2	7,020 inhabitants
ROUTE 2			
SORT	Pallars Sobirà	105.1 km^2	1,851 inhabitants
ALT ÀNEU	Pallars Sobirà	217.8 km^2	407 inhabitants
EL PONT DE SUERT	Alta Ribagorça	148.1 km^2	2,048 inhabitants
NAUT ARAN	Vall d'Aran	255.8 km^2	1,444 inhabitants
ROUTE 3			
RIBERA D'URGELLET	Alt Urgell	107.0 km^2	811 inhabitants
OLIANA	Alt Urgell	32.4 km^2	1,880 inhabitants

CUSÍ HOUSE
SINGLE-FAMILY DWELLING

Josep Maria Sostres
1952-1954

C/ Sant Ermengol, 67 - La Seu d'Urgell

The configuration of the house is determined by a deliberate desire to provide a simple response to a modest brief. The floor plan is laid out in two displaced volumes of identical dimensions that at once define the ground and upper floors. This displacement defines the image of the house as seen from the street. The small entrance porch and the dark-painted stairwell are given timber outlines that define this façade as a composition intended to differentiate the two constructions. The entrance hall and the corridor on the upper floor occupy both volumes and generate a cross circulation that is independent of the two-bay construction. Sostres took as his reference Jacobsen's small mass-produced houses and the way he enhanced domestic architecture by using very simple programmes.

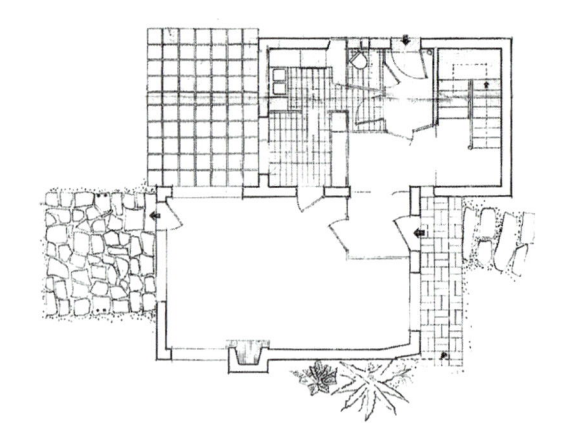

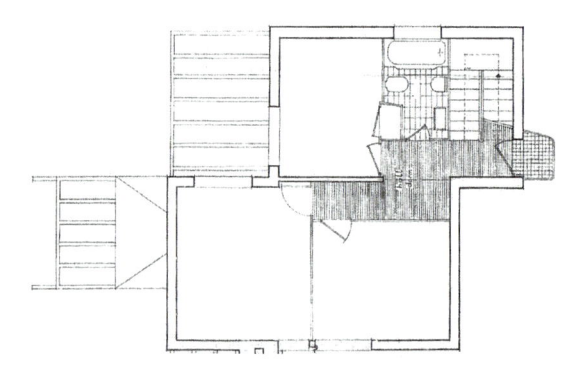

GALINDO HOUSE
SINGLE-FAMILY DWELLING

Marc Paré, Néstor Piriz, Ricard Paré, Carles Pubill
1995-1996

C/ Sant Ermengol, 90 - La Seu d'Urgell

The arrangement of the house makes the most of the possibilities offered by the urban planning regulations of La Seu d'Urgell. The house is positioned perpendicular to the street, leaving the 3-metre entrance in the west façade. In the east façade, this leaves half the plot free of building to be occupied by a garden delimited by the main façade. The walls are covered with different types of timber cladding. These surfaces invade the house and combine with the stucco of the overall volume. The door and windows frames, of matt silver anodised aluminium, adopt a range of different positions, allowing the house to present different appearances or situations. Rather than defining the surfaces or the house, the façades or the walls, they accompany and define the inhabitants' movements on their way around the house.

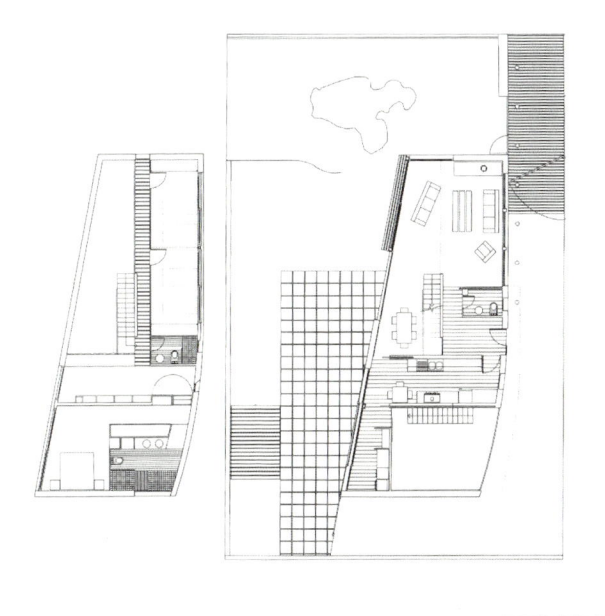

NEW VILLAGE OF EL PONT DE BAR

Lluís M. Vidal i Arderiu
1983-1988

El Pont de Bar

The floods in Catalonia in 1982 washed away much of the old village and produced landslides that revealed serious lesions in the subsoil of the nearby mountainside, to the extent of endangering attempts to reconstruct the village. The new centre stands on land 1000 metres from the original village, on the north mountainside, facing south. The programme for the new village is the same as the original: eleven dwellings, the village hall, the chapel and a hostel. The new village adopts a rigid urban structure due to geotechnical reasons, cost and the use of prefabricated elements. Nonetheless, the result is marked by a rhythm and a cadence that ensure its integration into its surroundings. The project either maintains or addresses a series of pre-existing elements that record the passage of humankind through this place, which are used as guidelines for some of the new constructions.

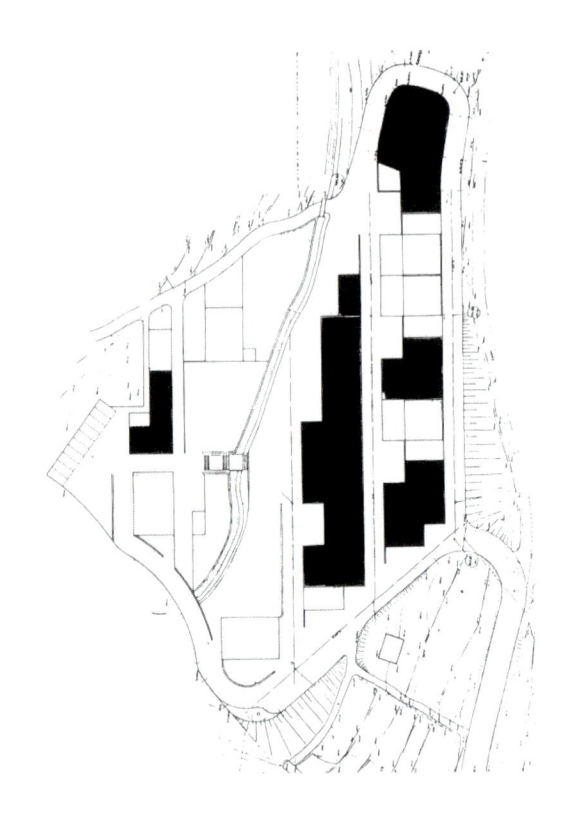

GARRIGA-POCH HOUSE
SINGLE-FAMILY DWELLING

Arturo Frediani
1999-2003

Pça. de Sant Pere - Lles de Cerdanya

The house is built on the ruins of the former smithy, and the project is based on an interpretation of planning regulations in which the principal materials shaping the place (stone, timber and channel tiles) are used in their most authentic sense. Though the house has a façade on one of the village's main squares, its configuration turns its back on the square to create its own exterior space, a stretch of grass raised above street level. Entrance to the house is via this garden, beneath a projecting volume that completes the volumetric arrangement of the house without hindering access to the garden. In terms of construction, the house weighs up the appropriate thickness of the stone walls, the judicious use of structural concrete (for the projection) and the use of timber as a skin that defines the main façade under the appearance of a plane of cladding. The house therefore respects strict planning regulations, at the same time presenting a modern image thanks to the authenticity with which the traditional materials are implemented. The project also includes an unusual take on the place, shunning traditional typologies and basing its configuration around an updated version of an ancestral element, the threshing ground.

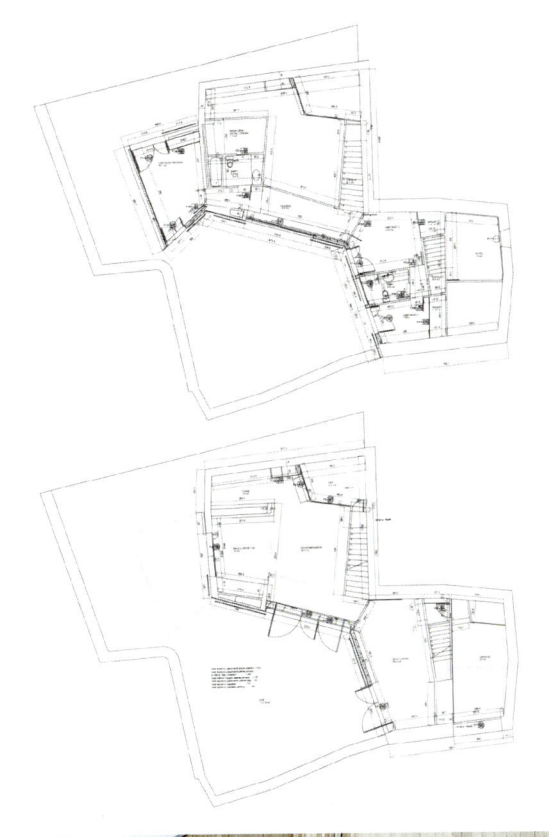

ELIAS HOUSE NO. 6
HOUSES ON CAMÍ DE TALLÓ
"BELGIAN HOUSES"

Josep Maria Sostres
1948-1950

Pg. de Pere Elias, 39 - Bellver de Cerdanya

Of the series of houses Sostres designed on Camí de Talló, all for a single client, this is the only one that takes as its reference the experiences of the modern movement and its interest in the work of Aalto. Being on the end plot, it is the only one to command south-facing views and it uses a small difference in level of the plot to adopt the configuration of two interrelated volumes. The living room is in an independent south-facing body at an angle to the road, though turned away from it. The larger volume on the lower level, which holds the other rooms, returns to the perpendicular and is laid out on intermediate floors. The materials used to clad the exterior respond to this configuration. Here, Sostres combined experiences of organic architecture with attention to vernacular architecture, a combination that he was to maintain in subsequent work.

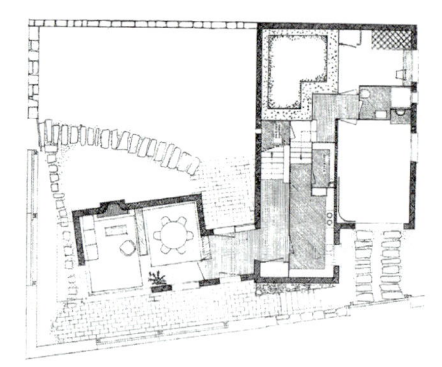

FONTANALS GOLF COURSE CLUB HOUSE

Josep Miàs
2004

Soriguerola - Fontanals de Cerdanya

The large surface required by the programme includes a building placed onto the topography, mimicking its relief. The building's basement houses the health and sports amenities, and an above-grade floor houses the more social aspects, with meeting rooms, a bar and a restaurant. The lower spaces are lit by means of skylights and do not form part of the landscape. The upper level is covered by a dark timber surface, laid like a sheet over the bearing structure without reaching the ground and therefore offering views of the surrounding countryside. The roof structure is supported by a system of metal pillars with a very small section. The building offers no resistance to the existing topography, instead allowing its contemplation alongside the new construction.

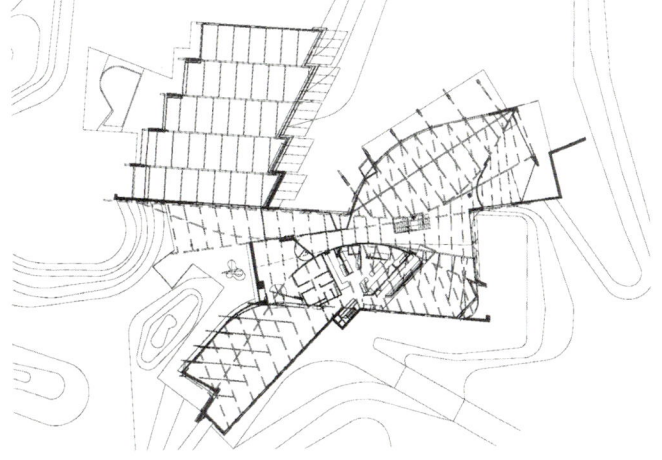

HOTEL MARIA VICTÒRIA

Josep Maria Sostres
1952-1956

C/ Querol, 7 - Puigcerdà

The shape of this plot in the old town determines the layout of the bays, and the three façades respond independently to their various uses and relation to the street. The wall structure of the bedroom floors is supported by a system of circular-sectioned pillars on the ground floor. Sostres endowed this space with great pliability by seeking out south-facing views of Cerdanya, creating small spaces by means of false ceilings, colour and slight differences in floor levels, and using the light well on the upper floors to project subdued overhead lighting into the entrance hall and the reception.

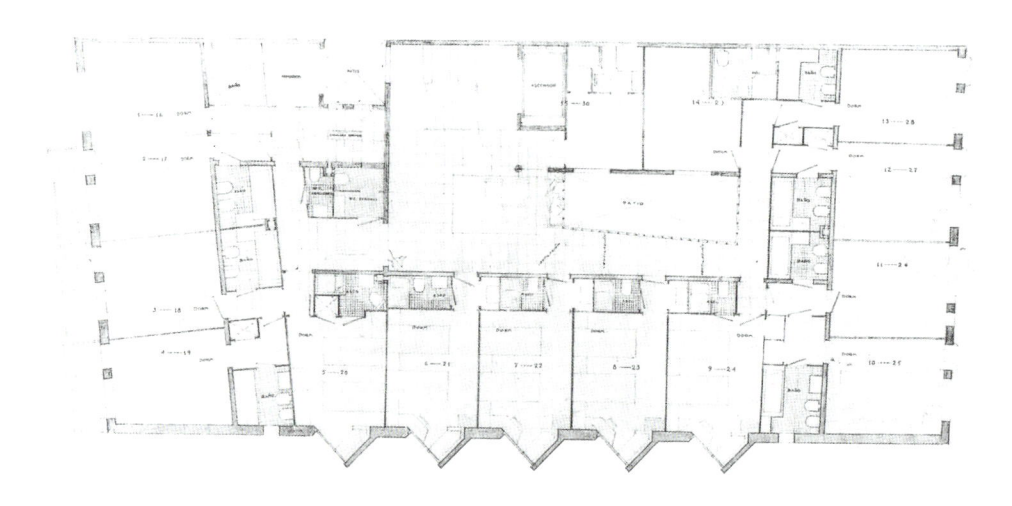

26 DWELLINGS IN THE COLÒNIA SIMÓN

Francesc Hereu, Joaquim Español
1994-1997

Colònia Simón 28, A-B - Puigcerdà

The site is located in a superlative landscape near the river Carol, on the southern edge of the Colònia Simón. This social housing block has a rectangular floor plan and stands on the south of the site, freeing up an area for a public square and avenue between the existing neighbourhood and the new building. The complex is laid out with four entrances and heights of three or four storeys, in keeping with the district. The construction materials and procedures hold no secrets: a concrete structure, tile cladding, stucco renders and double-glazing with aluminium frames. The steeply sloping roof is tiled with slate in accordance with planning regulations.

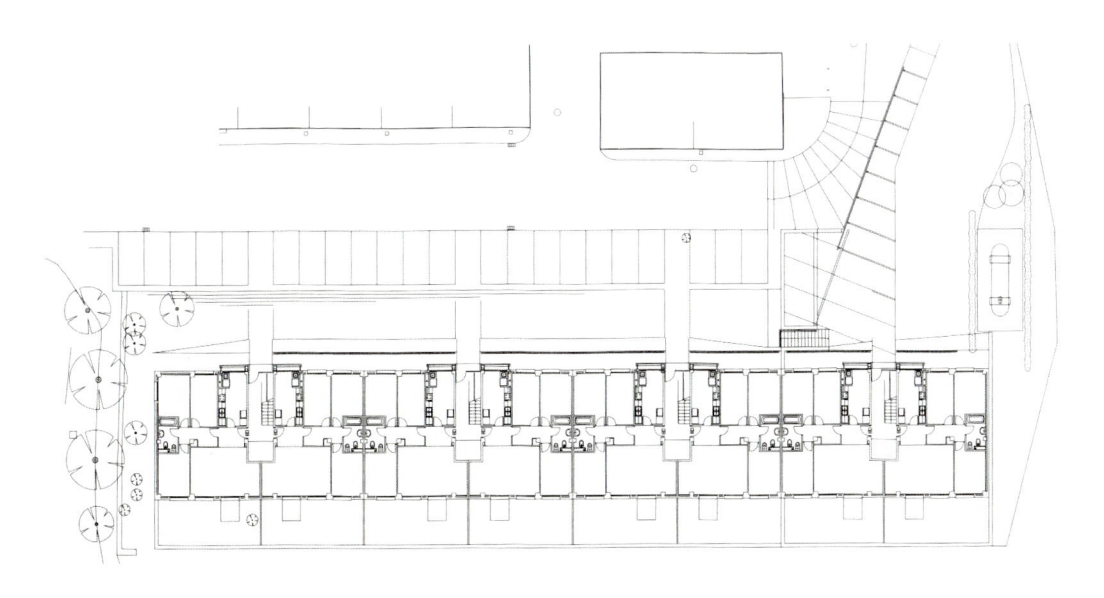

COMPLEX OF 62 APARTMENTS

Esteve Bonell, Ramon Artigues
1976-1978

Llessui (Sort)

The new intervention is located on a tract of land between Llessui and Torre, which are 200 metres apart. These two places are the product of the gradual construction of two- and three-storey buildings, sometimes with the addition of a further attic floor, with courtyards, adjoining stables and other small constructions associated with stock-keeping. The new building houses a series of apartments for winter tourism. The complex is divided into two blocks laid out to receive optimum sunlighting, separated by an orthogonal stairway that establishes continuity with the footpaths connecting the two villages. The lower block gives onto a new street that communicates the two. This façade combines shaded open spaces with the masonry and eaves of the building, minimizing visual impact by means of a less dense, higher-rise operation than the existing constructions.

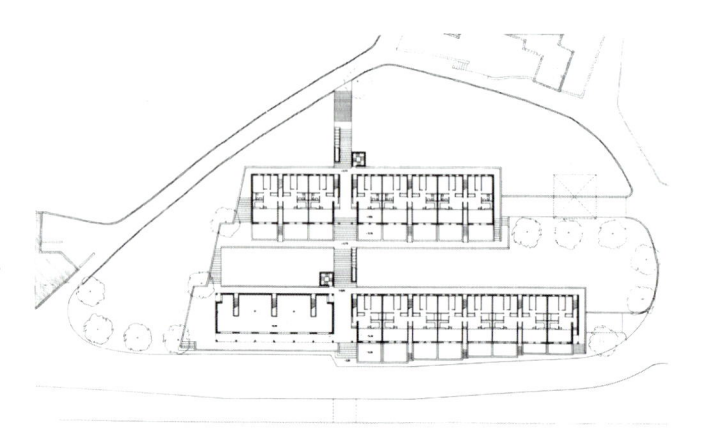

LLADÓ HOUSE
SINGLE-FAMILY DWELLING

Marta Gabàs, Anna Ribas
1995-1996

Solar de l'Antiga Rectoria - Saurí (Sort)

The house is situated at the top of a small hamlet in the Pyrenees, set on a sloping site marked by steep zigzagging streets. The site stands at the junction of two streets on the edge of the village, giving way at the rear to open countryside. The house adopts a slightly concave configuration, looking south and leaving a flat esplanade in front of the main façade. It comprises a single bay of thick stone walls, though the front wall is fragmented into two stretches, one thicker, one thinner. This point of fragmentation is marked by the front door. The narrow bay adapts to the programme for the master bedroom, and the broader bay houses the living room and kitchen. The upper floor is an attic that can be used for various purposes, accommodating large numbers of visitors at holiday times. Behind the house, an artificial embankment stands in place of a retaining wall and allows ventilation of the ground-floor rooms. The roof follows the lie of the land, sloping towards the esplanade, which is enclosed by a system of low walls built in keeping with the morphology of the rest of the village.

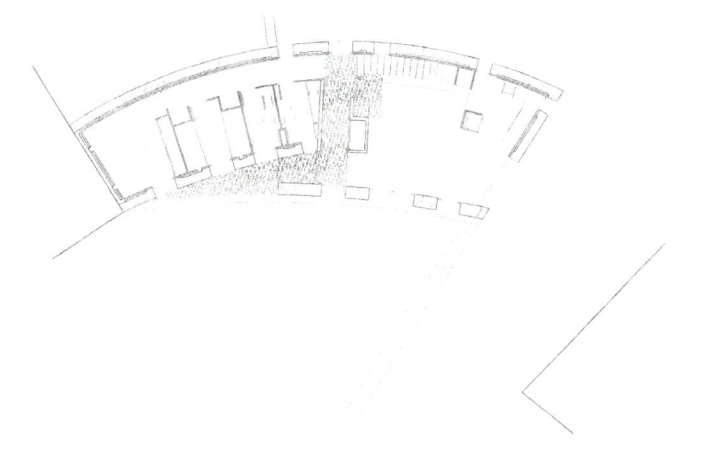

413

CENTRE FOR NATURE AND SUSTAINABLE DEVELOPMENT OF THE PYRENEES

Francesc Rius
1998-2002

Les Planes de Son - Valls d'Àneu (Alt Àneu)

414

CHURCH OF THE ASSUMPTION

José Rodríguez Mijares, Eduardo Torroja
1952-1954

Av. Victoriano Muñoz, 27 - El Pont de Suert

The church is one of the few examples in Spain of the integrated application of reinforced concrete procedures to religious architecture, a trend that became widespread in South America some time ago without being granted the approval of the Spanish ecclesiastic hierarchy. It comprises a single nave, built of a parallel series of pointed arches that define the section and are reflected in the outline of the façade. The side chapels are independent concrete shells, as are the Chapel of the Holy Sacrament and the baptistery, two exterior structures built against the main volumes. The bell tower, standing apart from the main body of the church, is a great concrete pillar with a trilobite section. Parts of the construction suggest an imitation of other materials, such as brick and stone, an effect produced by the treatment of the concrete surfaces.

415

HEREDERO HOUSE
SINGLE-FAMILY DWELLING

Oriol Bohigas, Josep Maria Martorell, David Mackay
1967-1968

Road from Vielha to Vaqueira (C-28), km 36
Tredòs - Vaqueira (Naut Aran)

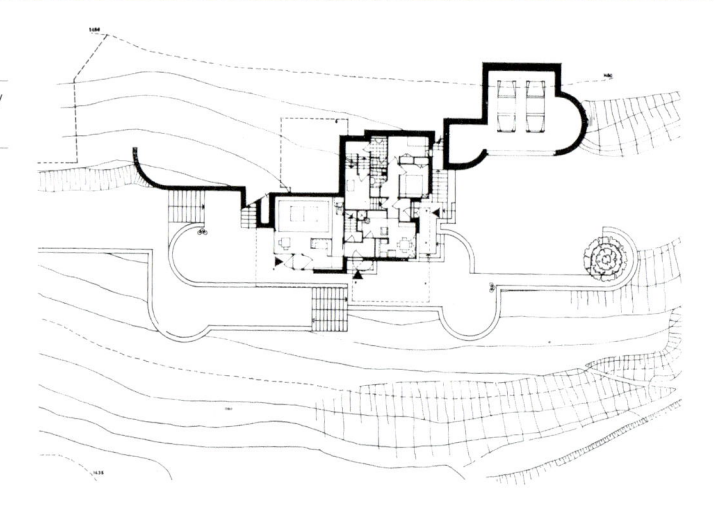

The programme for the centre is divided into three blocks: educational, residential and services. The aim of the centre, covering over 3000 square metres, is to provide information about the area and constitute an environmental education research facility. It has a single façade, and its section allows its construction partially underground, so that the roof becomes a prolongation of the meadow. The south-facing façade, commanding good views, contains photovoltaic thermal collectors to directly harness solar energy. The building is divided into three blocks, turned at an angle of 15 degrees, ensuring their adaptation to the relief and foreshortening the dimensions of the façade, thereby reducing its visual impact in a location of great landscape beauty.

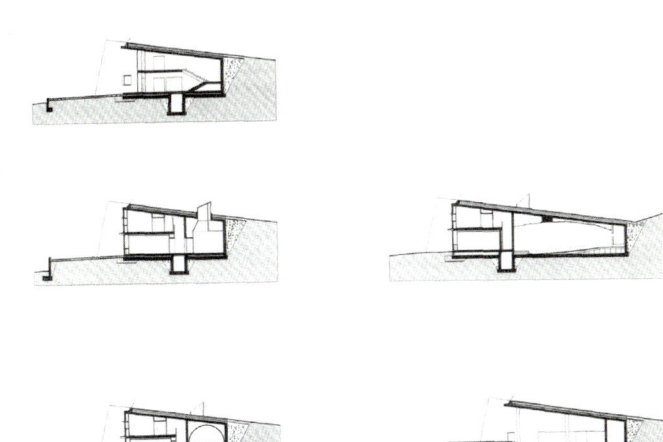

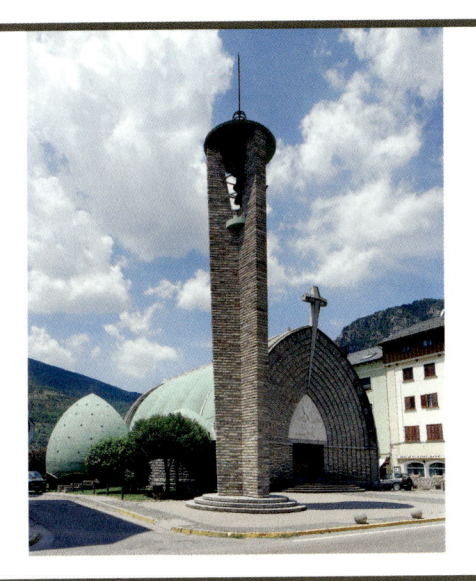

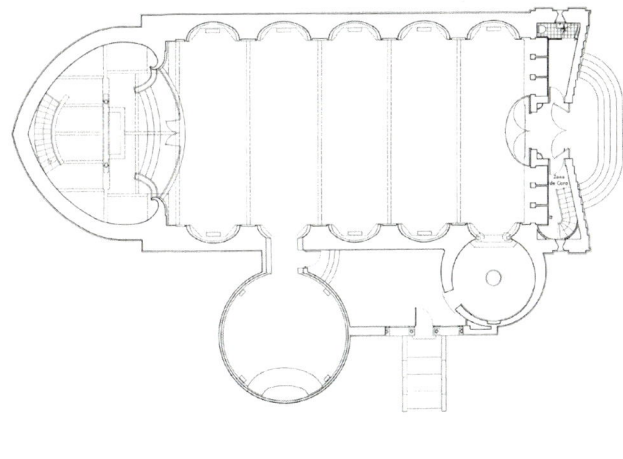

Tredòs is a village near the ski resort of Vaqueira, at an altitude of 1,200 metres. The house stands halfway up the mountain and is a holiday home for a large family. A series of terraces are laid out across the slope for greater ease of access on foot and to allow outdoor activities. The house itself comprises four square elements separated by a cross-shaped cut housing flights of stairs that fluidly connect all the areas of the house. The core is formed by four fireplaces on the lower floors and four bathrooms on the upper floor, and culminates in the four chimneys on the roof. The eight prismatic volumes stand out clearly in the exterior. The four-pitched roof and the earthy-grey facings make the house blend into the landscape with no need to imitate vernacular languages.

la Seu d'Urgell

CEIP SANT SERNI D'ARFA
INFANTS' AND PRIMARY SCHOOL
ONE-TEACHER SCHOOL

Conxita Balcells
1997-1998

Cap del Poble - Arfa (Ribera d'Urgellet)

The project responds to the education programme for a small Pyrenean village, involving the schooling of seven children by a single teacher. The new building stands at the end of a street, at the point where the existing village dies out and further construction could begin. The site designated for the building, a gently sloping north-facing plot of land, is connected to the backs of the outer-lying houses with their old threshing grounds and the incipient presence of a new street. The project is designed as a wall around the esplanade, comprising three single-storey constructions turned to face the village. The spaces between the three constructions serve to highlight the entrance and create a small triangular space of distribution. The constructions comprise concrete walls with timber-clad façades, topped by the slope of the roofs. The wall on the far side of the esplanade is lower, allowing good sunlighting conditions. The project follows the lie of the land, which it takes as the basis for construction, constituting a limit between the built village centre and the point where open countryside begins.

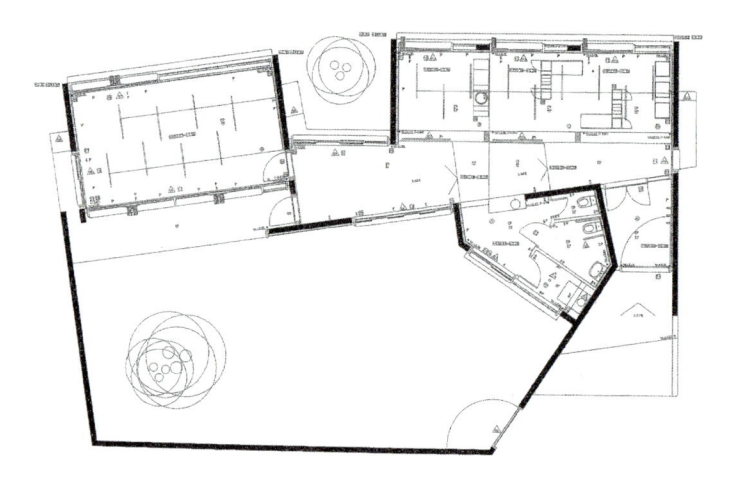

CAP OLIANA
HEALTH CENTRE

Ramon Fité, Julio José Mejón
1991-1993

C/ Girona, 8 - Oliana

The building stands on a corner, with a path to the north and a party wall to the west. The project responds to the characteristics of the programme and the location with great clarity in the floor plan, thereby resolving important issues such as the lighting of the waiting room, and privacy and lighting in the surgeries. The large contrasts in temperature and light advised protection of the building's true centre, the individual surgeries, by employing the service spaces, the double façade, the inspection floor and the space beneath the roof. The service spaces are used to compensate the irregularities of the site. The space beneath the roof is devoted to energy, as well as constituting a buffer and generating heat. The first- and ground-floor waiting rooms are communicated by a double-height space that runs along the façade, freeing up the building's two long façades from top to bottom.

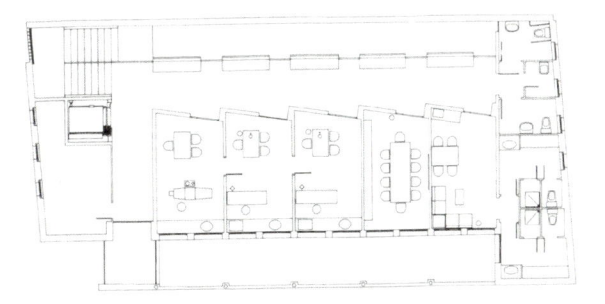

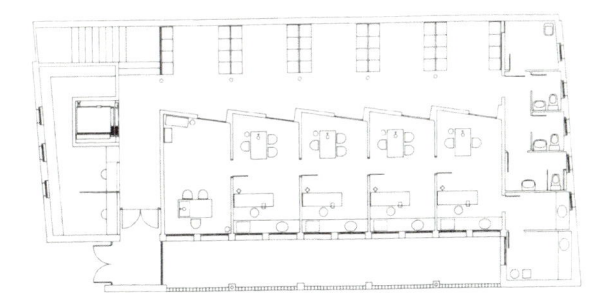

Index of buildings

The Figueres area

001 - ROGER HOUSE. Josep Azemar i Pont. 1896. C/ Monturiol, 9 - Figueres

002 - SALLERAS HOUSE. Josep Azemar i Pont. 1904. Rambla, 16 - Figueres

003 - FIGUERES MUNICIPAL ABATTOIR. Josep Azemar i Pont. 1907. Pl. de l'Escorxador, s/n - Figueres

004 - MAS I ROGER HOUSE. Josep Azemar i Pont. 1910. C/ Caamaño, 9 Pl. de la Palmera - C/ Monturiol, 10 Figueres

005 - GUILLAMET HOUSE. Emili Blanch. 1935. C/ Ample, 14 - C/ Sant Rafael, 22 C/ Santa Llúcia, 1 - Figueres

006 - DALÍ THEATRE AND MUSEUM. Salvador Dalí, Joaquín Ros de Ramis, Alejandro Bonaterra, Emilio Pérez Piñero. 1970-1974. Pl. Gala-Salvador Dalí Figueres

007 - ROZES HOUSE. José Antonio Coderch de Sentmenat, Manuel Valls. 1961-1962. Av. Díaz Pacheco, 184 - Roses

008 - CLOS-RAHOLA HOUSE. Víctor Rahola. 1971-1974. Cala La Pelosa - Cap de Norfeu - Roses

009 - VILLAVECCHIA HOUSE. Federico Correa, Alfons Milà. 1955. Riba del Pixot, s/n - C/ Eduard Marquina, 7 - Cadaqués

010 - SENILLOSA HOUSE. José Antonio Coderch de Sentmenat, Manuel Valls. 1955-1956. C/ Guillem Bruguera, 6 C/ Eliseu Meifrén, s/n - Cadaqués

011 - PÉREZ DEL PULGAR CHALET. Francesc Joan Barba i Corsini. 1957-1958. Terrenys de Torre Zariquiey Cadaqués

012 - MARY CALLERY HOUSE. Peter Harnden, Lanfranco Bombelli. 1961-1962. C/ Roses, 8 - Cadaqués

013 - FASQUELLE HOUSE. Peter Harnden, Lanfranco Bombelli. 1968. Portlligat (Cadaqués)

014 - JOVER-SALA HOUSE. Beth Galí, Màrius Quintana. 1990-1992. C/ Llevant Parcel·la 5 - Sector de les Figuerasses El Port de la Selva

015 - MARGARIDA FONTDEVILA HOUSE. Ignasi de Solà-Morales, Javier López del Castillo. 1997-1999. Carrer B - Parcel·la 24 - Urbanització Morasol - El Port de la Selva

016 - HEADQUARTERS OF THE UNIÓ MAÇANETENCA. Josep Azemar i Pont. 1906. Pl. de la Vila, 6 Maçanet de Cabrenys

017 - AGULLANA SCHOOLS. Josep Azemar i Pont. 1910. Ctra. de La Vajol, 4 Agullana

018 - HOUSE AND STUDIO FOR A PHOTOGRAPHER. Carles Ferrater. 1992-1993. Ctra. de Llampaies a Camallera (GI-623) Llampaies -Saus

019 - BIO VILLA. Enric Ruiz-Geli. 2003-2004. C/ Sant Jordi, 24 - Urbanització Montserrat - Llers

020 - MARE DE DÉU DE LA SALUT SOCIAL HEALTH CENTRE. Francesc Hereu, Joaquim Español. 1995-1998. Ctra. de la Salut, s/n - Terrades

021 - VILANOVA-CULLELL HOUSE. Albert Illescas, Jeroni Moner. 1972. Pg. Mossèn Constans, 217 - Banyoles

022 - HOUSING BLOCK NO. 10 IN THE OLYMPIC VILLAGE. Josep Fuses, Joan Maria Viader. 1990-1992. C/ Lluís Companys, 23-27 - Banyoles

023 - CEIP PLA DE L'AMETLLER. José Miguel Roldán, Mercè Berengué. 2001-2002. C/ Formiga, 117 - Banyoles

024 - PESQUERA D'EN MALAGELADA FISHING PAVILION. Jeroni Moner, Joaquim Figa, Josep Riera. 1990-1991. Pg. Darder - Pesquera núm. 16 - Estany de Banyoles - Banyoles

025 - ELS BANYS VELLS. BAR KIOSK. Josep Miàs. 1995-1996. Pg. de Lluís Maria Vidal, 25 - Estany de Banyoles Banyoles

026 - BOAT RACE FINISHING LINE PAVILION. Josep Cargol, Ricard Turon. 2001-2003. Zona d'Arribada del Camp de Regates - Estany de Banyoles Banyoles

The Girona area

027 - TEIXIDOR FLOUR MILL. Rafael Masó. 1910-1924. C/ Santa Eugènia, 42 Girona

028 - BATLLE HOUSE. Rafael Masó. 1909-1910. C/ Fontanilles, 2 - C/ Nou, 15 Av. Sant Francesc, 16 - Girona

029 - SALIETI HOUSE. Rafael Masó. 1910-1911. C/ Ciutadans, 8 - Girona

030 - NORAT HOUSE. Joan Roca i Pinet. 1912-1913. Rbla. Llibertat, 25 - Girona

031 - DALMAU HOUSE. Joan Roca i Pinet. 1917-1918. C/ Portal Nou, 17-19 Girona

032 - TEIXIDOR HOUSE, CASA DE LA PUNXA. Rafael Masó. 1918-1922. C/ Santa Eugènia, 19 - Girona

033 - GISPERT SAÜCH HOUSE. Rafael Masó. 1921-1923. C/ Alvarez de Castro, 9 - Av. Jaume I, 66 - Girona

034 - IGNASI IGLESIAS SCHOOL. Ricard Giralt. 1930-1932. Pjda. Montjuïc, 1 Girona

035 - BLANCH HOUSE. Emili Blanch. 1931-1932. C/ Bernat Boadas, 6 - Girona

036 - TARRÚS HOUSE. Josep Claret i Rubira. 1935. C/ Rutlla, 137 - Girona

037 - FORNÉ GARAGE. Joan M. de Ribot. 1957. Ctra. de Barcelona, 39 C/ Bisbe Lorenzana, 55 - Girona

038 - THE MARIST SCHOOL OF GIRONA. Joan M. de Ribot, Josep Maria Pla. 1972. Av. Josep Tarradellas, 5 - Girona

039 - HOUSING BLOCK IN FONTAJAU. Josep Fuses, Joan Maria Viader. 1990-1994. C/ Can Sunyer, 11 Girona

040 - OFFICIAL SCHOOL OF LANGUAGES. Víctor Rahola. 1991-1994. C/ Josep Viader i Moliner, 16 - Girona

041 - PLA-BARBERO HOUSE. Arcadi Pla. 1990-1993. C/ Serra de Bestracà, 4-6 Girona

042 - FIGUERES HOUSE. Àlex Sibils. 1995-1996. C/ Àngel, 5 - Girona

043 - PALAU DE JUSTÍCIA. Esteve Bonell, Josep Maria Gil. 1987-1992. Av. Ramon Folch, 1 - Girona

044 - GIRONA-FONTAJAU MUNICIPAL SPORTS CENTRE. Esteve Bonell, Josep Maria Gil. 1991-1993. C/ Josep Aguilera i Martí, 2 - Girona

045 - FACULTY OF ECONOMIC AND BUSINESS STUDIES. Arcadi Pla. 1988-1993. Av. Lluís Santaló, s/n - Campus de Montilivi - Universitat de Girona - Girona

046 - FACULTY OF EXPERIMENTAL SCIENCE. Josep Fuses, Joan Maria Viader. 1996-1997. Av. Lluís Santaló Campus de Montilivi - Universitat de Girona - Girona

047 - LAW FACULTY. Rafael Aranda, Carme Pigem, Ramon Vilalta. 1997-1999. Av. Lluís Santaló, s/n - Campus de Montilivi - Universitat de Girona - Girona

048 - WORKSHOP AND GREENHOUSE BUILDING. David Baena, Toni Casamor, Josep Maria Quera. 2000-2002. Av. Lluís Santaló, s/n - Campus de Montilivi - Universitat de Girona - Girona

049 - UNIVERSITY LIBRARY. Javier San José. 1998-2007. Av. Lluís Santaló Campus de Montilivi - Universitat de Girona - Girona

050 - APARTMENT BUILDING IN SANT PONÇ. Arcadi Pla. 1996-1999. C/ Esport, 3-5 - Girona

051 - CAP MALUQUER SALVADOR. Jaime Coll, Judith Leclerc. 2001-2003. C/ Castell de Solterra, 11-17 - Girona

052 - IES CARLES RAHOLA. Enric Massip-Bosch, Marc Rifà, Minoru Suzuki, Cornelia Memm. 2003-2006. C/ Joan Miró i Ferrà, 10 - Fontajau - Girona

053 - ELS QUÍMICS RESIDENTIAL COMPLEX. Eduard Gascón, Carles Martí Arís. 2001-2006. C/ Migdia, 137-139 C/ Marquès de Caldes de Montbui, 70-104 Pujada de la Creu de Palau, 2-4 Girona

054 - CEIP SANTA FE. Jordi Ros. 1986-1990. Pujada al Castell, s/n - Medinyà (Sant Julià de Ramis)

055 - JORDI CANTARELL HOUSE. Lluís Jubert, Eugènia Santacana. 1996-1997. C/ Migjorn, 1 - Púbol -La Pera

056 - MONTGRÍ SPORTS PAVILION. Carles Ferrater, Jeroni Moner, Arcadi Pla. 1982-1985. Rda. Pau Casals, s/n Torroella de Montgrí

057 - L'ESTARTIT YACHT CLUB. Carles Ferrater, Gerardo Rodríguez, Juan Díaz. 1988-1991. Port de l'Estartit - L'Estartit Torroella de Montgrí

058 - EL GUIX DE LA MEDA, SINGLE-FAMILY DWELLING. Carles Ferrater. 1983-1984. C/ Cap de la Barra, 31 L'Estartit - Torroella de Montgrí

059 - SINGLE-FAMILY DWELLING. Gustau Gili i Galfetti. 2002-2005. Camí de Gaüses de Dalt a Gaüses de Baix, Gaüses - Vilopriu

060 - APARTMENT COMPLEX AT PALS GOLF COURSE. Oriol Bohigas, Josep Maria Martorell, David Mackay. 1971-1973. C/ del Golf, 78 - Platja de Pals - Pals

061 - CANTARELL HOUSE. Josep Pratmarsó. 1962. Punta d'en Toni, 6 Port des Pins - Sa Riera - Begur

062 - CRUYLLES HOUSE. Antoni Bonet i Castellana, Josep Puig i Torné. 1967-1968. Ctra. del Port d'Esclanyà, 5 Paratge d'Aiguablava - Begur

063 - LLINÀS HOUSE. Josep Llinàs. 1978-1980. Ctra. de Begur a Sa Tuna (GIV-6534), km. 0,8 - Begur

064 - JORI-MISERACHS HOUSE. Ignasi de Solà-Morales. 1988-1990. C/ Port dels Orats, 9 - Paratge d'Aiguablava Begur

065 - CASTANERA HOUSE. Antoni Bonet i Castellana. 1963-1964. C/ Golfet, 12 Calella de Palafrugell

066 - RAVENTÓS HOUSE. Antoni Bonet i Castellana, Josep Puig i Torné. 1973-1974. C/ Golfet, 22 - Calella de Palafrugell

067 - REGÀS HOUSE AND VANTAGE POINT - Lluís Clotet, Oscar Tusquets. 1970-1971. Mas Catalanet Paratge Sobirà - Llofriu - Palafrugell

068 - BOFILL HOUSE. Ricard Bofill. 1973. C/ de la Font, 20 - Mont-ras

069 - MAS VIDAL HOUSE. Josep Pratmarsó. 1958. C/ Raval de Baix, s/n Vall-llobrega

070 - MAS GARBÀ HOUSE. Josep Pratmarsó. 1959. C/ Roca de Gria, 1 Vall-llobrega

071 - FOUR SINGLE-FAMILY ROW HOUSES. Lluís Nadal. 1987-1989. C/ Josep Pla, 11 - Platja de la Fosca Palamós

072 - HOUSE AT LA FOSCA. Jordi Garcés. 2003. Pg. de la Fosca, 22 - Platja de la Fosca - Palamós

073 - HOUSE AT THE GOLF CLUB. Lluís Clotet, Oscar Tusquets. 1978-1979. Urbanització Golf Costa Brava La Masia - Santa Cristina d'Aro

074 - HOUSE-CUM-STUDY FOR THE CARTOONIST CESC. Esteve Bonell, Josep Maria Gil. 1979-1982. Av. de l'Església, s/n - Santa Cristina d'Aro

075 - CENDRÓS HOUSE. Manuel Ribas i Piera. 1968. Rambla Vidal, 1-5 - Pg. del Mar, 24 - Sant Feliu de Guíxols

076 - APARTMENT BUILDING. Ramon Muñoz, Robert Pallí, Rodrigo Prats, Antonio Sanmartín. 1990-1992. C/ Gravina, 49-59 - C/ Fortuny, 26-36 C/ Bourg de Peage, 25 - Sant Feliu de Guíxols

077 - SALGOT HOUSE. Jordi Garcés, Enric Soria. 1988-1989. Parcel·les 6 i 8 Urbanització Vista Alegre - Paratge de St. Telm - Sant Feliu de Guíxols

078 - COURTS BUILDING. Jordi Moliner, Josep Lluís Mateo. 1990-1993. C/ Antoni Campmany, 15-21 - Sant Feliu de Guíxols

079 - IES SANT FELIU. Rafael Aranda, Carme Pigem, Ramon Vilalta. 1997-2001. C/ Canigó, 41 - Sant Feliu de Guíxols

080 - "ESCOLA DEL VEÏNAT". Oriol Bohigas, Josep Maria Martorell, David Mackay, Albert Puigdomènech. 1988-1991. C/ Enric Granados, 8 - Salt

081 - SANTA CATERINA GENERAL HOSPITAL. Manuel Brullet, Albert de Pineda, Alfonso de Luna, Albert Vitaller. 1995-2005. C/ Doctor Castany, 90 Parc Hospitalari Martí i Julià - Salt

082 - DIVÍ-BAENA HOUSE. Josep Maria Birulés, Frederic Cabré, Pià Romans. 1992-1993. C/ Eugeni D'Ors, 24 Fornells de la Selva

083 - HOTEL SANT MARCH. Joan M. de Ribot. 1955. Av. del Pelegrí, 2 Tossa de Mar

084 - NICOLÁS VALENZUELA HOUSE. Eva Jiménez, Xavier Llobet. 2003-2007. C/ dels Satèl·lits, 38 - Urbanització Lloret Residencial - Lloret de Mar

085 - BLANES COUNTY LIBRARY. Ramon Artigues, Ramon Sanabria. 2001-2002. Pg. Catalunya, 2 - Blanes

The Barcelona area

086 - CAFÉ-RESTAURANT OF THE 1888 WORLD FAIR. Lluís Domènech i Montaner. 1887-1888. Passeig Picasso, s/n (Parc de la Ciutadella) - Barcelona

087 - "ELS QUATRE GATS" PERE AND FRANCESC MARTÍ I PUIG HOUSE. Josep Puig i Cadafalch. 1895-1896. C/ Montsió, 3 bis - Barcelona

088 - PALAU GÜELL. Antoni Gaudí. 1885-1889. C/ Nou de la Rambla, 3-5 Barcelona

089 - CALVET HOUSE. Antoni Gaudí. 1898-1904. C/ Casp, 48 - Barcelona

090 - BATLLÓ HOUSE. Antoni Gaudí. 1904-1906. Pg. de Gràcia, 43 - Barcelona

091 - ANTONI AMATLLER HOUSE. Josep Puig i Cadafalch. 1898-1900. Pg. de Gràcia, 41 - Barcelona

092 - LLEÓ MORERA HOUSE. Lluís Domènech i Montaner. 1903-1905. Pg. de Gràcia, 35 - Barcelona

093 - MONTANER I SIMON PUBLISHING HOUSE. Lluís Domènech i Montaner. 1881-1884. C/ Aragó, 255 Barcelona

094 - CASIMIR CASARAMONA TEXTILE MILL. Josep Puig i Cadafalch. 1909-1911. Av. Marquès de Comillas, 6-8 Barcelona

095 - MILÀ HOUSE, "LA PEDRERA" (THE QUARRY). Antoni Gaudí. 1906-1910. Pg. de Gràcia, 92 - C/ Provença, 261-265 - Barcelona

096 - EXPIATORY TEMPLE OF THE SAGRADA FAMÍLIA. Antoni Gaudí. 1882-1926. C/ de la Marina, 253 - Barcelona

097 - HOSPITAL DE LA SANTA CREU I SANT PAU. Lluís Domènech i Montaner. 1902-1911. Av. Sant Antoni Maria Claret, 167-171 - Barcelona

098 - VICENS HOUSE. Antoni Gaudí. 1878-1885. C/ Carolines, 18-24 Barcelona

099 - GÜELL ESTATE. Antoni Gaudí. 1884-1887. Av. Pedralbes, 7-15 Barcelona

100 - MACARI GOLFERICHS HOUSE. Joan Rubió i Bellver. 1900-1901. Gran Via de les Corts Catalanes, 491 - Barcelona

101 - PALAU DE LA MÚSICA CATALANA. Lluís Domènech i Montaner. 1905-1908. C/ Sant Francesc de Paula, 2 Barcelona

102 - SCHOOL, ORIGINALLY A TERESIAN CONVENT. Antoni Gaudí. 1888-1890. C/ Ganduxer, 95-105 Barcelona

103 - TALLERS MANYACH. Josep Maria Jujol. 1916-1922. C/ Riera Sant Miquel, 39 Barcelona

104 - "BELLESGUARD", FIGUERES HOUSE. Antoni Gaudí. 1900-1909. C/ Bellesguard, 16-20 - Barcelona

105 - QUERALT HOUSE. Josep Maria Jujol. 1916-1917. C/ Pineda, 1 - Barcelona

106 - PLANELLS HOUSE. Josep Maria Jujol. 1923-1924. Av. Diagonal, 332 Barcelona

107 - SANT JORDI TOWNHOUSE. Francesc Folguera i Grassi. 1929-1931. C/ Pau Claris, 81 - C/ Casp, 24-26 Barcelona

108 - MASANA HOUSE. Ramon Reventós. 1928. C/ Lleida, 7-11 C/ Olivera, 78 - C/ Tamarit, 70 Barcelona

109 - APARTMENT BUILDING. Carles Martínez. 1932. Via Augusta, 12 Barcelona

110 - HOUSING BLOCK. Josep Lluís Sert, Josep Torres i Clavé, Joan Baptista Subirana. 1932-1936. Pg. Torras i Bages, 91-105 - Barcelona

111 - TUBERCULOSIS CLINIC. Josep Lluís Sert, Josep Torres i Clavé, Joan Baptista Subirana. 1934-1938. Ptge. Sant Bernat, 10 - Barcelona

112 - BUILDING WITH SIX DUPLEX APARTMENTS. Josep Lluís Sert. 1930-1931. C/ Muntaner, 342-348 - Barcelona

113 - APARTMENT BUILDING. Germán Rodríguez Arias. 1930-1931. Via Augusta, 61 - Barcelona

114 - BARANGÉ HOUSE. Ricardo de Churruca. 1931-1935. Plaça de Mons, 4 Barcelona

115 - BUILDING OF 40 APARTMENTS. Germán Rodríguez Arias. 1933-1934. C/ París, 193-199 - Barcelona

116 - APARTMENT BUILDING. Sixt Illescas. 1934-1935. C/ Pàdua, 96 Barcelona

117 - APARTMENT BUILDING. Raimon Duran i Reynals. 1933-1935. C/ Camp d'en Vidal, 16 - C/ Aribau, 243 Barcelona

118 - APARTMENT BUILDING. Francesc Mitjans. 1941-1943. C/ Amigó, 76 Barcelona

119 - "CASA DE LA MARINA", APARTMENT BUILDING. José Antonio Coderch de Sentmenat, Manuel Valls. 1951-1955. Pg. Joan de Borbó, 43 Barcelona

120 - HOTEL PARK. Antoni de Moragas. 1950-1953. Av. Marquès de l'Argentera, 11 Barcelona

121 - HOUSING FOR "LA MAQUINISTA" WORKERS' COOPERATIVE . José Antonio Coderch de Sentmenat, Manuel Valls. 1951-1953. Pl. del Llagut, 1-11 Barcelona

122 - GUSTAVO GILI PUBLISHING HOUSE. Francesc Bassó, Joaquim Gili. 1954-1961. C/ Rosselló, 87-89 Barcelona

123 - ARCHITECTS' INSTITUTE OF CATALONIA. Xavier Busquets. 1958-1962. Plaça Nova, 5 - Barcelona

124 - LAW FACULTY. Guillermo Giráldez, Pedro López Iñigo, Xavier Subías. 1958-1959. Av. Diagonal, 684 - Barcelona

125 - UNIVERSITY SCHOOL OF BUSINESS STUDIES. Javier Carvajal, Rafael García de Castro. 1955-1961. Av. Diagonal, 694 - Barcelona

126 - CAMP NOU, FC BARCELONA STADIUM. Francesc Mitjans, Josep Soteras, Lorenzo García-Barbón. 1954-1957. C/ Arístides Maillol, 12-18 Barcelona

127 - MERIDIANA GREYHOUND STADIUM, Antoni Bonet i Castellana, Josep Puig i Torné. 1962-1963. C/ Concepció Arenal, 165 - Barcelona

128 - HORTA MUNICIPAL CYCLE TRACK. Esteve Bonell, Francesc Rius. 1983-1984. Pg. Vall d'Hebron, 185-201 - Barcelona

129 - PALLARS HOUSING BLOCK BUILDING OF 130 SOCIAL DWELLINGS. Oriol Bohigas, Josep Maria Martorell. 1958-1959. C/ Pallars, 299-317 Barcelona

130 - MITRE BUILDING BLOCK OF 298 APARTAMENTS. Francesc Joan Barba i Corsini. 1960-1964. Rda. General Mitre, 1-13 - Barcelona

131 - SEIDA BUILDING BLOCK OF 96 DWELLINGS. Francesc Mitjans. 1959-1967. Av. Sarrià, 130-152 - Barcelona

132 - 26-DWELLING APARTMENT BUILDING. José Antonio Coderch de Sentmenat, Manuel Valls. 1957-1961. C/ Johann Sebastian Bach, 7 - Barcelona

133 -APARTMENT BUILDING. Emili Bofill, Ricard Bofill. 1962-1963. C/ Johann Sebastian Bach, 28 - Barcelona

134 - APARTMENT BUILDING. Emili Bofill, Ricard Bofill. 1962-1963. C/ Johann Sebastian Bach, 2-4 - C/ Francesc Pérez-Cabrero, 6 - Barcelona

135 - APARTMENT BUILDING. Emili Bofill, Ricard Bofill. 1962-1965. C/ Nicaragua, 97-99 - Barcelona

136 - APARTMENT BUILDING. Manuel de Solà-Morales i Rosselló, Manuel de Solà-Morales i Rubió. 1964-1967. C/ Muntaner, 271 - C/ Avenir, 35-37 Barcelona

137 - BUILDING OF 121 SOCIAL DWELLINGS. Oriol Bohigas, Josep Maria Martorell, David Mackay. 1959-1965. Av. Meridiana, 312-318 - Barcelona

138 - APARTMENT BUILDING. Antoni de Moragas, Francesc de Riba i Salas. 1966-1968. Via Augusta, 128-132 - C/ Brusi, 37-45 - C/ Sant Elies, 11-19 - Barcelona

139 - LA VINYA HOUSING COMPLEX. Lluís Nadal, Vicenç Bonet, Pere Puigdefàbregas. 1966-1968. C/ Alts Forns, 85-87 - C/ Ferrocarrils Catalans, 71-85 - Barcelona

140 - HISPANO-OLIVETTI OFFICES. Ludovico Belgiojoso, Enrico Peressutti, Ernesto N. Rogers. 1960-1964. Ronda Universitat, 18 - Barcelona

141 - BANCA CATALANA - Josep Maria Fargas, Enric Tous. 1965-1968. Pg. de Gràcia, 84 - Barcelona

142 - TÀPIES HOUSE. José Antonio Coderch de Sentmenat, Manuel Valls. 1960-1962. C/ Saragossa, 57 Barcelona

143 - OFFICES AND PRINT SHOPS OF EL NOTICIERO UNIVERSAL. Josep Maria Sostres. 1963-1965. C/ Roger de Llúria, 35 - Barcelona

144 - BANCO ATLÁNTICO. Francesc Mitjans, Santiago Balcells. 1965-1969. C/ Balmes, 168-170 - Barcelona

145 - TRADE BUILDINGS. José Antonio Coderch de Sentmenat, Manuel Valls. 1965-1969. Av. Carles III, 84-98 Barcelona

146 - TORRE ATALAYA. Federico Correa, Alfons Milá, José Luis Sanz Magallón. 1966-1971. Av. Diagonal, 523 - Barcelona

147 - MONITOR BUILDING. Federico Correa, Alfons Milà. 1968-1970. Av. Diagonal, 490 - Barcelona

148 - BANCO URQUIJO HOUSING COMPLEX. José Antonio Coderch de Sentmenat, Manuel Valls. 1968-1973. C/ Raset, 21-29 - C/ Modolell, 29-31 - C/ Freixa, 22-30 - C/ Vico, 12-18 Barcelona

149 - LES ESCALES PARK RESIDENTIAL COMPLEX. Josep Lluís Sert. 1967-1973. C/ Sor Eulalia de Anzizu, 46 Barcelona

150 - FRÉGOLI APARTMENT BUILDING. Esteve Bonell. 1972-1975. C/ Madrazo, 54-56 - Barcelona

151 - CAN BRUIXA APARTMENT BUILDING. Gabriel Mora, Helio Piñón, Albert Viaplana. 1974-1976. C/ Galileu, 281-285 - Barcelona

152 - FUNDACIÓ JOAN MIRÓ. Josep Lluís Sert. 1972-1975. Av. Miramar, 1 (Parc de Montjuïc) - Barcelona

153 - THAU SCHOOL. Oriol Bohigas, Josep Maria Martorell, David Mackay. 1972-1975. Carretera d'Esplugues, 49-53 Barcelona

154 - FRENCH INSTITUTE IN BARCELONA. José Antonio Coderch de Sentmenat, Manuel Valls. 1972-1975. C/ Moià, 8 - Barcelona

155 - CEIP LA TAXONERA. Emili Donato, Uwe Geest. 1978-1982. C/ Farnés, 60 Barcelona

156 - HORTA GERIATRIC HOME. Emili Donato, Miguel Jiménez, Ramon Martí. 1988-1992. C/ Josep Sangenís, 75 Barcelona

157 - BARÓ DE VIVER HOUSING BLOCK. Emili Donato, Miguel Jiménez, Ramon Martí. 1985-1988. Pg. Santa Coloma, 94-112 - Pl. Baró de Viver, 1-15 - C/ Campins, 5-19 - Barcelona

158 - JOAN GÜELL BUILDING. Josep Lluís Mateo, Jaume Arderiu, Josep Maria Crespo. 1989-1993. C/ Joan Güell, 213 C/ Joaquim Molins, 5 - C/ Les Corts, 22-38 - Barcelona

159 - BARCELONA PAVILION RECONSTRUCTION OF THE GERMANY PAVILION OF THE 1929 GREAT EXHIBITION. Ignasi de Solà-Morales, Cristian Cirici, Fernando Ramos. 1981-1986. Av. Marquès de Comillas, s/n Barcelona

160 - MONTJUÏC TELECOMMUNICATIONS TOWER. Santiago Calatrava. 1989-1992. Pg. Minici Natal, s/n (Anella Olímpica de Montjuïc) - Barcelona

161 - COLLSEROLA COMMUNICATIONS TOWER . Norman Foster. 1989-1992. Turó de Vilana (Tibidabo) - Barcelona

162 - PALAU SANT JORDI STADIUM. Arata Isozaki. 1985-1990. Pg. Minici Natal, s/n (Anella Olímpica de Montjuïc) Barcelona

163 - REGIONAL METEOROLOGICAL CENTRE OF CATALONIA. Alvaro Siza Vieira. 1990-1992. C/ Arquitecte Sert, 1 Barcelona

164 - NOVA ICÀRIA MUNICIPAL PAVILION. Franc Fernández, Moisés Gallego. 1990-1994. Av. Icària, 167 Barcelona

165 - APARTMENT BLOCK IN THE OLYMPIC VILLAGE. Albert Viaplana, Helio Piñón, Ricard Mercadé. 1989-1992. C/ Arquitecte Sert, 18-20 - Av. Icària, 174-184 - Av. Bogatell, 1-3 - C/ Frederic Mompou, 6 (Vila Olímpica) - Barcelona

166 - TIRANT LO BLANC HOUSING COMPLEX . José Antonio Martínez Lapeña, Elías Torres. 1989-1992. Pl. Tirant lo Blanc, 1-9 - C/ Salvador Espriu, 89-91 (Vila Olímpica) - Barcelona

167 - SWIMMING POOLS AT THE SANT SEBASTIÀ BATHS. José Antonio Martínez Lapeña, Elías Torres. 1988-1995. Pl. Mar, 1 - Barcelona

168 - NEW MARKET IN LA BARCELONETA. Josep Miàs. 2002-2007. Pl. Poeta Boscà, s/n - Barcelona

169 - L'ILLA DIAGONAL. Rafael Moneo, Manuel de Solà-Morales i Rubió. 1986-1993. Av. Diagonal, 545-575 - Barcelona

170 - CATALAN CONGRESS CENTRE. Carles Ferrater, Josep Maria Cartañá. 1996-2000. Av. Diagonal, 661 - Barcelona

171 - BARCELONA CONTEMPORARY ARTS CENTRE. Albert Viaplana, Helio Piñón. 1990-1993. C/ Montalegre, 5 Barcelona

172 - BARCELONA MUSEUM OF CONTEMPORARY ART. Richard Meier. 1988-1995. Pl. dels Àngels, 1 - Barcelona

173 - BARCELONA AUDITORIUM. Rafael Moneo. 1988-1998. C/ Lepant, 150 Barcelona

174 - GRAN TEATRE DEL LICEU, RECONSTRUCTION, REMODELLING AND EXTENSION OF THE OLD OPERA HOUSE. Ignasi de Solà-Morales i Rubió, Lluís Dilmé, Xavier Fabré. 1990-1998. La Rambla, 51-59 - Barcelona

175 - APARTMENT BUILDING. Josep Llinàs. 1989-1994. C/ Carme, 55 Barcelona

176 - VILA DE GRÀCIA PUBLIC LIBRARY. Josep Llinàs, Joan Vera. 2000-2002. C/ Torrent de l'Olla, 104 - Barcelona

177 - HOUSE IN LA CLOTA. Enric Miralles, Benedetta Tagliabue. 1998-1999. Ptge. Feliu, 15-17 (Barri de la Clota) Barcelona

178 - NEW MARKET OF SANTA CATERINA. Enric Miralles, Benedetta Tagliabue. 1998-2003. Av. Francesc Cambó, 16 - Barcelona

179 - BARCELONA INTERNATIONAL CONVENTION CENTRE. Josep Lluís Mateo. 2000-2004. Rambla Prim, 1-17 Barcelona

180 - FORUM BUILDING. Jacques Herzog, Pierre de Meuron. 2001-2004. Rambla Prim, 2-4 - Barcelona

181 - AGBAR TOWER. Jean Nouvel. 2000-2005. Av. Diagonal, 209-211 - Barcelona

182 - APARTMENT BUILDING IN DIAGONAL MAR. Lluís Clotet, Ignacio Paricio. 2001-2005. C/ Selva de Mar, 2 Parc de Diagonal Mar - Barcelona

183 - TORRE DEL GAS. Enric Miralles, Benedetta Tagliabue. 1999-2006. Pg. Marítim de la Barceloneta, 15 (Parc de la Barceloneta) - Barcelona

184 - FORT PIENC STREET BLOCK. Josep Llinàs. 2001-2003. C/ Ribes, 12-18 (Pl. Fort Pienc), C/ Sardenya, 101-147 Barcelona

185 - JAUME FUSTER PUBLIC LIBRARY. Josep Llinàs, Joan Vera. 2001-2005. Pl. Lesseps, 20-22 - Barcelona

186 - ENRIC PAVILLARD HOUSE. Joan Amigó i Barriga. 1906. Av. Martí Pujol, 23-25 - Badalona

187 - ENRIC MIR HOUSE. Joan Amigó i Barriga. 1908. Av. Martí Pujol, 45-47 Badalona

188 - MR-1 HOUSES. Miguel Donada, Josep Maria Massot, Alfons Soldevila. 1971. Av. dels Castanyers, 14 Urbanització Mas Ram - Badalona

189 - IES LA LLAUNA. Enric Miralles, Carme Pinós. 1984-1986. C/ Sagunt, 11 Badalona

190 - BADALONA BASKETBALL STADIUM. Esteve Bonell, Francesc Rius. 1987-1991. Av. Alfons XIII, s/n - Badalona

191 - CEMETERY OF SANT PERE. Albert Viaplana, Helio Piñón. 1984. Ctra. de la Conreria (Badalona - Mollet) - Camí del Xiprer - Badalona

192 - HOUSE B. Alfred Arribas. 1997-2003. Camí de la Font, s/n - Urbanització La Caritat - Premià de Dalt

193 - CEIP VAIXELL BURRIACH - IES VILATZARA. 1990-1993. Manuel Brullet, Alfonso de Luna. Av. Arquitecte Eduard Ferrés, 81 - Vilassar de Mar

194 - LA MASSA THEATRE, EXTENSION AND REHABILITATION OF THE OLD THEATRE. Ignasi de Solà-Morales i Rubió, Lluís Dilmé, Xavier Fabré. 1998-2002. Pl. del Teatre, 3 - Vilassar de Dalt

195 - PUIG I CADAFALCH HOUSE. Josep Puig i Cadafalch. 1897-1905. Pl. de Vendre, 8 - Argentona

196 - JOAQUIM COLL I REGÀS HOUSE. Josep Puig i Cadafalch. 1896-1897 C/ Argentona, 55-57 - Mataró

197 - PUIG I CADAFALCH HOUSING BLOCK. Lluís Clotet, Oscar Tusquets. 1970-1975. C/ Joan Maragall, 2-12 Mataró

198 - UGALDE HOUSE. José Antonio Coderch de Sentmenat, Manuel Valls. 1951-1953. C/ Torrenova, 16 Caldes d'Estrac

199 - ESCOLA SANT JORDI. Oriol Bohigas, Josep Maria Martorell, David Mackay. 1967-1969. C/ Jacint Verdaguer, 15 - Pineda de Mar

200 - EL PALAUET STADIUM. Arata Isozaki. 1990-1996. Ribera de la Burgada C/ Ramon Turró - Palafolls

201 - IES LA BASTIDA. Eduard Bru, Josep Lluís Mateo. 1981-1983. C/ Santa Eulàlia, s/n - Santa Coloma de Gramenet

202 - LA LLAGOSTA MUNICIPAL CEMETERY. Conxita Balcells, Santiago Vives. 1997-2001. Camí de Can Donadeu, s/n - La Llagosta

203. SHOOTING RANGE. Esteve Terradas, Robert Terradas. 1990-1992. Ctra. N-152, km. 20 - Mollet del Vallès

204 - CAN BORRELL HOUSING BLOCK. Oriol Bohigas, Josep Maria Martorell, David Mackay. 1983-1987. C/ Gallecs, 50 Av. Rivoli, 22 - C/ Salvador Espriu, 1-5 Ptge. Mestre Vinyas, 1-9 - Barri de Can Borrell - Mollet del Vallès

205 - PENINA HOUSE. Lluís Clotet, Oscar Tusquets. 1968-1969. Av. Adolfo Agustí, 46 - Cardedeu

206 - SINGLE-FAMILY DWELLING. Jaume Valor, Fidela Frutos, Josep Maria Sanmartín. 1994-1995. C/ del Cirare, 7 Llinars del Vallès

207 - GRANOLLERS MUSEUM. Andreu Bosch, Josep Maria Botey, Lluís Cuspinera. 1971-1976. C/ Anselm Clavé, 40-42 - Granollers

208 - CEIP FERRER I GUÀRDIA. Jordi Badia. 2003-2006. C/ Roger de Flor, 123 Granollers

209 - 170-APARTMENT SOCIAL HOUSING DEVELOPMENT. Lluís Cantallops, José Antonio Martínez Lapeña, Elías Torres, Miguel Usandizaga. 1977-1980. C/ Molí de la Sal, 90-94 - C/ Setcases, 1-67 - C/ Molló, 1-69, 2-12 Barri Joan Miró - Canovelles

210 - SERRAS HOUSE. Oriol Bohigas, Josep Maria Martorell, David Mackay. 1977-1981. C/ Bellmunt, 4 - Urbanització Bellulla - Canovelles

211 - PUIG HOUSE. Gabriel Mora, Helio Piñón, Albert Viaplana. 1972-1973. C/ Sant Sebastià, 22 - L'Ametlla del Vallès

212 - IRIS HOUSE. CECÍLIA REIG HOUSE. Manuel Joaquim Raspall. 1910-1911. El Passeig, 1 - La Garriga

213 - "LA BOMBONERA", CECÍLIA REIG HOUSE. Manuel Joaquim Raspall. 1910-1911. El Passeig, 3 - La Garriga

214 - JULI BARBEY HOUSE. Manuel Joaquim Raspall. 1910-1911. C/ Manuel Joaquim Raspall, 1 - El Passeig, 5 La Garriga

215 - JIMÉNEZ DE PARGA HOUSE. Gabriel Mora, Helio Piñón, Albert Viaplana. 1974. Ctra. de La Garriga a L'Ametlla del Vallès (BP-1432) - Can Busquets - Polígon 7 Parcel·la 7 - La Garriga

216 - CH HOUSE. Jordi Badia, Mercè Sangenís. 2001-2002. C/ Les Alzines, 21 La Garriga

217 - LLORET HOUSE. Tonet Sunyer. 2001. C/ Guinardó, 33 - La Garriga

218 - APARTMENT COMPLEX. Lluís Clotet, Oscar Tusquets. 1976-1979. C/ Jaume Mimó i Llobet, 14-16 Cerdanyola del Vallès

219 - M&M HOUSES. José Miguel Roldán, Mercè Berengué. 1999-2001. C/ Mercè Rodoreda, 11-11b - Bellaterra Cerdanyola del Vallès

220 - CENTRAL SPORTS SERVICES BUILDING. Josep Lluís Mateo, Ferran Cardeñas. 1987-1993. Campus de Bellaterra - Universitat Autònoma de Barcelona - Cerdanyola del Vallès

221 - FACULTY OF TRANSLATION AND INTERPRETATION. Jordi Bosch, Joan Tarrús, Santiago Vives. 1995-1998. Campus de Bellaterra - Universitat Autònoma de Barcelona - Cerdanyola del Vallès

222 - LUQUE HOUSE. José Antonio Coderch de Sentmenat, Manuel Valls. 1964-1966. Av. Canadà, 35 Sant Cugat del Vallès

223 - ROGNONI HOUSE. Lluís Clotet, Oscar Tusquets. 1976-1978. Pg. de l'Habana, 59 - Sant Cugat del Vallès

224 - MARTÍ L'HUMÀ STREET BLOCK. Oriol Bohigas, Josep Maria Martorell, David Mackay. 1974-1979. C/ Martí l'Humà, 1-9 - Av. Barberà, 290-300 - C/ Doctor Roges, 2-4 - C/ Cerdanyola, 1-3 Sabadell

225 - CAN BACIANA 2 APARTMENT BLOCKS. Felip Pich-Aguilera. 1995-2000. Pl. Aurora Bertrana, 14A-14D, 16 Sabadell

226 - MILLENNIUM TOWER. Enric Batlle, Joan Roig, Juan Manuel Sanahuja, Ricardo Sanahuja. 1999-2002. Av. Francesc Macià, 62 - Sabadell

227 - VAPOR SAMPERE APARTMENT AND OFFICE BUILDING. Rafael Moneo, José Antonio Martínez Lapeña, Elías Torres. 2001-2005. C/ Tres Creus, 88-104 - C/ Sallarès i Pla, 3 - Sabadell

228 - AYMERICH, AMAT I JOVER FACTORY. Lluís Muncunill. 1907-1908. Rbla. Egara, 254-270 - Terrassa

229 - MASIA FREIXA. Lluís Muncunill. 1907-1910. Pl. Josep Freixa i Argemí, s/n Terrassa

230 - TERRASSA CENTRAL LIBRARY. Josep Llinàs. 1995-1998. C/ Sant Gaietà, 94 - Terrassa

231 - LES PALMERES HOUSING COMPLEX. Josep Lluís Mateo. 1994-1998. Av. Béjar, 222-232 - Ctra. de Matadepera, 295-315 - Pg. Lluís Muncunill, 45-57 - Pl. de Montserrat Alavedra - Terrassa

232 - TERRASSA MUNICIPAL FUNERAL SERVICES. Jordi Badia. 2001-2002. Ctra. N-150 - Complex Funerari Terrassa

233 - S-T HOUSE. Iñaki Alday, Margarita Jover. 1999-2001. C/ Murcia, 46 Terrassa

234 - CEIP PALAU. Conxita Balcells, Santiago Vives. 1999-2001. C/ Arquitecte Falguera, 37 Palau de Plegamans

235 - CAP CASTELLAR - Carles Muro, Charmaine Lay, Quim Rosell. 1995-1999. C/ Ripollet, 30 - Castellar del Vallès

236 - 6 SINGLE-FAMILY DWELLINGS. Alfons Soldevila, Josep Ignasi de Llorens. 1977-1979. C/ Poeta Maragall, 27-35 Urbanització La Muntanyeta Matadepera

237 - MMI HOUSE. Josep Maria Sostres. 1955-1957. C/ Apel·les Mestres, 19 Esplugues de Llobregat

238 - IRANZO HOUSE. Josep Maria Sostres. 1955-1956. C/ Apel·les Mestres, 8-10 - Esplugues de Llobregat

239 - WALDEN 7, RESIDENTIAL COMPLEX. Ricard Bofill. 1970-1975. Av. Indústria, s/n - Sant Just Desvern

240 - LA BONAIGUA SPORTS COMPLEX. Jaime Coll, Judith Leclerc. 1997-2001. Pg. de la Muntanya, s/n - Sant Just Desvern

241 - GIBERT HOUSE. Josep Maria Jujol. 1913-1916. Pg. Canalies, 12 Sant Joan Despí

242 - "CAN NEGRE". Josep Maria Jujol. 1915-1930. Pl. Catalunya, s/n Sant Joan Despí

243 - LA SALUT HOUSING BLOCK, Oriol Bohigas, Josep Maria Martorell, David Mackay. 1969-1973. C/ Falguera, 94-102 C/ Prolongació de Falguera, 1-15 C/ Sant Josep, 74-84 - Pl. Falguera, 3-5 Barri de la Falguera - Sant Feliu de Llobregat

244 - MONTSERRAT ROIG PUBLIC LIBRARY. Albert Viaplana, Helio Piñón, Ricard Mercadé. 1990-1993. C/ Verge de Montserrat, 3 - Sant Feliu de Llobregat

245 - CHURCH CRYPT AT COLÒNIA GÜELL. Antoni Gaudí. 1898-1914. C/ Reixac, s/n - Colònia Güell Santa Coloma de Cervelló

246 - PONS HOUSE. Ramon Puig i Gairalt. 1931-1933. Ctra. de Collblanc, 43 L'Hospitalet de Llobregat

247 - HESPERIA TOWER. Richard Rogers, Lluís Alonso, Sergi Balaguer. 1999-2006. Av. Mare de Déu de Bellvitge, 1 L'Hospitalet de Llobregat

248 - LA RICARDA VILLA. Antoni Bonet i Castellana. 1953-1962. Camí de l'Albufera - El Prat de Llobregat

249 - EL PRAT ROYAL GOLF CLUB. Robert Terradas i Via, José Antonio Coderch de Sentmenat, Manuel Valls. 1954. Camí de la Volateria, Zona Camp de Golf núm. 1 - El Prat de Llobregat

250 - EL LLOBREGAT SPORTS PARK. Alvaro Siza Vieira. 2002-2006. Av. del Baix Llobregat, s/n - Cornellà de Llobregat

251 - L'OLIVERA CIVIC CENTRE AND SPORTS FACILITY. Moisés Gallego. 1995-1998. Pl. Montserrat Roig, 1 Sant Boi de Llobregat

252 - "EL BOLET", SINGLE-FAMILY DWELLING. Blai Pérez. 1992-1997. C/ Hortènsies, 6-8 - Urbanització Alba Rosa - Viladecans

253 - CAMY-NESTLÉ FACTORY BRIDGE. Enric Miralles. 1991-1994. Ctra. de Llobatona, 18 - Zona Industrial Centre Viladecans

254 - CEIP LLUÍS VIVES. Carme Pinós. 2003-2007. Pg. del Ferrocarril, 266 Castelldefels

255 - GÜELL WINE CELLAR IN GARRAF. Francesc Berenguer, Antoni Gaudí. 1895-1900. Ctra. de les Costes (C-246), km. 25 - El Garraf - Sitges

256 - CASABÓ HOUSE. Francesc Mitjans. 1934-1935. Pg. Marítim, 64-65 - Sitges

257 - CATASÚS HOUSE. José Antonio Coderch de Sentmenat, Manuel Valls. 1956-1958. C/ Josep Carner, 32 C/ Pintor Casas, 5 - Barri del Vinyet Sitges

258 - GILI HOUSE. José Antonio Coderch de Sentmenat, Manuel Valls. 1965-1966. C/ Salvador Casacuberta, s/n C/ Torres Quevedo, s/n - Barri del Vinyet Sitges

259 - KAFKA'S CASTLE DEVELOPMENT OF 112 HOLIDAY HOMES. Ricard Bofill. 1966-1968. Pg. Pujadas, 1 - Urbanització Vallpineda - Sant Pere de Ribes

260 - IES ALEXANDRE GALÍ - Pere Joan Ravetllat, Carme Ribas. 1992-1994. C/ Miquel Servet, s/n - Barri de Roquetes Sant Pere de Ribes

The Tarragona area

261 - TEATRE METROPOL. Josep Maria Jujol. 1908-1910. Rbla. Nova, 46 Tarragona

262 - MUNICIPAL ABATTOIR. Josep Maria Pujol de Barberà. 1895-1902. C/ Escorxador, s/n - Tarragona

263 - TARRAGONA CENTRAL MARKET. Josep Maria Pujol de Barberà. 1911-1915. Pl. Corsini, s/n - Tarragona

264 - XIMENIS HOUSE. Josep Maria Jujol. 1914. Via Imperi Romà, 17 - Tarragona

265 - MALÉ HOUSE. Josep Maria Monravà. 1930. Rambla Vella, 15 - C/ Portalet, 8 Tarragona

266 - CASA BLOC APARTMENT BUILDING. Josep Maria Monravà. 1940-1945. C/ Marquès de Guad-El-Jelú, 1-10 Tarragona

267 - INSTITUT POLITÈCNIC SCHOOL OF INDUSTRIAL PROFESSIONALS. Josep Maria Monravà. 1931. Ptge. Soler i Morey, s/n - Tarragona

268 - VERGE DEL CARME APARTMENT COMPLEX. Joan Zaragoza i Albí, José Antonio Coderch de Sentmenat. 1949. C/ Salou, 6-12 - C/ Lepanto, 1-7 Tarragona

269 - TARRAGONA LABOUR UNIVERSITY. Antonio de la Vega, Manuel Sierra, Luis Peral. 1952-1956. Autovia de Tarragona a Salou (C-31B) - Complex Educatiu - Tarragona

270 - HEADQUARTERS OF THE CIVIL GOVERNMENT IN TARRAGONA. Alejandro de la Sota. 1954-1957. Pl. Imperial Tarraco, 3 - Tarragona

271 - YXART HOUSE COMPLEX OF 2 APARTMENT BLOCKS. Lluís Nadal, Vicenç Bonet, Pere Puigdefàbregas. 1966-1969. Pg. de Sant Antoni, 16 - Tarragona

272 - CAN GASSET, APARTMENT BUILDING. Jaume Bach, Gabriel Mora. 1984-1987. C/ Santiyan, 7-9 Tarragona

273 - HEADQUARTERS OF THE TARRAGONA BRANCH OF THE COAC. Rafael Moneo. 1983-1992. C/ Sant Llorenç, 22 - Tarragona

274 - NEW HEADQUARTERS OF THE REIAL CLUB NÀUTIC DE TARRAGONA. David Baena, Toni Casamor, Josep Maria Quera, Carles Casamor. 1995-1997. Port Esportiu de Tarragona - Tarragona

275 - SANT SALVADOR SPORTS COMPLEX. Moisés Gallego, Pau Pérez, Anton Banús. 1998-2002. C/ Estadium, s/n - Tarragona

276 - SCHOOL OF CHEMICAL ENGINEERING. Manuel Brullet, Alfonso de Luna. 1997-2001. Av. Països Catalans, 26 - Campus Sescelades - Universitat Rovira i Virgili - Tarragona

277 - UNIVERSITY LIBRARY. José Antonio Martínez Lapeña, Elías Torres. 1999-2003. Av. Països Catalans, 26 Campus Sescelades - Universitat Rovira i Virgili - Tarragona

278 - FERRÁNDIZ HOUSE. Rafael de Cáceres. 1970-1971. Camí de l'Ermita de Sant Antoni - Altafulla

279 - CEIP LA PORTALADA. Pau Pérez, Jordi Bergadà. 1987-1991. Pl. Portalada, s/n - Altafulla

280 - COMPLEX OF FOUR MOTELS. Josep Maria Sostres. 1954-1957. C/ Aragó, 11 - Torredembarra

281 - IES TORREDEMBARRA. Josep Llinàs. 1994-1995. Av. Sant Jordi, 62-64 Torredembarra

282 - L'ESTEL DE MAR NURSERY. Manuel Bailo, Rosa Rull. 1998-2000. C/ Onze de Setembre, 4 - Creixell

283 - HORTAL HOUSE. Vicente Guallart. 2001-2003. C/ Santa Isabel, 72 Urbanització Nirvana 2 - Coma-ruga El Vendrell

284 - GARCIA HOUSE. José Antonio Martínez Lapeña, Elías Torres. 1968-1970. Av. de França, 27-29 - Segur de Calafell Calafell

285 - IES L'ARBOÇ. Emili Donato, Miguel Jiménez. 1993-2000. C/ Pompeu Fabra, s/n - L'Arboç

286 - OFFICE AND APARTMENT BUILDING. Josep Llinàs. 1988-1990. Av. Tarragona, 35 - Vilafranca del Penedès

287 - COVERED SPORTS COURT. Esteve Aymerich, Ton Salvadó. 1995-1997. Zona Esportiva - Vilafranca del Penedès

288 - CODORNIU WINERY. Josep Puig i Cadafalch. 1904. Av. Codorniu, s/n Sant Sadurní d'Anoia

289 - RAVENTÓS BLANC CELLARS. Jaume Bach, Gabriel Mora. 1985-1988. Pl. del Roure, s/n - Sant Sadurní d'Anoia

290 - MAS BOFARULL. Josep Maria Jujol. 1914-1931. C/ Barcelona, 11-13 Els Pallaresos

291 - CHURCH OF SANT BARTOMEU IN VISTABELLA. Josep Maria Jujol. 1918-1924. Pl. de Josep Gaspé i Blanc, s/n Vistabella - La Secuita

292 - COOPERATIVE CELLAR OF THE SINDICAT AGRÍCOLA DE SANT ISIDRE. Cèsar Martinell. 1918-1919. C/ Estació, s/n - Nulles

293 - SANCTUARY OF THE BLESSED VIRGIN OF MONTSERRAT. Josep Maria Jujol. 1926-1930. Camí del Correlot Montferri

294 - NAVÀS HOUSE. Lluís Domènech i Montaner. 1901-1907. Pl. del Mercadal, 7 - Reus

295 - RULL HOUSE. Lluís Domènech i Montaner. 1900-1901. C/ Sant Joan, 27 Reus

296 - GASULL HOUSE. Lluís Domènech i Montaner. 1911-1912. C/ Sant Joan, 29 Reus

297 - PERE MATA INSTITUTE. Lluís Domènech i Montaner. 1897-1919. Ctra. de l'Institut Pere Mata, 1 - Reus

298 - LAGUNA HOUSE. Pere Caselles i Tarrats. 1904. C/ Monterols, 15 - Reus

299 - GRAU HOUSE. Pere Caselles i Tarrats. 1910-1911. C/ Sant Joan, 32 Reus

300 - SERRA VILLA. Joan Rubió i Bellver. 1911. Ctra. de Reus a Castellvell (TP-7049), 20 - Reus

301 - HOUSE FOR DOCTOR DOMÈNECH. Josep Simó i Bofarull. 1930. C/ Frederic Soler, 55 - Reus

302 - HIPÒLIT MONTSENY HOUSE. Antoni Sardà i Moltó. 1934. C/ Colón, 1 Reus

303 - REUS CENTRAL MARKET. Antoni Sardà i Moltó. 1934-1949. C/ Josep Sardà i Cailà, s/n - Reus

304 - GAUDÍ DISTRICT. Ricard Bofill. 1964-1968. Av. Comerç - Av. Saragossa Pg. de la Boca de la Mina - Reus

305 - FACULTY OF ECONOMICS AND BUSINESS STUDIES. Pau Pérez, Anton Pàmies, Anton Banús. 1994-1996. Av. Universitat, 1 - Campus de Bellisens Universitat Rovira i Virgili - Reus

306 - MAITE VILLA. Mamen Domingo, Ernest Ferré. 1998-2000. Av. dels Pins, 21 - Urbanització El Pinar - Reus

307 - REUS CEMETERY CREMATORY. Pau Pérez, Anton Banús. 2001-2003. Av. de la Pau, s/n - Cementiri de Reus Reus

308 - SÍLVIA VILLA. Mamen Domingo, Ernest Ferré. 1997-2000. Ctra. de Castellvell del Camp a Almoster (TP-7049) - Castellvell del Camp

309 - SERRA HOUSE. Emili Donato, Uwe Geest. 1986. Av. Catalunya, 47-49 Alforja

310 - IES VILA-SECA. Jordi Sardà, Jordi Bergadà. 1995-1997. Av. Alcalde Pere Molas, s/n - Vila-seca

311 - VILA-SECA TOWN HALL.. Josep Llinàs. 1994-1997. Pl. de l'Església, 26 Vila-seca

312 - VILA-SECA MUNICIPAL FUNERAL SERVICES. Mamen Domingo, Ernest Ferré. 2001-2003. Av. de la Vila del Comú, s/n - Polígon Industrial L'Alba - Vila-seca

313 - JOSEP CARRERAS AUDITORIUM. Pau Pérez, Anton Banús. 1996-2002. Pl. Frederic Mompou, 1 - Vila-seca

314 - XIPRE APARTMENTS. Antoni Bonet i Castellana, Josep Puig i Torné. 1960-1962. Punta del Cavall - Cap de Salou Salou

315 - RUBIÓ HOUSE. Antoni Bonet Castellana, Josep Puig i Torné. 1960-1962. Cala Crancs, 38 - Cap de Salou Salou

316 - SALOU MUNICIPAL SPORTS CENTRE. Esteve Bonell, Josep Maria Gil, Francesc Rius. 1986-1991. C/ Milà, 5 - Salou

317 - SALOU MUNICIPAL LIBRARY. Pau Pérez. 1988-1992. C/ Ponent, 16 - Salou

318 - IES SCHOOL OF CATERING AND TOURISM. Víctor Rahola. 1986-1988. C/ L'Estel, s/n - Cambrils

319 - SAVALL HOUSE. Tonet Sunyer. 1998-1999. C/ Consolat de Mar, 5 Cambrils

320 - POBLAT HIFRENSA. Antoni Bonet i Castellana, Josep Puig i Torné. 1967-1975. Via Augusta - C/ Ramon Berenguer IV - Via fèrria - L'Hospitalet de l'Infant

The Tortosa area

321 - TORTOSA MUNICIPAL ABATTOIR. Pau Monguió i Segura. 1905-1908. Rbla. Felip Pedrell, 5 - Tortosa

322 - GREGO HOUSE. Pau Monguió i Segura. 1906-1911. Pl. Nostra Senyora de la Cinta, 6 - Tortosa

323 - PIÑANA HOUSE. Pau Monguió i Segura. 1914. Av. de la Generalitat, 105 Tortosa

324 - MANGRANÉ HOUSES. Emili Donato. 1965-1966. Sector 1-C, Parcel·la 32 Urbanització Calafat - L'Ametlla de Mar

325 - DOCTOR ARGANY HOUSES. Ramon Maria Puig i Andreu. 1975-1977. Quarta Avinguda, 81-A - Urbanització Sant Jordi d'Alfama - L'Ametlla de Mar

326 - CEIP RIUMAR. Manuel Ruisánchez, Xavier Vendrell. 1994-1996. C/ Ignasi, 26 Deltebre

327. IES RAMON BERENGUER IV. Oriol Bohigas, Josep Maria Martorell, Francesc Bassó, Joaquim Gili. 1955-1957. C/ Músic Sunyer, 1-37 - Amposta

328 - HOUSE FOR A PHOTOGRAPHER IN THE EBRE DELTA. Carles Ferrater, Carlos Escura. 2003-2006. Pg. del Mar, s/n - Les Cases d'Alcanar - Alcanar

329 - MÓRA D'EBRE COUNTY HOSPITAL. José Antonio Martínez Lapeña, Elías Torres. 1982-1987. C/ Benet Messeguer, 2 - Móra d'Ebre

330. COOPERATIVE CELLAR OF THE FARMS COOPERATIVE AND OIL MILL. Cèsar Martinell. 1919-1922. C/ del Pilonet, 10 - El Pinell de Brai

331 - CELLAR OF GANDESA FARMS COOPERATIVE. Cèsar Martinell. 1919-1920. Av. Catalunya, 28 - Gandesa

332 - LA FATARELLA, ECOLOGICAL HOUSE. Esteve Aymerich, Ton Salvadó, Joaquim Gascó. 1993-1999. Camí de la Mare de Déu del Carme - La Fatarella

333 - CAP LA SÈNIA. Esteve Aymerich, Ton Salvadó, Gerard Puig. 2001-2004. Pg. de Clotada, 60 - La Sènia

The Olot area

334 - SACREST FACTORY, CAN JOANETES. Joan Roca i Pinet. 1927-1929. Pg. Bisbe Guillamet, 10 - Olot

335 - MASRAMON HOUSE. Rafael Masó. 1913-1914. C/ Vayreda, 6 - Olot

336 - BASSOLS FACTORY. Joan Roca i Pinet. 1916-1917. C/ Escultor Llimona, 1 Olot

337 - SERRA HOUSE, CASA DELS NASSOS. Bartomeu Agustí. 1931-1933. C/ Nou, 13 - Olot

338 - AUBERT HOUSE, EL CAFETÍN. Joan Aubert i Camps. 1936. C/ Sant Cristòfol, 3 - C/ Pont de la Salut, 2 - Olot

339 - ARTUR SIMON FACTORY. Joan Aubert i Camps. 1940. C/ Josep Ayats, 10 C/ Pou del Glaç, 6 - C/ Pere Lloses, 11 Olot

340 - IES BOSC DE LA COMA. José Antonio Martínez Lapeña, Elías Torres. 1992-1995. C/ Toledo, 12 - Olot

341 - MARGARIDA HOUSE. Rafael Aranda, Carme Pigem, Ramon Vilalta. 1989-1993. C/ Sant Julià del Mont, 12 Olot

342 - MIRADOR HOUSE. Rafael Aranda, Carme Pigem, Ramon Vilalta. 1997-1999. Ctra. d'Olot a Banyoles (GI-524), km. 0,85 - Olot

343 - M-LIDIA HOUSE. Rafael Aranda, Carme Pigem, Ramon Vilalta. 2000-2003. C/ Sant Grau, 15 - Urbanització La Cometa - Montagut

344 - CENDRA HOUSE. Rafael Masó. 1913-1915. C/ Girona, 7-9 - Anglès

The Vic area

345 - TOWN COURT. Pere Llimona, Xavier Ruiz Vallès. 1967. C/ Bisbe Morgades, 2 - Vic

346 - PUIG-PORRET APARTMENT BUILDING. Manuel Anglada. 1971. C/ Verdaguer, 15-17 - Vic

347 - HEADQUARTERS OF THE OSONA BRANCH OF THE COAC. Dolors Ylla-Català, Joan Forgas. 1993-1994. Pl. Bisbe Oliva, 2 - Vic

348 - EPISCOPAL MUSEUM OF VIC. Federico Correa, Alfons Milà. 1996-2002. Pl. Bisbe Oliva, 3 - Vic

349 - CAP SANT HIPÒLIT. Albert Viaplana, Helio Piñón. 1984-1986. C/ Vinya, s/n - Sant Hipòlit de Voltregà

350 - APARTMENT BUILDING. Josep Lluís Mateo. 1992-1995. C/ Capsavila, 13-17 - Torelló

351 - RETIREMENT HOME. Josep Lluís Mateo. 1991-1994. C/ Girona, 9 Campdevànol

352. CHAPEL OF SANT MIQUEL DE LA ROQUETA. Joan Rubió i Bellver. 1912. C/ Indústria, 1 - Ripoll

353 - CAMPAÑÀ HOUSE. Josep Maria Sostres. 1971-1974. Ventolà - Ribes de Freser

354 - XAMPENY HOUSE. Josep Maria Sostres. 1971-1974. Ventolà - Ribes de Freser

355 - HOSTALETS DE BALENYÀ CIVIC CENTRE. Enric Miralles, Carme Pinós. 1986-1993. C/ Pista, 2 - Els Hostalets de Balenyà - Balenyà

356 - MARTÍN HOUSE. Emili Donato, Uwe Geest. 1972-1974. C/ Romaní, s/n Urbanització Serrabanda - Aiguafreda

The Manresa area

357 - SANATORIUM OF SANT JOAN DE DÉU. Germán Rodríguez Arias. 1931. C/ Dr. Joan Soler, s/n - Manresa

358 - RENAIXENÇA SCHOOL COMPLEX. Pere Armengou. 1934. Pl. de la Independència, 1 - Manresa

359 - DWELLINGS AROUND A SQUARE. Enric Massip-Bosch, Joan Sabaté, Horacio Espeche. 1996-2002. Primera fase: C/ Santa Llúcia, 18-22 - Pl. de la Immaculada - C/ Codinella, 11-15. Segona fase: Via de Sant Ignasi, 1 Pl. de la Immaculada - Manresa

360 - IES GERBERT D'AURILLAC. Jordi Bosch, Joan Tarrús. 1997-2000. Av. Lluís Companys, s/n - Sant Fruitós de Bages

361 - SINGLE-FAMILY DWELLING. Antoni Poch, Jordi Moliner. 1998. C/ Bruc, 19 Sant Fruitós de Bages

362 - ASLAND FACTORY. Rafael Guastavino. 1901-1904. Paratge del Clot del Moro, s/n - Castellar de n'Hug

363 - CABANÍ HOUSE. Eduard Bru. 1992-1994. Parcel·la 2 - Barri de Cal Ros Castellar de n'Hug

364 - CERVERA FLOURMILL. Cèsar Martinell. 1920-1922. Antic camí de Castellnou, s/n - Cervera

365 - BLOCK OF 16 SOCIAL DWELLINGS. Eva Prats, Ricardo Flores. 2001-2004. C/ Sant Pol, 15-17 - Guissona

366 - THE NEW CEMETERY, IGUALADA. Enric Miralles, Carme Pinós. 1985-1991. Polígon Industrial Les Comes - Igualada

367 - HOTEL CIUTAT D'IGUALADA. Manuel Bailo, Rosa Rull. 2003. Pg. Mossèn Verdaguer, 167 - Igualada

368 - IGUALADA HOSPITAL. Emili Donato, Julio Alberto Pueyo, Miguel Jiménez. 2002-2006. Av. Catalunya, 11 Igualada

The Lleida area

369 - HOTEL PAL·LAS. Francesc de Paula Morera i Gatell. 1900-1915. Pl. de la Paeria, 11 - Lleida

370 - RAVENTÓS RAÏMAT CELLARS. Joan Rubió i Bellver. 1924-1925. Ctra. d'Osca (N-240), km. 15 - Raïmat Lleida

371 - GOMÀ-PUJADAS HOUSE. Marià Gomà. 1945-1947. Rambla d'Aragó, 5 Lleida

372 - MODEST ULIER HOUSE APARTMENT BUILDING. Lluís Domènech i Torres. 1955-1957. C/ Vila de Foix, 2-4 - Lleida

373 - HOME OF THE LITTLE SISTERS OF THE POOR. Ramon Maria Puig i Andreu, Lluís Domènech i Girbau, Lauri Sabater, Jaume Sanmartí. 1965-1968. Ctra. de la Vall d'Aran (N-230), km. 5,5 Lleida

374 - CASIMIR DRUDIS HOUSE APARTMENT BUILDING. Marià Gomà. 1968-1970. Av. Alcalde Rovira Roure, 34 Lleida

375 - SANTA MARIA MAGDALENA PARISH PREMISES. Ramon Maria Puig i Andreu, Lluís Domènech i Girbau, Lauri Sabater. 1966-1970. C/ Ramon Llull, 10 Lleida

376 - CLUB RONDA BUILDING, Antoni Sas, Ramon Maria Puig i Andreu, Lluís Domènech i Girbau, Lauri Sabater. 1970-1974. Pg. de Ronda, 84 - Lleida

377 - LAVEDA HOUSE. Ramon Maria Puig i Andreu. 1975-1978. Camí de Boixadors, s/n - Lleida

378 - SOCIAL HOUSING COMPLEX WITH 56 APARTMENTS. Ramon Maria Puig i Andreu. 1977-1980. C/ Sant Agustí, 2-4 - C/ Solsona, 5 - C/ Isern, 1 Av. Artesa, 62 - Lleida

379 - HEADQUARTERS OF THE LLEIDA BRANCH OF THE COAATC. Franc Fernández, Moisés Gallego. 1981-1984. C/ Enric Granados, 5 - Lleida

380 - LLEIDA PARK RESIDENTIAL COMPLEX. Miquel Espinet, Antoni Ubach. 1983-1986. Av. Alcalde Rovira Roure, 163-165 - C/ Monestir de les Avellanes, 1-5 - Lleida

381 - CEIP CERVANTES. Roser Amadó, Lluís Domènech i Girbau. 1990-1995. C/ Canyeret, s/n - Lleida

382 - SCHOOL OF AGRICULTURISTS OF CATALONIA. Miquel Espinet, Antoni Ubach. 1982-1985. Av. Alcalde Rovira Roure, 191 - Campus d'Agrònoms Lleida

383 - UNIVERSITY OF LLEIDA. Miquel Espinet, Antoni Ubach, Ramon Maria Puig i Andreu. 1983-1992. Rambla d'Aragó, 37 - Lleida

384 - LAW COURTS AND COMMUNICATIONS TOWER. Roser Amadó, Lluís Domènech i Girbau. 1984-1990. C/ Canyeret, s/n - Lleida

385 - ENRIC GRANADOS MUNICIPAL AUDITORIUM. Ramon Artigues, Ramon Sanabria. 1983-1995. Pl. Mossèn Cinto Verdaguer, s/n - Lleida

386 - CAP PARDINYES. Ramon Maria Puig i Andreu. 1987-1991. C/ Alcalde Recasens, s/n - Lleida

387 - CAP CAPPONT. Ramon Fité, Julio Mejón. 1999-2001. C/ Marquès de Leganés, s/n - Lleida

388 -TORRE VICENS VOCATIONAL TRAINING INSTITUTE. Ramon Maria Puig i Andreu, Carles Sáez. 1986-1994. Av. Torre Vicens, 3 - Secà de Sant Pere Lleida

389 - OFFICIAL SCHOOL OF LANGUAGES. Ramon Artigues, Ramon Sanabria. 1991-1996. C/ Corregidor Escofet, 53 - Lleida

390 - CEIP SANT JORDI. Marta Gabàs, Anna Ribas. 1993-1995. Partida de Montcada, 22 - Ctra. de Vielha (N-230) Lleida

391 - ARTS CENTRE OF THE ESTUDI GENERAL AND LIBRARY. Kristian Gullichsen. 1998-2004. C/ Jaume II, 67 Campus de Cappont Universitat de Lleida - Lleida

392 - POLYTECHNIC UNIVERSITY SCHOOL OF INFORMATION TECHNOLOGY. Miquel Espinet, Antoni Ubach. 1993-1997. C/ Jaume II, 69 Campus de Cappont Universitat de Lleida - Lleida

393 - UNIVERSITY HALL OF RESIDENCE. Ramon Artigues, Ramon Sanabria. 1997-2000. C/ Jaume II, 75 - Campus de Cappont Universitat de Lleida - Lleida

394 - FACULTY OF EDUCATION SCIENCE. Alvaro Siza Vieira. 2003-2007. Av. Estudi General, s/n - Campus de Cappont - Universitat de Lleida - Lleida

395 - HEADQUARTERS OF THE LLEIDA BRANCH OF THE COAC. Francisco Burgos, Luis de Pereda. 1993-1996. C/ Canyeret, 2 Lleida

396 - MONTULL HOUSE. Ramon Fité, Julio Mejón. 2002-2003. C/ Castell de Formós, 4 - Lleida

397 - HOME FOR THE ELDERLY ON THE ESTATE OF THE HOUSE OF THE DUKE AND DUCHESS OF ALBA. Lluís M. Vidal i Arderiu. 1991-1994. Plaça Major, s/n Castelló de Farfanya

398 - IES LA SERRA. Carme Pinós. 1998-2001. Ctra. de Mollerussa a Torregrossa (LV-2001) - La Serra - Mollerussa

399 - CEIP GUILLEM ISARN. Maria Àngels Negre, Félix Solaguren-Beascoa. 1991-1994. Av. Catalunya, s/n - La Fuliola

400 - TÀRREGA MUNICIPAL SWIMMING POOLS. Moisés Gallego, Àlex Gallego. 2002-2004. C/ Joan Brossa, s/n Parc Esportiu - Tàrrega

401 - SINGLE-FAMILY DWELLING. Roser Amadó, Lluís Domènech i Girbau, Lauri Sabater. 1972-1976. Ctra. d'Alcarràs a Vallmanya (L-800) - Alcarràs

402 - SIX DWELLINGS IN A FARMING COMMUNITY. Lluís Domènech i Girbau, Ramon Maria Puig i Andreu, Lauri Sabater, Jaume Sanmartí. 1965-1968. C/ Únic, s/n - Santa Maria de Gimenells Gimenells

The La Seu d'Urgell area

403 - CUSÍ HOUSE. Josep Maria Sostres. 1952-1954. C/ Sant Ermengol, 67 La Seu d'Urgell

404 - GALINDO HOUSE. Marc Paré, Néstor Piriz, Ricard Paré, Carles Pubill. 1995-1996. C/ Sant Ermengol, 90 La Seu d'Urgell

405 - NEW VILLAGE OF EL PONT DE BAR. Lluís M. Vidal i Arderiu. 1983-1988. El Pont de Bar

406 - GARRIGA-POCH HOUSE. Arturo Frediani. 1999-2003. Pl. de Sant Pere, s/n - Lles de Cerdanya

407 - HOUSES ON CAMÍ DE TALLÓ. Josep Maria Sostres. 1948-1950. Pg. de Pere Elias - Bellver de Cerdanya

408 - FONTANALS GOLF COURSE CLUB HOUSE. Josep Miàs. 2004. Soriguerola Fontanals de Cerdanya

409 - HOTEL MARIA VICTÒRIA. Josep Maria Sostres. 1952-1956. C/ Querol, 7 Puigcerdà

410 - 26 DWELLINGS IN THE COLÒNIA SIMÓN. Francesc Hereu, Joaquim Español. 1994-1997. Colònia Simón 28, A-B - Puigcerdà

411 - COMPLEX OF 62 APARTMENTS. Esteve Bonell, Ramon Artigues. 1976-1978. Llessui - Sort

412 - LLADÓ HOUSE. Marta Gabàs, Anna Ribas. 1995-1996. Solar de l'Antiga Rectoria - Saurí -Sort

413 - CENTRE FOR NATURE AND SUSTAINABLE DEVELOPMENT OF THE PYRENEES. Francesc Rius. 1998-2002. Les Planes de Son - Valls d'Àneu Alt Àneu

414 - CHURCH OF THE ASSUMPTION. José Rodríguez Mijares, Eduardo Torroja. 1952-1954. Av. Victoriano Muñoz, 27 El Pont de Suert

415 - HEREDERO HOUSE. Oriol Bohigas, Josep Maria Martorell, David Mackay. 1967-1968. Ctra. de Vielha a Vaqueira (C-28), km. 36 - Tredòs - Vaqueira Naut Aran

416 - CEIP SANT SERNI D'ARFA. Conxita Balcells. 1997-1998. Cap del Poble - Arfa Ribera d'Urgellet

417 - CAP OLIANA. Ramon Fité, Julio José Mejón. 1991-1993. C/ Girona, 8 Oliana

Index of architects

AGUSTÍ i VERGÉS, Bartomeu
(1904-1944)
337

ALONSO i CALLEJA, Lluís
(n.1955)
247

AMADÓ i CERCÓS, Roser
(n.1944)
093, 381, 384, 401

AMIGÓ i BARRIGA, Joan
(1875-1958)
186, 187

ANGLADA i BAYÉS, Manuel
(1925-1999)
346

ARANDA i QUILES, Rafael
(n.1961)
047, 079, 341, 342, 343

ARDERIU i SALVADÓ, Jaume
(n.1951)
158

ARGENTÍ i SALVADÓ, Víctor
(n.1947)
097

ARMENGOU i TORRA, Pere
(1905-1991)
358

ALDAY SANZ, Iñaki
(n.1965)
233

ARRIBAS i CABREJAS, Alfred
(n.1954)
192

ARTIGUES i CODÓ, Ramon
(n.1936)
085, 385, 389, 393, 411

AUBERT i CAMPS, Joan
(1902-2004)
338, 339

AYMERICH i SERRA, Esteve
(n.1962)
287, 332, 333

AZEMAR i PONT, Josep
(1862-1914)
001, 002, 003, 004, 016, 017

BACH i NÚÑEZ, Jaume
(n.1943)
103, 272, 289

BADIA i RODRÍGUEZ, Jordi
(n.1961)
208, 216, 232

BAENA i ASENCIO, David
(n.1961)
048

BAILO i ESTEVE, Manuel
(n.1965)
282, 367

BALAGUER i BARBADILLO, Sergi
(n.1953)
247

BALCELLS i BLESA, Conxita
(n.1962)
202, 234, 416

BALCELLS i GORINA, Santiago
(1913-2007)
144

BANÚS i TELLA, Antoni
(n.1958)
275, 297, 305, 307, 313

BARBA CORSINI, Francisco Juan
(n.1916)
011, 095, 130

BASSÓ i VIDAL, Carles
(n.1947)
092

BASSÓ i BIRULÉS, Francesc
(n.1921)
122, 327

BATLLE i DURANY, Enric
(n.1956)
226

BELGIOJOSO, Ludovico Barbiano di
(1909-2004)
140

BENAVENT DE BARBERÀ i ABELLÓ, Pere
(1899-1974)
297

BERENGUÉ i IGLESIAS, Mercè
(n.1962)
023, 219

BERENGUER i MESTRES, Francesc
(1866-1914)
255

BERGADÀ i MASQUEF, Jordi
(n.1958)
279, 310

BERGNES DE LAS CASAS i SOTERAS, Antoni
(n.1945)
126

BIRULÉS i BERTRAN, Josep Maria
(n.1959)
082

BLANCH i ROIG, Emili
(1897-1996)
005, 035

BOFILL i LEVÍ, Ricard
(n.1939)
068, 133, 134, 135, 239, 259, 304

BOFILL i BENESSAT, Emili
(1907-2000)
133, 134, 135

BOHIGAS i GUARDIOLA, Oriol
(n.1925)
060, 080, 129, 137, 153, 199, 204, 210, 224, 243, 327

BOMBELLI, Lanfranco
(n.1921)
012, 013

BONATERRA MATAS, Alejandro
(1916-2006)
006

BONELL i COSTA, Esteve
(n.1942)
043, 044, 074, 097, 128, 150, 190, 316, 411

BONET i CASTELLANA, Antoni
(1913-1989)
062, 065, 066, 127, 248, 314, 315, 320

BONET i FERRER, Vicenç
(n.1928)
139, 271

BONET i GARÍ, Lluís
(1893-1993)
096

BOSCH i GENOVER, Jordi
(n.1949)
032, 221, 360

BOSCH i PLANAS, Andreu
(n.1943)
207

BOTEY i GÓMEZ, Josep Maria
(n.1943)
207

BRU i BISTUER, Eduard
(n.1950)
201, 363

BRULLET i TENAS, Manuel
(n.1941)
081, 193, 276

BURGOS RUIZ, Francisco Jesús
(n.1959)
395

BUSQUETS i SINDREU, Xavier
(1917-1990)
123

BUXADÉ i RIBOT, Carles
(n.1942)
228

CABRÉ i SEGARRA, Frederic
(n.1959)
082

CÁCERES ZURITA, Rafael de
(n.1944)
278

CALATRAVA i VALLS, Santiago
(n.1951)
160

CANTALLOPS i VALERI, Lluís
(n.1934)
209

CARDEÑAS i PARÉS, Ferran
(n.1961)
220

CARDONER i BLANCH, Francesc de Paula
(1929-1997)
096

CARGOL i NOGUER, Josep
(n.1968)
026

CARTAÑÁ i GUBERN, Josep Maria
(n.1951)
170

CARVAJAL FERRER, Francisco Javier
(n.1926)
125

CASADEVALL i DALMAU, Jordi
(n.1953)
003

CASALS i BALAGUÉ, Albert
(n.1941)
245

CASAMOR i MALDONADO, Carles
(n.1957)
274

CASAMOR i MALDONADO, Antoni
(n.1961)
048, 274

CASELLES i TARRATS, Pere
(1864-1936)
298, 299

Índex d'autors 479

CAVALLER i SOTERAS, Francesc
(n.1932)
126

CHURRUCA DOTRES, Ricardo de
(1900-1963)
114

CIRICI i ALOMAR, Cristian
(n.1941)
159

CLARET i RUBIRA, Josep M.
(1908-1988)
036

CLOTET i BALLÚS, Lluís
(n.1941)
067, 073, 182, 197, 205, 218, 223

CODERCH DE SENTMENAT, José Antonio
(1913-1984)
007, 010, 119, 121, 132, 142, 146, 148, 154, 198, 222, 249, 257, 258, 268

COLL LÓPEZ, Jaime
(n.1964)
051, 240

COREA AIELLO, Mario Luis
(n.1939)
111

CORREA RUIZ, Federico
(n.1924)
009, 146, 147, 348

CRESPO i LLOBET, Josep Maria
(n.1956)
158

CUSPINERA i FONT, Lluís
(n.1942)
207

DALÍ, Salvador
(1904-1989)
006

DÍAZ i GÓMEZ, Carles M.
(n.1946)
101

DÍAZ SUÑER, Juan
(n.1959)
057

DILMÉ i ROMAGÓS, Lluís
(n.1960)
174, 194

DOMÈNECH i GIRBAU, Lluís
(n.1940)
093, 369, 373, 376, 381, 384, 401, 402

DOMÈNECH i MONTANER, Lluís
(1849-1923)
086, 092, 093, 097, 101, 294, 295, 296, 297

DOMÈNECH i TORRES, Lluís
(1911-1992)
372

DOMINGO i DOMINGO, Mamen
(n.1963)
306, 308, 312

DONADA i GAJA, Miquel
(n.1934)
188

DONATO i FOLCH, Josep Emili
(n.1934)
155, 156, 157, 285, 309, 324, 356, 368

DURAN i REYNALS, Raimon
(1895-1966)
092, 117

ESCURA BRAU, Carlos
(n.1952)
328

ESPAÑOL i LLORENS, Joaquim
(n.1945)
020, 031, 410

ESPECHE SOTAILO, Horacio Osvaldo
(n.1954)
359

ESPINET i MESTRE, Miquel
(n.1948)
380, 382, 383, 392

FABRÉ i CARRERAS, Francesc Xavier
(n.1959)
174, 194

FARGAS i FALP, Josep Maria
(n.1926)
141

FERRATER i LAMBARRI, Carles
(n.1944)
018, 056, 057, 058, 170, 328

FERRÉ i RICART, Ernest
(n.1960)
306, 308, 312

FERRER i LÓPEZ, Miquel
(1958-2006)
035

FERNÁNDEZ i EDUARDO, Francesc
(n.1954)
164, 379

FERNÁNDEZ i PRAT, Armand
(n.1960)
264

FIGA i MATARÓ, Joaquim
(n.1949)
024

FITÉ i FONT, Ramon Antoni
(n.1958)
387, 396, 417

FLORES, Ricardo Daniel
(n.1965)
365

FOLGUERA i GRASSI, Francesc
(1891-1960)
107

FORGAS i COLL, Joan
(n.1959)
347

FOSTER, Norman
(n.1935)
161

FREDIANI SARFATI, Arturo
(n.1964)
406

FREIXA i JANÀRIZ, Jaume
(n.1942)
152

FREIXES i MELERO, Daniel
(n.1946)
006

FRUTOS i SCHWÖBEL, Fidela
(n.1965)
206

FUSES i COMALADA, Josep
(n.1954)
022, 039, 046

GABÀS i GONZALO, Marta
(n.1959)
390, 412

GALÍ i CAMPRUBÍ, Elisabeth
(n.1950)
014

GALLARDO-BRAVO ORTEGA, Francisco
(n.1950)
111

GALLEGO i URBANO, Àlex
(n.1971)
400

GALLEGO OLMOS, Moisés
(n.1947)
164, 251, 275, 379, 400

GARCÉS i BRUSÉS, Jordi
(n.1945)
072, 077

GARCÍA-BARBÓN FERNÁNDEZ DE HENESTROSA, Lorenzo
(1915-1999)
126

GARCÍA DE CASTRO PENA, Rafael
(n.1923)
125

GARRIGA i ROCA, Miquel
(1804-1888)
174

GASCÓ i PALACÍN, Joaquim
(n.1950)
332

GASCÓN i CLIMENT, Eduard
(n.1958)
053

GAUDÍ i CORNET, Antoni
(1852-1926)
088, 089, 090, 095, 096, 098, 099, 102, 104, 245, 255

GEEST, Uwe
(n.1941)
155, 309, 356

GIL i GUITART, Josep Maria
(n.1950)
043, 044, 097, 316

GILI i MOROS, Joaquim
(1916-1984)
122, 327

GILI i GALFETTI, Gustau
(n.1963)
059, 122

GIRÁLDEZ DÁVILA, Guillermo
(n.1925)
124

GIRALT i CASADESÚS, Ricard
(1884-1970)
034

GOMÀ i PUJADAS, Marià
(1915-1990)
371, 374

GONZÁLEZ i MASCLANS, Eulàlia
(n.1959)
006

GONZÁLEZ MORENO-NAVARRO, Antoni
(n.1943)
097, 245

GONZÁLEZ-MORENO NAVARRO, Josep Lluís
(n.1945)
097, 245

GUALLART FURIÓ, Vicente
(n.1963)
283

GUASTAVINO i MORENO, Rafael
(1842-1908)
194, 362

GULLICHSEN, Kristian
(n.1932)
391

HARNDEN, Peter G.
(1913-1971)
012, 013

HEREU i PASCUAL, Francesc
(n.1946)
020, 031, 410

HERNÁNDEZ-CROS, Josep Emili
(n.1939)
095

HERZOG, Jacques
(n.1950)
180

HOM i SANTOLAYA, Cinto
(n.1957)
264

ILLESCAS DE LA MORENA, Albert
(n.1940)
021

ILLESCAS i MIROSA, Sixt
(1903-1986)
116

ISOZAKI, Arata
(n.1931)
094, 162, 200

JIMÉNEZ i GÓMEZ, Eva
(n.1969)
084

JIMÉNEZ EROLES, Luis Miguel
(n.1951)
156, 157, 285, 368

JUBERT i ROSICH, Lluís
(n.1965)
055

JUJOL i GIBERT, Josep Maria
(1879-1949)
103, 105, 106, 241, 242, 261, 264, 290, 291, 293

JOVER BIBOUM, Margarita
(n.1969)
233

LAY, Charmaine
(n.1967)
235

LECLERC, Judith
(n.1967)
051, 240

LLIMONA i TORRAS, Pere
(n.1929)
345

LLINÀS i CARMONA, Josep Antoni
(n.1945)
063, 124, 175, 176, 184, 185, 230, 261, 270, 281, 286, 311

LLOBET i RIBEIRO, Xavier
(n.1963)
084

LLORENS i DURAN, Josep Ignasi de
(n.1946)
236

LÓPEZ DEL CASTILLO, Francisco Javier
(n.1961)
015

LÓPEZ IÑIGO, Pedro
(1926-1997)
124

LUNA FERNÁNDEZ, Roberto
(n.1949)
094

LUNA i COLLDEFORS, Alfonso de
(n.1960)
081, 193, 276

MACKAY GOODCHILD, David John
(n.1933)
060, 080, 137, 153, 199, 204, 210, 224, 243, 415

MANNINO VILA, Faustino Edgardo
(n.1944)
111

MARGARIT i CONSARNAU, Joan
(n.1938)
228

MARTÍ ARÍS, Carles
(n.1948)
053

MARTÍ i PUZO, Ramon
(n.1952)
156, 157

MARTINELL i BRUNET, Cèsar
(1888-1973)
292, 330, 331, 364

MARTÍNEZ LAPEÑA, José Antonio
(n.1941)
166, 167, 209, 227, 277, 284, 329, 340

MARTÍNEZ i SÁNCHEZ, Carles
(1896-1988)
109

MARTORELL i CODINA, Josep Maria
(n.1925)
060, 080, 129, 137, 153, 199, 204, 210, 224, 243, 327, 415

MASÓ i VALENTÍ, Rafael
(1880-1935)
027, 028, 029, 032, 033, 335, 344

MASRAMON i ORDIS, Josep Maria
(1947-1979)
031

MASSIP i BOSCH, Enric
(n.1960)
052, 359

MASSOT i BELTRAN, Josep Maria
(n.1947)
188

MATEO i MARTÍNEZ, Josep Lluís
(n.1949)
078, 158, 179, 201, 220, 231, 350, 351

MEIER, Richard
(n.1934)
172

MEJÓN ARTIGAS, Julio José
(n.1958)
387, 396, 417

MERCADÉ i ROGEL, Ricard
(n.1956)
165, 244

MESTRES i ESPLUGAS, Josep Oriol
(1815-1895)
174

MEURON, Pierre de
(n.1950)
180

MIÀS i GIFRÉ, Josep
(n.1966)
025, 168, 408

MIES VAN DER ROHE, Ludwig
(1886-1969)
159

MILÀ i SAGNIER, Alfons
(n.1924)
009, 146, 147, 348

MIRALLES i MOYA, Enric
(1955-2000)
177, 178, 183, 189, 253, 355, 366

MIRANDA BLANCO, Vicente
(n.1940)
006

MITJANS i MIRÓ, Francesc
(1909-2006)
118, 126, 131, 144, 256

MITJANS PERELLÓ, Juan Pablo
(n.1949)
126

MOLINER i SALINAS, Jordi
(n.1957)
078, 361

MONEO VALLÉS, José Rafael
(n.1937)
169, 173, 227, 273

MONER i CODINA, Jeroni
(n.1940)
021, 024, 056

MONGUIÓ i SEGURA, Pau
(1865-1956)
321, 322, 323

MONRAVÀ i LÓPEZ, Josep Maria
(1905-1999)
265, 266, 267

MORA i GRAMUNT, Gabriel
(n.1941)
103, 151, 211, 215, 272, 289

MORAGAS i GALLISSÀ, Antoni de
(1913-1985)
120, 138

MORERA i GATELL, Francesc de Paula
(1869-1951)
369

MUNCUNILL i PARELLADA, Lluís
(1868-1931)
228, 229

MUÑOZ i JORDÁN, Ramon
(n.1959)
076

MURO i SOLER, Carles
(n.1964)
235

NADAL i OLLER, Lluís
(n.1929)
071, 139, 271

Índex d'autors 481

NEGRE i BALSAS, Maria Àngels
(n.1957)
399

NOUVEL, Jean
(n.1945)
181

PALLÍ i VERT, Robert
(n.1958)
076

PÀMIES i MARTORELL, Antoni M.
(n.1951)
305

PARÉ i LEZCANO, Marc
(n.1969)
404

PARÉ i LEZCANO, Ricard
(n.1973)
404

PARICIO i ANSUATEGUI, Ignasi
(n.1944)
182

PERAL BUESA, Luis
(n.1921)
269

PERESSUTTI, Enrico
(1908-1976)
140

PEREDA FERNÁNDEZ, Luis de
(n.1964)
395

PÉREZ i JOVÉ, Pau
(n.1947)
275, 279, 297, 305, 307, 313, 317

PÉREZ i GONZÁLEZ, Blai
(n.1965)
252

PÉREZ PIÑERO, Emilio
(1935-1972)
006

PICH-AGUILERA i BAURIER, Felip
(n.1960)
225

PIGEM i BARCELÓ, Carme
(n.1962)
047, 079, 341, 342, 343

PINEDA i ÁLVAREZ, Albert de
(n.1953)
081

PINÓS i DESPLAT, Carme
(n.1954)
189, 254, 355, 366, 398

PIÑÓN PALLARÉS, Heliodoro
(n.1942)
151, 165, 171, 191, 211, 215, 244, 349

PÍRIZ i BERNAL, Néstor
(n.1969)
404

PLA i MASMIQUEL, Arcadi
(n.1945)
027, 041, 045, 050, 056, 334

PLA i TORRAS, Josep Maria
(n.1933)
038

POCH i VIVES, Antoni
(n.1955)
361

PRATMARSÓ i PARERA, Josep
(1913-1985)
061, 069, 070

PRATS i GÜERRE, Eva
(n.1965)
365

PRATS i SAN ROMAN, Rodrigo
(n.1959)
076

PUBILL i POCIELLO, Carles
(n.1969)
404

PUEYO DELL'ORO, Julio Alberto
(n.1945)
368

PUIG i FREIXAS, Gerard
(n.1973)
333

PUIG i ANDREU, Ramon Maria
(n.1940)
325, 369, 373, 375, 376, 377, 378, 383, 386, 388, 402

PUIG i BOADA, Isidre
(1891-1987)
096

PUIG i CADAFALCH, Josep
(1867-1956)
087, 091, 094, 195, 196, 288

PUIG i GAIRALT, Ramon
(1886-1937)
246

PUIG i TORNÉ, Josep
(n.1929)
062, 127, 314, 315, 320

PUIGDEFÀBREGAS i BASERBA, Pere
(1926-2003)
139, 271

PUIGDOMÈNECH i ALONSO, Albert
(1944-2004)
080

PUJOL DE BARBERÀ, Josep Maria
(1871-1949)
262, 263

QUERA i ARREGUI, Josep Maria
(n.1960)
048

QUINTANA i CREUS, Màrius
(n.1954)
014

RAHOLA i AGUADÉ, Víctor
(n.1945)
008, 040, 318

RAMOS GALINO, Fernando Juan
(n.1944)
159

RASPALL i MAYOL, Manuel Joaquim
(1877-1937)
212, 213, 314

RAVETLLAT i MIRA, Pere Joan
(n.1956)
100, 260

REVENTÓS i FARRARONS, Ramon
(1892-1976)
108

RIBA DE SALAS, Francesc de
(1910-2000)
138

RIBAS i PIERA, Manuel
(n.1925)
075

RIBAS i SEIX, Anna
(n.1959)
390, 412

RIBAS i SEIX, Carme
(n.1956)
100, 260

RIBOT DE BALLE, Joan M. de
(n.1919)
037, 038, 083

RIERA i MICALÓ, Josep
(n.1950)
024

RIUS i CAMPS, Francesc
(n.1941)
128, 190, 316, 413

ROCA i PINET, Joan
(1885-1973)
030, 031, 334, 336

ROGERS, Ernesto Nathan
(1909-1969)
140

ROGERS, Richard G.
(n.1933)
247

RODRÍGUEZ ARIAS, Germán
(1902-1987)
113, 115, 357

RODRÍGUEZ MIJARES, José
(1910-1990)
414

ROIG i DURAN, Joan
(n.1954)
226

ROLDÁN i ANDRADE, José Miguel
(n.1961)
023, 219

ROMANS DE FONSDEVIELA, Maria Pilar
(n.1958)
082

ROS i BALLESTEROS, Jordi
(n.1956)
054

ROS DE RAMIS, Joaquín de
(1911-1988)
006

ROSELL i GRATACÒS, Joaquim
(n.1961)
235

RUBIÓ i BELLVER, Joan
(1871-1952)
100, 300, 352, 370

RUISÁNCHEZ i CAPELASTEGUI, Manuel
(n.1957)
326

RUIZ i GELI, Enric
(n.1968)
019

RUIZ i VALLÈS, Xavier
(1931-2000)
345

RULL i BERTRAN, Rosa M.
(n.1964)
282, 367

SABATÉ i PICASÓ, Joan
(n.1960)
359

SABATER i ANDREU, Laureà
(1940-1975)
369, 373, 375, 376, 401, 402

SÁEZ i LLORCA, Carles
(n.1955)
388

SALVADÓ i CABRÉ, Anton M.
(n.1962)
287, 332, 333

SANABRIA i BOIX, Ramon
(n.1950)
085, 385, 389, 393

SANAHUJA ESCOFET, Juan Manuel
(n.1964)
226

SANAHUJA ESCOFET, Ricardo
(n.1970)
226

SANGENÍS i VINTRÓ, Mercè
(n.1957)
216

SAN JOSÉ MARQUÉS, Javier
(n.1949)
049

SANMARTÍ i VERDAGUER, Jaume
(n.1941)
110, 373

SANMARTÍN GABÁS, Antonio
(n.1958)
076

SANMARTÍN i BURGUÉS, Josep Maria
(n.1957)
206

SANTACANA i VERDET, Eugènia
(n.1967)
055

SANZ MAGALLÓN, José Luis
(n.1926)
146

SARDÀ i FERRAN, Jordi
(n.1951)
310

SARDÀ i MOLTÓ, Antoni
(1901-1978)
302, 303

SAS i LLAURADÓ, Antoni
(1936-2002)
376

SEGUÍ i SANTANA, Víctor
(n.1947)
110

SERT i LÓPEZ, Josep Lluís
(1902-1983)
110, 111, 112, 149, 152

SIBILS i ENSESA, Àlex
(n.1957)
042

SIERRA NAVA, Manuel
(1923-2007)
269

SIMÓ i BOFARULL, Josep
(1889-1966)
301

SIZA VIEIRA, Alvaro
(n.1933)
163, 250, 394

SOLAGUREN-BEASCOA DE CORRAL, Félix
(n.1956)
399

SOLÀ-MORALES i ROSSELLÓ, Manuel de
(1910-2003)
136

SOLÀ-MORALES i RUBIÓ, Ignasi de
(1942-2001)
015, 064, 159, 174, 194

SOLÀ-MORALES i RUBIÓ, Manuel de
(n.1939)
136, 169

SOLDEVILA i BARBOSA, Alfons
(n.1938)
188, 236

SÒRIA i BADIA, Enric
(n.1937)
077

SOSTRES i MALUQUER, Josep Maria
(1915-1984)
143, 237, 238, 280, 353, 354, 403, 407, 409

SOTA MARTÍNEZ, Alejandro de la
(1913-1996)
270

SOTERAS i MAURI, Josep
(1907-1989)
126

SUBÍAS i FAGES, Xavier
(n.1926)
124

SUBIRACHS i SITJAR, Josep Maria
(n.1927)
096

SUBIRANA i SUBIRANA, Joan Baptista
(1904-1978)
110, 111

SUGRAÑES i GRAS, Domènec
(1879-1938)
096

SUNYER i VIVES, Antoni
(n.1954)
217, 319

TAGLIABUE, Benedetta
(n.1963)
177, 178, 183

TARRÚS i GALTER, Joan
(n.1945)
032, 221, 360

TERRADAS i MUNTAÑOLA, Esteve
(n.1950)
203

TERRADAS i MUNTAÑOLA, Robert
(n.1944)
203

TERRADAS i VIA, Robert
(1916-1976)
249

TORRES i CLAVÉ, Josep
(1906-1939)
110, 111

TORRES i TORRES, Raimon
(n.1934)
110

TORRES i TUR, Elías
(n.1944)
166, 167, 209, 227, 277, 284, 329, 340

TORROJA MIRET, Eduardo
(1899-1961)
414

TOUS i CARBÓ, Enric
(n.1925)
141

TUSQUETS i GUILLÉN, Oscar
(n.1941)
067, 073, 092, 101, 197, 205, 218, 223

TURON i VICH, Ricard
(n.1971)
026

UBACH i NUET, Antoni
(n.1944)
380, 382, 383, 392

USANDIZAGA CALPARSORO, Miguel
(n.1954)
209

VALLS i VERGÉS, Manuel
(1912-2000)
007, 010, 119, 121, 132, 142, 154, 148, 154, 198, 222, 249, 257, 258

VALOR i MONTERO, Jaume
(n.1965)
206

VEGA MARTÍNEZ, Antonio de la
(n.1902)
269

VENDRELL i SALA, Xavier
(n.1955)
326

VERA i GARCÍA, Joan
(n.1961)
176, 185

VIADER i MARTÍ, Joan M.
(n.1953)
022, 039, 046

VIAPLANA i VEA, Albert
(n.1933)
151, 165, 171, 191, 211, 215, 244, 349

VIDAL i ARDERIU, Lluís Maria
(1939-2000)
397, 405

VILA i RODRÍGUEZ, Rafael
(n.1950)
095

VILALTA i PUJOL, Ramon
(n.1960)
047, 079, 341, 342, 343

VILLAR i LOZANO, Francesc de Paula del
(1828-1901)
096

VITALLER i SANTIRÓ, Albert
(n.1966)
081

VIVES i SANFELIU, Santiago
(n.1948)
032, 202, 221, 234

YLLA-CATALÀ i PUIGREFAGUT, Dolors
(n.1960)
347

ZARAGOZA i ALBÍ, Joan
(1912-2006)

**The architecture of Catalonia.
Regional and city guides.
Background.**

1973. HERNÁNDEZ-CROS, J. Emili; MORA, Gabriel; POUPLANA, Xavier: *Arquitectura de Barcelona. Guia*. Publicaciones del Colegio de Arquitectos de Cataluña y Baleares. Ed. La Gaya Ciència. Barcelona, 1973.

1977. TARRÚS, Joan; COMADIRA, Narcís: *Guia de l'arquitectura dels segles XIX i XX a la província de Girona*. Col·legi Oficial d'Arquitectes de Catalunya. Ed. La Gaya Ciència, Barcelona, 1977.

1978. ESPAÑOL, Joaquim; FÀBREGA, Jaume; FUSES, Josep; PARÉS, Fina: *Guia d'Arquitectura d'Olot*. Publicació de la Delegació de Girona del Col·legi Oficial d'Arquitectes de Catalunya. Ed. La Gaya Ciència, Barcelona, 1978.

1980. BUQUERAS, Josep M.: *Arquitectura de Tarragona. Siglos XIX y XX*. Llibreria Guardias. Tarragona, 1980.

1980. FUSES, Josep; FÀBREGA, Jaume; PARÉS, Fina; CASTELLS, Ramon Mª; PANELLA, Llorenç; REDONDO, Ernest: *Guia d'arquitectura de Girona*, Delegació de Girona del Col·legi Oficial d'Arquitectes de Catalunya. Ed. La Gaya Ciència, Barcelona, 1980.

1985. HERNÁNDEZ-CROS, Josep Emili; MORA, Gabriel; POUPLANA, Xavier: *Guía de arquitectura de Barcelona*. Demarcació de Barcelona del Col·legi d'Arquitectes de Catalunya, Ajuntament de Barcelona. Barcelona, 1985.

1990. HERNÁNDEZ-CROS, Josep Emili; MORA, Gabriel; POUPLANA, Xavier: *Arquitectura de Barcelona*. Demarcació de Barcelona del Col·legi d'Arquitectes de Catalunya. Barcelona, 1990.

1990. LACUESTA, Raquel; GONZÁLEZ, Antoni: *Guía de Arquitectura modernista en Catalunya*. Ed. Gustavo Gili. Barcelona, 1990.

1991. JUVÉ, Àngel; GISPERT, Joan: *Guia d'Arquitectura de la Seu d'Urgell*. Institut d'Estudis Ilerdencs, 1991.

1991. PLA, Arcadi: *Itineraris d'Arquitectura Catalana 1984-1991*. Quaderns d'Arquitectura i Urbanisme, COAC. Barcelona, 1991.

1995. AA.VV.: *Arquitectura del Camp. Guia*. Centre de Documentació de la Demarcació de Tarragona del Col·legi d'Arquitectes de Catalunya. Autoritat Portuària de Tarragona. Tarragona, 1995.

1995. LACUESTA, Raquel; GONZÁLEZ, Antoni: *Barcelona. Guía de arquitectura 1929-1994*. Ed. Gustavo Gili. Barcelona, 1995.

1996. BIRULÉS, Josep M.: *Girona ciutat. Guia d'arquitectura*. Demarcació de Girona del Col·legi d'Arquitectes de Catalunya. Girona, 1996.

1996. PIZZA, Antonio: *Guía de la arquitectura moderna en Barcelona (1928-1936)*. Ediciones del Serbal. Barcelona, 1996.

1997. LACUESTA, Raquel; GONZÁLEZ, Antoni: *Barcelona. Guía de arquitectura 1929-1996*. Ed. Gustavo Gili. Barcelona, 1997.

1998. CABRÉ, Tate: *Reus, ciutat modernista*. Ajuntament de Reus, Ed. Mediterrània. Barcelona, 1998.

1999. BERNADÓ, Jordi; BORDES, Francesc; LLOP, Carles; PUIGDEMASA, Josep M.: *Arquitectura contemporània. Terres de Lleida. 1948-1998*. Demarcació de Lleida del Col·legi d'Arquitectes de Catalunya, Diputació de Lleida. Lleida, 1999.

1999. LACUESTA, Raquel; GONZÁLEZ, Antoni: *Barcelona. Guía de arquitectura 1929-2000*. Ed. Gustavo Gili, Barcelona, 1999.

2001. GAUSA, Manuel; CERVELLÓ, Marta; PLA, Maurici: *Barcelona: Guía de Arquitectura Moderna 1860-2002*. Ed. ACTAR, Ajuntament de Barcelona. Barcelona, 2001.

2001. STRUM, Suzanne: *Barcelona. A guide to recent architecture*. Ellipsis London Limited. Londres, 2001.

2002. LÓPEZ I DAUFÍ, Antoni: *Guia d'Arquitectura de la Demarcació de l'Ebre*, Demarcació de l'Ebre del Col·legi d'Arquitectes de Catalunya, Fundació Caixa Penedès. Tortosa, 2002.

2003. SERRA i MASDEU, Anna Isabel: *Recorregut per la Tarragona modernista*. Cossetània Edicions, Ajuntament de Tarragona. Valls, 2003.

2004. MÀRIA, Magdalena; MARTÍN, Helena: *Guia d'Arquitectura de L'Hospitalet. L'obra dels germans Puig Gairalt*. Enginyeria i Arquitectura La Salle, URL. Barcelona, 2004.

2006. MÀRIA, Magda; RECIO, Manel: *Guia d'Arquitectura de Mataró. Obra contemporània*. Enginyeria i Arquitectura La Salle, URL. Barcelona, 2006.

2006. MÀRIA, Magda; ADAM DURAN, Josep M.: *Guia d'Arquitectura de Campdevànol*. Enginyeria i Arquitectura La Salle, URL. Barcelona, 2006.

COL·LEGI D'ARQUITECTES DE CATALUNYA (COAC)

BOARD OF DIRECTORS

President
Jordi Ludevid i Anglada

Vice President and Barcelona Branch Chairman
Lluís Comerón i Graupera

Branch Chairmen
Girona
Josep Riera i Micaló
Tarragona
Jordi Bergadà i Masquef
Lleida
Montserrat Giné i Macià
Ebre
Joan Josep Curto i Reverté

Secretary
Carles Crespo i Veigas

Treasurer
Josep M. Gutiérrez i Noguera

Board Members
Ramon M. de Puig i Andreu
Ramon Sanabria i Boix
Fernando Marzá i Pérez
Rosa Rull i Bertran

TRIANGLE EDITORIAL

Director
Ricard Pla

Production
Imma Planas
Mercè Camerino
Joan Montserrat

Coordination
Paz Marrodán

Digital retouching
Pere Vivas
Biel Puig
Laia Moreno

Publishers
Col·legi d'Arquitectes de Catalunya
Triangle Postals, S L

Author
Maurici Pla

Photographs
José Hevia

Other photographies
Arxiu Històric del Col·legi d'Arquitectes de Catalunya: 012, 034, 069, 070, 122, 315, 357, 358, 369
Arxiu Llimona-Ruiz Vallès: 345
Aleix Bagué: 328
Conxita Balcells: 202
Lluís Casals: 018, 067, 077, 382
Francesc Català-Roca: 249, 257, 415
Ramon Domènech: 372, 401
Ferran Freixa: 064, 380
Jordi Puig: 054, 084
Hisao Suzuki: 192, 342
Oscar Tusquets: 073
Pilar Vilaraso: 278
Pere Vivas: 088, 188, 191, 294

Coordination
Servei de Publicacions del COAC

Selection, documentation, database and routes by devised
Joan Jordi Obiols

Documentation and database
Laura Badell
Martina Garreta
Ernest Ruiz

Graphic design
Joan Barjau
Julià B. van den Eynde

Translation and correction
Anna Campeny
Elaine Fradley
Núria Gil
Jordi Palou
Marta Rojals

Source of statistics:
Institut d'Estadística de Catalunya, 2006

Printing
Grafos SA

ISBN: 978-84-8478-009-0
DL: B-42816-2007

© of this edition

Col·legi d'Arquitectes de Catalunya,
Plaça Nova 5, 08002 Barcelona
Tel. +34 93 306 78 06 | www.coac.net

Triangle Postals, S.L.
Carrer Pere Tudurí 8, 07710 Sant Lluís (Menorca) | Tel. +34 971 15 04 69
www.trianglepostals.com

© of the texts, the authors
© of the images, the photographers

Acknowledgments
The library of the COAC

The library of the Escola Tècnica Superior d'Arquitectura de Barcelona

The library of the Escola Tècnica Superior d'Arquitectura del Vallès

The Historical Archive of the Col·legi d'Arquitectes de Catalunya

The technical services of town and city halls throughout Catalonia

The architects and administrative staff of the architecture practices in Catalonia

Distribution
Midac Llibres SL
Tel. +34 93 746 41 10
Fax + 34 93 746 41 11
pedidos.midac@telefonica.net

International distribution
Actar D
Roca i Batlle 2 · 08023 Barcelona
Tel. +34 93 418 77 59
Fax +34 93 418 67 07
office@actar-d.com
www.actar-d.com